Vygotsky and education

Vygotsky and education

Instructional implications and applications of sociohistorical psychology

Edited by
LUIS C. MOLL

CAMBRIDGE
UNIVERSITY PRESS

Published by the Press Syndicate of the University of Cambridge
The Pitt Building, Trumpington Street, Cambridge CB2 1RP
40 West 20th Street, New York, NY 10011-4211, USA
10 Stamford Road, Oakleigh, Victoria 3166, Australia

First published 1990
First paperback edition 1992

Printed in the United States of America

Library of Congress Cataloging-in-Publication Data

Vygotsky and education: instructional implications and applications
of sociohistorical psychology / edited by Luis C. Moll.
p. cm.
ISBN 0-521-36051-X.
1. Learning, Psychology of. 2. Constructivism (Education)
3. Cognition and culture. 4. Teaching. 5. Vygotskii, L. S. (Lev
Semenovich), 1896–1934. I. Moll, Luis C.
LB1051.V94 1990
370.15′23 – dc20   90-31037
                                                                 CIP

British Library Cataloguing in Publication Data

Vygotsky and education : instructional implications and
applications of sociohistorical psychology.
1. Education. Theories of Vygotskii, L. S. (Lev
Semenovich) 1896–1934
I. Moll, Luis C.
370.1

ISBN 0-521-36051-X hardback
ISBN 0-521-38579-2 paperback

Contents

List of contributors   *page* vii
Preface   ix
Acknowledgments   xi

Introduction   1
Luis C. Moll

Part I   Historical and theoretical issues

1   Vygotsky: The man and his cause   31
    Guillermo Blanck

2   The historical context of Vygotsky's work: A sociohistorical
    approach   59
    Alberto Rosa and Ignacio Montero

3   Cognitive development and formal schooling: The evidence from
    cross-cultural research   89
    Michael Cole

4   The voice of rationality in a sociocultural approach to mind   111
    James V. Wertsch

5   The social origins of self-regulation   127
    Rafael M. Díaz, Cynthia J. Neal, and Marina Amaya-Williams

6   Vygotsky, the zone of proximal development, and peer
    collaboration: Implications for classroom practice   155
    Jonathan Tudge

Part II   Educational implications

7   Teaching mind in society: Teaching, schooling, and literate
    discourse   175
    Ronald Gallimore and Roland Tharp

v

8   A Vygotskian interpretation of Reading Recovery   206
    Marie M. Clay and Courtney B. Cazden

9   Vygotsky in a whole-language perspective   223
    Yetta M. Goodman and Kenneth S. Goodman

10 The development of scientific concepts and discourse   251
    Carolyn P. Panofsky, Vera John-Steiner, and Peggy J. Blackwell

Part III   Instructional applications

11 Changes in a teacher's views of interactive comprehension instruction   271
    Kathryn H. Au

12 Learning to read and write in an inner-city setting: A longitudinal
    study of community change   287
    Gillian Dowley McNamee

13 Writing as a social process   304
    Joan B. McLane

14 Creating zones of possibilities: Combining social contexts
    for instruction   319
    Luis C. Moll and James B. Greenberg

15 The zone of proximal development as basis for instruction   349
    Mariane Hedegaard

16 Detecting and defining science problems: A study of video-
    mediated lessons   372
    Laura M. W. Martin

17 Assisted performance in writing instruction with learning-
    disabled students   403
    Robert Rueda

Name index   427
Subject index   433

Contributors

Marina Amaya-Williams
Educational Foundations Department
University of New Mexico
Albuquerque, NM

Kathryn H. Au
Kamehameha Early Education Program
Honolulu, HI

Peggy J. Blackwell
Educational Foundations Department
University of New Mexico
Albuquerque, NM

Guillermo Blanck
University of Buenos Aires
Buenos Aires, Argentina

Courtney B. Cazden
Graduate School of Education
Harvard University
Cambridge, MA

Marie M. Clay
University of Auckland
Auckland, New Zealand

Michael Cole
Laboratory of Comparative Human
   Cognition
University of California, San Diego
La Jolla, CA

Rafael M. Díaz
School of Education
Stanford University
Stanford, CA

Ronald Gallimore
Department of Psychiatry and
   Biobehavioral Sciences
University of California
Los Angeles, CA

Kenneth S. Goodman
Division of Language, Reading, and
   Culture
College of Education
University of Arizona
Tucson, AZ

Yetta M. Goodman
Division of Language, Reading, and
   Culture
College of Education
University of Arizona
Tucson, AZ

James B. Greenberg
Bureau of Applied Research in An-
   thropology
University of Arizona
Tucson, AZ

Mariane Hedegaard
Institute of Psychology
University of Aarhus
Risskov, Denmark

Vera John-Steiner
Department of Linguistics
University of New Mexico
Albuquerque, NM

Joan B. McLane
Erikson Institute
Chicago, IL

Gillian Dowley McNamee
Erikson Institute
Chicago, IL

Laura M. W. Martin
Bank Street College of Education
New York, NY

Luis C. Moll
Division of Language, Reading, and
    Culture
College of Education
University of Arizona
Tucson, AZ

Ignacio Montero
Facultad de Psicología
Universidad Autónoma de Madrid
Cantoblanco, Madrid

Cynthia J. Neal
Educational Foundations Department
University of New Mexico
Albuquerque, NM

Carolyn P. Panofsky
School of Education
Rhode Island College
Providence, RI

Alberto Rosa
Facultad de Psicología
Universidad Autónoma de Madrid
Cantoblanco, Madrid

Robert Rueda
School of Education
University of Southern California
Los Angeles, CA

Roland Tharp
Provost and Vice-President for
    Academic Affairs
United States International University
San Diego, CA
and
Professor of Psychology, Emeritus
University of Hawaii
Honolulu, HI

Jonathan Tudge
Department of Child Development and
    Family Relations
School of Human Environmental
    Sciences
University of North Carolina
Greensboro, NC

James V. Wertsch
Department of Psychology
Clark University
Worcester, MA

Preface

In 1977 I spent a few months at the Laboratory of Comparative Human Cognition, now at the University of California, San Diego, then at Rockefeller University in New York City. The Lab was directed then, as it is now, by Michael Cole. I went as a predoctoral student to learn about the Lab's work and to finish my dissertation. As a graduate student at UCLA I had become very interested in the cross-cultural cognitive research (with the Kpelle in Liberia) conducted by Cole and colleagues (see Cole, Gay, Glick, & Sharp, 1971; Gay & Cole, 1969; Glick, 1974) and was eager to explore the relevance of that work to issues of minority education in this country. In particular, I was captivated by their studies of the relationship between culturally organized activities and thinking and by their clever methodological moves, combining ethnographic-like observations with manipulations of experimental tasks. Their findings, highlighting how cognition is embedded within the social and cultural world, indicated the paramount importance of contextual factors to thinking, a point neglected then in education and, I believe, still neglected today.

What I did not realize then was that this work would also serve as my introduction to Vygotsky's ideas – quite appropriately, a mediated introduction, as it turned out. I later learned that Cole had studied with Luria prior to the Kpelle research and that the work in Liberia was, to an extent, inspired by Luria's (and Vygotsky's) famous research in Central Asia (Luria, 1976). Subsequent interpretations of the Kpelle studies (see Cole & Scribner, 1974) and later work by Sylvia Scribner and Michael Cole (see Scribner & Cole, 1981) and by the Lab (Laboratory of Comparative Human Cognition, 1983) made much clearer the connection of this research to the sociohistorical school of psychology. My stint in the Lab in New York also coincided with the publication of Vygotsky's (1978) *Mind in Society,* an edited compilation of his writings. Reading that book helped me understand "firsthand" the relationship between the empirical work I was studying (and was fascinated with), my own research in minority education, and broader theoretical considerations. The great importance of Vygotsky's ideas to education began to become obvious to me.

As Vygotsky's ideas started gaining some newfound visibility in the 1980s, and influencing a new generation of scholars, the dearth of writings related directly to education became evident. This scarcity is ironic, as I point out in my Introduction, not only because Vygotsky assigned great importance to the role of formal schooling in cognitive development, with its special modes of discourse and potential for forging new modes of thinking, but because education in all its forms, human pedagogy, is so central to his theory. Why this scarcity existed became clearer later on. The immediate precursor to this volume, however, came in 1986 when I was asked to organize a seminar on Vygotsky and education for graduate students and colleagues in the College of Education at the University of Arizona, my new academic home. My compilation of articles for that seminar's readings contained only a handful on educational practice, again revealing the lack of articles on the topic. What became obvious during the seminar were the reasons for this lack of education-related work: It is not only that few educators know about Vygotsky but that most of the psychologists (and others, but more obvious in the work of psychologists) writing about Vygotsky know very little about education. This volume, therefore, is intended to inform educators and to help fill this "education gap" in the Vygotskian literature.

My intent is also to interest new readers, especially from the field of education, in the ideas of the sociohistorical school in general and Vygotsky's work specifically. As editor, I strove to make the education theme come through clearly, and the bulk of the book is devoted to studies utilizing Vygotskian ideas in practice. But I did not want to ignore seasoned Vygotskians. I, therefore, combined articles by well-known "senior" scholars and by "junior" authors making among their first contributions to this literature. The topics addressed by these authors are quite diverse, but I believe that they cohere nicely around the central education theme. I must add that every author contributed something new to the literature. Every article in this volume is an original contribution, prepared specifically for this book. I am very grateful to my colleagues for their time and effort, and for sharing their thinking with me and with the readers of this volume.

References

Cole, M., Gay, J., Glick, J., & Sharp, D. (1971). *The cultural context of learning and thinking: An exploration in experimental anthropology.* New York: Basic.

Cole, M., & Scribner, S. (1974). *Culture and thought: A psychological introduction.* New York: Wiley.

Gay, J., & Cole, M. (1969). *The new mathematics and an old culture: A study of learning among the Kpelle of Liberia.* New York: Holt, Rinehart & Winston.

Glick, J. (1974). Culture and cognition: Some theoretical and methodological concerns. In G. S. Spindler (Ed.), *Education and cultural processes: Toward an anthropology of education* (pp. 373–382). New York: Holt, Rinehart & Winston.

Laboratory of Comparative Human Cognition (1983). Culture and cognitive development. In W. Kessen (Ed.), *Handbook of child psychology* (Vol. 1, pp. 295–356). New York: Wiley.

Luria, A. R. (1976). *Cognitive development: Its cultural and social foundations.* Cambridge, MA: Harvard University Press.

Scribner, S. & Cole, M. (1981). *The psychology of literacy.* Cambridge, MA: Harvard University Press.

Vygotsky, L. S. (1978). *Mind in society.* Cambridge, MA: Harvard University Press.

Acknowledgments

Any book, especially an edited volume, is the product of the efforts of many people. This one is certainly no exception. My first thanks go to the colleagues who contributed the chapters that make up this book. I benefited enormously from reading their work; I am sure the readers of this volume will derive just as much pleasure and benefit from reading their essays. I owe much to the students who participated in two seminars on Vygotsky and education that I offered at the College of Education of the University of Arizona. Their great interest in Vygotsky's ideas and our class discussion did much to motivate the preparation of this volume. Thanks as well to Esteban Díaz and Elizabeth Howard for their editing suggestions and assistance. Lauren García translated the chapter by Guillermo Blanck, and Karen Goodman translated the one by Alberto Rosa and Ignacio Montero. Many thanks to them for agreeing to help on such short notice. I'd like to express my appreciation to my colleagues, past and present, at the Laboratory of Comparative Human Cognition of the University of California, San Diego, for providing the context for my study of Vygotsky's ideas. I hope this book contributes to the mission of the Lab.

A very special thanks to my family, Ana, Carlos, and Eric, for their patience and support, and to my parents, Olga Rita and Carlos, for their faith and encouragement.

I dedicate this volume to the memory of the "troika," the founders of the sociohistorical school of psychology: Lev Semenovich Vygotsky, Alexander Romanovich Luria, and Alexei Nikolaevich Leontiev.

Introduction

Luis C. Moll

> I am for practicing psychologists, for practical work, and so in the broad sense for boldness and the advance of our branch of science into life.
> L. S. Vygotsky (quoted in Leontiev & Luria, 1968, p. 367)

In his introduction to the first English translation of Vygotsky's *Thought and Language* (1962), Jerome Bruner remarked that "Vygotsky's conception of development is at the same time a theory of education" (p. v).[1] It is noteworthy that 25 years later, in his Prologue to the English edition of Vygotsky's *Collected Works*, Bruner (1987) elaborated on this same central theme of Vygotsky's work: "When I remarked a quarter century ago that Vygotsky's view of development was also a theory of education, I did not realize the half of it. In fact, his educational theory is a theory of cultural transmission as well as a theory of development. For 'education' implies for Vygotsky not only the development of the individual's potential, but the historical expression and growth of the human culture from which Man springs" (pp. 1–2).

Vygotsky regarded education not only as central to cognitive development but as the quintessential sociocultural activity. That is, he considered the capacity to teach and to benefit from instruction a fundamental attribute of human beings. As Premack (1984) has pointed out, the "presence of pedagogy in human affairs introduces a cognitive gap that is not found in other animals. If the adult does not take the child in tow, making him the object of pedagogy, the child will never become an adult (in competence)" (p. 33). Vygotsky (1978, 1987) viewed the filling of this "cognitive gap" as the development of higher or uniquely human psychological processes. Although he was clearly interested in how these human forms of thinking developed phylogenetically and socioculturally, the main focus of his work was on the social origins and cultural bases of individual development (see Cole, this volume; Scribner, 1985). He argued that these higher psychological processes develop in children through enculturation into the practices of society; through the acquisition of society's technology, its signs and tools; through education in all its forms.

For Vygotsky, as Rivière (1984) has observed, schools (and other informal educational situations) represent the best "cultural laboratories" to study thinking: social settings specifically designed to modify thinking. He particularly emphasized

1

the *social organization of instruction,* writing about the "unique form of cooperation between the child and the adult that is the central element of the educational process," and how by this interactional process "knowledge is transferred to the child in a definite system" (Vygotsky, 1987, p. 169). Given Vygotsky's emphasis on the social context of thinking, the study of educational change has important theoretical and methodological significance within his approach: It represents the reorganization of a key social system, and associated modes of discourse, with potential consequences for developing new forms of thinking.

Vygotsky also emphasized educational change as a practical objective of his psychology. In part, this concern with the importance of practical change stemmed from his Marxist orientation. But perhaps more important, practical change was especially relevant in the context within which Vygotsky developed his work, that of the Russian Revolution and the serious problems confronting the country (see Blanck, this volume; Luria, 1978; Rosa & Montero, this volume; Valsiner, 1988; Wertsch, 1985a, 1985b). As Wertsch (1985a, p. 10) has noted, Vygotsky and his followers devoted their lives to ensuring that the new socialist state would succeed. Their primary, practical contribution was to develop concrete solutions to problems in education.

Additionally, however, as several authors have pointed out (e.g., Levitin, 1982; Rivière, 1984), Vygotsky was unusual because he was an educator turned psychologist. He was a teacher throughout his life, from his days as a youngster in Gomel to his professional activities at various pedagogical and psychological institutes. His writings clearly reflected his pedagogical concerns. Blanck (this volume; also see Rosa & Montero, this volume) points out that seven of Vygotsky's first eight writings on psychology (between 1922 and 1926) discussed problems in education such as methods of teaching literature, the use of translation in language comprehension, and the education of blind, deaf, retarded, and physically handicapped children. As his most celebrated collaborators, A. N. Leontiev and A. R. Luria (1968), observed, "Vygotskii demanded that psychology become more than a scientific study of education and go beyond abstract theoretical knowledge and intervene in human life and actively help in shaping it" (p. 367). A psychologist must be not only a thinker, they added, but a practitioner as well.

Curiously, despite the pedagogical emphasis in Vygotsky's theory and praxis, little of what has been written recently about Vygotsky is devoted to education and less still to empirical applications of Vygotsky's ideas (see, however, Hedegaard, Hakkarainen, & Engeström, 1984; Markova, 1979; Newman, Griffin, & Cole, 1989; Talyzina, 1981; Tharp & Gallimore, 1989).[2] Of these recent volumes, only two address contemporary issues of education in the United States (Newman, Griffin, & Cole; Tharp & Gallimore). Although several recent doctoral dissertations have highlighted Vygotsky's work, some related to education (e.g., Appel, 1986; Nunn, 1984; Zebroski, 1983), I found none that examined classroom teaching or applied Vygotsky's theory in instruction.

This volume is devoted to analyzing educational implications and applications of

Vygotsky's ideas as a means of bringing to light the relevance of Vygotskian concepts to education.[3] Bruner is right to insist that Vygotsky's theory of development is simultaneously a theory of education, but education, itself a sociohistorically determined activity (see Cole, this volume), has changed radically since Vygotsky's time (see Rosa & Montero, this volume). What does Vygotsky have to say about modern educational issues such as equity, achievement, literacy learning, computerization, and teacher training? In short, what does Vygotsky's approach have to offer education?

There are several ways of presenting a Vygotskian approach to education. Instead of providing a list of relevant concepts or issues, I have opted to discuss Vygotsky's most influential concept, the *zone of proximal development*. Not only is this concept of obvious relevance to education and already well known, but it is a "connecting" concept in Vygotskian theory. As Bruner (1987) put it, the zone of proximal development "serves to give connectedness to a wide range of Vygotsky's thought" (p. 4). I agree with Blanck (this volume) that the Vygotskian theoretical structure is a habitable building. But, as with any important building, it may need renovations and improvements, without altering significantly its classical structure. Through the present text we hope to make it a hospitable and accommodating building for educators as well.

The zone as a social system

The concept of the zone is usually introduced in relation to Vygotsky's concerns with instruction or psychological testing, or as part of a broader discussion of the relationship of learning and development (see Vygotsky, 1978, chap. 6). And, in fact, Vygotsky developed the concept of the zone, in part, as a critique and as an alternative to static, individual testing, namely IQ testing. He claimed that static measures assess mental functioning that has already matured, fossilized, to use Vygotsky's term (1978); maturing or developing mental functions must be fostered and assessed through collaborative, not independent or isolated activities. He emphasized that what children can perform collaboratively or with assistance today they can perform independently and competently tomorrow; as Cazden (1981) put it, the zone makes possible "performance before competence."

The problem with introducing the concept as such is that it not only leaves implicit the important relationship of the zone of proximal development to other Vygotskian ideas but starts, so to speak, in the middle of the story. Minick (1987a), for example, has identified three related but distinct phases in the development of Vygotsky's thought. The first phase emphasized sign-mediated activity, focusing primarily on individuals in experimental settings; the second phase concentrated on the development of interfunctional psychological systems and word meaning as a key unit of analysis; and the third phase highlighted the importance of situating individuals within specific social systems of interactions. Within this last phase, shortly preceding his death, Vygotsky proposed the concept of the zone of proximal development. Thus the zone must be thought of as more than a clever instructional heuristic; it is a key theoretical construct, capturing as it does the individual within the concrete social situation of learning and development. Valsiner (1988) has made a similar point; the basic message of the zone is the "interdependence of the process of child development and the socially provided resources for that development" (p. 145).

Minick (1987a) is careful to point out the continuity in Vygotsky's work. In a way, Vygotsky came full circle. His original arguments, those which established his prominence in the psychology of his time (see, e.g., Blanck, this volume; Rosa & Montero, this volume), had to do with the inseparability of consciousness and human (socially and culturally mediated) behavior. In particular, he criticized approaches that retained a conceptual isolation of mind and behavior, and much of his work can be understood as developing concepts and theories to overcome this chasm. After some important divergences, he returned in his later (and last) work, equipped with more sophisticated concepts, to address and integrate the analysis of psychological processes and social actions. Important for our purposes is that among his conceptual equipment Vygotsky now possessed a more detailed understanding of sign- and tool-mediated behaviors. This semiotic emphasis on the importance of sign use brings with it a focus on meaning as central to human activity (see, e.g., Bakhurst, 1986), a focus that is often lost in subsequent reformulations of the zone (Moll, 1989).

A careful reading of *Mind in Society* (1978) also reveals that the zone is an important extension of Vygotsky's "functional method of double stimulation" (pp. 74–75). Vygotsky set out to develop a general method of study that would be faithful to his theory. Particularly, he wanted to study the formation of psychological processes through the analysis of sign-mediated activity. He did not want to study processes (behaviors) that were fossilized; he wanted to study the formation of processes by analyzing the subjects engaging in activities.

The general logic of his method is what is of interest here. He would present the subjects with a task beyond their present capabilities, a task that could not be solved using existing skills or tools. An object (or several objects) would be introduced into the task to observe how, in what ways, the object became part of the problem-solving task. That is, he would offer the subjects a second set of stimuli in order to study how the subjects accomplished the task with the aid of new auxiliary means. As Valsiner (1988) has pointed out, the focus of "the observations of the child's problem-solving efforts is put on the child's construction of new means that can help to solve the problem and that restructure the whole task situation" (p. 137).

The emphasis, then, is on the child's active creation or use of new means to accomplish or to reorganize the experimental task. Vygotsky claimed that in contrast to traditional experiments his method supplied him with access to "hidden processes" that became manifest only in a subject's interactions with the environment. Valsiner (1988) put it as follows: "It is the observation of the process by which solution is reached that constitutes the Vygotskian equivalent of the 'dependent variable' in traditional psychological experiments'' (p. 137).

The concept of the zone of proximal development is an extension of this method into a new social domain, but the emphasis of making "hidden processes" visible is the same. Minick (1987b) has pointed out that Vygotsky was concerned "with the *qualitative* assessment of psychological processes and the dynamics of their development'' (p. 119, italics added). He was interested in identifying the *social* dynamics of change. Perhaps more important, the move from the "method of double stimulation" to the "zone of proximal development" represents, in my view, an important transition or transformation in the theory itself: a change of focus from sign-mediated to socially mediated activity. This transition added a real social context to the research: It shifted the emphasis from sign use to social practice and development. However, Vygotsky did not discard his emphasis on the importance of instruments. The concept of the zone of proximal development integrated social activity into the theory while retaining the significance of sign and tool mediation in understanding human learning and development.

In this transition in unit of study, from what Minick (1985) has called the individual-as-such to the individual-in-social-activity, it becomes clear that other aspects of the theory are not peripheral, isolated insights but that they form part of the coherent whole in Vygotsky's formulation. In what follows, I discuss three aspects of Vygotsky's theory that I believe essential to understanding his zone of proximal development and important in clarifying the contributions of his approach to education: holistic analysis, mediation, and change (for additional discussions, see del Rio & Alvarez, 1988; Gallimore & Tharp, this volume; Griffin & Cole, 1984; Hedegaard, this volume; Minick, 1985, 1987b; Moll, 1989; Palacios, 1987; Rogoff & Wertsch, 1984; Tudge, this volume; Valsiner, 1988; Wertsch, 1984, 1985a).

Holistic analysis

Vygotsky was a "critical" psychologist. He started his career as a psychologist by providing a strong, historical critique of what he called the "crisis" in psychology, the atomistic divisions of the field (see Blanck, this volume; Rosa & Montero, this volume). Bakhurst (1986) explains that there were three primary considerations in Vygotsky's critique: (1) Prevailing approaches, especially the stimulus–response model, conceived human behavior as simply reactive. (2) These approaches accepted the innateness of psychological faculties, or that children come into the world already equipped and that the social world simply elicits, does not create, what is already present. (3) These approaches represented reductionist approaches to psychology, assuming that the accumulation of primitive psychological mechanisms eventually constitute higher mental functions. All three points, addressing disparities in the field of psychology, are also an apt critique of contemporary educational practice. Consider the emphasis on teaching methods primarily characterized by "recitation" (Gallimore & Tharp, this volume), ability grouping (with its assumptions of innateness), the relative passivity in student learning, and the reductionist emphasis on developing "basic" skills (see, e.g., Goodlad, 1984; Oakes, 1986). From my perspective, a Vygotskian approach to education should advance, first of all, a critical view on current instructional practices.

Accordingly, in this section I want to elaborate on the last of Vygotsky's considerations, and among the most neglected aspects of his theory, particularly as it relates to instructional applications of his ideas: his warnings against atomistic, reductionist approaches (see Vygotsky, 1987, chaps. 1, 7). Vygotsky argued against reducing the phenomenon of interest into separate elements studied in isolation. He offered the following analogy:

> This mode of analysis can be compared with a chemical analysis of water in which water is decomposed into hydrogen and oxygen. The essential features of this form of analysis is that its products are of a different nature than the whole from which they are derived. The elements lack the characteristics inherent in the whole and they possess properties that it did not possess. When one approaches the problem of thinking and speech by decomposing it into its elements, one adopts the strategy of the man who resorts to the decomposition of water into hydrogen and oxygen in his search for a scientific explanation of the characteristics of water, its capacity to extinguish fire. . . . This man will discover, to his chagrin, that hydrogen burns and oxygen sustains combustion. He will never succeed in explaining the characteristics of the whole by analyzing the characteristics of its elements. (p. 45).[4]

Instead, Vygotsky insisted on the dialectical study of what we could call *whole activities*. For example, he wrote as follows:

> A psychology that decomposes verbal thinking into its elements in an attempt to explain its characteristics will search in vain for the unity that is characteristic of the whole. These characteristics are inherent in the phenomenon only as a unified whole. Therefore, when the whole is analyzed into its elements, these characteristics evaporate. In his attempt to reconstruct these characteristics, the investigator is left with no alternative but to search for external, mechanical forces of interaction between elements. (1987, p. 45)

Vygotsky proposed partitioning the whole into what he called units (see Vygotsky, 1988; Wertsch, 1985a, chap. 7). In contrast to atomistic elements, units designated a product of analysis that contained all the basic characteristics of the whole. The unit, then, is an irreducible part of the whole. As Bakhurst (1986) has suggested, paraphrasing Vygotsky (1987, p. 46), in the "water analogy the H_2O molecule, and not the properties of hydrogen and oxygen considered separately, should be taken as the unit of analysis when attempting to explain water's propensity to extinguish fire" (p. 110). In short, Vygotsky rejected artificial divisions and abstractions and insisted on what we would call a holistic approach: The unit of study must be psychological activity in all its complexity, not in isolation. Wertsch (1985a) has noted that the unit of study "could not be derived through artificial divisions or abstractions of real psychological activity. It had to be a microcosm of the complex interfunctional processes that characterize actual psychological activity" (p. 185).

Vygotsky (1987, chaps. 6, 7) proposed the *meaning* of the word as a key unit of study, reflecting the unity of thinking and speech; or, as he stated, "word meaning is a unity of both processes that cannot be further decomposed" (p. 244). Word meaning was a pivotal concept through which to study the internal relations of speech and thinking. But as Bakhurst (1986) explains, Vygotsky's proposal of word meaning as a key unit of study is a hypothesis based on the proposition that meaning is a necessary condition for both thinking and speech. The selection of word meaning is "neither given nor is it backed by any logical guarantee. The selection will be vindicated only by the degree to which it contributes to the explanatory power of the genetic account of which it will be a crucial part" (p. 112). Without entering into a debate on the merits of Vygotsky's proposal regarding word meaning (see Wertsch, 1985a, chap. 7), it is important to note that the search for meaning and significance plays a prominent role in Vygotsky's theorizing, particularly in his ontogenetic account. Aside from his analysis of speech and thinking, Vygotsky's writings (1978) on the development of perception in children, the cognitive uses of signs and tools, the development of writing, and play all highlight the role of meaning and significance.

How can we relate these views on holism and meaning to the concept of the zone of proximal development? Griffin and Cole (1984), for example, have suggested that "English-speaking scholars interpret the concept more narrowly than Vygotsky intended, robbing it of some of its potential for enabling us to understand the social genesis of human cognitive processes and the process of teaching and learning in particular" (p. 45). Our work also suggests that to enhance a critique of instruction and develop feasible strategies for educational change we must surpass current definitions and uses of the zone (Moll, 1989; Moll & Greenberg, this volume; see also Gallimore & Tharp, this volume; Hedegaard, this volume; Tudge, this volume). One way is to reject conceptualizing the zone as the teaching or assessment of discrete, separable, skills and subskills. For example, a problem in applying the concept of the zone to the analysis of classroom instruction is that a definition of the zone emphasizing the transfer of knowledge, and especially of skills, by those knowing more to those knowing less, may characterize virtually any instructional practice. Consider the following three characteristics of the zone as usually presented. The zone is:

1. Establishing a level of difficulty. This level, assumed to be the proximal level, must be a bit challenging for the student but not too difficult.
2. Providing assisted performance. The adult provides guided practice to the child with a clear sense of the goal or outcome of the child's performance.
3. Evaluating independent performance. The most logical outcome of a zone of proximal development is the child performing independently.

It is misleading to assume that classroom activities containing these three characteristics represent zones of proximal development. For example, it seems reasonable to go from Vygotsky's basic definition and discussion of the zone to believing that the rote drill-and-practice instruction offered working-class students (see, e.g.,

Anyon, 1980) is an acceptable example of a zone of proximal development. After all, drill-and-practice instruction is usually meant to provide students with help in developing skills they do not have and the end result is often some individual evaluation or test of learning. The same could be said about the atomistic, skills-based practices that characterize most classroom instruction (see, e.g., Goodlad, 1984). This reductionism is hardly what Vygotsky had in mind. Clearly, standard instructional practices do not represent what Vygotsky meant by a zone of proximal development (also see Engeström, Hakkarainen, & Hedegaard, 1984; Henderson, 1986).

Cole and Griffin (1983) have pointed out that, from a Vygotskian or sociohistorical perspective,

> we should be trying to instantiate a basic *activity* when teaching reading and not get blinded by the basic *skills*. Skills are always part of activities and settings, but they only take on meaning in terms of how they are organized. So, instead of basic skills, a socio-historical approach talks about *basic activities* and instantiates those that are necessary and sufficient to carry out the whole process of reading in the general conditions of learning. (p. 73, italics in original)

The same point applies to the teaching of writing or other subject matter (see, e.g., Brown, Collins, & Duguid, 1989; Hedegaard, this volume; McLane, this volume; McNamee, this volume; Moll & Greenberg, this volume; Rueda, this volume). By focusing on isolated skills and subskills, the essence of reading and writing, or of mathematics, as a "whole activity" evaporates, to use Vygotsky's metaphor.

It is easy to miss this point when applying the concept of the zone to the study of classroom instruction because a "skills" perspective is so pervasive that, as Edelsky (1986, 1989) has pointed out, it is taken for granted that reading and writing skills and subskills are accurate or authentic instantiations of literacy. Perhaps no other researchers have been as concerned with "authentic" or socially meaningful educational activities as those associated with a "whole-language" approach (see, e.g., Goodman & Goodman, this volume). For example, central to this approach is a view of literacy as the understanding and communication of meaning. Consequently, whole-language educators emphasize that reading comprehension and written expression must be developed through functional, relevant, and meaningful uses of language. One of their major instructional recommendations is to make classrooms literate environments in which many language experiences can take place and different types of "literacies" can be developed and learned. Teachers who follow this approach reject rote instruction or reducing reading and writing into skill sequences taught in isolation or in a successive, stagelike manner. Rather, they emphasize the creation of social contexts in which children actively learn to use, try, and manipulate language in the service of making sense or creating meaning. As Goodman, Smith, Meredith, and Goodman (1987) put it: "Oral language is learned holistically in the context of speech acts; written language is learned holistically in the context of literacy events" (p. 398).

These "events" consist of a series of interrelated but diverse learning activities, usually organized around a specific theme or topic. The role of the teacher in these social contexts is to provide the necessary guidance, mediations, in a Vygotskian sense, so that children, through their own efforts, assume full control of diverse purposes and uses of oral and written language.[5] In these classrooms reading and writing occurs in many ways, usually integrated as part of a broader activity; for example, children read individually, they are read to, or they read and write to prepare a report, write for fun, or write in journals and logs. The topics and activities are very often of the children's own choosing. Each of these activities also represents a social situation where teachers can assess children's performance, the type of help they need; and whether the children are taking over the activity, making it their own (Moll, 1988, 1989). What Goodman et al. (1987; Goodman & Goodman, this volume; see also Brown et al., 1989) refer to as events or "authentic," meaningful activities represent, in my view, an appropriate holistic unit of study for understanding and applying the concept of the zone of proximal development to instruction.

Mediation

"The central fact about our psychology," Vygotsky wrote, "is the fact of mediation" (1982, p. 116, cited in Wertsch, 1985a, p. 15). Especially in his analysis of formal instruction, Vygotsky placed great emphasis on the nature of social interactions, particularly between adult and child. As mentioned earlier, he wrote about the forms of cooperation central to instruction and how knowledge is transferred to the child "in a definite system" (Vygotsky, 1987, p. 169). By a "definite system," Vygotsky referred to the social organization of instruction and how it provided a special socialization of children's thinking. In particular, he emphasized two characteristics of instruction. One was the development of conscious awareness and voluntary control of knowledge, which he thought of primarily as a product of instruction. He illustrated the importance of voluntary control by differentiating between what he called "scientific" and "everyday" concepts (see Gallimore & Tharp, this volume; Hedegaard, this volume; Martin, this volume; Panofsky, John-Steiner, & Blackwell, this volume; Vygotsky, 1987, chaps. 5, 6). The key difference is that scientific concepts (e.g., mammals and reptiles), as compared to everyday concepts (e.g., boats and cars), are systematic; that is, they form part of and are acquired through a system of formal instruction. As such, Gallimore and Tharp (this volume; also see Wertsch, this volume) have called them "schooled" concepts, because they arise through the social institution of schooling. According to Vygotsky (1987), the strength of scientific concepts is in the child's capacity (developed through instruction) to use these concepts voluntarily, what he called their "readiness for action" (p. 169; cf. Au, this volume). In contrast, the weakness of everyday concepts is the child's incapacity to manipulate them in a voluntary manner, their lack of systematicity.

In particular, Vygotsky concentrated on the manipulation of language as an important characteristic of formal schooling and of the development of scientific concepts. As Minick (1987b) has written, Vygotsky felt that formal instruction in writing and grammar, for instance, by refocusing attention from the content of communication to the means of communication, provided the foundations for the development of conscious awareness of important aspects of speech and language. Although both everyday and scientific concepts develop in communication, one out of school and one in school, schooled discourse represents a qualitatively different form of communication because words act not only as means of communication, as they would in everyday discourse, but as the object of study. In classroom interactions, the teacher directs the children's attention to word meanings and definitions and the systematic relationships among them that constitute an organized system of knowledge. Formal instruction, with its special organization and discourse, through its social and semiotic mediations, helps develop a general, self-contained system of words and their relationships (see Gallimore & Tharp, this volume). Through formal instruction, children develop the capacity to manipulate consciously this symbolic system.

Vygotsky also emphasized that everyday and scientific concepts are interconnected and interdependent; their development is mutually influential. One cannot exist without the other. It is through the use of everyday concepts that children make sense of the definitions and explanations of scientific concepts; everyday concepts provide the "living knowledge" for the development of scientific concepts. That is, everyday concepts *mediate* the acquisition of scientific concepts. However, Vygotsky (1987) proposed that everyday concepts also become dependent on, are mediated and transformed by the scientific concepts; they become the "gate" through which conscious awareness and control enter the domain of the everyday concepts (p. 193). Thus, he wrote, scientific concepts grow down into the everyday, into the domain of personal experience, acquiring meaning and significance, and in so doing "blaze the trail for the development of everyday concepts" upward toward the scientific and facilitate "mastery of the higher characteristics of the everyday concepts" (p. 219).

In this formulation of the consequences of schooling, Vygotsky introduced a more expansive notion of the zone of proximal development. For one, he highlighted the importance of everyday activities and content in providing meaning, the "conceptual fabric" for the development of schooled concepts. To make schooling significant one must go beyond the classroom walls, beyond empty verbalisms; school knowledge grows into the analysis of the everyday. And, in an almost Freirean sense, Vygotsky proposed that the children's perception and use of everyday concepts is transformed by interacting with schooled concepts; everyday concepts now form part of a system of knowledge, acquiring conscious awareness and control.

Ironically, little of what Vygotsky described as key psychological characteristics of schooling, development of conscious awareness and volition into various conceptual domains of life, forms part of contemporary schooling. In fact, little of what he called "living knowledge" enters the classroom, much less forms the basis for the acquisition and development of schooled concepts. Formal schooling, as alluded to in the previous section, is characterized by forms of discourse called by Gallimore and Tharp (this volume) a "recitation" script. Students generally sit silently, follow directions, read assigned texts, fill out work sheets, and take tests. Little dialogue or interactive teaching, as would characterize a zone of proximal development, forms part of the routines of schooling. This situation is exacerbated in working-class classrooms, where instruction is typified by rote practices (Anyon, 1980; Oakes, 1986). Interestingly, according to Davydov (1988), instead of "active" teaching methods, "passive" practices also characterize formal instruction in the Soviet Union; the "main method of instruction is the *illustration-explanation method,* or, alternatively, the *receptive-reproductive method,* which is thoroughly evident in teaching methods" (p. 31, italics in original).

We should note, however, that Vygotsky never specified the forms of social assistance to learners that constitute a zone of proximal development (Wertsch, 1984; Minick, 1987b). He wrote about collaboration and direction, and about assisting children "through demonstration, leading questions, and by introducing the initial elements of the task's solution" (Vygotsky, 1987, p. 209), but did not specify beyond those general prescriptions. Nevertheless, he considered what we would now call the characteristics of classroom discourse (see Cazden, 1988) as central to his analysis. Vygotsky (1981) claimed that the intellectual skills children acquire are directly related to *how* they interact with others in specific problem-solving environments. He posited that children internalize and *transform* the help they receive from others and eventually use these same means of guidance to direct their subsequent problem-solving behaviors (Díaz, Neal, & Amaya-Williams, this volume). Therefore, the nature of social transactions is central to a zone of proximal development analysis (Moll, 1989; Tudge, this volume).

The above suggests that we should think of the zone as a characteristic not solely of the child or of the teaching but of the child engaged in collaborative activity within specific social environments. The focus is on the *social system* within which we hope children learn, with the understanding that this social system is mutually and actively created by teacher and students. This interdependence of adult and child is central to a Vygotskian analysis of instruction.

Vygotsky also emphasized that social interactions are themselves mediated through auxiliary means (most prominently by speech). These auxiliary means, Leontiev and Luria (1968) have pointed out, were regarded by Vygotsky not only as aids developed historically to mediate relationships with society (see Cole, this volume) or reflections of the external world but as "main means of mastering psychological processes that have a decisive influence on the formation of man's psychological activity" (p. 342). These means, they added, always pack cognitive significance and meaning. Humans use cultural signs and tools (e.g., speech, literacy, mathematics) to mediate their interactions with each other and with their surroundings. A fundamental property of these artifacts, Vygotsky observed, is that they are social in origin; they are used first to communicate with others, to mediate contact with our social worlds; later, with practice, much of it occurring in schools, these arti-facts come to mediate our interactions with self; to help us think, we internalize their use (see, e.g., Vygotsky, 1978, chaps. 1–4; Wertsch, 1985a, chaps. 2–4; Wertsch, this volume).

Therefore, from a Vygotskian perspective, a major role of schooling is to create social contexts (zones of proximal development) for mastery of and conscious awareness in the use of these cultural tools. It is by mastering these technologies of representation and communication (Olson, 1986) that individuals acquire the capac-ity, the means, for "higher-order" intellectual activity. Thus Vygotskian theory posits a strong, dialectic connection between external (i.e., social and, as we noted above, extracurricular) practical activity mediated by cultural tools, such as speech and writing, and individuals' intellectual activity. As Wertsch (1985a) has written, Vygotsky "defined external activity in terms of semiotically mediated social pro-cesses and argued that the properties of these processes provide the key to under-standing the emergence of internal functioning" (p. 62).

Change

A major theme of Vygotsky's approach is a reliance on a genetic or developmental analysis, the claim that psychological processes must be studied in transition (Cole & Scribner, 1978; Vygotsky, 1978; Wertsch, 1985a). As Wertsch (1985a) explains it, "Vygotsky's major focus in genetic analysis was on developmental processes as they normally occur, but he also examined the effects of disruption and interven-tions" (p. 18). These disruptions and interventions are what is of interest here. That is, a Vygotskian approach to education must not only analyze teaching and learning as part of extant instructional practices but create fundamentally new, advanced instructional activities; in other words, produce learning by facilitating new forms of mediation.

Change within a zone of proximal development is usually characterized as indi-vidual change, that the child can do something independently today that she or he could do only with assistance yesterday. It is, in part, Vygotsky's examples that have led to this formulation. He wrote: "What lies in the zone of proximal devel-opment at one stage is realized and moves to the level of actual development at a second. In other words, what the child is able to do in collaboration today he will be able to do independently tomorrow" (Vygotsky, 1987, p. 211).

The essence of the zone of proximal development concept, however, is the qual-itatively different perspective one gets by contrasting students' performance alone with their performance in collaborative activity. Vygotsky also used the zone to emphasize the importance of social conditions in understanding thinking and its development (Vygotsky, 1978, 1987; Wertsch, 1985a). Hence, he viewed thinking as a characteristic not of the child only but of the child-in-social-activities with others (Minick, 1985). In terms of classroom learning, as mentioned above, Vy-gotsky specifically emphasized the relationship between thinking and the social or-ganization of instruction. That is why the zone of proximal development, beyond a practical heuristic, is also of great theoretical interest: It provides a unit of study that integrates dynamically the individual and the social environment.

I want to suggest, based on Vygotsky's qualitative emphasis, on factors discussed in the previous sections, and on the work presented in this volume, a different perspective of change within the zone of proximal development. The focus would be on the appropriation and mastery of mediational means, such as writing, assessed not only or necessarily through independent performance after guided practice but by the ability of children to participate in qualitatively new collaborative activities (for examples, see Moll, 1989; cf. Minick, 1985, pp. 252–253). The focus, therefore, is not on transferring skills, as such, from those who know more to those who know less but on the collaborative use of mediational means to create, obtain, and communicate meaning (see Clay & Cazden, this volume; Goodman & Goodman, this volume; McLane, this volume; McNamee, this volume; Rueda, this volume). The role of the adult is not necessarily to provide structured cues but, through exploratory talk and other social mediations such as importing everyday activities into the classrooms, to assist children in appropriating or taking control of their own learning (see Au, this volume; Hedegaard, this volume; Martin, this volume; Moll & Greenberg, this volume). The goal is to make children consciously aware of how they are manipulating the literacy process and applying this knowledge to reorganize future experiences or activities.

An example is in order. Here I borrow from recently published work analyzing the classroom instruction of outstanding teachers of Hispanic students (Moll, 1988, 1989). The most prominent characteristic of these classrooms was not the teaching of specific skills but the constant emphasis on creating meaning. In our terms, developing meaning was the key barometer to movement in the zone. The teachers ensured that making meaning permeated every instructional activity in these classrooms, regardless of topic or the children's level of bilingualism.

These teachers always made comprehension the goal of reading, including helping the students analyze the author's writing. As part of their questioning, the teachers helped the students examine the writer's strategies and the relationship of these strategies to the reading process: for example, how we interpret what we are reading, our feelings about the characters and why, predictions about the unfolding events in a story, and how writers utilize descriptions or dialogue to influence readers. Consider the following example from a fifth-grade classroom (from Moll, 1989). The story the group was reading was about a panther that kills a boy's (Lonny's) dog. The teacher asked the group to predict what would happen next:

1. Mary: I think Lonny is going to kill the cat.
2. John: I think Lonny is not going to kill the cat. . . .
3. Barb: The reason why he is not going to kill the cat is because she has babies.
4. Juan: I think that he is going to kill the panther and his dad is going to help him.
(Other children give their opinion of whether Lonny is going to kill the panther.)
5. Teacher (*interrupting*): I just want to explain what we just did in the group.

The teacher points out that Mary (the first student to respond) offered the prediction that the panther will be killed, and others shared their ideas on what might happen to the panther. She then emphasized to the students that, as readers, we are always predicting.

The lesson continued with the teacher asking, "We have been predicting what will happen; how about anything else? About the author or something that struck you about the story?" Roberto raised his hand and explained that he enjoyed the author's description of the dog's death because he could "see" exactly how it happened and "see" the wound in the dog. Manuel said that he could feel the sadness because the author described how Lonny's tears were dropping on the dog's body.

This teacher not only helped children become consciously aware of the writer's strategies but encouraged the children to develop their own strategies and use strategies from other authors to develop their own writing. For instance, the teacher asked the students to share what they were writing (the students wrote daily), an activity that was part of the students' writing routines. Two students, Lisa and Ernesto, volunteered. The rest of the class moved to the front of the room to listen to them. The teacher asked Lisa to read but first verified that Lisa understood the process: "Why are you doing this?" Lisa responded, "To see if it [the story she had written] is OK." Lisa read a fairly lengthy story, and when she finished the teacher asked the audience, "What worked well?" Some of the students responded that Lisa let them know her characters by providing a physical description and used the dialogue to describe the characters' thoughts. Another student pointed out that Lisa began her story with "The bus was coming . . . ," a more interesting beginning than the typical "Once upon a time . . ." Another student noted that by having the story's characters use different languages (Spanish and English) Lisa interested her readers and defined her characters.

The children in this class were used to reflecting and commenting on writing by pointing out strategies used by authors, including themselves. In a Vygotskian sense, these children had "internalized" ways of using and analyzing language. They had made this knowledge their own and were able to "reapply" this knowledge in various activities: to shape their own and their peers' writing, to make sense of text, or simply to derive more enjoyment from literacy.

The emphasis in these lessons, then, was not on transmitting knowledge or skills in prepackaged forms in the hope that these skills would be internalized in the form transmitted; the emphasis was on joint literacy activities mediated by the teacher intended to help children obtain and express meaning in ways that would enable them to make this knowledge and meaning their own (Moll, 1989; also see Clay & Cazden, this volume; Goodman & Goodman, this volume; McLane, this volume; McNamee, this volume; Rueda, this volume). In such a teaching system, within these zones of proximal development, children develop what Bruner (1986) calls "reflective intervention" in the knowledge encountered: the ability to control select knowledge as needed (p. 132).

This perspective is consistent with what Vygotsky (1987, chap. 6) felt was the essential characteristic of school instruction: the introduction of conscious awareness into many domains of activity; that is, children acquiring control and mastery of psychological processes through the manipulation of tools of thinking such as reading and writing. As Bruner (1986, p. 132) has put it, it is this "loan of consciousness" that gets children through the zone of proximal development.

Summary

Vygotsky's primary contribution was in developing a general approach that brought education, as a fundamental human activity, fully into a theory of psychological development. Human pedagogy, in all its forms, is the defining characteristic of his approach, the central concept in his system. And as part of his approach he provided the necessary theoretical concepts, the instruments with which to apply and elaborate his insights in practice.

I concentrated in this Introduction on developing some ideas about the zone of proximal development because, as a "connecting" concept in Vygotsky's theory, it embodies or integrates key elements of the theory: the emphasis on social activity and cultural practice as sources of thinking, the importance of mediation in human psychological functioning, the centrality of pedagogy in development, and the inseparability of the individual from the social. The concept of the zone posits active individuals as the object of study, with all the complexities that such a unit of study implies. As Minick (1985) has written: "To study psychological characteristics within this framework is to study the kinds of social activities that the individual can and does engage in and to study the psychological characteristics that emerge in the individual when he or she is engaged in those actions" (p. 286).

Applied to the study of education, this focus means the need to study how current educational practices constrain or facilitate thinking, and the need to create new, more advanced, amplifying practices for the teachers and children with whom we work. Many examples are provided in the present volume. The power of Vygotsky's ideas is that they represent a theory of possibilities. The construct of the zone of proximal development reminds us that there is nothing "natural" about educational settings (and about educational practices such as ability groupings, tracking, and other forms of stratification). These settings are social creations; they are socially constituted, and they can be socially changed. It warns us how easy it is to underestimate children's and teachers' abilities when we analyze them in isolation, in highly constrained environments, or in less than favorable circumstances. And it points to the use of social and cultural resources that represent our primary tools, as human beings, for mediating and promoting change.

The organization of this book

This volume is divided into three parts. Part I is devoted to historical and theoretical issues, including an attempt to place Vygotsky himself, his societal context, and his theory in historical perspective. A general theme of the chapters is that, if the full potential of a Vygotskian approach to education is to be fulfilled, one must not only consider the theoretical particulars, the individual concepts, but grasp Vygotsky's general approach, what Bakhurst (1986) called Vygotsky's "unified theoretical vision." It is also by understanding his theory as an "integral whole" that we can assimilate critically and correctly into the theory insights from other researchers and approaches.

Guillermo Blanck begins the volume with a biographical account of Vygotsky and a summary of his theory. We learn, for example, of Vygotsky's early socialization, his parents' emphasis on scholarly matters, his multilingualism, and his affinity for literature and art. We also learn about his early schooling, consisting primarily of individual tutoring that Blanck speculates might have been the source for his subsequent pedagogical ideas, such as the zone of proximal development. In summarizing the theory, Blanck points out the ambitiousness of Vygotsky's theoretical work: creating a unified psychology; a General Psychology that would provide a common methodological guide for the various psychological disciplines. And Blanck argues that Vygotsky was quite successful, his theory being much more than isolated insights or an incomplete attempt at a sociohistorical account of mind. Instead, it is a formidable and coherent formulation of a conscious program to develop a sociohistorical psychology. As Blanck writes: "Although Vygotsky's ideas did not constitute a perfect corpus, neither are they limited to being simply the beginnings of an approach. . . . The sociohistorical-cultural psychological theory is a satisfactorily habitable building, constructed on the work of Vygotsky himself." Its power, Blanck suggests, is in how it may fulfill Vygotsky's original program of providing an integrated, general science of thinking and human development.

Alberto Rosa and Ignacio Montero present a historical analysis of Vygotsky's work. Borrowing concepts from historians and philosophers of science, they analyze the consequences of the extremely complex, stimulating, and often disastrous social and political circumstances under which Vygotsky lived and worked. As the authors point out, "this period gave rise to scientific contributions of great interest, one of which was that of the Vygotskian school of psychology, at the same time both fruit and victim of the convulsive history of Russia during this century." As does Blanck, these authors suggest that we should not get lost in the particulars, the tip of the iceberg, and lose sight of Vygotsky's broader goal of developing a general theory of psychology. The Vygotskian approach, they conclude, holds enormous potential for furthering our knowledge about psychology and education and for the transformation of individuals and the social contexts within which they develop.

Michael Cole presents a framework for understanding formal education based on Vygotsky's historical emphases. He outlines basic postulates of the sociohistorical school, highlighting the special role of cross-cultural research in the development of the theory. In particular, he emphasizes that central to the theory, as well as central to the study of education, is taking into account changes occurring simultaneously at four historical levels: phylogeny, social history, ontogeny, and microgenesis. Cole then examines the cross-cultural evidence for the cognitive consequences of schooling and suggests caution in attributing to schooling a causal role in producing general cognitive effects on students. In his words, "I am unimpressed by the possibility that the specific cognitive strategies necessary for mastery of the curriculum have wide applicability across contexts, or that children master meta-cognitive abilities in school that transfer broadly." He argues, instead, that the consequences of schooling must be understood in relation to the distinctive social and historical features of educational activity, including the concrete instructional practices that make up the schooling experience.

James Wertsch discusses the theoretical advantages of combining the insights of Vygotsky, especially those having to do with the semiotic mediation of human activity, with those of the Soviet linguist M. M. Bakhtin. As do other authors in this volume, Wertsch emphasizes issues that integrate rather than isolate scholarly orientations. He proposes using Bakhtin's ideas on dialogic speech activity, such as "social speech types" and "voice," in elaborating the Vygotskian notion about the critical role of human communication in developing thinking, particularly in schooling contexts. In this respect, Wertsch discusses the emergence of what he calls the voice of "decontextualized rationality," the representation of objects and events in terms of formal (abstract) categories, and the prominence of this social speech type in formal schooling. Why has this specific voice been privileged in particular contexts, most prominently schools, even when other forms of representation would do equally well or better? The answer to this question, Wertsch suggests, cannot be found in psychological factors alone. "Instead," he writes, "it is at this point that psychologists interested in a sociocultural approach to mind must turn to analyses of institutional and cultural factors." To accomplish this broader analysis, psychologists need to surpass the confines of their discipline, as Vygotsky did, to search for interdisciplinary collaborations that help make a link between institutional, historical, and cultural factors and individual mental functioning. Wertsch proposes that combining Vygotsky's and Bakhtin's insights represents one such possible, fruitful collaboration that may extend in new ways the notion of semiotic mediation while retaining the advantages of a Vygotskian approach.

Rafael Díaz, Cynthia Neal, and Marina Amaya-Williams review the literature and present their recent empirical research on self-regulation, the child's ability to plan and regulate his or her own actions. The social development of this capacity is a key Vygotskian postulate, as it implies the use and internalization of speech, a major aspect of Vygotsky's theory (see Vygotsky, 1987). The authors set out to clarify the concept of self-regulation, particularly in contrast to the related concept of self-control, and to specify some social-interactional strategies that encourage and facilitate its development. Díaz and his colleagues propose that differences in self-regulatory capacity can be traced to differences in the quality of caregiver–child interactions. Their review reveals considerable work in related areas such as parenting styles and training studies of private speech. Few if any of the studies, however, have examined directly specific teaching strategies that facilitate children's use of self-regulatory language. The training studies involved a variety of procedures, including modeling and rehearsal, and have yielded positive results within experimental situations, but these results have seldom generalized elsewhere. The authors' own research extends the previous work and is based firmly on Vygotsky's and Luria's theoretical formulations, especially on a more elaborate understanding of the notion of internalization. Their work found a weak relationship between maternal talk and children's independent verbalizations but a strong positive relationship between what they called "relinquishing strategies" (less maternal physical and verbal control of the task, more conceptual questions) and the child's self-regulations. In brief, the key factor in facilitating self-regulation was a shift in the active control of the activity from mother to child. As the authors put it, "The most exciting finding was that the relinquishing factor . . . was significant and positively correlated to the child's takeover of the regulatory role." This finding, we should add, contradicts most classroom instructional practices, which are predicated on teacher control and manipulation of tasks and activities.

Jonathan Tudge presents his research on peer collaboration and discusses it in terms of Vygotsky's concept of the zone of proximal development. He points out that much of the research on the zone is limited to the examination of adult–child interactions and that implicit in this work is a certain unidirectional conception of development that assumes that participation in the zone invariably leads children to acquire more advanced, adult-sanctioned practices. Tudge suggests a more dynamic and context-specific conception: "Vygotsky's theory may be more compatible with a conception of a zone that extends not solely in advance of children but all around them, so that in different circumstances they can be led either to develop or to regress in their thinking, depending on the nature of their social interactions." The author presents a series of studies on peer collaboration in which children predict the working of a mathematical balance beam. By combining "more competent" with "less competent" peers, Tudge shows how, depending on the specific characteristics of the participants and task, children either progress or regress in their learning. Several factors are highlighted: the children's confidence in their knowledge, their reasoning, and the role of feedback in facilitating learning. Tudge's suggestions are important for educators: Simply facilitating peer interactions or pairing less and more competent students may be insufficient in promoting learning. We must pay more attention to the process of collaboration and the specific conditions that may help some but hinder others.

Part II presents chapters based on the analysis of classroom practices, including "neo-Vygotskian" interpretations of major innovations, such as the Kamehameha Early Education Project (KEEP), Reading Recovery, and the whole-language approach. As such, this work may be characterized as research *on* practice; the effort is to analyze existing systems from a Vygotskian perspective to draw implications for the delivery of instruction and for clarifying and developing the theory.

Ronald Gallimore and Roland Tharp start by presenting a "neo-Vygotskian" interpretation and extension of the well-known Kamehameha Early Education Project. KEEP has rightfully earned praise as a highly successful educational innovation. In the present chapter, the authors propose no less than a theory-driven system for the redesign and reformulation of schools. Central to this reformulation is the Vygotskian concept of assisted performance, prominent in his notion of the zone of proximal development, as well as other related ideas such as the development of activity settings, internalization, and the role of speech in thinking. The authors also borrow from other psychological concepts, such as feedback and contingency management, to propose an expanded model of progression through the zone of proximal development as constituted by stages ranging from assisted performance, to self-assisted behavior, to internalization and automatization, and a final recursiveness through previous stages when needed to enhance performance. Their model of schooling would incorporate these mechanisms for learning at all levels of the system: "One of the duties of each individual in a school system should be to assist the performance of the person next down the line: The superintendent assists the principal, the principal assists the teacher, the teacher assists the pupil. It is surely reasonable that the central responsibility of the teaching organization should be providing assistance for the performance of each member." Gallimore and Tharp provide multiple examples of the application of their far-reaching ideas in developing instruction and, in particular, in developing a social environment for the support and enhancement of teaching in schools.

Marie Clay and Courtney Cazden analyze various elements of the successful tutorial program, Reading Recovery. Reading Recovery is a systematic, integrated, reading and writing program for students who have experienced difficulty with literacy learning in their first year of schooling. Its main characteristic is that the children, with the deliberate and planned assistance of the teacher, develop strategies to become active, conscious, interactants with text. As the authors put it, "the teacher creates a lesson format, a scaffold, within which she promotes emerging skill, allows for the child to work with the familiar, introduces the unfamiliar in a measured way, and deals constructively with slips and errors." The goal is to coax and guide children into independent, constructive activity, for children to acquire and develop a self-improving system of reading and writing. As the authors discuss, the Reading Recovery system represents an instantiation of several Vygotskian principles: for example, the use of symbols, and text, as mediating devices; conscious realization and control of literate activity; assisted performance; and a combining of instruction and diagnosis. The authors also present examples that illustrate the types of social interactions that make up Reading Recovery and show how the system facilitates the development of new cognitive activities in the child.

Yetta and Kenneth Goodman present a description of the "whole-language" teaching philosophy, relating and contrasting it to a Vygotskian approach. In fact, as they explain it, whole-language approaches are based partly on Vygotsky's ideas, particularly his notions about the role of language in thinking and the importance of social interaction in learning. Throughout the chapter the Goodmans describe specific aspects of their approach and explain how their key concepts are related to Vygotsky's ideas and to the work of other researchers, such as Halliday, Dewey, and Piaget. There are many similarities between whole language and a Vygotskian perspective: the importance of developing "authentic" reading and writing opportunities for children, the centrality of social transactions in learning, the role of play in development, and the role of teachers as mediators of learning, to name a few. There are also differences; the Goodmans disagree with Vygotsky's dichotomy of spontaneous and scientific learning, considering this differentiation unnecessarily exaggerated. There is also their perspective that teachers cannot control or create zones of proximal development. The Goodmans' view is more child-centered: The role of the teacher is not to create zones but to observe learners insightfully in order to facilitate conditions that will let learners exhibit and make the most use of their zones of proximal development. In their words: "In defining themselves as mediators, whole-language teachers understand that less can be more. They realize that helping a learner solve a problem is better than giving him or her an algorithm or a solution. In reading and writing, teachers interfere as little as possible between the text and the reader. Teachers mediate by asking a question here, offering a useful hint there, directing attention at an anomaly, calling attention to overlooked information, and supporting learners as they synthesize what they are learning into new concepts and schemas. They provide just enough support to help the learner make the most of his or her own zone of proximal development."

Carolyn Panofsky, Vera John-Steiner, and Peggy Blackwell examine empirically Vygotsky's notions of the development of scientific and spontaneous concepts. They begin their chapter by defining the concepts and by contrasting Piaget's similar but more internally oriented notions with Vygotsky's socially and culturally oriented emphasis. They were particularly interested in examining the process of interweaving or relating the two concepts because it is central to understanding the concepts and Vygotsky's use of them. This process is characterized by the development of intermediate concepts as a stage in the acquisition of scientific concepts. To analyze this process they introduced two experimental activities as classroom lessons, a concept-sorting task and a film-retelling task. Their results highlight, among other factors, the fluidity of the children's use of concepts: "Children appear to have different ways of mixing concepts, but all of these have a kind of explanatory power for the child. Such mixtures are not just stopping points on the way to acquiring the adult and mature form. Rather, they reflect an active and frequently creative exploration by the child looking for the way things are connected." The authors conclude with suggestions for teaching and emphasize that exploring children's thinking provides teachers with valuable information that will help them assist the children's development of conceptual thinking.

Part III is devoted to original research applying Vygotskian concepts in practice. The studies, attempts to change instruction based on Vygotsky's theoretical concepts, address several topics, including teacher training, combining community resources with teaching, and using technology in instruction. All of the studies highlight the complex mediating role of teachers in structuring situations within which children can advance their learning.

Kathryn Au begins Part III with a case study of the transformation of a novice teacher into an expert teacher, In particular, Au concentrates on depicting the relationship between the development of the teacher's knowledge of practice and changes in her thinking. The author traced this development through data gathered in a series of meetings with the teacher, the analysis of videotapes collected in the teacher's classroom and of a "master teacher" at work. Au applied, and elaborated, three of Vygotsky's formulations in her analysis: the relationship between spontaneous and scientific concepts, the role of speech in thinking, and the development of consciousness. Although usually used to analyze instruction aimed at children, Au shows how these concepts are equally relevant and useful in understanding changes in adult thinking. She writes: "The results of this study suggest that the development of practical knowledge of teaching is an intellectually demanding process. Vygotsky's work provides a theoretical framework that allows researchers to acknowledge and deal with these complexities while still seeking general principles of development."

Gillian Dowley McNamee describes research based on her long-term involvement with teachers, students, and parents of an inner-city preschool. She reports on her attempts, in close collaboration with teachers and parents, to develop literacy activities that take full advantage of the children's language, experiences, and social relations. Influenced by Vygotsky's writings on the role of play in development and in literacy learning, McNamee helped develop the preschool into a supportive social context for the sharing of ideas, storytelling, and the reading of books. She emphasizes the importance, and the difficulties, of creating a truly joint, collaborative venture among all participants: "The challenge for establishing a [zone of proximal development] with them was to create a sense of 'our' work in order to create a joint venture. . . . We began to help each other achieve things with children that neither party could do alone. I did not know the children, their families, and the more subtle cultural practices in this community regarding ways of interacting, speaking, writing, and reading. They were unsure about what they were doing or not doing that might make a difference to the long-term literacy development of their children." Her analysis captures this interrelationship between the children's literacy development, the teachers' work, the researcher's contributions, and the parents' support. The development of this "community" of readers, writers, and language users was greatly facilitated by the exchange of written communications among the participants. Teachers wrote regularly to parents, and the parents reciprocated; the researcher wrote to the teachers and the students wrote to each other and to the adults. Literacy became the object of study and the medium through which to create conditions for its development.

Joan McLane presents her work with students at a community-based, after-school program. As part of a broader research effort to analyze children's writing outside of school, she describes her efforts to facilitate and support a broad range of writing for the students at the after-school day-care program. Building on Vygotskian notions about developing writing as a complex cultural activity, she developed activities, in collaboration with teachers, within which print would play a prominent role in communicating with others. As students acquired control over the situations for writing, they began to explore what they could do with print, using writing to play, to experiment, to develop or maintain social relationships, and even to fight with one another. As McLane put it, ''They found that writing could serve their own interests and purposes; they could do things with writing that they could not do – or could not do as effectively or that would not be as interesting – without it. In this sense, they were discovering that writing is a 'complex cultural activity.' ''

Luis C. Moll and James B. Greenberg combine an analysis of households with the teaching of literacy in classrooms. The study builds on the idea that to develop an advanced classroom pedagogy, one must fully understand the way students' households express their own pedagogy. The findings highlight the social relations that connect households to each other and facilitate the transmission of ''funds of knowledge'' among participants. The content and manner of this transmission, the households' zones of proximal development, are the central feature of the household study. As the authors view it, ''there are various household zones of proximal development, manifested in different ways depending on the social history of the family and the purpose and goal of the activity. These zones are clearly content- or knowledge-based and rarely trivial. They usually matter; that is, they are authentic. It is when the content of the interactions is important or needed that people are motivated to establish the social contexts for the transfer or application of knowledge and other resources. It follows that it is by creating similar authentic activities in schools that we can access these funds of knowledge and investigate their relevance for academic instruction.'' Two case studies illustrate how teachers may be able to harness these social and intellectual resources to develop innovations in the teaching of literacy. The studies describe the development of social networks for teaching that allow parents to contribute substantively to lessons and students to acquire resources beyond the classroom in extending the limits of their learning.

Mariane Hedegaard describes a teaching experiment conducted in a Danish elementary school. Hedegaard borrows from the work of Vygotsky, as well as other sociohistorical psychologists such as Elkonin, Leontiev, and, especially, Davydov, in applying and elaborating the concept of the zone of proximal development. The experiment emphasizes the careful planning and development of instructional activities to facilitate the development of children's ''empirical'' and ''theoretical'' knowledge.'' As Hedegaard explains it, empirical knowledge ''deals with differences and similarities among phenomena'' whereas theoretical knowledge ''deals with a connected system of phenomena and not the separate, individual phenomenon.'' The author considers the children's development of theoretical knowledge as key in developing and generalizing their thinking. She describes the different instructional methods, the moves, that the teacher used in the classroom, in particular, the use of models as tools to guide the teacher's instruction and the students' analysis and thinking. Hedegaard also presents an analysis of problems in teaching, what the children learned, and ways to develop the students' motivation and interest in the academic activity.

Laura Martin reports on attempts to use sophisticated video programs in the teaching of science. She focuses on the mediating role of these materials in educational activity and the consequences for the students. Three case studies analyze lessons in which teachers use the video to facilitate an interface between scientific knowledge and problem solving and the students' knowledge and experiences, what she called, following Vygotsky, the convergence of the everyday and the scientific. Her analysis captures the varied roles of the teachers in structuring the children's experience with the video program: "The variations emphasize the critical nature of the teacher's conceptualization of the everyday as well as of the scientific for the development of scientific meaning among children. This is because such a development process is essentially one of socialization, not merely learning." In general, the teachers defined and constrained the problem and brought student responses into conformity with their (the teachers') vision of the problem. Lessons went beyond the surface to the extent that the teacher was able to create a connectedness between aspects of the everyday and scientific experiences.

Robert Rueda analyzes the implications of a Vygotskian approach to the education of mildly retarded and learning-disabled children. He first compares a sociohistorical approach to other contemporary cognitive and developmental approaches to writing and reviews the literature on the writing instruction of mildly handicapped students, including social, cognitive, and instructional factors that influence the way these students are taught. Rueda points out that current approaches suggest that "beginning writing and/or writing activities for learning-handicapped students should be structured to minimize the cognitive demands in the face of [the students'] limited cognitive-processing capacity"; this position contrasts with that of a Vygotskian approach, which suggests that "mild learning or developmental delays should not preclude the introduction of and stress on writing at an early point in the curriculum." Rueda then combines ideas from Vygotsky with other "interactive" approaches to writing, especially the use of dialogue journals and the use of microcomputers for writing to facilitate the production and exchange of written messages between students and teachers. Among other findings, the author reports that the most elaborate and sustained exchanges were those concerning opinions, expressing feelings, and requesting personal information. In this social context, the students began to grasp the notion of written language as a communicative tool. Rueda shows how writing difficulties usually attributed to within-child disabilities can be successfully remedied under more appropriate and dynamic social conditions for writing.

Notes

1 In a recent electronic message (XLCHC Network, February 15, 1989), Michael Cole comments on the problems of translation and uses the same remark by Bruner as an example. I quote from Cole's message: "This apparently straightforward statement is in fact dependent upon the interpretation we give to the terms 'development' and 'education,' or more particularly, the interpretation we give to the translations of the Russian words, 'razvitie' and 'obrazovanie.' The matter is by no means straightforward. For example, 'razvitie' is often translated as in the 1962 version of Vygotsky's monograph

as 'evolution' in context where Minick [in his translation of Vygotsky's "Thinking and Speech"; see Vygotsky, 1987] uses the term, 'development.' Bruner's statement is substantially changed by the substitution 'Vygotsky's conception of evolution is at the same time a theory of education,' suggesting how easily the use of near-equivalent terms can change one's interpretation of concepts accessible only in translation. Taken out of their historical-cultural-linguistic context, even presumably non-problematic translation of individual terms can lead to undetected misunderstanding."

Cole continues as follows: "This point is further illustrated by considering the meaning of the Russian term translated (correctly!) as education, 'obrazovanie.' The etymology of English reveals that education is derived from the English word, 'educe' which means to draw out or extract. How different that is from obrazovanie, which my four volume Russian dictionary introduces with the example, 'The ocean also participated in the obrazovanie of that strip of land.' Given this context, we see a marked difference from the English which views education as a 'drawing out' of what was in the child already, whereas the Russian emphasizes a process of formation provoked by external forces. To complicate matters further, 'obrazovanie' has as its major root morpheme 'obraz' which in other contexts is the word for 'image,' so it is akin to image making and when we look for the definition of 'obrazovanie' we are provided with the term 'obuchenie.' The term 'obuchenie' . . . although often translated . . . as 'teaching' in fact can be used for both the activities of students and teachers, implicating a double sided process of teaching/learning, a mutual transformation of teacher and student. . . . Hence, while Bruner was certainly correct that for Vygotsky there is an intimate link between education and development, when we get into the guts of the Russian, we see that he [Bruner] can be correct and [we can] still be provided with an impoverished representation of the concepts that Russian readers take for granted, e.g., that American discussion about 'learning and development' are about obuchenie and development in the USSR."

For a discussion about the translation of the Russian term *obuchenie,* referred to above by Cole, and its importance in understanding Vygotsky's arguments, see Valsiner, 1988.

2 Recent educational research inspired by Vygotsky's ideas include work on teachers' self-regulation and thinking (Gallimore, Dalton, & Tharp, 1986), teacher explanations (Roehler & Duffy, 1986), students' private speech and task performance (Berk, 1986), peer interactions (Forman & Cazden, 1985), diagnosis (Brown & Ferrara, 1985), reading instruction (Palincsar, 1986), composition (Trimbur, 1987), and math instruction (Henderson, 1986).

3 Although most of the chapters in this volume highlight the contributions of Vygotsky, many theorists influenced Vygotsky's own formulations (see, e.g., Blanck, this volume; Cole, this volume; Griffin & Cole, 1984; Rosa & Montero, this volume; Van Der Veer & Valsiner, 1988; Wertsch, 1985a, 1985b, this volume); additionally, sometimes the contributions of Vygotsky are difficult to distinguish from those of his colleagues, especially A. R. Luria and A. N. Leontiev (see Kozulin, 1986). In paying homage to Vygotsky, in no way do we mean to slight or diminish the contributions of his peers, students, and colleagues.

4 Bakhurst (1986, p. 126) suggests that Vygotsky based this analogy on a similar one proposed by Marx. See Valsiner (1988) for a more extended discussion, including the influence of the Soviet psychologist Mikhail Basov on Vygotsky's formulation.

5 This approach is consistent with the recommendations of recent studies of effective literacy and language learning, which point out the importance of students interacting frequently, purposefully, and meaningfully with language and text (see, e.g., Clay & Cazden, this volume; Farr, 1986; Goodman & Goodman, this volume; Langer, 1987).

References

Anyon, J. (1980). Social class and the hidden curriculum of work. *Journal of Education, 162*(1), 67–92.

Appel, G. (1986). L1 and L2 narrative and expository discourse production: A Vygotskian analysis. *Dissertation Abstracts International, 47,* 4373.

Bakhurst, D. J. (1986). Thought, speech, and the genesis of meaning: On the 50th anniversary of Vygotsky's *Myslenie i Rec'* [Speech and thinking]. *Studies in Soviet Thought, 31,* 102–129.

Berk, L. (1986). Relationship of elementary school children's private speech to behavioral accompaniment to task, attention, and task performance. *Developmental Psychology, 22*(5), 671–680.

Brown, A. L., & Ferrara, R. A. (1985). Diagnosing zones of proximal development. In J. V. Wertsch (Ed.), *Culture, communication, and cognition: Vygotskian perspectives* (pp. 273–305). Cambridge: Cambridge University Press.

Brown, J. S., Collins, A., & Duguid, P. (1989). Situated cognition and the culture of learning. *Educational Researcher, 18*(1), 32–42.

Bruner, J. (1962). Introduction. In L. S. Vygotsky, *Thought and language* (pp. v–xiii). Cambridge, MA: MIT Press.

Bruner, J. (1986). *Actual minds, possible worlds.* Cambridge, MA: Harvard University Press.

Bruner, J. (1987). Prologue to the English edition. In L. S. Vygotsky, *Collected works* (Vol 1., pp. 1–16) (R. Rieber & A. Carton, Eds.; N. Minick, Trans). New York: Plenum.

Cazden, C. (1981). Performance before competence: Assistance to child discourse in the zone of proximal development. *Quarterly Newsletter of the Laboratory of Comparative Human Cognition, 3*(1), 5–8.

Cazden, C. (1988). *Classroom discourse: The language of teaching and learning.* Portsmouth, NH: Heinemann.

Cole, M., & Griffin, P. (1983). A socio-historical approach to re-mediation. *Quarterly Newsletter of the Laboratory of Comparative Human Cognition, 5*(4), 69–74.

Cole, M., & Scribner, S. (1978). Introduction. In L. S. Vygotsky, *Mind in society* (pp. 1–14). Cambridge, MA: Harvard University Press.

Davydov, V. V. (1988). Learning activity: The main problems needing further research. *Multidisciplinary Newsletter for Activity Theory, 1*(1–2), 29–36.

del Rio, P., & Alvarez, A. (1988). Aprendizaje y desarollo: La teoría de actividad y la zona de desarollo proximo [Learning and development: Activity theory and the zone of proximal development]. In C. Coll (Ed.), *Psicología de la educación* [Psychology of education] (pp. 1–34). Madrid: Alianza.

Edelsky, C. (1986). *Writing in a bilingual program; Había una vez.* Norwood, NJ: Ablex.

Edelsky, C. (1989). Bilingual children's writing: Fact and fiction. In D. Johnson & D. Roen (Eds.), *Richness in writing: Empowering ESL students* (pp. 165–176). New York: Longman.

Engeström, Y., Hakkarainen, P., & Hedegaard, M. (1984). On the methodological basis of research in teaching and learning. In M. Hedegaard, P. Hakkarainen, & Y. Engeström (Eds.), *Learning and teaching on a scientific basis* (pp. 119–189). Risskov: Aarhus University.

Farr, M. (1986). Language, culture, and writing: Sociolinguistic foundations of research on writing. In E. Z. Rothkopf (Ed.), *Review of research in education* (pp. 195–224). Washington, DC: American Educational Research Association.

Forman, E., & Cazden, C. (1985). Exploring Vygotskian perspectives in education: The cognitive value of peer interactions. In J. V. Wertsch (Ed.), *Culture, communication, and cognition: Vygotskian perspectives* (pp. 323–347). Cambridge: Cambridge University Press.

Gallimore, R., Dalton, S., & Tharp, R. (1986). Self-regulation and interactive teaching: The effects of teaching conditions on teachers' cognitive activity. *Elementary School Journal, 86*(3), 613–631.

Goodlad, J. (1984). *A place called school.* New York: McGraw-Hill.

Goodman, K. S., Smith, E. B., Meredith, R., & Goodman, Y. M. (1987). *Language and thinking in school: A whole-language curriculum.* New York: Owen.

Griffin, P., & Cole, M. (1984). Current activity for the future: The Zo-ped. In B. Rogoff & J. Wertsch (Eds.), *Children's learning in the "zone of proximal development"* (pp. 45–64). San Francisco: Jossey-Bass.

Hedegaard, M., Hakkarainen, P., & Engeström, Y. (1984). *Learning and teaching on a scientific basis.* Risskov: Aarhus University.

Henderson, R. (1986). Self-regulated learning: Implications for the design of instructional media. *Contemporary Educational Psychology, 11,* 405–427.

Kozulin, A. (1986). The concept of activity in Soviet psychology: Vygotsky, his disciples and critics. *American Psychologist, 41*(3), 264–274.

Langer, J. (1987). A sociocognitive perspective on literacy. In J. Langer (Ed.), *Language, literacy, and culture: Issues in society and schooling* (pp. 1–20). Norwood, NJ: Ablex.

Leontiev, A. N., & Luria, A. R. (1968). The psychological ideas of L. S. Vygotskii. In B. B. Wolman (Ed.), *The historical roots of contemporary psychology* (pp. 338–367). New York: Harper & Row.

Levitin, K. (1982). *One is not born a personality: Profiles of Soviet educational psychologists.* Moscow: Progress.

Luria, A. (1978). *The making of mind: A personal account of Soviet psychology* (M. Cole & S. Cole, Eds.). Cambridge, MA: Harvard University Press.

Markova, A. K. (1979). *The teaching and mastery of language.* White Plains, NY: Sharpe.

Minick, N. (1985). *L. S. Vygotsky and Soviet activity theory: New perspectives on the relationship between mind and society.* Unpublished doctoral dissertation, Northwestern University, Evanston, IL.

Minick, N. (1987a). The development of Vygotsky's thought: An introduction. In L. S. Vygotsky, *Collected works* (Vol 1., pp. 17–36) (R. Rieber & A. Carton, Eds.; N. Minick, Trans.). New York: Plenum.

Minick, N. (1987b). Implications of Vygotsky's theories for dynamic assessment. In C. S. Lidz (Ed.), *Dynamic assessment: An interactional approach to evaluating learning potential* (pp. 116–140). New York: Guilford.

Moll, L. C. (1988). Key issues in teaching Latino students. *Language Arts, 65*(5), 465–472.

Moll, L. C. (1989). Teaching second-language students: A Vygotskian perspective. In D. Johnson & D. Roen (Eds.), *Richness in writing: Empowering ESL students* (pp. 55–69). New York: Longman.

Newman, D., Griffin, P., & Cole, M. (1989). *The construction zone: Working for cognitive change in school.* Cambridge: Cmabridge University Press.

Nunn, G. (1984). Peer interaction during collaborative writing at the 4th/5th grade level. *Dissertation Abstracts International, 45,* 105.

Oakes, J. (1986). Tracking, inequality, and the rhetoric of school reform: Why schools don't change. *Journal of Education, 168,* 61–80.

Olson, D. (1986). Intelligence and literacy: The relationship between intelligence and the technologies of representation and communication. In R. Sternberg & R. Wagner (Eds.), *Practical intelligence: Nature and origins of competence in the everyday world* (pp. 338–360). Cambridge: Cambridge University Press.

Palacios, J. (1987). Reflexiones en torno a las implicaciones educativas de la obra de Vigotski [Reflections in terms of the educational implications of Vygotsky's work]. In M. Siguán (Ed.), *Actualidad de Lev S. Vigotski* [Actuality of Lev S. Vygotsky] (pp. 176–188). Barcelona: Anthropos.

Palincsar, A. S. (1986). The role of dialogue in providing scaffolded instruction. *Educational Psychologist, 21*(1, 2), 73–98.

Premack, D. (1984). Pedagogy and aesthetics as sources of culture. In M Gazzaniga (Ed.), *Handbook of cognitive neuroscience* (pp. 15–35). New York: Plenum.

Rivière, A. (1984). La psicología de Vygotski [The psychology of Vygotsky]. *Infancia y Aprendizaje, 27–28*(3–4), 7–86.

Roehler, L., & Duffy, G. (1986). What makes one teacher a better explainer than another. *Journal of Education for Teaching, 12*(3), 273–284.

Rogoff, B., & Wertsch, J. (Eds.) (1984). *Children's learning in the "zone of proximal development"* (pp. 7–18). San Francisco: Jossey-Bass.

Scribner, S. (1985). Vygotsky's uses of history. In J. V. Wertsch (Ed.), *Culture, communication, and cognition: Vygotskian perspectives* (pp. 119–145). Cambridge: Cambridge University Press.

Siguán, M. (Ed.) (1987). *Acutalidad de Lev S. Vigotski* [Actuality of Lev S. Vygotsky]. Barcelona: Anthropos.

Talyzina, N. (1981). *The psychology of learning.* Moscow: Progress.

Tharp, R., & Gallimore, R. (1989). *Rousing minds to life: Teaching, learning, and schooling in social context.* Cambridge: Cambridge University Press.

Trimbur, J. (1987). Beyond cognition: The voices of inner speech. *Rhetoric Review, 5*(2), 211–221.

Valsiner, J. (1988). *Development psychology in the Soviet Union.* Sussex: Harvester Press.

Van Der Veer, R., & Valsiner, J. (1988). Lev Vygotsky and Pierre Janet: On the origin of the concept of sociogenesis. *Developmental Review, 8,* 52–65.

Vygotsky, L. S. (1978). *Mind in sociey*. Cambridge; MA: Harvard University Press.

Vygotsky, L. S. (1981). The genesis of higher mental functions. In J. V. Wertsch (Ed.), *The concept of activity in Soviet psychology* (pp. 144–188). White Plains, NY: Sharpe.

Vygotsky, L. S. (1982). *Sobranie sochinenii: Tom vtoroi. Problemy obshchei psikhologii* [Collected works: Vol. 1. Problems in the theory and history of psychology]. Moscow: Izdatel'stvo Pedagogika.

Vygotsky, L. S. (1987). Thinking and speech. In L. S. Vygotsky, *Collected works* (vol. 1, pp. 39–285) (R. Rieber & A. Carton, Eds.; N. Minick, Trans.). New York: Plenum.

Wertsch, J. V. (1984). The zone of proximal development: Some conceptual issues. In B. Rogoff & J. Wertsch (Eds.), *Children's learning in the "zone of proximal development"* (pp. 7–18). San Francisco: Jossey-Bass.

Wertsch, J. V. (1985a). *Vygotsky and the social formation of mind*. Cambridge, MA: Harvard University Press.

Wertsch, J. V. (Ed.) (1985b). *Culture, communication, and cognition: Vygotskian perspectives*. Cambridge: Cambridge University Press.

Zebroski, J. (1983). Writing as "activity": Composition development from the perspective of the Vygotskian school. *Dissertation Abstracts International, 44*, 94.

Part I

Historical and theoretical issues

1   Vygotsky: The man and his cause

Guillermo Blanck

"Not everything that was must pass." This line from a poem by Tyutchev that Lev Vygotsky loved to recite can also serve as a metaphor for Vygotsky himself. Although he died more than 50 years ago, Vygotsky left an impressive body of work that, as is the case with most geniuses, becomes more modern as time goes by. Vygotsky gave a new configuration to psychology's past, proposed theoretical alternatives to its present, and suggested solutions that became projects for the future. It is only now that the impact of his work is beginning to be felt in the scientific community. His theory is offering answers to questions that seemed insoluble and is setting a course for us to follow. Vygotsky, as Jerome Bruner (1987) has said, speaks to us from the future.

Vygotsky did not write his memoirs, and none of his contemporaries wrote them for him, and a war that destroyed half a continent buried many of his life's documents. He seemed condemned to have no biography; his history, therefore, must be reconstructed from fragments that form pieces of a puzzle. Those wanting to assemble this puzzle have two main sources available: those who knew him personally and the biographical sketches drawn by those with access to his work or to his collaborators. Among the former, the best sources are Semyon Dobkin, his childhood friend; Vygotsky's sisters; his colleague and follower Alexander Luria; his disciples Rosa Levina, Natalia Morozova, Piotr Galperin, and Bluma Zeigarnik; and his daughter Gita Vygodskaya. I have had personal access to the last four and access to Vygotsky's private archives, thanks to the generosity and patience of Gita Vygodskaya, as well as access to the writings of others who have collected information on Vygotsky. Two especially important sources are Karl Levitin, who has been the inevitable conduit for all who have written biographical accounts of Vygotsky and with whom I recently (October 23, 1988, Moscow) discussed the methodological difficulties of his recasting of Vygotsky's early years, and James Wertsch, with whom I exchanged materials when I was writing my first article on Vygotsky in 1984 (Blanck, 1984).

Given these constraints, and within the restricted space of one chapter, I will attempt to provide the reader with a personal history of Vygotsky, as well as a

This chapter is dedicated to Adriana.

31

history of his ideas. Who was this man of blue eyes[1] and yellow voice[2] who speaks to us from the future?

The life of a genius

According to the old Russian calendar – 12 days behind the present one – Vygotsky was born to a middle-class Jewish family on November 5, 1896, in Orsha, a town in the northern part of the Byelorussia Republic, located within the western limits of the European portion of the Soviet Union. A year later his family moved to Gomel, a small town of greater cultural vitality. Gomel was located in southern Byelorussia, next to the Republic of the Ukraine and within the Pale – restricted territory where Jews were confined in Czarist Russia, the Imperial Russia of Nicholas and Alexandra. Vygotsky lived in Gomel during his infancy and his youth.

His father, Semyon L'vovich Vygodsky, was an executive of the United Bank of Gomel, and some years after the October Revolution of 1917 he went on to head a section of the Commercial Bank of Moscow (Vygodskaya, 1984). Together with his wife, Cecilia Moiseievna, a licensed teacher, he helped make his family one of the most cultured in the city and organized an excellent public library which was used exhaustively by his children and colleagues. Perhaps the strong repression suffered by Jews in prerevolutionary Russia – the territorial restrictions, the strict quotas for entrance to the university, the prohibition from many professions, the permanent threat of the pogrom – contributed to the closeness of the family and to the prominent intellectual character of his home.

Vygotsky's mother, who had a gentle personality, devoted her life to the rearing of her eight children. Lev was the second child and was especially close to his sister Zinaida, 18 months younger than Lev. He learned German from his mother and it is believed he acquired a permanent interest in Spinoza from his sister. Dobkin (1982) stated that Lev's parents were able to create a warm climate for their children in their six-room apartment. His father's study was available to Lev, his siblings, and his friends for playing and studying. Many interesting conversations took place in the dining room, site of the traditional evening tea around the samovar. These conversations would play a decisive role in the children's cultural formation.

Vygotsky received primary education at home with Solomon Ashpiz, a private tutor who had been exiled in Siberia due to his revolutionary activism. Although Ashpiz was a mathematician, he also taught other disciplines. He accepted only talented disciples, with the purpose of further developing their capacities. Ashpiz was a kind and good-humored person who conducted the educational process with a technique based on ingenious Socratic dialogues. Perhaps this experience was one of the roots of Vygotsky's conception of the zone of proximal development, which would play a central role in his pedagogical ideas.

After completing his tests at the primary level through independent studies, Vygotsky entered the public gymnasium but completed the final 2 years in a private

Jewish school of higher academic caliber. It was then that he began to show the exciting peculiarities of his genius. He expressed great interest in all subjects, and his abilities were such that each of his professors believed Vygotsky should follow his specialty. Thus his mathematics professor predicted for him a brilliant future in that area, as did his Latin professor in the area of classical studies. But by that time his main interest was already oriented toward the theater, literature, and philosophy (Vygodskaya, 1984).

Throughout his life Vygotsky expressed great love for the theater and poetry. I always believed that Vygotsky's relationship with the theater had two aspects. One was his work in dramaturgy, from his initial theater reviews to his mature works on the psychology of actors. And the other was his romantic and theatrical behavior, such as his childhood predilection for tragic poems, his dazzling recitations, his tendency during adolescence to play the most varied roles, his electrifying irruption in the Psychoneurological Congress where he was first introduced publicly as psychologist, and as recounted in so many other anecdotes of his life (Dobkin, 1982; Luria, 1979).

Like all Russian children, Lev was well acquainted with Pushkin, but unlike his friends, who preferred lyrical poems, he always chose the most tragic ones. Dobkin remembered that Vygotsky singled out the lines that he felt captured the essence of the poem and skipped the rest. For example, from Pushkin's *Mozart and Salieri* he recited only these lines: "They say: there is no justice here on earth. But there is none – hereafter. To my mind this truth is elementary as a scale." Whereas these lines are not the most significant in Salieri's monologue, in Vygotsky's opinion they were nonetheless sufficient to capture its essence. Wertsch (1985) rightly points out that this notion of the heightened significance of an abbreviated linguistic form was destined to play an essential role in Vygotsky's account of language and mind.

This distinctive quality is also demonstrated by Lev Semenovich's modification of his surname in the early 1920s. He believed that his name derived from the name of the town of Vygotovo (where his family originated); consequently, he replaced the *d* in his name with *t*. The reader will notice that his cousin and his daughter preserve the *d* in their surnames (Levitin, 1982).

Besides German and Russian, Vygotsky read and spoke Hebrew, French, and English; and, complementing his studies at the gymnasium, he learned Latin and Greek. He also knew Esperanto thoroughly.

A cognitive peculiarity of Vygotsky's was his exceptional speed in reading. Luria used to say that he read diagonally and that it would have been fruitful to investigate this special ability in processing information. He remarked that "what Vygotsky read were not exactly adventure novels" (Luria, n.d., p. 210).

Another outstanding cognitive characteristic of Vygotsky was his extraordinary memory. He used to begin his courses by asking a couple of students to write on the board many arbitrarily chosen words, while he faced away. After reading them carefully he would again turn his back to the board and repeat them, without error, in any order, from beginning to end or vice versa, from the middle to the end, and so forth. As a mnemonic technique, Vygotsky had memorized a chronological list of authors with whom he associated each word (Puzirei, 1986).

By the time Vygotsky turned 15 he was called "little professor" because he generated intellectual discussions among his friends. He explored the historical contexts of thoughts, debating the roles of personalities such as Napoleon or Aristotle in mock trials and other role-playing games where he and his friends represented historical figures. His interests in theater, history, and philosophy were thus integrated.

During that same time period, Fanya and Semyon Dobkin and Vygotsky's sister Zinaida invited him to preside over a Jewish history study circle. This activity lasted for 2 years and eventually led to the study of the philosophy of history. Here Vygotsky met Hegel, whose conception of history enraptured him. This strong identification must have stimulated his subsequent adherence to Marx, a connection not at all arbitrary (see Cohen, 1978).

Vygotsky completed his preparatory studies in 1913. Although only 3% of the students at the universities in Moscow and Petersburg (later called Petrograd and, from 1924, Leningrad) could be Jews, those who graduated by passing the admissions test with gold medals were admitted wherever they chose. Vygotsky, because of his talent, earned a gold medal. Nevertheless, the Czarist minister of education decreed a change in the selection criteria. Although the quota was preserved, admissions would be decided by casting lots. The objective of this strategy was to diminish the intellectual quality of Jewish students in the best universities. Dobkin (1982) recalls that Vygotsky showed him the notice bearing the bad news and said he would have no chance. His friend, irritated by the injustice and knowing that Lev was a wagerer, assured him that he would enter and dared him to bet a good book on the outcome. Vygotsky passed the examinations with his gold medal and, despite his fear, was favored by good luck: A telegram informed him that according to the drawing he would be admitted to Moscow University. That same day Lev gave his friend a book of Ivan Bunin's poetry, inscribed "To Senya, in memory of a lost bet."

Vygotsky was interested in studying history or philology, but these areas of study led to a teaching career, and as a Jew he could not be a government employee. So he entered medical school, an option encouraged by his parents because it guaranteed a modest but safe professional life. After a month, however, Vygotsky transferred to the law school, an option more suited to his interest in the humanities. Ironically, years later, after he was already a renowned psychologist, Vygotsky once again entered medical school as a modest first-year student. Life is a road with many curves.

Moscow was an exciting place for an intellectual young man. Innovative trends in the sciences, humanities, and arts were emerging. Kozulin (1986) keenly perceives that Vygotsky seemed to pursue them all. To satisfy his true inclination, Vygotsky decided in 1914 to study simultaneously at Moscow and at Shaniavsky

People's University. The latter was an unofficial institution, created in 1906 by Alfons Shaniavsky after the Ministry of Education expelled from Moscow's Imperial University most of the students who had participated in an anticzarist revolt. In protest, about a hundred leading scholars left the university, among them Timiryazev, Lebedev, and Vernadsky. Most of them took refuge at the Shaniavsky University; as a result, the highest intellects in Moscow gathered there. Vygotsky obtained a solid foundation in history, philosophy, and psychology and pursued studies in literature, which continued to be his primary interest.

In 1915, at the age of 19, Vygotsky finished an essay on *Hamlet,* which he had begun during his early adolescence. Dobkin attested to the deep impression the tragedy had made on Vygotsky when he was still a child. According to my sources, there is still no English publication of this precocious 200-page essay of unusual literary quality. Vygotsky, who while still a schoolboy staged Gogol's play *The Marriage,* was now publishing literary critiques in several magazines (Vygodskaya, 1984). Less than 10 of the many he wrote ever reached us. His opinion that Andrei Bely's *Petersburg* was a milestone in the narrative of the century is noteworthy.

In 1917 Vygotsky graduated simultaneously from both universities and returned to Gomel where his family was still living. There he worked as a teacher, a profession he was now able to practice due to the abolition of the anti-Semitic legislation after the October Socialist Revolution. Professor Edward H. Carr (1956) has stated that the Russian Revolution of 1917 may be considered by future historians as the major turning point of the 20th century. In Wertsch's (1985) opinion, the available documentation does not permit us to determine its impact on Vygotsky. However, we can say, without any doubt, that Vygotsky considered himself fully a Soviet (Vygodskaya, personal communication, October 21, 1988). His carnet of deputy of the soviet of the Frunze district of Moscow – of which I have a copy – strongly supports this contention. Vygotsky spent the next 7 years in Gomel, where he actively pursued his intellectual interests. He taught literature and Russian at the Labor School, at adult schools, at courses for the specialization of teachers, at the Workers' Faculty, and at technical schools for pressmen and metallurgists. At the same time, he taught courses in logic and psychology at the Pedagogical Institute, in aesthetics and art history at the Conservatory, and in theater at a studio. He edited and published articles in the theater section of a newspaper (Vygodskaya, 1984).

Semyon Dobkin was 3 years younger than Vygotsky. During their adolescent years they had formed a trio with David Vygotsky, a cousin of Lev's who was several years older and had great influence over him. Destined to become a brilliant linguist – and to die in one of Stalin's concentration camps – David familiarized Lev with the works of Roman Jakobson, Viktor Shklovsky, and Lev Jakubinsky, famous members of the Formalist school. These lingusits became common references in Vygotsky's work. The year 1918 reunited the three friends once more in a publishing venture called Ages and Days, which printed literary work in inexpensive editions. Its first book was *Fire,* poems of Ilya Ehrenburg solicited by Vygotsky. Despite their ambitious plans, they published just one other book before the national paper shortage forced them to close the business in 1919. Not long afterward, Dobkin (1982) left to continue his studies in Moscow, David went to Petrograd in search of work, and Vygotsky remained in Gomel.

Vygotsky's activities during his years in Gomel were part of one of the most important intellectual movements of our century. Futurist and suprematist paintings, as well as constructivist sculptures hung on streets, trains, trucks, and ships. Not only did the innovative intellectuals devote themselves to their specific creative work, they participated at institutions. For example, Kandinsky was vice-president of the Arts and Sciences Academy in Moscow; Malevich presided over the one in Petrograd, where the architect Tatlin, author of the famous project of the Monument for the Third International, headed a department. Chagall was the fine arts minister in Vitebsk. The versatile Rodchenko organized art instructional programs. In Petrograd the "Week of Sergei Prokofiev" was celebrated. Shostakovich represented his country in international contests. Meyerhold was director of the Theatrical Section of the Commissariat of the People for Education, and Stanislavsky presided over the Theater of Art of Moscow. Gabo and his brother Pevsner represented the constructivists' group, Mayakovsky the Leftist Front for the Arts (LEF). Eisenstein, who due to his knowledge in engineering organized the construction of defenses during the Civil War, was to become the directing professor of the State's Institute of Cinematography. The pedagogue Makarenko (1985) founded the Gorky Colony for the reeducation of homeless juvenile delinquents.

We must add to these names, representing diverse fields, those of El Lissitzky, Vertov, Gorky, Bulgakov, and Sholokhov, who in this period wrote his masterpiece *And Quiet Flows the Don,* which would earn him a future Nobel Prize in Literature. The Petrograd Formalist school was revolutionizing literary theory with its investigations. Bakhtin and his circle, from other perspectives, were producing in the same fields. Lenin was heading the state, and Lunacharsky was the minister of culture and education. With Stalin in power and with bureaucrats of the likes of Zhdanov in charge of the administration of culture, almost all of this movement would be swept away. A thorough analysis of this period may be found in Sánchez Vázquez (1970; see also Argan, 1970; Ehrenburg, 1962; Fitzpatrick, 1970; Shklovsky, 1979).

I have always been puzzled that such a magnificent cultural revolution was accomplished in the tragic atmosphere of the postrevolutionary period of invasions,[3] famine, and lack of the most basic products. John Reed (1920), the American journalist, attested to this situation: "There was no heating during all of winter. People died of cold in their rooms." The Vygodsky family suffered from hunger and tuberculosis.

Vygotsky was at the center of Gomel's intellectual avant-grade. He initiated "Literary Mondays" where new prose and poetry were discussed and was one of the founders of the magazine *Veresk.* His erudition astounded those who went to his lectures on Shakespeare, Chekhov and Pushkin, Esenin and Mayakovsky. Decades later some still recalled his lecture on Einstein and the theory of relativity (Vygodskaya 1984).

Immersed in teaching and writing, he avidly read literary works and essays: Dostoyevsky and Tolstoy, Tyutchev and Blok, Bunin and Mandelstam, Gumilyov and Pasternak, and numerous authors cited in his writings. But other readings suggest the new directions in which Vygotsky's thoughts were headed. His first two readings in psychology were Freud and James (Dobkin, 1982). He then began to explore Pavlov and others representing the principal schools of his time. Since childhood he had read the linguist Potebnya (1913). His *Thought and Language* of 1850 is actively present in Vygotsky's last book, *Thinking and Speech* (1934/1987b). He also studied Humboldt's hypothesis of linguistic relativity, later developed by Sapir and Whorf. Vygotsky was very interested in the works of V. A. Vagner, a Russian specialist in evolution and in the comparative study of animal behavior. The two men carried on an extensive correspondence (Luria, 1979), but I have been unable to discover the whereabouts of these letters. Such divergent sources as Bacon, Descartes, Spinoza, Feverbach, Hegel, Marx, and Engels contributed to Vygotsky's deliberations as he developed his philosophical concepts. As we shall see, Marxism became the governing influence on his thought.

It has been said that Vygotsky was concerned only with behavior and cognitive processes, setting aside human affect. In his book *The Psychology of Art,* Vygotsky (1971) has written that feelings were an obscure field. In a recent publication of an incomplete unpublished work, Vygotsky (1933/1984a; see also Van der Veer, 1987) argued that a philosophical-methodological restatement opened the door to a scientific investigation of affect. Vygotsky saw Descartes's (1649) dualism as the ominous obstacle to the integration of the various areas in psychology. The Cartesian view of humans as possessing a machinelike body and a spiritual mind was for centuries the basis for the subsequent conflict between a scientific materialistic psychology and a philosophical-speculative idealistic one. In the ideas of the philosopher Baruch de Spinoza (see 1675/1979), Vygotsky saw a monist solution to the body–mind problem. Although it is usually unnoticed, Vygotsky also referred to this topic in *Thinking and Speech* when among other things he wrote that conscience is a complex whole of cognition, motivations, and emotional feelings. In any case, this field of study was not pursued by him or by later Soviet psychologists, with the exception of Jakobson (1959, 1965, 1968, 1969, 1972). This neglect is due not only to the high degree of difficulty of the subject but to the importance given to behavior and cognition in the psychology of the 20th century.

In 1919 Vygotsky contracted the tuberculosis that would kill him 15 years later. Despite his illness, he continued working tenaciously, even during the most difficult periods. He knew he was irrevocably sentenced to death and on several occasions was convinced that death was imminent. After a severe attack in 1920, he asked Dobkin (1982), who was about to move to Moscow, to visit Yuly Aikhenvald, a literary critic and his former professor at Shaniavsky University, and to persuade him to publish the manuscripts he, Vygotsky, would leave when he died.

In 1924 he married Rosa Noevna Smekhova, a determined and intelligent woman who kept her high spirits during the many difficult times she shared with Vygotsky and during her subsequent widowhood. In this latter phase she worked up to 16 hours a day taking care of handicapped children. She died in Moscow in 1979. Vygotsky and Smekhova had two daughters. The elder, Gita Levovna, graduated as an educational psychologist. She is now retired and living in Moscow. The younger, Asya, a specialist in biophysics, died in 1985.

By the time he married, Vygotsky's interest in psychology had become his central concern. Some say that his real interest was in solving problems of art and culture, that he turned to psychology in order to solve them and eventually was captured by it (see, e.g., Schedrovitsky, 1982). Without underestimating Vygotsky's interest in those matters, matters that he would continue addressing all his life, albeit from a psychological perspective, I think that he was genuinely interested in the establishment of psychology as a science and in its potential for solving practical problems. As a matter of fact, his concern about pedagogical psychology is always present in his work. This opinion is supported by Moll (this volume) when he states that pedagogy is the essential route of Vygotsky's approach to psychology. Mecacci (1983) expresses a similar opinion. These affirmations are supported by the fact that seven of Vygotsky's first eight writings on psychology between 1922 and 1926 have to do with problems in education, such as methods of teaching literature, the use of translation in language comprehension, and the education of blind, deaf-mute, retarded, and physically handicapped children (see the bibliographical listing reconstructed by Shakhlevich-Lifanova, 1978). Vygotsky organized a psychological laboratory at the Pedagogical Institute in Gomel, where several investigations were conducted with preschool and school children. These experiences were, in fact, some of the basic material for his first book, on the psychology of art.

In 1924 Vygotsky traveled to Leningrad to participate in the Second Psychoneurological Congress, then the most important congress on psychology in Russia. According the program, he gave a full account of three of the Gomel investigations and made his first public appearance before the Russian psychological community. Luria (1979), who was present, has described Vygotsky's influential presentation. The date of this lecture, January 6, 1924, marks the beginning of the second period of Vygotsky's biographical trajectory, devoted almost exclusively to psychology. Vygotsky's lecture, "The Methodology of Reflexologic and Psychological Investigations," was remarkably impressive. Without following any written text, he spoke with extraordinary fluency. Instead of selecting a minor topic, which would have been expected of a young man addressing the graybeards of his profession for the first time, Vygotsky addressed the relationship between conditioned reflexes and conscious behavior. His thesis was that scientific psychology cannot ignore the facts of conscience. Several future disciples of Vygotsky who were present also recalled the electrifying effect of his presentation. Kornilov, director of the Institute of Psychology of Moscow, was sufficiently impressed to invite him to join the institute as a research fellow. Vygotsky accepted and several weeks later left Gomel in order to begin a new career. Many have wondered how someone without formal training in psychology could make such an original contribution to the discipline. I believe that it was precisely his newness to the field coupled with his strong insights from other fields (philosophy, linguistics, semiotics, historical materialism) that illuminated for Vygotsky fresh answers to perplexing questions. Schedrovitsky (1982) provides a similar interpretation.

Rivière (1985) has written that Vygotsky crossed through this century's psychology like a swift fury and left behind a long trail of influence that has not yet been exhausted. During his last decade, Vygotsky's activities were even more intensive and productive than any of his earlier work. When Vygotsky and his wife arrived in Moscow, they initially established themselves in the basement of the Institute of Experimental Psychology, in a very small room where they lived for a year, until their daughter's birth.

Around that time Walter Benjamin (1980) walked about Moscow and wrote in his diary that, underneath the appearance of serenity provided by the snow and the small amount of traffic, this was a city of much activity, unlike other capitals such as Berlin. And Vygotsky wasted no time in becoming part of the dynamic nature of the capital city of the USSR. The morning after his arrival he met with Luria and Leontiev to plan an ambitious project that was in marked contrast to the modest position of second-class assistant with which Vygotsky began his career: the creation of a new psychology. They built on the critical assimilation of the theories of Werner, Stern, Karl and Charlotte Bühler, Köhler, Piaget, James, Thorndike, and many others (see Luria, 1979). This is how the famous Vygotsky–Luria–Leontiev troika was formed, Vygotsky assuming the natural leadership. Each of the principal concepts of cognitive psychology was revised radically. At the beginning they met twice a week in Vygotsky's room to organize the investigations necessary to develop their ideas. In a couple of years they were joined by students Alexander Zaporozhets, Liya Slavina, Lidia Bozhovich, Natalia Morozova, and Roso Levina. The "eight," as they were christened by their colleagues, met in a one-room apartment on Bolshaya Serpukhova Street, where Vygotsky now lived and would spend the rest of his life. They carried out their investigations in the laboratory at the Krupskaya Academy, under Luria's direction.

According to many who worked with him, Vygotsky possessed a strong magnetism. Rosa Levina recalled her first meeting with Vygotsky as completely overwhelming. As Toulmin (1978) wrote, Vygotsky had a Mozartian aura of genius, recognized by those who knew him only through his work. Bruner (1985) has said that he was plainly a genius. Of a similar opinion are Bogdan Suchodolsky (1984), George Miller (1978), James Wertsch (1984), Rubén Ardila (1984a), and Juan Azcoaga (1984a). Luria's (1979) famous comment that Vygotsky was a genius and that his own work was nothing but the development of Vygotsky's ideas is paralleled by Zeigarnik's (1982) statement, "My humble contribution is nothing but the continuation of Vygotsky's thoughts through fifty years."

Vygotsky's enormous activity – he would lecture for up to 5 hours without rest – reflected the boundless energy in the Soviet Union during the decade following the Revolution. Vygotsky and his circle were caught up in the excitement of the greatest experiment in the social sciences in history: creating the first society based on socialist principles (Bernal, 1964). This excitement led Chagall to adorn Vitebsk with 10 miles of red cloth and was evident in the agitation of Vygotsky's entourage every time he left on a trip: They hardly slept; they gathered in masses and wrote and recited poems in honor of his journey (Luria, 1979, p. 52).

There are several interpretations of Vygotsky's objectives during the last stage of his life. As I commented earlier, Vygotsky intended, on the one hand, to reorganize psychology on Marxist fundamentals; on the other hand, he sought solutions to the serious problems of Soviet society, such as education to counter a high rate of illiteracy and the neglected problems of defectology (roughly, research on disabilities, e.g., deafness, blindness, mental retardation). Wertsch (1985) concurs with this opinion but cautions against categorizing Vygotsky as a psychologist, at least in the present meaning of the term. He characterizes him as a social theoretician. In my opinion, because Vygotskian reformulation of psychology can be characterized as a *sociohistoric theory of the mind*, with deep considerations of social and cultural factors, we can very well classify him as a psychologist, more specifically as a *Marxist psychologist*.

The presence of Marx is key in the possibility of structuring a scientific theory of the human mind. There can be no scientific theories of mind without a scientific theory of human beings, and there can be no accurate conception of humans without Marx; that was the critical element perceived by Vygotsky (Blanck, 1983a). Facing the apparent deadlock of psychology at the time, Vygotsky was convinced that to devise an authentically scientific psychology its bases had to be restated from a Marxist perspective: "I want to find out how science has to be built, to approach the study of the mind having learned the whole of Marx's method" (Cole & Scribner, 1978, p. 8). Marxist philosophy could provide the highest type of methodological organization. Vygotsky adopted not only Marx's methodological stance but the essential theses of historical materialism. Toulmin (1978) engagingly explains these productive consolidations.

Luria (1979) remembers that Vygotsky was the chief Marxist theoretician among their study group. The severe distortions that Marxism has suffered are the reason why today many intellectuals think of it as the degraded scholasticism of Stalinism or the limited Critical Theory of Frankfurt. Both are alien to the nature of Marxism. Vygotsky's reliance on Marx's *Capital,* Engels's *Dialectics of Nature,* and Lenin's *Philosophical Notebooks* demonstrates his classical orientation to Marxism.

From a Marxist perspective, the line of reasoning selected by Vygotsky was not the only possible one. Wertsch (1985) cites Sève (1978, also see 1980), a renowned Marxist philosopher, as an example of an alternative. Nevertheless, after reviewing Vygotsky's work, Sève (1984) himself acknowledged: "I consider Vygotsky as the true initiator of a Marxist way of thinking in psychology."

Vygotsky wrote his first works on defectology in 1924. His concerns with this field, with changes in learning and problems of education, remained as one of his major focuses. He headed the Section of Defective and Retarded Children of the

Department of Public Education. In 1925 he became the first director of the Psychology Laboratory for Abnormal Childhood in Moscow, presently the Institute of Defectology of the Academy of Pedagogical Sciences.

In the summer of 1925 Vygotsky was sent by Lunacharsky as the Russian delegate to the International Congress on the Teaching of Deaf Mutes, held in England. He then visited institutes concerned with defectology in Germany, France, and Holland to learn about their work (Vygodskaya, 1984). Upon his return to the USSR he suffered a bout of tuberculosis, and the Medical Control Commission confined him to bed. While confined, he finished *The Psychology of Art,* which he submitted as his doctoral thesis. In his preface he wrote: ''My intellect has been shaped under the sign of Spinoza's words, and it has tried not to be astounded, not to laugh, not to cry, but to understand'' (Vygotsky, 1972, p. 20).

In the fall of 1925 Vygotsky was to defend his dissertation, but because of his worsening illness the evaluating committee exempted him from so doing (Vygodskaya, 1984). Due to the deterioration of his condition, he was confined from November until the spring of the following year. While at the hospital, he wrote his metatheoretical essay *Historical Meaning of the Crisis in Psychology,* the most accurate analysis of the condition of psychology at that time. Its basic concepts are still relevant to contemporary psychology.

When he recovered his health, he continued his scientific investigations and lectured at the Department of Social Sciences at Moscow University, the Russian Psychoanalytic Society, the Krupskaya Academy of Communist Education, the institute for Child and Adolescent Health, the Pedagogical Department of the Moscow Conservatory, the second Medical Institute, and the Karl Liebknecht Industrial-Pedagogical Institute. He also held professorships and headed departments in these institutions (Vygodskaya, 1984).

In early 1929 Vygotsky traveled for several months to Tashkent, a remote city in the Asiatic part of the USSR, to train teachers and psychologists at the First Central Asian State University. On April 15, in Tashkent, Vygotsky wrote to the five students who had joined him when the ''eight'' were formed. A section of the letter reveals his passion for what he considered to be his historical mission:

> A sense of the enormity of the tasks facing contemporary psychology (we are living in an epoch of cataclysm in this field) is my most basic feeling. And that places an infinite responsibility – a most serious, almost tragic (in the finest, most genuine sense of the word) burden on the shoulders of those few who are conducting research in any new branch of science – and specially the science of the person. You must test yourself a thousand times and endure countless ordeals before you make a decision, because this torturous path demands total devotion of self. (Levitin, 1982, p. 322)

Vygotsky's activities are evidence of his devotion. Besides researching and teaching, he continued to write frenetically and to sponsor new projects. He wrote almost 50 works during the years 1929–1930.

He was still interested in the psychology of art. After 1930 he gave lectures on this topic at the Chamber Theater of Moscow. He codirected with Luria, film director Eisenstein, and linguist Nicolai Marr a seminar in the field of art, which was considered outstanding (Vygodskaya, 1984). He met frequently with Eisenstein to discuss how the abstract ideas of historical materialism could be depicted in movie images. Zaporozhets, who had been an actor, also participated (Cole, 1979).

In 1930 he and Luria wrote *Studies in the History of Behavior: Ape, Primitive, Child.* His interest in variations in the higher mental processes of people from different cultures led to the planning of a cross-cultural investigation conducted in Uzbekistan in 1931 and 1932. Vygotsky did not participate in the expeditions, which were led by Luria (1976, 1979). An interesting fact is that Kurt Koffka, the famous Gestalt psychologist, participated briefly in the second expedition before returning to Germany due to illness.

Vygotsky also held several sociopolitical positions at the Scientific State Council, the Society of Materialistic Neuropsychologists, the Presidium of the Krupskaya Academy, and at all kinds of plenary meetings and conventions on public education (Vygodskaya, 1984).

In 1931 the Department of Psychology of the Ukrainian Psychoneurological Institute was founded in Kharkov. Vygotsky was invited to join. Because of the better working conditions at the institute, Vygotsky and his colleagues moved part of their research there, despite repercussions for their personal lives. Leontiev and Bozhovich left their families in Moscow. Luria and Zaporozhets also moved to the distant Ukrainian city, joining the new members P. I. Zinchenko and P. Galperin. Vygotsky did not move permanently but traveled regularly to direct investigations and to lecture. During this time Vygotsky's interest in neurological disturbances of thought and language led him to become a medical student in Moscow and in Kharkov. He took his tests in the latter city during his visits and was able to complete 3 school years. However, because of increasing tensions between Vygotsky and some of his Kharkov colleagues, he shifted his attention elsewhere.

Vygotsky continued his work in Moscow with Levina, S. L. Slavina, B. V. Zeigarnik, and N. A. Menchinskaya. At the same time, he began visiting Leningrad on a regular basis to work with D. B. Elkonin and S. L. Rubinstein and to lecture at the Herzen Pedagogical Institute. The city of Poltova was also added to his itinerary because Bozhovich and her group had moved there from Kharkov. Considering the distances between these cities and the primitive means of transportation in the 1930s, I agree with Wertsch (1985) that these people were motivated not only by scientific concerns but by an exceptional ethical sense of commitment to the creation of a new society.

Vygotsky's vertiginous pace accelerated during his final years. His work schedule in Moscow began very early in the morning and ended late at night. He wrote after 2:00 a.m., when he had some time to himself. Toward the end, Vygotsky acquired the habit of dictating his ideas to a stenographer, who would return them typed a couple of days later. From his deathbed, he dictated the last chapter of *Thinking and Speech* (1934/1987a), in my opinion one of the most beautiful pieces of psychological literature of all time.

Dobkin (1982) recalls visiting Vygotsky in the early 1930s. Vygotsky had been invited to study the behavior of monkeys at the Primates Center founded by Voitonis in Sukhumi and asked Dobkin to accompany him, but Vygotsky's worsening illness prevented him from carrying out these plans in this remote city of Georgia.

It was also during this time that Vygotsky's personal encounter with Kurt Lewin took place. With Hitler's ascension to power, Lewin decided to leave Germany and went to Moscow in 1933. Zeigarnik (1982) described this "historical encounter of the two geniuses, a very polemic discussion" in which she participated. Of all the great encounters in the field of psychology, this was one that Bruner (conversation, May 7, 1987) always imagined and would not have missed for anything in the world. During the time Lewin spent in Moscow, he used to visit Vygotsky often.

During his last months, Vygotsky was named director of the Psychological Section of the National Institute of Experimental Medicine, but death prevented him from carrying out his work plans. In the spring of 1934 he suffered the last assault of tuberculosis. Doctors insisted on hospitalizing him, but Vygotsky refused because he wanted to complete as many of his works as possible. Those who knew him agree that this decision precipitated his end. His daughter tells us that "on May 9, while Vygotsky was at work, he suffered a throat hemorrhage; he was brought home and he could not get up again; toward the end of May he had another similar hemorrhage, and on June 2nd he was hospitalized; late in the evening of the 10th or in the early hours of the 11th of June he died" (Vygodskaya 1984). During his last days his wife and Bluma Zeigarnik took turns caring for him at the Serebrany Bor Sanatorium (Vygodskaya, conversation, October 19, 1988). His last words were, "I am ready." Vygotsky was buried at the Novodevechy Cemetery in Moscow, near the final resting place of Chekhov and Mayakovsky. He was only 37 years old.

Vygotsky's final manuscripts were published a year after his demise, but shortly thereafter a systematic persecution of intellectuals, part of the Stalinist degenerations, resulted in his writings being banned for 20 years. Starting in 1956, however, Vygotsky's work began to be reissued. Currently, the publication of his collected works is being completed, and the last shadows of Stalinism are beginning to dissipate (Gorbachev, 1987). Despite the slow pace of the nightmare's disappearance, we can state that the premises of the social objectives for which people like Vygotsky struggled have been achieved and that his cause has not been frustrated. Recently, the *UNESCO Courier* published a photograph of three Soviet citizens, deaf, mute, and blind from birth, who had just obtained doctoral degrees in psychology, an image that the pioneer of Soviet defectology would have perceived in its heightened significance, much like the child who selected those lines from Salieri's monologue.

The Vygotskian theory of psychology: A synthesis

Vygotsky's work is vast, not only because his writing extends to thousands of pages – in total there are over 180 works written by Vygotsky[4] – but because he was an innovator in multiple fields and acted as the nucleus of an intellectual circle. In addition, he created a school that to this day has inspired followers to continue developing his theory.

His work has been diversely interpreted and applied. In part, this is because many of his ideas went unpublished. Also, Vygotsky modified his proposals over time, often enriching them. These vacillations were due to the ambitiousness of his project and to the fact that his work was carried out in a tragic battle with time. Where some see a coherent development of Vygotsky's theory by his followers, others find irreconcilable antagonisms (see Blanck & Van der Veer, in press; also Kozulin, 1986). Although Vygotsky's ideas did not constitute a perfect corpus, neither are they limited to being simply the beginnings of an approach, as Leontiev affirmed (see Leontiev, 1982). The sociohistorical-cultural psychological theory is a satisfactorily habitable building, constructed on the work of Vygotsky himself. In what follows I will summarize Vygotsky's work. I also include interpretations by the members of his circle and by his followers.

What are the basic assertions of the Vygotskian theory? Mental activity is uniquely human. It is the result of social learning, of the interiorization of social signs, and of the internalization of culture and of social relationships. Mental development is, in essence, a sociogenetic process (Bain, 1983; Blanck, 1977). Culture is internalized in the form of neuropsychic systems that form part of the physiological activity of the human brain. The superior nervous activity, using Pavlovian terms, allows the formation and development of higher mental processes in humans, in contrast to other phylogenetically advanced animals. The higher neural activity of human beings is not, as it was once considered, simply "superior nervous activity," but superior nervous activity that has internalized social meanings derived from the cultural activity of human beings and mediated by signs. This process occurs during the course of ontogenetic development as carried out in the social activities of children with adults, the conveyors of social experience. Social activity and practical actions also facilitate the internalization of sensorimotor schemas, important in grasping social meanings.[5] Finally, the process of internalizing the higher mental functions[6] is historical in nature. The structures of perception, voluntary attention and memory, emotions, thought, language, problem solving, and behavior acquire different forms according to the historical context of the culture, its relationships, and its institutions. I will now briefly elaborate the Vygotskian conclusions I have just summarized.

Neither the naturalist nor the mentalist schools of early 20th-century psychology scientifically explained the higher mental processes (Vygotsky, 1926/1982d). Naturalists adhered to the methods of the natural sciences. Citing philosophical principles and/or historical limitations of the technology available for research, this approach limited itself to the study of relatively simple psychological processes – such as sensations – or observable behaviors. When this approach faced complex functions it dissected them into simple elements; or, in other cases, it adopted dualism, which opened doors to arbitrary speculation. Mentalists considered phenomena of the "spirit." From the stance of phenomenological apriorism or philosophical idealism they described the higher mental processes but argued that it was impossible to explain them. Or they explained them in an arbitrary and speculative manner.

Not satisfied with these options, Vygotsky held that psychology should not waive the scientific, determinist, and causal explanation of the higher mental functions. He refused, as did the Gestalt psychologist, to break complex forms into simple elements that did not conserve all properties of the whole. Convinced of the correctness of the Marxian conception that the human essence is constituted by social relations (Marx, 1845), Vygotsky refused to search for explanations of higher mental processes in the depth of the brain or in the ethereal characteristics of a soul detached from the physical. To explain the spirit, it was necessary to go beyond the confines of the body. Paradoxically, in order to find the soul it was first necessary to lose it.

Luria (1979) recalled that Vygotsky referred to his psychology as instrumental, cultural, and historical. Vygotsky placed this quotation from Bacon as an epigraph in one of his 1930 works: "Neither the unarmed hand nor the intellect left to itself is much value: things are carried out with instruments and means" (Vygotsky & Luria, 1930). "Instruments" alludes to the mediation of the higher mental processes. Humans actively modify the stimuli they encounter, utilizing them as instruments to control surrounding conditions and to regulate their own behavior. Vygotsky's investigations tried to establish how people, with the help of instruments and signs, direct their attention, organize conscious memorization, and regulate their conduct. The essence of human behavior resides in its mediation by tools and signs. Tools are oriented outward, toward the transformation of the physical and social reality. Signs are oriented inward toward the self-regulation of conduct itself (see Vygotsky, 1978). "The knot made in a handkerchief to remember" became for Vygotsky the prototype of the mediation of complex behavior.

As humans we live in a universe of signs; our conduct is determined not by objects themselves but by the signs attached to the objects. During the different situations of life, we incorporate auxiliary stimuli which break the immediacy of the stimulus–response formula. Schedrovitsky (1982, p. 63) points out that we attach meanings to the objects that surround us and act according to those meanings. We label everything: A "good" person is to be loved; a "bad" person is to be hated. Vygotsky argued that signs restructure the consciousness of humans and influence the consciousness of others. Vygotsky's contemporary, M. Bakhtin (see Silvestri & Blanck, 1990; Voloshinov, 1973; Wertsch, this volume), reached, independently, similar conclusions about the semiotic mediation of the mind. There are currently several studies elaborating the work of both authors.

Cultural influences means that society provides the child with goals and structured methods to achieve them. Language is one of the key tools created by humankind for the organization of thinking. Language bears concepts that belong to experience and to the knowledge of humankind. Tools such as language have developed throughout history; the cultural condition joins the historical one. Vygotsky (1981a) mentioned the following as "examples of psychological tools and their complex systems: language; various systems for counting; mnemonic techniques; algebraic symbol systems; works of art; writing; schemes; diagrams; maps and mechanical drawings; all kind of conventional signs" (p. 137). One implication is that, if a study were made of thinking in places where illiteracy is due to history, a different organization of the higher mental functions would be found. And that is precisely what was claimed by Vygotsky and Luria in their transcultural or, as Wertsch (1985) called it, transhistorical research.

In the early 1930s, accelerated social transformations were taking place in Soviet Central Asia. The feudal mode of production was replaced through a socialist re-structuring of the economy, including an intensive literacy plan. This seemed the right place and the right time to test the notion that the higher mental processes were not universal, static, or immutable but that their structure changed according to the mode of social life and the presence or absence of mediating systems such as writing or syllogistic modes of reasoning. The details of this Uzbekistan investigation can be found in Luria (1976). The following subpopulations were studied: illiterate women isolated from social life due to ancient Islamic customs, illiterate men, male and female political activists who had some schooling, and subjects with more advanced schooling. Their processes of perception, generalization and abstraction, reasoning, problem solving, self-analysis, and self-consciousness were analyzed. The results confirmed the hypothesis that semiotic mediation systems act as deter-minants of higher mental processes. Not only did the specific results differ from those of Europeans, but the Uzbekis' mental processes were changing due to schooling and to new forms of social organization.

Vygotsky also termed his psychology *genetic,* in the developmental sense. The term connotes the Marxist notion that the essence of any phenomenon can be cap-tured only through studying its origin and development. In studying mental pro-cesses, Vygotsky considered their social and cultural evolution and the individual's ontogenetic development. From birth, children interact with adults, who socialize them into their culture: their stock of meanings, their language, their conventions, and their way of doing things. Children, according to Vygotsky, utilize lower-order mental processes, elementary attention, perception, and memory within a "natural" line of development. Through constant interaction with adults, however, the low processes are transformed radically into higher mental processes. Here Vygotsky utilizes the Hegelian concept that saturates all the texts of Marx, Engels, and Lenin. The elementary processes are superseded by cultural ones. The term *supersede (sni-mat)* is commonly translated into Russian with the aid of the word *skhoronit,* which has both a negative and a positive meaning: *liquidation* and *conservation* (Vygot-sky, 1987a, p. 126). Thus Vygotsky implies not that the higher mental processes can be reduced to the inferior ones but that in meeting culture the natural line of development is restructured and reorganized. The problem of the natural line of development is one of the most obscure aspects of his work (see the different inter-pretations in Leontiev & Luria, 1956; Scribner, 1985; Wertsch, 1985). In my opinion, Vygotsky emphasized the cultural line of development because of his profound belief in the social determination of mental activity.

Internalization is one of Vygotsky's key concepts relevant to social determination: "Any higher mental function necessarily goes through an external stage in its development because it is initially a social function" (1981b, p. 162). The internalization process is not simply the transferral of an external activity to a preexisting internal stage of consciousness but the process through which said internal stage is formed (Leontiev, 1978). Vygotsky (see 1981b) shared the idea of the French psychologist Pierre Janet that interpersonal processes transform into intrapersonal ones. In the first stage mental functions exist on the level of interaction of children with adults; they are interpsychological. As these processes are internalized to exist inside children, they become intrapsychological (Vygotsky, 1978). This conception implies that culture is not simply an entity independent of individuals with which they must transact (Freud, 1927–1931). Humans are internalized culture. Culture, the accumulation of humankind's historical legacy outside the boundaries of the organism, is interiorized as mental activity, thus becoming internal to the organism. The articulation of Vygotsky's conceptions with those of Wright Mills (see, e.g., his *Character and Social Structure*) and G. H. Mead (1934) constitutes a promising field of investigation (see Blanck & Van der Veer, 1990).

After affirming the social, cultural, and historical nature of the higher mental processes, Vygotsky studied ontogenetic development and its dynamic changes. He envisioned ontogenetic development not as a straight path of quantitative accumulations but as a series of qualitative, dialectic transformations. Higher mental functions form in stages, each a complex process of disintegration and integration. Each stage is distinguished by a particular organization of the psychological activity. For example, Vygotsky considered the acquisition of language as the most significant moment in the course of cognitive development. When language begins to serve as a psychological instrument for the regulation of behavior, perception changes radically, new varieties of memory are formed, and new thought processes are created (Luria, 1961). Vygotsky (1987b) and his collaborators (see Luria, 1981) focused on the relations between thinking and speech, formulating a theory of semantic and systemic organization of consciousness (see Blanck, 1989). The whole structure of consciousness and the higher mental processes vary through the different stages of development. As Vygotsky (1978) suggested, in the early stages children think the way they perceive and remember; in subsequent ones they perceive and remember the way they think.

Vygotsky's theory had revolutionary implications for neurophysiology and its relationship with psychology. His ideas inspired new models of the cerebral organization of psychological activity, the object of study of neuropsychology,[7] a discipline of which Vygotsky can be considered the legitimate founder (Blanck, 1985). Death prevented Vygotsky from reading his paper on psychology and the theory of the localization of psychological functions (1965) before the First Ukrainian Congress on Psychoneurology. The title of this paper reflects his idea that a psychological physiology must prevail over a physiological psychology (Vygotsky, 1983c, p. 15). The problem of localization concerns the relationship between structural and functional units in brain activity. Vygotsky pointed out that the dominant psychological theory influences the manner of conceiving this relationship.

At the time, two theories of this relationship dominated. The old atomist theory posited a rigorous correspondence between structural and functional units: Each "center," located strictly within the geography of the cerebral cortex, carried out a specific function. Extremely naturalist, this theory homogenized complex mental functions with simpler ones while attempting to localize all levels of functions in an assumed strict center. On the other hand, the holistic tendency proposed the equivalence of all the centers, because their functions were not specific. The holistic theory maintained that complex phenomena such as "categorical conduct" were not elementary functions of particular areas of the cerebral tissue but the result of the undifferentiated work of the whole brain.

According to Vygotsky, changes in the relationship among the higher mental processes necessarily lead to changes in the relationship between systems in the cortex. He proposed the notion of neuronal constellations of work. According to Luria (1974), these are organized in systems of zones that work in concert, each zone performing its work within a complex functional system, with other zones located in completely different and frequently very distant areas of the brain.

Researchers such as N. A. Bernshtein had already suggested the existence of functional organs in the human body, different from the morphological, anatomical organs. When Vygotsky (1960) spoke of an "extracortical organization of the higher mental functions," he was referring to the historical and cultural construction of such functional organs, with the help of external, auxiliary instruments. Thanks to these instruments, functional connections are established in the brain between previously independent areas of the cortex, building a unique functional system. Procedures invented through history to organize behavior "tie new functional knots" in people's cerebral cortex (Luria, 1974), without the appearance of new morphological formations. According to Leontiev (1982), the cerebral cortex is an organ that creates organs, a morphological organ that is able to form functional organs. Vygotsky had already considered the higher mental processes as functional organs or systems.

He also concluded that the "localization" of higher mental functions varies during the ontogenetic development. The following example shows that the biological support of the higher mental processes is not static; in ontogenesis different zones perform the same psychological function. Writing depends initially on the memorization of each letter's graphic form, which is carried out through a chain of isolated motor impulses. Each impulse executes only one element of graphic structure. The organization of this process is modified with practice. According to Luria, writing transforms into a kinetic melody not dependent on the visual form of each isolated letter or on individual motor impulses to design each stroke. This is the process behind the common and seemingly simple act of signing one's name.

If during early childhood the visual cortex is injured, interrelated areas are altered and an underdevelopment of visual thought takes place. In an adult, the same lesion would cause only partial defects in the visual processing, without altering the complex forms of thought. This differential effect on cognitive performance confirms the Vygotskian postulate that during ontogeny the higher mental processes change in their structure, in their interrelationship, and in their interfunctional organization.

I believe that from the synthesis I have made of the Vygotskian conceptualizations we can infer that social relationships and culture are the *sources* of the mind, the working brain only its *organ,* and the unique social activity of each subject how it *originates.* In this way, we can clarify a second misunderstanding. Those who are unfamiliar with the Vygotskian production and the philosophical framework from which it acquires its exact meaning believe that, when one discusses the mind–body problem and assigns psychological processes their precise status, one falls into a Cartesian-like dualism, similar to the one Popper and Eccles (1977) recently defended. In Vygotsky's systemic approach, psychological processes are a *function* of the cerebral activity and not an autonomous emergence.

I have summarized the essential aspects of Vygotsky's psychological work, but his ideas extend much farther. Areas of research influenced by Vygotsky include play (Elkonin, 1980), the evolution of children's drawing (e.g., Vygotsky, 1982a), literate codes (Azcoaga, 1982), and the nature of thought disturbance in certain schizophrenias (Goldstein, 1958). Ivanov (1971) considers Vygotsky's work a precursor to cybernetics, the science of control, communication, and information, and semiotics. Vygotsky also developed new disciplines: neuropsychology (Blanck, 1989a), neurolinguistics (Luria, 1980), psycholinguistics (Azcoaga, 1984b), and the psychology of art (Blanck, 1989b; Vygotsky, 1971). His theories have had implications in the fields of aesthetics (Morawski, 1977), literary criticism (Ambrogio, 1975), the psychology of creativity (Vygotsky, 1936, 1982a), defectology (Meshchernyakov, 1985), transcultural psychology (Scribner & Cole, 1981), cognitive anthropology (Goody, 1977), and education (Bruner, 1971), not excluding his important metatheoretic contributions (Puzirei, 1986; Rivière, 1985). I will consider further the last two.

Vygotsky and education

We have already seen that Vygotsky was a pedagogue before becoming a psychologist. A profound relationship exists between these professions, because an essential element of his theory is that higher mental functions are formed during children's enculturation. At the time of birth the organism is completely hominidized (its biological structure is already formed), yet it is not humanized at all. We become human through the internalization of culture. For Vygotsky, formal education was an essential tool of enculturation, which is not to imply that informal education was not considered important. He considered school the best laboratory of human psychology (see Vygotsky, 1926). Within the context of an active, systematic interaction between the child and the pedagogue, children are provided, in an organized way, with the psychological tools that will determine the reorganization of their mental functions.

In Azcoaga's (1988) opinion, Vygotsky's most important contribution was to acknowledge children as active agents in the educational process. Children have been contradictorily viewed as agents *and* as the objects of the educational process. They are agents because they internally elaborate pedagogical activity. This elaboration may or may not have much relationship with the contents of the pedagogical plan. Children also are conceived as the objects or receivers of instruction. Pedagogy has usually operated on the supposition that children are "receivers" of instruction and not, as they certainly are, *elaborators* of the contents presented to them (Vygotsky, 1978).

The polemical relationship between learning and development, crucially important to educators, was highlighted in Vygotsky's work. Psychologists such as Piaget and educators have emphasized biological maturity as an inevitable condition for learning. Vygotsky disagreed, holding that the developmental process was towed by the learning process and any pedagogy that did not respect this fact was sterile. For Vygotsky, pedagogy creates learning processes that *lead* development, and this sequence results in zones or areas of proximal (nearest) development. Vygotsky defined this zone as the distance between the real level of development and the potential level of development (Vygotsky, 1978, p. 85). The concept of the zone of proximal development typifies Vygotsky's method of research in education: A difficult goal is offered; the child receives orientation from an adult; he reaches that goal and another one is offered; he tackles it and solves it independently, if possible, or with the help of the adult. This concept has had a major influence in education (e.g., Gallimore & Tharp, this volume; Hedegaard, this volume; Rogoff & Wertsch, 1984; Tudge, this volume).

Among Vygotsky's (1978) fundamental contributions, his ideas regarding play are of vital importance in the preschool educational processes. In fact, he considered play to be the principal activity for the interiorization and appropriation of reality during the first years. Vygotsky's writings on the connections among play, language, and thought, among many other topics, have become a rich source of inspiration and motivation for the development of a new psychology of education.

The Vygotskian legacy for a unified psychological science

At present, most scholars agree that psychology is in a state of crisis. Sève (1972) described psychology as an immature science. A Kuhnian (1962) analysis would classify psychology as pre-paradigmatic. From another point of view, Leontiev (1978) pointed to the increased contradictions between results obtained in laboratories and the poor state of psychology's theory and methodology. Staats (1983) made an important study of the crisis of separatism in psychology, and Ardila (1984b), notwithstanding his optimism, has recognized that a unified conceptualization of psychology does not exist. The lack of a unifying theory is evident. Vygotsky (1987b) explained that, without a system accepted by everyone to incorporate available knowledge, any new discovery would inevitably lead to the creation of a new theory to make it understandable. Through this process, atomization has proliferated in schools and psychological systems.

Although scholars agree that a crisis exists, their attitudes toward it vary greatly. Some hold that the integration of psychology is not convenient, even unacceptable (S. Koch, conversation, September 5, 1984). Others, such as orthodox psychoanalysts, insist on maintaining the restricted, separatist positions of their schools.[8] On the other hand, I detect an increasing agreement by scholars on the need for a theoretical framework that may unify all of psychology, that searches for points of contact, and that creates a common language. The problem arises when deciding which theory will govern the desired unification. Staats proposes, for example, a basically neobehaviorist theory with marked eclectic traits (Blanck, 1983b). At the international congress on psychology in 1984, I supported the integration and proposed Vygotskian theory as the framework for the unification of psychological science (Blanck, 1987; International Union of Psychological Science, 1984, p. 39).

Vygotsky's metatheoretical contribution to the creation of a unified science of psychology has been underestimated. In my opinion, the present crisis is essentially similar to the one analyzed by Vygotsky in 1926. He was right not only as to the diagnosis but as to the prognosis; history proved him right. A few months after Vygotsky concluded his *Historical Meaning of the Crisis in Psychology,* Karl Bühler (1927) published *Die Krise der Psychologie,* and in 1928 Politzer (see 1964) published his *Critique de fondements de la psychologie.*

Vygotsky stated that his purpose was to make a methodological, that is to say, metapsychological, analysis of the crisis. I have already discussed his conclusion: the division of psychology into two fundamentally opposing fields. He also concluded that the division between psychological systems was so serious that one could speak of different sciences rather than of different schools within a science and that some schools did not deserve classification as a science. Vygotsky (1928) called for a General Psychology to supply a common methodological guide for all the psychological disciplines, maintaining that the historical goal of psychology was the unification within a unique scientific system of all knowledge obtained in its history.

The problem of psychology's unification in a general theoretical framework is as much metatheoretical-epistemological as it is philosophical-ontological (*ontology* in the sense described by Lukács, 1976; Pinkus, 1975). An examination, neither rigid nor absolutist, of the history of science in general, and of Vygotsky's work in particular, suggests a methodology that is broad as well as objective, productive and dynamic, which includes all the procedures that lead to sensible knowledge and which states the facts and allows us to transform the reality we care about. The

Vygotskian vision of instruments was broad-based in its epistemology, incorporating both inductive and hypothetical-deductive thought processes, a dialectical model of reasoning, a flexible conception of experimental design.[9]

Vygotsky was an expert in the delicate dialectics of continuity and disruption in science. Zinchenko and Davydov (1985) were correct in highlighting this passage of Vygotsky's:

> The very attempt to approach the soul scientifically . . . contains in itself the entire past and future path of psychology because science is the path to truth, albeit one that passes through periods of error. . . . We do not suffer from illusions of grandeur, thinking that history begins with us. . . . We want a name on which the dust of centuries settles. In this we see our historical right, an indication of our historical role, the claim of realizing psychology as science. (Vygotsky, 1982b, p. 428)

Vygotsky demanded amplitude without eclecticism or dogmatism but with flexibility. A main instrument in his scientific attitude was what I have called *critical assimilation*. This intellectual posture incorporates valid contributions of different psychological systems while eliminating proposals having no real correlation with facts. Few works like Vygotsky's have been written in permanent dialogue with so many psychologists from such a range of orientations. His assertions result from creative counterpoints. Critical assimilation is different from eclecticism in that it allows coherent integration. Eclecticism, in contrast, is just the incoherent coexistence of contradictory assertions under an allegedly unifying structure.

Self-critique was absent neither in Vygotsky's work nor in its subsequent development. Although proposing the sociohistorical theory as an integrating theoretical framework, I am aware that subsequent investigators have seriously questioned basic statements of Vygotsky's theory. Scribner and Cole's (1981) transcultural investigations have reilluminated important aspects of the historical-cultural research of higher mental processes. Wertsch's (1985) analysis and redefinition of aspects of Vygotsky's theory deserve earnest evaluation and critical assimilation. Similarly, Leontiev and Puzirei, Valsiner and Van der Veer have made suggestions that must be considered. Overall, I believe that, despite these critiques, the essential elements of Vygotsky's theory stand.

The sociohistorical theory as a general theoretical framework could integrate the valid nuclei of various schools: many postulates of classic and operant conditioning, ethological discoveries about animal behavior, many facts put in evidence in the Piagetian consideration of ontogenesis, and even many "colorless green ideas" of Chomsky. Some examples from Chomsky's work may be a case in point. At first glance it may appear that a Cartesian innatist like Chomsky may have nothing in common with Vygotsky. However, Luria (1980) incorporated transformational generative grammar as a tool in his detailed analysis of the transition from thought to oral expression and vice versa. Critical assimilation is evidenced in that Chomsky's belief in the innateness of cognitive structures is not incorporated because it is incompatible with Vygotskian theory. However, Chomsky's dynamic description of message production is incorporated. In a similar manner, Azcoaga (1984b) has incorporated Chomskian transformational semantics into a Vygotskian perspective.

I believe we are marching on a difficult but transitable road. We move toward a unified conceptualization of psychology as science and as profession, both in its philosophy and in its praxis: The goal is a paradigmatic conceptualization that will integrate psychology. The future will tell whether we are right and if, being part of the problem, we can become part of the solution.

Notes

1 Zeigarnik (1982), who dealt with Vygotsky daily during his final years, gave this testimony: "Vygotsky had that special gift of knowing how to listen to someone else; he almost always remained seated, in an apparently absorbed manner; he would very frequently remain silent, and the only way to penetrate his thoughts was through the shine or the force of his blue eyes. At that time the speaker was fully aware that he was participating actively in the matter being dealt with. He was a respectful and at the same time delicate person, undoubtedly a very categorical and arduous defender of his ideas."

2 S. V. Sherashevsky, the famous mnemonist studied by Luria, possessed an eidetic-synesthetic type of memory: He converted every impression, even the words he heard, into an association of sonorous, gustative, tactile, etc., sensations. Luria (1979) recalled one day when they had gone together to the laboratory of L. A. Orbeli. When Vygotsky greeted him, Sherashevsky told him: "You have such a yellow and crumbly voice."

3 The Russian Revolution, between 1918 and 1922, was fought not only against contrarevolutionaries but against foreign troops from 14 nations (English, French, American, Japanese, etc.) which invaded its territory. This episode was called the Civil War.

4 The first anthology of Vygotsky's writings was published in 1956. Since then his books and works have been published continuously in the USSR as well as in other countries (Vygotsky, 1960, 1962, 1964, 1971, 1972, 1974, 1977, 1978, 1982a, 1985, 1986, 1987a). Recently in the USSR the publication of six volumes of his *Collected Works* (Vygotsky, 1982b, 1982c, 1983a, 1983b, 1984b, 1984c) was finally completed; nevertheless, some important manuscripts are still unpublished. Other material was lost in a fire during the Nazi invasion that almost entirely destroyed the European part of the USSR (see Salisbury, 1978). In 1987 Vygotsky's *Collected Works* (1987b) began to be published in the United States. In 1990 they will begin to be published in Spain.

5 Hasty interpretations of humans' internalization of culture sometimes portray the subject as simply a passive blank page over which culture is printed, ignoring in this process the role of the subject's social activity. For Vygotsky, personality begins forming at birth, developing in a dialectic manner. Once the first sketch of internal organization is formed, it is then, from this structure, that the subject actively begins to select the elements he or she will incorporate. This is the role of the subject in constructing his or her own personality configuration. (Of course, this does not mean that the selection is deliberate.) Therefore, we are different from one another not just because we have been impressed by different aspects of the extensive environment but because we have internalized them in a fashion consonant with our developing personality structure, from a personal sense, and in the context of our specific, unique, and individual social activity.

6 In this work, *higher mental functions* and *higher mental processes* are used as synonyms. Actually, mental activity is at the same time a process and a function.

7 This is the Vygotskian conception of *neuropsychology* as a science. In other current theories the term is given a more diffuse meaning.

8 With a more open attitude, people like Fromm (1967) consider that psychoanalysis should be placed at the height of its competitors: "Names like those of Goldstein, Piaget, Vygotsky and Lorenz are just some of the contributors relevant today."

9 In the Anglo-Saxon world, strict rules have been established in this field which are generally not shared beyond its boundaries. A detail of Vygotsky's conception of experimentation of psychology can be seen in Cole and Scribner (1978).

References

Ambrogio, I. (1975). *Ideologías y técnicas literarias* [Ideologies and literacy techniques]. Madrid: Akal.

Ardila, R. (1984a). Letter to G. Blanck, February 9, 1984. Private collection.

Ardila, R. (1984b). Escuelas y sistemas psicológicos y la síntesis experimental del comportamiento [Schools and psychological systems and the experimental synthesis of behavior]. In G. Blanck & R. Ardila (Eds.), *Crisis e integración de la psicología como ciencia.* Buenos Aires: C. & C.

Argan, G. C. (1970). *L'arte moderna* [Modern art] (Vol. 2). Florence: Sasoni.

Azcoaga, J. E. (1982). *Aprendizaje fisiológico y aprendizaje pedagógico* [Physiological learning and pedagogical learning]. Buenos Aires: El Ateneo.

Azcoaga, J. E. (1984a). Comment. In G. Blanck (ed.), *Vigotski: Memoria y vigencia* (p. 206). Buenos Aires: C. & C.

Azcoaga, J. E. (1984b). Vigotski y la psicolingüística actual [Vygotsky and current psycholinguistics]. In G. Blanck (Ed.), *Vigotski: Memoria y vigencia* (pp. 139–145). Buenos Aires: C. & C.

Azcoaga, J. E. (1988). Letter to G. Blanck, January 27, 1988. Private collection.

Bain, B. (Ed.) (1983). *The sociogenesis of language and human conduct.* New York: Plenum.

Benjamin, W. (1980). *Moskaver Tagebuch.* Frankfurt: Suhrkamp.

Bernal, J. D. (1964). *Science in history.* London: Watts.

Blanck, G. (1977). *La determinación social de la actividad psíquica específicamente humana* [Social determination of specifically human mental activity]. Booklet. Buenos Aires: Stokoe.

Blanck, G. (1983a, June). Carlos Marx y la psicología. *Contexto, 25.*

Blanck, G. (1983b, November). La teoría del conductismo social de A. W. Staats [The theory of social behaviorism of A. W. Staats]. *International Newsletter of Social Behaviorism, Selección en Español,* Buenos Aires.

Blanck, G. (1984). Vida y obra de Vigotski [The life and work of Vygotsky]. In G. Blanck (Ed.), *Vigotski: Memoria y vigencia* [Vygotsky: Memory and actuality]. Buenos Aires: Cultura y Cognición.

Blanck, G. (1985, fall). Review of *Neuropsicología* by J. Azcoaga. *Cuadernos de cultura.*

Blanck, G. (1987). Teoría y método para una ciencia psicológica unificada [Theory and method for a unified psychological science]. In M. Siguán (Ed.), *Actualidad de Lev S. Vigotski* [Actuality of Lev S. Vygotsky] (pp. 102–127). Barcelona: Anthropos.

Blanck, G. (1989a, September). La neuropsicología de Vigotski a Luria [Neuropsychology from Vygotsky to Luria]. *Perspectivas Sistématicas, 8.*

Blanck, G. (1989b). Psicología del arte [The psychology of art]. In Centro de Investigaciones y Crítica de Arte, *Diccionario de estética marxista* [Dictionary of Marxist aesthetics]. Buenos Aires: Dialéctica.

Blanck, G., & Van der Veer, R. (1990, January). Vigotski y Mead: Una psicología social de los procesos cognitivos [Vygotsky and Mead: A social psychology of cognitive processes]. *Boletín Argentino de Psicología, 9.*

Blanck, G., & Van der Veer, R. (in press). *Vigotski: Una introducción crítica* [Vygotsky: A critical introduction]. Buenos Aires: Dialéctica.

Bruner, J. S. (1971). *The relevance of education.* New York: Norton.

Bruner, J. S. (1985). Vygotsky: A historical and conceptual perspective. In J. Wertsch (Ed.), *Culture, communication, and cognition: Vygotskian perspectives* (pp. 21–34). Cambridge: Cambridge University Press.

Bruner, J. S. (1987, May). *Vygotsky revisited.* Paper presented at the Graduate School and University Center, City University of New York.

Buhler, K. (1927). *Die Krise der Psychologie* [The crisis in psychology]. Stuttgart: Fischer.

Carr, E. H. (1956). *The Bolshevik Revolution, 1917–1923.* London: Penguin.

Cohen, G. A. (1978). *Karl Marx's theory of history: A defense.* Oxford: Oxford University Press.

Cole, M. (1979). Afterword. In A. Luria, *The making of mind*. Cambridge, MA: Harvard University Press.

Cole, M., & Scribner, S. (1978). Introduction. In L. S. Vygotsky, *Mind in society*. Cambridge, MA: Harvard University Press.

Descartes, R. (1649). *Les passions de l'âme*. Paris: Henri Le Gras.

Dobkin, S. (1982). Ages and days. In K. Levitin, *One is not born a personality* (pp. 23–38). Moscow: Progress.

Ehrenburg, I. (1962). *Men, years, life*. Cleveland: World.

Elkonin, D. B. (1980). *Psicología del juego* [The psychology of play]. Madrid: Visor.

Fitzpatrick, S. (1970). *The Commissariat of Enlightenment: Soviet organization of education and the arts under Lunacharsky, October 1917–1921*. Cambridge: Cambridge University Press.

Freud, S. (1927–1931). "The future of an illusion" and "Civilization and its discontent." In J. Strachey (Ed.), *Freud* (Vol. 21) (Standard Ed.).

Fromm, E. (1967). La crisis actual en el psicoanálisis [The current crisis in psychoanalysis]. *Revista de Psicoanálisis, 7,* 6–30.

Goldstein, K. (1958). El desorden del pensamiento esquizofrénico [The disorder of schizophrenic thought]. In J. Kasanin (Ed.), *Lenguaje y pensamiento en la esquizofrenia*. Buenos Aires: Hormé.

Goody, J. (1977). *The domestication of the savage mind*. Cambridge: Cambridge University Press.

Gorbachev, M. (1987). *Perestroika*. New York: Harper & Row.

International Union of Psychological Science (1984). *XXIII International Congress of Psychology*. Abstracts (Vol. 2).

Ivanov, V. V. (1971). Commentary. In L. S. Vygotsky, *The psychology of art*. Cambridge, MA: MIT Press.

Jakobson, P. M. (1959). *Psicología de los sentimientos* [The psychology of emotions]. Montevideo: EPU.

Jakobson, P. M. (1965). *Los sentimientos en el niño y en el adolescente* [Emotions in the child and adolescent]. Montevideo: EPU.

Jakobson, P. M. (1968). *La vida emocional del alumno* [The emotional life of the student]. Montevideo: EPU.

Jakobson, P. M. (1969). *La educación de los sentimientos en el niño* [The education of emotions in the child]. Montevideo: EPU.

Jakobson, P. M. (1972). *La motivación de la conducta humana* [The motivation for human behavior]. Montevideo: EPU.

Kozulin, A. (1986). Vygotsky in context. In L. S. Vygotsky, *Thought and language* (pp. xi–lvi) (A. Kozulin, Ed.). Cambridge, MA: MIT Press.

Kuhn, T. S. (1962). *The structure of scientific revolutions*. Chicago: University of Chicago Press.

Leontiev, A. N. (1978). *Activity, consciousness, and personality*. Englewood Cliffs, NJ: Prentice-Hall.

Leontiev, A. N. (1982). *Problems in the development of mind*. Moscow: Progress.

Leontiev, A. N., & Luria, A. R. (1956). Introduction. In L. S. Vygotsky, *Izbrannye psikhologicheskie issledovaniya* [Selected psychological investigations.] Moscow: Izdatel'stvo Akademii Pedagogicheskikh Nauk SSSR.

Levitin, K. (1982). *One is not born a personality*. Moscow: Progress.

Lukács, G. (1976). *Ontologia dell'esere sociale* [Ontology of the social being] (3 vols.). Rome: Riuniti.

Luria, A. R. (1961). *The role of speech in the regulation of normal and abnormal behavior*. New York: Irvington.

Luria, A. R. (1974). *El cerebro en acción* [The working brain]. Barcelona: Fontanella.

Luria, A. R. (1976). *Cognitive development*. Cambridge, MA: Harvard University Press.

Luria, A. R. (1979). *The making of mind: A personal account of Soviet psychology*. (M. Cole & S. Cole, Eds.). Cambridge, MA: Harvard Univesity Press.

Luria, A. R. (1980). *Fundamentos de neurolingüística* [Foundations of neurolinguistics]. Barcelona: Labor.

Luria, A. R. (1981). *Language and cognition* (J. Wertsch, Ed.). New York: Wiley.

Luria, A. R. (n.d.). Comment. In G. Blanck (Ed.) (1984), *Vigotski: Memoria y vigencia* [Vygotsky: Memory and actuality]. Buenos Aires: C. & C.

Makarenko, A. S. (1985). *The road to life* (2 vols.). Moscow: Progress.

Marx, K. (1845). Thesis on Feuerbach. In K. Marx & F. Engels, *Selected works*. Moscow: Progress.

Mead, G. H. (1934). *Mind, self, and society* (C. Morris, Ed.). Chicago: University of Chicago Press.

Mecacci, L. (1983). Introduzione [Introduction]. In L. Mecacci (Ed.), *Vygotskij: Antologia di scritti*. Bologna: Mulino.

Meshchernyakov, A. (1985). *Awakening to life*. Moscow: Progress.

Miller, G. A. (1978). Comment. In L. S. Vygotsky, *Mind in society*. Cambridge, MA: Harvard University Press.

Morawski, S. (1977). *Reflexiones sobre la estética marxista* [Reflections about Marxist aesthetics]. Mexico, D. F.: Era.

Pinkus, T. (Ed.) (1975). *Conversations with Lukács*. Cambridge, MA: MIT Press.

Politzer, G. (1964). *Crítica de los fundamentos de la psicología* [Critique of the foundations of psychology]. Buenos Aires: Carlos Hernández.

Popper, K., & Eccles, J. (1977). *The self and its brain*. New York: Springer.

Potebnya, A. A. (1913). *Mysl i yazyk* [Thought and language]. Kharkov: Mirny Trud.

Puzirei, A. A. (1986). *The cultural-historical theory of L. S. Vygotsky and contemporary psychology* [in Russian]. Moscow: MGU.

Reed, J. (1920). Soviet Russia now. *Liberator, 3*, 9–12.

Rivière, A. (1985). *La psicología de Vygotski* [The psychology of Vygotsky]. Madrid: Visor.

Rogoff, B., & Wertsch, J. V. (Eds.) (1984). *Children's learning in the "zone of proximal development."* San Francisco: Jossey-Bass.

Salisbury, H. E. (1978). *The unknown war*. New York: Bantam.

Sánchez Vázquez, A. (Ed.) (1970). *Estética y marxismo* [Aesthetics and Marxism] (2 vols.). Mexico, D. F.: Era.

Schedrovitsky, G. (1982). Comment. In K. Levitin, *One is not born a personality* (pp. 59–63). Moscow: Progress.

Scribner, S. (1985). Vygotsky's uses of history. In J. Wertsch (Ed.), *Culture, communication and cognition* (pp. 119–145). Cambridge: Cambridge University Press.

Scribner, S., & Cole, M. (1981). *The psychology of literacy*. Cambridge, MA: Harvard University Press.

Sève, L. (1972). *Marxisme et théorie de la personnalité* [Marxism and the theory of personality]. Paris: Editions Sociales.

Sève, L. (1978). *Man in Marxist theory and the psychology of personality*. Sussex: Harvester Press.

Sève, L. (1980). *Une introduction a la philosophie marxiste* [An introduction to Marxist philosophy]. Paris: Editions Sociales.

Sève, L. (1984). Letter to G. Blanck, July 7, 1984. Private collection.

Shakhlevich-Lifanova, T. M. (1978). Vygotsky's works. In L. S. Vygotsky, *Mind in society* (pp. 141–151). Cambridge, MA: Harvard University Press.

Shklovsky, V. (1979). *Testimone de un'epoca* [Testimony of an era]. Rome: Riuniti.

Silvestri, A., & Blanck, G. (1990). *Bajtín y Vigotski: La organización semiótica de la conciencia* [Bakhtin and Vygotsky: The semiotic organization of mind]. Barcelona: Anthropos.

Spinoza, B. de (1979). *Etica* [Ethics]. Madrid: Editora Nacional. (Original work published 1675)

Staats, A. W. (1983). *Psychology's crisis of disunity*. New York: Praeger.

Suchodolsky, B. (1984). Comment. In G. Blanck (Ed.), *Vigotski: Memoria y vigencia* (p. 229). Buenos Aires: Cultura y Cognición.

Toulmin, S. (1978, September). The Mozart of psychology. *New York Review of Books*.

Van der Veer, R. (1987). El dualismo en psicología: Un análisis vygotskiano [Dualism in psychology: A Vygotskian analysis]. In M. Sigúan (Ed.), *Actualidad de Lev S. Vigotski* (pp. 87–101). Barcelona: Anthropos.

Voloshinov, V. N. (1973). *Marxism and the philosophy of language*. New York: Seminar.

Vygodskaya, G. L. (1984). *Lev Semenovich Vigotskii (1986–1934 gg.)*. Unpublished manuscript.

Vygotsky, L. S. (1926). *Pedagogical psychology* (in Russian). Moscow: Worker of Education Publishing House.

Vygotsky, L. S. (1928). Psychological science in the USSR. In *Social sciences in the USSR, 1917–1927.* Moscow. (Original work in Russian)

Vygotsky, L. S. (1936). The problem of creativity in actors. In P. M. Jakobson (Ed.), *The psychology of the stage feelings of an actor.* Moscow: Government Publishing House. (Original work written in 1932)

Vygotsky, L. S. (1960). *Razvitie vysshykh psikhicheskikh funkstii* [The development of higher mental functions]. Moscow: Izdatel'stvo Akademii Pedagogicheskikh Nauk.

Vygotsky, L. S. (1962). *Thought and language* (E. Hanfmann & G. Vakar, Eds. & Trans.). Cambridge, MA: MIT Press.

Vygotsky, L. S. (1964). *Pensamiento y lenguaje* [Thought and language]. Buenos Aires: Lautaro.

Vygotsky, L. S. (1965). Psychology and localization of functions. *Neuropsychologia, 3,* 381–386.

Vygotsky, L. S. (1971). *The psychology of art.* Cambridge, MA: MIT Press.

Vygotsky, L. S. (1972). *Psicologiá del arte* [The psychology of art]. Barcelona: Barral.

Vygotsky, L. S. (1974). *Storia dello sviluppo delle funzioni psichiche superiori* [History of the development of higher psychological functions] (M. Serena Veggetti, Trans.). Florence: Giunti-Barbera.

Vygotsky, L. S. (1977). *Denken und Sprechen* [Thinking and speech]. Frankfurt: Fischer.

Vygotsky, L. S. (1978). *Mind in society: The development of higher psychological processes* (M. Cole, V. John-Steiner, S. Scribner, & E. Souberman, Eds.). Cambridge, MA: Harvard University Press.

Vygotsky, L. S. (1981a). The instrumental method in psychology. In J. V. Wertsch (Ed.), *The concept of activity in Soviet psychology* (pp. 134–143). White Plains, NY: Sharpe.

Vygotsky, L. S. (1981b). The genesis of higher mental functions. In J. V. Wertsch (Ed.), *The concept of activity in Soviet psychology* (pp. 144–188). White Plains, NY: Sharpe.

Vygotsky, L. S. (1982a). *La imaginación y el arte en la infancia* [Imagination and art in infancy]. Madrid: Akal.

Vygotsky, L. S. (1982b). *Sobranie sochinenii: Tom pervyi. Voprosy teorii i istorii psikhologii* [Collected works: Vol. 1. Problems in the theory and history of psychology]. Moscow: Izdatel'stvo Pedagogika.

Vygotsky, L. S. (1982c). *Sobranie sochinenii: Tom vtroi. Problemy obschei psikhologii* [Collected works: Vol. 2. Problems of general psychology]. Moscow: Izdatel'stvo Pedagogika.

Vygotsky, L. S. (1982d). *Historical meaning of the crisis in psychology.* In L. S. Vygotsky, *Sobranie sochinenii: Tom pervyi. Voprosy teorii i istorii psikhologii* [Collected works: Vol 1. Problems in the theory and history of psychology]. Moscow: Izdatel'stvo Pedagogika. (Original work written in 1926)

Vygostky, L. S. (1983a). *Sobranie sochinenii: Tom tretii. Problemy razvitiya psikhiki* [Collected works: Vol. 3. Problems in the development of mind]. Moscow: Izdatel'stvo Pedagogika.

Vygostky, L. S. (1983b). *Sobranie sochinenii: Tom pyatyi. Osnovy defektologii* [Collected works: Vol. 5. Foundations of defectology]. Moscow: Izdatel'stvo Pedagogika.

Vygostky, L. S. (1983c). From the notebooks of L. S. Vygotsky. *Soviet Psychology, 21*(3).

Vygotsky, L. S. (1984a). The theory of emotions: An historical and psychological investigation (in Russian). In L. S. Vygotsky, *Sobranie sochinenii: Tom shestoi. Nauchnoe nasledtvo* [Collected works: Vol. 6. Scientific legacy]. Moscow: Izdatel'tsvo Pedagogika. (Original work written in 1933)

Vygotsky, L. S. (1984b). *Sobranie sochinenii: Tom shestoi. Nauchnoe nasledtvo* [Collected works: Vol. 6. Scientific legacy]. Moscow: Izdatel'tsvo Pedagogika.

Vygotsky, L. S. (1984c). *Sobranie sochinenii: Tom chetvertyi. Detskaya psikhologiya* [Collected works: Vol. 4. Child psychology]. Moscow: Izdatel'tsvo Pedagogika.

Vygotsky, L. S. (1985). *Pensée et langage* [Thinking and speech] (F. Sève, Trans.). Paris: Editions Sociales.

Vygotsky, L. S. (1986). *Thought and language* (A. Kozulin, Ed.). Cambridge, MA: MIT Press.

Vygotsky, L. S. (1987a). *Historia del desarrollo de las funciones psíquicas superiores* (L. Ruiz, Trans.). Havana: Científico Técnica.

Vygotsky, L. S. (1987b). Thinking and speech. In L. S. Vygotsky, *Collected Works* (Vol 1, pp. 39–285) (R. Rieber & A. Carton, Eds.; N. Minick, Trans.). New York: Plenum. (Original work published in Russian in 1934)

Vygotsky, L. S., & Luria, A. (1930). *Etyudy po istorii povedeniya: Obez'yana, primitiv, rebenok* [Studies in the history of behavior: Ape, primitive, child]. Moscow and Leningrad: Gosudarstvennoe Izdatel'stvo.

Wertsch, J. V. (1984). Comment. In G. Blanck (Ed.), *Vigotski: Memoria y vigencia* [Vygotsky: Memory and actuality] (pp. 205–206). Buenos Aires: C. & C.

Wertsch, J. V. (1985). *Vygotsky and the social formation of mind.* Cambridge, MA: Harvard University Press.

Zeigarnik, B. V. (1982). Comment. In M. Golder (Ed.) (1986), *Reportajes contemporáneos a la psicología soviética* [Contemporary reports on Soviet psychology]. Buenos Aires: Cartago.

Zinchenko, V. P., & Davydov, V. V. (1985). Foreword. In J. V. Wertsch, *Vygotsky and the social formation of mind* (pp. vii–xi). Cambridge, MA: Harvard University Press.

2   The historical context of Vygotsky's work: A sociohistorical approach

Alberto Rosa and Ignacio Montero

In recent years the Western world has witnessed an increasing interest in Vygotsky's contribution to psychology and education. It might even be said that Vygotsky is "in." What has happened to make the work of a psychologist who has been dead for over 50 years so relevant now? What is it in Vygotsky's works that invites psychologists and educators to scrutinize his writings when in the normal course of events they would be subject matter mainly for historians of science? It may be that the recent translations of some of his writing and the work of researchers inspired by the sociohistorical approach have a lot to do with it, but these causes alone cannot fully explain why so much attention is given to an approach to psychology that had been forgotten for so long.

It would be prolix, even pretentious, to try to answer these questions adequately. The goal of this chapter is more modest. It will try to outline a sociohistorical approach to Vygotsky's contribution to psychology and education.

Vygotsky's conception of history and the use he makes of it in relation to science, to psychology, and to the history of psychology are something we think worth taking seriously. As Scribner (1985) points out, Vygotsky's uses of history are not exhausted by the phylogenetic history of the species, the history of the development of cultures, or the history of the ontogenetic individualization of each person. This chapter starts by offering some Vygotskian ideas about the historical development of psychology – in conjunction with the contributions of contemporary authors – in order to develop some conceptual tools for a historical analysis of science which, in turn, will be applied to the analysis of the Vygotskian system of psychology.

Lev Semenovich Vygotsky was a man of his country and time. His genius was in building the basis of a new psychological system from materials borrowed from the philosophy and social sciences of his time. Many of the main concepts of Vygotskian psychology, such as mediation, practice and activity, or the historical nature of higher psychological processes, were adapted from ideas previously developed by Marx and Engels. What is more, to a great extent Vygotsky's psychology is an application of dialectical and historical materialism to the psychological realm. Therefore, if we agree with the fundamental tenets of the Vygotskian view of psychology, then we have to approach his own contribution historically. We shall do that, first, by devoting a part of this chapter to showing how Vygotsky's work is

59

framed – and partly explained – by the immediate context of his time; in other
words, how the events that took place in postrevolutionary Russia affected the development of Soviet psychology. Then we shall offer some ideas about how the
Vygotskian approach fits today into the current state of psychology and education.
Finally, we shall argue that Vygotsky's system currently retains its potential, although it has to be considered within the framework of the knowledge accumulated
over the last 50 years.

Some conceptual tools for the history of science

One of Vygotsky's contributions worth revitalizing is the use he makes of history
and of metatheoretical analysis of psychology as an orientation to his psychological
research. His research program developed from an essay (Vygotsky, 1982) in which
he analyzed the psychology of his time from the point of view of his philosophical
ideas about history and science. A great many of his psychological ideas were
already present in this early piece of work.

This section presents some contemporary conceptual tools for the historical analysis
of science, which we believe are not only coherent with the Vygotskian approach
but also develop some of his ideas. The ideas described here form the basis for the
rest of the chapter.

From a Marxist viewpoint, history is not simply a narrative that permits an understanding of the past; rather, history relies on material bases to explain the events
that have affected a particular society. In the case of the history of a science such
as psychology, in order to explain the appearance of a given theory and its fate one
must refer to its conceptual development, its empirical discoveries, the theoretical
instruments it generates, and the external history of the discipline itself, as well as
to the social or personal events that favor its development or stifle its progress.

History of science is no longer considered to be merely a narrative of past events
that justifies the progress of science from its more backward beginnings to the present time. This is an idea, currently denominated *justificationist presentism,* that has
virtually disappeared with the diminished importance of positivism. Today the history of science is considered to be a discipline related symbiotically to the theory of
science. As Lakatos (1970) points out, philosophy of science without history of
science is empty, and history of science without theory of science is blind.

Theory of science has the purpose of dealing with the validity of scientific knowledge; to do this, it sometimes draws on information offered by history of science.
But, in addition to this theoretical plane, there is a psychological one that attempts
to explain how individuals acquire knowledge from their social medium and make
new contributions to the collective enterprise of the construction of knowledge that
we call science. A historian of psychology who is at the same time a psychologist
and who believes in the unity of nature and its operating principles should, at the
very least, try to unite the vision of history with that of psychology, so that the
historical explanations he or she makes use of include a form of psychological

explanation coherent with the former and vice versa. This obliges him or her to take a specific theoretical position and to create data, reconstruct the past, and view individuals, society, knowledge, and science in a particular manner.

As Chalmers (1976) points out, there are two ways of looking at the relationship between philosophy of science and history of science. The first consists of starting with a set of prescriptions regarding what science is and then constructing a history of science that tries to justify it, without concern for previously developing a theory of history. The second, in contrast, begins with a theory of history that includes an analysis of the diverse conceptions of science that have developed over time. In this way, the knowledge of history contributes to the understanding of why and how science has been undertaken in the past; and in addition to explaining why we have arrived at the current state of knowledge, it may illuminate the options we have for the future. The position presented here clearly favors this second option.

Human actions carried over time are the subject of history. In this sense, history is not far from psychology. This similarity has been noted frequently. For example, Dilthey said that man had a historical nature and that psychology needs history to understand man, while at the same time history requires psychology to explain the human actions that produce historical change. R. I. Watson (1972) said that both history and psychology refer to the same object, human actions, although in a different way. The role of the historian, then, is in some way similar to that of the psychologist, although it is more difficult, because the behavior that historians try to explain happened sometime in the past. Vygotsky also gives history a central role in his psychological system, since for him the higher mental processes are a result of the internalization of cultural means of regulating human behavior. Given that these socially organized activities change over time and space, it becomes difficult to maintain the belief that higher psychological activities have identical characteristics in different cultures.

Given that science is the result of a social activity, we must consider the nature of this activity. Althusser (1965; Althusser & Balibar, 1967) characterizes society as a set of interrelated practices, defining *practice* as any process of transforming raw material into a finished product. This transformation is carried out by human effort through specific means of production. One can speak of practices that are, among other things, agricultural, industrial, commercial, political, ideological, or epistemological – in the latter three cases, the action is produced on conceptual or power structures in order to transform them. Each society reveals a particular interrelationship among the diverse practices, so that each practice is maintained by the others as long as it fulfills the role it is supposed to play within the social body. If it does not, it disappears or is transformed. These actions come to be collective modes of activity governed by specific rules, at times clearly explicit and at other times tacit but nonetheless real; in either case, they are susceptible to being reconstructed axiomatically. Hübner (1983) calls each of these rules a "historical system," or simply "system." There are as many rule systems as there are social practices or facets of human life. These systems often do not have an ideal formal precision, but they are exact enough to be applied in specific situations and thus to guide human activities in society. To this structural methodological construct (the system) that corresponds to a functional one (the practice), another also suggested by Hübner (1983) must be added: a "system ensemble" that corresponds to the set of practices. A system ensemble is the set of rule systems that are formed within a given society and that constitute its culture. The individual systems are not independent but, rather, interrelated, although not in a perfectly coherent way, since many of them are incompatible, contradictory, or simply incommensurate.

Historical systems are the result of social practices. The rules happen to be the internal structure of practices that have been developed historically to respond to the needs of the physical or social environment and evolve according to their own dynamics. These rules help to organize social life, but at the same time they are internalized by each individual group member so that they govern his or her behavior in specific situations. Current psychological theories have some theoretical tools available that can explain this interiorization of behavioral norms, as is the case with *schema, script,* or the notion of *activity* developed by the sociohistorical school, in particular Leontiev (1978).

When a social group is faced with a new problem, it has to devise a particular means of solving it; that is, it must create a new practice with its inherent rule system. But as Paris (1982) states, referring to Marx (1859), humanity does not take on more problems than it can solve. From this reference Paris extracts a methodological tool he calls the "kairological principle" (from the Greek *kairos,* the opportune moment). Two further principles are derived from this: the subprinciple of "conjunctural urgency" – a society at a particular moment is faced with an imperative to solve a problem – and the subprinciple of maturity – in order to solve this problem, the society must manifest certain requisites, a certain conceptual apparatus and resources that can be mobilized to confront the new situation. This principle, applied here to the history of science, has a close similarity to the Vygotskian notion of the zone of proximal development in the explanation of the relationship between learning and development. The application of this principle to scientific practice can help to explain some behaviors in the history of science. It allows us to understand why the solution to a problem not yet viewed as such by the scientific community can be ignored and remain forgotten until the same problem becomes urgent.

The impulse for historical change can be found in environmental necessities as understood by individuals and societies at a given historical moment. Hübner (1983) describes a second impulse that helps to facilitate change: the incoherence in the system ensemble. As previously noted, the equilibrium in the system ensemble is somewhat unstable. At a specific historical moment the systems are structured hierarchically in a particualr fashion, so that certain sets of rules are considered primordial and others assume a position subordinate to them. This occurs at both a societal and an individual level. One of the objectives of change, then, is that the system ensemble as a whole appears more coherent in some way. According to

Hübner, historical progress follows a tendency toward the harmonization of the system ensemble of a given society and culture.

However, even if change is produced within a social group, we cannot forget that the role of a particular personality may have a strong impact on historical events. Before deciding what to do in a given situation, a person must conceptualize the problem and decide which of the available resources she or he will employ to solve it. In other words, he or she must decide which script to use or which rule to apply or, where appropriate, which of the systems that occupy his or her mind are at the vertex of the hierarchy, to which the rest must yield. An approach such as that of Leontiev (1978) links social practice, individual activity, and personality so that categories of historical and psychological analysis can be managed in a coherent fashion.

The image of science presented here is that of a type of historically conditioned knowledge. Let us consider, then, that science is made up of knowledge systems that result from practice that follows certain rules. Consequently, science does not explain the world as it is; instead, it presents an image of the world "as if" things were as theory presents them. Thus we have, as Chalmers (1976) points out, a real world (of things as they are, in themselves), the world as we conceive it (the image of the world that we perceive through phenomena that theory or prior experience allows us to perceive), and a theoretical world (the more or less rational reconstruction of reality that science offers us). The real world does not present itself to us in a direct way – as in the Kantian *noumenon* – whereas the other two worlds relate to each other in a dialectical manner through scientific practice or, in other words, through the process of transformations by the action of conceptual tools and the facts that they allow us to examine.

Chalmers also points out that practices give way to a structure that has an objective existence, so that, even though science is a result of human activity, it is at the same time a process without a subject; thus the systems that result from practice have implications that often go far beyond the understanding of their authors themselves, and they may even apply the rules erroneously. In the language of Lakatos, the positive heuristics of a research program has no subject. It constitutes a property of the program and not of an individual or a community.

Within the system of each science we can differentiate between the set of theories that comprise the body of knowledge on the subject matter of that science and the theory of the practice of that science, that is, the formal requisites that the practice of that science must fulfill at a particular historical moment in order to be considered scientific. Each of these aspects is formed by interconnected rules. The concept of the theory of practice is of special interest to the historian because, on the one hand, it provides an understanding of the way in which scientific knowledge has been produced at a given moment in time and, on the other, it makes it possible to examine the basic assumptions on which the theoretical structure of a science has been built. This yields a tool critical to the analysis of different theories and systems.

This conception of science confers a central role to the history of science, since its practice provides the only possible means of justifying scientific knowledge, through the explanation of how theoretical tools have been generated over time and the way empirical verification has been understood. But history of science must therefore be included in the history of culture, since the sciences come to be "historical systems." A particular science can be characterized as a system or a set of systems of rules developed by scientific practice and applied to a defined area of reality, the limits of which have been established at a particular historical moment. The history of the sciences, then, can be constructed using the previously mentioned historical categories, and the succession of theories and systems within a given science can be described by means of "explications" and "mutations,"[1] always within the context of the system ensemble that comprises the culture by which it is nurtured and which it serves. The opposition between internal and external history of science therefore loses its meaning since it is impossible to separate science from its causes and its function, which are within society and culture. The role of the history of science is a central one, as it permits us to explain what a particular science is and provides the foundation for the knowledge that science offers.

At the same time, however, science attempts to study reality, verifying the empirical validity of the concepts it studies. Vygotsky (1982) offers an elegant exposition of the relationship between the history of knowlege and empirical verification:

> The regularity in the change and development of ideas, the appearance and death of concepts, even the change in classifications, etc., can all be explained scientifically based on the connection of the science in question with (1) the sociocultural substratum of the time, (2) the general laws and conditions of scientific knowledge, (3) the objective demands the nature of the phenomena currently under investigation make on scientific cognition, in other words, with the demands of the objective reality studied by the science in question. Scientific cognition must adapt itself, accommodate to the peculiarities of the facts under study, be structured in accordance with their demands. (p. 302)

Later, Vygotsky discusses the psychological and at the same time historical character of scientific cognition:

> Scientific interpretation, together with other activities, is one of the forms of activity of social man. Therefore, scientific cognition, considered as a facet of the cognition of nature and not as ideology, is a certain variety of labor and, like any form of labor, is above all a process of interaction between man and nature in which man, as a force of nature, has to face nature. This is a process that is conditioned by the properties of elaborated nature and by the producing force of nature; that is [in the case of psychology], a process conditioned by the nature of psychological phenomena and by the cognitive properties of man (G. V. Plejanov). But it is evident that unmodified natural phenomena cannot explain the development, the movement, the change in the history of science. However, at any given level of development we can point out, differentiate, abstract the requirements that nature makes on the phenomena to be studied at the current level of cognition, a level that is determined not by the nature of the phenomena but by the history of man. This is so because the natural properties of psychological phenomena are a purely historical category at the current level of cognition. Since these properties vary in the process of cognition, and the totality of specific properties is a historical dimension,

they may be considered as the cause, or as one of the causes, of the historical development of science. (1982, p. 306)

Following this conception of the history of science, we shall go on to contextualize the meaning of the contribution of Vygotsky's work both at the time he lived and at the current moment. But to do this we must first address the historical evolution of postrevolutionary Russia, the country and the time in which he lived.

The external historical context: Postrevolutionary Russia

As is well known, following the October Revolution Russia entered into a tumultuous period characterized by civil war, foreign intervention, and an asphyxiating economic situation that the new regime tried to combat with what was called the "Communism of War." In 1921 under Lenin's leadership the New Economic Policy was adopted, which allowed a market economy. At the same time, political and ideological polemics arose among diverse party factions, focusing mostly on the problems of resource distribution and the priority of either agricultural or industrial development.

One of the great challenges facing the new state was education. According to Downing (1988), the average literacy rate in the USSR at the time of the Revolution was about 30%, with regions in which there were virtually no literates. In spite of the tremendous difficulties that existed, the fight against illiteracy was begun immediately. On October 29, 1917, a few days after the installation of the revoutionary government (Council of National Commissars), Lunacharsky, the first national commissar of education, calling for all citizens to achieve complete literacy, created a national system of schools and a system for teacher training (Nazarova, 1988). On December 26, 1919, Lenin signed the decree "On the liquidation of illiteracy amongst the population of the Russian Soviet Federal Socialist Republic." Lenin himself, his wife, Krupskaia, and other distinguished leaders gave this undertaking top priority. Lenin's aim was to mobilize every literate in the fight against illiteracy, and 400,000 volunteers responded to his call. Classes were established in factories and barracks, and teachers even followed nomadic tribes migrating through Central Asia.

In 1922 Moscow hosted the first All-Russian Congress for the Elimination of Illiteracy. At this congress, the results of the first 2 years of program implementation were evaluated. Although there had been some important successes – for example, the illiteracy rate in the Red Army had dropped from 65% to 6% – there was still much work to be done. The program continued for a long time; among the difficulties faced was the circumstance that some of the languages spoken in the USSR did not have a written alphabet. It is noteworthy that Lenin himself insisted on having pupils choose the language in which they preferred to receive instruction (Downing, 1988).

On December 11, 1917, a decree transferred the control of education from the Ecclesiastical Department to the National Commissariat for Education. One of the commissariat's tasks was to appeal to teachers who were divided between the conservative antisoviet faction, the Teachers' All-Russian Union, and the recently created Union of Internationalist Teachers. In 1918 the former organization was dissolved and the latter became an organization of the masses (Nazarova, 1988).

The recommendations of the National Commissariat for Education were focused on the integration of academic work with physical activity and the natural environment – fields, people, garden work, factory visits, and so on – without stressing adherence to a preestablished curriculum. In this way substantial latitude was given to the creativity of teachers at the local level. From 1923 to 1925 an experimental program based on the same principles was implemented, this time providing materials and suggestions to teachers (Nazarova, 1988).

The most ardent advocate of this kind of progressive education was V. N. Shulgin, director of the Marx–Engels Institute of Pedagogy. To him formal education was merely a complement to spontaneous education; when the authentic socialist society was established the school would disappear to give way to the social environment.

In regard to the academic and intellectual world, the new Bolshevik state inherited an important network of academic institutions, although the majority of their members did not approve the new state of things. Nevertheless, at this early stage intellectuals enjoyed complete independence in their work, as long as they did not go against party politics. Evidence of this is the fact that until January 1929 there were no Communist Party militants in the Academy of Sciences, and only one of the members of the Academy, the linguist N. I. Marr, identified himself as a Marxist, whereas many others, including Pavlov, did not hide their open hostility toward the system. Until 1928 there was freedom of literary creation; an example of this is a declaration by the Central Committee in 1925, apparently inspired by Bukharin, that maintained a willingness to tolerate a multiplicity of approaches in literature and even a certain disinclination to express a preference for any particular one (Carr, 1981).

However, this initial absence of control over intellectual life is not an indication of a lack of interest in science and culture on the part of the new state. From the beginning there was an attempt to create a new science and a scientific policy. What happened was that the tumultuous period of power struggle that arose with Lenin's illness and that lasted through most of the 1920s did not allow this policy to proceed in a definite direction almost until the decade of the 1930s with Stalin's consolidation in power.

As early as 1918 the Socialist Academy was created (renamed the Communist Academy in 1923); it was dedicated primarily to social science research, but with time it attempted to widen its sphere of influence to include natural sciences (Graham, 1972). The first objective of this institution was to create a treatise on dialectical materialism and on historical materialism, but the scarcity of qualified personnel prevented this task from being carried out. The manual in use for the training of new generations of Marxists, for lack of a better one, was the one by Bukharin, heavily criticized both in the USSR and abroad by such distinguished Marxists as Gramsci and Lukàcs. When the institution changed its name, attacks, which were fundamentally ideological, began against the "bourgeois scientists" of the Academy of Sciences, including Pavlov; these attacks were always made indirectly in a manner that maintained respect to support the work of the Academy of Sciences, even though it produced "bourgeois science," while giving the Communist Academy the task of establishing the foundations of a Soviet science with a unified system of research methods, theories, and organizational principles (Vucinich, 1984).

Another institution that had an important role in the polemics of the postrevolutionary period was the Society of Militant Materialist Dialecticians founded in 1924. Although it had no scientific production of its own, it exercised considerable critical activity directed at scientists considered to be opposed to Marxist philosophy and official ideology, stressing the need for central planning of research policy. Some of these actions will be discussed later.

In this early phase, psychologists who had begun their work prior to the Revolution, as is the case of the so-called idealists (Lopatin, Nechaev, Chelpanov), conserved their position although they began to be attacked in 1921. In contrast, those known as objectivists (Pavlov, Bekhterev), rooted in the tradition of biological materialism, were in a theoretical position compatible with the new regime. Pavlov, whose position toward the revolutionary regime was not exactly sympathetic, received explicit support nonetheless. In 1921, a year characterized by severe famine and by which time Moscow and Petrograd had lost almost half of the prerevolutionary population, the Council of People's Commissars approved a declaration signed by Lenin that created a commission presided over by Gorki and charged with facilitating Pavlov's work and editing his writing.

In 1922 Stalin was named general secretary of the party, an event that placed him in an advantageous position in the struggle to succeed Lenin that began in 1923. At that time there arose a bitter political battle with ideological overtones that had far-reaching consequences for psychology and education in the USSR.

In January 1923 the First Pan-Russian Psychoneurological Conference was held, in which Kornilov, an old disciple of Chelpanov, proposed a program for establishing a psychology based on dialectical materialism. As a result, Kornilov replaced his old teacher as the director of the State Institute of Experimental Psychology of Moscow.

At the second conference, held a year later, a conflict arose between the objectivists, who were on good terms with the powers that be, and the psychologists, who were searching for a space between physiology and the idealist concepts of the old psychology. It is here that Vygotsky appeared on the scene with a presentation that won him an invitation from Kornilov to join the team at the institute he directed. There he met Luria and Leontiev, and they formed what they liked to call the "troika"; they were soon joined by the "pyatorka," made up of Bozhovich, Levina, Morozova, Slavina, and Zaporozhets.

In 1925 Engels's *Dialectics of Nature* and some of Lenin's writings were published by the Marx–Engels Institute; this reactivated the polemics between two ideological factions of the Soviet Communist Party who were involved in a political and theoretical struggle that was enmeshed in the process of Stalin's rise to power.

As Bauer (1959) and Vucinich (1984) report, an old controversy existed among Russian Marxists over the interpretation of materialism. On one side were the "mechanicists," who maintained an explanation of change in genetic terms, emphasizing the importance of objective conditions and the limitations they impose on political action. This group argued that science is self-sufficient and discovers its own laws through the process of research. They had even come to believe that dialectics could be reduced to mechanical expressions. This interpretation received explicit support from Bukharin – the party ideologue and director of *Pravda* – in his *Historical Materialism,* published in 1922. On the other side, the "dialecticians" supported an open and nondeterministic explanatory principle, believing that the course of events was open to human action, which could transform the world in the desired direction. This second position implicitly attributed great importance to consciousness as the human characteristic that propitiated the will to build socialism in a single country, according to the Stalinist interpretation of Leninism.

This theoretical polemic was of great importance, as much in politics as in its consequences for the development of psychology. For one thing, it was one of the causes of the split that occurred in 1903 between the Mensheviks, who favored the first position, and the Bolsheviks. Lenin, it goes without saying, was aligned with the second position, consistent with his notion of an elitist and highly ideologized party that would be the vanguard of the proletariat in the transformation of society. This position led him to reduce the number of militants from 600,000 to 350,000 at the CP congress in 1921.

But after Lenin's illness in 1923 and his death in 1924, Stalin undertook a profound transformation of the party in line with his particular interpretation of Leninism. His first measure, after his first victory over Trotsky, was the "Lenin Recruitment," through which he increased the party base by 240,000 militants, along with the first purge.

The theoretical polemic was focused at this time on economic issues. Whereas the left wing of the party (the dialecticians), led by Trotsky, advocated a rejection of the New Economic Policy and the introduction of central planning, the rightwingers, led by Bukharin and Tomsky (the leader of the unions), opposed a program of forced industrializatioin at the expense of the peasants, since, according to them, the objective conditions did not exist to carry it out successfully.

Stalin's role in this regard is well known. While continuing to favor the New Economic Policy, he purged the leftists in a process that lasted from 1925 to 1928 when Trotsky was expelled from the USSR. At the same time, as early as 1926, the draft of the First Five-Year Plan appeared, which followed the line advocated by the leftists; this plan was officially approved in 1929. In short, Stalin liquidated the Left and then implemented the policies it advocated, eliminating the rightwing faction.

In this context the first All-Union Conference on Pedology was held in November 1928. There, Bukharin, Kromskaia, and Lunacharsky pointed out the need to apply psychology and other disciplines to research on children and education, recommending that psychologists begin to develop plans for pedology and psychotechnics to be included in the First Five-Year Plan. Three journals were created that year devoted to psychology, pedology, and psychotechnics.

The same year, while continuing their work in Kornilov's institute, the troika became involved in the research projects of the psychology laboratory at the Institute of Communist Education and formed the Institute of Defectology.

To return to the ideological polemic of the time, it must be noted that mechanistic materialism rested on the notion of environmental adaptation and equilibrium, a notion that by this time had come to be considered as "right-wing opportunism" since it was identified with Bukharin and Tomsky, who lost their political power in 1929. It was at this time that reflexology came under attack as "bourgeois materialism." In the same month that Bukharin was defeated, a resolution was approved by the Second Conference of Marxist-Leninist Scientific Institutes of the USSR accusing mechanistic approaches of comprising a clear deviation from the Marxist-Leninist philosophical position. A short time later, the Central Committee of the CP approved a decree instructing the Communist Academy to impose dialectical materialism in the natural sciences. It can be said that at this moment ideology started to exert pressure on scientific research and to be used as a weapon in any type of argument.

The results were not long in coming. As early as 1928 the Central Committee of the CP had issued a decree that placed all literary publications under party control. Between 1929 and 1932 the Academy of Sciences was renovated and placed under the control of the CP. At the same time, the Communist Academy held the first All-Union Conference on Human Behavior in Moscow in January 1930.

The psychological position of Vygotsky and his associates cannot be considered in contradiction with the outcome of the theoretical polemic described above. However, it was soon overcome by the Left, becoming the object of attacks by persons close to the official position.

The 1930 psychological conference proclaimed that the psyche could not be reduced to physiology and maintained the primordial importance of consciousness. It can be said that psychology was secured against reductionist positions. But the growing influence of the CP was soon evident in the course of the development of this science. Around 1931 the position of the militant dialectical philosophers who advocated the need to subordinate theory to the practical necessities of the moment triumphed. This, along with the doctrine that the party must watch over all activities for their implications concerning the political agenda, led to a situation in which any theoretical deviation from the official line was branded a "political error" that fed arguments to enemies of the party, the state, and socialism. As a result, all psychological schools came under ideological scrutiny (Bauer, 1959).

At this point the emphasis was on the importance of consciousness; the so-called two-factor theory (heredity and environment) was attacked on the grounds that it perpetuated the capitalist mentality through a fatalism that prevented the active construction of the new socialist man. To these two factors a third was added: instruction. Education was to promote the individual's self-consciousness and sense of responsibility.

The decade of the 1930s is marked by the progressive strengthening of Stalin's power. The Second Five-Year Plan changed the emphasis from industrialization to the formation of cadres. Whereas the motto of the first plan was "Technique decides everything," that of the second was "Cadres decide everything." State policy was shifted to the control of the individual. In 1934 writers were asked to create a revolutionary romanticism; in 1935 Stajanovism was created as a system for rewarding individual productivity; and, finally, the new constitution of the USSR was promulgated in 1936 (Bauer, 1959).

Although psychologists were called upon again in 1930 to participate in pedology, the period from 1932 to 1936 made evident a growing crisis in the latter discipline as well as increasing difficulties in psychology in the light of dominant political forces.

In 1931, following a debate initiated in 1927 over claims of deficient academic achievement among school children, a closed curriculum was imposed on the schools and the system of projects was suppressed. At the same time, pedologists were relieved of their directive role in the schools, and this responsibility was given to pedagogues and teachers. According to Bauer (1959), this conflict partially concealed a power struggle between educators and pedologists, which was resolved with the triumph of the former. Shulgin was accused of being left-wing in form, due to his ultraradicalism, and right-wing at the core, because his approach led to inaction in education. As a result he was removed from his post and deported.

The same year the ideological controversy over the rejection of mechanicism reached the Moscow Institute of Psychology, and Kornilov lost the directorship due to attacks on reactology. Vygotsky and his associates were at that time attempting to achieve an independent institutional position and, not being successful in Moscow, they accepted an offer from the Psychology Department of the Ukrainian Psychoneurological Institute located in Kharkov. At this time, Luria, Leontiev, Zaporozhets, Galperin, Zinchenko, and Bozhovich relocated to this city. Luria returned to Moscow after a short time, and Vygotsky coordinated his work in Moscow and Leningrad with visits to Kharkov. Those who remained in that city were later known as the Kharkov school.

By the end of 1932 attacks on psychology and pedology became stronger, and as a result the journals *Psychology* and *Pedology* and that of Bekhterev's institute had disappeared, though *Psychotechnics* survived until 1934. From that time on the only journals in which psychological papers appeared were *Soviet Pedagogy, Problems of Philosophy,* and *Under the Banner of Marxism,* until *Voprossi Psichologuii* began to be published in 1955.

Peak political interference in psychology came in 1936 with the famous decree "On the Pedological Perversions in the System of the People's Commissariat for

Education.'' There is no room here to explore the details of the arguments behind this decree (see Bauer, 1959), but the consequences were dismal for psychology. Not only did tests and industrial psychology disappear, but psychologists suffered a definitive loss of their dominant position in the educational system; many of them ended up blacklisted by the powers that be, among them Vygotsky, who had died in 1934.

How is it possible that the psychologist who is universally recognized as having produced the most important contribution to Soviet psychology could be ostracized by the very system he served? If we examine the history of Stalinism this question almost appears as a macabre joke; to attempt an answer we must refer to the theoretical and, of course, political polemic that arose as of 1931.

After the triumph of the psychology of consciousness in the 1930 conference, a strong emphasis was placed on the individual capacity for autonomous action independent of environmental influence. Although it may be surprising, Vygotsky came under attack from this position. For example, he was accused of ''right-wing opportunism'' for defending the notion that development occurs through equilibrium with the environment; he is also accused of believing that consciousness cannot be modified except by indirect means through manipulation of the environment. Also under attack was the research that Luria conducted in Uzbekistan. The results were labeled pseudoscientific, reactionary, anti-Marxist and antiproletariat, and conducive to the notion that the USSR was governed by a class that was incapable of abstract thought. In addition, his frequent references to Western psychology also made him a target for criticism (Bauer, 1959).

As a result of the 1936 decree, a substantial number of psychological institutions disappeared, and the teaching of the discipline was restricted to teacher-training colleges. As Bauer (1959) points out, psychologists were in a state of confusion and panic, not knowing what to teach. The situation was such that the journal *Under the Banner of Marxism* called for the creation of a working group to develop the line that should be followed. This group, made up of Kornilov, Blonsky, Kolbanovski, Leontiev, Luria, Teplov, and others, beginning in 1938 published a series of articles indicating the correct position to follow; at the same time, they prepared a detailed and closed curriculum for the teaching of psychology and a manual full of omissions justified by the ''lack of adequate empirical evidence.'' Rubinshtein's book of 1940 later came to be considered the official position.

Also in 1936, the Communist Academy was closed by government order, and some of its institutes, among them that of philosophy, were transferred to the Academy of Sciences. The main task of these philosophers became the elaboration of a philosophy that would yield to Stalinist ideology and the development of a supposedly Leninist scientific methodology. This did not preclude the generation of important contributions in an attempt to make dialectical materialism a philosophy of science with a broad scope (Vucinich, 1984).

A year later Bukharin was jailed as an ''enemy of the people,'' the label Stalin gave to those who got in his way; he was executed in 1938.

The rest of the history is well known. Following Stalin's consolidation of power, the USSR entered World War II – in Soviet terminology the "Great Patriotic War" – and, after that, the period of maximum Soviet chauvinism coinciding with the cold war. At this time, there arose a curious scientific nationalism that exalted Soviet science as the most advanced in the world.

After the war some of the prior tradition began to be restored. Once the general political objectives had changed, it was possible to recuperate some theoretical aspects, especially within the wave of Russian nationalism that followed the triumph over Germany. But the worst moment of Stalinism was yet to come, this being the period of greatest ideological control over science, considering that centralized control over both research and teaching had been in effect since before the war.

The best-known phenomenon was the imposition of a very peculiar interpretation of dialectical materialism on biology through the work of Lysenko, among whose merits must be noted his important contribution to discrediting this philosophical approach to science. In any case, it must be noted that Lysenkoism shows how ideological control can not only harm a science but also impair the reputation of the very philosophy it attempts to impose.

Biology was not the only field ravaged by Stalinist ideology. Following Stalin's well-known article on linguistics – assailing Marr's thesis, until that time considered the official position in that discipline – the Pavlovian conference of 1950 was held. At this conference, Pavlov's work became the new official doctrine of Soviet psychology.

After Stalin's death in 1953 there was an ideological and cultural thaw and a period of de-Stalinization. The event that opened this period was the 20th Congress of the Soviet CP, held in 1956, in which Khrushchev denounced Stalinism and the cult of personality. That year witnessed the first publication of Vygotsky's work after the long period of ostracism.

It may be said, as Graham (1972) points out, that from the middle of the decade of the 1950s science entered a process of progressive normality without ideological interference.

In 1966 the Department of Psychology of the Lomonosov State University of Moscow was founded. There, some former Vygotsky collaborators, such as Luria, Leontiev, and Galperin, were among the members of the faculty.

From all that has been presented it should not be concluded, as has been all too frequently the case, that Soviet scientists adhere to dialectical materialism only in a formal manner to defend themselves from ideological attacks. In fact, this period gave rise to scientific contributions of great interest, one of which was that of the Vygotskian school of psychology, at the same time both fruit and victim of the convulsive history of Russia during this century.

An interpretation of the influence of external history on the development of Soviet psychology

Some conclusions can be drawn from the history outlined above. After the triumph of the Revolution, Russia found itself in a lamentable state. In addition to its backwardness relative to the West, there was the destruction left by the First World War and still more produced by the Civil War. But even under these circumstances the leading party of the new state had a profound desire for renovation that motivated it to undertake a program of action of unprecedented amplitude. In other words, the objective of the revolutionary activity went far beyond the reconstruction of the country; the goal was the construction of a new society and, within it, a new science.

Knowledge would have to be one of the pillars of the new society since, according to Marxist theory, it prevents alienation in work and makes man free. But, as mentioned previously, Marxist philosophy contains a materialist epistemology and a dialectical logic that call for the development of a new conception of science.

One of the problems faced by those who had to carry out this revolutionary concept was that for the construction of a new socialist science thay had available only a set of general theoretical prescriptions extracted from the formulations of Marxist philosophers. Applying the previously mentioned "kairological principle," we can say that there was a situational urgency, since scientists were expected to devise formulas that would further the rapid construction of the socialist state, but sometimes without sufficient maturity in the elaboration of the theoretical tools.

In Hübner's terms, the situation of the new Soviet science was that of a gigantic mutation, the meaning of which varied as a function of the attitude that diverse groups of scientists had toward it. In some cases, Marxist philosophy guided the scientific practice of groups of researchers who believed in the potential of the new system, even though it might at first be difficult to reconcile the state of knowledge of that science with the theoretical tools derived from Marxist philosophy. In other instances this mutation was ignored in the scientific work carried out by researchers, although they risked attack from official spheres of influence. In still other cases, the new terms and corresponding citations were incorporated into theoretical systems that had little to do with the philosophy they were supposed to be derived from, becoming no more than verbosity that added nothing to previously existing scientific systems.

In conclusion, the scientific practice of researchers depended on the goals they hoped to achieve through their actions, and this led to distinct forms of development of scientific systems, influenced in one way or another by Marxist thinking.

Another factor entered this picture to complicate things even more. Stalin embarked on a national policy of accelerated industrialization and diverted all resources toward this end. Furthermore, and very much in the tradition of Russian despotism, he exercised absolute power, attempting to justify this by drawing on the ideology of the new state. The excesses that were committed have already been mentioned, and science did not escape them.

The political and ideological practice of Stalinism led to a search for coherence in the system ensemble surrounding the dictates of a monolithic political power to which scientific practice had to yield. The result was that sometimes ideology substituted for science.

In this context it is not surprising that the Vygotskian program was attacked for being, among other things, idealistic and removed from practical reality as it was viewed by the powers that be, in other words, for not bending to ideological dictates that were presented in dogmatic and unscientific fashion.

Vygotsky himself criticized the attempt to create a false Marxist psychology by gathering references that supported propositions with theoretical bases removed from dialectical materialism.

> My thesis is that the analysis of the crisis and the structure of psychology indis-
> putably witnesses that no psychological system can directly dominate psychology
> as a science without the help of methodology, that is, without creating a general
> science. The only legitimate adaptation of Marxism to psychology would be the
> creation of a general psychology with its concepts formulated in direct relation to
> general dialectics; that is, the dialectics of psychology. Any application of Marxism
> to psychology that follows other paths will inevitably lead to scholastic, verbal
> constructions, to dissolving dialectics in questionnaires and tests, to reasoning about
> things on the bases of external, casual, secondary features, to losing any objective
> criteria, to trying to negate any historical trend in the development of psychology,
> to a terminological revolution, in short, to a coarse deformation of Marxism and
> psychology. (1982, p. 419)

Later on he adds: "A theory of materialist psychology has to be built, handbooks of dialectical psychology cannot still be written" (p. 421).

For Vygotsky it was essential to develop, first, a set of methodological tools that would enable the collection of data in the diverse theoretical disciplines so that, once these disciplines had achieved the required maturity, the elaboration of a general psychology could be approached. This position is consistent with the parsimony of the true scientist. The proposal for the elaboration of a general psychology is of great importance to the understanding of Vygotsky's work, and we shall return to it later.

Vygotsky: A man of his time

It has frequently been claimed that Vygotsky was ahead of the time in which he lived. However, his work can only be understood within the historical context in which he developed.

From the beginning of his professional career, Vygotsky was involved in educational issues, first as a teacher of literature and later as a lecturer at a teacher-training college. That much of his psychological effort was related to pedology and defectology during the years of his intellectual maturation is evidence that his interests coincided with the priority given to education by the Soviet government. In fact, his concept of practical psychology is largely along these lines.

Also noteworthy is his background in Marxist philosophy – declared by Luria to be the most extensive among the members of the Moscow Institute of Psychology – along with his interest in literature, art, semiotics, and linguistics. In fact, Vygotsky never received formal training in psychology, and, as far as it is known, his interest in psychology was stimulated, at least in part, by his literary concerns.

Kozulin (1986) points out how Vygotsky's interest in psychology stems from his interest in the humanities.

> First, the very title of Vygotsky's book [*Psychology of Art*] suggests that to him Psychology was a method of uncovering the origins of higher forms of human consciousness and emotional life rather than elementary behavioral acts. This preoccupation with specifically *human* functions, in opposition to merely *natural* or *biological* ones, was to become a trademark of Vygotsky's lifework. Moreover, it suggests that Vygotsky never believed that psychological inquiry should be considered as a goal in itself. For him, culture and consciousness constituted the actual *subject* of inquiry, while Psychology remained a conceptual tool, important but hardly universal.
>
> Second, in the very beginning of "The Psychology of Art" Vygotsky argued that Psychology cannot limit itself to direct evidence, be it observable behavior or accounts of introspection. Psychological inquiry is *investigation,* and like the criminal investigator, the psychologist must take into account indirect evidence and circumstantial clues, which in practice means that works of art, philosophical arguments, and anthopological data are no less important for Psychology than direct evidence. (pp. XV–XVI)

Kozulin goes on to make the suggestion – with which we agree – that Vygotsky is an outsider in psychology. In fact, his work agenda in psychology, proposed early in his text *The Historical Meaning of the Crisis in Psychology,* arose from a historical analysis of psychology made within a Marxist theoretical framework and with an intention that was practical rather that descriptive; he was attempting to find in historical criticism a solution to the problem of the discipline. Vygotsky himself (1982) called for a degree of distance from psychological practice in order to understand its methodological meaning.

> Only those who in their analysis rise above the level of critical discussion on this or that system of conceptions to a higher plane of research on principles, with the help provided by the general science, will be able to orient themselves toward what is happening in psychology in crisis. They will be able to see the consistencies within the confrontations of ideas and opinions being put forward, which themselves are conditioned by the development of the science and by the nature of the reality under study within the current state of knowledge. Instead of chaotic heterogeneous opinion, instead of variegated discrepancies of opinions, a harmonious picture of the fundamental criteria about the development of the science will be offered, as will be the system of objective trends that are necessarily locked into the historical tasks required by the development of the sciences, trends which act with the strength of a steel spring behind the backs of isolated researchers and theoreticians. (p. 324)

It may have been this outsider status, along with his solid background in philosophy, that allowed Vygotsky to contribute such a novel approach. But there is another factor that should not be forgotten. The Revolution had displaced some of the traditonal figures in Russian psychology and education. Not only was there a tremendous impetus for renewal in the young state, but also, in the early phase, young people had opportunities for action that are not easily repeated in other circumstances. The transformation of old institutions and the creation of new ones offered career opportunities to members of the younger generation who supported the new state. This allowed Vygotsky's group to achieve in a short time considerable visibility in Soviet psychology and pedology, although they remained outside positions of power throughout the Stalinist period.

This outsider status, however, should not by any means be understood as a kind of dilettantism. Vygotsky's career in psychology started with a thorough review of the state of the art in psychology and other sciences. Indeed, his approach to psychology developed from the study of thesè sources and from the elaboration he made of the knowledge they offered when interpreted from the point of view of Marx's and Engels's philosophy.

Vygotsky's sources were, mainly, German, Russian, and North American. Authors frequently quoted were Wundt, Brentano, Stumpf, Ebbinghaus, Ach, Bühler, Meinong, Lipps, Stern, Husserl, Binswanger, Dilthey, Münsterberg, Freud, Adler, Uexküll, Wertheimer, Köhler, and Koffka, among the Germans; Chelpanov, Bekhterev, Pavlov, Kornilov, Blonski, and Vagner, among the Russians; and James, Dewey, Baldwin, Thorndike, and Watson, among the North Americans. Together with these authors, psychologists of diverse nationalities are also quoted, such as Titchener, Claparède, Janet, and Piaget. There are also references to physicists of the time such as Einstein and Planck. All these names, which do not exhaust the list of his references and the depth of the analysis Vygotsky makes of some of their contributions, show the breadth of Vygotsky's acquaintance with the psychology of his time. He himself contributed to the diffusion of science in his country through the writing of forewords to many Russian translations of the works of the aforementioned authors.

The purpose of Vygotsky's work in psychology was very ambitious. He aimed to build a system of Marxist psychology. In order to do this he started research both on specific psychological and educational issues and on psychological metatheory. All this effort followed the thread of a conscious program, on which we will now focus our attention.

The significance of the Vygotskian program in psychology

When Vygotsky entered the psychological scene in 1924 he had two issues clearly in mind: to identify the problems that psychological research should address and to approach this research in a radically new and different way. He believed that the subject matter of psychology was consciousness and that the way to approach its study was through research on how higher psychological processes – namely, those of a sociohistorical, "artificial" nature – develop from "natural" psychological processes. The methodology that lies at the basis of his research technique was developed from Marxist philosophy. In other words, the task that Vygotsky set for himself was the elaboration of a new system of psychology based on historical and dialectical materialism, that is, a "mutation" of psychology by means of an "explication" from Marxist philosophy.

A short time after beginning his work at the Moscow Institute of Psychology,

Vygotsky undertook a review of the contemporary psychological literature, the result of which is the work published recently under the title *The Historical Meaning of the Crisis in Psychology,* written in 1926.

The argument that runs through *The Historical Meaning of the Crisis in Psychology* concerns the creation of a General Psychology, the subject matter of which is "what is general, what is characteristic of all the subject matters of that particular science" (1982, p. 228). The importance that Vygotsky places on this general discipline can be gathered from the following quotation:

> Unity is achieved through subordination, through supremacy, through renouncing the sovereignty of the particular disciplines in favor of the general science. Within the new ensemble the independent disciplines do not simply coexist but are arranged in a hierarchical system with a main center and some secondary centers, as in a solar system. Thus it is unity that gives the role, the sense, the meaning to each isolated sphere; that is, unity determines not only the content but also the form of explanation, the generalization principle, which as science develops will become its explanatory principle. (1982, p. 300)

The general concepts of the general science are provided by the particular sciences, but it is the general science working with the same facts that the particular sciences work with that produces new facts. In Vygotsky's own words:

> General science continues the task of the particular science. When the material produced by a particular science reaches the maximum degree of possible generalization within the limits of that particular science, a further generalization is only possible beyond its limits, when the material of that particular science is compared with that offered by a series of bordering sciences. . . . That is the reason why the relationship between the general science and the particular science is the same as the relationship between the theory of that particular science and its own laws; that is, it is a function of the degree of generalization of the phenomena under study. General science arises from the need to further the labor of the particular sciences beyond their limits. The relationship between the general science and the laws, hypotheses, methods of the particular sciences is the same as the relationship between these and the reality they study. (1982, p. 323)

Elaborating on this theme, Vygotsky says that in order to develop a general theory of psychology it is necessary to begin by developing its tools of knowledge. Vygotsky compared the production of these conceptual tools through scientific action with the production of the means of production. From this notion it follows that the creation of the conceptual tools by means of an adequate methodology is of central importance. With regard to this he points out that in order to overcome dualism – the separation between the objective and the subjective – a molar approach has to be taken; a psychological unit of analysis and a methodology have to be developed, together with intermediate concepts adapted to that science, since there is no universal application of dialectics to all sciences, but each must develop its own methodology.

> Only by following each principle to its far-reaching conclusions, taking each concept to its limits, exhausting each phase of thought, sometimes taking the author's thoughts, can the methodological nature of the phenomena under study be determined. For this reason, a concept is used, not blindly but in a conscious way,

> within the science where it was created, developed and explored to its limits. When we transfer that concept to another science it becomes blind, it leads nowhere. Such a blind transportation of the biogenetic principle, of the experiment, of the mathematical method, taken from the natural sciences has given psychology the appearance of something scientific, while hidden underneath there is total impotence when faced with the phenomena for study. (p. 354)

It is not surprising that after this "manifest program" Vygotsky and his associates launched a research program specifically designed to develop this.

It is not the objective of this chapter to examine the systematic development of Vygotsky's program or his contributions to psychology and education in the form of the previously mentioned intermediate concepts, units of analysis, methodological tools, or explanatory principles. A number of papers have been dedicated to this theme (Iaroshevsky & Gurguenidze, 1982; Leontiev, 1982; Minick, 1987; Wertsch, 1985), including the chapter by Blanck in this volume, so no further development of these lines is required here.

Vygotsky was aware of his limited time and did not have the opportunity to complete his program. His closest collaborators (Luria, Leontiev, Elkonin, Zaporozhets, Galperin, etc.) and those who might be called second-generation Vygotskians (Davydov, Zinchenko, etc.) have continued to develop his program. Works such as those of Wertsch (1981a, 1981b, 1985), Rogoff and Wertsch (1984), Cole (1978), Cole and Maltzman (1969), Cole, Gay, Glick, and Sharp (1971), Cole and Scribner (1974), Scribner and Cole (1981), Laboratory of Comparative Human Cognition (1982, 1984), journals such as *Soviet Psychology,* and a growing number of translations are furthering the familiarity of Western psychologists and educators with the contributions of the sociohistorical school and the continuing research based on the assumptions of this system.

Familiarity with the work of the sociohistorical school has been late in coming to the West, but it has not been totally absent. For example, Luria's work has been known and respected for several decades; nevertheless, it has not been until recently that Western scholars have begun to recognize the profound implications of the Vygotskian approach, a fact that might be related to the current state of psychology.

However, the Vygotskian contribution is not exhausted by the conceptual tools so far developed by followers of the sociohistorical approach who have become known to psycholgists and educators. His work holds much potential for furthering our knowledge of psychology and education.

Some contributions from the sociohistorical model to current educational psychology

Although, obviously, it is not our goal to try to summarize in a few lines what this volume as a whole deals with, it has to be stressed that some of the Vygotskian contributions to developmental and educational psychology – in addition to supplying some tools for educational practice – may offer us today, as they did half a century ago, the answers to some of the questions faced by basic psychology.

Vygotsky's analysis of the relationship between learning and development may be among the ideas that are better known to Western educational psychology. His starting point was the consideration that the higher psychological processes have a cultural origin. In order to develop this principle he elaborated a theory of how the developing individual acquired these processes from his or her culture.

Starting from a critical review of some of the more relevant developmental theories in existence at the time – Thorndike, Piaget, Koffka – Vygotsky established an alternative path to those postulated by these authors, stating that ''the developmental process does not coincide with learning; rather, it follows learning'' (Vygotsky, 1984, p. 116). The relationship between the two processes takes shape in the zone of proximal development, which is the distance between the ''effective development'' of the individual and his or her ''potential development.'' ''The difference between the level of the tasks that can be performed with the help of adults and the level of the tasks that can be solved with independent activity is what defines the zone of proximal development of the child'' (1984, p. 112).

However, what appears not to have penetrated the thoughts of Western psychologists is the fact – pointed out by Vera John-Steiner and Ellen Souberman (1978) – that social learning through the zone of proximal development is only the tip of the iceberg, composed of a general theory of the social origin of the uniquely human psychological functions, the transmission of which, to the individual in formation through ontogenesis, constitutes development; that transmission is carried out through dialectical interaction mediated by the use of sign systems between the individual and the sociocultural context; and that the fruits of such interaction are both the transformation of the individual by internalization – phylogenetically the most recent form of learning – and the modification and change of the very context within which interaction occurs.

We emphasize this because when one reviews today the theories on development and learning that have been elaborated in the West over the last two decades – during which time Vygotskian theory was becoming known – it is clear that, although interaction is frequently acknowledged, its use does not seem to have substantially affected conceptions of development; often, it seems to be an ad hoc addition that reveals eclecticism.

If we now address the issue of motivation, either from a general perspective or from the most specific area of school activity, we find a quite disintegrated panorama.

Currently, there is a clear separation between the approaches used for the analysis and study of what traditionally have been called basic or primary motivations and the approach used for so-called secondary or social ones. Whereas the former are the responsibility of psychobiologists and ethologists, the latter are the responsibility of educational and social psychologists (Montero, 1989). This reality reflects perfectly the Cartesian dualism that applies a mechanistic model for animal behavior and a rational one for human actions.

In the only work of his we know on the issue of emotion and motivation, Vygotsky (1987) begins with a criticism of the Cartesian positions as being responsible for the inconsistencies that appear when counterposing the theories of James-Lange and Canon (see Bruner, 1987; Leontiev, 1982; Van der Veer, 1987).

In the specific case of motivation, particularly in reference to its educational importance, Vygotsky implicitly revealed the role of motivation in relation to learning and development in his writing on the importance of play for child development. As he points out, "if we ignore the child's needs, the incentives which are effective in getting him to act, we will never be able to understand his advance from one developmental stage to the next, because every advance is connected with a marked change in motives, inclinations, and incentives" (Vygotsky, 1978, p. 92). This idea acquired central importance in development as seen by Leontiev as part of activity theory (see Wertsch, 1981b).

Vygotsky's concern for educational activity is not exhausted by these theoretical concepts; his work has important practical implications for instructional design, the evaluation of educational efficacy, and the use of standardized tests.

Recent works concerned with the area of learning and instruction, such as those of Reigeluth (1983), Dillon and Sternberg (1986), and Pozo (1987), reveal that the research and applications currently being developed by Western psychologists share some characteristics that demand the attention of anyone who is familiar with Vygotsky's work. We shall focus on three of these characteristics in order to contrast them with notions included within the sociohistorical model.

First, analyses currently are being developed that attempt to explain how the isolated subject learns, and, in keeping with this, teaching strategies are being developed for isolated individuals. Perhaps the best exponents of this idea are the theorists of learning by discovery, whose most important instructional strategy is the creation of contexts for discovery. In opposition to this type of analysis, recent works (among them those of Campione, Brown, & Ferrara, 1982; Echeita, 1987; Forman & Cazden, 1985; and some of the chapters of this volume) demonstrate how communication in the learning process and cooperation among participants in the teaching–learning process (teacher–student or students among themselves) prove to be a tremendously effective instructional strategy.

Second, although there are those who label the process that characterizes human learning as meaningful learning (Ausubel, Novak, & Hanesian, 1978; Novak & Gowin, 1984), in these theories one finds a systematic omission of what gives meaning to learning, that is, motivation. Even though there is some mention of motivational designs for instruction (Keller, 1983), what actually is presented is a simple list of motives studied in relation to the educational setting, without making clear what it is that makes learners motivated in one way or another and what role the academic context plays in this.

This theme, however, is fully integrated in Leontiev's activity theory (1978). Research recently undertaken in Spain (Pardo, 1988) shows not only how the development of more adaptive motivational patterns depends on how the activity is presented but that such patterns are better learned in a cooperative work context than in an individual one.

Third and finally, another issue we would like to highlight regarding authors who do research in particular curricular areas (see the review of Dillon & Sternberg, 1986) is the strategy they use to determine what knowledge should be transmitted by the curriculum. Use of an empiricist model always leads to the conclusion that what should be taught is what has been learned by those who know most. Such a proposal appears perfectly logical; nevertheless, it ignores an aspect that Vygotsky considered important, particularly in the context of postrevolutionary Russia. We refer to the possibility, from a sociohistorical point of view, of reaching beyond, of advancing the processes of human knowledge, in a way, helping to form a new person. This has a particular relevance when innovative educational programs are developed.

Finally, we do not wish to conclude this brief review without alluding to two themes that today are of great educational importance and that had a central part in the scientific-political discussions of postrevolutionary Russia. These are the issues of assessment in the educational context and the psychology and education of the handicapped.

With reference to the former, we have pointed out how Vygotsky's notion of the zone of proximal development went beyond the customary logic of the use of standardized tests, since they provide information only on the child's current development and not on his or her potential development. It is noteworthy that current trends in the West for evaluating intelligence in the educational setting are beginning to coincide with the Vygotskian proposals made so long ago. A review of the existing literature on this theme (Alonso, 1983; Campione et al., 1982; Feuerstein, 1980) shows the utility of Vygotsky's ideas.

The Soviet decree of 1936, in which the use of tests was suppressed, may have had questionable consequences for Soviet psychology of that era (as pointed out previously), but it was still in advance of the criticisms currently being made in the West of the use of testing in educational practice.

Aside from the issue of the evaluation of intelligence, today's professionals in education are discussing the use of assessment models that are centered more on process than on product, with more reference to criteria than to norms, focused more on qualitative than on quantitative aspects (Fernández Ballesteros, 1983; Montero, 1989). In this area too, Vygotsky was ahead of his time, as such proposals are developed in his writings on the zone of proximal development and the experimental genetic method (Vygotsky, 1978).

In relation to the education of the handicapped, productive research based on the Vygotskian approach is currently being carried out in an attempt to examine such areas as the psychology of blindness (Rosa & Ochaita, 1988), auditory deficiencies (Marchesi, 1987), cerebral palsy (Rosa & Montero, 1988), and autism (Rivière, 1983). Vygotskian educational theory – with such concepts as the zone of proximal development, the use of mediational tools, or the remediation of psychological functions – and his writings on what in his time was called defectology turn out to be of utility when it comes to proposing solutions applicable to the education of this type of learner as well as collecting data for theoretical use in basic psychology.

From what has been said so far in this section, it could be concluded that Vygotsky's contribution maintains its vitality today in both the theoretical and the applied practices of developmental and educational psychology. This relationship between theoretical and applied science (what he called practical psychology) was given prime methodological importance by Vygotsky. According to this idea, practical psychology is the supreme test that psychology has to pass in order to adjust its theoretical principles.

This concept of practical psychology can be seen within the context of Marxist philosophy. It has to be remembered that Marx in his *Thesis on Feuerbach* pointed out that the objective of knowledge should be not to understand the world but to transform it. Within the context of the elaboration of Soviet educational practice in postrevolutionary Russia, this idea took the form of an attempt to construct a new socialist man. The same concept of science geared to action is acknowledged by John Dewey in the form of an ethical principle.

But practical psychology has also an epistemological function. "Practice belongs to the deepest roots of scientific operation and restructures it from beginning to end. It is practice that poses the tasks and is the supreme judge of theory; practice is the criterion of truth; it is practice which dictates how to build concepts and how to formulate laws" (Vygotsky, 1982, pp. 388–389).

For Vygotsky, the way out of the crisis in psychology was in the methodology of applied psychology, in other words, in a philosophy of practice. It is in practice where the most complicated contradictions of psychological methodology are resolved. If the method is a road to knowledge, the objective of the knowledge determines the method. For this reason, practice restructures all of the scientific methodology.

Viewing the Vygotskian program from the present

Since the crisis of positivism, there has been no shortage of calls for a changing conception of science. Some of these proposals are sympathetic to contributions of a dialectical origin, in particular the Vygotskian approach. It appears that the sociohistorical framework provides answers to some of the questions generated by the present state of development of the human sciences.

Scholars such as Gergen (1984) point out the preeminence in Western thought of the metaphysics of permanence relative to the metaphysics of change – in short, the dominance of Parmenides over Heraclitus. According to these authors, in all sciences this emphasis has led to a search for invariant explanatory models – in other words, mechanistic types of explanations arising from a series of basic laws that are considered eternal and immutable, leaving aside the ontological or epistemological

types of explanation produced at different moments. The metaphysics of permanence has brought with it the reduction of the phenomena of change to a mere
development of invariant mechanisms. This is common to most of the sciences, and
psychology is no exception.

There are also those who advocate the necessity of recognizing that social contact
is one of the basic human needs, required even for the very formation of the human
individual. Henriques, Hollway, Urwin, Venn, and Walkerdine (1984) criticize the
existence in psychology of an individual–society dualism that is reflected in the use
of terms such as *socialization,* and revealing an underlying Hobbesian view of social pacts among isolated individuals. As these authors point out, this view implies
a conception of the individual as opposed to the social realm.

The Vygotskian approach, on the contrary, shatters this dualism and emphasizes
the development of the individual in social interaction; specifically, the individual
is formed through the internalization of activities carried out in the bosom of society
and through the interaction that occurs within the zone of proximal development.
Cognition is a social product that is achieved through interaction. This position
reflects a model that attempts to integrate the various psychological disciplines within
a general theory in which each fulfills a specific, meaningful explanatory function
within the whole, rather than an unconnected fragmentation among the diverse fields.

Even distinguished scholars of the natural sciences advocate change in the orientation of the conception and practice of the sciences. Ilya Prigogine, 1977 Nobel
Prize winner in physics, in his most interesting book *La nouvelle alliance* (see
Prigogine, 1984) points out the historical preeminence of mechanistic thinking in
physics and the current incoherence of this explanatory mode both within the discipline and in relation to others. As he indicates, thermodynamics has demonstrated, with the concept of entropy, that time is not reversible and that chemistry
reveals the undeniable existence of objects with negative entropy. This leads to the
impossibility of applying an automatic and deterministic causality to all physical
phenomena and reveals the existence of random behaviors in matter and points of
bifurcation in the history of matter. This amounts to nothing other than the emergence of new behavioral modes of matter that contradict existing knowledge in
various disciplines of the physical sciences, in short, the appearance of a historical
dimension in matter and in the very laws that govern the way it functions. As
Prigogine states, this puts physics in a position similar to that of the human sciences. It is essential to look for a *new alliance* among the diverse branches of
knowledge once we see that they are all faced with the same challenge: the existence
of an irreversible time that changes the behavioral modes of matter and a world
open to random behavior with points of bifurcation in which human activity can
play a central role.

It is somewhat surprising that, when psychology has spent a good part of its
history as a science trying to imitate explanatory models derived from physics, one
of the most distinguished physicists of our day indicates the necessity of incorporating explanatory models from social sciences into physics and calls for an integra-

tion of sciences and humanities. It appears that the gap between natural sciences and social sciences created in the last century is ready to be bridged.

But psychology at the end of the 20th century is very different from that of the 1920s and early 1930s. The lineal mechanistic conceptions and the reflexologic and behavioristic reductionism so much criticized by Vygotsky have given way to the new cognitive psychology. The development of other disciplines such as computer science, neuroscience, anthropology, and linguistics has revolutionized the state of current science, to such an extent that Gardner (1985) ventures to state that we are at the fringe of a new scientific revolution in which a new discipline – cognitive science – opens a new view that could be compared to that of the scientific revolution of the 17th century.

However, there are opinions that differ with such optimism. Fodor (1983) points out the impossibility of modeling global nonencapsulated cognitive processes in a computational way, that is, higher processes that fix belief or knowledge. He goes as far as stating that cognitive science has no idea how to develop computational mechanisms to describe them.

It is significant, as Rivière (1987) states, that information-processing psychology, in spite of its important contributions to the understanding of many cognitive processes, is limited in its progress precisely in the study of some of the higher psychological processes. On the other hand, this approach to psychology comes from a solipsist notion of the human individual to which it is difficult to fit the social dimensions of learning and development. But it is precisely on these higher psychological processes that Vygotsky and his associates concentrated their work, offering a thought-provoking approach to their study. However, sociohistorical psychology does not say anything about the cognitive processes studied by current Anglo-Saxon cognitive psychology. In addition, Rivière points out that the Soviet conception of science is very far from the Western aesthetics of science.

The appeal of the contribution of Vygotsky and his associates might be in their suggestive approach to questions that resist the attack of the paraphernalia of current cognitive psychology. As Siguán (1987) says, "Vygotsky's work keeps attracting our interest because his diagnosis of the crisis of psychology maintains its validity today, and because the basic problems he tried to answer are still our problems" (p. 19). But profiting from the Vygotskian contribution, given the current state of the historical development of psychology, presents wide-ranging problems.

Epilogue

All that has been said so far suggests that the main proposals of Vygotsky's work can be, or already are, of use to the development of basic psychology and educational practice.

When one looks at the current state of psychology as a discipline, it may be concluded that it is still in a pre-paradigmatic state of development – in the terminology of Kuhn (1962) – or even that it is a multiparadigmatic science because of its own nature. Leahey (1980) considers definitive the failure of psychology to achieve a synthesis and goes as far as saying that it is chimerical to await the advent of a Newton in psychology. The way out, according to this author, is in the discipline's division into distinct sciences. Others, such as George Miller (1982), however, do not give up hope for the formation of a discipline that unifies psychology as a whole. Stagner (1988) in keeping with this opinion, points out the advantage of such unification, although he acknowledges its difficulties at a time in which the disciplinary structure of psychology and its institutional basis tend toward a growing specialization, resulting in an increasing fragmentation of the field under study. To solve this state of affairs – Stagner goes on – a determined intellectual and institutional effort is needed.

We have been trying to show that the idea of a General Psychology was the backbone of Vygotsky's work and that all his contributions stem from this idea. However, we also have pointed out that the current state of psychology is very different from that of his time. On the other hand, there are signs of an attempt to find new nonreductionist general frameworks to approach the study of processes that today are beyond the range of study of Western psychology due to a lack of methodological tools. This leaves room for hope for a unifying effort.

The reappearance of interest in dialectical and emergentist approaches makes room for an integration of the knowledge accumulated by Western psychology and by those who have developed Vygotsky's seminal ideas. However, this is not going to be an easy task if it is ever approached. On the one hand, Vygotsky's work was unfinished, and as Iaroshevski and Gurguenidze (1982) said, in spite of all the subsequent Soviet work the formation of a general psychology, as Vygotsky meant it to be, has not been achieved. On the other hand, Western psychological discoveries are the result of epistemological models difficult to reconcile with the theoretical premises that are at the base of a sociohistorical psychology. Even the very notion of science is not identical in both cases.

Two factors, at least, are essential in order to be able to profit from the Vygotskian contribution: first, to develop a ''practical psychology'' in the sense we have been talking about (this book is a good example); second, as Kozulin (1986) suggested, to elaborate on methodology through philosophical work.

Vygotsky was very explicit on this second point:

> The methodology of a particular science is formed under the influence of philosophy, but it has its own rules determined by the nature of the subject matter of that science, by the historical development of its conceptual structures. That is why methodological research on psychological concepts, methods, explanatory principles is not a philosophical ''loft'' added to science. It appears as a consequence of the requirements of a particular science; it is an integral part of that science. (1982, p. 451)

In the same work Vygotsky emphasized that ''psychology is pregnant with a general discipline, but it has not yet given birth to it'' (p. 297). A critical examination of the current state of psychology could allow us to determine its stage of gravidity and even to contribute to its delivery. Perhaps this birth is not far off, or maybe it will still be long in coming. But what we are sure of is that in Vygotsky's methodological contribution resounds the heartbeat of an offspring of our time. Whether it enters the world or not depends on our labor.

Note

1 Hübner (1983) differentiates two types of historical change: "explication" or "progress I" and "mutation" or "progress II."

Explication is a form of development in which a system evolves without changing its foundations; that is, for particular situations specific rules are deduced from previously existing ones (in the same way that openings or moves intended to respond to a given situation in chess can be deduced from the rules of the game). In any case, the system does not change in its basic rules but is enriched with new rules deduced from the prior ones.

Mutation or progress II, on the contrary, is a change in the premises and basic assumptions of the system and, consequently, is the development of a new system on new foundations. The old system is contemplated in a critical manner, and its elements can be assimilated by the new one, although the structure of the new system is completely different from that of the old one.

What differentiates the mutations of scientific systems from Kuhn's "revolutions" is the existence of an explanation of the change. According to Hübner, a mutation is not produced in an arbitrary manner or exclusively as a consequence of an internal crisis of the paradigm, which would isolate a system (science, for example) from the system ensemble in which it is immersed; on the contrary, the mutation finds its explanation in the cultural complex to which the system belongs. This kind of change would be the result of an attempt to make it more coherent within the system ensemble as a whole. In other words, the basic rules on which the new system is formed do not appear out of nowhere, nor are they just a result of the evolution of the rules of the old system; their origin must be found in the system ensemble. The new rules are taken or derived from those existing in other systems, so that the result is a state of greater coherence within the whole of the cultural complex.

References

Alonson, J. (1983). Alternativas actuales en la evaluación de la inteligencia. In R. Fernández Ballesteros (Ed.), Psicodiagnóstico: Unidades didácticas. Madrid: Universidad Nacional de Educación a Distancia.

Althusser, L. (1965). Pour Marx. Paris: Librairie François Maspero.

Althusser, L., & Balibar, E. (1967). Lire le Capital. Paris: Librairie François Maspero.

Ausubel, D. P., Novak, J. D., & Hanesian, H. (1978). Educational psychology: A cognitive view. New York: Holt, Rinehart & Winston.

Bauer, A. R. (1959). The new man in Soviet psychology. Cambridge, MA: Harvard University Press.

Bruner, J. S. (1987). Prologue to the English edition. In R. W. Rieber & A. A. Carton (Eds.) (1987), The collected works of L. S. Vygotsky (Vol. 1). New York: Plenum.

Campione, J. C., Brown, A. L., & Ferrara, R. A. (1982). Mental retardation and intelligence. In R. J. Sternberg (Ed.), Handbook of human intelligence. Cambridge: Cambridge University Press.

Carr, R. B. (1981). La revolución rusa de Lenin a Stalin (1917–1929). Madrid: Alianza Editorial.

Chalmers, A. F. (1976). What is that thing called science? Sidney: University of Queensland Press.

Cole, M. (1978). Soviet developmental psychology. White Plains, NY: Sharpe.

Cole, M., Gay, J., Glick, J., & Sharp, D. (Eds.) (1971). The cultural context of learning and thinking. New York: Basic.

Cole, M., & Maltzman, I. (Eds.) (1969). Handbook of contemporary Soviet psychology. New York: Basic.

Cole, M., & Scribner, S. (1974). Culture and thought: A psychological introduction. New York: Wiley.

Davydov, V. V., & Radzikhovskii, L. A. (1985). Vygotsky's theory and the activity-oriented approach in psychology. In J. V. Wertsch (Ed.), *Culture, communication, and cognition*. Cambridge: Cambridge University Press.

Dillon, R. F., & Sternberg, R. J. (1986). *Cognition and instruction*. New York: Academic Press.

Downing, J. (1988). Comparative perspectives on the development of the cognitive psychology of reading in the USSR. In J. Downing (Ed.), *Cognitive psychology and reading in the U.S.S.R.* Amsterdam: North-Holland.

Echeita, G. (1987). La interacción entre alumnos: Una herramienta educativa. *Boletín del Instituto de Ciencias de la Educación de la Universidad Autónoma de Madrid, 10*, 33–51.

Fernández Ballesteros, R. (1983). Concepto de psicodiagnóstico. In R. Fernández Ballesteros (Ed.), *Psicodiagnóstico: Unidades didácticas*. Madrid: Universidad Nacional de Educación a Distancia.

Feuerstein, R. (1980). *Instrumental enrichment: An intervention program for cognitive modifiability*. Baltimore: University Park Press.

Fodor, J. A. (1983). *The modularity of mind*. Cambridge, MA: MIT Press.

Forman, E. A., & Cazden, C. B. (1985). Exploring Vygotskian perspectives in education: The cognitive value of peer interaction. In J. V. Wertsch (Ed.), *Culture, communication, and cognition*. Cambridge: Cambridge University Press.

Gardner, H. (1985). *The mind's new science*. New York: Basic.

Gergen, K. (1984). An introduction to historical social psychology. In K. J. Gergen & M. M. Gergen, *Historical social psychology*. Hillsdale, NJ: Erlbaum.

Graham, L. R. (1972). *Science and philosophy in the Soviet Union*. New York: Knopf.

Henriques, J., Hollway, W., Urwin, C., Venn, C., & Walkerdine, V. (1984). *Changing the subject*. London: Methuen.

Hübner, K. (1983). *Critique of scientific reason*. Chicago: University of Chicago Press.

Iaroshevski, M. G., & Gurguenidze, G. S. (1982). Epilogue. In A. R. Luria & M. G. Iaroshevski (Eds.), *L. S. Vygotsky: Collected works* (Vol. 1). Moscow: Pedagogika. (In Russian)

John-Steiner, V., & Souberman, E. (1978). Epilogue. In L. S. Vygotsky, *Mind in society: The development of higher psychological processes*. Cambridge, MA: Harvard University Press.

Keller, J. M. (1983). Motivational design of instruction. In C. M. Reigeluth (Ed.), *Instructional design theories and models: An overview of their current status*. Hillsdale, NJ: Erlbaum.

Kozulin, A. (1986). Vygotsky in context. In L. S. Vygotsky, *Thought and language* (A. Kozulin, Ed.). Cambridge, MA: MIT Press.

Kuhn, T. S. (1962). *The structure of scientific revolutions*. Chicago: University of Chicago Press.

Laboratory of Comparative Human Cognition (1982). Culture and intelligence. In R. J. Sternberg (Ed.), *Handbook of human intelligence*. Cambridge: Cambridge University Press.

Laboratory of Comparative Human Cognition (1984). Culture and cognitive development. In W. Kessen (Ed.), *Carmichael's manual of child psychology: History, theories, and methods*. New York: Wiley.

Lakatos, I. (1970). Falsification and the methodology of scientific research programs. In I. Lakatos & A. Musgrave, *Criticism and the growth of knowledge*. Cambridge: Cambridge University Press.

Leahey, T. H. (1980). *A history of psychology*. Englewood Cliffs, NJ: Prentice-Hall.

Leontiev, A. N. (1978). *Activity, consciousness, and personality*. Englewood Cliffs, NJ: Prentice-Hall.

Leontiev, A. N. (1982). Introduction. In A. R. Luria & M. G. Iaroshevski (Eds.), *L. S. Vygotsky: Collected works* (Vol. 1). Moscow: Pedagogika. (In Russian)

Luria, A. R. (1976). *Cognitive development: Its cultural and social foundations*. Cambridge, MA: Harvard University Press.

Marchesi, A. (1987). *El desarrollo cognitivo y linguistico de los niños sordos*. Madrid: Alianza Psicología.

Marx, K. (1859). *Zur Kritik der politischen Okonomie*.

Miller, G. A. (1982). The constitutive problem of psychology. In S. Koch & D. E. Leary (Eds.), *The century of psychology as science*. New York: McGraw-Hill.

Minick, N. (1987). The development of Vygotsky's thought: An introduction. In *The collected works of L. S. Vygotsky: Vol. 1. Problems of general psychology*. New York: Plenum.

Montero, I. (1989). *Motivación de logro: Concepto y medida en el ámbito de la enseñanza*. Unpublished doctoral dissertation, Universidad Autónoma de Madrid.

Nazarova, L. K. (1988). An outline of the history of methods of teaching psychology in Soviet Russia. In J. Downing (Ed.), *Cognitive psychology and reading in the U.S.S.R.* Amsterdam: North-Holland.

Novak, J. D., & Godwin, D. B. (1984). *Learning how to learn.* Cambridge: Cambridge University Press.

Pardo, A. (1988). *Motivación de logro y enriquecimiento motivacional.* Unpublished doctoral dissertation, Universidad Pontificia de Comillas, Madrid.

Paris, C. (1982). Posición de la ciencia en el complejo cultural: Contra la autonomía de la ciencia. In *Actas del primer congreso de teoría y metodología de las ciencias.* Oviedo: Sociedad Asturiana de Filosofia, Pentalfa Ediciones.

Pozo, J. I. (1987). *Aprendizaje de la ciencia y pensamiento causal.* Madrid: Aprendizaje-Visor.

Prigogine, I. (1984). *Order out of chaos: Man's new dialogue with nature.* Toronto: Bantam. (First published in French under the title of *La nouvelle alliance*)

Reigeluth, C. M. (Ed.) (1983). *Instructional design theories and models: An overview of their current status.* Hillsdale, NJ: Erlbaum.

Rivière, A. (1983). Interacción y simbolo en autistas. *Infancia y Aprendizaje, 22,* 3–26.

Rivière, A. (1987). *El sujeto de la psicología cognitiva.* Madrid: Alianza Psicología.

Rogoff, B., & Wertsch, J. V. (1984). *Children's learning in the "Zone of proximal development": New directions for children's development.* San Francisco: Jossey-Bass.

Rosa, A. (1985). Entrevista con Michael Cole. *Estudios de Psicología, 21,* 3–20.

Rosa, A., & Montero, I. (1988). Aplicación de las teorias de la instrucción y la motivación a la enseñanza de los niños con trastornos motores. In Centro Nacional de Recursos para la Educación Especial, *Alumnos con necesidades educativas especiales, módulo 2.* Madrid: Centro Nacional de Recursos para la Educación Especial.

Rosa, A., & Ochaita, E. (1988). ¿Qué aportan a la psicología cognitiva los datos de la investigación evolutiva en sujetos ciegos? *Infancia y Aprendizaje, 41,* 95–102.

Scribner, S. (1985). Vygotsky's uses of history. In J. V. Wertsch (Ed.) *Culture, communication, and cognition.* Cambridge: Cambridge University Press.

Scribner, S., & Cole, M. (1981). *Psychology of literacy.* Cambridge, MA: Harvard University Press.

Siguán, M. (Ed.) (1987). *Actualidad de Lev S. Vygotski.* Barcelona: Anthropos.

Stagner, R. (1988). *A history of psychological theories.* New York: Macmillan.

Toulmin, S. (1978). The Mozart of psychology. *New York Review of Books, 25*(14), 51–57.

Van der Veer, R. (1987). El dualismo en psicología: Un análisis vygotskiano. In M. Siguán (Ed.), *Actualidad de Lev S. Vygotski.* Barcelona: Anthropos.

Vucinich, A. (1984). *Empire of knowledge: The Academy of Sciences of the U.S.S.R.* Berkeley: University of California Press.

Vygotsky, L. S. (1978). *Mind in society: The development of higher psychological processes.* Cambridge, MA: Harvard University Press.

Vygotsky, L. S. (1982). The historical meaning of the crisis in psychology. In A. R. Luria & M. G. Iaroshevski (Eds.), *L. S. Vygotsky: Collected works* (Vol. 1). Moscow: Pedagogika. (In Russian)

Vygotsky, L. S. (1984). Aprendizaje y desarrollo intelectual en la edad escolar. *Infancia y Aprendizaje, 27–28,* 105–116.

Vygotsky, L. S. (1987). Emotions and their development in childhood. In R. W. Rieber & A. S. Carton (Eds.), *The Collected Works of L. S. Vygotsky* (Vol. 1). New York: Plenum.

Watson R. I. (1972). The role and use of history in the psychology curriculum. *Journal of the History of the Behavioral Sciences, 8,* 64–69.

Wertsch, J. V. (1981a). *The concept of activity in Soviet psychology.* Armonk, NY: Sharpe.

Wertsch, J. V. (1981b). Trends in Soviet cognitive psychology. *Storia e Critica della Psicologia, 2*(2), 219–295.

Wertsch, J. V. (Ed.). (1985). *Culture, communication, and cognition: Vygotskian perspectives.* Cambridge: Cambridge University Press.

Zinchenko, V. P. (1985). Vygotsky's ideas about units for the analysis of mind. In J. V. Wertsch (Ed.), *Culture, communication, and cognition.* Cambridge: Cambridge University Press.

3 Cognitive development and formal schooling: The evidence from cross-cultural research

Michael Cole

> It is the dilemma of psychology to deal as a natural science with an object that creates history.
> Ernst Boesch

My goal in this chapter is to summarize the implications for understanding cognitive development of the past three decades of intensive cross-cultural research on the cognitive consequences of formal educational experience during middle childhood. Furthermore, in concert with the theme of this book, I will approach this topic from the perspective of the sociohistorical school associated with the names of Lev S. Vygotsky, Alexei N. Leontiev, Alexander R. Luria, and their followers.

Some basic presuppositions

As described by Luria (1979), the sociohistorical school of psychology emerged in the 1920s as an explicit attempt to resolve the widely perceived dilemma commented on by Ernst Boesch in the epigraph with which this chapter begins: Scientific psychology, conceived as an experimental discipline, depends upon the assumption that the processes it studies are universal (and hence not dependent upon the exigencies of time and place), yet human beings manifestly are creatures who create history, rendering psychological processes historically contingent (and thus inappropriate objects of study using experimental methods).

Wilhelm Wundt, titular father of scientific psychology, was acutely aware of this problem. His solution was to declare that psychology must be two sciences. The first, experimental psychology, was to be an experimental, explanatory science, in the mold of the natural sciences such as physics. Its task was to be the analysis of the contents of individual human consciousness into its elements and a specification of the universal laws according to which these elements combine. But, he argued, an experimental psychology, so conceived, could not in principle be applied to the study of "higher psychological functions," which include the everyday processes of human reasoning and memory. These characteristics of human thought, he argued, had to be studied as part of a historical, descriptive science that he called *Volkerpsychologie.*

89

Wundt believed that the two enterprises need to supplement each other; only a synthesis of the respective insights they afford could provide a full account of human psychological processes. To those who argued (as did adherents of both the behaviorist and gestaltist schools who superseded Wundt) that *Volkerpsychologie* could be entirely subsumed under experimental psychology, Wundt replied that although attempts had frequently been made to study complex mental phenomena using "mere introspection,"

> these attempts have always been unsuccessful. Individual consciousness is wholly incapable of giving us a history of the development of human thought, for it is conditioned by an earlier history which cannot itself give us any knowledge. (1921, p. 3)

Because of its historical nature, Wundt also believed in a close affinity between *Volkerpsychologie* and the study of development. "Folk psychology," he declared, "is in an important sense, genetic psychology," which implied that psychological analysis would have to go beyond the individual to investigate "the various stages of mental development still exhibited by mankind" (1921, p. 4).

Wundt's injunctions about the limitations of the study of individual psychological processes using experimental methods and his declared sympathy for including the methods of ethnography and folklore in a study of the history of mind certainly provide the cross-cultural approach to mind with an authoritative pedigree. However, Wundt's ideas about the development of scientific psychology were rather quickly rejected; not only did the experimental method come to be the accepted yardstick for evaluating the scientific merits of psychological research, but attempts to make culture (the history-creating aspect of human nature) a fundamental category in theories of the constitution of mind were largely marginalized as part of a semiautonomous enterprise referred to as a cross-cultural psychology.

This situation has not sat well with cross-cultural psychologists, who have (correctly, in my opinion) insisted that evidence of cultural variation is of cardinal importance to the development of a coherent psychological approach to human nature (see, for example, Triandis & Lambert, 1980). However, as Wundt forewarned, the barriers to including the category of culture in a unified science of psychology are exceedingly difficult to overcome. In my opinion, eventual solution of this problem requires that one formulate an approach to human nature that provides a clear conception of the role played by culture in general as a theoretical/methodological foundation for the assessment of cultural variations. To my knowledge, the only existing school of psychology that has developed such a formulation is that of the sociohistorical school. Hence, it is to this set of ideas that I turn in order to provide the foundation for assessing the topic of this paper: How does formal schooling impact the process of cognitive development?

Basic postulates of the sociohistorical school

The central role of culture in the sociohistorical school's approach to mind and the special role that cross-cultural data played in the development of its theories were clear in the earliest English publications of its ideas in the late 1920s and early 1930s (Leontiev, 1930; Luria, 1928, 1932; Vygotsky, 1929). Briefly (for a more extended discussion, see Cole, 1988), the fundamental postulate of their approach is that human psychological functions differ from the psychological processes of other animals because they are *culturally mediated, historically developing,* and arise from *practical activity.* Each term in this formulation is linked to the other. Taken as a whole, they provide a starting point for considering the special features of formal schooling as an activity context within which some human beings, in some cultural circumstances, and some historical eras develop.

1. *Cultural mediation:* The basic idea here, which can be traced back into antiquity and which forms the basis for a good deal of anthropological theorizing, is the notion that human beings live in an environment transformed by the artifacts of prior generations, extending back to the beginning of the species. The basic function of these artifacts is to coordinate human beings with the physical world and each other. As a consequence, human beings live in a "double world," simultaneously "natural" and "artificial." Culture, in this sense, must be considered the unique *medium* of human existence.

Cultural artifacts are simultaneously ideal (conceptual) and material. They are ideal in that they contain in coded form the interactions of which they were previously a part. They exist only as they are embodied in material. This applies to the language/speech as well as the more usually noted forms of artifact.

In that they mediate interaction with the world, cultural artifacts can also be considered tools. As Luria (1928) put the matter early on,

> Man differs from animals in that he can make and use tools. [These tools] not only radically change his conditions of existence, they even react on him in that they effect a change in him and his psychic condition. (pp. 493, 495)

2. The fact of cultural mediation fundamentally changes the structure of human psychological functions vis-à-vis animals.

> Instead of applying directly its natural function to the solution of a particular task, the child puts between that function and the task a certain auxiliary means . . . by the medium of which the child manages to perform the task. (Luria, 1928, p. 495)

3. Cultural and therefore human psychological functions are historical phenomena.

> The history of one man's mastery over the regulation of the behavior of another repeats in many points his mastery over tools. It presupposes a change in the structure of behavior, which turns behavior directed to an end into behavior directed circuitously. (Leontiev, 1930, p. 59)

4. The basic unit for the study of psychological processes is practical activity. This idea, taken from Hegel by way of Marx and Engels, is basic to what Vygotsky called the "cultural method" of thinking:

> human psychology is concerned with the activity of concrete individuals, which takes place either in a collective or in a situation in which the subject deals directly with the surrounding world of objects – i.e., at the potter's wheel or the writer's desk. . . . if we removed human activity from the system of social relationships, it

would not exist. . . . the human individual's activity is a system in the system of
social relations. It does not exist without these relations. (Leontiev, 1981, pp. 46–
47)

5. Cultural mediation and grounding of thought in activity imply the context
specificity of mental processes. As Vygotsky (1978) put it, "the mind is not a
complex network of [general] capabilities, but a set of specific capabilities. . . .
Learning . . . is the acquisition of many specialized abilities for thinking" (p. 83).

Four streams of history, four levels of development

In the early statements of their ideas, and in later applications, the founders of the
sociohistorical school emphasized that a full theory of human development must
take account of changes occurring simultaneously on four historical levels: the development of the species (*phylogeny*), the *history* of human beings since their emergence as a distinct species, *ontogeny* (the history of individual children), and *microgenesis,* the development of particular psychological processes in the course of
experimental interactions in a single experimental session (e.g., the "psychological
task").

Applied to the problem of cognitive development and formal schooling, this approach provides a rather well specified framework of inquiry. First, one must inquire, at the phylogenetic level, what is the special, general characteristic of homo
sapiens that underpins the specific form of activity called formal education? Second,
at the historical level one must answer such questions as: Under what historical
conditions did formal education arise? What are the social tasks that it evolved to
fulfill, and what special means does it employ? Third, at the ontogenetic level one
asks: What is the impact of involvement in formal school activity on individual
development? Fifth, at the microgenetic level (which is the focus of the vast majority of research in educational psychology), how does the actual process of change
in individual behavior occur within specific formal educational activity settings?
Put differently, how is one to understand the moment-by-moment process of teach-
ing/learning?

The phylogenetic level

For current purposes, this level is probably well enough specified in my brief summary of the basic postulates of the sociohistorical school. The special phylogenetic
capacity of homo sapiens is cultural mediation, the ability to act indirectly on the
world via material/ideal artifacts and to communicate adaptively advantageous
modifications to subsequent generations. Although isolated examples of embryonic
forms of such capacities are reliably found in nonhuman species (Kawai, 1963;
Premack, 1983; Tomasello, 1989), the high-level pervasiveness of the capacity to
create and use artifacts is a phylogenetic universal that attests to the "psychic unity"
of our species, as Waitz (1863) argued very persuasively more than a century ago.

The historical level

Though it must be argued that cultural mediation is a universal fact of our species, the development of specific forms of mediation (particular forms of activity employing particular mediational means) clearly is not. All cultures known to man have elaborated the basic potential of language and tool use, but not all cultures have developed the forms of activity that we refer to as formal schooling or the forms of mediation that we call literacy and numeracy.

Literacy and numeracy are direct extensions of the basic mediating capacity of language; sounds disappear as soon as they are spoken, and even the loudest speakers can only project their voices over a short distance. Language can be elaborated in myth and ritual to preserve information and make it available to later generations. In some systems (e.g., the tradition for teaching the large collection of hymns and rituals known as the Indian Vedas, Oliver, 1979; Street, 1984), great accuracy can be achieved by oral recitation techniques, but at a tremendous cost of time and effort.

The essential advantage shared by all written notation systems is that they extend the power of language in time and space (Goody, 1977). Words that are written down can be carried great distances with no change in their physical characteristics. In like manner, writing systems freeze words in time; once written down, ideas and events can be returned to and contemplated time and again in their original form. In this respect, written notations are a form of memory. However, as both common sense and the evidence from research show, the actual way in which the potential of writing is realized depends crucially on the way in which it represents language and the way in which it enters into the mediation of activity.

A new mode of representation

When we look into the archaeological record, we can discern two distinct purposes of reading and writing: to regulate people's interactions with the physical world, and to regulate people's interactions with each other. The first of these purposes is illustrated by the bits of bone discovered in the vicinity of Lascaux, in southern France, which was inhabited approximately 40,000 years ago. In the 1960s Alexander Marshak (1972) began to take an intense interest in these artifacts because of their patterned inscriptions. Previous scholars had assumed that they were used as decorations or perhaps represented no more than a form of doodling by people inhabiting the caves. By sitting at the mouth of the cave evening after evening and observing the rising moon, Marshak discovered that the cave dwellers were not doodling; they were making calendars.

A calendar is an excellent example of the way that written symbol systems can be used to regulate people's interactions with the physical environment. The key purpose of a calendar is prediction: How many days until winter? How many days until salmon return from the sea? Prediction is essential to control. Knowing when the salmon will arrive allows one to build fish traps and to set them in time to catch the fish; knowing when winter will arrive provides time to lay in provisions that enable one to survive the winter. Marshak's discovery is not an isolated one. Throughout the world archaeologists have discovered a variety of sophisticated calendrical devices – for example, Stonehenge – that were important for organizing people's activities.

A more immediate precursor of modern literacy is to be found in that part of the world now called the Middle East, where farming and the domestication of animals began some 10,000 years ago (Pfeiffer, 1972; Schmandt-Besserat, 1978). Once people discovered that they could collect and raise the seeds of food-bearing plants and that they could raise animals in captivity, they began to make permanent settlements. Permanent settlements permitted people to accumulate surplus goods to use in trade for things they could not grow or make themselves. It was in such early agricultural villages that archaeologists discovered a variety of small clay objects, such as the tokens found in the ancient Near East (Schmandt-Besserat, 1978). These tokens illustrate both of the fundamental features of writing systems in their most primitive aspect. First, because they "stood for" the actual objects – a circular token with lines on it might represent wool, for example, and a cone-shaped token might represent bread – they enabled people to keep track of their goods over time without having to count them over and over again. Second, because they were small and sturdy, they could be carried from one place to another as a kind of promissory note for purposes of trade. In either case, they were artificial signs that represented natural objects, allowing people more effectively to regulate their economic and social activities.

What makes these tokens of central importance to understanding the role of literacy and numeracy in human development is evidence that they are the direct antecedents of our system of writing. Moreover, the conditions under which this crude system of marked tokens became a full-blown writing system are the same ones that eventually gave rise to schools.

The origins of "Western" formal schooling

The system of tokens remained unchanged for several thousand years, during which time people continued to live in small villages or as nomads. Then, around 4000 B.C., people discovered a means of smelting bronze that revolutionized their economic activities and social lives. Plows could be used to till the earth more deeply; extensive canals could be built to irrigate fields, and armies could be equipped with more effective weapons. For the first time, people could regularly grow substantially more food than they needed for their own use and could compel large numbers of other people to work for them. City-states arose where large numbers of people lived in close proximity to each other and separate from their sources of food.

The new form of life that arose with cities required a substantial division of labor. This made it impossible for everyone to interact on a face-to-face basis as they had when they lived in small, self-sufficient villages and greatly increased the importance of their primitive systems of record keeping.

Side by side with the development of these early cities token-based record-keeping systems rapidly evolved, allowing kings to monitor the wealth of their lands, the size of their armies, and the tax payments of their subjects. Under these new conditions, the early token system expanded to keep pace with the increased variety of things to be counted. This increase in the number of tokens made the entire system cumbersome. As a solution to this problem, people began to make pictures of the tokens on clay tablets instead of using the tokens themselves. This practice gave rise to cuneiform (*cuneiform* means, literally, to etch in clay).

This transformation in the medium of recording enabled a crucial change in how people began to relate inscribed symbols to objects. In the case of tokens, the tokens literally "stood for" objects. But when complicated transactions began to occur in the newly complex political and economic conditions of cities, the need arose to represent relationships among objects (such as *owe* or *paid*) as well as objects themselves. In these conditions, a revolutionary discovery was made. It is possible to represent the sounds of language using marks in clay just as it is possible to represent objects. (See Goody, 1987; Harris, 1986; Larsen, 1986, for more extended discussions of early writing systems, cuneiform in particular.)

The system of cuneiform writing that resulted from this discovery could not be mastered in a day. It required long and systematic study. Nevertheless, so important was the power associated with this new system of written communication that societies began to support young men who otherwise might be engaged directly in a trade or farming with the explicit purpose of making them "scribes," people who could write. The places where young men were brought together for this purpose were the earliest schools.

Fragmentary records of the activities in these early schools show that although they were very restricted and specialized in some ways they appear startlingly modern in others. As in modern schools, students were asked to copy out lists containing the names of various objects deemed important by their teachers and to spend a great deal of time memorizing the facts contained on such lists (see Table 3.1). In addition to learning the rudiments of writing and reading, these early students were learning something about the basic contents of the records that they were asked to keep so that they could act as civil servants once they graduated. Besides the financial benefits that derive from schooling, the ancients also believed that there was power to be had from the knowledge it produced. The basis of this knowledge is the ability to read, write, and solve problems in the economic and social spheres of life.

Modern children in elementary school in the 1980s still make lists, although they are more likely to be lists of the presidents of the United States or the spelling words in which *e* comes before *i*. But the purposes to which this practice is to be put and the presumed advantages to be gained from study, no matter how boring, remain very much the same. As one father admonished his son, several thousand years ago,

Table 3.1. *Examples from lists memorized in ancient and modern schools*

Ancient		Modern	
Subject	Number	Subject	Number
Trees	84	Presidents of the U.S.	40
Stones	12	States of the Union	50
Gods	9	Capitals of the states	50
Officials	8	Elements in the periodic table	105
Cattle	8	Planets in the solar system	9
Reeds	8		
Personal names	6		
Animals	5		
Leather objects	4		
Fields	3		
Garments	3		
Words compounded with *gar*	3		
Chairs	3		

Source: Adapted from Goody, 1977, p. 95.

> I have seen how the belaboured man is belaboured – thou shouldst set thy heart in pursuit of writing. . . . behold, there is nothing which surpasses writing. . . .
> I have seen the metalworker at his work at the mouth of his furnace. His fingers were somewhat like crocodiles; he stank more than fish-roe. . . .
> The small building contractor carries mud. . . . He is dirtier than vines or pigs from treading under his mud. His clothes are stiff with clay. . . .
> Behold, there is no profession free of a boss – except for the scribe: he is the boss. . . .
> Behold, there is no scribe who lacks food from property of the House of the King – life, prosperity, health! (Quoted in Donaldson, 1978, pp. 84–85)

I have sketched only one line in the history of formal schooling, and it is certainly true that a great deal can be learned from comparison with systems that arose in different parts of the world using different means of representing language and privileging different social functions. However, the system in question represents a tradition of special relevance for the developing countries of Africa and South America with which I am familiar because its practices can be traced down to the present day via the later civilizations of Greece and Rome.

If I restrict myself to the case at hand, several points concerning the special organization of behavior peculiar to formal schooling stand out:

1. There is an intimate link between the development of schooling and the development of large urban centers engaged in trade and technologically sophisticated means of production.
2. There is a special mediational means, writing, that is essential to the activity of schooling. Writing is used to represent both language and physical systems (e.g., mathematics).
3. The activity settings where schooling occurs are distinctive in that they are removed from contexts of practical activity, and the requisite skills that will become the means of later activity are the goal.

4. There is a peculiar social structure to formal schooling in which a single adult interacts with many (often as many as 40 or 50, sometimes as many as 400) students at a time. Unlike most other settings for socialization, this adult is unlikely to have any familial ties to the learner, rendering the social relations relatively impersonal.
5. There is a peculiar value system associated with schooling that sets the educated person above his or her peers and which, in secular versions of formal education of the type I am focusing on, values change and discontinuity over tradition and community.

This characterization of the distinctive nature of the activity settings associated with formal schooling does not do justice to the full range of contexts that distinguish formal schooling from other contexts of socialization that might be considered educational in the broad sense (for more extended discussions, see Greenfield & Lave, 1982; Scribner & Cole, 1973). However, it is sufficient to permit us to pose more clearly the question before us: How does schooling influence cognitive development?

That issue can now be rephrased as follows. What are the consequences for later cognitive development of participation in contexts that have the characteristics of formal schooling in a society where formal schooling is an integral part of the political economy and a major institution for the socialization of children? Assuming that identifiable influences on cognitive development can be demonstrated, a series of subsequent questions can be addressed: Are the cognitive consequences of involvement in formal schooling general or specific? What aspects of schooling are responsible for such effects? Since it has already been shown that schooling arose historically as part and parcel of wider sociocultural changes, an inquiry into the cognitive impact of schooling naturally leads us to attempt to "unpackage" features of the experience of schooling such as its socioeconomic context, mediational means, etc., all of which might be expected to influence cognitive development. (See Whiting, 1976, for the general notion of "packaged" variables in research on culture and development.)

The ontogenetic level

Barbara Rogoff's (1981) review of the literature on schooling and cognitive development provides a handy framework for discussion of the cognitive consequences of schooling as it has been studied in standard cross-cultural research.

> Schooled individuals have gained skills in the use of graphic conventions to represent depth in two-dimensional stimuli and in the fine-grained analysis of two-dimensional patterns. They have increased facility in deliberately remembering disconnected bits of information, and spontaneously engage in strategies that provide greater organization for the unrelated items. Schooled people are more likely to organize objects on a taxonomic basis, putting categorically similar objects together, whereas nonschooled people often use functional arrangements of objects that are used together. Schooled groups show greater facility shifting to alternative dimensions of classification and in explaining the basis of their organization. Schooling appears to have no effect on rule learning nor on logical thought as long

as the subject has understood the problem in the way the experimenter intended. Nonschooled subjects seem to prefer, however, to come to conclusions on the basis of experience rather than relying on the information in the problem alone.

I will attempt to unpack this summary beginning with the cases where schooling was said to have no impact, because these are the cases where the common phylo-genetic heritage of the species results in forms of interaction with the world during ontogeny that are universal. The major body of research referred to here focuses on the development of operational thought in the Piagetian tradition.

Schooling and the development of logical operations

I believe that Rogoff is correct in her conclusion about the development of logical operations, but, as she is at some pains to point out, the matter has to be considered controversial. For purposes of discussion, I will assume that the logical operations in question are those that form the basis for Piagetian theory (Rogoff herself con-centrated on cultural variations in response to logical syllogisms and concept learn-ing based on logical relations). According to Inhelder and Piaget (1958):

> Although concrete operations consist of organized systems (classifications, serial ordering, correspondences, etc.) [children at this age] proceed from one partial link to the next in a step-by-step fashion, without relating each partial link to all the others. Formal operations differ in that all of the possible combinations are con-sidered in each case. Consequently, each partial link is grouped in relation to the whole; in other words, reasoning moves continually as a function of a "structured whole." (p. 16)

If we address first the question of concrete operations as embodied in the conser-vation tasks, it appears to be the case that schooling has no consistent influence on performance, although in a few well-publicized cases (e.g., Greenfield & Bruner, 1966) the steady development of conservation among schooled children and its absence among noneducated adults led to speculation that schooling might do more than accelerate rates of development (as Piaget, 1970, speculated, it might actually be necessary for the development of concrete operations). This kind of result was picked up by Hallpike (1979), who claimed that adults in nonliterate societies, as a rule, fail to develop beyond pre-operational thought (a conclusion hotly denied by, among others, Jahoda, 1980).

The crucial phrase in Rogoff's review pertaining to performance on concrete operations tasks is "as long as the subject has understood the problem in the way the experimenter intended." A number of years ago Dasen (1977) suggested that performance factors might interfere with the expression of concrete operational competence. In many, but not all, cases, modest amounts of conservation training were sufficient to improve performance markedly; it remained an open question if different kinds of training, or more training, would reveal the hypothesized com-petence (Dasen, Ngini, & Reschitzki, 1979). Greenfield's own research also points to situational factors that interfere with conservation judgments; when Wolof chil-dren poured water themselves, conservation performance improved markedly.

Most notably, when university-trained African psychologists have conducted studies with Piagetian conservation tasks, they have found rates of development to be similar for schooled and nonschooled populations (Kamara & Easley, 1977; Nyiti, 1976). Nyiti (1982) found a similar result when he contrasted the performance of Micmac (Canadian) children tested in English and Micmac.

Although there is room for disagreement, I believe that it is sensible to conclude that concrete operational thinking is not influenced by schooling; what is influenced is subjects' ability to understand the language of testing and the presuppositions of the testing situation itself.

At the level of formal operations, it is far more often concluded that schooling is a necessary, but not sufficient, condition for development. However, there is ample reason to question this conclusion as well. First, formal operations are rarely manifested by nonschooled subjects, and even highly schooled subjects are none too proficient (Neimark, 1975). Second, as Jahoda (1980) points out, when one moves outside of the narrow realm of the procedures used by Inhelder and Piaget (1958) in their monograph on formal operations, there is anecdotal, but persuasive, evidence that subjects can use formal operations.

My own beliefs appears to be close to that of Piaget (1972) (and, I believe, Jahoda, 1980). Formal operations are a universal achievement accompanying the change in social status from child to adult, but they will be manifest in specific domains of dense practice. As Jahoda notes, such practice is likely to be most dense in the domain of social relations. Consequently, it should come as no surprise that when Eric Erikson defines the process of identity formation, which is a hypothesized universal feature of the transition to adulthood, he seems to capture rather precisely the conception of a "structured whole" underpinning formal operations:

> In psychological terms, identity formation employs a process of simultaneous reflection and observations, a process taking place on all levels of mental functioning, by which the individual judges himself in the light of what he perceives to be the way others judge him in comparison to themselves and to a typology significant to them; while he perceives himself in comparison to them and to types that have become relevant to him. (1968, pp. 22–23)

Outside of contexts where individuals are actively thinking about their identities, in the absence of recording devices, full-blown formal operational thinking is probably a rarity in any culture. It will be associated with schooling as a normative part of scientific activities, but it almost certainly does not describe the actual thinking of trained scientists except under special circumstances where they need to check on their results or are working with auxiliary tools that help them to record and keep straight information (Latour, 1986). In the special sense that schooling expands the contexts of its use, then, formal operational thinking can be said to be influenced by schooling.

An interesting line of evidence in favor of this context-specific interpretation of formal logical skills comes from reasoning about logical syllogisms. In an early study, Luria (1934, 1976) demonstrated what appeared to be a strong relationship between formal schooling and syllogistic reasoning. Nonschooled Central Asian peasants responded to the syllogisms he posed in terms of their everyday knowledge, not the logical terms of the problem (the phenomenon referred to by Rogoff at the end of her summary). To take a famous example, when presented a syllogism of the form, "In Siberia all the bears are white; my friend Ivan was in Siberia and saw a bear; what color was it?" nonschooled subjects answered to the effect, "I have never been to Siberia, so I cannot say what color the bear was; Ivan is your friend, ask him." This kind of response has now been recorded in many cultures among nonschooled peoples and has been shown to diminish quickly with a few years of schooling in favor of a response based on the logical requirements of the task (Cole, Gay, Glick, & Sharp, 1971; Scribner, 1975; Tulviste, 1979). To judge from such evidence, it appears that formal schooling promotes a distinctive kind of theoretical thinking, in line with expectations of the sociohistorical school as developed in the USSR.

Unhappily for the view that "empirical" thinking is replaced by "theoretical" thinking as a consequence of schooling, a substantial literature collected among college students in Great Britain and the United States shows that for slightly more complicated syllogisms responses are highly content-dependent. For example, Wason (1960) found that college students could solve a particular syllogism when it was embodied in a realistic question about postage stamps and envelopes but not when it was embodied in a hypothetical question about quality control at work. This same problem did not work for students in the United States, where one based on rules about the age of drinking worked quite well (D'Andrade, 1982).

Following D'Andrade, it seems best to conclude that cultural variations in the outcome of logical thinking are primarily the result of differences in the supply of well-formed content-based schemata that are brought to the task, for example, differences in cognitive content, not the presence of generalized thinking skills in one group that are absent in the other.

Information-processing skills

Within this category I include those tasks that Rogoff refers to as "fine-grained analysis of two-dimensional patterns," memory for disconnected bits of information, and classification. In each of these areas there is substantial evidence that exposure to schooling brings about changes in cognitive performance which are taken to be indicative of cognitive development when they are observed among children raised in industrially advanced countries where schooling and psychological testing are ubiquitous.

Analysis of two-dimensional patterns

Early research on perception of depth (summarized in Jahoda & McGurk, 1982) seemed to show that, whether they attended school or not, people from a wide variety of African cultures had difficulty perceiving two-dimensional representations of three-dimensional space. However, using more carefully constructed materials, Jahoda and McGurk found little difference across cultures, with even very small children displaying sensitivity to depth cues. In some cases (e.g., Dawson, 1967), there is evidence of improved performance for schooled populations, but performance was generally poor, and I am uncertain if schooling can be said to be a major factor in the development of the associated perceptual skills.

Other lines of evidence provide more support for Rogoff's generalization that formal schooling promotes skills in fine-grained analysis of two-dimensional figures. One source of support comes from research on the Ponzo illusion (two converging straight lines that are seen as parallel if interpreted three-dimensionally, as in the representation of railroad track). Wagner (1982) found that susceptibility to illusions increases as a consequence of schooling. Research on the embedded-figures test and other perceptual tasks using two-dimensional drawings also indicates a significant impact of schooling (Berry, 1976; Serpell, 1976).

Memory

A variety of evidence supports Rogoff's generalization that schooling promotes memory for unrelated materials (Cole & Scribner, 1977; Stevenson, 1982; Wagner, 1982). For example:

1.   In repeated trials of free recall of common items that fall into culturally recognized categories, children with 6 or more years of schooling (Cole et al., 1971) and adults with varying years of schooling (Scribner & Cole, 1981) remember more and cluster items in recall more than nonschooled comparison groups.
2.   Short-term recall of item location increases as a function of schooling but not of age (Wagner, 1982).
3.   Paired-associate learning of randomly paired items increases with schooling (Sharp, Cole, & Lave, 1979).

In addition, Stevenson (1982) reports a small positive effect of very small amounts of schooling on a battery of tasks that included various kinds of memory problems a well as visual analysis.

By contrast, schooling effects are generally absent in cases of recall of well-structured stories (Mandler, Scribner, Cole, & De Forest, 1980). They are also absent when the items to be paired in a paired-associate task are strongly associated with each other (Sharp et al., 1979). Very short-term memory also seems unaffected by schooling; in Wagner's studies, most recently probed locations show no education effects (Wagner, 1974, 1978).

Classification and concept formation

A wide variety of studies have shown that schooled subjects are more likely to classify objects and pictures according to form (when such attributes as form, color, and function are used as possible bases for classification) and more likely to create categories that map onto taxonomic rather than functional attributes when these dimensions are put in competition with each other (Bruner, Olver, & Greenfield, 1966; Childs & Greenfield, 1982; Cole & Ciborowski, 1971; Serpell, 1976; Sharp et al., 1979).

Interpretation: Are the effects specific or general?

The central question about such results is whether they signal something general about the cognitive capacities of educated children or relatively restricted outcomes of practice in specific cognitive skills explicitly trained in schools.

During the 1940s and 1950s, it was assumed that formal schooling promoted quite general forms of cognitive development. This assumption was widely shared by the founders of the United Nations (UNESCO, 1970) and underpinned the policies of developmental economics for several decades (Lerner, 1957; Inkeles & Smith, 1974).

Among academic researches, the "general change" position is represented by Greenfield and Bruner's (1966) early speculation (subsequently abandoned; see Greenfield, 1976) that schooling is a major institution by means of which some cultures "push cognitive development faster and further than others," but especially relevant to the present discussion is A. R. Luria's interpretation of his cross-cultural research, which is squarely in the "general cognitive change" camp. Luria (1976) characterized the goal of the research as an attempt to demonstrate that "many mental processes are social and historical in origin [and] that important manifestations of human consciousness have been directly shaped by the basic practices of human activity and the actual forms of culture" (p. 3).

Luria presents many interesting results in support of this thesis; in the areas of classification (colored threads, geometric figures, and various objects), logical deduction, and self-evaluation (roughly equivalent to what is now referred to as metacognition), traditional people responded to his tasks in ways systematically different from their neighbors who had been involved in collective agriculture and schooling.

Greatly simplified, the following conclusions are almost central: In the change from traditional agricultural life to collectivized labor in literate/industrialized circumstances:

1. "Direct graphical-functional thinking" is replaced by at least the rudiments of "theoretical thinking."
2. The basic forms of cognitive activity go beyond fixation and reproduction of individual practical activity and cease to be purely concrete and situational, becoming a part of more general, abstractly coded, systems of knowledge.
3. These changes give rise not only to new forms of reasoning, restricted to logical premises free of immediate experience, but new forms of self-analysis and imagination as well.

Without dwelling on the complexities involved, I can point to two features of Luria's cross-cultural research that fail to fulfill the methodological requirements of the sociohistorical school. First, as we have commented elsewhere (Cole & Griffin, 1980), Luria neither studied nor modeled in his experiments the practical activity systems of the Uzbeki and Kazaki people and the psychological processes associated with them; hence, his interpretations were not grounded in an analysis of culturally organized activities. Instead, for purposes of psychological diagnosis he introduced distinctly Western European activity systems, in the form of psychological tests and interviews, which did not model local reality but served instead as measurements of generalized psychological tendencies for which there was a developmental interpretation in Western European societies.

Using this approach, Luria found that contact with European culture through either schooling or participation in Soviet-run collective enterprises increased the likelihood that traditional peasants would respond appropriately to his intellectual puzzles in Russian terms, but these results are basically silent with respect to possible analogues in indigenous practices. Such analogues might or might not exist, but the research Luria engaged in would, in principle, not be able to tell us which case fits reality.

The second, closely related problem, which becomes the focus when the sociocultural tradition is taken up in cross-cultural research by American investigators, is Luria's failure to restrict his conclusions to particular domains, instead appearing to claim that in general there is a change in the complexity of mediational mechanisms of cognition in the socioeconomic change from agricultural to industrial modes of production. Too often he seems to be concluding that the results he reports are independent of problem content and activity context, for example, generalized cognitive changes. This kind of conclusion simultaneously undermines the well-established principles of the dependence of psychological process on living activity systems and renders adults who display such behaviors childlike in (inappropriate) terms.

As we have argued elsewhere, my colleagues and I believe that the data on the cognitive consequences of schooling at the level of individual behavior are best interpreted in context-specific terms (Cole et al., 1971; Laboratory of Comparative Human Cognition, 1983). I will not repeat this argument in detail here. Suffice it to say that, insofar as the task environments used by psychologists to assess consequences of schooling for cognitive development take their structure and content from school-like tasks, it can hardly be surprising that people with extensive experience in school outperform those who have no pertinent practice.

As discussed elsewhere (Jahoda, 1980; Laboratory of Comparative Human Cognition, 1983), a major shortcoming of the context-specific approach is that it fails to account for the apparent generality of cognitive change associated with context-specific experience. I will return to this important issue presently, but first we must address the final level of developmental change needed for a full account of schooling and cognitive development, the *microgenetic developments* that occur within formal educational activity settings.

The microgenetic level

Analyses of teaching/learning interactions in classrooms throughout the world yield a picture of very broad similarities, modified to some extent in some places by local practices (see, e.g., Spindler, 1980).

Four distinctive features of educational activity, already present in the schools of ancient Summeria briefly described earlier, capture a good deal of the contemporary ethnographic picture.

First, formal schooling uses a distinctive mediational means, written symbol systems. In many discussions of the consequences of formal schooling in the past, literacy acquisition itself has been credited with causing advances in cognitive development, but in all such discussions literacy and schooling have been totally confounded. The conclusion we have reached on the basis of our analysis of literacy acquired in nonschools, Quranic schools, and English-style schools is that writing is a necessary, but not sufficient, explanation of schooling effects, be they context-specific or general.

This conclusion is based on the work of Scribner and Cole (1981) among the Vai people of northwestern Liberia. Many Vai (primarily men) are literate in an indigenous syllabic script, which they use mainly to write letters and to keep records either for personal use or for the affairs of small communities. Others are literate in the Quran, at least to the extent of being able to copy and recite verses, if not to use Arabic productively for nonreligious purposes. Still others have attended school where they acquired literacy in English.

Though indigenous Vai literacy is clearly useful, and has a notable impact on Vai life, it is not used to master large bodies of knowledge that would otherwise be inaccessible to the individual, and the tested cognitive consequences of Vai literacy are correspondingly modest; the only item from Rogoff's summary that shows an impact of Vai literacy is the way that geometric figures are categorized – Vai literates sort such figures according to form and number more often than nonliterates.

The consequences of schooling summarized by Rogoff seem to depend on repeated practice in learning new material and mastering new information-processing procedures (''cognitive strategies''). The sheer mass of this knowledge requires that students learn how to commit large amounts of information to memory, to be used later to gain still more information, with no clear connection to everyday activities outside of school. Moreover, this information is structured according to category systems that are a part of the tradition that created modern science and bureaucratic institutions. It privileges the taxonomic/paradigmatic form of organization over the thematic/syntagmatic.

This aspect of the contexts of schooling appears, in my opinion, to be sufficient to explain most of the tested results comparing schooled and nonschooled children on memory and classification tasks.

The second conspicuous fact about schooling is the participant structure and the form of discourse that goes on there. Overwhelmingly, not just in the Arab world

(Wagner & Lofti, 1980) but in American classrooms as well, a single teacher organizes recitations for large numbers of students. The material to be learned is broken down into units with a particular sequence, and the students must master lower-level steps to achieve higher-order ones. The larger purposes of this activity are observed; learning is for short-term information mastery goals.

Detailed studies of the way that language is used in schools reveal a distinctive pattern called instructional discourse. Instructional discourse differs from other ways in which adults and children speak in both its structure and its content. The central goals of instructional discourse are to give children information about the content of the curriculum and feedback about their efforts while providing teachers with information about their students' progress (Mehan, 1979).

One of the distinctive indicators of instructional discourse is the presence of the initiation–reply–evaluation sequence. This pattern starts when the teacher initiates an exchange, usually by asking a question; a student replies, and then the teacher provides an evaluation. An important feature of the initiate–reply–evaluate sequence is a form of questioning that is very rarely encountered outside of school, the "known-answer question" (Searle, 1969). When a teacher asks, "What does this say?" she is seeking information about what the child has learned, not about the state of the content in question. Children can ask questions just as they would at home, but very often when the teacher asks a question it is really a covert way to evaluate the student's progress. Learning to respond easily to known-answer questions, in addition to learning about the academic content of the curriculum, is an important early lesson of schooling (Mehan, 1979).

The special nature of language in school-based learning is also manifested in the emphasis that teachers place on linguistic form. Sometimes this emphasis on form may even occur at the expense of accuracy about content, making the entire exercise appear rather strange.

This set of practices, I believe (along with Rogoff, 1981, and Scribner, 1977), helps to account for the fact that only a very few years of schooling are sufficient to bring about a marked change in response to verbal logical problems. Such verbal logical problems map neatly onto the discourse of school with its motivated exclusion of everyday experience and its formal mode. Subjects who have attended school recognize the form and reply appropriately in its terms so long as the form of the syllogistic problem is simple enough. However, when the question becomes difficult, even educated adults, as D'Andrade (1982) clearly shows, fall back on everyday knowledge and modes of interpretation.

Sources of general cognitive effects

So far, the distinctive features of the microenvironment of schooling I have discussed motivate a context-specific interpretation of schooling's impact on cognitive development. It is important to ask if there is anything in the microenvironment that might reasonably be expected to have context-independent consequences. However, this discussion cannot get very far unless we complete the circle and inquire into the larger historical/cultural context within which schooling activity is embedded. General effects, according to the view our group has adopted, will depend crucially upon the extent to which forms of cognition mastered in one context are relevant in other contexts; put differently, "transfer" of school-based knowledge should be sought in the environment as well as in the transformed capacities within children's heads.

Three factors of educational activity have prima facie generality in the sense that they are relevant to behavior in a wide range of contexts (at least within industrially advanced countries). First, the medium of instruction, writing, is the medium of public life, aiding performance in a great many settings. Second, insofar as the content of the curriculum allows them more broadly to understand their particular historical circumstances, it will lead students to be more effective problem solvers when they are not in school. Third, the lexicon of every language carries within it the culture's theory about the nature of the world. Insofar as children's linguistic resources are expanded by exposure to words in many contexts, they gain access to the meaning systems of which those words are a part, meaning systems that have applicability beyond the school walls.

This is a very content-oriented view. The only quasi-cognitive process involved is the mastery of the written medium. Relatively speaking, I am unimpressed by the possibility that the specific cognitive strategies necessary for mastery of the curriculum have wide applicability across contexts, or that children master metacognitive abilities in school that transfer broadly. I am quite impressed, on the other hand, with evidence of greatly restricted transfer of problem-solving strategies and of the dependence of the quality of problem solving and other kinds of cognitive activity on content-based knowledge (for a more detailed justification of both these views, see Laboratory of Comparative Human Cognition, 1983).

General implications

If my view of the cognitive consequences of formal schooling is approximately correct, it cautions against the position, still easy to encounter in international development circles, that education will develop the minds of the world's nonliterate populations, thereby serving as the engine of economic and political development. Education provides new "tools of the intellect," to be sure. But without contexts of use, these tools appear to "rust" and fall into disuse.

It is my reading of the earliest origins of schooling in Summeria that formal education could not be conceived of as a cause of the momentous sociopolitical-economic changes that took place there. Nor was it a simple effect; rather, it was an enabling condition along with many others. Schools evolved over many centuries, perhaps a thousand years, along with the social forms that they served and mediational means that made them possible. In short, formal schooling was an integral part of the social process.

That history is incredibly different from the situation of less-developed countries today, where schooling is an alien form, inserted into the social process by powerful outsiders within the past several decades, or at most 100 years. Less-developed countries have had no choice but to adopt formal schooling; it seemed to represent both a passkey to the modern world and the only hope of regaining national independence. But I think there is little doubt that widespread adoption of formal schooling has also been a source of social disruption and human misery.

Surveying the world today we witness a number of attempts by less-developed countries to modify their educational systems, free of both the value systems and political control of outsiders. The ideology of development that underpinned development efforts in the 1950s and 1960s, including educational development, has been forcefully rejected by Muslim fundamentalism in the Near East. In a different form, that ideology is being rejected in West Africa in favor of a strategy of development consistent with the countries' own resources and national heritages. Perhaps the first shock wave of widespread formal schooling is passing. If this is so, perhaps a reevaluation of the relation between cognitive development and education along the lines suggested here will also provide useful ideas for policy makers who must be able not only to criticize the shortcomings of the past but to find a usable route to the future.

References

Berry, J. M. (1976). *Human ecology and cultural style.* New York: Sage-Halstead.

Bruner, J. S., Olver, R., & Greenfield, P. M. (1966). *Studies in cognitive growth.* New York: Wiley.

Childs, C. P., & Greenfield, P. M. (1982). Informal modes of learning and teaching: The case of Zinacanteco weaving. In N. Warren (Ed.), *Studies in cross-cultural psychology* (Vol. 2). New York: Academic Press.

Cole, M. (1988). Cross-cultural research in the socio-historical tradition. *Human Development, 31,* 137–157.

Cole, M., & Ciborowski, T. (1971). Cultural differences in learning conceptual rules. *International Journal of Psychology, 6,* 25–37.

Cole, M., Gay, J., Glick, J. A., & Sharp, D. (1971). *The cultural context of learning and thinking.* New York: Basic.

Cole, M., & Griffin, P. (1980). Cultural amplifiers reconsidered. In D. Olson (Ed.), *Social foundations of language and thought.* New York: Norton.

Cole, M., & Scribner, S. (1977). Developmental theories applied to cross-cultural cognitive research. *Annals of the New York Academy of Sciences, 285,* 366–373.

D'Andrade, R. (1982). *Reason vs. logic.* Paper presented at the Symposium on the Ecology of Cognition, Greensboro, NC.

Dasen, P. R. (Ed.) (1977). *Piagetian psychology: Cross-cultural contributions.* New York: Gardner.

Dasen, P. R., Ngini, L., & Reschitzki, L. (1979). Cross-cultural studies of concrete operations. In L. H. Eckensberger, W. J. Lonner, & Y. H. Poortinga (Eds.), *Cross-cultural contributions to psychology.* Amsterdam: Swetz & Zeitlinger.

Dawson, J. L. M. (1967). Cultural and physiological influences upon spatial-perceptual processes in West Africa (Pt. 1). *International Journal of Psychology, 2,* 115–128.

Donaldson, M. (1978). *Children's minds.* New York. Norton.

Erikson, E. H. (1968). *Identity: Youth and crisis.* New York: Norton.

Goody, J. (1977). *Domestication of the savage mind.* Cambridge: Cambridge University Press.

Goody, J. (1987). *The interface between the written and the oral.* Cambridge: Cambridge University Press.

Greenfield, P. M. (1976). Cross-cultural research and Piagetian theory: Paradox and progress. In K. F. Riegel and J. A. Meacham (Eds.), *The developing individual in a changing world: Historical and cultural issues* (Vol. 1). Chicago: Aldine.

Greenfield, P. M., & Bruner, J. S. (1966). Culture and cognitive growth. *International Journal of Psychology, 1,* 89–107.

Greenfield, P. M., & Lave, J. (1982). Cognitive aspects of informal education. In D. A. Wagner & H. Stevenson (Eds.), *Cultural perspectives on child development.* San Francisco: Freeman.

Hallpike, C. R. (1979). *The foundations of primitive thought.* New York: Oxford University Press.

Harris, R. (1986). *The origin of writing.* London: Duckworth.

Inhelder, B., & Piaget, P. (1958). *The growth of logical thinking from childhood to adolescence.* New York: Basic.

Inkeles, A., & Smith, D. H. (1974). *Becoming modern.* Cambridge, MA: Harvard University Press.

Jahoda, G. (1980). Theoretical and systematic approaches in cross-cultural psychology. In H. C. Triandis & W. W. Lambert (Eds.), *Handbook of cross-cultural psychology: Vol. 1. Perspectives.* Boston: Allyn & Bacon.

Jahoda, G., & McGurk, H. (1982). The development of picture perception in children from different cultures. In D. A. Wagner and H. W. Stevenson (Eds.), *Cultural perspectives on child development.* San Francisco: Freeman.

Kamara, A. I., & Easley, J. A., Jr. (1977). Is the rate of cognitive development uniform across cultures? A methodological critique with new evidence from Themne children. In P. R. Dasen (Ed.), *Piagetian psychology: Cross-cultural contributions.* New York: Gardner.

Kawai, M. (1963). Newly acquired pre-cultural behavior of the natural troop of Japanese monkeys on Koshima islet. *Primates, 6,* 1–30.

Laboratory of Comparative Human Cognition (1983). Culture and cognitive development. In P. H. Mussen (Ed.), *Carmichael's handbook of child development* (Vol. 1). New York: Wiley.

Laboratory of Comparative Human Cognition (1986). The contribution of cross-cultural research to educational practice. *American Psychologist, 41,* 1049–58.

Larsen, M. (1986). Writing on clay: From pictograph to alphabet. *Quarterly Newsletter of the Laboratory of Comparative Human Cognition, 8*(1), 3–10.

Latour, B. (1986). *Laboratory Life: The construction of scientific facts.* Princeton, NJ: Princeton University Press.

Leontiev, A. N. (1930). Studies of the cultural development of the child: 3. The development of voluntary attention in the child. *Journal of Genetic Psychology, 37,* 52–81.

Leontiev, A. N. (1981). *Problems in the development of mind.* Moscow: Progress.

Lerner, D. (1957). *The passing of traditional society.* New York: Free Press.

Luria, A. R. (1928). The problem of the cultural development of the child. *Journal of Genetic Psychology, 35,* 493–506.

Luria, A. R. (1932). *The nature of human conflicts.* London: Liveright.

Luria, A. R. (1934). The second psychological expedition to Central Asia. *Journal of Genetic Psychology, 41,* 255–259.

Luria, A. R. (1976). *Cognitive development.* Cambridge, MA: Harvard University Press.

Luria, A. R. (1979). *The making of mind.* Cambridge, MA: Harvard University Press.

Mandler, J. M., Scribner, S., Cole, M., & De Forest, M. (1980). Cross-cultural invariance in story recall. *Child Development, 51,* 19–26.

Marschak, A. (1972). *The roots of civilization: The cognitive beginnings of man's first art, symbol, and notation.* New York: McGraw-Hill.

Mehan, H. (1979). *Learning lessons.* Cambridge, MA: Harvard University Press.

Neimark, E. D. (1975). Intellectual development during adolescence. In F. D. Horowitz (Ed.), *Review of child development research* (Vol. 4). Chicago: University of Chicago Press.

Nyiti, R. (1982). The validity of "cultural differences explanations" for cross-cultural variation in the note of Piagetian cognitive development. In D. A. Wagner & H. W. Stevenson (Eds.), *Cultural perspectives on child development*. San Francisco: Freeman.

Nyiti, R. M. (1976). The development of conservation in the Meru children of Tanzania. *Child Development, 47*, 1122–1129.

Pfeiffer, J. (1972). *The emergence of man*. New York: Harper & Row.

Piaget, J. (1970). Piaget's theory. In P. H. Mussen (Ed.), *Carmichael's handbook of child psychology* (3rd ed.). New York: Wiley.

Piaget, J. (1972). Intellectual evolution from adolescence to adulthood. *Human Development, 15*, 1–12.

Premack, D. (1983). Pedagogy and aesthetics as a source of culture. In M. S. Gazzaniga (Ed.), *Handbook of cognitive neurosciences*. New York: Plenum.

Rogoff, B. (1981). Schooling and the development of cognitive skills. In H. C. Triandis & A. Heron (Eds.), *Handbook of cross-cultural psychology* (Vol. 4). Boston: Allyn & Bacon.

Schmandt-Besserat, D. (1978). The earliest precursor of writing. *Scientific American, 238*, 50–59.

Scribner, S. (1975). Recall of classical syllogisms: A cross-cultural investigation of errors on logical problems. In R. Falmagne (Ed.), *Reasoning: Representation and process*. Hillsdale, NJ: Erlbaum.

Scribner, S. (1977). Modes of thinking and ways of speaking: Culture and logic reconsidered. In P. N. Johnson-Laird & P. C. Wason (Eds.), *Thinking: Readings in cognitive science*. Cambridge: Cambridge University Press.

Scribner, S., & Cole, M. (1973). Cognitive consequences of formal and informal education. *Science, 182*, 553–559.

Scribner, S., & Cole, M. (1981). *The psychology of literacy*. Cambridge, MA: Harvard University Press.

Searle, J. (1969). *Speech acts*. Cambridge: Cambridge University Press.

Serpell, R. (1976). *Culture's influence on behavior*. London: Methuen.

Sharp, D. W., Cole, M., & Lave, C. (1979). Education and cognitive development: Evidence from experimental research. *Monographs of the Society for Research in Child Development, 44* (Serial No. 178).

Spindler, G. D. (1980). *Doing the ethnography of schooling*. New York: Holt, Rinehart and Winston.

Stevenson, H. W. (1982). Influences of schooling on cognitive development. In D. A. Wagner and H. W. Stevenson (Eds.), *Cultural perspectives on child development*. San Francisco: Freeman.

Street, B. V. (1984). *Literacy in theory and practice*. Cambridge: Cambridge University Press.

Tomasello, M. (1989, Winter). Chimpanzee culture? *SRCD Newsletter*, pp. 1–3.

Triandis, H. C., & Lambert, W. W. (Eds.) (1980). *Handbook of cross-cultural psychology: Vol. 1. Perspectives*. Boston: Allyn & Bacon.

Tulviste, P. (1979). On the origins of theoretic syllogistic reasoning in culture and the child. *Quarterly Newsletter of the Laboratory of Comparative Human Cognition, 1*(4), 73–80.

UNESCO. (1970). *Literacy 1967–9: Progress throughout the world*.

Vygotsky, L. S. (1929). The problem of the cultural development of the child (pt. 2). *Journal of Genetic Psychology, 36*, 414–434.

Vygotsky, L. S. (1978). *Mind in society*. Cambridge, MA: Harvard University Press.

Wagner, D. A. (1974). The development of short-term and incidental memory: A cross-cultural study. *Child Development, 45*, 389–396.

Wagner, D. A. (1978). The effects of formal schooling on cognitive style. *Journal of Social Psychology, 106*, 145–151.

Wagner, D. A. (1982). Ontogeny in the study of culture and cognition. In D. A. Wagner and H. W. Stevenson (Eds.), *Cultural perspectives on child development*. San Francisco: Freeman.

Wagner, D. A., & Lofti, A. (1980). *Learning to read by "rote" in the Quranic schools of Yemen and Senegal*. Paper presented at the meeting of the American Anthropological Society, Washington, DC.

Waitz, T. (1863). *Introduction to anthropology*. London: Longmans Green, Longman, & Roberts.

Wason, P. C. (1960). Regression in reasoning. *British Journal of Psychology, 4*, 471–480.

Wertsch, J. V. (Ed.) (1985). *Culture, communication, and cognition*. Cambridge: Cambridge University Press.

Whiting, B. (1976). The problem of the packaged variable. In K. F. Riegel & J. A. Meacham (Eds.), *The developing individual in a changing world: Historical and cultural issues* (Vol. 1). The Hague: Mouton.

Wundt, W. (1921). *Elements of folk psychology*. London: Allen & Unwin.

4 The voice of rationality in a sociocultural approach to mind

James V. Wertsch

Over the past decade there has been a growing tendency among cognitive, developmental, and educational psychologists to view human mental functioning in terms of an aggregate of skills or an aggregate of contextually situated processes. This contrasts with the dominant tendency toward viewing mental functioning as some kind of unified entity, a tendency clearly manifested in notions of general intelligence or in the metaphor of a central processor. Some of the impetus for this change has come from new theoretical orientations such as Leont'ev's (1981) ideas about activity (e.g., LCHC, 1983), but it also stems from a host of other factors such as a general dissatisfaction with standard measures of intelligence (e.g., Gardner, 1983).

Much of this new orientation has grown out of a desire to expand the focus of research beyond the kinds of mental functioning privileged in formal instructional settings. In this connection, whole new areas of inquiry have emerged. For example, the recent emphases on "everyday cognition" (Rogoff & Lave, 1984) and on "cognition in practice" (Lave, 1988) have been motivated by a desire to examine forms of social and psychological functioning that are explicitly contrasted with practices found in formal educational settings.

Although there is clearly a growing tendency to espouse an approach that recognizes various forms of mental functioning, there remains a tendency to view one form of mental functioning as somehow more basic, more "cognitive," or more important than others. The usual candidate for this is rational, logico-deductive reasoning of the sort found in formal instructional settings. In my view the reasons for this are twofold. First, we are still a long way from producing a theoretical framework that would specify how various forms of mental functioning are systematically interrelated. As a result, the debate often continues to disintegrate into arguments about why one form of functioning is more interesting or fundamental or important than another instead of focusing on relationships that may exist among different but equally necessary forms of functioning.

An earlier version of this chapter was presented as my inaugural lecture for the Belle van Zuilen Professorship at the University of Utrecht, The Netherlands. I wish to express my appreciation for the support, intellectual and otherwise, provided by the University of Utrecht and particularly by my colleagues in the Department of Development and Socialization. The research for this chapter was also assisted by the Spencer Foundation. The statements made and the views expressed are solely the responsibility of the author.

111

Second, we have all too often tried to resolve these issues within the confines of psychology. Notable exceptions to this can be found in the writings of authors such as Lave (1988) and Scribner and Cole (1981), but we need to go farther in trying to understand how forms of mental functioning are tied to various social and cultural contexts. In the end, the identification of various forms of mental functioning and an account of how they are organized will be grounded in such contextual issues as much as in issues ordinarily considered under the heading of psychology.

In this chapter I shall address these questions from the perspective of a developmental, sociocultural approach to mind. By *development* I mean an approach grounded in the assumption that one can fully understand mental functioning only by understanding its origins and the genetic (i.e., developmental) transitions it has undergone. By *sociocultural* I mean an approach that focuses on the institutional, cultural, and historical specificity of mental functioning rather than on universals. I want to pursue a sociocultural approach not because I believe there are no universals but because I believe that universalism has come to dominate psychological theory today to such a degree that little attention has been given to the historical, cultural, and social situatedness of mind. One of the results of this is that psychology has often produced ethnocentric conclusions, thereby avoiding some of the most complex and interesting issues that we should be addressing.

Although my orientation is that of a developmental psychologist, I wish to stress that the issues raised here cannot be adequately addressed if one adheres to a narrow disciplinary perspective. In that spirit I have found it useful to turn to ideas from semiotics, literary analysis, and social theory. This reflects a general belief that it is only by organizing our scholarly efforts around issues such as socioculturally situated forms of representation – that is, issues that integrate rather than isolate various forms of mental functioning and various scholarly orientations – that we will be able to overcome the debilitating effects of disciplinary specialization. The ideas I shall propose here owe a great deal to several scholars, but the work of two Soviet scholars is particularly important: L. S. Vygotsky (1896–1934) and M. M. Bakhtin (1895–1975).

Over the past decade or so the ideas of Vygotsky and other Soviet psychologists have come to play an increasingly important role in the thinking of Western developmental psychologists. Furthermore, as scholars in political science (e.g., Cook, 1985), literary studies (e.g., Clark & Holquist, 1985), and other disciplines have come to recognize, Vygotsky's ideas have more general implications for the humanities and social sciences. This is not surprising, given that he lived and worked in a setting where most scholars had little patience for the kinds of disciplinary divisions and disputes that characterize so much of today's academic scene. During his career, cut short by his death from tuberculosis, Vygotsky wrote extensively on issues of philosophy, semiotics, psychology, aesthetic theory, pedagogy, the rehabilitation and pedagogy of the handicapped, and literature, all in pursuit of developing a sociocultural theory of mind.

Vygotsky's theoretical framework

Vygotsky's sociocultural approach to mind can be characterized briefly in terms of three general themes that run throughout his writings: (1) a reliance on genetic (i.e., developmental) analysis; (2) the claim that higher mental functions in the individual have their origins in social life; and (3) the claim that an essential key to understanding human social and psychological processes is the tools and signs used to mediate them.

Vygotsky's insistence on using genetic analysis when examining human mental functioning meant that for him the major route to understanding mind is to specify the origins and genetic transformations it has undergone, a point that can be summarized in his acceptance of the statement by his Soviet colleague P. P. Blonskii (1921) that "behavior can be understood only as the history of behavior." In Vygotsky's view, by failing to employ genetic analysis we run the risk of being misled by the appearance of "fossilized behaviors" (1978). That is, we run the risk of trying to explain a phenomenon on the basis of fossilized phenotypic appearances that mask its underlying nature.

Vygotsky employed genetic analysis in a variety of "genetic domains" (Wertsch, 1985b). In addition to ontogenesis, where he carried out his most extensive empirical studies, he examined issues in phylogenesis, social history, and "microgenesis" (Wertsch, 1985b). His writings on issues of social history played such a central role in his account (cf. Scribner, 1985) that in the USSR his approach is often labeled *sociohistorical* or *cultural-historical* (Smirnov, 1975). In incorporating various genetic domains into his overall account he explicitly rejected recapitulationist notions, arguing that each domain is characterized by unique forces and mechanisms of change. For him, the issue was ultimately one of how the various forces of change act in tandem in human activity (cf. Vygotsky & Luria, 1930).

Vygotsky was clearly influenced by the writings of Marx, Engels, and Hegel in formulating his ideas about genetic analysis. However, as I have argued elsewhere (Wertsch, 1985a), he was also heavily influenced by other psychologists of his day, including Blonskii, Piaget, and Werner.[1] It was by building on the ideas of such figures that he was able to deal with the "methodological" (Zinchenko & Smirnov, 1983) problem of translating Marxist claims into a psychological theory.

The second theme in Vygotsky's approach, a theme that presupposes the first, is that higher (i.e., uniquely human) mental functioning in the individual has its origins in social activity. His most general formulation of this claim appears in his "general genetic law of cultural development."

> Any function in the child's cultural development appears twice, or on two planes. First it appears on the social plane, and then on the psychological plane. First it appears between people as an interpsychological category, and then within the child as an intrapsychological category. This is equally true with regard to voluntary attention, logical memory, the formation of concepts, and the development of volition. . . . It goes without saying that internalization transforms the process itself and changes its structure and function. (1981, p. 163)

This theme in Vygotsky's work, which bears a striking resemblance to some of G. H. Mead's (1934) claims, entails some ideas whose importance is often not recognized at first glance. For example, higher mental processes such as voluntary attention, logical memory, and thinking are not attributed to individuals alone; they are also appropriately attributed to dyads and other groups. Conversely, mental functioning on the intrapsychological plane reflects its interpsychological percursors to such a degree that it retains a "quasi-social" nature (Vygotsky, 1981).

On the basis of Vygotsky's claims about interpsychological functioning or "socially distributed consciousness" (Bruner, 1985), it follows that one should examine phenomena such as "adult–child problem-solving systems" (Wertsch, McNamee, McLane, & Budwig, 1980) as well as mental functioning in the individual. Vygotsky's claim about interpsychological functioning is not a claim about the kind of group mind that has been discounted in social psychology. Instead, it is a claim that forms an essential and coherent part of the theoretical system Vygotsky was trying to develop.

When tracing the origins of this theme in Vygotsky's work, one can again turn to the ideas of Marx. Indeed, at certain points in Vygotsky's writings he explicitly stated that his work on this topic represented an attempt to outline the psychological correlates of Marx's *Sixth Thesis on Feuerbach*. However, it is also important once again to recognize the impact of other psychologists on Vygotsky's ideas here. In particular, the writings of the French psychiatrist Janet (1926–1927, 1928) and the early writings of Piaget (1932) were important in this connection.

The third theme in Vygotsky's writings is the claim that higher mental functioning is mediated by tools and signs. This theme is grounded partly in the ideas of Engels and others about the role of tools in hominidization, but its elaboration reflects Vygotsky's lifelong interest in semiotics, linguistics, and literary analysis (three disciplines that were not so isolated in Vygotsky's day as they are now). The fundamental claim here is that human activity (on both the interpsychological and the intrapsychological plane) can be understood only if we take into consideration the "technical tools" and "psychological tools" or "signs" that mediate this activity. These forms of mediation, which are products of the sociocultural milieu in which they exist, are not viewed as simply facilitating activity that would otherwise take place. Instead, they are viewed as fundamentally shaping and defining it.

As I have argued elsewhere (Wertsch, 1985b), the mediational theme in Vygotsky's writings is analytically prior to the other two. In the case of genetic analysis, Vygotsky defined domains and transitions in terms of the appearance or transformation of some form of mediation. In the case of his claim about the social origins of higher mental functioning in the individual, his very definition of social (i.e., interpsychological) and hence intrapsychological activity rested on their being mediated by signs.

In addition to its analytic priority, there is another reason for paying special attention to the mediational theme in Vygotsky's approach: It is here that he made his most unique and important contribution. As noted earlier, it is not difficult to find strong similarities between the writings of other authors and Vygotsky's claims about genetic analysis and the social origins of individual mental functioning. He certainly had theoretical precursors when it came to the mediational theme as well, but the ways he extended others' ideas on this topic were unique. Furthermore, the ways he integrated notions about mediation with the other two themes meant that they were transformed into something different from what they were in other authors' hands.

Vygotsky's primary emphasis when examining mediation was on the sign systems used in human communication, in particular, speech. In this connection, it is essential to keep in mind that the object of analysis was human communicative activity, or speech, not language as a system abstracted from use. This is a frequent source of confusion among Western readers, something that has been exacerbated by the use of *language* rather than the correct term, *speech,* in the title of his best-known work in English (Vygotsky, 1962). In today's terminology, his writings might be termed *discourse analysis* or *pragmatics* rather than linguistics. However, unlike many contemporary discourse and pragmatic analyses, which separate semiotic from other aspects of activity, his concern was always with how speech is interrelated with other aspects of social and individual activity. For example, instead of focusing on issues such as given and new information (Wertsch, 1979) in isolation from problem solving, he was concerned with ways in which this semiotic distinction can inform analyses of reasoning and other forms of goal-directed action.

The task of Vygotsky's sociocultural approach to mind was to specify how human mental functioning reflects and constitutes its historical, institutional, and cultural setting. In my opinion he clearly succeeded in producing an approach that is consistent with this goal, but he did relatively little in the way of specifying how his approach would apply to concrete settings. This is partly attributable to his early death, which prevented him from examining many issues, but it is also in part due to the fact that most of his concrete research on interpsychological functioning focused on dyadic or small-group interactions rather than broader institutional or cultural phenomena. There is evidence, however, that he was becoming more concerned with these phenomena near the end of his life.

In this connection it is instructive to compare chapters 5 and 6 in his volume, *Thinking and Speech* (1987). Both of these chapters deal with the ontogenetic transition from "complexes" to "genuine" or "scientific" concepts,[2] a transition that is one instantiation of the process of the "decontextualization of mediational means" (Wertsch, 1985b). In chapter 5 (written in the early 1930s) concept development is treated primarily from the perspective of individual psychology, that is, children's conceptual development as they move from "unorganized heaps" to "complexes" to "concepts," whereas in chapter 6, which was probably written in 1934, there is an essential shift in perspective. Though Vygotsky clearly continued to be interested in intrapsychological functioning, he now approached concept development from the perspective of how it emerges in institutionally situated activity. Specifically, he was concerned with how the forms of discourse encountered in the social institution of formal schooling provide the underlying framework within which concept development occurs. He did this by focusing on the forms of teacher–child interpsychological functioning found in this setting rather than on the child's intrapsychological functioning alone.

The trend in Vygotsky's thinking near the end of his life is clear. He was searching for a way to relate the psychological functioning of the individual with particular sociocultural settings, specifically with the setting of formal instruction. The theoretical mechanism that he used to specify this relationship was grounded in his theme of semiotic mediation; his line of reasoning was to identify the forms of speech or discourse characteristic of particular sociocultural settings and examine the impact their mastery has on mental functioning (on both the interpsychological and the intrapsychological plane). It is in this connection that the writings of M. M. Bakhtin become relevant.

Bakhtin's contribution to a sociocultural approach to mind

Even though Bakhtin and Vygotsky were contemporaries, there is no evidence that they actually met (Clark & Holquist, 1985), and neither seems to have referred to the work of the other.[3] However, partly because they lived and worked in the same general intellectual milieu, their ideas are quite compatible on several counts. This compatibility makes it possible to use several elements in Bakhtin's theoretical framework to extend Vygotsky's formulation of a sociocultural approach to mind. I shall focus on four such elements here: *utterance, voice, social speech type,* and *dialogue.*

Unlike most linguists, who concern themselves primarily with linguistic form and meaning abstracted from actual conditions of use, Bakhtin focused his analytic efforts on the *utterance,* or "the *real unit* of speech communication" (1986, p. 71). That is, he was concerned with speech activity that is contextualized in terms of historical, institutional, cultural, and individual factors. His motivation for focusing on this unit of analysis was that he believed other scholars of language often lose sight of the fact that "speech can exist in reality only in the form of concrete utterances of individual speaking people[,] . . . in the form of an utterance belonging to a particular speaking subject" (1986, p. 71).

Bakhtin's emphasis on the need to study utterances did not mean that he viewed them in terms of the randomness linguists traditionally have associated with "parole" or "performance." Instead, he sought to provide an account of the principles that organize utterances and their contexts. One of the building blocks in this effort is the notion of voice. "Individual speaking people" and "particular speaking subject" are ways of referring to voice. When utterances are produced by a voice (the only way they can be produced), they can be characterized in terms of a number of dimensions that cannot be reduced to the abstract phenomena usually examined by linguists. They have a "will" or "intention," as well as an "accent" or "timbre," associated with them.

The intention and accent of an utterance are not random. Furthermore, they are not simply selected or created by the speaking subject acting in isolation. Rather, they reflect the intention and accent of other voices. This occurs through "ventriloquation" (Bakhtin, 1981; Holquist, 1981), or the process whereby one voice speaks *through* another.

> The word in language is half someone else's. It becomes "one's own" only when the speaker populates it with his own intention, his own accent, when he appropriates the word, adapting it to his own semantic and expressive intention. Prior to this moment of appropriation, the word does not exist in a neutral and impersonal language (it is not, after all, out of a dictionary that the speaker gets his words!), but rather it exists in other people's mouths, in other people's contexts, serving other people's intentions; it is from there that one must take the word, and make it one's own. (Bakhtin, 1981, pp. 293–294)

Thus, in addition to the unique circumstances of the concrete speech event, the intention and accent a voice has in producing an utterance may depend on another particular voice's being appropriated or ventriloquated. These aspects of the utterance are not reducible to socially established categories or types, something that would be incompatible with Bakhtin's ideas about the "unfinalizability" of human consciousness. However, there are other patterns of organization that involve processes whereby voices ventriloquate through "national languages" (i.e., Dutch, Russian, Japanese, etc.) and through "social speech types."

Bakhtin's notions of languages and social speech types provide further means for identifying the organizational principles that govern what otherwise appears to be the randomness of utterances in human communication. He included in his list of social speech types "social dialects, characteristic group behavior, professional jargons, generic languages, languages of generations and age groups, tendentious languages, languages of the authorities of various circles and of passing fashions, languages that serve the specific sociopolitical purposes of the day" (1981, p. 262). One of the items on this list that he explicated in some detail is the notion of generic language or "speech genre." Among the speech genres he mentioned are military commands, everyday genres of greeting, farewell, and congratulation, salon conversations about everyday, social, aesthetic, and other subjects, genres of table conversation, intimate conversations among friends, and everyday narration. In Bakhtin's view,

> We speak only in definite speech genres, that is, all our utterances have definite and relatively stable typical *forms of construction of the whole*. Our repertoire of oral (and written) speech genres is rich. We use them confidently and skillfully *in practice*, and it is quite possible for us not even to suspect their existence *in theory*. Like Molière's Monsieur Jourdan who, when speaking in prose, had no idea that was what he was doing, we speak in diverse genres without suspecting that they exist. (1986, p. 78)

Bakhtin's claims that we must appropriate the words of others and that individual voices ventriloquate through speech genres reflect a concern with his most fundamental category: dialogicality. In his account, dialogue is a much broader phenomenon than face-to-face turn-taking interaction. While recognizing this as the "primordial dialogism of discourse" (1981, p. 275) arising from the interanimation of utterances within a single language and speech type, he also was concerned with various forms of ventriloquation, with the interanimation of social speech types within a single national language, and with the contact of different national languages within a single culture.

The inherent nature of dialogicality in human communication derives from the observation that "any utterance is a link in the chain of speech communication" (1986, p. 84). As a result of this fact,

> Utterances are not indifferent to one another, and are not self-sufficient; they are aware of and mutually reflect one another [e.g., through ventriloquation]. These mutual reflections determine their character. Each utterance is filled with echoes and reverberations of other utterances to which it is related by the communality of the sphere of speech communication. Every utterance must be regarded primarily as a *response* to preceding utterances of the given sphere (we understand the word "response" here in the broadest sense). (1986, p. 91)

Dialogicality in its various forms served as the foundation for Bakhtin's analysis of novelistic discourse (1981), his observations on the origins of the novel in the carnival (1968), his reinterpretation of the psychoanalytic method (Voloshinov, 1987), his approach to human consciousness and understanding (Voloshinov, 1973), and his claims about Dostoevsky's "polyphonic" novel (1984).

Because Bakhtin grounded his notions of voice and social speech type in the category of dialogue, these notions have an interpretation distinct from those found in other linguistic, sociolinguistic, or stylistic analyses. For this same reason, his account also has implications for extending a sociocultural approach to mind in essential new ways. A review of his analysis of fundamental aspects of the utterance can reveal some of these.

Bakhtin argued that one must take into consideration an utterance's relation to the speaker and its relation to other utterances and participants in speech communication. Under the heading of the former, he distinguished between (1) the "referentially semantic content," which provides the primary characterization of an utterance, and (2) the expressive aspect of the utterance. When dealing with the referentially semantic content or "referentially semantic sphere" of an utterance, Bakhtin was concerned primarily with issues of content, meaning, and reference as they are typically examined in linguistics. Indeed, it would appear that this is a phenomenon that he would have been willing to leave, at least in part, to linguistics, as opposed to the properties of concrete utterances that were to be examined by "metalinguistics" (1984).

Bakhtin's account of the expressive aspect of the utterance (the aspect that has traditionally been the focus of stylistics) concerns "the speaker's subjective emotional evaluation of the referentially semantic content of his utterance" (1986, p. 84). Beginning with the assumption that "there can be no such thing as an absolutely neutral utterance" (1986, p. 84), Bakhtin notes that "the speaker's evaluative attitude toward the subject of his speech . . . determines the choice of lexical, grammatical, and compositional means of the utterance" (1986, p. 84).

Although Bakhtin might not have agreed with such a proposal, I shall expand the notion of the expressive aspect of the utterance to include a wider range of phenomena than those commonly associated with an analysis of the speaker's subjective emotional evaluation. Specifically, I would like to include aspects of the utterance having to do with the more general category of perspective or point of view as outlined by authors such as Uspensky (1973). This makes it possible to deal with many complex issues in a sociocultural approach to mind having to do with the socialization of cognitive skills. For example, it allows one to address issues of "referential perspective" (Wertsch, 1980) that play such a central role in the dynamics of the "zone of proximal development" (Cole, 1985; Vygotsky, 1978; Wertsch, 1985b).

Bakhtin's account of the utterance's relation to other participants in speech communication is of course grounded in the notion of dialogicality. In his view, "each utterance is filled with various kinds of responsive reactions to other utterances of the given sphere [i.e., referentially semantic content] of speech communication (1986, p. 91). These reactions may be to prior utterances, or they may reflect the anticipation of future utterances. They may also take many forms. For example, they may repeat or refer to others' utterances, or they may be more subtle reflections of others' words such as may be found in the way an argument is shaped in order to anticipate and preclude counterarguments.

In all these cases the issue is how voices may or may not come into dialogic contact and "interanimate" one another. The aspects of dialogicality Bakhtin outlined in this and other connections form the core of his unique insights into how dialogical principles organize speech communication. In order to understand the full implications of his account of the utterance, one must integrate his ideas about the relationships between the speaker and other voices with his observations about the relationship of the speaker to the utterance (i.e., referentially semantic content and expressive aspect or perspective). However, it is in connection with his ideas about the dialogicality between a speaker and other voices that his ideas have the most to offer a sociocultural approach to mind. This is not only because it is on this topic that he made his most original contributions, it is also because social science accounts are particularly weak on this point.

The implications of Bakhtin's ideas for a sociocultural approach to mind are enormous. His analyses of utterance, voice, social speech type, and dialogue suggest major new ways to extend the notion of semiotic mediation, while retaining the basic advantages of a Vygotskian approach. Of particular importance in this connection is that Bakhtin's analyses focus on socioculturally situated communicative phenomena. That is, he was focusing on forms of discourse that allow the investigator to make a concrete link between institutional, historical, and cultural factors on the one hand and the mental functioning of the individual on the other. Furthermore, the fact that he grounded his approach in the notions of utterance and voice, rather than in an abstract analytic category such as role (something more akin to Mead), means that the genetic precursors of intrapsychological functioning are concrete social processes. This, of course, is a major desideratum for the kind of sociocultural approach to mind being proposed here.

The voice of decontextualized rationality

As an example of how the notion of voice can play a role in a sociocultural approach to mind, consider some characteristics of what I shall call the voice of "decontextualized rationality." The historical emergence of this voice is usually associated with the Enlightenment, and its use continues to be an issue today with regard to phenomena such as gender differences in moral reasoning (e.g., Gilligan, 1982). In terms of Bakhtin's analysis of the utterance, the voice of decontextualized rationality is primarily concerned with the perspective a speaker takes toward the referentially semantic content, and in actuality it often involves a social speech type rather than a voice in the strict sense. The social speech type involved is one that simultaneously reflects several of the "stratifications" of language (e.g., generic, professional, gender) that Bakhtin (1981) outlined.

The defining characteristic of the voice of decontextualized rationality is that it represents objects and events (i.e., the referentially semantic content) in terms of formal, logical, and, if possible, quantifiable categories. The categories used in this form of representation are decontextualized in the sense that their meaning can be derived from their position in abstract theories or systems that exist independently of particular speech contexts. For example, the meaning of *five* or *electron* or *interpsychological* can be and often is established by definitions that are abstract (i.e., independent of particular use) and hence identical across various contexts.

Such decontextualized meanings are sometimes thought to have some kind of primordial existence that underlies our ability to use language in concrete discourse, but authors such as Linell (in press), Olson (1977), Rommetveit (1979), and Scribner (1977) have argued quite convincingly that they actually have grown out of specific modes of discourse associated with the rise of literacy. That is, these are forms of discourse that rely on the "semiotic potential" (Wertsch, 1985b) of linguistic and other kinds of sign types to enter into relationships.

The voice of decontextualized rationality contrasts with "contextualized forms of representation" (Wertsch, 1987a) in that the latter represents events and objects in terms of their concrete particularity. For example, a listener may need to have access to information from the unique context in which an expression is used in order to understand its reference. Or the particular speaker's emotional orientation toward the objects and events being talked about may play a crucial role in determining the significance of an utterance. In general, contextualized forms of representation foreground issues of perspective that derive from the interlocutors' identity and the concrete communicative context, whereas the voice of decontextualized rationality strives to represent phenomena in terms of their referentially semantic content such that information from the communicative context is backgrounded or even made to seem irrelevant.

The willingness and ability to use the voice of decontextualized rationality have been the object of a great deal of psychological research in the USSR. For example, Vygotsky (1987) focused on this issue in his analysis of the emergence of "spontaneous" versus scientific concepts in ontogenesis, and Luria (1976) and Tulviste (1978) examined it in their analysis of schooled and nonschooled subjects' use of concrete (i.e., experience-based) versus more abstract (e.g., syllogistic) reasoning. While sometimes seeming to assume that the voice of decontextualized rationality is developmentally more advanced than more contextualized forms of representation, these authors have also made the point that humans who have mastered this voice do not always invoke it. For example, Vygotsky (1987) specifically noted that adults who are capable of using scientific conceptual discourse often do not rely on it in solving everyday problems, and Tulviste (1987) makes a similar point in his review of Levy-Bruhl's ideas on the "heterogeneity" of human thinking.

This brings us back, then, to the issue of how several different forms of mental functioning (on either the interpsychological or the intrapsychological plane) are related to one another. Specifically, it raises the question of when and why one voice or one form of mental functioning, such as the voice of decontextualized rationality, is "privileged" (Wertsch, 1987a) in a particular context. If a voice is only one of several possible voices a speaker can appropriate, what are the factors that determine its selection? The answer to this question cannot be found in psychological factors alone. Instead, it is at this point that psychologists interested in a sociocultural approach to mind must turn to analyses of institutional and cultural factors. With regard to the voice of decontextualized rationality, this has led several investigators (e.g., Scribner & Cole, 1981) to examine the institution of formal schooling. Such research suggests that a great deal of the activity of formal instruction focuses on encouraging children to master discourse grounded in decontextualized forms of representation. As Wertsch and Minick (1987) have noted, this may be true even when other forms of representing the objects and operations at issue would do equally well or better. This suggests that one of the messages of formal schooling is that, whenever possible, one should privilege decontextualized, rational modes of discourse over others.

This pattern of privileging the decontextualized, rational voice is not limited to formal instructional settings, however. Instead, it reflects a wider tendency in modern society. Namely, it reflects a general tendency for this voice to occupy a privileged position and hence to dominate and silence other voices, something that has been the topic of a great deal of debate among social theorists. For example, Lukàcs (1971) has examined it under the heading of "reification," and Habermas (1970) has dealt with it in his analysis of "instrumental rationality." Furthermore, with regard to specific areas of contemporary public discourse (e.g., the nuclear arms debate), it has been observed (Wertsch, 1987a) that a decontextualized form of representation has traditionally been dominant even though its efficacy has often been called into question.

From a psychological perspective, it is interesting that the general tendency to privilege the voice of decontextualized rationality exists in spite of the fact that empirical evidence (e.g., Kahneman & Tversky, 1973; Tversky & Kahneman, 1974) indicates that people who have mastered relevant abstract reasoning processes often do not use these processes, even when the situation clearly calls for them to do so. Instead, they seem to rely on processes of making analogies with what they regard as representative examples from their concrete experience. Similarly, researchers such as Cicourel (1984) and Mehan (1986) have demonstrated that decision making in small groups is often not characterized by the use of decontextualized rationality, although this voice may be invoked to support or defend these decisions. Such findings suggest that the reason for privileging the voice of decontextualized rationality cannot be found in psychological factors alone. Instead, this is obviously a topic on which psychology needs to collaborate with other disciplines such as history, sociology, and anthropology.

The problem of voices for developmental psychology and education

The issue of voice raises a host of intriguing issues and opportunities for developmental psychologists interested in a sociocultural approach to mind. For example, if we wish to deal with the problem of ''patterns of privileging'' particular voices over others, we must begin to focus on the issue of how children develop the ability to make judgments about what voice is appropriately invoked in particular settings. The notion of privileging, rather than the metaphor of possession, becomes central in such an account. It is what can be seen as implicitly lying at the foundation of many researchers' claims about differences between sexes (Gilligan, 1982), between schooled and nonschooled people (Cole, Gay, Glick, & Sharp, 1971; Luria, 1976), and between cultures (Wertsch, 1987c).

In order to produce an account of privileging and to deal with other issues raised by the notion of voice in developmental psychology, we will need to confront several other research questions as well. Among these are (a) the development of a new theory of meaning, and (b) the formulation of typologies of the voices and social speech types that characterize particular sociocultural settings. Each of these projects is ambitious in itself.

For those interested in mental functioning in educational settings, the tasks raised by a sociocultural approach of the sort I have outlined are both formidable and exciting. As far as typologies of social speech types in educational settings go, we already have a good start. At least since Cazden, John, and Hymes published *Functions of Language in the Classroom* in 1972, there has been a great deal of informed debate about the kinds of discourse found in formal instructional settings. This tradition has been greatly enriched by the contributions of scholars such as Heath

(1983) and Mehan (1979). One of the major issues facing someone interested in formulating an analysis of these findings from a Vygotskian/Bakhtinian perspective is to clarify the theories of meaning inherent in what these investigators have said. There are many important points of similarity between what they have done and what Vygotsky and Bakhtin had in mind, but there is also a great deal of room for all the participants in this discussion to grow as we try to identify differences and similarities.

One area where such growth could be most exciting concerns the process of mastering or internalizing particular social speech types. Many sociolinguistic and ethnographic accounts have produced insightful accounts of discourse as it occurs in classrooms, but few have tried to go on to identify ways in which these forms of semiotically mediated interpsychological functioning might be related to forms of intrapsychological functioning. One exception to this can be found in the research of Brown and Palincsar on "reciprocal teaching" (Palincsar & Brown, 1984, 1988). These authors have explicitly argued that patterns of individual psychological functioning can be understood as internalized social interactional routines. Although studies of reciprocal teaching are not usually conceptualized in terms of discourse modes, social speech types, or voice, they can profitably be viewed as dealing specifically with these issues.

The challenges posed by a Vygotskian/Bakhtinian approach would appear to take developmental psychology out of its normal sphere of activity. In my opinion this is precisely what the discipline needs if it is to make some of the most important contributions it can make to our understanding of human mental life. As long as we continue to study development as it occurs within individuals in a cultural and historical vacuum, we will continue to overlook major issues of how mental life develops in specific sociocultural settings. This means we will continue to encounter major stumbling blocks in our attempts to develop accounts of intelligence and mental functioning that recognize a multiplicity of skills. Furthermore, it means that we will continue to cut ourselves off from a dialogue with other areas of scholarly inquiry (e.g., history) and with the general public. The price of this isolation is very high indeed, not only for the discipline of developmental psychology but for our understanding of some of the most pressing problems of our time.

Notes

1 Vygotsky was extremely interested in Piaget's writings. This is reflected in chapter 2 of *Thinking and Speech,* a chapter that originally appeared as a long introductory essay to the Russian translation of Piaget's *Langage et la pensée chez l'enfant.*

2 *Scientific* here is a translation of *nauchnii,* a term that could also be translated as *academic* or *scholarly.* The latter terms make even clearer the connection Vygotsky saw between conceptual discourse and the social institution of formal instruction.

3 Ivanov (1974) has claimed that there was a connection between Vygotsky and Bakhtin, but I believe that the evidence he uses to support this claim really reflects Vygotsky's debt to Yakubinskii.

References

Bakhtin, M. M. (1968). *Rabelais and his world.* Cambridge, MA: MIT Press.

Bakhtin, M. M. (1981). *The dialogic imagination* (M. Holquist, Ed.). Austin: University of Texas Press.

Bakhtin, M. M. (1984). *Problems of Dostoevsky's poetics* (C. Emerson, Ed.). Minneapolis: University of Minnesota Press.

Bakhtin, M. M. (1986). *Speech genres and other late essays* (C. Emerson & M. Holquist, Eds.; V. W. McGee, Trans.). Austin: University of Texas Press.

Blonskii, P. P. (1921). *Ocherki po nauchnoi psikhologii* [Essays in scientific psychology]. Moscow: Gosudarstvennoe Izdatel'stvo.

Bruner, J. S. (1985). Vygotsky: A historical and conceptual perspective. In J. V. Wertsch (Ed.), *Culture, communication, and cognition: Vygotskian perspectives* (pp. 21–34). Cambridge: Cambridge University Press.

Cazden, C. B., John, V. P., & Hymes, D. (Eds.) (1972). *Functions of language in the classroom.* New York: Teachers College Press.

Cicourel, A. V. (1984). *The reproduction of objective knowledge: Common sense reasoning in medical decision making.* Paper prepared for the conference on "The impact of scientific knowledge on social structure," Technical University of Darmstadt.

Clark, K., & Holquist, M. (1985). *M. M. Bakhtin.* Cambridge, MA: Harvard University Press.

Cole, M. (1985). The zone of proximal development: Where culture and cognition create each other. In J. V. Wertsch (Ed.), *Culture, communication, and cognition: Vygotskian perspectives* (pp. 146–161). Cambridge: Cambridge University Pres.

Cole, M., Gay, J., Glick, J. A., & Sharp, D. W. (1971). *The cultural context of learning and thinking.* New York: Basic.

Cook, T. E. (1985). The bear market in political socialization and the costs of misunderstood psychological theories. *American Political Science Review, 79,* 1079–1093.

Gardner, H. (1983). *Frames of mind: The theory of multiple intelligences.* New York: Basic.

Gilligan, C. (1982). *In a different voice: Psychological theory and women's development.* Cambridge, MA: Harvard University Press.

Habermas, J. (1970). *Toward a rational society: Student protest, science, and politics.* Boston: Beacon.

Heath, S. (1983). *Ways with words: Language, life, and work in communities and classrooms.* Cambridge: Cambridge University Press.

Holquist, M. (1981). The politics of representation. In S. Greenblatt (Ed.), *Allegory in representation: Selected papers from the English Institute.* Baltimore: Johns Hopkins University Press.

Ivanov, V. V. (1974). The significance of M. M. Bakhtin's ideas on sign, utterance, and dialogue for modern semiotics. In H. Baran (Ed.), *Semiotics and structuralism: Readings from the Soviet Union.* White Plains, NY: International Arts and Sciences Press.

Janet, P. (1926–1927). *La pensée intérieure et ses troubles.* Course given at the Collège de France.

Janet, P. (1928). *De l'angoisse à l'extase: Etudes sur les croyances et les sentiments.* Paris: Alcan.

Kahneman, D., & Tversky, A. (1973). On the psychology of prediction. *Psychological Review, 80*(4), 237–251.

Karmiloff-Smith, A. (1979). *A functional approach to child language.* Cambridge: Cambridge University Press.

Lave, J. (1988). *Cognition in practice: Mind, mathematics, and culture in everyday life.* Cambridge: Cambridge University Press.

LCHC (Laboratory of Comparative Human Cognition) (1983). Culture and cognitive development. In W. Kessen (Ed.), *Mussen's handbook of child psychology* (4th ed., Vol. 1). New York: Wiley.

Leont'ev, A. N. (1981). The problem of activity in psychology. In J. V. Wertsch (Ed.), *The problem of activity in Soviet psychology.* Armonk, NY: Sharpe.

Linell, P. (in press). The impact of literacy on the conception of language: The case of linguistics. In R. Saljo (Ed.), *The written word.* Berlin: Springer.

Lukàcs, G. (1971). *History and class consciousness: Studies in Marxist dialectics.* Cambridge, MA: MIT Press.

Luria, A. R. (1976). *Cognitive development: Its cultural and social foundations*. Cambridge, MA: Harvard University Press.

Mead, G. H. (1934). *Mind, self, and society from the standpoint of a social behaviorist*. Chicago: University of Chicago Press.

Mehan, H. L. (1979). *Learning lessons*. Cambridge, MA: Harvard University Press.

Mehan, H. L. (1986). *Oracular reasoning*. Paper presented at the meeting of the International Sociological Association, New Delhi.

Olson, D. R. (1977). From utterance to text: The bias of language in speech and writing. *Harvard Educational Review, 47*, 257–281.

Palincsar, A. S., & Brown, A. L. (1984). Reciprocal teaching of comprehension-fostering and comprehension-monitoring activities. *Cognition and Instruction, 1*(2), 117–175.

Palincsar, A. S., & Brown, A. L. (1988). Teaching and practicing thinking skills to promote comprehension in the content of group problem solving. *RASE, 9*(1), 53–59.

Piaget, J. (1932). *Rech' i myshlenie rebenka* [The speech and thinking of the· child]. Moscow and Leningrad: Gosizdat. (Russian translation of J. Piaget (1923), *Le langage et la pensée chez l'enfant*, Paris).

Rogoff, B., & Lave, J. (Eds.) (1984). *Everyday cognition: Its development in social context*. Cambridge, MA: Harvard University Press.

Rommetveit, R. (1979). On negative rationalism in scholarly studies of verbal communication and dynamic residuals in the construction of human intersubjectivity. In R. Rommetveit & R. M. Blakar (Eds.), *Studies of language, thought, and verbal communication*. London: Academic Press.

Scribner, S. (1977). Modes of thinking and ways of speaking. In P. N. Johnson-Laird & P. C. Wason (Eds.), *Thinking: Readings in cognitive science*. Cambridge: Cambridge University Press.

Scribner, S. (1985). Vygotsky's uses of history. In J. V. Wertsch (Ed.), *Culture, communication, and cognition: Vygotskian perspectives* (pp. 119–145). Cambridge: Cambridge University Press.

Scribner, S., & Cole, M. (1981). *The psychological consequences of literacy*. Cambridge, MA: Harvard University Press.

Smirnov, A. N. (1975). *Razvitie i sovremennoe sostoyanie psikhologicheskoi nauki v SSSR* [The development and current state of psychology in the USSR]. Moscow: Izdatel'stvo Pedagogika.

Tulviste, P. (1978). On the origins of theoretic syllogistic reasoning in culture and in the child. In *Problems of communication*. Tartu: Tartu University Press.

Tulviste, P. (1987). L. Levy-Bruhl and problems of the historical development of thought. *Soviet Psychology, 25*(3), 3–21.

Tversky, A., & Kahneman, D. (1974). Judgment under uncertainty: Heuristics and biases. *Science, 185*, 1124–1131.

Uspensky, V. (1973). *A poetics of composition: The structure of the artistic text and typology of a compositional form* (V. Zavarin & S. Wittig, Trans.). Berkeley: University of California Press.

Voloshinov, V. N. (1973). *Marxism and philosophy of language* (I. Matejka and I. R. Titunik, Trans.). New York: Seminar Press.

Voloshinov, V. N. (1987). *Freudianism: A critical sketch*. Bloomington: Indiana University Press.

Vygotsky, L. S. (1962). *Thought and language*. Cambridge, MA: MIT Press.

Vygotsky, L. S. (1978). *Mind in society: The development of higher psychological processes* (M. Cole, V. John-Steiner, S. Scribner, & E. Souberman, Eds.). Cambridge, MA: Harvard University Press.

Vygotsky, L. S. (1981). The genesis of higher mental functions. In J. V. Wertsch (Ed.), *The concept of activity in Soviet psychology*. Armonk, NY: Sharpe.

Vygotsky, L. S. (1987). *Thinking and speech* (N. Minick, Trans.). New York: Plenum.

Vygotsky, L. S., & Luria, A. R. (1930). *Etyudy po istorii povedeniya: Obez'yana, primitiv, rebenok* [Essays on the history of behavior: Ape, primitive, child]. Moscow and Leningrad: Gosizdat.

Wertsch, J. V. (1979). The regulation of human action and the given-new organization of private speech. In G. Zivin (Ed.), *The development of self-regulation through private speech* (pp. 79–98). New York: Wiley.

Wertsch, J. V. (1980). *Semiotic mechanisms in joint cognitive activity*. Paper presented at the Joint

U.S.–USSR Conference on the Theory of Activity, Institute of Psychology, USSR Academy of Sciences, Moscow.

Wertsch, J. V. (1985a). Introduction. In J. V. Wertsch (Ed.), *Culture, communication, and cognition: Vygotskian perspectives* (pp. 1–18). Cambridge: Cambridge University Press.

Wertsch, J. V. (1985b). *Vygotsky and the social formation of mind.* Cambridge, MA: Harvard University Press.

Wertsch, J. V. (1987a). Modes of discourse in the nuclear arms debate. *Current Research on Peace and Violence, 2–3.*

Wertsch, J. V. (1987b). *Sociocultural setting and the zone of proximal development: The problem of text-based realities.* Paper presented at the Tel-Aviv Annual Workshop in Human Development, "Culture, schooling, and psychological development," Tel-Aviv University.

Wertsch, J. V. (1987c). *Worlds of discourse in the nuclear arms debate.* Paper presented at the Colloquium on Cultural and Historical Perspectives on Nuclear Policy, University of Chicago.

Wertsch, J. V., McNamee, G. D., McLane, J. G., & Budwig, N. A. (1980). The adult–child dyad as a problem solving system. *Child Development, 51,* 1215–1222.

Wertsch, J. V., & Minick, N. (1987). *Negotiating sense in the zone of proximal development.* Paper presented at the conference "Thinking and problem solving in the developmental process: International perspectives," Rutgers University, New Brunswick, NJ.

Zinchenko, V. P., & Smirnov, S. D. (1983). *Metodologicheskie voprosy psikhologii* [Methodological problems in psychology]. Moscow: Izdatel'stvo Moskovskogo Universiteta.

5 The social origins of self-regulation

Rafael M. Díaz, Cynthia J. Neal, and
Marina Amaya-Williams

A central theme in Vygotsky's development theory is that cognitive development can be understood as the transformation of basic, biologically determined processes into higher psychological functions. According to the theory, the human child is endowed by nature with a wide range of perceptual, attentional, and memory capacities, such as the capacity to perceive contrast and movement, the capacity for eidetic memory, and arousal/habituation responses to environmental stimuli, to name a few. Such basic processes (also referred to by Vygotsky as "biological," "natural," or "elementary"), however, are substantially transformed in the context of socialization and education, particularly through the use of language, to constitute the higher psychological functions or the unique forms of human cognition.

Our readings of Vygotsky suggest that this "transformation" from basic to higher functions consists mostly of an increasing self-regulation of processes and capacities that are originally bound to and controlled by the concrete, immediate stimulus field. In development, the infant's eidetic, rudimentary memory processes are gradually transformed into the capacity for voluntary memory and the use of mnemonic strategies; the capacity to perceive salient stimulus features develops into the capacity for selective attention; arousal/habituation patterns develop into the capacity for vigilance, concentration, and sustained attention. The common denominators of these transformations or developmental changes are the decreasing power of immediate environmental contingencies and the increasing role of self-formulated plans and goals in the regulation of behavior and cognitive activity.

An example is in order. Originally, the child attends to whatever is perceptually salient in the environment; that is, what the child perceives is totally determined by and can be successfully predicted from the properties of the stimuli in the child's immediate perceptual field. Later on, however, with the development of selective attention, the child becomes capable of reorganizing the perceptual field according to a plan, goal, or specific task. If she or he so desires, the child can attend to specific features of the stimulus field, regardless of the perceptual salience of such features. Similar changes, from externally regulated inborn processes to self-regulated capacities, can be observed in memory, attention, and problem solving.

A major premise of Vygotsky's theory is that the transformation of basic processes into higher psychological functions occurs within the child's social interac-

127

tions and through the use of culturally determined tools and symbols. Specifically, Vygotsky suggests that early on the caregiving adult environment mediates and regulates the child's interactions with his or her immediate environment. The caregiver's words, signs, and gestures regulate the child's behavior, for example, by directing the child's attention away from perceptually salient features, socially reorganizing the child's perceptual field in a culturally relevant manner. Thus higher psychological functions have social origins in two related ways. First, higher functions, such as voluntary attention, appear first in the interpersonal, social plane before they appear as part of the child's cognitive/behavioral repertoire in the intrapsychological plane. Second, higher psychological functions can be understood as the internalization of social regulating interactions or, more appropriately, as the internalization of culturally determined adaptations that mediate the child's relation to his or her environment.

Vygotsky's theory suggests that higher psychological functions, such as selective attention and voluntary memory, can be distinguished from basic processes in four different ways. Unlike basic processes, higher functions are (1) self-regulated rather than bound to the immediate stimulus field; (2) social or cultural rather than biological in origin; (3) the object of conscious awareness rather than automatic and unconscious; and (4) mediated through the use of cultural tools and symbols (Wertsch, 1985). The present chapter focuses on and attempts to integrate conceptually the first two properties of higher psychological functions: their self-regulatory organization and their social origin. Based on and inspired by Vygotskian concepts of development, the chapter argues first that the capacity for self-regulation is, indeed, a major outcome of development that accounts for a radical transformation of children's cognitive and social skills. Second, in an attempt to elaborate Vygotsky's theory, the chapter proposes that self-regulatory development not only originates in but must be encouraged and facilitated by specific caregiver–child social interactions.

In developmental psychology, the capacity for self-regulation appears as a central organizational construct in both cognitive and social development. Cognitive advances in the school years, for example, are marked by increased "executive control" (Sternberg, 1984) and self-regulation of perceptual, attentional, and memory processes. Within the social realm, successful discipline and socialization are measured by the child's capacity to self-regulate in a socially appropriate fashion and in the relative absence of adult supervision or other external supporting structures. In addition, neuropsychologically, the development of self-regulation can be described as the onset and development of functions attributed to the prefrontal cortex, such as the capacity to guide behavior according to a verbalized plan and the capacity to modulate arousal to meet the demands of different tasks or situations (Luria, 1973; Passler, Isaac, & Hynd, 1985; Stuss & Benson, 1984).

A major purpose of the present chapter is to establish that self-control and self-regulation represent different capacities and different levels of behavioral organization (see, e.g., Kopp, 1982). In self-control, the child complies with a command or request in the absence of the caregiver; that is, the child complies with and responds to an internalized caregiver command. In self-regulation, on the other hand, a self-formulated plan of action, rather than an internalized command, guides the child's activity. Although current developmental literature has given some attention to children's self-control capacities, such as the capacity to wait and delay gratification upon the experimenter's request (see, e.g., Mischel & Patterson, 1976), little information exists on the origins and development of self-regulation proper.

In line with Vygotsky's and Luria's formulations, we believe that the regulation of a child's behavior is, first, a shared act, an interpersonal phenomenon. Since the human infant is immersed from birth in a sociocultural environment, the child's functioning and behavior are externally regulated by the adult caregiving interactions. We propose further that self-regulatory capacities develop within the context of adult–child interactions, especially when the caregiver sensitively and gradually withdraws from joint activity, allowing, promoting, and rewarding the child's take-over of the regulatory role. Our perspective builds on Vygotsky's theory by postulating that individual differences in self-regulatory capacities can be expected from differences in the quality of caregiver–child interactions. To date, unfortunately, we do not have a clear description of how the caregiver's sensitive withdrawal and the corresponding takeover of the regulatory function by the child actually occur.

In order to accomplish our purposes we have divided the rest of the chapter into four sections. First, we will define self-regulation in contrast to self-control, as a new level of behavioral organization emerging during the preschool years. Second, we will review and summarize different perspectives on how self-regulation develops, including Vygotsky's and Luria's, especially their ideas about the use and internalization of private speech. In the third section, we will review two sets of developmental findings related to the issues at hand. Specifically, we will review findings about maternal teaching strategies and the training of self-regulatory language; these findings suggest ways in which self-regulation can or cannot be facilitated in the context of social interactions. Finally, we will report pilot findings from our own laboratory, documenting the search for teaching strategies that facilitate and promote children's self-regulatory behavior in the context of mother–child teaching interactions.

Self-control and self-regulation

Self-regulation can be defined, in contrast to self-control, in the following manner. Following Kopp (1982), we understand self-control as the capacity to comply with the caregiver's commands and directives in the absence of the caregiver. In other words, self-controlled behavior implies the capacity to behave, in the relative absence of supporting external structures, according to a directive or command that was originally given externally. Behavior of this kind (e.g., a child playing alone says to himself, "Don't touch that," when approaching an electrical outlet and withdraws) can be seen as organized in a rigid stimulus–response (S–R) manner, where the internalized command (i.e., "Don't touch") is the stimulus, and the compliance with such command (i.e., withdrawing from outlet) is the response.

Up to the development of self-control, the child's behavior has been controlled by the caregiver in a similar S–R fashion. The difference between adult control and self-control is, therefore, that the child (the self) is now the source of both S and R. The basic structure and organization of the behavior, however, remain the same: Self-controlled behavior is still a somewhat rigid response to an outside-given, externally determined command or directive that is now internalized and emitted by the child.

The capacity for self-regulation, on the other hand, is defined as the child's capacity to plan, guide, and monitor his or her behavior from within and flexibly according to changing circumstances. An example of self-regulated behavior can be described as follows: A child constructing a castle with wooden blocks, after consulting a pictured model, says: "I need two red ones for the tower tops." The child then goes to the block pile but, after searching for a while, realizes that there is only one red block left. Looking around at his different toys, the child sees a box of crayons and says, "I'll make it red." Somewhat clumsily, the child colors a white block red and places it on the top of the second tower.

In self-regulation, unlike self-control, the child's behavior follows a plan or goal formulated by the self. Furthermore, unlike the rigidity of S–R-organized behavior, self-regulated behavior is flexibly adjusted (according to changing circumstances) in order to accomplish such self-formulated goals or objectives. In what follows, and in very schematic form, we propose three major differences between the organization of self-control and self-regulation:

Self-control	*Self-regulation*
1. Behavior is displayed in response to internalized command or directive.	1. Behavior is guided according to self-formulated plan or goal.
2. Behavior is organized in rigid S–R connections.	2. Behavior, organized as a functional system, is changed and adjusted according to changing goals and situations.
3. Environmental cues serve as stimuli for behavioral responses.	3. Child uses aspects of the environment as tools and mediators to attain goals.

A central point in the distinction between self-control and self-regulation is that, in self-regulation, the child has not merely internalized the caregiver's commands and directives but has taken over effectively the caregiver's regulating role. The developmental question remains, of course, as to how this transition happens.

In the next section we will review, first, the current available description of the developmental antecedents of self-regulation, as formulated by Claire Kopp (1982). As will be discussed below, Kopp's description does not directly address the mechanisms by which children attain self-regulatory capacities. We will then turn to Soviet developmental theory, as represented in the works of Vygotsky and Luria, in search of some clarifying answers.

The development of self-regulation

In an excellent review of research findings and theoretical orientations regarding the emergence and development of self-regulatory capacities, Kopp (1982) outlined four major antecedents of self-regulation, including earlier forms of regulation such as the infant's modulation of arousal and toddlers' compliance with maternal verbalized dictates. Specifically, Kopp suggests that the development of self-regulation is accomplished through the following five phases.

1. *Neurophysiological modulation:* The first forms of organismic control can be observed in the infant's attempts to modulate arousal states through organized patterns of behavior that include reflex actions, such as the "hand-to-mouth movement that the neonate utilizes for thumb–finger sucking" (Kopp, 1982, p. 202). Such modulations, or self-soothing capacities, are regulatory in nature since they function as a stimulus barrier protecting the infant's immature nervous system from excessive stimulation. Even though infants are capable of such self-soothing behaviors, the modulation of arousal states and the regulation of incoming stimuli are accomplished mostly in interaction with the caregiver. In fact, caregivers' routines in the first 3 months of life can be understood as assisting the baby in achieving such modulation of neurophysiological functions and protecting the immature organism from a potentially intrusive environment.

2. *Sensorimotor modulation:* The next phase signals the infant's capacity to coordinate nonreflexive motor actions in response to different environmental situations. The behaviors observed during this phase are similar to Piaget's (1952) secondary circular reactions, where new patterns of behavior are developed and organized in response to interesting events and consequences in the infant's environment. Sensorimotor modulations, however, are immediately tied to "motivational and perceptual sets that arise as a function of stimuli characteristics" (Kopp, 1982, p. 203). The newly acquired behavioral sequences are totally dependent on their environmental effects; there is no conscious awareness or cognitive intent in these patterns of behavior during this phase.

3. *Control:* During the third phase, children show the capacity to initiate, maintain, or cease actions in response to caregivers' verbalized signals. This phase signals the onset of infants' capacity to obey or comply with caregivers' requests. Needless to say, during this phase of control and compliance, the control and modulation of the child's behavior require the immediate presence of external signals. Even though there is greater flexibility in the regulation of behavior, the sources of such regulation are not within the child but in the caregiving environment.

4. *Self-control:* The child has the capacity to comply with the caregiver's commands and directives in the absence of the caregiver. Self-control signals, indeed, a newly acquired independence from external structures. However, as described in the preceding section, in self-control the command was at one point externally given, even though now the child is able to emit the command (overtly or covertly) and comply with it in the relative absence of external monitors and structures.

5. *Self-regulation:* Finally, the child is capable of self-regulation proper. According to Kopp's developmental review, self-regulation involves the flexible guiding of behavior according to internalized contingency rules. It is different from self-control mostly in its flexible adjustment of behavior to changing situations and also in the active use of reflection and metacognitive strategies.

Kopp's integrative account of the antecedents of self-regulation has given us a very useful guide to understanding the continuity and relations among earlier forms of control, social forms of regulation, and the emergence of self-regulatory capacities. The review is especially enlightening because it integrates cognitive and social accomplishments, such as the onset of symbolic-representational capacities and the increasing awareness of social demands, as they interact to create new levels of behavioral organization. In our opinion, however, Kopp's account was aimed at outlining the antecedents of self-regulatory capacities rather than formulating a model of how self-regulation develops. Therefore, as a developmental model of self-regulation, Kopp's integrating review is limited in two ways. First of all, for Kopp self-regulation is not qualitatively distinct from self-control capacities. Self-regulation is portrayed simply as a more flexible form of self-control. In her own words:

> What sets self-control apart from self-regulation is a difference in degree, not in kind. Self-control and self-regulation are linked conceptually because both depend on the development and use of representational thinking and recall memory. However, the term self-control means that the child has limited flexibility in adapting to acts to meet new situational demands and a limited capacity for delay and waiting. In contrast, self-regulation is considered to be adaptive to changes. It is a distinctly more mature form of control and presumably implicates the use of reflection and strategies. (1982, p. 207)

Considering our earlier distinction between self-control and self-regulation, we should like to argue that self-control and self-regulation represent two qualitatively distinct levels of behavioral organization. Also, we have argued that self-control and self-regulation are different on other important dimensions besides the increased flexibility of adaptation to changing circumstances.

A second limitation of Kopp's account is that there is no indication as to how self-control develops into self-regulation. The actual developmental processes that account for the increased flexibility or the active use of plans and strategies, for example, are not specified. It is clear that further conceptual and empirical work is needed in order to formulate and test a developmental model of self-regulatory capacities. Vygotsky's ideas on the role of private speech in development, as well as Luria's elaboration and testing of Vygotsky's ideas, below, provide an excellent starting point to fill in the gaps in current developmental accounts of self-regulation.

Vygotsky's contribution

One of the most detailed accounts of the development of self-regulation or, more appropriately, of the increasing self-regulation of cognitive functions can be found in the works of Vygotsky. In his essay "The Genesis of Higher Mental Functions"

(1960/1981), Vygotsky describes four major milestones or "stages" of cognitive development, describing the changing relation between the child and his or her concrete stimulus environment. The major theme underlying this developmental progression is children's increasing mastery of and eventual independence from the stimulus field, accompanied by an increasing mastery over their own behavior, through the active use of signs.

In the first stage, "a stage of natural and primitive responses" (Vygotsky, 1960/1981, p. 177), children respond to the environment, simply and directly, according to the dictates, states, capacity, and limitations of their nervous system. Behavior is controlled by environmental contingencies, on the basis of natural laws of stimulus–response. At this stage, the social (caregiver) regulation of the child's behavior is possible only by controlling the concrete, immediate stimuli that, in turn, control the child's behavior.

At a later point in time, the child becomes capable of some beginning mediation by using external signs as an aid to their responses. During this second stage, for example, the child is able to press a key in response to a given light, using a picture that meaningfully guides the key-selection process. The picture, as an external sign, mediates the relation between the stimulus light and the child's key-pressing response. At this stage, however, the child has not fully mastered the mediational properties of signs. Only the external, concrete, and actual connections between signs and stimuli can affect the child's behavior. Nonetheless, the child's use of auxiliary signs creates a new freedom from the stimulus field:

> The use of auxiliary signs breaks up the fusion of the sensory field and the motor system and thus makes new kinds of behavior possible. A "functional barrier" is created between the initial and final moments of the choice response; the direct impulse to move is shunted by preliminary circuits. The child who formerly solved the problem impulsively now solves it through an internally established connection between the stimulus and the corresponding auxiliary sign. (Vygotsky, 1978, p. 35)

As children become more experienced in the use of auxiliary signs to help them attend, respond, or remember, they also become more *aware* of the role and functions of signs in cognitive activity. At this point, children "no longer operate superficially with signs; rather, they *know* that the presence of such signs helps them carry out the operation" (Vygotsky, 1960/1981). This new awareness and understanding of the possible role and utility of signs lead to a third and new stage, where children begin to create and actively to manipulate signs in order to achieve a given desired response. Thus, during the third stage, children can properly regulate their own behavior by actively organizing their stimulus field in order to achieve a desired response. This stage is limited, however, by the fact that the child's regulation of his or her own behavior is still dependent on the arrangement or organization of external stimuli.

The last or fourth stage in this developmental progression toward self-regulation is characterized by the *internalization* of the external relations among stimuli, signs, and behavior. At this point the child begins to reject the external stimuli that at one point helped him or her to emit a given response; now the child can achieve the same desired response without the aid of external auxiliary signs. In Vygotsky's words:

> We can see what has happened: any external operation has, so to speak, its internal representation. What does this mean? We make a certain movement and rearrange certain stimuli in various contexts. All of this corresponds to some kind of inner brain process. As a result of several such experiences in the transition from an external operation to an internal one, all the intermediate stimuli turn out to be no longer necessary, and the operation begins to be carried out in the absence of mediating stimuli. (Vygotsky, 1960/1981, p. 183)

By postulating a final stage of "internalization of external operations," Vygotsky suggests a very important aspect in the development of self-regulation, namely that, in development, the new levels of activity achieved through the use of external signs become part of the child's own internal organization (brain organization?) to the extent that original mediating signs can be discarded. The new relation between the child and his or her environment, established once through the use of external mediators, is now an intrapsychological property of the child, that is, an internally organized way of responding and relating to the environment. In this context, in a true Vygotskian meaning, internalization refers not to a mere mental image or mental representation of the external relation but actually to a new level of behavioral organization that was once possible only with the help of external signs and mediators. The external signs, having created a new way of functioning in the world, a new level of behavioral organization, can now be discarded. The freedom from the immediate, concrete stimulus field is now the child's psychological function, a property of the child's behavioral repertoire.

In Vygotsky's developmental theory, the child achieves self-regulatory capacities by actively manipulating the environment with the use of signs. This active manipulation of the environment leads ultimately to control of the child's own behavior. Vygotsky's logic, in this case, raises a very important question: How does the child's manipulation of the external environment lead to the child's control over his or her own behavior? Vygotsky (1978) answered the question by stating that signs have the property of "reverse action" (p. 40). Signs, unlike tools, do not change the objective properties of the external environment but rather are meant to alter the subject's operations on that environment. Even though signs can be considered as "tools" for the child's cognitive activity, they are distinct from tools in very substantial ways; above all, the sign changes the nature and structure of the activity itself.

> A most essential difference between sign and tool, and the basis for the real divergence of the two lines, is the different ways that they orient human behavior. The tool's function is to serve as the conductor of human influence on the object of activity; it is externally oriented; it must lead to changes in objects. It is a means by which human external activity is aimed at mastering, and triumphing over, nature. The sign, on the other hand, changes nothing in the object of a psycholog-

ical operation. It is a means of internal activity aimed at mastering oneself; the sign is internally oriented. (Vygotsky, 1978, p. 55)

So far, we have portrayed Vygotsky's account of the development of self-regulation in terms of the individual child as an active manipulator of the environment through the use of signs. As Wertsch (1981) has pointed out, this perspective represents a typical bias of Western psychology, where the subject is conceived as an independent cognitive agent. In truth, our account so far leaves out a major aspect of Vygotsky's theory, namely, that the developmental progression described above is indeed a culturally determined social process, that is, an interpersonal process that becomes internalized as an intrapsychological function.

The developmental progression on the road to self-regulation can be seen as a social process, as formulated by Vygotsky, in four specific ways: First, from the very beginning, auxiliary signs are brought in and given to the child by the social environment in order to control, direct, and regulate the child's behavior. Second, the child actively begins to use signs in order to influence other people and act on others around him. Third, the word, as a sign with socially shared meaning, is the most useful sign in children's attempts to master their environment. Finally, basic processes are transformed mostly as a function of children's use of speech as a tool for planning and guiding their activity; the same speech that mediates social interaction is used as the main mediator of cognitive activity.

Indeed, a major theme in Vygotsky's developmental theory is that, at one point, children begin to use language not only to communicate but to guide, plan, and monitor their activity. The child's speech is used initially to label different aspects of the environment and describe his or her ongoing activity, probably in an attempt to engage and establish a meaningful connection with the adult social environment. Gradually, however, the timing of such speech changes with respect to the ongoing activity. Speech ceases merely to accompany the child's activity and begins to precede it. At this later stage, the child's speech, now as the starting point of the activity, takes on a planning and guiding function.

The use of private speech as a tool of thought transforms the structure of practical activity, creating and giving birth to the "purely human forms of human intelligence" (Vygotsky, 1978, p. 24). Specifically, with regard to self-regulatory development, this use of language has three major consequences: First, the child's cognitive operations gain greater flexibility, freedom, and independence from the concrete stimulus field. For example, with the use of speech, children can bring to their problem solving elements that are not immediately present. Also, through the use of language, children can structure their perceptual field and restructure their perceptions in terms of their own goals and intentions:

> By means of words children single out separate elements, thereby overcoming the natural structure of the sensory field and forming new (artificially introduced and dynamic) structural centers. The child begins to perceive the world not only through his eyes but also through his speech. As a result, the immediacy of "nat-

ural'' perception is supplanted by a complex mediated process; as such, speech becomes an essential part of the child's cognitive development. (Vygotsky, 1978, p. 32)

Second, through the use of speech, the child's operations and actions become less impulsive. Speech breaks down the immediate, spontaneous connection between the stimuli and the child's responses, allowing the child to act reflectively according to a plan rather than responding impulsively to the objective properties of the stimuli at hand. Finally, speech allows not only for a control of the stimulus field but for an increasing mastery over the child's own behavior. To summarize in Vygotsky's own words: "The specifically human capacity for language enables children to provide for auxiliary tools in the solution of difficult tasks, to overcome impulsive action, to plan a solution to a problem prior to its execution, and to master their own behavior" (1978, p. 28).

Needless to say, Vygotsky's theory provides the most detailed and fascinating answer to our major question regarding how self-regulatory capacities develop. It is the child's symbolic activity, specifically the child's use of language in private speech, that creates a new level of behavioral organization characterized by independence from the stimulus field and by increasing mastery and control of the child's own operations. Empirical studies of private speech in this country and in Europe (see, e.g., Berk & Garvin, 1984; Díaz, 1986; Goudena, 1987; Zivin, 1979) have generally supported Vygotskian perspectives on the significance and functions of children's private speech.

Luria's contribution

Vygotsky's colleague, student, and collaborator Alexander R. Luria addressed the development of self-regulation in terms of humans' capacity for conscious, voluntary action:

> The structure of the voluntary act has remained for centuries one of the most complex problems of psychology. The problem is as follows. It is quite apparent that in addition to performing instinctive reflex acts, we can carry out conscious, voluntary acts. Humans can prepare a plan and carry it out. They may wish to raise their hand and they do so. This is self-evident. The main difficulty for psychologists has been to find a scientific explanation for it. (Luria, 1982, p. 88)

Rejecting both mechanistic and idealistic positions and taking Vygotsky's sociogenetic position, Luria argued that the voluntary act is first a shared social event. The argument goes as follows: It is clear that, at the beginning, children are not capable of voluntary action; rather, they are at the mercy of environmental contingencies and reflexive patterns of action. Caregivers, however, gradually gain power over the child's behavior by instructing, guiding, and directing the child's actions with the help of speech. At the beginning, the voluntary act is a shared event because the action begins with the adult command and is completed by the child's motor action in response to such command. At a later point in time, Luria argues, the child "learns to speak and can begin to give spoken commands to himself/herself" (1982, p.89). At this point, the child takes over the caregiver's role by repeating to himself the caregiver's commands and directives with his external speech. Finally, the child's external speech is internalized to constitute inner speech, the main regulating tool of human behavior. Through the use of first external and then internal speech, the child carries out the voluntary functions that were once shared by two people.

Luria's research on the self-regulatory functions of speech revealed some interesting and important aspects in the development of these functions. Most notably, Luria found that at first, for both the caregiver's and the child's speech, the acoustic and not the semantic properties of speech performed the regulatory functions. For example, for very young children, the strong command "Don't press!" emitted after several commands to press a rubber bulb would lead children to press the bulb still more forcefully. At this point, children's motor activity is guided by the sheer physical force of the caregiver's speech. Only later and very gradually do children begin to attend to the semantic properties of the caregiver's and their own speech. When the child is guided semantically rather than physically by his or her own speech, speech need no longer be external or emitted overtly and, therefore, becomes internalized. In Luria's view, self-regulatory capacities are finally established with the internalization of private speech.

An important aspect of Luria's theory is that the origins of private speech are to be found in the caregiver's verbal commands and directives. Luria (1982) argues, however, that the child does not simply repeat the caregiver's commands and directives; rather, "self-regulation is realized through the child's expanded speech" (p. 103). As Vygotsky had suggested earlier, Luria argues that, during a cognitive task, children begin to speak mostly when they encounter some impediment or difficulty. When presented with some difficulty, the child first attempts to solve the problem with his practical activity. If unsuccessful, the child transfers his efforts and attempts to the verbal sphere. In that context, the child's external speech begins as a social dialogue with the experimenter or other person in the room, sometimes asking for help, sometimes expressing frustration. Children's speech begins by describing the situation and stating the difficulties and then gradually develops into planning a possible course of action. The planning, guiding, regulating functions of speech stem from a social dialogue but do not simply mirror or model the adult's guiding speech; in fact, children's planning and regulating speech actually appears as the child makes active attempts to solve the problem at hand.

In both Vygotsky's and Luria's writings, the increasing self-regulation of cognitive functions has been treated appropriately as a universal phenomenon of development. It is a well-known fact, however, that children vary in their capacity to regulate effectively different aspects of their perception, attention, memory, and problem-solving activity. In addition, current research has uncovered large individual differences in children's use of private speech (see, e.g., Frauenglass & Díaz, 1985). Therefore, one aspect of Vygotsky's theory that needs to be elaborated, both conceptually and empirically, is to understand the nature and origins of individual differences in the attainment of self-regulatory capacities.

Another major and closely related question that needs further elaboration is the one openly addressed in this chapter: How could the progression toward self-regulation be facilitated by the child's social-caregiving environment? This question has very special relevance to the present volume on Vygotsky and education. As educators, we are concerned with intervening and facilitating different aspects of this process. If, as Vygotsky and Luria suggested, self-regulation has social origins, then the quality of the social-caregiving environment must have a major impact on the attainment of self-regulatory capacities. Moreover, if we understand how self-regulatory development is facilitated by the social environment, then we might be able to understand some of the sources of individual differences in this developmental achievement.

In search of some tentative answers, we now turn to two different sets of developmental literature that contain findings relevant to our question. In what follows, we will review findings on maternal teaching strategies that might promote self-regulation and also findings regarding the training of private speech. The chapter will then conclude with a brief description of our own research endeavors.

Teaching for self-regulation

A substantial number of studies have investigated parental teaching and discipline strategies that promote children's competent social and cognitive behaviors. None of the studies has directly examined the construct of self-regulation or examined the effects of teaching on children's spontaneous use of private speech. Nevertheless, some investigators have examined the effects of teaching strategies on constructs closely related to self-regulation, such as instrumental competence, self-assertion, and internal locus of control. We believe some of these findings are relevant to our question regarding the social origins and facilitation of self-regulation.

In Diane Baumrind's (1973) classic study of parental child-rearing styles, three specific parenting patterns were identified: *Authoritarian* parents value obedience as a virtue and believe in the need to restrict the child's autonomy. The child is expected to accept the parents' word as final, with no encouragement for verbal give-and-take. Authoritarian parents tend to be less nurturant and sympathetic than other types of parents and can be characterized as detached, controlling, and affectively cold. On the other hand, *permissive* parents behave in a markedly less controlling manner; they tend to be disorganized and ineffective in running a household. These parents see themselves neither as having control over their child's behavior nor as having much overall influence on their child. Permissive parents prefer to use love withdrawal and ridicule rather than overt physical punishment. They can be seen as being at the opposite pole from authoritarian parents on the dimensions of control and nurturance; authoritarian parents are high in control and low in nurturance whereas permissive parents are low in control and high in nurturance.

In contrast to the first two types, *authoritative* parents are seen as both controlling and nurturant; their parenting style has been characterized as a healthy combination of love and limits. Although the use of corporal punishment is not uncommon for this pattern, these parents rarely use love withdrawal and ridicule when disciplining their children. Authoritative parents are seen as encouraging and nurturing while placing a constant pressure for mature and obedient behavior. Above all, authoritative parents accompany their control efforts with verbal reasoning, willingly providing the rationale for their requests, commands, and directives.

Baumrind's work is important for our question in that the authoritative parenting style was strongly related to children's instrumental competence. Instrumental competence was defined by a combination of social responsibility, independence, achievement orientation, and self-reliance variables. Children of authoritative parents were characterized by a combination of socially responsible behaviors and a sense of purposiveness, nonconformity, and autonomous self-assertion. These children's capacity for both compliance and self-assertion, expressed in a socially appropriate manner, suggests the flexibility of a self-regulated level of organization.

Along the same lines, the works of Hoffman (1970) and Johnson (1983) have underscored the effectiveness of providing children with overt verbal rationales for parental directives, commands, and discipline. Hoffman suggested that parental discipline strategies characterized by *induction* (i.e., giving reasons and explanations for parental commands and directives) resulted in children with more mature moral development and altruistic behavior. Along similar lines, Johnson found that maternal *cognitive-structuring* behaviors (i.e., explanations) predicted children's ability to delay gratification. In addition, Johnson's study suggested that maternal relinquishing of control and lack of intrusiveness was a predictor of child self-control variables.

In sum, studies of parental teaching styles and child-rearing patterns suggest that three characteristics of caregiver–child interactions promote capacities related to self-regulatory functions: the use of reasoning and verbal rationales, the gradual relinquishing of control, and these two combined with a sense of affective nurturance and emotional warmth. In fact, these three variables characterize the parents of children who have an internal locus of control, that is, children who see themselves as active and effective agents in their environment. In a study of mother–child interactions around a task designed to produce dependency behaviors (Gordon, Nowicki, & Wichern, 1981), mothers of internals offered fewer directives and helped their children less but engaged in more verbal descriptions of their child's on-task behavior. Not surprisingly, internal children exhibited more autonomy and emitted more self-descriptions during the task than their external counterparts.

Based on Jerome Bruner's concept of ''scaffolding,'' Wood and colleagues have studied the tutor's or teacher's role in helping children move from joint to independent problem solving (Wood, Bruner & Ross, 1976; Wood & Middleton, 1975). As the analogy implies, scaffolding refers to the gradual withdrawal of adult control and support as a function of children's increasing mastery of a given task. The work of Wood has shown that successful scaffolders focus children's attention on the task and keep them motivated and working throughout the session. They also divide the task at hand into simpler and more accessible components, directing the child's attention to the essential and relevant features. Finally, the scaffolding tutor demonstrates and models successful performance while keeping the task at a proper level of difficulty, avoiding unnecessary frustration and encouraging children's independent functioning. Research shows that children's increasing mastery and competence on a given task, therefore, depend on detailed adult interventions that are tailored to and determined by children's level of mastery and need for external assistance (Reeve, 1987).

Based on Vygotsky's notion of the zone of proximal development (ZPD), several investigators have examined the role of the adult as teacher within the ZPD. Vygotsky defined the ZPD as "the distance between the actual developmental level as determined by independent problem solving and the level of potential development as determined through problem solving under adult guidance or in collaboration with more capable peers" (1978, p. 86). In line with Vygotsky's formulations, within the ZPD the child is not a mere passive recipient of the adult's teachings, nor is the adult simply a model of expert, successful behavior. Instead, the adult–child dyad engages in joint problem-solving activity, where both share knowledge and responsibility for the task. Rather than simply modeling, the adult teacher must create first a level of "intersubjectivity" (Wertsch, 1984, p. 13), where the child redefines the problem situation in terms of the adult perspective. Once the child shares the adult's goals and definition of the problem situation, the adult must gradually and increasingly transfer task responsibility to the child (Rogoff & Gardner, 1984; Wertsch, McNamee, McLane, & Budwig, 1980). Parental efforts to give explanations and rationales for their commands and directives, described above, can be seen as attempts to create such levels of intersubjectivity. Even though Wertsch (1984) has discussed at length the role of language in the creation of a given level of adult–child intersubjectivity, little is known about the process involved in the successful transfer of task responsibility from adult to child.

The studies reviewed so far seem to converge on two important adult teaching characteristics that promote self-regulatory development: the verbalization of plans, rationales, and goals, and the adult's gradual and sensitive withdrawal from the regulatory role. Furthermore, observational studies of teaching strategies, inspired by concepts such as *scaffolding* and the *zone of proximal development*, suggest three major facts that must be taken into account regarding the social origins of self-regulation. First, the child's cognitive or problem-solving activity is first socially regulated by the adult in joint interaction. Second, the child's successful takeover of the regulatory role involves the active redefinition of the problem situation in terms of the adult's goals and perspective, with a gradual increase in child responsibility for the task at hand. Third, the process from other- to self-regulation, from joint to independent problem solving, does not simply happen automatically or by chance but rather involves very specific teaching interactions on the part of the adult.

As discussed in the previous section, Vygotsky and Luria suggested that children's takeover of the regulatory role occurred mostly as a function of children's increasing use of language for self-regulatory functions. Unfortunately, none of the studies reviewed has examined specific teaching strategies that promote children's use of the self-regulatory language in a teaching situation. We now turn our attention to studies that have attempted actively to train children's use of private speech to regulate their own behavior.

The training of private speech

In order to improve children's ability to control and regulate their own behavior, researchers and clinicians have trained verbal self-regulatory capacities by modeling self-talk and self-instructional strategies (see, e.g., Camp, 1977; Kendall & Braswell, 1985; Meador & Ollendick, 1984; Meichenbaum & Goodman, 1979). Self-instructional training has been attempted with different types of childhood disorders including hyperactivity, impulsivity, learning disabilities, and mental retardation. Attempts to train private speech and self-instructional strategies have been inspired not only by Soviet developmental theory but also by findings about children's increased reliance on verbal mediation in the performance of different cognitive tasks. Somewhat parallel to the Soviet tradition, studies in this country have demonstrated the effectiveness of verbal mediational strategies in delaying gratification and coping with highly distracting stimuli (Mischel & Patterson, 1976; Patterson & Mischel, 1976).

As a rule, training studies involve a multifaceted intervention technique that combines procedures such as modeling self-talk, training the use of overt and covert verbal rehearsal, instruction in self-monitoring strategies using a variety of prompts, and, of course, reinforcement for appropriate behavior (see Cole & Kazdin, 1980, for a critical review). Although there is no agreed-upon common procedure, the major goal of most studies remains the same: to provide the child with a self-regulatory technique, usually verbal, that can be used as a planning, guiding, and self-monitoring tool. The expectation is that the use of such a tool should increase children's awareness of their own actions, diminish impulsive responding, and promote a general pattern of more reflective behavior.

In general, as discussed in more detail below, training studies have demonstrated the effectiveness of self-instructional strategies in decreasing impulsive responding and in promoting more successful patterns of cognitive performance. However, for the most part, improvement has been shown only for the experimental tasks and only within the experimental situation. Treatment effects have not generalized to situations outside the experiment, such as at home or in the classroom. Most likely, training studies have promoted children's self-control abilities in the context of specific tasks and situations but have failed to develop a new level of self-regulatory organization that could be used flexibly across different tasks and situations.

Kendall and Braswell (1985) have divided the literature on self-instructional training into two major categories, according to the training procedures employed: interactive or noninteractive. The noninteractive intervention is typically brief and consists of telling the child to repeat a given verbal command, directive, or statement for a specific purpose or in a specific situation. For example, noninteractive techniques have been used frequently in delay-of-gratification studies, where the child is told to tell himself or herself something such as ''If I wait, I can get a better reward.'' Taking into account our earlier distinction between self-control and self-regulation, noninteractive studies train and demand a self-control level of organization, where the child is asked to repeat and comply with the experimenter's commands in the absence of the experimenter. Therefore, in our opinion, noninteractive studies do not provide much information on how to train for self-regulation.

Interactive studies, on the other hand, follow Luria's three-stage model of self-regulation and require a more active role on the part of the experimenter. Typically, in interactive studies, the trainer first models the use of speech in planning, guiding, and monitoring activity. At this first stage of training, the experimenter performs the task while talking to himself or herself in a self-regulatory fashion. The trainer then repeats the self-instructions while the child is performing the task. The child is then asked to perform the task again; this time, however, the child is asked to repeat overtly the self-instructions while working at the task. Finally, the child is asked to perform the task while repeating covertly the self-instructions.

A classical study in the use of interactive techniques is Meichenbaum and Goodman's (1971) study with impulsive children. The sample was selected from a special ''opportunity remedial class'' that included children who had academic and behavior problems such as poor self-control and hyperactivity. Children were randomly assigned to three different conditions: an experimental condition for cognitive self-instruction training and two control conditions. One control condition, the ''attentional'' group, met with the experimenter for the same amount of time as the experimental children. This control group, however, did not receive any particular training; they just received the experimenter's ''attention'' for the same amount of time as the experimental group. The second control group, an ''assessment'' condition, received only the pre-post battery of tests. Children in the sample were tested on selected subtests of the Wechsler Intelligence Scale for Children, the Porteus Mazes (a test of planning vs. impulsive behavior, where the subject is required to trace a path out of a maze without lifting the pencil, crossing any lines, or erasing), and the Matching Familiar Figures Test (MFFT) immediately preceding and following the training procedures, as well as one month later in a follow-up session. In addition, after training was completed, observations of classroom behaviors and teacher's ratings of children's self-control were obtained.

Children in the training condition were trained on four half-hour sessions within a 2-week period. The training followed the interactive pattern that Meichenbaum and colleagues have developed and used extensively, based on Luria's stages of self-regulation. As summarized later by Meichenbaum and Goodman (1979), the treatment regimen consists of the following four steps:

1. An adult model performing a task while talking aloud to himself (cognitive modeling).
2. The child performing the task under the directions of the model's instructions (overt guidance).
3. The child whispering the instructions to himself as he went through the task (faded self-guidance).
4. The child performing the task while guiding his performance by way of private speech (covert self-instruction). (p. 350)

The modeled self-instructions were a series of statements that, among other things, stated the goal of the task, described the ongoing activity, reminded the child to go slowly and carefully, verbalized errors and corrections, and provided self-praise and positive feedback. For example, during a task that required copying line patterns, the experimenter would say:

> Okay, what is it that I have to do? You want me to copy the picture with the different lines. I have to go slowly and carefully. Okay, draw the line down, down, good; then to the right, that's it; now down some more and to the left. Good, I'm doing fine so far. Remember, go slowly. Now back up again. No, I was supposed to go down. That's okay. Just erase the line carefully. . . . Good. Even if I make an error I can go on slowly and carefully. I have to go down now. Finished. I did it! (Meichenbaum & Goodman, 1971, p. 117)

The results indicated that children in the experimental self-instructional training condition performed better at posttest in the Porteus Mazes and in the MFFT, as well as in the Picture Arrangement subtest of the WISC. The advantages of the experimental group were also evident at the 1-month follow-up. Since the Mazes and the MFFT are well-established measures of impulsivity-reflectivity, the investigators claimed that modeling self-instructions in an interactive procedure can modify impulsivity and create a more reflective pattern of responding. However, this conclusion might be overly optimistic. The study failed to show training effects on children's classroom behaviors. Timed-sampled observations of children's on-task and appropriate behavior in the classroom failed to show improvement over time due to the training procedures. Also, no treatment effects were observed for teachers' ratings of children's self-control and impulsivity.

Camp and her colleagues (e.g., Camp, Blom, Herbert, & van Doornick, 1977) have developed a program to improve self-control called Think Aloud. Training involves a "copycat" method (i.e., modeling) where, through a series of cartoons, children are taught to use the following questions when approaching a problem or task situation:

1. What is my problem?
2. How can I do it?
3. Am I using my plan?
4. How did I do?

Through the use of these questions, the Think Aloud program teaches children a series of self-regulatory skills such as how to analyze a situation, define a plan of action, and assess their behavior in a self-monitoring fashion. In the Camp et al. (1977) study, training was given to a group of highly aggressive boys ages 6–8. The authors reported positive training effects on posttest measures of WISC-R Mazes and MFFT scores. However, similar to Meichenbaum and Goodman's (1971) findings, the training resulted in no improvement of classroom aggressive behavior, as assessed through teachers' ratings.

The pattern of findings for the two studies described above, that is, improvement on the experimental tasks without generalization to other tasks outside the experimental situation, is a typical outcome of studies that model self-instructional training. We should like to propose that failure to generalize treatment outcomes is indeed an indication that the training is not affecting the self-regulatory system. Repetition of adult commands and instructions (i.e., the modeled verbalizations) in a specific task or situation is a clear indication of functioning at the self-control level. The fact that children did not act in a more self-regulated and less impulsive manner outside the confines of the experimental situation suggests the training's failure to promote a self-regulatory behavioral organization in children. It is precisely a high degree of flexibility and adjustment to different circumstances that characterize a self-regulated system. The failure to generalize treatment effects outside the experiment situation witnesses the lack of such flexibility.

Other studies, using different kinds and variations of self-instructional training, have claimed more successful outcomes. For example, Drabman, Spitalnik, and O'Leary (1973) claim that teaching disruptive boys self-evaluative and self-reinforcement skills prevented the deterioration of behavior after the withdrawal of a token economy. Similarly, Neilans and Israel (1981) have shown that the training of self-instruction and self-regulation skills reduced disruptive behavior after training in both reading and math tasks. The researchers found that, unlike the token economy intervention, training of self-instruction and self-regulation skills led to maintenance of positive treatment effects over time.

Even though these two studies seem to claim generalization effects of modeled self-instructions, it should be noted that generalization was obtained because in both studies children were encouraged to keep using some external structures that were originally provided during the training sessions. For example, in the Drabman et al. study, children were still doing some paper-and-pencil evaluations of their own behavior; in the Neilans and Israel study, children were asked to use any overt self-regulatory strategy (learned in training) they so desired during the posttraining observation session. We should like to argue that in these studies generalization was obtained because children still carried with them and used, in a self-control fashion, an overt external strategy given to them in the training. Moreover, in the Neilans and Israel study, posttraining observations of behavior were done with the same tasks (reading and math) used in the training; it is questionable whether such observations truly indicate a generalization of training effects.

In summary, results from studies that have modeled self-regulatory verbalizations are far from being encouraging. There is enough indication that such studies might be affecting and promoting a self-control level of organization, resulting in positive effects that are circumscribed to specific training tasks and situations. It is possible that even the limited positive effects may result because the children in those studies already possessed some degree of self-control. When similar training studies have been done with truly hyperactive children (as measured by the Conners scale), that is, children with well-documented deficits in both self-regulation and self-control, self-instructional training has no demonstrated positive outcomes in comparison to other control conditions (Cohen, Sullivan, Minde, Novak, & Helwig, 1981; Eastman & Rasbury, 1981).

In our own laboratory, after a careful review of the literature, we decided to train a group of normal children in the use of self-regulatory private speech. The study (Padilla & Díaz, 1986) was designed to address three specific research gaps noted in self-instructional training studies. First, most training studies have modeled extremely elaborate statements, questions, and monologues, using language that has no resemblance to spontaneously occurring private speech. We decided, then, to model two simple types of verbalization taken verbatim from transcriptions of spontaneous private-speech protocols. We modeled a frequently used form of private speech, that is, labeling of experimental materials such as "the red flower," "the big bird." We also modeled the use of a less frequent verbalization that we call transitional statements: "OK, I am done . . . now another one." In the past, (Gaskill & Díaz, 1989), we have shown that children's spontaneous labels and descriptions of task materials facilitate performance in classification tasks. Also, the use of spontaneous transitional statements helps the child move from one task item to another, requiring minimal adult intervention. Both labeling and transitional statements are verbal tools that children use to help regulate their task performance. We argued that the failure of previous training studies could be attributed in part to the use of difficult experimenter-formulated verbalizations.

Second, we argued that, in order to assess the effects of training on the self-regulatory system, we should evaluate not simply posttraining task performance but posttraining use of spontaneous self-regulatory language. In our study, therefore, we took pre- and posttraining measures of children's spontaneous verbalizations during classification and block design tasks. Training was given using a completely different type of task that required matching figures from memory. We argued that an increase in the use of self-regulatory speech on different tasks as a result of training was our best indicator of affecting the self-regulation system in a generalized way.

Third, the majority of training studies in the field have used school-aged children. If the self-regulatory system is being organized and developed during the preschool years, as suggested by a peak in the frequency of private speech between the ages of 4 and 5 (Díaz, 1986), training efforts should be more efficacious during the preschool years. A system that is rapidly changing in the process of development is presumably more open to environmental input and external intervention. We decided, therefore, to train the use of self-regulatory language in a group of 10 preschoolers, ages 3–5, over three 15-minute sessions on three different days within a week's period; the experimental group was compared to a randomly chosen "attentional" control group ($N = 10$) that met with the experimenter for the same amount of time for shared activities that involved no modeled self-verbalizations.

It should be kept in mind that the purpose of our study was to assess the possibility of promoting the *spontaneous* use of private speech through modeling self-verbalizations, rather than to reduce impulsive or aggressive behavior, as in many of the studies reviewed above. Also, because we were interested in affecting the use of overt verbalizations, our training procedures consisted of modeling overt verbalizations and asking the child to repeat the verbalization overtly while working on the task in the experimenter's presence; our study did not involve training the gradual fading or whispering of private speech, nor did it train children to use covert verbalizations. By training the use of labeling and transitional statements, we were not teaching children to use a particular verbalization that they should repeat in the experimenter's absence; rather, we attempted to model the more general rule that language can be used for self-regulatory functions.

The results of our study can be summarized very briefly. We found absolutely no effects of self-verbalization training on the spontaneous use of private speech. In comparison to the control group, the experimental group showed no advantages in their use of spontaneous labeling and transitional statements in their private speech. In addition, we did not find any improvement due to training in children's overall private speech or, for that matter, in their performance scores for the classification and block design tasks.

Considering the previous literature and the findings from our modest training study, we have concluded that modeling self-verbalizations has no demonstrated effects on the development or organization of the self-regulatory system. Moreover, in light of the findings, we would like to argue that, to date, there is no empirically proven method, training, or treatment that can affect and promote the level of behavioral organization that we have termed self-regulation.

In our opinion, a major conceptual problem in training studies is a misunderstanding of Vygotsky's concept of internalization. As described above, both Vygotsky and Luria believed that the internalization of private speech was a necessary final stage in the formation and consolidation of the self-regulatory system. Unfortunately, most training studies have interpreted the internalization of private speech simply as a developmental progression from overt to covert verbalizations. Even though children do indeed become capable of subvocalizing and of "hearing the little voice inside" (personal communication from a preschool subject), as Wertsch and Stone (1985) suggest, Vygotsky's concept of internalization has a much broader meaning.

In Vygotsky's theory, internalization refers primarily to the transferring of a function from the social plane to the psychological plane:

> Any higher mental function necessarily goes through an external stage in its development because it is initially a social function. This is the center of the whole problem of internal and external behavior. . . . When we speak of a process, "external" means "social." Any higher mental function was external because it was social at some point before becoming an internal, truly mental function. (1960/1981, p. 162)

Moreover, Vygotsky (1962, 1978) argued that private (egocentric) speech was the bridge that linked social and individual functioning. Not surprisingly, language, as mediator of both social interactions and mental functioning, has a privileged role in the internalization process. Internalization, the movement of a function from the social to the mental plane, occurs, therefore, when children begin to use for themselves the signs that adults used to regulate their activity. Internalization refers to the child's final mastery and control of social signs, especially of those signs used in the social regulation of behavior. This mastery and control of signs is manifested in the increasing adult–child shared word meanings but, more specifically, in children's active and spontaneous use of the sign system to regulate their own activity.

In our opinion, training children to repeat covertly adult-given verbalizations in order to develop self-regulatory functions represents a somewhat misguided interpretation of Vygotsky's theory. In fact, as the studies reviewed in this section show, there is no indication that such training promotes children's spontaneous use of language for self-regulation.

In order to begin our exploration of the social origins and facilitation of self-regulation, and following Vygotsky's lead regarding the self-regulatory functions of private speech, we formulated the following related questions: How can children's spontaneous use of private speech be promoted, taught, facilitated? What specific teaching strategies, training techniques, social experiences might promote children's greater use of self-regulatory language in their cognitive activity? How can a teacher or caregiver, during a joint problem-solving task, help the child move from social dialogue and the use of descriptive statements to the use of planning, self-regulatory language?

From social dialogue to private speech

In order to examine teaching strategies that promote children's use of self-regulatory language in a teaching situation, 51 mothers and their 3-year-old children were videotaped during a 5-minute teaching session at their children's preschool. Mothers were asked to teach either a classification or a story-sequencing task "so that the child can do it on his/her own at a later time." In order to ensure a wide variability of teaching styles, approximately half of the sample (24 dyads) were recruited from a high-risk population serviced by a therapeutic preschool program. High-risk mothers were characterized by lower socioeconomic status, lower levels of education, younger age, and a high incidence of child abuse and substance abuse. The teaching interaction was then later transcribed and coded to obtain the following measures:

Maternal verbal teaching

Mothers' utterances during the teaching session were classified under the following mutually exclusive categories:

> Commands (imperatives: "Put the card here!")
> Directives (softer commands: "Let's take the red one.")
> Directive questions ("Can you put this one here?")
> Perceptual questions (questions where the answer is present in the immediate stimulus field: "What color is this one?")
> Conceptual questions (questions that cannot be answered by simply attending to the immediate perceptual field but rather require a mental representation of the rules or goals of the task: "How are these two alike?" in a classification task, or "What goes next?" in a sequencing task)
> Praises ("Boy, you sure did a good job!")
> Direct relinquishing ("Now you show Mommy how to do it.")
> Other speech
> Whispers/inaudible utterances

Child task-relevant speech

Children's utterances during the task were categorized under the following mutually exclusive categories:

1. Imitations/repetitions of maternal speech
2. Verbal responses to maternal questions
3. Questions to the mother about the task
4. Independent task-relevant verbalizations

where each category from 1 to 4 represents a higher degree of children's active self-regulatory participation. Category 4 was not labeled *private speech* because of the difficulties in establishing the distinction between private and social speech in an essentially interactive social situation. However, the category of *independent verbalizations* reflected children's spontaneous use of language about the task, not specifically addressed to the mother. In our opinion, this category captures the beginnings of children's active and spontaneous use of language to master independently the task at hand.

Physical manipulation of task materials

Using a time-sampling procedure, with observations every 30 seconds, the amount of time the child and the mother manipulated the task during the session was calculated.

Maternal withdrawal

The teaching session was divided into two equal-time halves. The following questions were asked from the videotaped interactions and the transcribed protocols:

1. Was there a decrease (from first to second half) in maternal commands?
2. Were there more directives than commands overall?
3. Were there more questions than directives and commands?
4. Were there more conceptual than perceptual and directive questions?
5. Was there a decrease in maternal overall speech?
6. Was there a decrease in maternal manipulation of task materials?
7. Was the mother a high user of whispers?
8. Was the mother a high user of praises?
9. Was the mother a high user of direct relinquishing?

Questions were answered as yes or no and coded as 1 and 0, respectively. A high score indicates high maternal withdrawal during the teaching session. For item 3, the three types of questions were combined to calculate the total number of questions the mother used; since questions promote the child's active participation, the use of questions indicates a higher level of maternal withdrawal than the use of commands and directives. For questions 7–9 the sample was divided into high and low users of a given type of utterance through a median split according to the number of whispers, praises, and direct relinquishing utterances in the sample.

Children's takeover of regulatory role

Once the teaching session was divided into two equal-time halves, the following questions were asked:

1. Was there an increase (from first to second half) in the child's manipulation of task materials?
2. Was there an increase in the child's task-relevant speech from first to second half?
3. Did the child ask task-relevant questions?
4. Did the child use independent verbalizations?
5. Were there more task-relevant questions and independent verbalizations than imitations and responses?

Questions were answered yes or no and coded as 1 or 0, respectively. A high score indicates a high degree of child takeover of responsibility during the task.

Two sets of correlational analyses were done in order to examine maternal verbal and withdrawal strategies that promoted the child's use of independent verbalizations and the child's takeover of the regulatory role during the teaching task. The first set of analyses investigated the relation between maternal verbal teaching and the child's use of task-relevant utterances during the teaching session; we also included in this analysis the amount of time mothers and their children physically manipulated the task materials. The second set of analyses investigated the relation among our measures of maternal withdrawal, the child's task-relevant verbalizations, and the child's takeover of the regulatory role.

Relation between maternal and child verbalizations

The nine categories of maternal speech were submitted to a principal components factor analysis with varimax rotation. The analysis yielded the following three factors with eigenvalues greater than 1, explaining 59% of the variance:

Table 5.1. *Correlations between maternal verbal teaching/manipulation and children's task-relevant speech/manipulation*

	Maternal variables			
Child variables	Verbal Directing	Verbal Focusing	Verbal Relinquishing	Manipulation of Task
Imitations/ repetitions	.38[a]	.39[a]	−.36[a]	.27[b]
Verbal responses	.04	.35[a]	.31[a]	−.10
Questions to mother	−.08	.13	.01	.10
Independent verbalizations	−.08	.18	.10	−.24[b]
Manipulation of task materials	.17	−.21	.22[b]	−.48[c]

[a]$p < .01$. [b]$p < .05$. [c]$p < .001$.

1. Verbal Directing: commands, directives, and directive questions
2. Verbal Focusing: perceptual questions and other speech
3. Verbal Relinquishing: conceptual questions, praises, and direct relinquishing

Table 5.1 reports Pearson correlation coefficients between maternal verbal factors and children's verbalizations, as well as the physical manipulation variables. Unfortunately, no specific maternal verbal factor predicted children's independent verbalizations. On the other hand, maternal manipulation of the task materials, as an idex of maternal intrusiveness and lack of withdrawal, discouraged the use of independent verbalizations. As expected, the most facilitating verbal strategy for children's active participation in the teaching session is the Verbal Relinquishing factor; this factor predicted both children's verbal responses and their increased manipulation of task materials. Interestingly, children's imitations and repetitions of maternal speech were negatively correlated with the relinquishing factor, whereas they were positively related to maternal directing and physical manipulation. These findings suggest that children's verbal imitations and repetitions represent a different and more passive type of verbal participation, not conducive to a true takeover of the regulatory role. We should like to argue that this finding is consistent with our distinction between self-control and self-regulation.

Relations among maternal withdrawal, child task-relevant speech, and child takeover

The nine questions in the maternal withdrawal measure were submitted to a principal components factor analysis with varimax rotation. The factor analysis yielded

Table 5.2. *Correlations between maternal withdrawal factors and*
children's task-relevant speech/takeover of regulatory role

Child variables	Maternal variables		
	Decline in Control	Engaging Strategies	Relinquishing
Repetitions/ imitations	.07	−.29[a]	−.28[a]
Verbal responses	−.14	.31[b]	−.16
Questions to mother	.14	.05	.01
Independent verbalizations	−.07	.13	.14
Takeover of regulatory role	−.02	.08	.27[a]

[a]$p < .05$. [b]$p < .01$.

the following withdrawal factors with eigenvalues greater than 1, explaining 52%
of the variance:

1. Decline in Control: decrease in commands and decrease in overall maternal speech
2. Engaging Strategies: more directives than commands, more questions than directives and commands, and high use of praises
3. Relinquishing Strategies: more conceptual than directing or perceptual questions, decline in maternal manipulation of task materials, and high use of direct relinquishing verbalizations.

Table 5.2 reports the Pearson correlation coefficients between the maternal withdrawal factors and the items from the child's takeover measure. Unfortunately, no specific withdrawal factor predicted children's independent verbalizations. Similarly to the first set of analyses, children's imitations and repetitions of maternal verbalization correlated negatively with engaging and relinquishing strategies. The most exciting finding was that the relinquishing factor, as a true index of maternal sensitive withdrawal during the teaching task, was significant and positively correlated to the child's takeover of the regulatory role.

The results from the present study should be considered mostly as pilot and exploratory data, considering this was our first attempt to tackle the issues at hand. Specifically, the results should be considered with caution because the 5-minute period was simply not enough time for children to learn the task and, therefore, not enough time to observe a proper level of maternal withdrawal and the corresponding child takeover of task responsibility. Nonetheless, the study was successful in identifying a pattern of verbal teaching and withdrawal, both labeled relinquishing, that is significantly related to children's active participation and takeover of the regulatory role during the teaching task.

Conclusion

This chapter has described and elaborated Vygotsky's notions regarding the social origins and self-regulation of higher cognitive functions. Specifically, we have considered Vygotsky's theory from the point of view of individual differences in development, suggesting that the quality of social interactions a child experiences might have a significant effect on the development of self-regulation. We then reviewed the relevant literature and presented our own findings in search of specific adult teaching strategies that might promote a higher level of self-regulatory functioning in young children.

We have argued that the question regarding the social origins and facilitation of self-regulation must be operationalized as follows: What specific adult teaching interventions promote and facilitate the child's spontaneous use of language for self-regulation? At this point we recognize that there is no satisfactory answer to this question, even though we know that modeling self-verbalizations and children's corresponding imitations seem quite ineffectual in promoting self-regulation. However, so far and very tentatively, four specific strategies have emerged as promoting the child's active participation in a teaching task and the gradual takeover of the regulatory role: (1) the use of praise and encouragement, (2) conceptual questions, (3) direct relinquishing statements, and (4) a true physical withdrawal as manifested in the adult's decreased manipulation of task materials.

Not surprisingly, the adult's physical withdrawal, accompanied by the use of direct relinquishing statements, places the child at the center of the action and exerts a subtle pressure and demand for the child to take over responsibility for the task. Conceptual questions, in contrast to directing and perceptual questions, force the child to function at the level of mentally represented plans and rules, promoting a symbolic detachment from the immediate perceptual field. Finally, praises and encouragement communicate to the child a pleasurable sense of effective competence and mastery over his or her environment. We would like to present the effects of these teaching strategies on the development of self-regulation as hypotheses that should be tested with further scientific observations.

References

Baumrind, D. (1973). The development of instrumental competence through socialization. In A. D. Pick (Ed.), *Minnesota Symposia on Child Psychology*. Minneapolis: University of Minnesota Press.

Berk, L. E., & Garvin, R. A. (1984). Development of private speech among low-income Appalachian children. *Developmental Psychology, 20,* 271–286.

Camp. B. W. (1977). Verbal mediation in young aggressive boys. *Journal of Abnormal Psychology, 86,* 145–153.

Camp, B. W., Blom, G. E., Herbert, F., & van Doornick, W. J. (1977). "Think aloud": A program for developing self-control in young aggressive boys. *Journal of Abnormal Child Psychology, 7,* 169–177.

Cohen, N. J., Sullivan, J., Minde, K., Novak, C. I., & Helwig, C., (1981). Evaluation of the relative effectiveness of methylphenidate and cognitive behavior modification in the treatment of kindergarten-aged hyperactive children. *Journal of Abnormal Child Psychology, 9*, 43–54.

Cole. M. P., & Kazdin, A. E. (1980). Critical issues in self-instruction training with children. *Journal of Child Behavior Therapy, 2*, 1–23.

Díaz, R. M. (1986). The union of thought and language in children's private speech. *Quarterly Newsletter of the Laboratory of Comparative Human Cognition, 8*(3), 90–97.

Drabman, R. S., Spitalnik, R., & O'Leary, K. D. (1973). Teaching self-control to disruptive children. *Journal of Abnormal Psychology, 83*, 10–16.

Eastman, B. G., & Rasbury, W. C. (1981). Cognitive self-instruction for the control of impulsive classroom behavior: Ensuring the treatment package. *Journal of Abnormal Child Psychology, 9*, 381–387.

Frauenglass, M., & Díaz, R. M. (1985). The self-regulatory functions of children's private speech: A critical analysis of recent challenges to Vygotsky's theory. *Developmental Psychology, 21*, 357–364.

Gaskill, M. N., & Díaz, R. M. (1989). *The relation between private speech and cognitive performance.* Manuscript submitted for publication.

Gordon, D., Nowicki, S., Jr., & Wichern, F. (1981). Observed maternal and child behaviors in a dependency producing task as a function of children's locus of control orientation. *Merrill-Palmer Quarterly, 27*, 43–52.

Goudena, P. P. (1987). The social nature of private speech of preschoolers during problem solving. *International Journal of Behavioral Development, 10*, 187–206.

Hoffman, M. L. (1970). Moral development. In P. H. Mussen (Ed.), *Carmichael's handbook of child psychology* (Vol. 2). New York: Wiley.

Johnson, K. (1983). Maternal behavior and self-control in young children. *Dissertation Abstracts International, 43* (10 = B) 3385.

Kendall, P. C., & Braswell, L. (1985). *Cognitive-behavioral therapy for impulsive children.* New York: Guildford Press.

Kopp, C. B. (1982). Antecedents of self-regulation: A developmental perspective. *Developmental Psychology, 18*(2), 199–214.

Luria, A. R. (1973). *The working brain: An introduction to neuropsychology.* New York: Basic.

Luria, A. R. (1982). *Language and cognition.* New York: Wiley.

Meador, A. E., & Ollendick, T. H. (1984). Cognitive behavior therapy with children: An evaluation of its efficacy and clinical utility. *Child and Family Behavior Therapy, 6*, 25–44.

Meichenbaum, D. H., & Goodman, J. (1971). Training impulsive children to talk to themselves: A means of developing self-control. *Journal of Abnormal Psychology, 2*, 115–126.

Meichenbaum, D. H., & Goodman, S. (1979). Clinical use of private speech and critical questions about its study in natural settings. In G. Zivin (Ed.), *The development of self-regulation through private speech.* New York: Wiley.

Mischel, W., & Patterson, C. J. (1976). Substantive and structural elements of effective plans for self-control. *Journal of Personality and Social Psychology, 34*, 942–950.

Neilans, T. H., & Israel, A. C. (1981). Towards maintenance and generalizations or behavior change: Teaching children self-regulation and self-instructional skills. *Cognitive Therapy and Research, 5*, 189–195.

Padilla, K. A., & Díaz, R. M. (1986). *The training of self-regulatory private speech.* Paper presented at the conference of the Minority Biomedical Research Program, New Orleans.

Passler, M. A., Isaac, W., & Hynd, G. W. (1985). Neuropsychological development of behavior attributed to frontal lobe functioning in children. *Developmental Neuropsychology, 1*(4), 349–370.

Patterson, C. J., & Mischel, W. (1976). Effects of temptation-inhibiting and task-facilitating plans on self-control. *Journal of Personality and Social Psychology, 33*, 207–217.

Piaget, J. (1952). *The origins of intelligence in children.* New York: International Universities Press.

Reeve, R. A. (1987). *The functional significance of parental scaffolding as a moderator of social influence on children's cognition.* Paper presented at the biennial meeting of the Society for Research in Child Development, Baltimore.

Rogoff, B., & Gardner, W. (1984). Adult guidance of cognitive development. In B. Rogoff & J. Lave (Eds.), *Everyday cognition: Its development in social context.* Cambridge, MA: Harvard University Press.

Sternberg, R. J. (1984). Toward a triarchic theory of human intelligence. *Behavioral and Brain Sciences, 7,* 269–315.

Stuss, D. T., & Benson, D. F. (1984). Neuropsychological studies of the frontal lobes. *Psychological Bulletin, 95,* 3–28.

Vygotsky, L. S. (1962). *Thought and language.* Cambridge, MA: MIT Press.

Vygotsky, L. S. (1978). *Mind in society.* Cambridge, MA: Harvard University Press.

Vygotsky, L. S. (1981). The genesis of higher mental functions. In J. V. Wertsch (Ed. & Trans.), *The concept of activity in Soviet psychology.* (pp. 144–188). New York: Sharpe. (Reprinted from *Razvitie vysshikh psikhicheskikh funktsii,* 1960, pp. 182–223)

Wertsch, J. V. (Ed.) (1981). *The concept of activity in Soviet psychology.* New York: Sharpe.

Wertsch, J. V. (1984). The zone of proximal development: Some conceptual issues. In B. Rogoff & J. V. Wertsch (Eds.), *Children's learning in the "zone of proximal development"* (pp. 7–18). New Directions for Child Development, No. 23. San Francisco: Jossey-Bass.

Wertsch, J. V. (1985). *Vygotsky and the social formation of mind.* Cambridge: Cambridge University Press.

Wertsch, J. V. (1986). *Culture, communication, and cognition.* Cambridge: Cambridge University Press.

Wertsch, J. V., McNamee, G. D., McLane, J. B., & Budwig, N. A. (1980). The adult–child dyad as a problem-solving system. *Child Development, 50,* 1215–1221.

Wertsch, J. V., & Stone, C. A. (1985). The concept of internalization in Vygotsky's account of the genesis of higher mental functions. In J. V. Wertsch (Ed.), *Culture, communication, and cognition* (pp. 162–182). Cambridge: Cambridge University Press.

Wood, D., Bruner, J., & Ross, S. (1976). The role of tutoring in problem-solving. *Journal of Child Psychology and Psychiatry, 17,* 89–100.

Wood, D., & Middleton, D. (1975). A study of assisted problem-solving. *British Journal of Psychology, 66,* 181–191.

Zivin, G. (Ed.) (1979). *The development of self-regulation through private speech.* New York: Wiley.

6 Vygotsky, the zone of proximal development, and peer collaboration: Implications for classroom practice

Jonathan Tudge

Vygotsky, when introducing the concept of the zone of proximal development, declared that "more competent peers," as well as adults, can aid children's development (1978, p. 86). Although there has been a recent upsurge of interest in Vygotsky's theory, fueled by several influential books (e.g., Wertsch, 1985a) and research based on Vygotskian theory (Rogoff & Wertsch, 1984; Valsiner, 1987; Wertsch, 1985a), most of this interest has centered on the role adults play in fostering children's development. The same focus is apparent in this book; not unnaturally, in a volume devoted to education, the role of adults is given a good deal of emphasis.

I have chosen, instead, to examine the effects of collaboration between peers. After all, in many classrooms children work in groups, either under the guidance of a teacher or aide or as members of a team, working together to solve a problem with little or no adult guidance. In some classes, children also act as tutors, helping less competent peers learn some relatively straightforward skill. Even where peer collaboration is not encouraged, the potential role of such collaboration should not be casually dismissed.

There is a theoretical, as well as a practical, motivation for examining peer collaboration. Because the research set within a Vygotskian framework has almost exclusively focused upon adult–child interaction and has supported the view that providing information within a child's zone of proximal development can be highly beneficial, the impression left is that development proceeds in the direction of current adult models of culturally appropriate practice. For example, researchers working in the Vygotskian tradition have examined the ways in which preschoolers come to be successful in model-copying tasks (Wertsch, 1979, 1980; Wertsch, Minick, & Arns, 1984) and learning numerical skills (Saxe, Gearhart, & Guberman, 1984; Saxe, Guberman, & Gearhart, 1988), and the ways children of school age solve

Much of this research was conducted as part of a doctoral dissertation in the Department of Human Development and Family Studies, Cornell University. The research was funded by: the College of Human Ecology (dissertation grant and Alumni Association award), the Committees of Soviet Studies and International Studies (all of Cornell University); the Institute for Intercultural Studies; the American Council of Learned Societies; Sigma Xi.

I am very grateful to the principals, staff, and children of Central Elementary School (Ithaca, NY), Yasli-sad No. 865 (Moscow), Ensign Elementary School, and Rosecrest Elementary School (both of Salt Lake City). My thanks also to Antoinette Levatich and Susan Bjorge for much of the data collection and coding and, for their critical reading, to Mary Larner and Barbara Rogoff.

tasks requiring use of memory, classification, and planning strategies (Ellis & Rogoff, 1982, 1986; Radziszewska & Rogoff, 1988; Rogoff & Gardner, 1984; Rogoff & Radziszewska, 1985). In all cases, children who collaborated with an adult (generally a mother) were most likely to complete the task successfully.

This research strongly suggests that children come to learn adult meanings, behaviors, and technologies in the process of collaboration. Implicit in much of this research is a teleological conception of development – not in the sense of some overall goal toward which development aims but a relativistic teleology, which holds that learning unfolds in the direction of culturally appropriate practices. The role that children play in the interaction is not ignored; their active role in this process is emphasized. Azmitia and Perlmutter (in press) argue that a good deal more attention should be paid to the children's contribution in the process of arranging types of interaction that best suit their needs, and indeed, Rogoff and her colleagues have examined the ways in which young children influence the adults who are in turn attempting to socialize them (Mosier & Rogoff, 1989; Rogoff, 1989; Rogoff, Malkin, & Gilbride, 1984; Rogoff, Mistry, Radziszewska, & Germond, in press). For the most part, however, the implicit assumption is that the adults carry the weight of responsibility for the learning process, children being helped to learn adult-sanctioned solutions to problems. In this way, children are socialized into the cultural norms of society.

However, if there are circumstances in which collaboration with others leads children to *regress,* doubt must be cast on an interpretation of the zone of proximal development in which development always leads to more advanced practices. Vygotsky's theory may be more compatible with a conception of a zone that extends not solely in advance of children but all around them, so that in different circumstances they can be led either to develop or to regress in their thinking, depending on the nature of their social interactions. I shall illustrate this view of the zone of proximal development with some of my research into peer interaction. First, however, I shall provide more information about what Vygotsky meant by the zone of proximal development and how it fits into his broader theoretical position.

The zone of proximal development in its theoretical context

The zone of proximal development, as a concept, cannot be separated from the broader theoretical system in which it is set (Cole, 1985; Griffin & Cole, 1984; Wertsch, 1985a). In fact, failure to see the connections between the zone and the theory as a whole means that it is difficult to differentiate Vygotsky's concept from any instructional technique that systematically leads children, with the help of an adult, through a number of steps in the process of learning some set of skills. The difference for Vygotsky is that the *context* in which the interaction occurs is of crucial importance.

Vygotsky proposed that each child, in any domain, has an "actual developmental level," which can be assessed by testing him or her individually, and an immediate potential for development within that domain. Vygotsky termed this difference between the two levels the zone of proximal development, which he defined as "the distance between the actual developmental level as determined by independent problem solving and the level of potential development as determined through problem solving under adult guidance or in collaboration with more capable peers" (Vygotsky, 1978, p. 86). Vygotsky gave the concept a clearly maturational slant:

> The zone of proximal development defines those functions that have not yet matured but are in the process of maturation, functions that will mature tomorrow but are currently in an embryonic state. These functions could be termed the "buds" or "flowers" of development rather than the "fruits" of development. (1978, p. 86)

Vygotsky also provided some indication of a seemingly teleological view of the developmental process, a process in which children come to be socialized into the dominant culture. Just as Marx wrote that the first use of tools mediated human beings' experience of the physical environment and had a huge impact on social relations among people, Vygotsky used the notion of "psychological tools" to explain the developmental revolution from "natural" processes to higher mental processes. Thus language, a tool of immense power, ensures that linguistically created meanings are shared meanings, social meanings. Words that already have meaning for mature members of a cultural group come to have those same meanings for the young of the group in the process of interaction.

Collaboration with another person, either an adult or a more competent peer, in the zone of proximal development thus leads to development in culturally appropriate ways. This conception is not teleological in the sense of some universal end point of development, but it may be in the more relative sense that the preexisting social world, embodied in the adult or more competent peer, is the goal to which development leads.

This view of the results of interaction within the zone of proximal development has been accepted at least in part because Vygotsky introduced the concept within the context of describing school-based instruction (Vygotsky, 1978, 1987). In this context he is clearly interested in discussing the ways in which instruction can be most useful to children. Elsewhere in his writings, however, Vygotsky discussed less beneficial interactional contexts.

As Vygotsky pointed out in his discussion of the education of physically and mentally handicapped children, changes in the context of education may have profound consequences for the developmental process. Vygotsky felt that children with either mental of physical handicaps should be mainstreamed rather than educated with children with the same handicap. He held that if blind, deaf, or mentally retarded children were educated separately from "normal" children their development would proceed in a totally different, and not beneficial, manner, which "would inevitably lead to the creation of a special breed of people" (in press, p. 178). For example, Vygotsky mentioned that when mentally retarded children are not exposed to abstract thought in their schooling (because they are supposedly capable only of concrete thinking) the result will be a "suppressing [of] the rudiments of any abstract thought that such children still have" (1978, p. 89). Similarly, deaf children who are educated only with other deaf children are highly likely to develop differently from their counterparts who are mainstreamed. "Everything in this environment accentuates [the deaf child's] handicap, everything fixes his attention on his deafness and traumatises him precisely for this reason. Here not only is there no development, but those forces in the child which would subsequently have helped him enter life become systematically atrophied" (in press, pp. 205–206).

It is clear that Vygotsky did not view the developmental process as unidirectional, with handicapped children merely being in some way less developed on a continuum of development, but believed that development could proceed along entirely separate lines (in press, p. 3). He felt that this would be particularly true when children were labeled, and treated differently because of that label. "Once branded a fool or handicapped, the child is placed in completely new social circumstances and his/her entire development proceeds in a completely new direction" (in press, p. 153).

Thus, in order to determine the nature and path of development, it becomes essential to examine the social environment in which development occurs and the type of instruction provided. This is true equally of children who are not "handicapped" in any way. Thus, just as ontogenetic development is dependent upon the broad social and cultural conditions in society that have developed over time, so children's microgenetic development is dependent upon the particular interactions they have with others. Development, far from being teleological or unidirectional, must be viewed as context-dependent. In this case, one must accept that if a child is interacting with another person who is less competent the result of that interaction may be regression. Examination of adult–child interactions is unlikely to provide much evidence of anything other than a unidirectional process. This is particularly apparent in cases in which instruction takes place in school, or when preschoolers are asked to classify materials or copy a model. The "approved," or culturally appropriate, solutions are well understood by the adults involved, and the children know that their performance will be judged in terms of its degree of approximation to these solutions.

When considering interactions between peers, however, the situation may be less clear-cut. Vygotsky implied that working with a more competent peer could lead to the development of the less competent child. But is it the case that the opinions of the more competent child always prevail? When two children are working to solve some problem one may be more advanced in her thinking, but it is an open question as to whether the other child is as willing to accept her partner's view as she would if her partner were an adult. To put it another way, when an adult provides information within a child's zone of proximal development, development may indeed result, but can we be as certain about the outcome when peers interact?

Peer collaboration and the zone of proximal development

Much of the research on peer collaboration would answer this question in the affirmative; interaction with a more competent peer has been shown to be highly effective in inducing cognitive development. The bulk of the research that has examined this topic has been set in a Piagetian, rather than Vygotskian, framework. I will discuss this research in some detail because equally strong claims have been made by new-Piagetian scholars for the beneficial and unidirectional effects of collaboration with a more competent peer as have been made by the Vygotskian researchers who have dealt with adult–child collaboration.

Over the last 15 years scholars working within the Piagetian framework have developed a model relating collaboration to cognitive development, in which the mechanism promoting development is "cognitive conflict" or "sociocognitive conflict" (see, e.g., Ames & Murray, 1982; Bearison, Magzamen, & Filardo, 1986; Doise & Mugny, 1984; Murray, 1972, 1982; Perret-Clermont, 1980). Research based on this model has indicated that social interaction between peers who bring different perspectives to bear upon a problem is a highly effective means of inducing cognitive development.

The task that has most commonly been used in the Piaget-inspired research is conservation. Typically, children are pretested to determine their status as conservers or nonconservers in some domain such as conservation of liquid. A nonconserver is then paired with one or more conservers, and the children are asked to reach agreement on the problem. Conservers declare that pouring liquid from one container to another whose dimensions are different does not change the amount of liquid whereas nonconservers are likely to hold that there is either more liquid or less in the new container, because of the change in dimensions. Hence a difference in perspectives is attained, along with the possibility for cognitive conflict. In this experimental situation, upward of 80% of nonconservers attain conservation in the course of discussing the problem with a peer, compared with a success rate of only about 50% in typical training studies (Murray, 1982).

These results have been taken as clear support for the neo-Piagetian position regarding the impact of peer interaction. However, they also are compatible with the Vygotskian model of development, for conservers clearly qualify as "more competent peers" in comparison to nonconservers. From a Vygotskian perspective, one would expect the nonconservers to come to an initial understanding of conservation when collaborating with a more competent peer and then to show evidence of conservation in later independent performance.

Some support for this view can be garnered from a number of studies which have taken not only conservers and nonconservers but conservers, "partial conservers," and nonconservers. From a Vygotskian position, we would expect that partial conservation is more likely to be within a nonconserver's zone of proximal development than conservation, and similarly that conservation should be more likely to be within the zone of proximal development of a partial conserver than a nonconserver.

Thus partial conservers paired with conservers should develop more than nonconservers, and nonconservers should gain more from being paired with a transitional conserver than with a conserver. The evidence seems to support this position (Mugny & Doise, 1978).

Competence or confidence?

Although the neo-Piagetian research and the work on peer tutoring have suggested that interaction with a more competent peer is beneficial to development, it is necessary to consider the nature of the relationship between the more and less competent partners in this type of interaction. When conservers are paired with nonconservers the relationship between partners is somewhat similar to the relationship between an adult and a child. One member of a dyad has access to the culturally appropriate means of solution (conservation, or knowledge of some mathematical concept, for example), and one does not. As I have argued elsewhere (Tudge, 1986a, 1986b, 1989), in this situation conservers are tantamount to experts within that domain and are, moreover, confident of their beliefs (Miller, 1986; Miller & Brownell, 1975; Miller, Brownell, & Zukier, 1977; Murray, 1982, 1987). Many instances of collaboration between children do not feature this type of expert–novice relationship, however. The focus of my research has been upon peer collaboration in which there is a difference in the level of ability of the partners but in which the more advanced partner is not necessarily more confident of his or her beliefs. The aim has been to disentangle competence and confidence. Two studies were undertaken to examine the extent to which development occurred when children were paired with another child whose level of thinking about the task of interest was at the same level, at a lower level, or at a higher level. The task on which the children worked required them to predict the working of a mathematical balance beam. This task, first employed by Inhelder and Piaget (1958) and then developed by Siegler (1976, 1981), allowed children's thinking to be distinguished on six levels (or "rules" for predicting the performance of the beam), each more cognitively sophisticated than the ones before. (For details of the rules, see Table 6.1.) The task was chosen because level of thinking and confidence were not confounded; children using one of the higher rules were not necessarily more confident than children using one of the lower rules.

The beam had eight sticks placed equidistant from each other, four on either side of a central fulcrum, and was held stable by wooden blocks supporting it at each end (see Figure 6.1). Metal nuts that fit over the sticks were used as the weights. In each of 14 different trials the weights were placed on only one stick on each side of the fulcrum, with a maximum of 6 weights on any one side and a maximum of 10 on both sticks.

Table 6.1. *Rules for predicting the working of the balance beam*

Rule 0. No understanding either of the idea of balance or of what will happen when one side of the beam has more weights. Children using this rule did not participate further.

Rule 1. No understanding of the idea of simple balance but a belief that the beam will tip to the side with the greater number of weights. Children using this rule attend only to the dimension of weight and can therefore predict with confidence all configurations in which one side of the beam has more weights. However, they are uncertain when the number of weights is identical.

Rule 2. A belief that the beam will tip to the side with the greater number of weights and that it will balance when the number of weights is equal. Children using this rule attend only to the dimension of weight and can predict with confidence all configurations.

Rule 3. A belief that the beam will tip to the side with the greater number of weights. When the weights are equal, some attention is paid to distance from the fulcrum but not in consistent fashion. For children using this rule, confident predictions can be made when one side of the beam has a greater number of weights; when the number is identical and the distance from the fulcrum is different, there is uncertainty.

Rule 4. The variables of distance and weight can be considered simultaneously. Distance is consistently treated as an important variable but only when the number of weights is equal. In other cases, there is a belief that the beam will tip to the side with the greater number of weights. For children using this rule all configurations can be predicted with confidence.

Rule 5. Distance is viewed as an important variable even when the number of weights is different. However, there is no means of ascertaining precisely under which conditions greater distance but fewer weights will overrule lesser distance but more weights; confident predictions cannot be made when children are presented with configurations of this type.

Rule 6. An understanding of what will happen in each configuration is gained by multiplying the number of weights by the distance from the fulcrum. All configurations can be predicted with confidence. No children used this rule.

Study 1

The subjects consisted of 154 children, aged from 5 to 9, from a public elementary school in Ithaca, New York. There were 51 children from the kindergarten, 56 6–7-year-olds, and 47 8–9-year-olds, approximately equally divided by gender.

Each child was pretested individually by being asked to predict the movement of the beam when differing configurations of weights were placed at differing distances from the fulcrum. The pattern of their predictions determined which of the six rules they were using. The treatment phase of the study consisted of four different conditions. Some children were again tested as individuals; they had no partner with whom to discuss their predictions. In the remaining three conditions, children were paired. In Condition 2 (equal rule partners) each child was paired with a partner who had used, at the pretest, the same rule. In Condition 3 (lower partners) each child was paired with a partner who had used a rule one or two higher. In Condition 4 (higher partners) each child was paired with a partner who had used a rule one or two lower. The partners took turns predicting the beam's movement. In the event of a disagreement in prediction, they were asked to discuss their predictions until they reached agreement. In each case the pairs consisted of children of

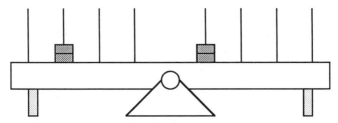

Figure 6.1. The balance beam

the same age, gender, and class in school. The sample of target children (not including those who served as their partners) consisted of 97 children.

Thus, in each condition the social contexts were different. In the first there was no partner with whom to discuss the problem. In the other three the superficial similarity of context (the presence of a partner) disguised major differences: discussion with a partner who had the same perspective on the problem; discussion with a more competent partner; and discussion with a partner who was less competent.

Following the experimental phase, there were two individual posttests, a minimum of 4 days and 28 days apart, to determine whether collaboration with a partner had induced thinking at a higher level, that is, whether the children had begun to use, independently, a more cognitively sophisticated rule.

The neo-Piagetian position is that cognitive conflict, based on a difference in perspectives, induces cognitive development. This model thus would predict that both lower partners (those paired with a partner who had used a more advanced rule) and higher partners would improve, for both have the same degree of cognitive conflict built into their interactions. The traditional, narrow, interpretation of the zone of proximal development would predict that the lower partners would be the only children to improve, for only they have the opportunity for discussion with more competent partners. Neither the neo-Piagetian view nor this interpretation of the zone of proximal development would predict regression. The broader interpretation of the zone of proximal development, that the zone exists not solely in advance of the child but all around him or her, would predict development for the lower partners but regression for the higher partners, for the social context in which the two types of partners are situated is quite different.

The results indicate a surprising amount of regression for all children except lower partners. As Table 6.2 shows, at the time of the treatment over one-third of the children whose partners used the same rule and almost half of those whose partners used a lower rule adopted a rule that was less sophisticated than the rule they had previously used. More significantly, having come to adopt this rule in conjunction with a partner, in virtually every case the children retained this rule during subsequent individual posttests. The collaboration had a powerful impact, therefore – but for many children the impact was anything but beneficial. Only the lower partners (those paired with a more competent partner) benefited from the interaction. Almost

Table 6.2. *Percentages of children in the 4 conditions who declined, retained the same rule, and improved upon their pretest rule*

	Indivs.	Equal rule	Lower ps.	Higher ps.
Treatment				
Improve	17.1	15.8	57.9	11.1
No movement	56.1	47.4	42.1	44.4
Decline	26.8	36.8	0	44.4
N	41	19	19	19
$X^2 (6) = 20.41$[a]				
1st posttest				
Improve	9.7	5.3	47.4	0
No movement	61.0	63.2	52.6	61.2
Decline	29.3	31.6	0	38.9
N	41	19	19	19
$X^2 (6) = 25.36$[b]				
2nd posttest				
Improve	18.8	10.5	57.9	5.9
No movement	57.9	52.6	36.8	52.9
Decline	26.3	36.8	5.3	41.2
N	38	19	19	17
$X^2 (6) = 21.67$[b]				

[a]$p < .005.$ [b]$p < .001.$

60% adopted a more sophisticated rule during the treatment phase and with few exceptions continued to use that rule during the posttests.[1] To test the generality of these findings, this study was replicated with a sample of children in the Soviet Union (Tudge, 1989). As was found in the Ithaca sample, the lower partners tended to improve, and the higher partners declined more than any other group.

This pattern of results in the two samples suggests that the consequence of collaboration on a task of this nature seems as likely to be regression as development. In Vygotskian terms, the impact of the immediate social context has both a powerful and a lasting effect. Children who were led to think at a higher level through being paired with a more competent peer achieved that higher level in the course of collaboration and generally retained it in subsequent independent performance. The same, unfortunately, was true of children who regressed in their thinking.

What occurred in the course of collaboration that determined whether a child would improve or regress? One factor of importance appears to be the degree of confidence each child brought to the interaction. Confidence was assessed indirectly, by the particular rule used at the time of the pretest. Three of the rules (Rules 1, 3, and 5) do not allow children to make confident predictions of all configurations (for details of the rules, see Table 6.1). For example, children using Rule 1 confidently predicted when one side of the beam had more weights (irrespective of their distance from the fulcrum). However, when the number of weights was equal they

Table 6.3. *The influence of type of pretest rule upon treatment performance, across conditions (Ithaca data only, percentages)*

	Rules (2, 4) allowing confident prediction ($N = 54$)	Rules (1, 3, 5) incorporating some uncertainty ($N = 43$)
Improved	25.9	20.9
No movement	59.3	37.2
Declined	14.8	41.9
$X^2 (2) = 9.1^a$		

$^a p < .05$.

were unsure whether the beam would tip to the left or to the right, because they did not have the concept of balance. Similarly, children using Rule 5 were aware that weight *and* distance had to be considered but had to resort to guessing what would happen when on one side of the beam fewer weights were placed at a greater distance from the fulcrum. Children using these rules were therefore necessarily lacking in confidence when trying to solve some of the problems. On the other hand, children using Rules 2 and 4 had access to a rule that allowed them to answer all problems with confidence. For example, children using Rule 4 believe that distance need be considered only when the number of weights is equal. This rule, although less sophisticated than Rule 5, allows children to predict the beam's performance with confidence.

As can be seen in Table 6.3 (which refers to the Ithaca data), children who used a rule that allowed confident prediction were far less likely to be shifted away from their position during the treatment than those whose rule did not allow confident prediction. So, for example, children using Rule 3 were highly likely to improve in their thinking if paired with a partner who used Rule 4 but were likely to regress if paired with one who used Rule 2.

The degree of confidence that partners brought to bear during the collaboration was not the only important factor determining whether children were likely to improve or regress. Another variable of significance was the reasoning that was brought up by the target children's partner in the course of the interaction. Pairing a child with a partner who, at the time of the pretest, had used a higher rule did not necessarily mean that he or she actually used reasoning indicative of that rule during the discussion. Nevertheless, when children's partners supported their predictions with reasoning at a higher level than that used by the target children the latter were highly likely to improve, whereas if their partners only presented reasoning indicative of a lower rule the target children were likely to regress (see Table 6.4). If their partners only presented reasoning at the same level, they were likely to continue to use the same rule themselves.

This study was designed to examine the impact of being paired with a more

Table 6.4. *The influence of partner's level of reasoning upon treatment performance, across conditions (Ithaca data only, percentages)*

	Lower-level reasoning ($N = 18$)	Same-level reasoning ($N = 20$)	Higher-level reasoning ($N = 15$)
Improved	0	15.0	86.7
No movement	44.4	75.0	6.7
Declined	55.6	10.0	6.7
$X^2 (4) = 42.4^a$			

$^a p < .0001.$

competent, a less competent, or an equally competent peer in a situation in which level of thinking and degree of confidence were not confounded. The results indicate that the effects of collaboration on cognitive development are less clear-cut than the neo-Piagetians have argued and than has been assumed by Vygotskian scholars. One child may be more competent than another, as measured in an individual pretest, but if this level of thinking is not held with some degree of confidence there is no reason to expect that she will be able to aid her partner's thinking, particularly if she does not actually introduce that higher level of thinking in the course of discussion.

In this study, the main comparison of interest was with Piaget-inspired research. When a conserver is paired with a nonconserver and the children are asked to reach a joint decision about the conservation problem, they receive no independent confirmation or disconfirmation of their views. The problem is resolved solely on the verbal plane. For this reason, the children working with the balance beam problems received no confirmation or disconfirmation of their predictions.

This methodology, while allowing a precise comparison with the neo-Piagetian research, does not allow the best assessment of many problem-solving situations that occur in school. When children are asked to solve a problem in the classroom, whether in groups or alone, they generally receive feedback; they find out whether their attempts at solution were successful. For this reason, a second study was conducted, in which feedback was provided after the children had reached agreement on their predictions.

Study 2

In the second study information was explicitly provided, in the form of feedback from the materials. With minor exceptions, the design was the same as in the earlier study. The main change was that, after the children had reached agreement in their predictions about the movement of the balance beam, the supports holding it in place were removed. One hundred and eighty children, aged 6–8, took part in this study. Two-thirds of them were assigned to the feedback condition, one-third to the no-feedback condition. Only children of the same age, gender, and class in school were paired, and assignment to feedback/no-feedback conditions was designed to ensure, wherever possible, a match in the two conditions of the child's pretest rule and his partner's pretest rule. Children were randomly designated as "target" children or "partners," and target children were randomly assigned to one of the four treatment conditions (individuals, equal rule, lower partners, and higher partners). A further change was that the range of problems given to the children during the treatment was restricted, half of the problems solvable by application of the target child's pretest rule and half solvable only by a rule one or two above the pretest rule. The reason for this change was to ensure that the children receiving feedback would not be exposed to information too far ahead of their current level of thinking; hence the performance of the children who did not receive feedback cannot be compared with those from the first study, in which children were presented with the full range of problems. As in the previous study, lower and higher partners differed by no more than two rules.

The main hypotheses were, first, that children receiving feedback would improve more than those who did not, because only in the feedback condition did the target children receive information relating to rules one or two above their current level of thinking, and second, that of the children who received feedback lower partners (those with more competent partners to help them) would improve the most.

To reveal the effect of receiving feedback, the analyses reported here used only the two subsamples matched by pretest rule and distinguished solely by whether or not they received feedback. There was clear support for the first hypothesis. At the time of the first posttest, of the 34 target children who had not received feedback only 13 improved, compared to 25 of the 34 children who had received feedback. The difference was even clearer at the time of the second posttest, when 7 of the 13 children not receiving feedback who had improved at the time of the first posttest had reverted to their pretest rule. By comparison, all 25 children in the feedback condition who had improved continued to do so, and one other child in this group also had moved up by this time.

On the other hand, lower partners did not improve significantly more than the other children. Feedback from the materials, when the problems to be solved were not far in advance of the children's current level of thinking, seems to have been sufficient to increase understanding of the problem irrespective of the effects of collaborating with a partner. The fact that children who had collaborated with a more competent partner did not benefit to a greater degree may have been because ceiling effects were reached too easily – although further research (currently under way) is needed to verify this conclusion. It is clear, however, that impersonal feedback (from the materials alone) may be as effective as interpersonal assistance in promoting development within the zone of proximal development.

The results of these two studies indicate that care has to be taken in specifying the likely consequences of peer collaboration. The neo-Piagetian research has demonstrated that children can gain markedly from being paired with a more competent partner. This research ties in well with traditional notions relating to the zone of proximal development, which provide additional theoretical support for the beneficial effects of this type of peer collaboration. Research into adult–child interaction conducted by scholars working in the Vygotskian tradition also supports the more traditional view that collaboration leads to development. It is clear, however, that adult–child interaction and peer collaboration in which the more competent partner is also more confident are not typical of all interaction, and that peer collaboration can lead to regression as well as to development. The results from Study 2 suggest that when children receive feedback from the materials they benefit. Further research is clearly necessary and too much weight should not be placed upon one study, but the indications are that when feedback is provided its impact overshadows any effects of discussion with a partner.

In general, these results suggest that any model of the effects of peer collaboration on cognitive development has to be more multifaceted than is implied by either the concept of cognitive conflict or the relativistically teleological view of the zone of proximal development. To talk simply about cognitive conflict, or about providing information within a child's zone of proximal development, is insufficient. It may be adequate when the more competent child of a pairing is also more confident, as when a conserver is paired with a nonconserver, or when a child who knows how to solve some problem in math is assigned to act as a teacher of another child who does not. But cases of peer interaction in which competence and confidence are not confounded are likely to be a good deal more variable in their consequences. In fact, children are likely to regress in their thinking when confronted with less competent partners who are not confident of their views and when feedback is not provided.

How far can a child be led to regress? One would expect that, just as information provided that is too far in advance of a child's thinking (i.e., not within his or her zone of proximal development) will not lead to development, so information too far below his or her thinking will not lead to regression. But when some area of knowledge is not well understood, we should expect to see regression if the child is working with a partner whose thinking in that domain is at a lower level.

The implication for teachers is that they must do more than merely ask children to collaborate to solve a problem, or even to pair a child who is more advanced in his thinking with one who is less advanced. It goes without saying that the children should be interested in the task and share the goal of solving it; in addition, however, the results of their attempted solutions should be both immediate and visible (Kamii & De Vries, 1978; Tudge & Caruso, 1988).

Toward a more complete model of the effects of peer collaboration

Although researchers have typically not examined factors likely to lead to regression as a result of peer collaboration, in recent years there has been increasing recognition of the complexity of the effects of peer interaction on cognitive development. For example, Azmitia and her colleagues (Azmitia, 1988; Azmitia & Perl-mutter, in press) have argued that models of the effects of collaboration on cognitive development have to take into account such factors as the age of the collaborators (older children being more skilled at verbal interaction) and the extent of engage-ment in the task. Damon and Phelps (1987) have argued that different types of peer interaction should be distinguished in terms of the degree of equality of relationship and degree of mutual involvement displayed by the peers. They distinguish peer tutoring, peer collaboration, and cooperative learning. They are not convinced of the value of cooperative learning but feel that peer tutoring can be effective for "the consolidation of insights already attained" whereas peer collaboration "can have lasting effects on children's understanding of difficult conceptual material" (Damon & Phelps, 1987, pp. 27, 29). Damon and Phelps's data seem supportive of the beneficial effects of collaboration, but their statement that "any peer dialogue is a cooperative, consensual, and nonauthoritarian exchange of ideas" seems overly optimistic.

Other researchers, notably Johnson and Johnson (1975; Johnson, Maruyama, Johnson, Nelson, & Skon, 1981) and Slavin (1980, 1983a, 1983b, 1987) have examined peer cooperation from a perspective that derives from neither Vygotsky not Piaget. Meta-analytical studies of research comparing individual learning with group learning suggest that motivational factors must be considered when discuss-ing the effectiveness of collaboration. If one member of a supposedly cooperative enterprise lacks interest in the group goal, there is no reason to expect him or her to benefit from it. Slavin (1983b) argues that extrinsic motivation, in the form of some type of reward for the group or partnership, and individual accountability are necessary if collaboration is to be successful. Research conducted in the classroom supports his contention: 25 of 28 studies of cooperative learning with group rewards found that children who were grouped fared significantly better than individuals (Slavin, 1983b).

However, although Slavin (1987) explicitly distinguishes research that focuses on motivational factors from research in the Vygotskian and Piagetian traditions, the most recent neo-Piagetian and Vygotskian research has stressed the importance of the participants' active involvement in collaborative problem solving (Bearison, in press; Damon and Phelps, 1987; Forman & Cazden, 1985; Kol'tsova, 1978; Light, 1986; Light & Perret-Clermont, 1989; Lomov, 1978; Martin, 1985; Rubtsov, 1981). Motivation, in this case the desire to construct joint or group solutions to problems, is viewed as highly relevant. This research has moved away from a focus upon pairing a more competent child with one who is less competent to greater attention to the processes of collaboration when two children of approximately equal levels collaborate. Bearison (in press), for example, argues that one has to attend to the ways in which children arrive at a common point of view rather than to the process of conflict itself, and Light and Perret-Clermont (1989) stress the impor-tance of arriving at shared meaning.

Researchers working within the Vygotskian tradition have also focused their at-tention upon the processes of collaboration rather than upon conflict, arguing that for interaction to be effective children have to work toward accomplishing joint goals. For example, Forman and her colleagues (Forman, 1986; Forman & Cazden, 1985; Forman, Gilman, Kaur, & McPhail, 1987; Forman & Kraker, 1985) have examined the ways in which young adolescents arrive at greater understanding of various tasks (including Piaget's chemicals task and a projection-of-shadows problem) in the course of collaboration. Forman argued that the most important aspect of this collaboration is the ability on the part of the partners to engage in "social coordination." Forman (1981, cited in Forman, 1986) found that fourth-graders initially did not attempt to coordinate their activities with those of their partners. However, over the course of a 7-month period many became increasingly able to work together and eventually to subordinate their individual roles to those of the partnership, in order to achieve a joint goal. Similarly, Martin (1985; Kol'tsova & Martin, 1985) has argued that the cognitive benefits derived from collaboration on a mathematical balance beam task were most likely to occur when children in a team set themselves a joint goal and worked toward it.

Recent studies of the effects of peer interaction conducted in the Soviet Union have also examined the degree of involvement in the collaborative process. Kol'tsova (1978), for example, argued that children were more likely to learn rich, precise, and well-developed historical concepts when working in groups than when working individually. Not all groups performed equally; Kol'tsova pointed to "active participation" in a group goal as being a necessary component. Another was the opportunity "for critical evaluation that emerged during the course of the joint discussion and to the refining of different views" (1978, p. 35). Similarly, Lomov (1978) found much the same results in his study of recall under individual and joint conditions, and Rubstov (1981; Rubtsov & Guzman, 1984–1985) has argued that children solved classification tasks and complex trajectory construction far better when working jointly to achieve their goals.

Although researchers are acknowledging that the effects of peer interaction on cognitive development are more complex than what is implied by typical conceptions of the zone of proximal development, this revision does not constitute a rejection of this concept. As I have argued, it is necessary to view the zone of proximal development in the context of Vygotsky's overall theoretical position. Vygotsky's position incorporates a view of the developmental process that stresses the joint attainment of meaning (Tudge & Rogoff, 1989). There is no guarantee that the meaning that is created when two peers interact will be at a higher level, even if one child is more competent than another and is providing information within the less competent peer's zone of proximal development. Rather than casually assuming the cognitive benefits of pairing a child with a more competent peer, we should pay more attention to the processes of interaction themselves.

Note

1 Some of this change from one rule to another may be attributable to regression artifacts – higher partners, on average, had necessarily used a higher rule at the time of the pretest than the lower

partners. But it should be noted that "higher" and "lower" are defined in terms of the pair; it was not the case that higher partners consistently used high rules. A Rule 2 user, paired with a child who used Rule 1, would be a higher partner; a Rule 4 user, paired with a child who used Rule 5, would be a lower partner. Irrespective of how high or low their initial rules were, lower partners tended either to retain their original rule or to improve whereas higher partners tended either to retain their original rule or to decline.

References

Ames, G. J., & Murray, F. B. (1982). When two wrongs make a right: Promoting cognitive change by social conflict. *Developmental Psychology, 18*, 894–987.

Azmitia, M. (1988). Peer interaction and problem solving: When are two heads better than one? *Child Development, 59*, 87–96.

Azmitia, M., & Perlmutter, M. (in press). Social influences on children's cognition: State of the art and future directions. In H. Reese (Ed.), *Advances in child development and behavior*. New York: Academic Press.

Bearison, D. J. (in press). Interactional contexts of cognitive development: Piagetian approaches to sociogenesis. In L. Tolchinsky (Ed.), *Culture, cognition, and schooling*. Norwood, NJ: Ablex.

Bearison, D. J., Magzamen, S., & Filardo, E. K. (1986). Socio-cognitive conflict and cognitive growth in young children. *Merrill-Palmer Quarterly, 32*, 51–72.

Cole, M. (1985). The zone of proximal development: Where culture and cognition create one another. In J. Wertsch (Ed.), *Culture, communication, and cognition: Vygotskian perspectives* (pp. 146–161). Cambridge: Cambridge University Press.

Damon, W., & Phelps, E. (1987, June). *Peer collaboration as a context for cognitive growth*. Paper presented at Tel Aviv University, School of Education.

Doise, W., & Mugny, G. (1984). *The social development of the intellect*. Oxford: Pergamon.

Ellis, S., & Rogoff, B. (1982). The strategies and efficacy of child versus adult teachers. *Child Development, 43*, 730–735.

Ellis, S., & Rogoff, B. (1986). Problem solving in children's management of instruction. In E. Mueller & C. Cooper (Eds.), *Process and outcome in peer relationships* (pp. 301–325). New York: Academic Press.

Forman, E. A. (1981). The role of collaboration in problem solving in children. *Dissertation Abstracts International, 42*, 2563B. (University Microfilms No. 81-25, 480)

Forman, E. A. (1986, April). *Learning through peer interaction: A Vygotskian perspective*. Paper presented at the annual meeting of the American Educational Research Association, San Francisco.

Forman, E. A., & Cazden, C. B. (1985). Exploring Vygotskian perspectives in education: The cognitive value of peer interaction. In J. V. Wertsch (Ed.), *Culture, communication, and cognition: Vygotskian perspectives* (pp. 323–347). Cambridge: Cambridge University Press.

Forman, E. A., Gilman, R., Kaur, B., & McPhail, J. (1987, April). The negotiation of task goals & strategies in a collaborative problem-solving activity. In C. Wallat (Chair), *Discourse in experimental contexts*. Symposium conducted at the annual meeting of the American Educational Research Association, Washington, DC.

Forman, E. A., & Kraker, M. J. (1985). The social origins of logic: The contributions of Piaget and Vygotsky. In M. W. Berkowitz (Ed.), *Peer conflict and cognitive growth* (pp. 23–39). San Francisco: Jossey-Bass.

Griffin, P., & Cole, M. (1984). Current activity for the future: The zo-ped. In B. Rogoff & J. V. Wertsch (Eds.), *Children's learning in the "zone of proximal development"* (pp. 45–64). San Francisco: Jossey-Bass.

Inhelder, B., & Piaget, J. (1958). *The growth of logical thinking from childhood to adolescence*. New York: Basic.

Johnson, D. W., & Johnson, R. T. (1975). *Learning together and more: Cooperation, competition, and individualization*. Englewood Cliffs, NJ: Prentice-Hall.

Johnson, D. W., Maruyama, G., Johnson, R., Nelson, D., & Skon, L. (1981). Effects of cooperative, competitive, and individualistic goal structures on achievement: A meta-analysis. *Psychological Bulletin, 89*, 47–62.

Kamii C., & De Vries, R. (1978). *Physical knowledge in preschool education: Implications of Piaget's theories.* Englewood Cliffs, NJ: Prentice-Hall.

Kol'tsova, V. A. (1978). Experimental study of cognitive activity in communication (with specific reference to concept formation). *Soviet Psychology, 17*(1), 23–38.

Kol'tsova, V. A., & Martin, L. M. W. (1985). Lichnostnie determinanti obshcheniya v usloviyakh sovmestnoi poznavatel'noi deyatel'nosti [Individual determinants of communication in the context of joint cognitive activity]. In B. F. Lomov, A. V. Belyaeva, & V. N. Nosulenko (Eds.), *Psikhologicheskie issledovaniya obshcheniya* [Psychological studies of communication] (pp. 207–219). Moscow: Nauka.

Light, P. (1986). Context, conservation, and conversation. In M. Richards & P. Light (Eds.), *Children of social worlds.* (pp. 170–190). Cambridge, MA: Harvard University Press.

Light, P., & Perret-Clermont, A.-N. (1989). Social context effects in learning and testing. In A. Gellatly, D. Rogers, & J. A. Sloboda (Eds.), *Cognition and social worlds* (pp. 99–112). Oxford: Oxford University Press.

Lomov, B. F. (1978). Pyschological processes and communication. *Soviet Psychology, 17*(1), 3–22.

Martin, L. (1985). The role of social interaction in children's problem solving. *Quarterly Newsletter of the Laboratory for Comparative Human Cognition, 7,* 40–45.

Miller, S. (1986). Certainty and necessity in the understanding of Piagetian concepts. *Developmental Psychology, 26,* 3–18.

Miller, S., & Brownell, C. (1975). Peers, persuasion, and Piaget: Dyadic interaction between conservers and nonconservers. *Child Development, 46,* 972–997.

Miller, S., Brownell, C., & Zukier, H. (1977). Cognitive certainty in children: Effects of concept, developmental level, and method of assessment. *Developmental Psychology, 13,* 236–243.

Mosier, C., & Rogoff, B. (1989). *Infants' instrumental use of their mothers.* Manuscript submitted for publication.

Mugny, G., & Doise, W. (1978). Socio-cognitive conflict and structure of individual and collective performance. *European Journal of Social Psychology, 8,* 181–192.

Murray, F. B. (1972). Acquisition of conservation through social interaction. *Developmental Psychology, 6,* 1–6.

Murray, F. B. (1982). Teaching through social conflict. *Contemporary Educational Psychology, 7,* 257–271.

Murray, F. B. (1987). Necessity: The developmental component in school mathematics. In L. S. Liben (Ed.), *Development and learning: Conflict or congruence?* (pp. 51–69). Hillsdale, NJ: Erlbaum.

Perret-Clermont, A.-N. (1980). *Social interaction and cognitive development in children.* London: Academic Press.

Radziszewska, B., & Rogoff, B. (1988). Influence of adult and peer collaborators on children's planning skills. *Developmental Psychology, 24,* 840–848.

Rogoff, B. (1989). *Apprenticeship in thinking: Cognitive development in social context.* New York: Oxford University Press.

Rogoff, B., & Gardner, W. (1984). Adult guidance of cognitive development. In B. Rogoff & J. Lave (Eds.), *Everyday cognition: Its development in social context* (pp. 95–116). Cambridge, MA: Harvard University Press.

Rogoff, B., Malkin, C., & Gilbride, K. (1984). Interaction with babies as guidance in development. In B. Rogoff & J. Wertsch (Eds.), *Children's learning in the "zone of proximal development"* (pp. 31–44). San Francisco: Jossey-Bass.

Rogoff, B., Mistry, J., Radziszewska, B., & Germond, J. (in press). Infants' instrumental social interaction with adults. In S. Feinman (Ed.), *Social referencing and the social construction of reality in infancy.* New York: Plenum.

Rogoff, B., & Radziszewska, B. (1985, April). *The influence of collaboration with parents versus peers in learning to plan.* Paper presented at the meetings of the Society for Research in Child Development, Toronto. (Reprinted in *Resources in Education* [ERIC], September, 1985)

Rogoff, B., & Wertsch, J. V. (Eds.) (1984). *Children's learning in the "zone of proximal development."* San Francisco: Jossey-Bass.

Rubtsov, V. V. (1981). The role of cooperation in the development of intelligence. *Soviet Psychology, 19*(4), 41–62.

Rubtsov, V. V., & Guzman, R. Y. (1984–1985). Psychological characteristics of the methods pupils use to organize joint activity in dealing with a school task. *Soviet Psychology, 23*(2), 65–84.

Saxe, G. B., Gearhart, M., & Guberman, S. B. (1984). The social organization of early number development. In B. Rogoff & J. V. Wertsch (Eds.), *Children's learning in the "zone of proximal development"* (pp. 19–30). San Francisco: Jossey-Bass.

Saxe, G. B., Guberman, S. R., & Gearheart, M. (1988). Social processes in early number development. *Monographs of the Society for Research in Child Development, 52*(2, Serial No. 216).

Siegler, R. S. (1976). Three aspects of cognitive development. *Cognitive Psychology, 4,* 481–520.

Siegler, R. S. (1981). Developmental sequences within and between concepts. *Monographs of the Society for Research in Child Development, 46*(2).

Slavin, R. E. (1980). Effects of student teams and peer tutoring on academic achievement and time-on-task. *Journal of Experimental Education, 48,* 252–257.

Slavin, R. E. (1983a). *Cooperative learning.* New York: Longman.

Slavin, R. E. (1983b). When does cooperative learning increase student achievement? *Psychological Bulletin, 94,* 429–445.

Slavin, R. E. (1987). Developmental and motivational perspectives on cooperative learning: A reconciliation. *Child Development, 58,* 1161–1167.

Tudge, J. R. H. (1986a, May). *Beyond conflict: The role of reasoning in collaborative problem solving.* Paper presented at the Jean Piaget Society, Philadelphia. (Reprinted in *Resources in Education* [ERIC], May 1987)

Tudge, J. R. H. (1986b, April). *Collaboration, conflict, and cognitive development: The efficacy of joint problem solving.* Paper presented at the Eastern Psychological Conference, New York. (Reprinted in *Resources in Education* [ERIC], February 1987)

Tudge, J. R. H. (1989). When collaboration leads to regression: Some negative consequences of socio-cognitive conflict. *European Journal of Social Psychology, 19,* 123–138.

Tudge, J. R. H., & Caruso, D. (1988). Cooperative problem solving in the classroom: Enhancing young children's cognitive development. *Young Children, 44,* 46–52.

Tudge, J. R. H., & Rogoff, B. (1989). Peer influences on cognitive development: Piagetian and Vygotskian perspectives. In M. Bornstein & J. Bruner (Eds.), *Interaction in human development* (pp. 17–40). Hillsdale, NJ: Erlbaum.

Valsiner, J. (1987). *Culture and the development of children's action: A cultural-historical theory of developmental psychology.* New York: Wiley.

Vygotsky, L.S. (1978). *Mind in society: The development of higher psychological processes.* Cambridge, MA: Harvard University Press.

Vygotsky, L. S. (1987). *The collected works of L. S. Vygotsky: Vol. 1. Problems of general psychology* (R. W. Rieber & A. S. Carton, Eds.; N. Minick, Trans.). New York: Plenum.

Vygotsky, L. S. (in press). *The collected works of L. S. Vygotsky: Vol 2. Problems of abnormal psychology and learning disabilities: The fundamentals of defektology* (R. W. Rieber & A. S. Carton, Eds.; J. E. Knox & K. Stevens, Trans.). New York: Plenum.

Wertsch, J. V. (1979). From social interaction to higher psychological processes. *Human Development, 22,* 1–22.

Wertsch, J. V. (1980) The significance of dialogue in Vygotsky: Account of social, egocentric, and inner speech. *Contemporary Educational Psychology, 5,* 150–162.

Wertsch, J. V. (1985a). *Vygotsky and the social formation of mind.* Cambridge, MA: Harvard University Press.

Wertsch, J. V. (Ed.) (1985b). *Culture, communication, and cognition: Vygotskian perspectives.* Cambridge: Cambridge University Press.

Wertsch, J. V., Minick, M., & Arns, F. J. (1984). The creation of context in joint problem solving action: A cross-cultural study. In B. Rogoff & J. Lave (Eds.), *Everyday cognition: Its development in social context* (pp. 151–171). Cambridge, MA: Harvard University Press.

Part II

Educational implications

7   Teaching mind in society: Teaching, schooling, and literate discourse

Ronald Gallimore and Roland Tharp

Time and again in this century the impulse to improve public schools has fallen short of reformist hopes. One reason for limited progress has been the absence of a basis for understanding and correcting teaching and schooling. Although the ideas of Vygotsky are having a profound influence on education, they are not alone sufficient to construct a fully satisfying theory of education. The achievements of social, cognitive, and behavioral science – achievements that have detailed the processes of learning in social interactions – must be brought into conjunction with the neo-Vygotskian understanding now being created. Such a union of neo-Vygotskian and behavioral/cognitive scientific principles can accelerate the impact of research on the practice of teaching and schooling and radically increase the explanatory power of neo-Vygotskian theory (Tharp & Gallimore, 1988).

Constructing a theory of education

For over 100 years, there has been ample evidence that recitation, not teaching, is the predominant experience of American school children. Sitting silently, students read assigned texts, complete "ditto" sheets, and take tests. On those rare occasions when they are encouraged to speak, teachers control the topic and participation. Connected discourse occurs so rarely that observation detects barely a trace (e.g., Durkin, 1978–1979; Goodlad, 1984). Even in more effective classrooms, teachers do little that meets any acceptable image of serious interactive teaching.

If we are to build a theory of teaching, evidence must come from elsewhere than schools. The most effective teaching occurs in other settings of socialization, from child rearing to employee-training programs. From these teaching–learning interactions in nonschooled settings, we can derive principles that schools should use to produce effective teaching. These same principles can guide the design of schools,

An elaborated discussion of the theory and research presented here can be found in R. G. Tharp and R. Gallimore (1988), *Rousing minds to life: Teaching, learning, and schooling in social context* (Cambridge: Cambridge University Press).

The research on which this paper is based was supported by the Princess Bernice Pauahi Bishop Estate/ Kamehameha Schools. Additional resources were provided by the National Institute of Child Health and Human Development, the Sociobehavioral Research Group of the Mental Retardation Research Center at UCLA, and the University of Hawaii.

175

so that their social organization will foster, rather than impede, the teaching and learning of all their members. Such a set of principles will constitute an integrated neo-Vygotskian theory of education.

A theory of teaching as assisted performance

Vygotsky argued that a child's development cannot be understood by a study of the individual. We must also examine the external social world in which that individual life has developed. Cognitive and linguistic skill appears "twice, or in two planes. First it appears on the social plane, and then on the psychological plane. First it appears between people as an interpsychological category, and then within the child as an intrapsychological category" (Vygotsky, 1978, p. 163).

In the following example of an excellent instructional conversation, a Navajo teacher assists some third-grade children to comprehend the concept of *hero*. The discussion began with John Kennedy and John Glenn, but the children's understanding of *hero* unfolds through the interaction and comes to include some surprising examples.

> Teacher: Jimmie, what would you call a hero? Who would you call a hero?
> Cindy: John Glenn.
> Jimmie: Superman!
> Teacher: What did he have to do to make him a hero?
> Nick: Apache Chief.
> Teacher: OK, what would Apache Chief have to do to be a hero?
> Jimmie: He-Man!
> Emma: John Glenn! John Glenn!
> Teacher: Or He-Man.

The nominations are useful: Superman, He-Man, Apache Chief, and John Glenn are all acceptable as members of the class "heroes" and can be used by the children to work out the concept. Unfortunately, they drift away from the task set by the teacher into some loose associations:

> Emma: A rocket, blah blah.
> Jimmie: Cartoons! Cartoons!
> Emma: Bugs Bunny! [Emma and Nick laugh.]

The teacher gets the children back on the track by refocusing the discussion.

> Teacher: What could Superman do that would make him a hero?
> Jimmie: Bullets . . . ! [In Navajo: He dodges the bullets!]
> Teacher: Oh, he doesn't dodge any bullets.
> Nick: Helps people.
> Teacher: Who helps people?
> Nick: Superman. }
>   }
> Jimmie: He-Man. }
> Teacher: Superman?
> Nick: And He-Man.
> Teacher: What about the chief you were talking about?

Nick: [Explains in Navajo that he saw "Apache Chief" on television.]
Teacher: What does he do?
Jimmie: [Explains in Navajo by giving an incident.]
Nick: He helps people.
Teacher: Yeah.
Nick: [Says softly in Navajo that Superman helps people too.]
Teacher: I think that it's good because . . . if somebody helps people, then I would think he's a hero.
Nick: A hero.
(Adapted from Tharp & Gallimore, 1988, pp. 67–69; Afton Sells, teacher)

The children had the bits of information necessary to construct a meaning, and the teacher assisted by providing the structure and the questions that provoked the assembly of that information and its organization. In the excerpt, all the components of the process are present, but they are assembled from the separate contributions of the children and the teacher. By adolescence, most children will have internalized the process of approaching a new concept. They will query themselves as to its possible meanings, match them against the text, try out new class members, and proceed until the sources are integrated. However, until internalization occurs, *performance must be assisted.*

Distinguishing the *proximal zone* from the *developmental level* by contrasting *assisted* versus *unassisted* performance has profound implications for educational practice. It is in the proximal zone that teaching may be defined in terms of child development. In Vygotskian terms, teaching is good only when it *"awakens and rouses to life those functions which are in a stage of maturing, which lie in the zone of proximal development."* (Vgyotsky, 1956, p. 278, quoted in Wertsch & Stone, 1985, italics in original)

We can therefore derive this general definition of teaching: *teaching consists of assisting performance through the Zone of Proximal Development. Teaching can be said to occur when assistance is offered at points in the ZPD at which performance requires assistance.* (Tharp & Gallimore, 1988, chap. 2)

The means of assisting performance

In the transition from other-assistance to self-assistance (internalization and automatization) there are variations in the *means by which assistance is provided.* By discussing the several qualitatively different means of assisting performance, we have the opportunity to connect neo-Vygotskian ideas with a broader literature of American and British psychology.

Psychology of this century has focused on six means of assisting performance: *modeling, contingency, managing, feeding back, instructing, questioning, and cognitive structuring.* The study of each of these means of assistance has "belonged" to different theories, different disciplines, and even to different nations. By considering them together, we can link large areas of Western psychology to the neo-Vygotskian theory, and the explanatory power of both is increased substantially.

In industrialized, urban society, the dominant means of assistance do appear to be linguistic. However, we risk distorting our understanding of human processes by considering only a narrow range of cultural interactions. Our own technological culture may seem to require verbal explanation before children can understand adult activities; but this is a requirement of a particular society, not a requirement of cognitive development (Nerlove & Snipper, 1981; Rogoff, 1982; Scribner & Cole, 1981).

> In non-technological societies, adult behaviors are learned and understood with only occasional verbal explanation. Such societies rely heavily on "observational" learning; this is practical where adult behaviors and role performances are available for prolonged and careful scrutiny by children – in cultures that are "within the direct reach of the sensory organs" of the child (Fortes, 1938; Pettit, 1946). This means that children are incorporated into the activity settings of the society. The process has been put succinctly by Margaret Tafoya, doyen of American Indian potters, herself both daughter and mother in a family of distinguished artists in clay:

>> My girls, I didn't teach them . . . they watched and learned by trying. I was taught to stay with the traditional clay designs, because that was the way it was handed down to my mother and me. I am thankful for my mother teaching me to make the large pieces (which require special skill and understanding). I watched her and tried to do like she did. And, I did. (Tafoya, 1983)

> John-Steiner & Oesterrich . . . discuss this Pueblo Indian culture and provide a link from typical interpersonal events to intra-psychological processes:

>> Children listening to the many legends of their people learn to represent these visually . . . because they are not allowed to ask questions or verbally reflect on what they hear. They are to say only *aeh hae* to acknowledge auditory attention. As a result, while the verbal representations of some of these legends are fairly simple nursery tales, the inner representations of the same legends, for older children and adults, are replete with highly abstract visual and symbolic articulations of cultural value. (John-Steiner & Oesterreich, 1975, p. 192)

> That which is modeled is internalized and represented by the learner as an image, a paradigm-icon, for self-guidance. The image of the expert's hands on the loom is transformed into an intra-psychological standard for comparison and feedback as the learning weaver watches her own fingers fly. (Quoted from Tharp & Gallimore, 1988; for a detailed discussion of these issues, see Jordan, Tharp, & Vogt, 1985; Tharp, 1985, 1987; White, Tharp, Jordan, & Vogt, 1987.)

Of course, modeling and feedback are means of assistance used in all societies, including our own. There are many examples, such as athletic coaching (Tharp & Gallimore, 1976a). Therefore, the means of assistance are not restricted to language. The full list also includes those nonlinguistic and paralinguistic means that have been identified over several decades of research in behaviorist and cognitive psychology. Although Vygotsky insisted on the primacy of linguistic means in the development of higher mental processes, this does not mean that all means of assisting performance are linguistic. We propose a list of six means of assistance, gleaned from research of this century. Others may well emerge; the list is surely not final. Each in turn will be briefly described.

Modeling. Modeling is the process of offering behavior for imitation. Not all imitated models are intentionally offered, of course. The socialization of children and other new members into cultures is largely accomplished by their imitation of mature members' culturally organized but unreflective acts. Most traditional and pre-technological cultures teach their offspring largely through modeling, rather than through a verbal emphasis (Scribner & Cole, 1973). These acts of modeling take place during activities created by the family's ecocultural niche – working the fields, caring for domestic animals, collecting and preparing food, caring for children, weaving, and other such tasks. Children take part in these activities through a process of guided participation (Rogoff, in press), in which opportunities to learn through modeling are seamlessly woven into subsistence and family maintenance, the fabric of everyday life.

Many parameters of the modeling/imitation process are now well known (Bandura, 1977). Whether or not imitation of models will occur is affected by the comparative age and sex of modeler and imitator; the presence of reinforcement for the behavior; whether or not the model is live or depicted; relationship factors among the actors; the generalized repertoire of imitation itself, which can be strengthened or weakened by reinforcement and punishment (Staats, 1968); and many other factors, all of which are complexly interactive.

Modeling is a powerful means of assisting performance, one that continues its effectiveness into adult years and into the highest reaches of behavioral complexity. In the educational setting, both expert teachers and peer models are highly important sources of assisted performance, for children and adults alike.

Contingency management. Contingency management is the means of assisting performance by which rewards and punishments are arranged to follow behavior, depending on whether the behavior is desired or not. It is composed of a set of techniques so well known by now that few readers will need another explication. Review can be had on a research level from Bandura (1969), or on the level of practice from Tharp and Wetzel (1969).

All manner of rewards have been used in contingency management – the social reinforcements of praise and encouragement, material reinforcements of consumables or privileges, tokens and symbolic rewards. In most educational prescriptions, punishments are restricted to the loss of some positive opportunity or to brief, firm reprimands. In effective teaching, contingency management is focused on positive behavior and positive rewards. When these prescriptions are followed, classrooms that employ contingency management as a means of assistance are productive and pleasant in emotional tone.

Widespread use of contingency management in the 1960s and 1970s led to many incompetent applications and considerable opposition to the concept – some in response to the mechanistic, reductive theory of conditioning by which contingency management was often and inappropriately justified. This is unfortunate because contingency management is not operant conditioning (Homme, 1966; Tharp & Wetzel, 1969). The effects of contingencies on behavior are strong; but they do not need to be explained by operant conditioning and indeed are as well explained by philosophical utilitarianism, cognitive science, game theory, and a host of competing theories.

Contingency management cannot be used to originate new behaviors. Novel skills must be elicited by other means of assistance – modeling, instructing, cognitive structuring, and questioning. But the rewards, praises, and encouragements that follow a behavior strengthen each point of advance through the zone of proximal development, preventing loss of ground. This bulwarking of gains already made is of vital assistance to performance.

Feeding back. Feeding back information on performance is a powerful means of assistance. Feedback alone can guide a student to substantial improvement in performance on the next try. Providing for feedback is the most common and single most effective means of self-assistance; this has been demonstrated for virtually all problematic behaviors in which self-regulation has been studied (Watson & Tharp, 1988). Feedback is such an ingrained part of normal life that it goes unnoticed; without feedback to the self, no correction – or even maintenance – is possible.

In educational programs, feedback on performance is vital to every participant, although the form it takes in current practice is often inconsistent or too remote to be useful. Feeding back performance information to students can be done in many forms: criterion-referenced test data, achievement test data, instantaneous teacher responses to children's conversation, and grade work sheets among others.

Feedback is a concept derived from cybernetics and must be understood in the context of other concepts of that system. Simply providing performance information is not feedback; there will be no performance assistance unless the information provided is compared to some standard. The self-regulation literature emphasizes the necessity for setting standards (as goals and subgoals) and for setting up specific procedures for regular comparison of feedback information to that standard (Carver & Scheier, 1981; Tharp, Gallimore, & Calkins, 1984; Watson & Tharp, 1988).

Feeding back occurs in interactive teaching. When the discussions have to do with matters of fact, it is important that students get feedback about accuracy. The setting of standards for accuracy is an important part of this process. How does that happen? Some of the ways it happens illustrate the interdependency of the means of assistance.

For example modeling provides standards. Students can observe peers who are *reinforced* for prompt completion of work and thereby have a standard set by example. Standards can be set by simple instructions (a means of assistance discussed below). Indeed, all the means of assisting performance can be used to regulate standard setting. Standards for performance can be exemplified by the teacher instructing the children to repeat the process until accuracy is achieved. The interdependence of the means of assisting performance is a topic to which we will return later and which will become clearer as we consider the remaining means of assistance.

Instructing. Instruction is surely the most ubiquitous of all the means of assisting in ordinary life. Compliance with instructions is not inevitable, since effective instructions must be embedded in a context of other effective means, notably contingency management, feeding back, and cognitive structuring.

In typical educational settings, instructions are used primarily in two contexts: on matters of deportment and in assigning tasks. It is unfortunately rare to see instructing used to assist the performance of the next specific act needed to move through the zone of proximal development. Instructions, like other forms of assistance, can be expected to occur only when teachers assume responsibility for assisting performance rather than expecting students to learn on their own.

Of course, too much instructing can be obnoxious to a learner. A measured use of instructing, however, does not create opposition. And it is important that instructing be included in teaching, because the instructing voice of the teacher becomes the self-instructing voice of the learner in the transition from apprentice to self-regulated performer. The noninstructing teacher may be denying the learner the most valuable residue of the teaching interaction: that heard, regulating voice, that gradually internalized voice, which then becomes the pupil's self-regulating "still, small" instructor.

Questioning. Questions assist performance in ways that lie below the surface. This point can be made by comparing the ways that questions assist and the ways that instructions assist. Ervin-Tripp (1976, 1977) considers both instructions and questions as subclasses of *directives.* For example, we may say to a child, "What flowers did you see yesterday?" or we may say, "Tell me what flowers you saw yesterday." These are functionally equivalent means of assisting the child by requiring recall and categorization. At one level of analysis, the question contains the implicit instruction, "(tell me) or (think of) what flowers did you see." According to Ervin-Tripp (1976, 1977), whether this regulation is phrased explicitly or not is a matter of courtesy, or role regulation, not of the process per se.

However, there are important distinctions between questions and instructions in the context of teaching. If the speaker wants action but phrases the directive as a question, "misfires" are a likely result (Ervin-Tripp, 1976, 1977). "Will you dance?" and "Dance!" are not the same, in that the interrogative form, in linguistic logic, *requests a reply in language.* If the dancers are asked "Will you dance?" they might shout "Yes!" but stand still. The instructional form "Dance!" requests a reply in action.

Questioning, in contrast to instructing, provides a distinct and valuable means of assisting performance. Questioning explicitly calls for an active linguistic and cognitive response: It provokes creations by the pupil. A teacher can either ask "What is the meaning of 'democracy'?" or give a lecture on the subject. If the teacher questions, two teaching advantages are gained. First, there is the mental and verbal activation of the pupils, which provides them with practice and exercise. Second, during this exercise of the pupils' speech and thought, the teacher will be able to assist and regulate the students' assembling of evidence and their use of logic. If the teacher only lectures, he or she will never know what the students are thinking (Tharp & Gallimore, 1988).

Not all questions assist performance. We must distinguish those that *assist,* from those that merely *assess.* Durkin (1978–1979), Hoetker and Ahlbrand (1969), Duffy and Roehler (1981), and Tharp and Gallimore (1988), among others, have noted the predominance of the assessment type in typical classrooms. We have already described assessment questions as the major interaction component of the recitation script. The *assessment question* inquires to discover the level of the pupil's ability to perform without assistance. When such questions are used to tailor instruction to the student's point in the zone of proximal development (ZPD), they are one part of competent instruction.

However, most teachers do not distinguish questions that assess from those that assist. This results in the teacher assuming that a request for information constitutes teaching. It does not. Though necessary to teaching, assessment is not itself a means for directly assisting performance. The *assistance question,* on the other hand, inquires in order to produce a mental operation that the pupil cannot or would not produce alone. The assistance provided by the question is the prompting of that mental operation.

Cognitive structuring. As a means of assisting performance, cognitive structuring refers to the provision of a structure for thinking and acting. It may be a structure for beliefs, for mental operations, or for understanding. It organizes, evaluates, and groups and sequences perception, memory, and action. In everyday life, cognitive structures may be more or less formalized, more or less conscious.

From the point of view of the teacher, various kinds of cognitive structures can be provided. They can be grand: world views, philosophies, ethical systems, scientific theories, and religious theologies. Or they can be as modest as giving a name to a thing.

A simple but useful distinction among kinds of cognitive structures can be offered: Type I, *structures of explanation;* and Type II, *structures for cognitive activity.* Type I may be an explanation that molecular activity increases with temperature as gases expand in a third-grade experiment. Or the teacher may say that the story for today is about heroes. In such cases, structure serves to organize perception in new ways. Ice and steam fall into the new science structure. In reading the new story, the readers can group their own feelings of admiration toward some others with the judgment of history on national figures. Evaluation, grouping, and sequencing of both old and new information are performances assisted by these newly developed cognitive structures.

Type II structures operate on the level of cognitive process. Children may be given structures for memorization, or for recall, or for rules for accumulating evidence, as in the following example: "So, whenever you are reading any place and you come to a word that is new to you and you are not sure what the word is, you first look for clues, then put the clues together with what you already know about the word and you decide on a meaning, and finally you check to see if that meaning fits in with the rest of the sentence" (Duffy, Roehler, Meloth, & Vavrus, 1986, p. 211).

The procedures for cognitive structuring are simple. The teacher assists the pupil to organize the raw stuff of experience – what is before them in the text or in the experiment – with other like instances. The assistance of cognitive structuring can often be achieved merely by making a general statement. Cognitive structures *organize* content and/or functions and (as a corollary) *refer to like instances*. These are the features that distinguish cognitive structuring from simple instructing.

> Cognitive structuring can be distinguished from the other forms of linguistic assistance by the following hypothetical examples which all deal with the same issue:
> *Instructing:* "Think about the main theme of this story."
> *Questioning:* "What do you think the main idea of this story is (or) will be?"
> *Cognitive structuring (Type I):* "All of this story's parts are connected to its main idea: the girl's feelings toward her cat. The word we use for her feelings is *loving*. She is loving toward her cat."
> *Cognitive structuring (Type II):* "Stories have main ideas. The pieces of any story are related to this main idea." (Tharp & Gallimore, 1988)

We do not yet know under what circumstances cognitive structuring is to be preferred over questioning, or vice versa; there is little evidence as to whether or not Type I or Type II structures are superior, or when one or the other is to be preferred (Tharp & Gallimore, 1985). As attested by instances of religious conversion, or the revolutionary effect on some people's thinking of a new idea, the power of cognitive structuring is potentially enormous. Advances in our understanding of these remarkable processes are increasing (Brown, Bransford, Ferrara, & Campione, 1983; Brown & Campione, 1986).

The means of assistance are drawn from social and behavioral science. Using these concepts provides a more differentiated analysis of "performance assistance" and moves teaching/learning analysis closer to a scientific base of understanding. In many ways, the linking of these concepts with Vygotskian developmental principles makes possible a science of teaching. However, the use of the means of assistance can never become narrowly prescriptive. Responsiveness to individual children's zones of proximal development requires individualization according to the exigencies of the moment and movement through the ZPD. The developmental level of the learner requires close accommodation.

There is ample room for the tastes, personalities, and different patterns of teaching skills of individual teachers. However scientific our analysis, teaching will always require some art.

Pathways through the zone of proximal development

> . . . *Teaching consists of assisting performance through the Zone of Proximal Development. Teaching can be said to occur when assistance is offered at points in*

> *the ZPD at which performance requires assistance.* (Tharp & Gallimore, 1988, (chap. 2)

This definition of teaching implies a developmental progress, an unfolding of potential through the reciprocal influence of child and social environment. Higher mental functions that are part of the social and cultural heritage of the child move from the social plane to the psychological plane, from the intermental to the intramental, from the socially regulated to the self-regulated. The child, through the regulating actions and speech of others, is brought to engage in independent action and speech.

The development of any performance capacity in the individual represents a changing relationship between self-regulation and social regulation. Gradually, over time, a child requires less performance assistance, as the capacity for self-regulation increases. Thus progress through the zone of proximal development – from assisted performance to unassisted and self-regulated performance – is gradual.

> Attentional processes may be used as an example. In the first days of school, even simple problems can be solved by the child only if attentional processes are brought into a new relationship with perception and memory. The attention capacity of the child entering kindergarten may be in the zone of proximal development, so that a five-year old is capable of attending to teacher instruction and direction, but only if a rich diet of teacher praise is available. The teacher's praise assists the child's attending by both cueing and reinforcing it. With time the necessary amount of praise may be expected to decline. (Tharp & Gallimore, 1976b)
>
> As the capacity for attending advances through the ZPD, assistance is often provided by peers, who may remind a daydreamer that attention to the teacher is wise. For most pupils, after third grade, assistance by either teachers or peers is rarely needed; attention processes can be invoked when the situation is judged appropriate; they have become self-regulated. (Tharp & Gallimore, 1988)

Progress through the zone of proximal development may be portrayed in a model of four stages (see Figure 7.1). The model focuses particularly on the relationship between self-control and social control. This discussion is necessarily abbreviated here; an extended description of the model and four stages is presented in Tharp and Gallimore (1988).

The four stages of the zone of proximal development

Stage I: where performance is assisted by more capable others. Before children can function as independent agents, they must rely on adults or more capable peers for other-regulation of task performance. The amount and kind of other-regulation a child requires depend on the child's age and the nature of the task, that is, the breadth and progression through the zone of proximal development for the activity at hand. During the earliest periods of the zone of proximal development, the child may have a very limited understanding of the situation, the task, or the goal to be achieved; at this level the parent, teacher, or more capable peer offers directions or

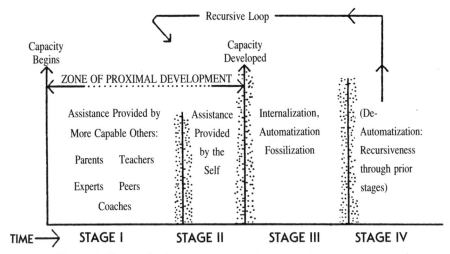

Figure 7.1. The genesis of a performance capacity: Progression through the zone of proximal development and beyond

modeling, and the child's response is acquiescent or imitative (Wertsch, 1978, 1979, 1981, 1985b).

The child gradually comes to understand how the parts of an activity relate to one another, or to understand the meaning of the performance. Ordinarily, this understanding develops through conversation during the task performance. When some conception of the overall performance has been acquired through language or other semiotic processes, the child can be assisted by other means – questions, feedback, and further cognitive structuring. To a child perplexed by a myriad of puzzle pieces, an adult might say, "Which part of the puzzle will you use first?" The child may respond by putting in the ears and thus seeing an elephant take shape.

Stage I is transited when the responsibility for tailoring the assistance, tailoring the transfer, and for the task performance itself has been effectively handed over to the learner. Of course, this achievement is a gradual one, with progress occurring in fits and starts. The shaded line between each of the stages Figure 7.1 represents a subzone itself.

Stage II: where performance is assisted by the self. If we look carefully at the child's statements during this transition, we see that the patterns of activity that allowed the child to participate in the problem-solving effort on the intermental plane now allow him or her to carry out the task on the intramental plane (Wertsch, 1979, p. 18). Thus, in Stage II, the child carries out a task without assistance from others. *However, this does not mean that the performance is fully developed or automatized.* Regulation may have passed from the adult to the child speaker, but the control function remains with the overt verbalization in the form of self-directed speech.

The phenomenon of self-directed speech reflects a development of profound significance. Once a child begins to direct or guide behavior with his or her own speech, an important stage has been reached in the transition of a skill through the zone of proximal development. It constitutes the next stage in the passing of control or assistance from the adult to the child, from the expert to the apprentice. Thus, for children, a major function of self-directed speech is self-guidance (Berk, 1986; Berk & Garvin, 1984; Meichenbaum, 1977; Tharp et al., 1984).

This remains true throughout life. In the acquisition of particular performance capacities, adults during Stage II consistently talk to themselves and assist themselves in all ways possible (Gallimore, Dalton, & Tharp, 1986; Tharp et al., 1984; Watson & Tharp, 1988). Vygotsky's available work principally concerns children, but *identical processes of self- and other-assistance in the ZPD can be seen operating in the learning adult* (see Tharp & Gallimore, 1988, chaps. 10, 11). Recognition of this fact allows the creation of programs for teacher training and offers guidance for organizational management of school and classroom systems of performance assistance (Tharp & Gallimore, 1988).

Stage III: where the performance is developed, automatized, and fossilized. Once evidence of self-regulation has vanished, the child has emerged from the zone of proximal development. Task execution is smooth and integrated. It has been internalized and automatized. Assistance, from the adult or the self, is no longer needed. It is in this condition that continued assistance by others is disruptive and irritating. Even self-consciousness itself is detrimental to the smooth integration of all task components. This is a stage beyond self-control and beyond social control. Performance here is no longer developing; it is already developed. Vygotsky described it as the ''fruits'' of development; but he also described it as ''fossilized,'' emphasizing its fixity and distance from the social and mental forces of change.

Stage IV: where deautomatization of performance leads to recursion through the zone of proximal development. The lifelong learning by any individual is made up of these same regulated, ZPD sequences – from other-assistance to self-assistance – recurring over and over again for the development of new capacities. For every individual, at any point in time, there will be a mix of other-regulation, self-regulation, and automatized processes. The child who can now do many of the steps in assembling a puzzle might still be in the zone of proximal development for the activities of reading.

Furthermore, once a child masters cognitive strategies he or she is not obligated to rely only on internal mediation. She or he can also ask for help when stuck, for example in the search for lost items of attire. During periods of difficulty, children may seek out controlling vocalizations by more competent others (Gal'perin, 1969). Cognitive strategy training emphasizes such action. Again, we see the intimate and shifting relationship between control by self and control by others.

Even for adults, the effort to recall a forgotten bit of information can be aided by the helpful assistance of another, so that the total of self-regulated and other-regulated components of the performance once again resembles commonplace shared functioning of parent and child. Even the competent adult can profit from regulation for the enhancement and maintenance of performance. A most important consideration is that deautomatization and recursion occur so regularly that they constitute a fourth stage of normal developmental process. What one formerly could do, one can no longer do.

It often happens that self-regulation is not sufficient to restore performance capacity, and a further recursion – the restitution of other-regulation – is required. The readiness of a teacher to repeat some earlier lesson is one mark of excellent teaching. Whatever the level of recursion, the goal is to re-proceed through assisted performance to self-regulation and to exit the zone of proximal development anew into automatization.

This theory of teaching, demonstrating how performance needs to be assisted by one or more means so that the learner proceeds through the zone of proximal development for one capacity after another, is both sensible and well demonstrated by empirical literature. How is it, then, that there is so little teaching of this kind in ordinary schooling? The answer is: Teacher capacities for assisting performance are not developed; teaching as assisted performance does not exist on the interpersonal plane of schooling sufficiently to support, maintain, or even recognize teaching when it occurs. A Vygotskian analysis of schools can lead to a theory of schooling itself that is as closely allied to the theory of teaching as two grasped hands.

Theory of schooling: The institutional organization of assisted performance

All performance assistance is embedded in complex organizations. The acquisition, enhancement, and maintenance of specific individual competencies are the conditions for the survival of all institutions, from the post office to the church to the school district. Regulation of new members begins immediately, through such systems as orientation and training programs. Many successful organizations also have settings for enhancement and maintenance of appropriate institutional behaviors, such as workshops, consultants, or retreats. But only these few settings are organized to "teach" by assisting performance in the zone of proximal development.

To be sure, there are organizational systems to ensure good performance, such as inspections, merit reviews, or performance incentives. These are not seen as "teaching" systems, even though all of them – from orientation programs to salesmen's incentives – involve means of assistance: modeling, contingencies, feedback, instructions, questions, cognitive structuring. These interpersonal transactions create patterns of meanings, values, and cognitive structures, thereby creating/perpetuating the culture of the institution.

Even so, most institutions accept a limited responsibility for "teaching" per se. The provision of assistance is limited. When performance weakens, and the usual dosage of instructions and incentives does not cure, employees or recruits can be dismissed. Perhaps because such institutions have a limited commitment to teaching, they rarely conceive their relationships to personnel as "teaching through assisting performance."

Regrettably, schools are too much like this general description of organizations. Schools also accept highly limited responsibility for assisting the performance of their personnel. This is paradoxical, since teaching is the sole formal purpose for the existence of schools, and thus schools bear a unique relationship to the act of teaching.

Therefore, schools should be in a position to understand a corollary of our theory of teaching: *A primary operational principle for schools should be to assist the performance of all their members,* from kindergartners to superintendent. Sadly, it is not so.

Organizing schools for teaching

Little actual teaching occurs in schools; this is characteristic of transactions within the entire educational apparatus. All the way down the educational ladder, teaching is peculiarly absent in transactions between children and teachers, teachers and administrators, students and professors. Each appears to believe that, somewhere below, someone is teaching someone. Each position attempts to create educational opportunities for those down the chain – good textbooks, good workshops, even good performance objectives – but no one attends to assisting the performance of those objectives.

Rather than assisting performance, the supervision usually means direction and evaluation. *This is organically related to the classroom practice of directing and assessing: the recitation script.* At neither level is there sufficient assistance, responsiveness, joint productive activity, or the building of common meanings and values. One reason why the recitation script is so firmly entrenched in the classroom (cf. Hoetker & Ahlbrand, 1969; Goodlad, 1984; Tharp & Gallimore, 1988) is that it is ubiquitous in the school.

An alternative model of supervision and school organization grows from the concepts discussed in this chapter. One of the duties of each individual in a school system should be to assist the performance of the person next down the line: The superintendent assists the principal, the principal assists the teacher, the teacher assists the pupil. It is surely reasonable that the central responsibility of the teaching organization should be providing assistance for the performance of each member. This assistance, with its accompanying cognitive and behavioral development, is the justifying goal of the school, and all other duties should be in its service. Supervision itself should be defined as assisting performance in precisely the terms we used to define teaching.

In this way, the superintendent can indirectly affect the work of teachers by assisting the principal to assist them. The primary responsibility of principals (or designated instructional leaders) should be to assist teachers to assist children. Thus the good work of each position lies in assisting the next position to assist the third, and so forth down the chain for the ultimate benefit of the student.

Nonsupervisory sources of assistance

Effective assistance does not require authority. In fact, it is more nearly the opposite: Teaching is the process upon which authority depends to achieve its aims. Peers are a major source of nonsupervisory assistance. Vygotsky emphasized that the zone of proximal development is extended through problem solving under adult guidance *or in collaboration with more capable peers.* At every level of schooling, nonsupervisory influences can be structured so as to maximize the coherence of the overall system of assistance provided by the school. This principle is foundational to the ''cooperative-learning'' movement.

Assistance and teaching do not flow in one direction. Employees also assist supervisors, pupils teach teachers, teachers assist principals. In any interaction, influences are reciprocal. Assistance most often flows from the more competent to the less competent participant – from teacher to learner, from trainer to trainee – but the interpersonal plane, created in joint activity, is a joint product.

> A central feature of the interpersonal plane is its intersubjectivity. In joint activity, the signs and symbols developed through language, the development of common understanding of the purposes and meanings of the activity, the joint engagement in cognitive strategies and problem solving – all these aspects of interaction influence each participant. While the more able member of a joint activity exercises more influence, through providing more assistance, it is one task of the teacher to understand the subjectivity of the learner, and – for the task at hand – to share it so as to influence it. As new members coalesce in a new activity, a new intersubjectivity is created, and for all members, it is internalized into a new cognitive development. (Tharp & Gallimore, 1988, p. 89)

Authority in the supervisory line should be used to create new activity settings in which joint productive activity will produce the assistance that will increase the competence of supervisees. All those who participate will be influenced, will be assisted, will develop a new intersubjectivity, and will advance in the development of capacities to assist. The basic principle for the design of effective assistance is to marshal the sources that will assist the performance of those down the supervisory chain and to eliminate the sources that hinder or obstruct that performance. Good design and management of assisted performance can be seen as the creation of appropriate activity settings.

The design of activity settings in schools

Those occasions when collaborative interaction, intersubjectivity, assisted performance occur – when *teaching* occurs – are referred to as *activity settings.* Activity setting is a concept that has multiple origins (Cole, 1985; Leont'ev, 1981; Tharp &

Gallimore, 1988; Weisner, 1984; Weisner & Gallimore, 1985; Wertsch, Minick, & Arns, 1984; Whiting & Whiting, 1975).

The name *activity setting* incorporates the two essential features: the cognitive and motoric action itself (activity); and the external, environmental, and objective features of the occasion (setting). They are the who, what, when, where, and why, the small recurrent dramas of everyday life, played on the stages of home, community, and workplace. All these features – personnel, occasion, motivations, goals, places, and times – cannot be unpackaged without drastically reducing the explanatory and practical utility of the concept of activity setting. It is true that social science has always separated these features, and consequently the concept requires some practice before its use is comfortable (Tharp & Gallimore, 1988). But all settings for activity in the school can be analyzed in these terms, from work centers in classrooms to independent teacher self-study groups.

Examples and principles of activity settings in the schools

Examples of important activity settings for students include whole-class settings, laboratory partnerships, cooperative-learning small groups, debates, drama rehearsals. Activity settings for adult members of school organizations include faculty committees, peer coaching groups, workshops, individual teacher consultation by outside experts, grade-level committee meetings, curriculum revision groups. We will exemplify the concept by discussing two activity settings in detail; one is designed to assist the performance of students, and the other assists the performance of teachers. Both examples are drawn from work at the Kamehameha Early Education Program (KEEP; see Tharp & Gallimore, 1988).

Center One. Center One accomplishes assistance of child learning by creating an activity setting in the classroom that maximizes opportunities for coparticipation and instructional conversation with the teacher. Center One is the central activity setting at KEEP for the teaching of literacy to children from kindergarten through third grade. It is the focal point of teacher–child interaction. The specific activities vary from one group to another and from day to day, but in each the children and teacher are engaged in a lively instructional conversation. The Center One lesson teaches not only reading but also listening, speaking, and thinking. The basic goal of instruction is the development of cognitive/linguistic abilities.

This direct daily instruction occurs in homogeneous ability groups of five to six children. The most common pattern is highly informal mutual participation by the teacher and students, co-narration, volunteered speech, instant feedback, and lack of penalty for "wrong" answers. (However, for vocabulary and decoding teaching, the pattern may be highly teacher-dominated, almost drill-like.)

During instruction in comprehension, the teacher follows a pattern of repeated thematic routines, labelled "E-T-R sequences" (Au, 1979, 1981). The teacher introduces content drawn from the child's experience (E), followed by text (T) material, followed by establishing relationships (R) between the two. These sequences may last from a few seconds up to several minutes. The teacher relies heavily on questioning that samples from the various levels of cognitive operations, extending from recall of specific detail through the higher orders of reference and extension (Crowell & Au, 1979; White & Tharp, 1988).

The teacher builds flexibly on the children's responses. Thus the teacher maintains goals for the discussion but often alters or even abandons the anticipated "script" for a given lesson. This technique engages the children's interest, and the result is a vigorous, enthusiastic discussion.

This activity setting occupies most of the teacher's interactive teaching time. The teacher only occasionally monitors the other 20 or so children who are busy working at other independent activity settings. (For more detailed discussions of Center One and of KEEP, see Au, 1979; Tharp, 1982; Tharp & Gallimore, 1988.)

Observation-and-conference activity settings. The second example, also drawn from KEEP, is a major activity setting designed to assist the performance of teachers. In the observation-and-conference activity, each teacher is observed at least once a week by an assigned consultant (or other supervisor), and some assessment is made of the teacher's performance on a teaching skill of current focus. An example is an observation of the proportion of time spent by the teacher on *comprehension instruction,* as opposed to decoding or sight vocabulary objectives. The results are fed back to the teachers immediately. Measurements of student on-task rate (or engaged time) are done periodically, or on request by the teachers or their supervisors. Rates of positive contingency management are also measured, especially for beginning teachers. Sample lessons or videotapes of direct instruction sessions are periodically reviewed by supervisors, and feedback is provided.

The activity setting for consultant–teacher interaction is also an instructional conversation, that of the *weekly conference,* where the two meet to discuss the feedback, to decide on the next goals for the teacher's own learning, and to work cooperatively in planning for the children in the classroom. Frequently, a videotape of one of the teacher's lessons is reviewed. Both participants comment on the tape, and the consultant uses this stimulus to provide feedback, instructions, reinforcement, questioning, or cognitive structuring. In the later stages of the zone of proximal development, the teacher provides most of this assistance in a pattern of "self-collaboration."

Though there are many possibilities for joint productive activity, in the typical school there are insufficient opportunities, personnel, time, and commitment for principals to interact with teachers, for superintendents to interact with principals, for district-level experts to interact with grade levels, for program designers to interact with program operators, or for any level of personnel to interact with peers. That is to say, in schools there is too seldom *joint productive activity.* Teachers, principals, curriculum specialists, and other authorities direct their subordinates to accomplish a task but do not participate in the productivity. A basic condition for effective activity settings is *jointness* (Tharp & Gallimore, 1988). Without joint-ness, the supervisor cannot assist performance, affect cognitive structures of learn-ers, or be affected by the emerging group intersubjectivity.

In schools' activity settings, there is too seldom a product at all. This removes another basic condition needed for good functioning of any human group. The ac-tivity of a group, the helpfulness of members to one another, the motivation to participate in the activity – all these indispensable conditions are, in ordinary life, *driven by the product itself*. When a curriculum specialist asks, ''What can I do to assist this teacher to become a better assister of his students?'' one answer is: ''Find a time and a place to work together, on a product that we will both value, and through which we can come to a common and advancing understanding.'' When that time and place are identified, the specialist will have begun to identify the teacher's zones of proximal development (for content, pedagogy, planning, etc.) and will have some idea of what means of assistance to employ and in what order.

Four basic principles can guide school personnel in evaluating and improving the structure of activity settings. First, the assister should at all times participate in at least one activity setting with the assistee(s). Second, the authority of the assister should be used to organize activity settings and to make resources of time, place, persons, and tools available to them. Third, authority should not override the emerging intersubjectivity and problem solving of the activity's members. Fourth, every member of the school community should be engaged in some setting of joint productive activity.

After sketching the theory of teaching, and the theory of schooling, we are now prepared to consider the third leg of a theoretical tripod: the theory of literacy.

A theory of literacy

Schools should teach students to be literate in the most general sense – capable of reading, writing, speaking, computing, reasoning, and manipulating verbal (and visual) symbols and concepts. Together, the three theoretical legs of teaching, schooling, and literacy support a *theory of education*. The term *three legs of a tripod* emphasizes the interconnectedness of these considerations: If one collapses, all fall down.

For each of the legs of this theory of education, there is a crucial concept. For the theory of teaching, the zone of proximal development is the cornerstone. For the theory of schooling, activity settings are key. For a theory of literacy, the key Vygotskian concept is *word meaning*.

Word, discourse, and meaning

Vygotsky considered *word meaning* the basic unit for the analysis of consciousness, because word meaning is both an intramental and an intermental phenomenon. Word meaning is the stuff of verbal thinking. It also resides in the community of language users. Through the use of language in activity settings, the dialectic between the intramental and the intermental planes produces constant, evolutionary development in word meaning.

Vygotsky uses *word* (the Russian *slovo*) in both the simple, lexical form as the symbol for a concept and in the larger sense of *discourse*. It refers to both vocabulary and discourse competencies, which develop in the context of social use in joint activity. The intersubjectivities of activity settings are created through the use of words in discourse; these signs and symbols take on new and shared meanings, as they are hallowed by use during joint productive activity. The social meanings of words are internalized by individuals through self-directed speech, taken underground, and stripped down to the lightning of thought. When we turn our attention to word meaning and a theory of knowledge development and expression, we are merely attending to another facet of the zone of proximal development and the activity setting. But this facet is a vital one; word meanings are the threads by which society weaves itself into one cloth.

Discourse in schooling

One of the characteristics of schooled discourse is its dependence on written language. When children learn to read, there is a major alteration in the entire form of thinking, and in the relationship of language to thinking. These developmental changes in the relationship may be observed on both a sociohistorical level (Ong, 1982) and an ontogenetic level.

Paralleling the difference between written and verbal discourse is the distinction between "everyday" concepts and "schooled" concepts. According to Minick, the Russian *nauchnoe ponyatie* may be translated (Vygotsky, 1987) as *scientific concepts*. It translates equally well as *scholarly concepts*. The kernel of the issue is that these concepts, unlike everyday concepts, are schooled and systematic. The most sensitive English term for the concept as we understand it today may be neither *scientific* nor *scholarly* but *schooled*. Schooled concepts arise through the social and historical development of formal education and its social institutions (Leont'ev, 1935/1983).

All concepts develop through language use accompanying joint activity. Everyday concepts are closely tied to the specific objects and conditions that their names represent. The word for an object is a part of the object, an attribute of the object as integral as its color, smell, or size. Words, in the everyday realm, cannot be detached and manipulated in the young child's mind separately from the image of the phenomenon represented.

In schooled concepts, words are wrested from their designata and manipulated in the mind independently of their images. Many of these new schooled words are themselves imageless and serve to link and manipulate other words. The student's attention shifts from sign–object relationships to sign–sign relationships (Wertsch,

1985a). A *system* of words develops, with units of decontextualized words, rules of use, rules of transformation, and an emphasis on these internal relationships.

Vygotsky argues that the unique route to higher-order verbal thinking is the experience of schooling. *Schooling detaches the word from its designatum and attaches it to a generalization.* This shift is of profound importance because *only if the word is freed of its sensory impedimenta can it be manipulated voluntarily and with conscious awareness.* Written speech must have more words, be more precise, and be more expanded than verbal speech, because it cannot rely on paralinguistic elements such as tone and gestures. This enforces an experience of language as system. This systematicity – self-contained and self–sufficient – is what allows language to be unhooked from the sensory world, to be taken in hand by the thinker, to be used as a tool for thought (Tharp & Gallimore, 1988).

The "system" of written discourse is far different from that used in practical activity settings of home and community. Vygotsky points out that everyday concepts are learned primarily through speech; schooled examples are learned primarily through written symbols. Everyday concepts are learned "upward" from sensory experience to generalization; schooled concepts are learned "downward" from generalization to palpable example.

The course of development of higher mental processes lies in bringing the two together, in allowing the synthesis of the opposites. Schooled concepts connect with the experienced world through the everyday concepts that have arisen through practical activity. Relating the two enriches and saves schooling from aridity; but this relating also profoundly changes the nature of the everyday concepts, making them more systematic, autonomous, and tool-like. Of course, everyday thinking continues, permanently. But the relating of the domains of everyday concepts and the system of schooled concepts requires the learner "to attend to aspects of linguistic activity that had earlier been mastered without conscious awareness" (Minick, 1985, p. 365). Their conjunction illuminates both.

Thus the dialectic between everydayness and the systematic tools of schooled discourse gives rise to consciousness of these symbols and makes possible their use in practical thinking. The instructional task of the school is to facilitate that developmental process by teaching the schooled language of reading and writing and facilitating the constant conjunction of these systems with those of everyday concepts (Tharp & Gallimore, 1988). "Effective instruction with young children involves a continuous integration of language and action" (Wood, 1980, p. 290).

Effective school instruction must provide the interface between emergent schooled concepts and everyday concepts. Only in this way will the highest order of meaning be achieved, and only in this way will teaching ensure that tools of verbal thought will be manipulated for the solution of practical problems of the experienced world. Reading and writing prepare the child for receiving schooled concepts. Reading is both the condition and the process of acquiring meaning. To learn to read is to learn to comprehend, and to teach reading means to teach comprehension.

Teaching reading and comprehension

Comprehending text means the weaving of new, schooled concepts with those of everyday life, a process that Wittrock (1974) described as generative. In Wittrock's conception, comprehension is "a function of the abstract and distinctive, concrete associations which the learner generates between his prior experience, as it is stored in long-term memory, and the stimuli" (1974, p. 89). Text becomes meaningful because it has become woven into the student's *system* of meanings and understandings. Extracting information from text, arraying and preparing it for weaving into existing cognitive systems are basic competencies that literate societies transmit. School-based instruction in comprehension of written text is our basic system for establishing the discourse meanings that create both the intermental and intramental capacity for verbal thinking (Vygotsky, 1987).

At the earliest levels of instruction – for children whose emergent literacy experiences in the home have been limited – it is necessary to build those cognitive competencies that are fundamental to eventual text comprehension. For the very young child, or for the child without early interactions with schooled parents – it is necessary first to build word meanings on the everyday, verbal level and to introduce gradually the linguistic stream of writing itself.

Thus comprehension is established by the weaving of new, schooled concepts with the concepts of everyday life. Textual material becomes meaningful because it has gained a new attachment – it is now hooked by *sense* to everyday concepts and hooked by *system* to the whole structure of meaning given by schooling. The homely "weaving" heuristic used by reading teachers is not only a short-term instructional strategy. Indeed, it is used consistently in the highest reaches of scientific and philosophical thought. Theoretical thought and discussion require a continual freshening by example and a testing against sensory data. This constant connecting of schooled concepts and everyday concepts is the basic process of understanding the world used by mature schooled thinkers.

The weaving of the schooled with the everyday is not only enhancing to the dialectical growth of concepts but also motivating. For example, we know that the *discourse of science* occurs in a particular register, with its distinct rules and formalities. In the *teaching of science,* however, these conventions are frequently violated by the interpolation of everyday discourse. These alternations are unmistakable, ordinarily being marked by tone of voice, laughter, asides, and so on. During these times, the attention of students is at its highest (Cazden, 1987; Lemke, 1982).

"Formal schooling is a place where the child is drawn into unique modes of social interaction and thinking that have their roots in the history of Western science and philosophy" (Minick, 1985, pp. 367–368). From kindergarten to graduate seminars, the small discussion group where text and personal understanding can be compared, discussed, and related is the prime opportunity for this "unique social interaction."

In contemporary schools, this social interaction is rare indeed (Goodlad, 1984; Hoetker & Ahlbrand, 1969; Sarason, 1983). For example, Durkin (1978–1979) observed 18,000 minutes of reading comprehension instruction and found that less than 1% dealt with units of meaning larger than words. Hiebert (1983) compared instruction of higher and lower ability groups. Children in the lowest reading groups receive more word-list drill but read less connected text; they are asked more simple, factual questions and fewer questions that require inference or synthesis. Opportunities for participation in the unique social interaction we call literate discourse are virtually nonexistent. Such patterns of instruction will only reinforce the problems of poor readers. It is known that poor readers are unlikely to make the inferences required to weave information in a text into a coherent overall mental model. Poor readers' beliefs about knowledge do not lead them to suppose that consistent interpretations of events are generally possible, or even desirable. For the poor reader, knowledge is a basket of facts (Anderson, 1984).

A group discussion, around a text, is a reflection of the larger society for which children are to be educated, in which pairs and groups of people in the workplace and at play interact around a text, the meaning of which influences their actions. When Minick (1985) argues that society, as the larger social context, influences schools to adopt relevant activity settings, he is arguing the ideal rather than the actual instance. Perhaps schools' failure to reflect the larger context of society is the reason for society's impatience with the schools. Society depends on the school to prepare students in ways more profound than learning "baskets of facts." For the child, the educational design of activity settings produces more than habits of action, more even than cognitive transformation. The school's activity settings bring about a fundamental restructuring in which all are transformed: actions, relationships, and thinking (El'konin, 1972).

The instructional conversation

> Discourse in which expert and apprentices weave together spoken and written language with previous understanding appears in several guises. It appears as literacy experiences in activity settings of successful students' homes, the ways that parents teach their children language and letters. It is disguised in many activity settings as the chat that accompanies action. It is the natural conversational method of language instruction. It can be the medium for teacher training. It can wear the mask of a third-grade reading lesson, or a graduate seminar. It's generic name is the *Instructional Conversation*. . . . The concept itself contains a paradox: "instruction" and "conversation" appear contrary, the one implying authority and planning, the other equality and responsiveness. The task of teaching is to resolve this paradox. To most truly teach, one must converse; to truly converse is to teach. (Tharp & Gallimore, 1988, p. 111)

Earlier, we spoke of the task of schooling as the creation of activity settings. That is because the language that accompanies joint productive activity is the major vehicle for the development of intersubjectivity, the internalization of concepts, the development of discourse meaning, and the development of higher cognitive processes. Joint productive activity is good in part because it allows the instructional conversation. Thus, in emphasizing this concept, we may characterize the task of schooling as creating and supporting instructional conversations among students, teachers, administrators, program developers, and researchers. Not only do babies learn to speak, and children to read, through the instructional conversation, but by this same means teachers learn to teach, researchers learn to discover, and all learn to become literate.

Instructional conversational exchanges among parents and children, and in a few classrooms, are fundamentally different from the recitation script. To *converse* is to assume that the learner may have something to say beyond the "answers" already known by the teacher. To grasp a child's communicative intent requires careful listening, a willingness to guess about the meaning of the intended communication, and responsive adjustments to assist the child's efforts. Instructional conversation in the school setting requires that "teachers" engage "learners" in discourse like that used by Ochs's (1982) literate caregivers:

> One of the most distinctive characteristics of middle-class Anglo caregivers is their willingness to engage in communicative exchanges [even] with the smallest of infants. . . . Long before the child has actually produced its first word, it is treated as if it in fact does have something to say. . . . When young children actually begin producing words, this set of assumptions by the caregiver continues. The caregiver, typically the mother, considers the young child to be expressing somewhat imperfectly a communicative intention. (pp. 88–89)

Later, a similar pattern is observed in storybook reading and other emergent literacy events (Heath, 1982; Teale, 1986).

This is very unlike the verbal exchanges students experience in their school lives. The teachers generally ignore children, talk over them, and dominate the proceedings (Goodlad, 1984; Wells, 1986; Wood, McMahon, & Cranstoun, 1980).

This kind of school discourse is particularly handicapping to children whose home activity settings do not include "meaningful discourse" in the language of schooling.

> The failure of many disadvantaged children in school is often explained by referring to their unfamiliarity with the middle-class ethos of school. But many schools operate in a way that is similar to the disadvantaged home in terms of using language and developing thinking skills. . . . teachers need a new understanding of the part they can play in children's education. They need insight into the role that language plays in learning and . . . the way in which children learn to use language through interaction with adults. . . . Teachers need to recognize that many children will not have experiences through which their thinking might be extended unless these are provided in school . . . and [teachers need] to recognize the critical importance of the experiences they themselves provide through their own talk with children. (Tough, 1982, pp. 14–15)

Rather than provide such programs, however, teachers usually blame families-and-culture for the failure to provide adequate language development at home. The incredible irony is this: Schools themselves have adopted the interactional patterns so often attributed to disadvantaged homes.

There is another irony: Most teachers are members of the literate middle class, where researchers have most often found the instructional conversation. Why, then, is this interactional pattern so seldom observed in classrooms run by teachers who talk to their own children in this way?

There are at least two main reasons. First, a teacher cannot provide assistance in the ZPD unless she knows where the learner is in the developmental process. Opportunities for such careful observation of the child's in-flight performance are rarely available in typical American classrooms. In individual tutorials, in private schools with classes of seven or less, such intimate knowledge of the learning process may be possible. But all involve a pupil–teacher ratio that society generally declines to provide. There is some cause for optimism in schools' increased use of small groups, maintenance of positive classroom atmosphere which increases independent task involvement of students, and new materials and technology with which students can interact independently of the teacher. But these positive developments do not speak to the second reason that assisted performance has not diffused into the schools. Although most parents do not need to be trained to assist performance, most teachers do because their task is more complex. Teachers cannot rely on skills that are sufficient for parental socialization of offspring. Lay or parental skills are a foundation, but teachers need a more elaborate set of skills in assistance, and they need to be more conscious of their application.

Teachers do not conduct instructional conversations because they do not know how. They do not know how, because they have never been taught. They almost never have opportunities to observe effective models or occasions for practicing and receiving feedback or for competent coaching by a skilled mentor. Like all learners, teachers themselves must have their performance assisted if they are to acquire the ability to assist the performance of their students. Teachers, like all learners, have zones of proximal development of professional skills. And teachers, like all learners in schools, seldom receive the performance assistance that is required for them to develop.

Teachers need to learn the "expert pedagogy" of which Berliner (1986) and others have written (see various chapters in Wittrock, 1986). They must learn professional skills of assisting performance and learn to apply them at a level far beyond that required in private life. Thus pedagogically expert teachers do not act exactly like parents. The large numbers of pupils, the restricted and technical curriculum, and the complexity of institutional restraints of schooling require that teaching be a highly deliberate, carefully structured, planned, professional activity. Unlike conversations in natal settings, teachers have a deliberate curriculum of literate knowledge and skills to impart.

Nevertheless, working with content-rich curricula teachers can and must move closer to the communicative styles of parents with their own children. What might appear to be "spontaneous" instructional conversations (see, e.g., Tharp & Gallimore, 1988, chaps. 3, 7, 8, 10) are not. We are not advocating casual, drifting classroom chatter. Rather, we mean instructional conversations that require highly refined interpersonal competencies in combination with a solid grasp of the substantive knowledge to be taught.

Teaching-as-assisted-performance and the arts of the instructional conversation can be taught (Tharp & Gallimore, 1988). We know that these skills are acquired in the interpsychological plane: Teachers acquire these skills through instructional conversations with trained consultants. With assisted performance in teachers' zones of proximal development, these teaching skills of the instructional conversation eventually are internalized and automatized as intrapsychological cognitive processes. These skills themselves are skills of thinking and decision making and are employed regularly and permanently as the skills are plied. In the intersubjectivities developed in instructional conversations, "teaching" takes on a different meaning. To produce these teacher-training conversations requires a different organization of schooling than is found in educational institutions today. It takes a different form of training. The uniting of Vygotskian concepts and perspectives with social and behavioral science provides a basis on which to proceed.

Conclusions: A unified theory of education

On the whole, contemporary teaching research is atheoretical (Good & Weinstein, 1986), thus suffering from what Price-Williams (1975) called the "Penelope complex," after the wife of Odysseus who each night undid her day's weaving. By unraveling, she put off finishing the cloak – and her promise then to choose among the suitors for her hand and the throne of Ithaca. So too in educational science: the threads of knowledge carded by investigators are not woven into a whole, durable cloak of principles that can be called a theory in the broader sense of the word. And without such a cloak, no new kingdom will come.

Consider "microteaching," a briefly fashionable teacher-training system that soon disappeared from citation indexes, despite ample evidence of its effectiveness (Walberg, 1986). In current discussions about improving teaching and teacher preparation, almost no writers even mention microteaching or make any effort to incorporate and explain the data that movement produced. If the vigorous interest in Vygotskian perspective follows this same pattern, then we can expect in a decade or so that it will be occasionally remembered as another in the long line of discarded educational fashions.

Microteaching is a particularly apt example of a lost thread because it no doubt seems an unlikely topic for this chapter on Vygotsky's contributions to a unified theory of education. It is our brief that a true theory of education must incorporate and account for robust germane phenomena. Microteaching grew out of research on observational learning; it employed modeling, one of the six means of assisting performance in the zone of proximal development. Microteaching works because it activates a fundamental, universal learning process. Microteaching may have lost favor, but the laws of human behavior on which it rests have not changed.

A theory of education must account for and predict how teachers can learn to truly teach; it must specify principles by which schools can be reformed to make possible such teacher experiences at the beginning and throughout their careers. All previous efforts to reform schools have been defeated by the failure to change teachers by changing the contexts in which they work (Sarason, 1971; Tharp & Gallimore, 1988). The problem now, as during earlier reform movements, is the lack of a theory of schooling, of training, and of professional development.

The uniting of Vygotskian and other perspectives provides the set of principles, the guiding theory, that has been missing:

> In Vygotskian terms, teaching is good only when it *"awakens and rouses to life those functions which are in a stage of maturing, which lie in the zone of proximal development"* (Vygotsky, 1956, p. 278, italics in original).
>
> Teaching consists of assisting performance through the zone of proximal development. Thus teaching can be said to occur at that point in the zone where performance can be achieved with assistance.
>
> Teachers, like their students, have zones of proximal development; they too require assisted performance; as with students, activity settings for teachers must create opportunities in which they receive all the six means of assistance. The sources and contexts of assistance are infinitely varied; it does not matter by whom or in what way it happens, as long as performance is assisted.
>
> Activity settings are contexts for assisted performance opportunities created by the concentration of personnel present, their goals, the tasks at hand, and the scripts which guide interaction. To create opportunities for assisted performance in joint productive activity requires keen attention to the components of which they are constructed. Each activity setting should have a product as its goal, a product that is motivating for all its participants.
>
> Schools must construct activity settings that assist teachers to truly teach: to adopt a role in which teachers assist students in the zone of proximal development.
>
> The purpose of schooling is teaching students to be literate in the most general sense of the word – capable of reading, writing, speaking, computing, reasoning, and manipulating visual as well as verbal symbols and concepts. Literacy is achieved through the creation of opportunities for students to be assisted in the use of word meanings, conceptual structures, and discourse itself – so that signs and symbols take on new and shared meanings as they are hallowed by use during joint productive activity, taken underground, and stripped down to the lightning of thought. (Tharp & Gallimore, 1988)

These principles allow us to define for teachers, as well as children, the most productive social contexts for teaching and learning: Productive interactions occur in goal-directed activity settings, which are jointly undertaken by apprentices and experts. They involve contributions and discoveries by learners, as well as the assistance of an "expert" collaborator. Instruction in such collaborative efforts is contingent on the apprentice's own activities and related to what he or she is currently trying to do. The assisting expert typically provides information relevant to furthering the apprentice's current goal-directed activity. Such information is provided in a way that is immediately responsive and proportionate to the apprentice's varying information needs. Departures from this evolved pattern of responsive, synchronous interaction create difficulties for learners (Fischer & Bullock, 1984; Wood, 1980). Yet such interactions are rare in the school lives of teachers and children alike (e.g., Duffy & Roehler, 1981; Durkin, 1978–1979; Goodlad, 1984; Hoetker & Ahlbrand, 1969; Joyce & Clift, 1984; Tharp & Gallimore, 1988).

With these principles, the fundamental barrier to reform of teaching and schooling can be identified: Most teachers work alone, in splendid isolation (Griffin, 1985; Jackson, 1968; Knoblock & Goldstein, 1971; Sarason, 1971). This isolation of teachers accounts for much of the problem of achieving school reform. Isolated teachers have limited opportunities for receiving assistance through modeling and feedback, two means of assistance crucial to acquisition of complex social repertoires. Ordinary means of teacher preparation and training can provide cognitive structuring, but that alone will not assist teachers to develop new repertoires of complex social behavior necessary to meet the criterion of teaching-as-assisted-performance in the zone of proximal development. Without performance assistance for themselves, there is no chance that teachers will ever learn to assist the performance of their students. Without assistance, there is no chance that teachers will ever abandon the viewpoint common in American classrooms, now and since the 19th century, that students are supposed to learn on their own (Tharp & Gallimore, 1988).

Adequate theory must address not only the individual processes of development and learning but the social contexts in which they transpire (Langer & Applebee, 1986). Such a comprehensive theory is made possible by a uniting of emergent Vygotskian perspectives with this century's achievements in social and behavioral science. This uniting insists that teaching will not be reformed until schools are reformed. Schools will not be reformed until it is understood that schools must be a context for teaching and that context must itself be a teaching context. Such a theory can also retrieve the lost knowledge of previous research, such as microteaching, and perhaps begin to weave our accumulated knowledge into a garment for more than one season.

Vygotsky – known for his interest in the arts and literature – might be pleased that his ideas contributed to a cure for the Penelope complex of American educational science.

References

Anderson, R. C. (1984). Some reflections on the acquisition of knowledge. *Educational Researcher, 13*(9), 5–10.

Au, K. H. (1979). Using the experience-text-relationship method with minority children. *Reading Teacher, 32*(6), 677–679.

Au, K. H. (1981). The comprehension-oriented reading lesson: Relationships to proximal indices of achievement. *Educational Perspectives, 20,* 13–15.

Bandura, A. (1969). *Principles of behavior modification.* New York: Holt, Rinehart & Winston.

Bandura, A. (1977). *Social learning theory.* Englewood Cliffs, NJ: Prentice-Hall.

Berk, L. E. (1986). Relationship of elementary school children's private speech to behavioral accompaniment to task, attention, and task performance. *Developmental Psychology, 22,* 671–680.

Berk, L. E., & Garvin, R. (1984). Development of private speech among low-income Appalachian children. *Developmental Psychology, 20,* 271–286.

Berliner, D. C. (1986). In pursuit of the expert pedagogue. *Educational Researcher, 15*(7), 5–13.

Brown, A. L., Bransford, J. D., Ferrara, R. A., & Campione, J. C. (1983). Learning, remembering, and understanding. In J. H. Flavell & E. M. Markman (Eds.), *Handbook of child psychology: Vol. 3. Cognitive development* (4th ed.) (pp. 77–166). New York: Wiley.

Brown, A. L., & Campione, J. C. (1986). Psychological theory and the study of learning disabilities. *American Psychologist, 41*(10), 1059–1068.

Carver, C. S., & Scheier, M. F. (1981). *Attention and self-regulation: A control-theory approach to human behavior.* New York: Springer-Verlag.

Cazden, C. B. (1987, January). *Text and context in education.* Paper presented at the Third International Conference on Thinking, Honolulu.

Cole, M. (1985). The zone of proximal development: Where culture and cognition create each other. In J. V. Wertsch (Ed.), *Culture, communication, and cognition: Vygotskian perspectives* (pp. 146–161). Cambridge: Cambridge University Press.

Crowell, D. C., & Au, K. H. (1979). Using a scale of questions to improve listening comprehension. *Language Arts, 56,* 38–43.

Duffy, G. G., & Roehler, L. R. (1981, December). *An analysis of instruction in reading instructional research.* Paper presented at the meeting of a Research Session on Reading Instructional Research, National Reading Conference, Dallas.

Duffy, G. G., Roehler, L. R., Meloth, M. S., & Vavrus, L. G. (1986). Conceptualizing instructional explanation. *Teaching and Teacher Education, 2,* 197–214.

Durkin, D. (1978–1979). What classroom observations reveal about reading comprehension instruction. *Reading Research Quarterly, 14,* 481–533.

El'konin, D. B. (1972). Toward the problem of stages in the mental development of the child. *Soviet Psychology, 10,* 225–251.

Ervin-Tripp, S. (1976). Is Sybil there? The structure of some American English directives. *Language in Society, 5,* 25–66.

Ervin-Tripp, S. (1977). Wait for me, roller skate! In S. Ervin-Tripp & C. Mitchell-Kernan (Eds.), *Child discourse* (pp. 165–188). New York: Academic Press.

Fischer, K. W., & Bullock, D. (1984). Cognitive development in school-aged children: Conclusions and new directions. In W. A. Collins (Ed.), *Development during middle childhood: The years from six to twelve* (pp. 70–146). Washington, DC: National Academy Press.

Fortes, M. (1938). Education in Taleland. *Africa, 11*(Suppl. 4), 4.

Gallimore, R., Dalton, S., & Tharp, R. G. (1986). Self-regulation and interactive teaching: The impact of teaching conditions on teachers' cognitive activity. *Elementary School Journal, 86*(5), 613–631.

Gal'perin, P. (1969). Stages in the development of mental acts. In M. Cole & I. Maltzman (Eds.), *A handbook of contemporary Soviet psychology* (pp. 249–273). New York: Basic.

Good, T. L., & Weinstein, R. S. (1986). Schools make a difference: Evidence, criticism, and new directions. *American Psychologist, 41*(10), 1090–1097.

Goodlad, J. (1984). *A place called school.* New York: McGraw-Hill.

Griffin, G. A. (1985). The school as workplace as the master teacher concept. *Elementary School Journal, 86*(1), 1–16.

Heath, S. B. (1982). What no bedtime story means: Narrative skills at home and school. *Language and Society, 11*(2), 49–76.

Hiebert, E. H. (1983). An examination of ability grouping for reading instruction. *Reading Research Quarterly, 18*(9), 231–255.

Hoetker, J., & Ahlbrand, W. (1969). The persistence of recitation. *American Educational Research Journal, 6,* 145–167.

Homme, L. (1966, November). Contingency management. *Clinical Child Psychology Newsletter, 4.*

Jackson, P. (1968). *Life in classrooms.* New York: Holt, Rinehart & Winston.

John-Steiner, V. P., & Oesterreich, H. (1975). *Learning styles among Pueblo children: Final report to National Institute of Education.* Albuquerque: University of New Mexico, College of Education.

Jordan, C., Tharp, R. G., & Vogt, L. (1985). *Compatibility of classroom and culture: General principles, with Navajo and Hawaiian instances* (Working Paper). Honolulu: Kamehameha Schools/ Bishop Estate, Center for Development of Early Education.

Joyce, B. R., & Clift, R. (1984). The phoenix agenda: Essential reform in teacher education. *Educational Researcher, 13*(4), 5–18.

Keenan, E. O., & Schieffelin, B. B. (1976). Topic as a discourse notion: A study of topic in the conversations of children and adults. In C. Li (Ed.), *Subject and topic* (p. 335–384). New York: Academic Press.

Knoblock, P., & Goldstein, A. P. (1971). *The lonely teacher*. Boston: Allyn & Bacon.

Langer, J. A., & Applebee, A. N. (1986). Reading and writing instruction: Toward a theory of teaching and learning. In E. Z. Rothkopf (Ed.) (1986), *Review of research in education* (Vol. 13). Washington, DC: American Educational Research Association.

Lemke, J. L. (1982). *Classroom communication of science: Final report* (Report No. (SEDR-79-18961). Washington, DC: National Science Foundation. (ERIC Document Reproduction Service No. ED 222 346)

Leont'ev, A. N. (1981). The problem of activity in psychology. In J. V. Wertsch, (Ed.), *The concept of activity in Soviet psychology* (pp. 37–71). Armonk, NY: Sharpe.

Leont'ev, A. N. (1983). The mastery of scientific concepts by students as a problem of educational psychology. In A. N. Leont'ev (Ed.), *Selected psychological works* (Vol. 2). Moscow: Pedagogika. (Original work published 1935)

Meichenbaum, D. (1977). *Cognitive behavior modification: An integrative approach*. New York: Plenum.

Minick, N. (1985). *L. S. Vygotsky and Soviet activity theory: New perspectives on the relationship between mind and society*. Unpublished doctoral dissertation, Northwestern University, Evanston, IL.

Minick, N. (1987). Implications of Vygtosky's theories for dynamic assessment. In C. S. Lidz (Ed.), *Dynamic assessment: An interactional approach to evaluating learning potential* (pp. 116–140). New York: Gilford.

Nerlove, S. B., & Snipper, A. S. (1981). Cognitive consequences of cultural opportunity. In R. H. Munroe, R. L. Monroe, & B. B. Whiting (Eds.), *Handbook of cross-cultural human development* (pp. 423–474). New York: Garland.

Ochs, E. (1982). Talking to children in Western Samoa. *Language in Society, 11*, 77–104.

Ong, W. *Orality and literacy: The technologizing of the world*. New York: Methuen.

Paris, S., Lipson, M., & Wixson, K. (1983). Becoming a strategic reader. *Contemporary Educational Psychology, 8*, 293–316.

Pettit, G. A. (1946). *Primitive education in North America*. University of California Publications in American Archeology and Ethnology, No. 43 (Whole No. 1).

Price-Williams, D. R. (1975). *Explorations in cross-cultural psychology*. San Francisco: Chandler.

Rogoff, B. (1982). Integrating context and cognitive development. In M. E. Brown & A. L. Brown (Eds.), *Advances in developmental psychology* (Vol. 2, pp. 125–170). Hillsdale, NJ: Erlbaum.

Rogoff, B. (in press). The joint socialization of development by young children and adults. In L. M. Feinman & S. Feinman (Eds.), *Social influences and behavior*. New York: Plenum.

Sarason, S. B. (1971). *The culture of the school and the problem of change*. Boston: Allyn & Bacon.

Sarason, S. B. (1983). *Schooling in America: Scapegoat and salvation*. New York: Free Press.

Schieffelin, B. B. (1985). Acquisition of Kaluli. In D. I. Slobin (Ed.), *The crosslinguistic study of language acquisition: Vol. I. The data* (pp. 525–593). Hillsdale, NJ: Erlbaum.

Schultz, J., Erickson, F., & Florio, S. (1982). Where's the floor? Aspects of the cultural organization of social relationships in communication at home and at school. In P. Gilmore & A. Glatthorn (Eds.), *Children in and out of school: Ethnography and education* (pp. 88–123) Washington, DC: Harcourt Brace Jovanovich and Center for Applied Linguistics.

Scribner, S., & Cole, M. (1973). Cognitive consequences of formal and informal education. *Science, 182*, 553–559.

Scribner, S., & Cole, M. (1981). *The psychology of literacy*. Cambridge, MA: Harvard University Press.

Sloat, K. C. M., Tharp, R. G., & Gallimore, R. (1977). The incremental effectiveness of classroom based teacher training techniques. *Behavior Therapy, 8*,810–818.

Staats, A. W. (1968). *Learning, language, and cognition.* New York: Holt, Rienhart & Winston.

Tafoya, M. (1983). The red & the black: Santa Clara pottery. Posterboard, Wheelwright Museum of the American Indian, Santa Fe.

Teale, W. H. (1986). Home background and young children's literacy development. In W. H. Teale & E. Sulzby (Eds.), *Emergent literacy: Writing and reading* (pp. 173–206). Norwood, NJ: Ablex.

Tharp, R. G. (1982). The effective instruction of comprehension: Results and description of the Kamehameha Early Education Program. *Reading Research Quarterly, 17*(4), 503–527.

Tharp, R. G. (1985, October). *Wholism and the "observational-learning complex": A comparative study of comprehension instruction among Navajo and Hawaiians.* Paper read at the meeting of the National Indian Education Association, Spokane, WA.

Tharp, R. G. (1987, January). *Culture, cognition, and education.* Symposium conducted at the Third International Conference on Thinking, Honolulu.

Tharp, R. G. (1989). Psychocultural variables and constants: Effects on teaching and learning in schools. *American Psychologist, 44*(2), 349–359.

Tharp, R. G., & Gallimore, R. (1976a). Basketball's John Wooden: What a coach can teach a teacher. *Psychology Today, 9*(8), 74–78.

Tharp, R. G., & Gallimore, R. (1976b). *The uses and limits of social reinforcement and industriousness for learning to read* (Tech. Report No. 60). Honolulu. Kamehameha Schools/Bishop Estate, Kamehameha Early Education Program.

Tharp, R. G., & Gallimore, R. (1985). The logical status of metacognitive training. *Journal of Abnormal Child Psychology, 13*(3), 455–466.

Tharp, R. G., & Gallimore, R. (1988). *Rousing minds to life: Teaching, learning, and schooling in social context.* Cambridge: Cambridge University Press.

Tharp, R. G., Gallimore, R., & Calkins, R. P. (1984). On the relationship between self-control and control by others. *Advances en Psicologia Clinical Latinoamericano, 3*,45–58.

Tharp, R. G., & Wetzel, R. (1969). *Behavior modification in the natural environment.* New York: Academic Press.

Tough, J. (1982). Language, poverty, and disadvantage in school. In L. Feagans & D. C. Faran (Eds.), *The language of children reared in poverty* (pp. 3–18). New York: Academic Press.

Vogt, L. A., Jordan, C. J., & Tharp, R. G. (1987). Explaining school failure, producing school success: Two cases. *Anthropology & Education Quarterly, 18,* 276–286.

Vygotsky, L. S. (1956). *Izbrannie psibhologicheskie issledovania* [Selected psychological research]. Moscow: Izdateel'stro Akademii Pedagogicheskikh Nak.

Vygtosky, L. S. (1978). *Mind in society: The development of higher psychological processes* (M. Cole, V. John-Steiner, S. Scribner, & E. Souberman, Eds. and Trans). Cambridge, MA: Harvard University Press.

Vygtosky, L. S. (1987). *Collected works of L. S. Vygtosky: Vol. 1. Problems of general psychology* (N. Minick, Trans.; R. W. Rieber & S. Carton, Series Eds.). New York: Plenum. (Original work published 1982 in Russian).

Walberg, H. J. (1986). Syntheses of research on teaching. In M. C. Wittrock (Ed.), *Handbook of research on teaching* (3rd ed.) (pp. 214–229). New York: Macmillan.

Watson, D. R., & Tharp, R. G. (1988). *Self-directed behavior* (5th ed.). Monterey, CA: Brooks/Cole.

Weisner, T. S. (1984). Ecocultural niches of middle childhood: A cross-cultural perspective. In W. A. Collins (Ed.), *Development during middle childhood: The years from six to twelve* (pp. 335–369). Washington, DC: National Academy of Sciences Press.

Weisner, T. S., & Gallimore, R. (1985). *The convergence of ecocultural and activity theory.* Paper read at the annual meeting of the American Anthropological Association, Washington, DC.

Wells, G. (1986). The language experience of five-year-old children at home and at school. In J. Cook-Gumperz (Ed.), *The social construction of literacy* (pp. 69–93). Cambridge: Cambridge University Press.

Wertsch, J. V. (1978). Adult–child interaction and the roots of metacognition. *Quarterly Newsletter of the Laboratory of Comparative Human Cognition, 2*(1), 15–18.

Wertsch, J. V. (1979). From social interaction to higher psychological process: A clarification and application of Vygtosky's theory. *Human Development, 22,* 1–22.

Wertsch, J. V. (1981). *The concept of activity in Soviet psychology.* New York: Sharpe.

Wertsch, J. V. (1985a). *Culture, communication, and cognition: Vygotskian perspectives.* Cambridge: Cambridge University Press.

Wertsch, J. V. (Ed.) (1985b). *Vygtosky and the social formation of mind.* Cambridge, MA: Harvard University Press.

Wertsch, J. V., Minick, N., & Arns, F. A. (1984). The creation of context in joint problem-solving. In B. Rogoff & J. Lave (Eds.), *Everyday cognition: Its development in social contexts* (pp. 151–171). Cambridge, MA: Harvard University Press.

Wertsch, J. V., & Stone, C. A. (1985). The concept of internalization in Vygtosky's account of the genesis of higher mental functions. In J. V. Wertsch (Ed.), *Culture, communication, and cognition: Vygotskian perspectives* (pp. 162–179). Cambridge: Cambridge University Press.

White, S., & Tharp, R. G. (1988). *Training handbook for coding teacher questions* (Tech. Rep. No. 141). Honolulu: Kamehameha Schools/Bishop Estate, Center for Development of Early Education.

White, S., Tharp, R. G., Jordan, C., & Vogt, L. (1987, January). *Cultural patterns of cognition reflected in the questioning styles of Anglo and Navajo teachers.* Paper presented at the Third International Conference on Thinking, Honolulu.

Whiting, B., & Whiting, J. (1975). *Children of six cultures.* Cambridge, MA: Harvard University Press.

Wittrock, M. C. (1974). Learning as a generative process. *Educational Psychologist, 11,* 87–95.

Wittrock, M. C. (Ed.) (1986). *Handbook of research on teaching* (3rd ed). New York: Macmillan.

Wood, D. J. (1980). Teaching the young child: Some relationships between social interaction, language, and thought. In R. Olson (Ed.), *The social foundations of language and thought* (pp. 280–296). New York: Norton.

Wood, D., McMahon, L., & Cranstoun, Y. (1980). *Working with under fives.* London: Grant McIntyre.

8 A Vygotskian interpretation of Reading Recovery

Marie M. Clay and Courtney B. Cazden

This is an analysis of one tutorial program, Reading Recovery (RR), for children who have been in school for 1 year and have not yet "caught on" to reading and writing. RR was designed and evaluated by Clay in New Zealand (1979, 1985; Clay & Watson, 1982) and will soon be available to children who need it throughout that country. Because of its success there, it is being tried out in the United States, notably through Ohio State University (Lyons, 1987; Pinnell, 1985, 1988). Cazden learned about RR while on extended stays in New Zealand during 1983 and 1987 and became interested in features of its instructional design after viewing videotapes of New Zealand RR lessons.

RR was designed from Clay's theory of the nature of reading, observations of children's behavior in learning to read, and collaboration with experienced New Zealand infant school teachers. Although no thought was given to Vygotsky's theories during this program development, it is possible to interpret features of RR in Vygotskian terms. At first it seemed to Cazden that RR was simply an elegant example of scaffolded instruction (Cazden 1979, 1988).[1] As we worked together on this chapter, more relationships to Vygotsky's ideas appeared.

After a brief introduction to the theory of reading that guides literacy instruction in both regular New Zealand classrooms and RR programs, we analyze features of RR that require teacher (T) and child (C) to collaborate in shared tasks – reading a new book and writing the child's story – and present evidence in both cases of a shift from T/C interindividual functioning to increasingly complex intraindividual functioning by the child. We then suggest Vygotskian interpretations of RR as a system of social interaction organized around the comprehension and production of texts that demonstrably creates new forms of cognitive activity in the child.

A theory of reading

According to Clay's theory of reading and writing instruction (1979, 1985), all readers, from 5-year-old children attempting their first book to proficient adults, have to monitor and integrate information from multiple sources. Readers need to use, and check against each other, four types of cues: semantic (text meaning),

206

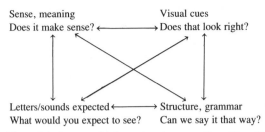

Figure 8.1. Sources of information about text (from Clay, 1985, p. 74)

syntactic (sentence structure), visual (graphemes, orthography, format, and layout), and phonological (the sounds of oral language) (see Figure 8.1).

The end point of early instruction has been reached when children have a *self-improving system:* They learn more about reading every time they read, independent of instruction. (Stanovich, 1986, calls this "boot-strapping.") When they read texts of appropriate difficulty for their present skills, they use a set of mental operations, strategies in their heads, that are just adequate for more difficult bits of the text. In the process, they engage in "reading work," deliberate efforts to solve new problems with familiar information and procedures. They are working with theories of the world and theories about written language, testing them and changing them as they engage in reading and writing activities.

By the age of 6, after 1 year of instruction, high-progress readers in New Zealand classrooms operate on print in this way. As cue users, not just oral language guessers, they read with attention focused on meaning, checking several sources of cues, one against the other, almost simultaneously. When such higher-level strategies fail, they can engage a lower processing gear and shift focus to one or another cue source in isolation – such as letter clusters or letter–sound associations – while maintaining a directing attention on the text message at all times.

Low-progress readers, on the other hand, operate with a more limited range of strategies – some relying too much on what they can invent from memory without paying attention to visual details, others looking so hard for words they know or guessing words from first letters that they forget what the message as a whole is about.

For all children, the larger the chunks of printed language they can work with, the richer the network of information they can use, and the quicker they learn. Teaching should dwell on detail only long enough for the child to discover its existence and then encourage the use of it in isolation only when absolutely necessary.

Overview of Reading Recovery

RR addresses a problem of concern to most Western educational systems. It selects young children who have the poorest performance in reading and writing and, in daily individual teaching sessions over 12–15 weeks, brings most of them to average levels of performance and teaches them how to improve their own reading and writing skills when they are no longer in the program.

Children are selected for the RR program by a diagnostic survey (Clay, 1985) administered by RR teachers and by consultation among the school staff. No child in ordinary classrooms is excluded because of intelligence, limited English proficiency, possible learning disability, or for any other reason.

The children's rate and amount of progress in the program in New Zealand (where 3-year follow-up research yielded evidence of continued average achievement) are similar to what is achieved in Bloom's one-to-one tutoring programs (Bloom, 1971, p. 60). With the exception of 1–2% of the entire age–class cohort who need more help than RR provides, pupils from the low end of the achievement distribution are moved into the average band of performance. In other words, a significantly different population becomes not statistically different from the average group.

In order to achieve such accelerated learning, attention of teacher and child must be on strategies or operations – mental activities initiated by the child to get messages from a text. If the teacher becomes involved in teaching items rather than strategies – particular letter–sound correspondences or sight vocabulary words, for example, rather than the strategy of checking a word that would make sense in the context against information in the print – the prospect of accelerated learning is seriously threatened. Letter–sound correspondences and spelling patterns are learned, but in the course of reading and, especially, writing meaningful text, RR teachers praise children for generative strategies, not for items learned.

The following activities, usually in this order, constitute the daily RR lesson:

1. rereading of two or more familiar books
2. independent reading of yesterday's new book while the teacher takes a running record
3. letter identification (plastic letters on a magnetic board)
4. writing a story the child has composed (including hearing sounds in words)
5. reassembling the cut-up story
6. introducing a new book
7. reading the new book

When a child no longer needs to work on letter identification, the third slot is deleted or used for other word-breaking or word-building work.

We will present a detailed analysis of reading activities (6) and (7) and writing activities (4) and (5). All examples are from videotapes of RR lessons in New Zealand and Ohio. The teachers, like all RR teachers, are regular classroom teachers (infant teachers in New Zealand, primary teachers in the United States) who have received a year of full-time training and practicum. Because of this training, and subsequent monthly meetings while on the job, there is much less variation among teachers than in most program implementations. The children – Melanie, Larry, and Premala – are all from the lowest 10% in their school cohort.

Reading a new book

During the first two weeks of a Reading Recovery program, the teacher does not try to teach the child anything new but initiates activities that allow the child to use and explore further the repertoire of behaviors he or she already controls. Teacher and child discover many things about each other during these two weeks. The teacher discovers what the child already knows; and the child learns how book sharing will occur in the lessons to come. A format for book-sharing interaction between this child and this teacher is created.

Excerpts from Melanie's book introduction illustrate this. Because the teacher takes the initiative in these early lessons, her moves are given on the left, categorized by kinds of help, with the child's responses on the right. Oral reading is transcribed in capital letters.

Melanie: Book introduction during the first week

Teacher	*Child*
Setting the topic THE CHOCOLATE CAKE. (T reads the title for M.)	
Maintaining interaction Let's read this together.	
Increasing accessibility (She provides a model:) "MM" and GRANDMA.	
Supporting performance (T and M complete the page together.) "MM, MM," SAID GRANDMA.	
Prompting constructive activity (T pauses . . .)	
	(and M continues reading the next two pages.) "MM, MM," SAID GRANDPA. "MM," SAID MA and "MM," SAID BABY.
Working with necessary knowledge And what did they do?	
	Eat it.
That's right. They all ate it (confirming M's response, while changing the verb tense to match the text).	
Providing a model and prompting completion And so they said, "IT'S ALL . . ."	
	(M anticipates and generates) . . . GONE. (Then she goes quickly to the next page and anticipates and generates a relevant oral text.) We want more.

Accepting partially correct response
(T accepts this but revises it in her re-
ply to match the sentence in the text.)
"MORE, MORE, MORE," THEY
SAID.

Maintaining shared interaction
(Pointing to the page, T invites M:)
Read it with me.

Calling for reflection or judgment
about the story
                  (T and M discuss what will happen –
                  will another cake be baked? – focusing
                  M's attention on comprehension of the
                  story as a whole.)

The teacher's introduction of a new text

In RR, the child is not usually expected to sight-read novel text without preparation; that is more appropriate after children have learned how to read. A new book is both carefully selected and carefully introduced. What may seem like casual conversational exchanges between teacher and pupil are based on deliberate teaching decisions for a particular child. These are based on the teacher's records, obtained from the daily individual teaching sessions, of each child's response repertoire – what Wood, Bruner, and Ross refer to as "performance characteristics" (1976, p. 97), the observable aspects of the child's reading and writing action system.

Setting the topic. The teacher has selected the new book to challenge the pupil in specific ways. She has previewed the story and its challenges. She sets the topic, title, and characters with minimal interaction; too much talk confuses. Titles are treated as labels; they often have tricks in them and tend to use language from which redundancy has been stripped. Discussion may relate to the conceptual context of the new story or to a related book the child has read.

Increasing accessibility. The teacher may sketch the plot, or the sequences in the text, up to any climax or surprise. Using new or unusual words in context, she introduces things the child might not understand or language the child might not be able to anticipate. She may carefully enunciate unusual syntax (for example, when the text uses a full form, *cannot,* where the child might expect *can't*). Or she may use a sentence pattern two or three times to help the child hold it in his or her mind. If the child generates a relevant phrase, T confirms it and alters it where necessary to match the text (as one teacher does when Melanie says "Eat it," above, and another teacher does when Larry makes the same error in the transcription below).

    In these ways, T and C rehearse what is novel in the story without the child actually hearing the text read. It is typical of all RR instruction that features of texts receive attention not in isolation but within the complexity of that text for this particular child.

Maintaining interactive ease. To repeat and amplify what the child says maintains interactive ease, but it also models for the child that discussion of the story is expected. It may create more conceptual context, add new information, or remove ambiguity and possible confusion.

Prompting the child to constructive activity. In general, the teacher urges the child to search actively for links: links within the story (pausing for the child to generate the ending: "It's all . . ." [*gone*] or to guess *grandpa* and *baby* by analogy with *grandma*); links within the print (asking, "How did you know . . . ?''); and links beyond the book into the child's experiences ("Have you ever done that?" "How do you think *X* felt?'').

Teachers may think that such questions are intended to arouse the child's interest and motivation, but they play a more instrumental role in beginning reading. Such questions provide signals to the child that reading requires active interaction with texts and brings relevant experiences and knowledge to the child's "context in the mind" (Cazden, 1982).

Working with new knowledge. The teacher checks to see whether the child has relevant knowledge and ensures that it has been "brought to mind" and is accessible for use in reading the book. When the teacher suspects that the child does not have the ideas or word needed for a particular text, she may explain some part of the story or contrast a feature of the story with something she knows the child knows in another book. For example, she may help the child discriminate between two things like a school desk and an adult-type writing desk. Such help may be either anticipatory or responsive to signals from the child. When teachers expect a word to be unfamiliar to a child, they first talk toward the meaning, describe some relevant object, setting, or use, and only then label or name the word; cognitive context is necessary in order for the child to "receive" the new word with understanding.

Because constructive activity is so important, the teacher gently pushes the child toward actively working with the new knowledge in some way – for example, by checking the new information with the pictures in the book.

Accepting partially correct responses. The teacher promotes emerging skill by accepting and reinforcing responses that are only partially correct. Rarely does the child's response come out of thin air; it is a response to some part of the text and/ or some part of his or her understanding. If a response is correct in some respect, it is in the interest of both the child's economy in learning and his or her increasing self-confidence as a reader for the teacher to recognize this and then help the child change where necessary. If the teacher cannot tell what strategy the child has used, her response will be deliberately general: "I liked the way you did that, but did you notice . . ." At other times, she praises the use of a particular feature or type of information (such as attention to the first letter).

In this way the teacher creates a lesson format, a scaffold, within which she promotes emerging skill, allows for the child to work with the familiar, introduces the unfamiliar in a measured way, and deals constructively with slips and errors. The teacher calls for the comprehension of texts and for the detection and repair of mismatches when they occur. She passes more and more control to the child and pushes the child, gently but consistently, into independent, constructive activity.

In the second example, Larry is introduced to a new book, *The Great Big Enormous Turnip,* in the ninth week of his daily lessons.

Larry: Book introduction during the ninth week

Teacher	*Child*
Setting the topic, theme, and characters	
Let's look at our new book. This story was about a big turnip, wasn't it? (T knew L had heard the story somewhere but had not read it.) THE GREAT BIG ENORMOUS TURNIP. Let's see what happened. Here's a little old man and he's . . .	
Prompting constructive activity	
What's he doing?	
	He's telling it to grow.
Accepting the child's involvement	
That's right! He's telling it to grow. Good!	
Prompting constructive activity	
And then what's he trying to do?	
	Pull it out.
Pull it out. Can he pull it out?	
	(Shakes his head.)
No. Who does he ask to help him?	
	The little old woman.
And what do they do?	
	Pull it?
Did they do it?	
	(Shakes his head.)
No. Who do they ask next?	
	(No reply.)
Working with new knowledge	
They're asking the granddaughter, aren't they?	
Prompting constructive activity	
And do they all pull? Does it come up?	
	No.
Who do they ask next?	
	The dog.

Accepting partially correct responses
The black dog, that's right.
And still it doesn't come up.

Prompting constructive activity
Who do they ask next?

> The cat.

Playing with the climax effect
And does it come up? Does it? I think
it might, and they all . . . (turns the
page). Oh, no! Not yet.

Prompting constructive activity
Who do they ask?

> The mouse.

The mouse, that's right. And they're
all pulling, aren't they? And then what
happened?

> It came out.

It came out, and what did they all do?

Accepting partially correct responses

> Eat it.

That's right. They all ate it.
You read it to me.

Following this introduction, the teacher expects Larry to read the book for the first time by problem solving as independently as possible.

Teacher–child interaction during the first reading

Over the course of each child's RR program, there are shifts in how much control of the task he or she is able to take as a result of such introductions, and how independent the first reading of a text can be. In the early weeks, the child will generate an oral utterance, inventing and reconstructing a text from the introduction or memory of past readings, the pictures, and what little is known about print. He or she will spend the next 12 to 15 weeks mapping oral language onto printed text. Through the child's constructive cognitive activity, visual perception of print, oral language, and world knowledge work together, with meaning as the goal and the teacher as monitor and guide.

Here is Larry's first reading of *The Great Big Enormous Turnip,* immediately after T's introduction. On two occasions, she directs his attention to the subword level of analysis, ''sw——''(*eet*) and ''str——''(*ong*), without losing the textual emphasis of the interchange. (Sometimes a first reading will contain more new teaching than this one does.) The teacher decides not to work on some errors and attends only to what she believes is critical for a correct reading of the text the next day.

Because the child now has the initiative, in this transcription his reading is placed on the left, with the teacher's responses on the right.

Larry's first reading of the new book

Child	*Teacher*
THE GREAT BIG ENORMOUS TURNIP. ONCE AN OLD MAN PLANTED A TURNIP.	
	Good. (T ignores the omission of "Once upon a time.")
HE SAID, GROW, GROW LITTLE TURNIP, GROW . . . (pauses at the next word).	
	How does that word start? Can I help you start it off? How does it start? s— — He tells it to grow sw—— sweet. (T could have anticipated this word in her introduction.)
(The child does not reread the prompted text but moves on.) GROW LITTLE TURNIP, GROW S—— (pauses at another word).	
	How else does he want it to grow? He wants it to grow sweet and he wants it to grow str——
(Child is now working at both word and story level) . . . STRONG.	
	Good boy, that's lovely. Grow strong.
AND THE TURNIP GREW UP SWEET AND STRONG AND . . .	
	(No attention to the omission of "big.") What's the other word that begins with *e*? Enor——
ENORMOUS.	
	Good.
AND THEN . . . (self-corrects) THEN ONE DAY THE OLD MAN WENT TO PULL IT UP. HE . . .	
	(No attention to the self-correction, so as not to detract from meaning.) What's he doing?
PULL . . .	
	That's right.
AND PULLED AGAIN BUT HE CAN'T	
	(Teacher ignores the uncorrected "pulled" and, attending to the present problem solving, accepts the partially correct response.) Nearly right. It starts like *can't* but he c——

COULDN'T

               (Models) could

COULD NOT PULL IT UP.

               That's right. He could not pull it up.

I can't . . .

               (Prompts story structure.) What did he do?

HE . . .

               Look! What is he doing, do you think? He . . .

HE CALLED THE OLD WOMAN.

               Right, he called the old woman.

THE OLD WOMAN PULLED . . .
THE OLD WOMAN PULLED THE OLD MAN

               Good, I like the way you went back and did that again (confirming check).

THE OLD MAN PULLED THE TURNIP AND THEY PULLED AND PULLED AGAIN BUT THEY COULD NOT PULL IT UP.

               Well done. We got that word (*they*). Jolly good.

SO THE OLD WOMAN CALLED HER GRANDDAUGHTER.

               Good boy!

THE GRANDDAUGHTER PULLED THE OLD WOMAN. THE OLD WOMAN PULLED THE OLD MAN. THE OLD MAN PULLED THE TURNIP AND THEY PULLED AND PULLED AGAIN BUT THEY COULD NOT PULL IT UP.

               (The teacher skips to the end. This is a timed session being recorded.) Right! Let's find where they pulled it up . . . and it came out.

THEN THEY . . .

               (Steadying.) That's right.

THEY PULLED AND PULLED AGAIN AND UP CAME THE TURNIP AT LAST.

               That's very good. Do you like that book? What would you like to do to finish off?

A running record would be taken when the child reads the book independently the next day, and this teacher could be reasonably confident that the child will read it at or above 90% accuracy. When this does not happen, then the teacher's choice of book, or the way she introduced it, or her teaching around the first reading has not been appropriate.

After this first reading, each book is reread several times during the first activity in subsequent lessons. During these rereadings, there will be opportunities for the child to return to, and discover, more aspects of the text than he understood the first day.

Writing a story

During each RR lesson, the child composes a "story" (usually just one sentence) and writes it, with help from the teacher, in an unlined notebook. Then a sentence-strip version of the same story, copied and cut up by the teacher, is given to the child to reassemble immediately and take home to reassemble again "for Mum." Much of the child's learning of sound–letter relationships and spelling patterns is prompted and practiced in these activities.

For one child, Premala, we have three videotapes taken near the beginning, middle, and end of her 15-week RR program (Premala I, II, and III). Here are the stories she composes:

I   *A little girl is cuddling a cat* (about a book).
II   *The little red hen made a cake* (about a book).
III *I am going swimming at school now* (about a personal experience; New Zealand children do swim at school).

The chart shows how these three sentences got written down. What the child (C) wrote is on the top line; what the teacher (T) wrote is underneath. If the child wrote the letter, but only after some kind of help from the teacher, the letter appears on the child's line with a circle around it. The "boxes" around letters in *hen* and *made* are explained below.

I   (C)   A Ⓛ   g   k   a   c t.
     (T)   ittle   irl   is   cuddling   a

II   (C)   The littl ⓔ   r Ⓔⓓ |h\e/n| |m|a|d/e| c
                                2 3 1   2 3 1 4

     (T)   some cakes.

III (C)   I ⓐm going s Ⓦⓘ m ⓜ ing at s Ⓒⓗⓞⓞ l now.

Premela's progress in transcribing her stories can be summarized in the increasing number of letters written correctly by the child, alone or with help, and the decreasing number written by the teacher (T):

	C alone	C with help	T	Total
I	5	1	19	25
II	9	10	9	28
III	19	8	0	27

To achieve this progress, the teacher gives various kinds of writing help that are analogous in function to her help in reading:

Calling attention to the sounds of words and spelling patterns in writing:

    I   "Do you know how to start writing *little?*"

    III (After P has written *s* for *swim*) "Let's listen to it. What can you hear?"

Prompting visual memory of previous experience with written words:

    II "Something needs to go on the end [of *little*], doesn't it?"

Drawing boxes (Clay, 1985; adapted from Elkonin, 1975) to correspond to the sounds (phonemes, not letters) in the word, and showing the child how to push counters into the boxes, left to right, while saying the word slowly: h-e-n, m-a-d-e.[2] When these boxes are first introduced, T accepts letters in any order, as long as they are in the correct place. The numbers under the boxes show that Premala placed the letter for the final sounds in both words first. Later T will encourage the child to fill in the letters in left to right order and will draw them to correspond to letters rather than sounds.

Asking the child to develop and use her visual memory: In II, T asked P to write *red* several times, first with a model available to copy, then with the model covered; then to walk over and write it on the blackboard from memory; and finally to finish it after T had erased the last two letters. In III, there was similar practice for a harder word, *school.*

Praising strategies, even if the result is only partially correct:

    I   "That's a good guess, because *cuddling* sometimes sounds like that" (when P has written a *k*).

    II   "Good thinking. You remembered that" (*e* on *little*).

    II   "I liked the way you checked it all through" (referring to the child's reassembly of her cut-up sentence).

    III "You don't need to look because you've got it inside your head, haven't you" (referring to writing *school* from memory).

Introducing new information:

    I   "Let's have a look and I'll show you what else *cuddling* can sound like."

Increasing the difficulty of the task: Because the child composes the sentence that is written during each RR lesson, the teacher cannot increase the challenge of the overall writing task as she does in selecting a new book. But she does increase the challenge of the reassembly of the child's sentence from sentence-strip pieces. Slash lines show her segmentation of the sentences for II and III (not done in I):

    II   The / little /r/ed /hen / made / some / cakes.

          (Note the relationship between the segmentation of *red* and the writing Premala did from memory at the blackboard.)

    III I / a/m / go/ing / swi/mm/ing / a/t / school / now. Although both sentences have seven words, T increases the number of segments for Premala to reassemble from 8 to 12. In both cases, Premala succeeds, rereading and checking as she goes.

General RR features

Generalizing from these examples of RR activities, we suggest features that distinguish RR from other reading programs and features that may apply to other curriculum areas.

For teachers in the United States, this program should be differentiated from both "whole language" (WL) and "phonics" (PH). It differs from most WL programs in recognizing the need for temporary instructional detours in which the child's attention is called to particular cues available in speech or print. It differs from PH in conceptualizing phonological awareness as an outcome of reading and writing rather than as their prerequisite, and in developing children's awareness of sounds in oral language rather than teaching letter–sound relationships. It differs from both in the frequent observation and recording of the reading and writing repertoire of the individual child as the basis for teacher initiative (as in choosing the next book) and response (in moment-to-moment decisions about when, and how, to help).

There are three reasons for these features. First, especially when children have limited strengths relevant to the task at hand, it is important to use those strengths. Five-year-old children have oral language resources; RR draws on those resources in developing the child's sound awareness, which can then be used to check against visual cues in print. Second, at-risk children who are taught letter–sound relationships often cannot use that information, because they cannot hear the sounds in words they say or read. So the harder skill must be taught, and the easier one seems to follow. The most pragmatic place to teach sound awareness is in writing, where segmentation is an essential part of the task.

Finally, in the case of vowels, teaching any one-to-one relationship between letters and sounds in English words must eventually be confusing to the child. Reading requires flexibility in handling such relationships, and writing provides rich practice. For example, children who learn to write five high- and medium-frequency words containing the vowel a – a, at, play, father, said – have implicitly learned a one-to-many letter–sound relationship (Clay & Watson, 1982, Pt. 2, p. 24). The teacher helps the child use this knowledge, first learned in writing, during reading.

RR was designed specifically to teach reading and writing to children who are still low achievers after 1 year of school. In developing programs of problem solving with adult guidance for other low-achieving learners in other curriculum areas, six pedagogical premises may have wider significance:

1. The teacher works with what she knows the children can do alone, or with assistance, and brings them by different paths to patterns of normal progress, with which she has had extensive experience.
2. The interactions occur daily for a substantial block of time, and daily records ensure that at any one time the teacher knows exactly what the child can now do independently, and what he or she is currently learning to do with support.
3. The lessons address a wide range of subroutines and types of learning, all of which have been shown in research on normal children to play a role in the desired outcome behaviors, even though they may not be highly interdependent at this particular stage of learning. Most obvious is the example of reading and writing: Both occur in the daily lessons from the beginning, although their reciprocal value may not be utilized by teacher or child until later in the program.
4. At all times, the achievement of a task requires that the child see it as meaningful, because only then can the child control the task and detect errors when the message doesn't make sense.
5. The child is encouraged to work independently in some way from the first week of the program.
6. Because task difficulty is constantly being increased, the types of interactions between the child and teacher do not change greatly throughout the program, even though the child assumes more control. What do change are the problem solving done by the child and the strategies that the child is called upon to use.

Vygotskian interpretations

The teacher's role as scaffold

The metaphorical term *scaffold,* though never used by Vygotsky, has come to be used for interactional support, often in the form of adult–child dialogue that is structured by the adult to maximize the growth of the child's intrapsychological functioning. In their shared activity, the teacher is interacting with unseen processes – the in-the-head strategies used by the child to produce the overt responses of writing and oral reading. For any one child, the RR program as a whole is such a scaffold. On a more micro level, we have seen many examples of the child functioning independently, in both reading and writing, where earlier collaboration between teacher and child was necessary.

But it would be a mistake to think of the scaffold as simply being removed as the child's competence grows. If we consider RR as a whole, that does happen, and the child becomes able to continue learning to read and write as a "self-improving system" within the regular classroom, without the finely tuned support of the RR teacher. But within the program, because the teacher selects texts on an increasing gradient of difficulty, the scaffold of teacher support continues, always at the cutting edge of the child's competencies, in his or her continually changing zone or proximal development.

Changes in the forms of mediation

According to Vygotsky, major turning points in development are connected with the appearance, or transformation, of new forms of mediation. Reading Recovery is designed to help the child accomplish just that: the integration of the semiotic codes of oral language and English orthography, plus world knowledge, into the complex operations of reading and writing. It includes the presence of stimuli created by the child (in the self-composed sentences) as well as those given to the child in teacher-selected texts. And it includes a shift from pointing as an external psychological tool (Wertsch, 1985, pp. 77–81), which the child is asked to use to focus his attention on each word in sequence, to later internalization, when the teacher judges the child to be ready to "Try with just your eyes" (as she said in Premala III).

The special case of conscious realization

Wertsch discusses four criteria that Vygotsky used to distinguish higher mental functions: their social origins, the use of sign mediation, voluntary rather than environmental regulation, and the emergence of conscious realization of mental processes (1985, p. 25). The role of the last in learning to read (perhaps in learning any skill) is not a simple linear development toward increasing consciousness.

It is true that during RR, as the child becomes familiar with lesson procedures and text-solving processes, the teacher imposes demands for conscious realization by asking "How did you know. . . ?" She needs to understand what information the child is using. And the child, by being prompted to talk briefly about text processing, learns that we can know about how we know and thereby control our mental processes more effectively.

But there are two qualifications to the growth of conscious realization in the RR teaching procedures and their outcomes. First, though conscious manipulation of signs to mediate higher mental functions should be available when needed for problem solving, it should recede into automatic processing when the reader/writer is attending to text meaning, which is most of the time. (We do not drive in low gear when we do not need to.)

Second, certain behaviors developed and checked initially at an explicit interpsychological level (such as directional behaviors and most visual perception learning of written language forms and formats) are properly run off as automatic subroutines without conscious attention. Most cognitive psychology models of reading capture the trend toward conscious manipulation in some form. What are often neglected are the perceptual, directional, sequential sign-processing operations that operate outside conscious awareness but must be learned since they are specific to the script in use. Learning to read and write can be considered a prototypical example of what Rommetveit calls "the cultural development of attention" (1985, p. 194).

Development, instruction, and diagnosis

Vygotsky applied the concept of a zone of proximal development to both instruction and diagnosis. In his well-known words, "the only good kind of instruction is that which marches ahead of development and leads it; it must be aimed not so much at the ripe as at the ripening function" (1962, p. 104).

Reading Recovery is designed for children younger than those in many "remedial" programs, and teachers may ask why children are placed in the program after only 1 year in school. Wouldn't some children "catch on" to reading and writing in the regular classroom in their own time? For a few, this might happen. But for most children identified as low achievers after 1 year in school, time will only bring an increasing gap between them and the rest of their age cohort and will reinforce their self-image as incompetent in important school skills. In short, many will learn – unnecessarily – to be "learning-disabled" (Clay, 1987). With RR, instruction supports emergent development rather than waiting for it.

With respect to diagnosis, Vygotsky and Soviet psychologists working with his ideas[3] use the concept of the zone of proximal development to differentiate among a group of underachieving learners. Though RR is most obviously and intentionally a program of instruction, it also can serve as a form of what Brown and Ferrara (1985) call "dynamic assessment."

According to the New Zealand experience, within the 10% of each 6-year-old cohort assigned to RR, the effects of 15 weeks of instruction lead to the differentiation of two groups of children. One group, approximately 9% of the age group, benefits sufficiently from the program to progress as average learners in the regular classroom, at least for the 3-year period for which follow-up research has been done. The other group, less than 1% of the original age cohort, needs further specialist help. Although the two groups of children have similar levels of independent performance at the time of the 6-year diagnostic survey, their response to RR instruction is very different:

> Reading Recovery is a programme which should clear out of the remedial education system all the children who do not read for many event-produced reasons and all the children who have organically-based problems but who can be taught to achieve independent learning status in reading and writing despite this, leaving a small group of children requiring specialist attention. (Clay, 1987, p. 169)

In the United States, the percentage of children requiring specialist attention may be somewhat different, but the benefits of making assessment decisions on the basis of the child's response to carefully designed instruction should be the same.

Notes

1 As far as we know, Wood, Bruner, and Ross (1976) were the first to apply the term *scaffold* metaphorically to instruction. But, surprisingly, their article does not cite Vygotsky at all, though Bruner had been familiar with his work at least since writing the introduction to *Thought and Language* (as recounted in Bruner, 1985).
2 Clay has found that in the training of RR teachers, the concept they find most difficult is the distinction between phonemes and letters, presumably because their mental representation of English word sounds has been so deeply influenced by experience with written text.
3 Cazden (1979) and Brown and Ferrara (1985) report Cazden and Brown's observations of Soviet psychologists V. I. Lubovsky and T. V. Rozanova's diagnostic use of "graduated aids" during a visit to the Institute of Defectology in Moscow (an institution founded by Vygotsky) in December 1978.

References

Bloom, B. (1971). Mastery learning. In J. H. Block (Ed.), *Mastery learning: Theory and practice*. New York: Holt, Rinehart & Winston.

Brown, A. L., & Ferrara, R. A. (1985). Diagnosing zones of proximal development. In J. V. Wertsch (Ed.), *Culture, communication, and cognition*. Cambridge: Cambridge University Press.

Bruner, J. (1985) Vygotsky: A historical and conceptual perspective. In J. V. Wertsch (Ed.), *Culture, communication, and cognition*. Cambridge: Cambridge University Press.

Cazden, C. B. (1979). Peekaboo as an instructional model: Discourse development at home and at school. In *Papers and reports on child language development* (No. 17). Stanford University, Department of Linguistics. Reprinted in B. Bain (Ed.), *The sociogenesis of language and human conduct*. New York: Plenum, 1983.

Cazden, C. B. (1982). Contexts for literacy: In the mind and in the classroom. *Journal of Reading Behavior, 14*, 413–427.

Cazden, C. B. (1988). *Classroom discourse: The language of teaching and learning*. Portsmouth, NH: Heinemann.

Clay, M. M. (1979). *Reading: The patterning of complex behavior*. Portsmouth, NH: Heinemann.

Clay, M. M. (1985). *The early detection of reading difficulties* (3rd ed.). Portsmouth, NH: Heinemann.

Clay, M. M. (1987). Learning to be learning disabled. *New Zealand Journal of Educational Studies,*
    22, 155–173.
Clay, M. M., & Watson, B. (1982). *The success of Maori children in the Reading Recovery programme.*
    Report prepared on research contract for the Director-General of Education, Department of Educa-
    tion, Wellington.
Elkonin, D. B. (1975). USSR. In J. Downing (Ed.), *Comparative reading: Cross-national studies of
    behavior and processes in reading and writing.* New York: Macmillan.
Lyons, C. A. (1987). *Reading Recovery: An effective intervention program for learning disabled first
    graders.* (ERIC Document Reproduction Service No. ED 284 170).
Pinnell, G. S. (1985, Spring). Helping teachers help children at risk: Insight from the reading recovery
    program. *Peabody Journal of Education,* pp. 70–85.
Pinnell, G. S. (1988, April). *Sustained effects of a strategy-centered early intervention program in
    reading.* Paper presented at the annual meeting of the American Educational Research Association,
    New Orleans.
Rommetveit, R. (1985). Language acquisition as increasing linguistic structuring of experience and
    symbolic behavior control. In J. V. Wertsch (Ed.), *Culture, communication, and cognition.* Cam-
    bridge: Cambridge University Press.
Stanovich, K. E. (1986). Matthew effects in reading: Some consequences of individual differences in
    the acquisition of literacy. *Reading Research Quarterly, 21,* 360–406.
Vygotsky, L. (1962). *Thought and language.* Cambridge, MA: MIT Press.
Wertsch, J. V. (1985). *Vygotsky and the social formation of mind.* Cambridge, MA: Harvard University
    Press.
Wood, D., Bruner, J. S., & Ross, G. (1976). The role of tutoring in problem solving. *Journal of Child
    Psychology & Psychiatry, 17,* 89–100.

9   Vygotsky in a whole-language perspective

Yetta M. Goodman and Kenneth S. Goodman

> The best method [for teaching reading and writing] is one in which children do not
> learn to read and write but in which both these skills are found in play situations.
> . . . In the same way as children learn to speak, they should be able to learn to
> read and write. (Vygotsky, 1978, p. 118)

In this passage, Vygotsky expresses his belief that written language develops, as
speech does, in the context of its use. It indicates his holistic inclinations and his
awareness of the need for learners to be immersed in language for literacy learning
to be easy.

Such a view is the essence of whole language. Whole language is more than
anything else a philosophy of education. It draws heavily on Vygotsky, among
others. As we relate the developing conceptualizations of whole language to the
work of Vygotsky, we will explore (1) what whole language is; (2) what it takes
from Vygotsky; (3) how whole language can contribute to the application and development of Vygotskian psychology; and (4) how it departs from or goes beyond
Vygotsky.

What is whole language?

Whole language is a holistic, dynamic, grass-roots movement among teachers. It is
spreading rapidly in the English-speaking countries of the world and moving beyond to other countries. Though some of the key concepts of whole language have
origins in the United States, particularly in the work of John Dewey (1938) and
other progressive educationists such as Kilpatrick (1926), Counts (1932), and Childs
(1956), and more recently in the work on reading and writing processes, other
English-speaking countries came to whole language earlier and more pervasively
than the United States. In Canada several provinces have whole-language policies,
and implementation is widespread. Whole language in Great Britain is building on
a number of holistic movements in education. The report of the Bullock committee,
A Language for Life (1975), played a major role in innovation in schools in Britain
as well as in Canada, Australia, and New Zealand. Though the term *whole language*
is not used widely in Great Britain, the integrated day, language across the curriculum, and other school movements have led to widespread holistic school practices.

223

In Australia, drawing on European and North American sources, whole-language policies, methods, and materials have become dominant. New Zealand, however, has the longest continuous tradition of progressive, holistic education. Since the 1930s New Zealand educators have developed learner-centered curricula and school practices (Penton, 1979). This small country, perhaps the world's most literate according to multinational studies, never abandoned Dewey's progressive education concepts, and it has provided models of application for the rest of the world (Clay & Cazden, this volume; Department of Education, 1985).

The development of whole language in the United States has been held back by the strong influence of behavioral psychology in American schools. This influence has been felt through textbooks, particularly those used in reading instruction, through mandated norm-referenced tests, and through curricula organized around testable, behavioral objectives. Though teachers in the United States have the most degrees and the most years of education of any country in the world, these behavioral curricula, policies, and materials control teachers and make it difficult for them to apply their professional knowledge to decision making in their classrooms. With these constraints, teachers find it particularly difficult to respond to the characteristics and needs of individual learners.

Ironically, whole-language teachers in the United States have been strengthened as a result of their struggle against the behavioristic mandates that govern their teaching. They have had to examine their professional beliefs and values and, at the same time, build a knowledge base to support and defend their innovations. That is why whole-language teachers are reading Vygotsky individually and in support groups, thinking about his concepts, applying them in their classrooms, and using his arguments to defend their teaching and to understand what their pupils are doing.

Whole language, as it is emerging, draws on the antecedent movements in education that have taken positive, humanistic views of teaching and learning (Y. Goodman, 1989). These can be traced at least as far back as Comenius, who advocated vernacular schools and brought pictures and the real world into instruction (see Comenius, 1887). But whole language also draws on knowledge from all of the foundational disciplines: psychology, linguistics, anthropology, and sociology. It draws on interdisciplinary work in psycholinguistics, sociolinguistics, language development, artificial intelligence, and communication theory; and it draws on all disciplines that are concerned with language: literary criticism, semiotics, semantics, and language philosophy. This is not to say that whole language is eclectic. Rather, it integrates what it draws from these sources into a practical philosophy that provides the criteria for making all the decisions teachers, as practitioners, must make. This is no small undertaking. But whole language is in fact developing in such a sophisticated way that practice is getting ahead of theory and consequently knowledgeable whole-language teachers have much to teach psychologists, linguists, anthropologists, and others.

Whole-language teachers, with their focus on authentic learning experiences (Edelsky, 1986) and integration of subject matter with the language arts, create nonreductionist school learning environments. These environments are quite different from those experimental psychologists create in their laboratories or contrive in traditional classrooms. In these nonreductionist classrooms we are just beginning to see the potential for human learning and for the kinds of teaching that most effectively support learning. Key ideas of whole language concerning social contexts and literacy development, learning in and out of school, teaching and learning, and the relationship between teaching and learning draw heavily on Vygotsky while differing from some of his concepts.

Learning literacy in the context of its use

Language, written language included, is learned most easily in the context of use. When language is whole, relevant, and functional, learners have real purposes for using language, and through their language use they develop control over the processes of language. In authentic literacy events (Edelsky, 1986), events that have personal and significant meaning for the language user, there are transactions between the reader and the text in which the reader is continuously solving new problems and building and extending psycholinguistic strategies. Through these transactions text serves to mediate the development of reading and writing. We use the concept of text, as defined by Halliday and Hasan (1976). To them, text is the basic semantic unit of linguistic interaction. "It has . . . a unity of meaning in context, a texture that expresses the fact that it relates as a whole to the environment in which it is placed" (pp. 293–295).

The whole-language view of literacy development is thus an immersion view. Children growing up in literate societies are surrounded by print. They begin to be aware of the functions of written language and to play at its use long before they come to school. School continues and extends this immersion in literacy. The school can be an even richer literate environment than the world outside of school. The teacher can serve as mediator between the learners and this literate environment. Each school experience can be an authentic speech or literacy event, "a complex cultural activity" (Vygotsky, 1978, p. 118). The teacher invites the participation of the learners and supports their transactions with language and the world.

Learning and teaching

In *Crow Boy* by Taro Yashima (1959), an insightful author and illustrator of children's books, we are introduced to Chibi, a tiny boy in a village school in Japan, who has been an isolate, a "forlorn little tag-along," for 6 years. Even the teachers are pictured as uninvolved and distant from Chibi. When the children are in the sixth grade, Mr. Isobe, a new teacher, "a friendly man with a kind smile," introduces innovative experiences for the children. He often "took his class to the hilltop behind the school." He responds to Chibi differently as well.

He [Mr. Isobe] was pleased to learn that Chibi knew all the places where the wild grapes and wild potatoes grew. . . .

He was amazed to find how much Chibi knew about all the flowers in our class garden. . . .

He liked Chibi's own handwriting, which no one but Chibi could read, and he tacked that upon the wall. . . .

And he often spent time talking with Chibi when no one was around. . . .

But when Chibi appeared on the stage at the talent show of that year, no one could believe his eyes. . . . "What can that stupid do up there?" . . .

Until Mr. Isobe announced that Chibi was going to imitate the voices of crows. (pp. 19–25)

Chibi learned from staring at ceilings, gazing out of windows, wandering the hills, and listening with great attention and interest to birds. But it wasn't until Mr. Isobe appeared in his sixth year of school that he found out that he could also learn in school and that what he had learned outside of school was important, valuable, and of interest to others. Mr. Isobe, like many teachers who call themselves whole-language teachers now, saw no clear distinction between teachers and learners. He saw himself as a learner and believed that even the least of his pupils knew a lot and had a lot to teach him. He was a kid watcher who evaluated his pupils by talking with them, observing them, and transacting with them. Like Chibi, all children are whole-language learners. Unfortunately, also like Chibi, they don't often encounter whole-language teachers.

A basic tenet of whole language is that kids learn when they are in control of their learning and know that they are in control. Here is another point where Vygotsky and whole language come together. When children are immersed in real reading and real writing, they can read and write for purposes of their own and they are empowered.

In whole language, each learner builds on his or her own culture, values, and interest. Each builds on his or her own strengths: There are no disadvantaged. Such a view about learners is essential to literacy development, but is also essential to truly democratic education. Whole language opens up what Frank Smith (1988) calls "the literacy club" for members of both sexes and all classes, races, and language groups.

Whole language views learners as strong not weak, independent not dependent, active not passive. We believe such views are consistent with Vygotsky's views. Learners are capable of learning relatively easily what is relevant and functional for them. So the purpose of schools is to help learners to expand on what they know, to build on what they can do, to support them in identifying needs and interests and in coping with old and new experiences.

John Dewey (1902) provided considerable insight into the relationship between learning in school and learning outside of school. We learn by doing, he showed us. It becomes important then that students are involved in functional authentic activities in school. School is not preparation for life; it is life. Children can learn much more easily, therefore, when the knowledge is immediately useful; learning is more difficult if it has a more distant purpose. In Dewey's pragmatic philosophy there is no useful separation between ends and means in learning; what we learn today is the means of further learning tomorrow. There are no end products, no mastery goals; rather, each goal is part of the means to a new goal, a new schema, a new concept, a new view of the world.

The transactional view of learners in whole-language classrooms owes much to Dewey's views of education. He recognized the importance of integrating language, thought, and content in the thematic solving of everyday problems. Such experiences are authentic for learners. Learning by doing means that we learn to read by reading and to write by writing as we are using literacy for purposes that are important to ourselves. Skills cannot be isolated from their use, in fact, they develop most easily in the context of their use.

We see inconsistencies in Vygotsky's discussion (1978) of the authenticity of learning experiences in schools in his exploration of the similarities and differences between in-school and out-of-school learning. We will explore these similarities and differences in relation to Vygotsky's position throughout this chapter. On the one hand, Vygotsky establishes his position when he states:

> School learning introduces something fundamentally new into the child's development. In order to elaborate the dimensions of school learning we will describe a new and exceptionally important concept without which the issue cannot be resolved: the zone of proximal development. (p. 84)

On the other hand, Vygotsky, contradicts his own statement that school learning alone activates the zone of proximal development when he discusses the role of play as a context in which the zone of proximal development is also activated.

> Play creates a zone of proximal development of the child. In play a child always behaves beyond his average age, above his daily behavior; in play it is as though he were a head taller than himself. As in the focus of a magnifying glass, play contains all developmental tendencies in a condensed form and is itself a major source of development. (p. 102)

The role of play

Vygotsky, like Dewey and Piaget, writes extensively about the power of play in the learning of children. In play children exercise their imaginations, but they also explore the roles of adults in common daily experiences.

When their play involves fantasizing, children draw on their experiences with stories, books, television, and films and on the special folklore that is passed on from each generation of children to the next. When our daughter Debra drove from Detroit to Tucson with her then 3-year-old son Reuben, she planned to stop at parks along the way for him to run and play to relieve the long stretches of sitting on the trip. She carefully packed toys and supplies for him to occupy himself. At the time his favorite playthings were the plastic figures from Masters of the Universe, which he also watched on television. Within minutes of arriving at a park he and other preschoolers were actively involved in imaginative play, easily fitting into the roles of He-man and She-ra as they opposed the imaginary forces of evil. They quickly lost any shyness and found common images and language to share their play.

At other times play appears more realistic as children play house or school or store or office. They pretend to be parents and children, teachers and pupils, gas station attendants, doctors and nurses, bus drivers, pilots, police officers, store clerks. As they do they adopt the appropriate language and engage in relevant activities. In both fantasy and realistic play situations children are involved in out-of-school experiences through which they are learning a good deal about the knowledge and culture of their peers and the adults in the society.

As Vygotsky suggests, play, itself, mediates the learning of children. Because they are "only" playing, they are free to risk doing things they are not yet confident they can do well. In social play, children transact with each other, mediating each other's learning. They learn to understand the meanings of the world as they play with their representations of the world. They build concepts of mathematics and science as well as language, including literacy. We believe that the concepts begun in play not only are the basis for scientific concepts but eventually become part of these concepts.

Social transaction

Vygotsky helps us understand that as children transact with their world they are capable of doing more than they appear to be and that they can get much more out of an activity or experience if there is an adult or more experienced playmate to mediate the experience for them. We believe that all social interactions, not only those involving expert peers and adults, provide the opportunity for children to learn more about the world. There is growing evidence that collaborative learning between peers, regardless of ability, activates the zone of proximal development (see Tudge, this volume). Pontecorvo and Zucchermaglio (1990) have shown that peers of similar knowledge or ability cause reorganization of concepts as students argue and negotiate their solutions to various problems. Teberosky (1990) has shown how bilingual children learn about language through interactions with peers as they explore literacy events together.

We believe that zones of proximal development are created within the learners in the context of activities. Caring adults are sensitive to the directions in which children's curiosity takes them, their attempts to express needs or understandings, and the meanings they are creating. These adults track the development of the learners, and they are eager to help them learn. In fact, they take delight in the learning and in the developing ideas and invented language of the children. Teachers, as professionals but still caring adults, can be insightful kid watchers who sense from what kids *are doing* what they are *capable of doing*. They are able to involve learners in relevant functional activities and experiences that will stretch their capabilities, and they mediate the learners' transactions with the world in minimally intrusive ways, supporting learning without controlling it. They find opportunities to encourage learners to work in collaboration on a variety of problems that are important and meaningful to them.

Dewey, Vygotsky, and the Soviet psychologists who built on Vygotsky's work all emphasize the importance of activity and learning in the process of doing. In whole language the importance of authentic activities in which language, both oral and written, serves in real and functional ways is always stressed. In fact, the popular term *whole language* derives at least partly from a concern for keeping language whole and in the context of functional use.

Piaget (1977) has demonstrated that children are active and intelligent learners. They expect the world to make sense, so they continually seek order in the world as they transact with it. In coping with the physical world they shape the world and are shaped by it, in processes of assimilation and accommodation. Learners adapt to the physical world by building schemas to which they assimilate new knowledge. If there is a disequilibrium, if they cannot assimilate because of contradictions between existing schemas and new experience, then they must accommodate by modifying existing schemas or developing new ones.

The process of adaptation is one that can be supported by caring and insightful teachers, but it cannot be forced or controlled by teachers. In fact, teachers must be careful that they support real learning rather than forcing superficial behavior which may satisfy school requirements without real learning. Vygotsky cautioned against such superficial behavior as well. He provided research evidence that raises questions about "pedagogical movements that emphasized formal discipline and urged the teaching of classical languages, ancient civilizations, and mathematics . . . regardless of the irrelevance of these . . . for daily living" (1978, pp. 81–82).

David Bloome (1987) in his ethnographic studies calls this superficial behavior "procedural display." School becomes a place where you display the expected behavior by acting in acceptable ways without any real adaptation, without any real learning.

Learning language and learning through language

If we accept the concept that learning is different in school and out of school and that scientific concepts are learned only in school and spontaneous concepts only out of school, then we are put in the position of accepting the notion that experiences should be substantively different for school-learned concepts.

We believe, rather, that learning in school and learning out of school are not different. The same factors that make concepts easy to learn out of school make them easy in school: Learners build on experience, expand on *schemas* and rely heavily on language for development. We cannot accept the notion that the two kinds of concepts develop differently. Whole language assumes a single learning process influenced and constrained by personal understandings and social impacts.

We believe that scientific concepts begin as personal concepts that develop in individuals. These personal concepts are influenced by the social community, including the school community, which may or may not be scientific in nature. We use the terms *public* or *folk concepts* (Goodman, Smith, Meredith, & Goodman, 1987) to contrast with scientific concepts. Scientific concepts are derived from activities of scholars in various fields of study as they carefully consider the results of research and theory and incorporate them into explanations of phenomena and expansions of their own knowledge and ideas. Folk concepts are those that are carried by public means of communication, which may vary from accurate accounts of events to hearsay passed along in public places of work and commerce. They are the "commonsense" notions of a society, probably much the same as those concepts Vygotsky considered to be spontaneous.

Folk concepts can also be held up to scrutiny by their developers. They may or may not be accepted and corroborated by the scientific community. Many folk remedies have been supported by scientists once ways to study certain features became more accessible. Uses of herbs and spider webs as home remedies are examples.

Teachers can mediate concept development by providing opportunities for pupils to test personal, spontaneous, and scientific concepts. The water and sand tables found in many kindergartens and some first grades provide opportunity for children to explore concepts of volume, density, states of matter, categorization, and math, among others. But the process of concept development is a unitary one. Whether concepts are spontaneous or scientific, they are all learned in much the same way. For learners, a teacher may label a concept as scientific, but that doesn't mean they can or will learn it differently.

Vygotsky (1986) argues that

> to learn a foreign language at school and to develop one's native language involve two entirely different processes. . . . While learning a foreign language, we use word meanings that are already well developed in the native language and only translate them; the advanced knowledge of one's own language also plays an important role in the study of the foreign one, as well as those inner and outer relations that are characteristic only in the study of a foreign language. (pp. 159–161)

This is a major point of departure between whole-language advocates and ideas expressed by Vygotsky. We see only one language-learning process whether in school or out. Second-language learning is indeed facilitated by the "advanced knowledge" of the first language, but the process of learning is no different. In the last few decades, second-language and foreign-language programs have moved away from dual views and are now trying to organize instruction in the new language so that it is as authentic, natural, and contextualized as possible. Organizing schools to be like the most supportive learning and spontaneous social environments outside of school makes schools much more effective for learning.

We believe that Vygotsky was expressing the complex relationship between different kinds of knowledge of language. In our own work we have been aware that there are complex differences between being able to read, being able to talk about reading, and understanding the reading process. But it is the knowledge learners bring to the making of meaning, the knowledge and the relationships between the people in the environment who interact with the learners, and the particular environment itself that influence how easily and how well reading develops.

In his study of language development, Michael Halliday (1975) uses the phrase "learning how to mean." He describes the development of a range of personal/social functions which then stimulate the development of the forms of language. As learners experience the wide variety of functions and forms of language, they internalize the way their society uses language to represent meaning. So they are learning language at the same time they are using language to learn. They also are learning about language. But all three kinds of language learning must be simultaneous (Halliday, 1980). Thinking that we can teach the forms of language as prerequisites to their use is a mistake schools often make.

Halliday, like Vygotsky, has a social theory of language. In his systemic-functional view, the very form that language takes derives from the fact that it is used socially and that, through its use, language users, including children, create and learn the language conventions or social rules of language to make communication easy and effective.

It is equally important to recognize the central role that language plays in human learning. Language makes it possible to share experience, to link our minds and produce a social intelligence far superior to that of any one individual. We can learn from shared vicarious experience through language. Language, oral and written, can never be simply a school subject.

Centrifugal force and centripetal force: Personal invention and social convention

A common interpretation of Vygotsky's view of language development is that social experience is internalized and social language shapes the language of the individual. Though there can be no doubt that eventually the language of each individual must fall within the norms of the social language and that the way society organizes meaning and represents it strongly shapes the way the individual makes sense of the world, we believe that language is as much personal invention as social convention. Human learners are not passively manipulated by their social experiences; they are actively seeking sense in the world. The individual and society both play strong roles in language development.

Vygotsky (1986) describes the process of internalization: "An operation that initially represents an external activity is reconstructed and begins to occur internally" (pp. 56–57). We don't disagree with this concept of internalization. But we believe that there are also internal efforts to represent experience symbolically and that the reconstruction of external activity is simultaneously a reconstruction of internal activity.

There are two seemingly opposing forces shaping the development of language in individuals and in communities. Although they are opposing in a sense, they operate in an integral fashion. The metaphor we use to describe these forces comes from the concept of centrifugal and centripetal forces of physics. If a ball is twirled on a string, there is a centrifugal force pulling it away from the center. If the twirler lets go, the ball flies off in a straight line. The string transmits an opposing, centripetal force pulling it back toward the middle. As long as these are in balance, the ball will orbit the center.

In language, the centrifugal force is the ability of people individually and collectively to create semiotic systems, to invent new language, to deal with new experience, feelings, and ideas. This creative force produces change and makes it possible for language continuously to meet the developing and changing needs of its users. But if this force were unchecked, language would expand so rapidly that it would lose its social utility. People would soon be unable to understand each other at all.

The centripetal force that provides the counterbalance and relative stability is the social nature of language. If language were static and unchanging it would quickly inhibit its users in learning and in communicating their responses to new experiences. Change in language, whether temporary or permanent, may be initiated by individuals, but it must be understood and accepted by others in order for language to be effective. To serve its functions it must be comprehensible by others, not just by the speaker or the writer. In social transactions with others, learners experience the conventions of the social language. When language changes there is always balance between the creative force and the need to communicate. So the inventor moves toward the social forms and uses the social resources in making new inventions. Thus there is a centripetal force that balances the outward thrust of personal language.

Language development, then, can be viewed as being shaped by these two forces. There is an almost explosive force from within the children that propels them to express themselves, and at the same time there is a strong need to communicate that pushes the direction of growth and development toward the language of the family and community. This shaping is accomplished through the myriad language transactions that involve children with others. The language is generated by the child, but it is changed in transactions with others by their comprehension or lack of comprehension and by their responses. Thus parents, teachers, caregivers, siblings, peers, and significant others play vital roles in the language development of children. They are essential communicative partners, less role models than respondents, less to be imitated than to be understood and understanding.

Another way to view these two opposing forces shaping language is as a balance between invention and convention. Both invention, personal creation of language, and convention, the socially established systems and norms, are necessary for learning. Language is not learned by imitating adults or learning rules out of the context of language use. It is invented by each individual, and in the context of its social use it is adapted to the social conventions. Every language must have within it devices for change, but innovators must use the devices for change the language provides or risk not being understood.

Learners are not resistant to the social force in language. In fact, language comes about at least partially as a means of social participation. Infants sense the social functions of language before they understand the communicative functions. As they begin to represent their own needs and experiences symbolically, they are eager to be understood and to understand others. So they are accepting of the social conventions of language. But these conventions are implicit, not explicit. The rules by which language is governed can be inferred by learners, but they are never directly observable, never imitatable. Any attempt by well-meaning adults to make the rules explicit can actually inhibit learning. Rather, the child keeps inventing rules and trying them out until they work – until they come into balance with social conventions.

We believe that maintaining the balance between invention and convention in developing reading and writing is a major factor in whether pupils come to consider themselves as insiders or outsiders, members of the literacy club or excluded from club benefits (Smith, 1988). If all students are subjected to rigid curricula and interventionist teaching, some will survive and make their way into the club anyway. As they do they will be permitted more latitude in their reading and writing and will be able to balance their inventive energy against the conventions they find in their authentic literacy events. Because they belong to the literacy club, their in-school activities begin to look more like what they do outside of school. Other pupils, defeated by the rejection of their inventions, will be confused by the rigid conventions of textbooks and by the inflexibility of prescriptive language rules. These pupils will be excluded from the literacy club. The less they succeed, the less authentic will be their experiences and the less control they will be permitted. School life becomes alien to their out-of-school experiences. Ironically, the interventionist program is given credit for those who make it into the literacy club whereas the pupils who do not make it are blamed for their own failure.

Society values the inventions of some but not others. Established artists, writers, and scientists are supported. Art shows, book, drama, and concert reviews often praise the creative aspects of artistic works or performances. New discoveries of scientists are extolled on the front pages of newspapers. But a scientist whose discovery breaks with the dominant paradigm will not be easily accepted by his or her peers. Which concepts are scientific is not self-evident. Consider how long it took for Darwin's ideas about the scientific nature of biology to become established. The French Impressionists were vilified and unappreciated because they broke with the conventions of their time. Eventually their inventive energy was so strong, and they themselves so persistent, that new conventions emerged. The fact that these artistic nonconformists were also nonconformist in their life styles did not help their acceptance.

To this day, we are likely to reject and minimize the creative invention of some groups more than others. Poor people, minorities, teenagers, those from cultures outside the mainstream, and nonconformists in general are not expected to contribute in valued ways. Their lack of conformity to some social conventions defined by reference to the dominant culture is interpreted as ignorance, incompetence, or anti-social behavior.

The inventive abilities of young people of all ages are often treated as disruptive and antisocial. So school practice in all respects has tended to treat difference as deficiency and inventive strength as random weakness. Instead of understanding the ability of all pupils to learn and the need for them to make their own way to an equilibrium between invention and convention, we treat some as lacking in the requirements for admission to the literacy club and use interventionist strategies that become self-fulfilling prophecies: Eventually many accept the view of themselves as incapable; those that don't rebel or drop out.

The process of balancing invention and convention works better for young people outside of school than in the traditional school setting. Schools have traditionally narrowly defined conventions of behavior, of learning, of language, of thinking, even of dress. We believe that the difference between learning in school and out of school is largely an imposed one and an undesirable one. It ought to be easier to learn in school than out of school because in school there are professional teachers to mediate the learning. But instead of adjusting school to the learners we require them to adjust to the school.

Scientific concepts can be considered a type of social convention; they are conventional views shared by the best informed and most enlightened within the society. The process by which concepts are validated as scientific is itself highly conventionalized. The status of scientists gives their concepts a special status in society. But that also makes them resistant to displacement by better, alternate concepts, which may have to break with or defy the conventions. We believe scientific concepts are learned in the same way as other concepts, through the push and pull of personal invention and social convention.

Vygotsky certainly recognized the tensions between the individual and society. Wertsch (1985) says Vygotsky discusses the child's cultural development on two planes. "First it appears between people as an interpsychological category and then within the child as an intrapsychological category." We see this as more a transaction than a one-way sequence, with the social first and the personal following. Rather, the child invents in the context of authentic social experiences in which conventions are implicit. Over time the inventions come to conform to the social conventions.

Aaron, at age 4, provided a powerful example of invention when he wrote his "GRAPA GHENE" a birthday card. The card contains much evidence to support our contentions about the relationship of invention to convention, including his awareness of card giving for birthdays and the general form of birthday cards. But his spelling of GRAPA GHENE is a very strong example of how invention works in language development. What he is inventing is a spelling for *Grandpa Kenny*, his most common term for his grandfather. English does not represent the aspiration of /k/ in the initial position in *Kenny* (contrast the breathiness of the /K/ in *Ken* with the /k/ in *skill*). Aaron perceives this aspiration and draws on his knowledge of how it is represented in his own last name, *Hood*. At the same time that he invents the spelling GHENE, he shows his knowledge of a number of phonological and orthographic conventions.

Traditional methods in schools may get willing students to echo verbalizations of language conventions and scientific concepts and even manipulate them in narrow and controlled contexts. But for these to become internalized and operationalized by learners – for the social to become the personal – there must be room to invent, to test out, to experiment, and to reach personal-social equilibrium.

Collaboration in whole-language classrooms

In whole language there is a reciprocal, transactional view of teaching and learning. Using transaction as Dewey did implies that in classroom transactions teachers and learners are changed. Wertsch (1985) quotes Vygotsky on this change in learners: "Internalization transforms the process itself and changes its structure and functions" (p. 81). The traditional idea that teaching can control learning or that each act of teaching results in a reciprocal act of learning in each learner is too simplistic. Teachers learn and learners teach, and as they transact each is changed. Both can resist this change by not committing themselves to the transactions. Whole-language teachers recognize the power of classroom transactions and plan for them.

One key to teachers' success is building an atmosphere of mutual respect in their classrooms. These become social communities where teachers value each learner, help the learners to value themselves and each other, and win the respect of their students.

Whole-language teachers don't abdicate their authority or responsibility. But they lead by virtue of their greater experience, their knowledge, and their respect for their pupils. They know their pupils, monitor their learning, and provide support and resources as they are needed. They recognize that there must be collaboration between themselves and their pupils if an optimal learning atmosphere is to be created. Whole-language teachers believe that experiences and literacy events must be as authentic in the classroom as they are outside of it. Pupils must feel a sense of purpose, of choice, of utility, of participation, and of shared ownership in their classrooms and in what happens there. Even as young beginners they need to participate in decision making and see relevance in what they are doing. The tenor of relationships between teachers and learners becomes one of trust and collaboration rather than conflict and domination.

New roles for teachers

In whole-language classrooms teachers are empowered. They are not reduced to powerless technicians administering someone else's work sheets, skill drills, and basal readers to powerless pupils. In turn they empower learners by valuing who they are and what they know, do, and believe. They support the learners in solving their problems and pursuing knowledge. The learners are involved and committed to the ongoing learning events in their classrooms because these events are authentic and relevant and because the learners are empowered participants.

The teacher is an initiator. Whole-language teachers are initiators. Their roles are in no sense passive. They create authentic contexts in their classrooms and participate with their students in order to stimulate learners to engage in solving problems and identifying and meeting their own needs. As they do so they insightfully observe the learners so that they can recognize and even anticipate the learners' potential. These teachers know how to create conditions that will cause learners to exhibit and make the most of their zones of proximal development.

The teacher is a kid watcher. The whole-language teacher is skilled at observing kids at play and at work, knowing where they are developmentally, and seeing the naturally occurring zones of proximal development. We believe it is a mistake to think that teachers can control or even create zones of proximal development in learners. But whole-language teachers know how to detect the evidence of what learners are ready to do with support. If the teacher is not a successful kid watcher the zones will be missed, and so will opportunities for growth and learning.

The teacher is a mediator. Redefining learning requires us to redefine teaching. Optimal learning requires teaching that supports and facilitates it without controlling, distorting, or thwarting the learning. Vygotsky's (1978) concept of mediation is a useful way to view a major component of optimal teaching. The learner is in a situational context in which problems need to be solved or experiences understood. The teacher is present as the learning transaction takes place but in the role of mediator – supporting the learning transactions but neither causing them to happen in any direct sense nor controlling the learning. In this way the forces of invention and convention are unfettered, and the teacher supports the learner in achieving equilibrium.

In defining themselves as mediators, whole-language teachers understand that less can be more. They realize that helping a learner solve a problem is better than giving him or her an algorithm or a solution. In reading and writing, teachers interfere as little as possible between the text and the reader. Teachers mediate by asking a question here, offering a useful hint there, directing attention at an anomaly, calling attention to overlooked information, and supporting learners as they synthesize what they are learning into new concepts and schemas. They provide just enough support to help the learner make the most of his or her own zone of proximal development. Whole-language teachers do assume, as Vygotsky (1978) said, that "even the profoundest thinkers never questioned that what children can do with the assistance of others might be in some sense even more indicative of their mental development than what they can do alone" (p. 85). But whole-language teachers also know that assisting pupils in doing something is different from doing it for them or controlling what they do. Consider two classroom episodes:

1. A group of black inner-city fourth-grade pupils have read Langston Hughes's poem "Mother to Son" (Hughes, 1963, p. 67). The pupils discuss the poem. The classroom procedure involves a pupil leading the discussion; the teacher is a codiscussant. The teacher wonders what they think about the mother's saying "Life for me ain't been no crystal stair." Some of the pupils point out other references to stairs in the poem. The teacher shares with them her knowledge of the author's life and political beliefs. She suggests that the stairs represent the author's view of this woman's attempt to raise herself up from her difficult conditions. One boy asks, "She talkin' 'bout climbin' up to heaven?" They decide that the mother is contrasting her hard life to the religious idea of life as a beautiful crystal stair leading to heaven. In doing so they draw on their own knowledge of the likely experiences and religious beliefs of the mother. They share stories of their own mothers. "I never thought of this poem in quite that way," says the teacher.

2. An eighth-grade group in a working-class suburb plans a unit on evolution. The discussion and webbing of their knowledge of the concept introduce the controversy over the biblical view of creation. Two weeks after the unit begins one student tells the teacher that his minister would like to come in and debate evolution with the teacher. The teacher declines, explaining that studying a theory is different than advocating it. The class discusses the situation and reaffirms that they are studying evolution as a theory. They decide to explore the role of theory in science and the difference between established fact and theory. The student is encouraged by the teacher and his classmates to bring into the study literature from creationists on the subject. The ensuing study is enlivened. The pupils search avidly for resources not only on evolution but on the history of the theory and the controversy over it. One group of students reads Irving Stone's (1979) biography of Charles Darwin and shares their responses.

In both of these examples, the teacher plays a crucial but not controlling role. The teacher is an initiator, selecting a poem to be shared, planning a unit, providing time for pupils to pursue a spontaneous question. The teacher is a kid watcher who considers not only where the pupils are but where they are capable of going in their learning. So one teacher is supportive and receptive as pupils relate their own schemas to Hughes's poem. The other teacher welcomes the fundamentalist challenge to the scientific concept. These teachers are not intervening in the learning; they are mediating it. The role of the teacher as mediator is an active one and reflects the teacher's understanding that teaching supports learning; it can't force it to happen.

In areas of controversy the teacher is not afraid to express belief but shows respect for the developing beliefs of the learners, whether they are based in personal, public, or scientific concepts. The teacher shares knowledge but knows that when learners can relate the new knowledge to what they already know and what they need to know they will understand why the knowledge is important, and they will be able to integrate the new knowledge with their existing schemas and conceptual systems. In building comprehension the teacher knows that the pupils' development of their own strategies is more important than whether they agree with the teacher. So the teacher helps the pupils to examine the available facts, to evaluate their own beliefs, and to find more information as they need it.

The teacher is by no means the only mediator in the whole-language classroom. By providing opportunities for pupils to self-evaluate, the power of reflective thinking as a mediating force is revealed. Reflecting on one's own learning is necessary for both the teacher and the learner. Dewey (Archambault, 1964), in his concern for reflective thinking, says: "Thinking enables us to direct our own activities with foresight and to plan according to ends-in-view, or purposes of which we are aware" (p. 212).

The teacher is a liberator. There is a vital difference between mediation and intervention. This difference controls whether the teacher liberates or suppresses the learners. In intervention the teacher takes control of learning, knows with great certainty in advance what learning will be acceptable, and thus undermines the learners' confidence in themselves; the teacher becomes the determiner of social conventions and the suppressor of invention. When invention is inhibited, risk taking is limited and zones of proximal development are unlikely to be revealed or explored.

Paolo Freire (1970) contrasts "banking" views of pedagogy with liberating views. The banking view treats learners as empty vessels. Teachers deposit bits of learning into their heads. Learners have no control over the process, nor are their needs or interests considered. Liberating pedagogy sees learners in a power relationship to society. If education is to help them to liberate themselves it must be empowering. The learners must own the process of their learning. They must see learning, including literacy and language development, as part of a process of liberation. Freire was successful in helping Brazilian peasants to become literate by using the ideas and concepts of their political movement in the texts they used in learning to read.

In a broader sense Freire was recognizing that learners learn best when they are free to control their own learning. This liberation is neither romantic nor abstract. Teachers cannot liberate pupils from society or from the constraints of social transactions. But they can remove the artificial controls of traditional schooling. They can encourage pupils to enter freely into speech and literacy events, authentic social transactions, in which language is a tool for communication. They can make their classrooms communities of learners in which a full range of language genres occur naturally and in which their own language and the language of their home cultures are completely accepted. In such a community pupils are free to invent ways of dealing with their functional needs and free to discover the conventions in authentic social language transactions.

Freeing pupils to take risks is a major concern of whole-language classrooms. In traditional classrooms, not only are pupils required to stay within arbitrary conventions in their oral and written expression, but they are penalized for their errors.

Whole-language classrooms liberate pupils to try new things, to invent spellings, to experiment with new genres, to guess at meanings in their reading, to read and write imperfectly, to challenge textbooks, to pursue inquiry.

Our research on reading and writing has strongly supported the importance of error in language development (K. Goodman & Gollasch, 1982; Y. Goodman & Wilde, 1985). Miscues represent the tension between invention and convention in reading. They show the reader's use of existing schemas in attempting to comprehend texts. They also show how the text itself mediates learning. In whole-language classrooms risk taking is not simply tolerated, it is celebrated. Learners have always been free to fail in school. However, in whole-language classrooms they are free to learn from their failures with the support of their teachers.

Dewey relates failure to the power of thought:

> While the power of thought, then, frees us from servile subjection to instinct, appetite, and routine, it also brings with it the occasion and possibility of error and mistake. In elevating us above the brute, it opens the possibility of failures to which the animal, limited to instinct, cannot sink. (Archambault, 1964, p. 217)

The role of text and the zone of proximal development

Whole-language teachers recognize that if their pupils are involved in authentic experiences the speech acts and literacy events will largely be self-mediating.

In the act of composing, for example, the writing of text mediates writing development as the language user seeks actively to make sense through the text being created.

For this self-development to take place, the written text must be authentic. That is, it must be whole with all the characteristics of real written texts created for real purposes in real contexts (keeping in mind Halliday and Hasan's [1976] definition of text as "a unity of meaning in context"). Vygotsky (1978) recognized writing as "a complex cultural activity." In contrast to his view on foreign-language teaching cited earlier, he says there is a "requirement that writing be taught naturally":

> Writing must be "relevant to life." . . . Writing should be meaningful for children, . . . an intrinsic need should be aroused in them, and . . . writing should be incorporated into a task that is necessary and relevant for life. Only then can we be certain that it will develop not as a matter of hand and finger habits but as a really new and complex form of speech. (p. 118)

In our studies of children's writing (Y. Goodman & Wilde, 1985), a research project that followed the writing of six Tohono O'odham Indian third- and fourth-graders over a 2-year period, we collected considerable evidence of how the developing written text mediates learning. We saw a continuously moving zone of proximal development in every piece of writing the children produced.

Gabriel, a third-grade Native American, decided that *foot* and *ball* needed to be placed closer together in the word *football* than the normal spacing between words. Observations of Gabriel in the act of composing over 2 years showed how he dealt with spacing and hyphenation as he gained control over the features of how compound words are represented in written English. In the act of producing text, Gabriel is inventing a way of representing in the written semiotic system phenomena that he knows he can represent in the oral semiotic system. In the process he discovers that there are not isomorphic conventions in the orthography for everything that can be represented in speech. In this research we found examples of the young writers developing control over genre variations, syntactic rules, spelling, and punctuation.

Another third-grader, Bill, also shows how the text serves as mediator. He invented a "sadlamation point" in a story about his pet dog who was killed in an automobile accident. He had realized there were no existing punctuation marks that represent sadness. When his classmates found out about his invention, they began to focus much more on the uses of punctuation in their writing. Bill's written text provided the opportunity for him to learn about the need for punctuation. Then Bill and the teacher became mediators for the other students' exploration of punctuation. Through writing conferences and other classroom discussions, all the members of the class became more conscious of the conventional uses of punctuation in their reading of books, advertisements, and signs in their environment.

In miscue research, where we analyze reading miscues (unexpected responses to written texts in oral reading), we became aware that every time we analyzed a reader's miscues in reading a whole story we saw learning and development (Goodman & Goodman, 1977). In miscue research, readers read a complete story aloud without aid from the researcher. Then each of the readers' miscues is analyzed using linguistic, psycholinguistic, and sociolinguistic criteria (Y. Goodman, Watson, & Burke, 1987). We have concluded that readers are developing new strategies, new vocabulary, new confidence in their ability to read during the reading itself without any discussion or aid from anyone else. In the reading of authentic texts, at all levels of reading proficiency, there are transactions between the reader and the text in which the reader is continuously solving new problems and building and extending psycholinguistic strategies.

Miscue research shows that reading is also a "complex cultural activity." John, a second-grader, was reading a story in which the word *oxygen* occurred a number of times (Y. Goodman & Burke, 1972). Each time he came to the word in his oral reading he omitted it but commented, "There's that word again," or "I think I'll skip that word." Later, during his retelling of the story, he was relating that men in the space station were feeling sleepy because the air was bad. He said, "They didn't have enough . . . oxygen! That's that word I didn't know! Oxygen!" Given the opportunity to think through the text while retelling the story, the meaning came together for him and he was able to identify a word that he thought he didn't know while he was reading earlier. At no time did the researcher give John specific information. The text mediated his learning.

Transactions with written texts provide the problem situations that readers need to deal with. During these transactions texts become mediators as the reader takes control of the learning. We've marveled watching readers, often labeled as problem readers, move toward control of complex conventions that linguists are still struggling to understand and explicate.

Another example of text as mediator during reading is revealed through our analysis of Peggy's oral reading of *The Man Who Kept House* (1964, pp. 282–283). Peggy was chosen by her teacher for this analysis because she was supposedly reading below grade level (Goodman & Goodman, 1977). Her reading of the story shows how she learns the metaphor *keeping house* as a result of reading the story. In the next segment where the text is shown on the left and Peggy's reading on the right, we see how she learns to read complex syntactic structure as she transacts with the text.

"If you stay home to do my work, you'll have to make butter, carry water from the well, wash the clothes, clean the house, and look after the baby," said the wife.	". . . , well you'll have to make bread, carry . . . carry water from the well, wash the clothes, clean the house, and look after the baby," said the wife.

We don't show in this example the problem Peggy has with the beginning of the clause since it is not relevant to this discussion. She inserts *well,* suggesting that she is aware that this is an argument between the husband and the wife. She substitutes *bread* for *butter,* an expected and common miscue in this context. Peggy, like most other children her age, is much more aware of the process of bread making in the home than butter making. The substitution not only reveals her background knowledge but suggests that she is monitoring the text for comprehension since making bread is an alternate choice in "keeping house." She then quickly reads *carry,* followed by a 7-second pause. She then very slowly says *carry* again and cautiously reads the phrase *carry water from the well.* At this point her reading speeds up once again, and she reads the rest of the sentence with confidence and without hesitation. For many who are not familiar with miscue analysis procedures, it is easy to conclude that Peggy's problem is that she is having some difficulty with the word *carry.* However, it is more likely that Peggy, who has heard stories read to her but had never read a seven-page story before in her life, is having problems with the syntactic complexity of the sentence. The series of five phrases that end the sentence are all connected to the verb stem of the sentence, *will have to.* Peggy has to know that each of the phrases must start with *will have to* – *will have to carry, will have to wash, will have to clean,* and *will have to look after* – in order to read and comprehend this sentence. When she comes to the first verb that does not have the *will have to* stem, she hesitates, pauses, wonders about what the language of the sentence might be. Her intonation as she reads first cautiously and then confidently suggests that she has worked out the problem by reading.

Miscue analysis reveals that texts not only mediate the meanings and syntactic structures but allow the reader to work out strategies for comprehension as well. In a study of word-level omissions in children's miscues (K. Goodman and Gollasch,

1980), a fourth-grade Navajo reader had a very high percentage of omission miscues during the reading of a 12-page text. A close examination of her reading showed that for the first 23 lines she had utilized a strategy of pausing frequently, apparently waiting for the researcher to tell her what the following word was. Finally, she seemed to accept that this was not going to happen, and for the next 22 lines the pauses got progressively shorter and she omitted the following words and went on. She had switched to a new strategy, which we came to call "deliberate omission." Her motto seemed to have become "When in doubt, leave it out." But that strategy gave way to a third strategy because for the remaining 10 pages there were no pauses longer than 5 seconds and virtually no omissions. She produced a number of miscues, but they all showed use of comprehending strategies.

This example, besides showing how authentic texts can mediate reading development, also illustrates the perils of intervention. Had we responded to her pauses by supplying the following words we would have been assuming that she was pausing because (1) she didn't know them (in some absolute sense) and (2) she was incapable of resolving her difficulty. And we would have supported her strategy that the safest thing to do in reading when you are unsure is to wait for the teacher to tell you what to do. By not intervening we helped her help herself. We liberated the reader to work through her own zone of proximal development.

The teacher's role in balancing invention and convention

Teachers have traditionally been seen as agents of conformity in the language use of their pupils. This role must be reconsidered to give sufficient room for invention and to let learners become aware of convention as it exists in social language. Too often teachers have rewarded conformity, punished experimentation and risk taking, and confused learners about conventions just as they were building some sense of them.

In fact, the rules taught in school were based on authority, a set of arbitrary rules established by textbooks or teachers, and not on scientific concepts about language in use. Learners often found it hard to apply the rules or confirm them in their own language experiences. For example, teachers have sometimes taught pupils that *and* and *but* may *not* be used to start sentences. *But* pupils often found examples of sentences that did start with these words in their reading. Too much intervention and direction by others, particularly teachers, can minimize invention and focus excessively and prematurely on the need for conventionality.

Everything we learn involves imperfection and error as we gain competence. Support for mistake making and hypothesis testing is one way teachers can mediate the balancing of invention and convention. "To err is human" is an old folk saying that illustrates how long people have been aware that error is a normal part of human learning. If language learning were purely imitative or purely innate it would be hard to explain the pervasiveness of error. But if we understand the role of invention then we can understand that as people move into equilibrium between invention and convention their errors reflect their progress. The 2-year-old who says "I taked it" has moved to a rule for past tense that is partway between his early inventions and the convention of adult grammar.

The 6-year-old who invents the spelling WAT for *went* has invented the alphabetic system whereby letter sequences represent sound sequences. Her spelling represents what she hears and her own articulatory system. The /n/ in *went* is nasalized, a feature that does not fit the phoneme she represents with ⟨n⟩. But spelling conventions in English are the same across dialects, and therefore standard spellings cannot be dependably generated. For the sake of standardizing spellings across dialects the system sacrifices conformity to rules. The invented spellings represent the child's control over the basic principles of the orthography but not the many exceptions.

If the teacher treats all nonstandard spellings as equally wrong the insight into the learner's control of English spelling is lost. If the teacher insists on conventional language at all stages of development and during every phase of the composing process, then the whole balance between invention and convention is destroyed and the strength and creativity of the pupils in language learning is neutralized.

No invention is wholly the creation of the inventor. Every invention, whether one by a famous scientist that has broad impact on society or the child's invention of something known to every adult in the community, is built on transactions with others. As we quoted earlier, Vygotsky (1978) emphasized the child's development from the outside in. Our view, supported by literacy development research in the last decade and a half, shows how children's inventions based on social transactions transform written language and are modified until they coincide with the social conventions of written language (Y. Goodman & Altwerger, 1981; Ferreiro & Teberosky, 1982; Goelman, Olberg, & Smith, 1984; Teale & Sulzby, 1986). Thus the social becomes the personal through the tension between invention and convention.

Eleanor Duckworth (1987) comes to similar conclusions regarding personal invention:

> I see no difference in kind between wonderful ideas that many other people have already had and wonderful ideas that nobody has yet happened upon. That is, the nature of creative intellectual acts remains the same, whether it is an infant seeing things and reaching for them . . . or an astronomer who develops a new theory of the creation of the universe. (p. 14)

Curriculum in whole-language classrooms

Traditionally, classrooms have been organized to pass on the conventional wisdom, usually the wisdom of an educated elite, that ignores the knowledge, the culture, and the wisdom of large groups of people representing the less powerful gender, races, languages, and ethnicities. Accepting this fund of knowledge and belief is rarely considered as legitimate for schooling. That was as true in Vygotsky's era as in ours. Even after social and political revolutions, it has often been deemed sufficient to provide access to schools for all people while continuing to accept the traditional closed curriculum.

With the focus in whole-language classrooms on authentic experiences, learners are engaged in purposeful and meaningful uses of language, both oral and written. There is no artificial breaking down of language learning into sequences of abstract skills and no synthetic language designed to control vocabulary or focus on the form of written language out of the context of its functional use. Teachers are knowledgeable empowered professionals who empower their pupils.

Because of the emphasis on using the whole of language in meaningful situational contexts there is no disruption of the two forces, personal and social, that shape language and facilitate learning. Teachers are free to learn collaboratively with their pupils and are there to support and mediate the learning. There are no artificial limits on what can be learned, nor are there any school-imposed barriers to the literacy club. The curriculum is broad and open. It brings learners into contact with a full range of social conventions as they naturally occur, but it does not reduce itself to arbitrarily imposed and narrowly interpreted conventions.

This chapter is not the vehicle in which to explore all the ramifications of a whole-language curriculum; however, we do want to touch on those aspects of curriculum which we believe inform whole language and which have been informed by Vygotskian theory.

The social nature of schooling

Social context is itself a powerful mediator. Classrooms are social organizations. They are necessarily different than other social groups pupils encounter since they bring numerous similarly aged people together. Their funding, staffing, and social-political status also constrain them. But it is possible to organize classrooms so that social interactions will be supportive, and bridges will be provided to the cultures and social values pupils bring to school. Students are capable of learning the conventions of new social contexts and new linguistic genres if the contexts are dynamic ones in which students are invited to participate and are free to be themselves. If, however, their learning in classrooms is too highly constrained, then all they will learn is a narrow set of behaviors. Some pupils will find themselves permitted to fail but not to be nonconformists.

Other pupils, highly motivated to do well in school, can literally play the "school game." They get satisfaction out of doing the school tasks and winning the praise of the teachers and the rewards of the system. And they continue to learn what they can in school and integrate it with what they learn outside of school. The success that many pupils have in traditional situations obscures the relationship between in-school and out-of-school learning. To understand the problems of traditional education and its failure to provide authentic learning situations we must look to those who do not succeed in the system. What we find is that disproportionate numbers of minorities, of the poor, of boys, and of nonconformists are among the low achievers. In all of these the inability of the system to adapt to the learners is the key. Pupils succeed in traditional controlled programs to the extent that they are willing and/or able to conform and accept nonfacilitative curriculum and teaching.

All human beings are capable of learning language and learning through language. If learning in school is as authentic as learning outside of school, then there are no disadvantaged groups. But not all groups are so motivated and culturally equipped for school that they can survive dysfunctional teaching and curricula.

Language empowerment by demystifying language processes

If the zone of proximal development is viewed as a source of positive development, then only certain kinds of teaching support the zone and in fact other attempts can disrupt, confuse, or negate the potential development. The informal literacy club (Smith, 1988) that exists in classrooms and schools accepts some pupils but excludes others. Social, cultural, and linguistic dues are required for membership.

Those pupils who find admission to the club easy learn to read and write with little trauma. They bring the right language and experience to school, and they can accept school experience even if it is somewhat dysfunctional. Others feel unwelcome, and the language and responses to school experience are interpreted as inappropriate. So they participate in a self-fulfilling prophecy: They appear to be stupid and unprepared for literacy. The school technology then classifies them as deficient, and a cycle of intervention begins that eliminates all invention and most of the authentic convention of functional language. The learners fail at this too.

These negative influences on the zone take many forms in schools and limit entry into the learning or literacy club. Often the negative influences come from particular views about the role of the teacher. One of these roles sees the teacher as diagnostician. In this role the teacher is involved in finding out what the learner doesn't know, letting the learner and the family know what is missing, and then setting up interventions that cause conflict with the learning because they are counterproductive.

Another view of the teacher disruptive to the development of the zone characterizes the teacher as an expert imparting knowledge and discipline. Teachers who accept this view make choices and assignments for students. They control what and how much is learned within a specified period of time. Specified skills in a particular sequence are considered prerequisite to learning, and the curriculum is, therefore, arranged to pass on information in specified ways. The teacher becomes so dominant that opportunities for mediation are lost and an autocratic social environment is fostered. The learner becomes dependent on the teacher for sources of information and for ways of thinking and doing. When the student responds as expected, learning is rewarded and students become more concerned with behaving in a particular way than learning through their own activated zone. Procedural display as described by Bloome (1987) is rewarded, invention becomes too risky, and learning is curtailed and moved toward a stultifying conformity, not simply toward social convention.

Behavioral learning theories support imitative, memorizing, and cloning activities that reduce the zone, trivialize it, narrowing the opportunities for students to expand on and develop to their fullest potential. Inauthentic activities become ends in themselves and are valued more than students' learning and development.

Views of learning often relate to theories of language. Teachers holding the narrow views of learning often have narrow and outdated models of the reading and writing processes. They therefore use artificial and conformist materials and methods that force students out of their naturally developing zones into transacting with artificially written texts. The students are forced into activities they are often unable to complete appropriately. Even students who have the sociocultural potential to join the literacy club can be excluded because they are not paying the proper classroom dues that include filling out work sheets, working quietly and alone, spending hours on meaningless homework, and doing what they are told without question or argument.

Because of unexamined beliefs about gender, race, or ethnicity, teachers' attitudes toward particular students often result in their *not* recognizing students' potential. In such situations, students' attempts at invention or interpretation of conventions are easily rejected because they do not fit the school's or the teacher's values, expectations, and knowledge.

A view of curriculum that rejects this negative teaching encourages teachers to organize the classroom environment so that students will have many opportunities to realize the extent to which they know and control language, the ways in which language controls them, and the significance of language to their lives. Such a curriculum not only supports the students' right to speak and read and write in their own variation of language but also helps students understand why there are those in society who are strongly opposed to multilingualism, multiculturalism, and multidialectalism in schools and in society.

The intuitive knowledge students have developed about language becomes more explicit as students examine the real things that they do with language as they use it. They are helped to view their errors in reading and writing as an important part of their learning and as part of the multiple interpretations that all readers and writers develop as they compose and comprehend texts. Students and teachers learn with each other and from each other as they explore each other's responses to literature and each other's attempts at composition.

In many schools in Great Britain, there is a language curriculum in place that includes many of the ideas suggested above. Introducing a text for students called *The Languages Book,* the editor writes:

> This book is about language and how people use it. . . . But everyone who reads this knows much more about language than can be put in a book. Everyone has managed the amazing job of learning at least one language – and, when you think about it, you use even one language in so many different ways that even one is a lot. So you're the expert; make sure you tell the others what you know about language and the way it works. (Raleigh, 1981, front matter)

Knowing that they know about language allows students to understand that language is not a mystery understood by only a few experts but a powerful tool to control and use in learning.

Authentic language experiences

With the focus in whole-language classrooms on authentic experiences, learners are engaged in purposeful and meaningful use of language, both oral and written. There is no artificial breaking down of language learning into sequences of abstract skills and no synthetic language designed to control the form of written language out of the context of its functional use. The form of language is examined as it is necessary to communicate to others. Reasons for language convention are explored so that students have opportunities to choose when they want to be conventional and when they are willing to take the risk to invent.

In one whole-language classroom such ideas were translated into students studying utopian societies and organizing the whole classroom into a town they wanted to establish. Class activities and daily routines were carried out by the students. Students searched the literature to discover what others had written about utopias and then wrote about their own. They had a town meeting on a regular basis to establish the laws of their classroom society. A publishing company, post office, library, museum, town meeting area, and store all became part of the community the students organized and reorganized, discussed and debated. The problems of the society such as noise abatement, traffic, and disease control were a few of the issues the students explored, and through their studies the students developed concepts concerning language, science, math, social studies, art, music, and other aspects of academic and real life. They also found many opportunities to talk, to read, and write, and to discover many conventions about how and why they used the various functions and forms of language in the ways they did.

Long before teachers began to use the term *whole language* there were whole-language teachers like the above and like Mr. Isobe, the Japanese teacher we introduced earlier. These were teachers who understood that schools existed for the pupils and who trusted in their ability to recognize their students' strengths and knowledge.

Largely, these teachers were successful because they cared about their pupils and knew them well. Their empathy provided them with an intuitive sense of what sort of support their pupils needed. What whole language adds is a scientific base of knowledge about language, learning, and teaching amassed over several decades. Teachers can respond to their intuitions as professionals who thoughtfully examine what they learn from their students.

Such teachers are aware they they need to know a great deal about their students and the communities in which their students live in order to provide for and support authentic opportunities for learning. Such teachers are sensitive to the total social context in which the student lives so that they know what criteria to use to establish authentic situations so that students' language learning is meaningful and functional to the students' life. This does not mean that a laissez-faire situation is allowed to exist. Rather, starting where the learner is assures that the teacher provides many different kinds of opportunities for the zones of proximal development to occur.

Dewey (1902) provides an important rationale for the need for a variety of opportunities for learning to occur. He explores the value of what he calls "the real symbols," which he states "are tools by which the individual pushes out most surely and widely into unexplored area." But then Dewey cautions that only when the symbol "stands for and sums up in shorthand actual experiences which the individual has already gone through can it really symbolize. . . . A symbol which is induced from without, which has not been led up to in preliminary activities, is . . . a bare or mere symbol; it is dead and barren" (pp. 24–25).

There are too many subjects, facts, and statements presented in school as symbols "induced from without." We believe that these kinds of presentations never allow learners to reach for the real concepts of any subject, and they are thereby seduced to remain with what Vygotsky (1986) might call pseudoconcepts.

Whole language represents a major departure from the kind of education that even Vygotsky seemed to take for granted. Schools have traditionally been regarded as places for inculcating conservative societal values and knowledge. The whole-language movement has historic roots in a continuous attempt since the beginning of formal schooling to move away from simplistic views of teaching and learning. In choosing to make schools fit learners, whole language draws on the best scientific knowledge of how learning and teaching work and how language relates to learning and teaching.

In a very real sense, now that there are appreciable numbers of classrooms and schools where whole language is developing, it is possible to reevaluate the whole discussion of in-school and out-of-school learning and the relationship between scientific and spontaneous concepts. When schools implement a whole-language philosophy, teachers are initiators, kid watchers, liberators, and professional mediators who support the pupils through their zones of proximal development. And even the most optimistic of theorists may have to admit that they have underestimated what learners are capable of achieving.

References

Archambault, R. D. (Ed.) (1964). *John Dewey on education.* Chicago: University of Chicago Press.

Bloome, D. (1987). Reading as a social process in a middle school classroom. In D. Bloome (Ed.), *Literacy and schooling* (pp. 123–149). Norwood, NJ: Ablex.

Bullock, A. (Chair) (1975). *A language for life: Report of the committee of inquiry.* London: Her Majesty's Stationery Office.

Childs, J. L. (1956). *American pragmatism and education.* New York: Holt.

Comenius, J. (1887). *The orbis pictus* (English ed.). Syracuse, NY: Bardeen.

Counts, G. (1932). *Dare the school build a new social order?* New York: Day.

Department of Education (1985). *Reading in junior classes.* Wellington, NZ.

Dewey, J. (1902). *The child and the curriculum.* Chicago: University of Chicago Press.

Dewey, J. (1938). *Experience and education.* New York: Macmillan.

Duckworth, E. (1987). *"The having of wonderful ideas" and other essays.* New York: Teachers College Press.

Edelsky, C. (1986). *Habia una vez: Writing in a bilingual classroom.* Norwood, NJ: Ablex.

Ferreiro, E., & Teberosky, A. (1982). *Literacy before schooling* (K. Goodman, Trans.). Portsmouth, NH: Heinemann.

Freire, P. (1970). *Pedagogy of the oppressed.* New York: Seabury.

Goelman, H., Olberg, A., & Smith, F. (Eds) (1984). *Awakening to literacy.* Exeter, NH: Heinemann.

Goodman K., & Gollasch, F. (1980). Word omissions: Deliberate and nondeliberate. *Reading Research Quarterly, 16:*(1), 6–31.

Goodman K., & Gollasch, F. (1982). *Language and literacy: The selected writings of Kenneth S. Goodman: Vol 2. Reading, language, and the classroom teacher* (F. V. Gollasch, Ed.). London: Routledge and Kegan Paul.

Goodman, K., & Goodman, Y. (1977). Learning about psycholinguistic processes by analyzing oral reading. *Harvard Educational Review, 40*(3), 317–333.

Goodman, K., Smith, E. B., Meredith, R., & Goodman, Y. (1987). *Language and thinking in school.* New York: Owen.

Goodman, Y. (1989, November). Roots of the whole language movement. *Elementary School Journal.* Vol. 90 No. 2 pp. 113–127.

Goodman, Y., & Altwerger, B. (1981). *Print awareness in preschool children* (Occasional Paper No. 4). Program in Language and Literacy. Tucson: University of Arizona, College of Education.

Goodman, Y., & Burke, C. (1972). *Reading miscue inventory: A procedure for diagnosis and evaluation.* New York: Richard C. Owen.

Goodman, Y., with Watson, D., & Burke, C. (1987). *Reading miscue inventory: Alternative procedures.* New York: Owen.

Goodman, Y., & Wilde, S. (1985). *Writing development: Third and fourth grade O'Odham (Papago) students* (Occasional paper No. 14). Program in Language and Literacy. Tucson: University of Arizona, College of Education.

Halliday, M. A. K. (1975). *Learning how to mean: explorations in the development of language.* London: Edward Arnold.

Halliday, M. A. K. (1980). Three aspects of children's language development: Learning language, learning through language, and learning about language. In Y. M. Goodman, M. Haussler, & D. S. Strickland (Eds.), *Oral and written language development research: Impact on the schools.* Urbana, IL: National Council of Teachers of English.

Halliday, M. A. K., & Hasan, R. (1976). *Cohesion in English.* London: Longman.

Hughes, L. (1963). Mother to son. In A. Bomtemps (Ed.), *American Negro poetry* (p. 67). New York: Hill & Wang.

Kilpatrick, W. (1926). *Foundation of method.* New York: Macmillan.

The man who kept house. (1964). In J. McInnes, M. Gerrard, & J. Ryckman (Eds.), *Magic and make believe.* Don Mills, Ont. Nelson.

Penton, J. (1979). *Reading in NZ Schools: A survey of our theory and practice.* Auckland: Department of Education.

Piaget, J. (1977). *The development of thought: Equilibration of cognitive structures.* New York: Viking.

Pontecorvo, C., & Zucchermaglio, C. (1990). A passage to literacy: Learning in a social context. In Y. Goodman (Ed.), *How children construct literacy: Piagetian perspectives.* Newark, DE: International Reading Association.

Raleigh, M. (Ed.) (1981). *The languages book.* London: ILEA English Centre.

Smith, F. (1988). *Joining the literacy club.* Portsmouth, NH: Heinemann.

Stone, I. (1979). *The origin.* New York: Doubleday.

Teale, W., & Sulzby, E. (Eds.) (1986). *Emergent literacy: Writing and reading.* Norwood, NJ: Ablex.

Teberosky, A. (1990). The language young children write: Reflections on a learning situation. In Y.

Goodman (Ed.), *How children construct literacy: Piagetian perspective*. Newark DE: International Reading Association.

Vygotsky, L. S. (1978). *Mind in society* (M. Cole, S. Scribner, V. John-Steiner, & E. Souberman, Eds.). Cambridge, MA: Harvard University Press.

Vygotsky, L. S. (1986). *Thought and language*. (A. Kozulin, Ed. & Trans.). Cambridge, MA: MIT Press.

Wertsch, J. W. (1985). *Vygotsky and the social formation of mind*. Cambridge, MA: Harvard University Press.

Yashima, T. (1959). *Crow boy*. New York: Viking.

10   The development of scientific concepts and discourse

Carolyn P. Panofsky, Vera John-Steiner,
and Peggy J. Blackwell

Vygotsky's writings on the development of scientific concepts have important implications for both psychology and education. Although his writing on scientific concepts has not been followed by as much research as some of his other ideas, it constitutes an important part of a central theme in his overall theory. For Vygotsky, the study of cognitive development included investigating the effect of formal school instruction on the development of thinking; he saw instruction as fundamentally different from spontaneous learning in everyday contexts, and he theorized that such experience would have a distinctive and transforming impact on the school child's mental development. In Vygotsky's view, the structure of school learning provides the kind of cultural experience in which the higher psychological processes, such as voluntary attention and logical memory, are formed.

Thus the distinction between spontaneous or everyday concepts and scientific concepts is central to a Vygotskian analysis. A spontaneous concept is purely denotative in the sense of being defined in terms of perceptual or functional or contextual properties of its referent. In contrast, "the relationship [of a scientific concept] to an object is mediated from the start by some other concept. . . . the very notion of scientific concept implies *a certain position in relation to other concepts, i.e., a place within a system of concepts*" (1962, p. 93, italics added).

The development of a system of concepts and the mediation of these concepts are seen as involving a kind of learning from which higher psychological functions develop. Like the learning of a second language in school compared with native language development, or the learning of written language in school compared with oral language at home, the development of scientific concepts begins with analytic procedures rather than concrete experiences. By contrast, spontaneous concepts and oral language develop in the context of the child's everyday experiences, with their rich immediacy of meanings, whereas scientific concepts or a second language are examples of "nonspontaneous speech development" (Vygotsky, 1987, p. 180). The learning of scientific concepts or a second language in school both rely on a

The authors gratefully acknowledge a grant that supported this study from the University of New Mexico Research Allocation Committee. In addition, we would like to express our thanks to Mrs. Stanfield, principal, Mrs. Ortega, fifth-grade teacher, and the fifth-grade students of Mora Avenue School, Las Vegas, New Mexico, for their enthusiastic participation in this project.

251

previously developed set of word meanings originating from the child's everyday experiences, and this spontaneously acquired knowledge mediates the learning of the new. In this way, everyday concepts stand "between the conceptual system and the world of objects" (p. 180), just as one's first language mediates between one's thoughts and a second language. Thus the development of scientific concepts both depends and builds upon an already existing set of everyday concepts.[1]

In the development of scientific concepts, Vygotsky saw a set of general principles that pervade all institutionalized or formal instruction. Foremost among these is that the child is put in the position of consciously regarding and manipulating the object of instruction. In this way conscious awareness and volition are bound up with the act of knowing, in contrast with the spontaneous quality of everyday concepts. The modality of school instruction in part accounts for the conscious and volitional nature of school knowledge, for formal instruction is above all verbal instruction. So, for example, the child learns to define terms, even though the referent of the term may be only vaguely apprehended. Such learning proceeds in the opposite direction of spontaneous learning, where the object is directly experienced but not verbally apprehended. Thus a child may have a rich understanding of the spontaneous concept *brother* but not be able to define it in a logical, conceptual way (e.g., "male sibling"). The same child may be able to define Archmiedes' law without having much sense of its concrete realization. Conscious verbal strategies have not been directed at the former but have at the latter, so that in a verbal task the child may perform more successfully with material that appears more difficult. The apparent paradox is resolved by the recognition that the scientific concept has been experienced in verbal, rationalized terms, whereas the spontaneous concept has not: "The teacher, working with the child on a given question, explains, informs, inquires, corrects, and forces the child himself to explain. All of this work on concepts, the whole process of their formation, is worked out by the child in the process of instruction in collaboration with an adult" (Vygotsky, 1987, pp. 215–216). The child's later use of this material depends on the now invisible earlier collaboration. "In the thinking of the child, one cannot separate the concepts that he acquires in school from those that he acquires at home. Nonetheless, these concepts have entirely different histories" (p. 219).

These different histories of the spontaneous and scientific concepts may be reflected in the ways the child uses or displays his or her knowledge. In the ideal case, the scientific concepts will eventually acquire concrete meanings for the child, and the spontaneous concepts in time will become rational and accessible to his or her conscious and volitional verbal strategies, and both kinds of concepts will be used in similar ways. This ideal development is not inevitable, of course, and depends on the characteristics of instruction.

Vygotsky's distinction between spontaneous and scientific concepts bears an obvious resemblance to distinctions made by others, although his explanatory theory is unique. Piaget's work on concepts, for example, has been used extensively in education. Like Vygotsky, Piaget also proposes intermediate stages. But there are some interesting differences as well as similarities between them. Piaget wrote,

> The child begins by utilizing only syncretic pseudo-concepts before elaborating true logical classes, because the operations formative of classes . . . require a system of definitions whose stability and generality transcend the personal point of view and its subjective attachments. . . . From this stems the conclusion that a deductive structure on the plane of reflective thought presupposes a mind freed from the personal point of view by methods of reciprocity inherent in cooperation or intellectual exchange, and that reason, dominated by egocentrism on the verbal and social plane, can only be "transductive," that is, proceeding through the fusion of preconcepts located midway between particular cases and true generality. (Gruber & Vonèche, 1977, p. 287)

Like Vygotsky, Piaget here referred to the importance of the development of logical or systematic concepts through social exchange, but for Piaget this comes in later development and relies on the prior development of logical classes. For Vygotsky, the development of systematic concepts is not dependent on such prior development but rather is supported by social experience in the context relevant to the domain of knowledge. For Piaget, the development of mental structures precedes the learning of logically or systematically organized concepts, whereas for Vygotsky, the learning of systematic concepts precedes the development of an elaborated logical structure. Piaget focuses on the internal structure of concepts, whereas Vygotsky views concepts as differing on the basis of their context of acquisition. This distinction between Vygotsky's contextually derived notion and an internal one has significant implications for the way in which concepts develop in the life of the learner. By contrast with Piaget, Vygotsky's view of concept formation has more to say about the cultural setting in which the child develops his or her concepts. For both Piaget and Vygotsky, "pseudo" or "spontaneous" concepts are primarily inductive and strongly based on the individual experiential history of the learner. However, for Vygotsky, the "scientific" set is systematically transmitted by knowledge-disseminating institutions within a particular society, rather than an elaboration "of true logical classes on . . . the plane of reflective thought" (Gruber & Vonèche, 1977, p. 287). The contrast between spontaneous and scientific concepts and the way in which they are woven together in the history of a learner needs to be examined to uncover the complexity which may be oversimplified in Vygotsky's original formulation.

Of central importance is the transition from the earlier reliance on spontaneous concepts to the later development of scientific concepts. To attempt to trace this transition, Vygotsky's distinction can be effectively related to the developmental research conducted by Katherine Nelson and her co-workers on the acquisition of the scriptlike knowledge that develops spontaneously from everyday experiences. Nelson (1983) defines scripts as generalized event representations of the child's earliest recurring experiences; they are contextualized wholes such as the "restaurant script" or the "preschool script" that consist of a sequence of events that join to form a meaningful script. Over time, concepts are derived from scripts by a process of analysis or partitioning.

Research such as Nelson's is one of the new approaches to the study of children's cognitive processes which effectively combines research conducted in the naturalistic settings of knowledge acquisition and in more structured laboratory tasks. Much research has been conducted on the transmission of highly organized concepts such as time and space, which are specifically required for the mastery of school-related knowledge, but less work has been done on conceptual knowledge that is embedded in daily life. It is in this regard that Katherine Nelson's work is so crucial to our understanding of concept development. In this study, to explore the shift from spontaneous to systematic conceptualizations, we have combined the Vygotskian framework with notions developed by Nelson.

We view Vygotsky's notion of spontaneous "concepts" as those which are derived from scripts in Nelson's scheme. Such concepts take their meaning from the perceptual, functional, and contextual aspects of their referents. In our study, we focused on biological referents, which can be classified in either script-based or scientific taxonomic ways. For example, a child may group *robin* and *butterfly* together because "both fly in the air," a script organization; alternatively, the child may group *robin* and *ostrich* taxonomically in the sense that within "a system of relationships of generality" (Vygotsky, 1962, p. 92) they are birds. In the child's movement from script to taxonomic groupings, "the emphasis has shifted away from those aspects of linguistic organization that involve contextualization to the capacity of linguistic signs to enter into decontextualized relationships, that is, relationships which are constant across contexts of use" (Wertsch, 1985, p. 103).

In his research into children's concepts, Vygotsky relied primarily on children's responses to a sorting task using nonsense words, rather than upon extensive observation of children's daily activities (1987, chapter 5). In that task, Vygotsky was especially interested in exploring the child's sense of the conceptual connections – those hierarchical and parallel relations – that underlie a set of concepts. According to Vygotsky, spontaneous concepts are not organized in a set of consistent, systematic relations; it is such relations that are the distinguishing mark of scientific concepts.

The very wide-ranging work of Katherine Nelson supplements Vygotsky's early work because it is based on the observation of everyday cognition. It reveals the significance of script-based concepts by showing that children construct regularities, connections, and systematicity in ongoing daily activity, even though such constructions are not as sophisticated as the later mastery of more scientific concepts. Vygotsky's idea about conceptual relations has considerable power, but it also is limited because the data he used were from an arbitrary setting using a specialized task.

Although his analysis of concept learning relied on a task that was unconnected with everyday activity, Vygotsky did apply the implications of the spontaneous/ scientific distinction to more ongoing and critical processes of learning. He saw analogous differences between speech and writing and between first- and second-language acquisition. In both of these examples he viewed the earlier knowledge as a more inductively based process of generalization and abstraction that becomes linked with a more deductively explored, systematic conceptual framework. In each of these examples Vygotsky stressed the complex interweaving of the two, and it is especially this powerful interweaving of the two lines of development that we wish to highlight because it is central to understanding changes in conceptualization. From this perspective, the role of transitional or intermediate concepts is of particular significance. Vygotsky has emphasized these dynamic intermediate structures in his writing, but little research has been done to explore them. Our approach stresses the notion that there is no single universal set of intermediate stages but, instead, that cultural and family experiences contribute to the way systematic and spontaneous concepts are woven together at different phases of development. The acquisition of science concepts in early schooling provided an opportunity for studying ongoing development in a typical context rather than in a laboratory setting removed from the children's everyday activity.

Method

Overview

The use of ethnographic methods and a minilongitudinal design enabled us to explore both the nature of children's involvement with scientific concepts in the school setting and the dynamics of their use of these concepts. As the work of Scribner and Cole (1981) has shown, ethnographic observations and interviews can be used to uncover the links between everyday cognition and general cognitive processes.

Setting, population, and background

The setting for this study was a school with limited resources. It was a small rural school, with only one classroom at each grade and no lunchroom, which necessitated busing the students every day to a central facility for lunch. We worked with the fifth-grade class, composed of 27 children, aged 10 to 11, during 2 months late in the school year. The school was located in a community of 15,000 in the high desert region of northern New Mexico. Ranching, farming, hunting, and fishing were common experiences for many of the children in the class, although their daily lives were lived "in town," with weekends spent "at the ranch," a reference to the family home of grandparents or other extended family members. Parents of some of the children were attending 2-year or 4-year programs at the local college, but most were employed in labor or service occupations. The ethnic composition of the school was 75% to 80% Hispanic and 20% to 25% Anglo. All the children in the fifth-grade class were native English speakers, though a number understood Spanish.

Science instruction was not emphasized at the elementary level in the district. Most teachers adopted a textbook-oriented approach, using science to "teach reading in the content area." However, the target classroom was selected for study because the teacher was noted for her interest in science and her dedication to teaching. She wanted the children to "really get involved with science and to love it." She had chaired the science curriculum committee in the district for several years and had favored the selection of the textbook series in current use, in part because of the kit materials that were available. Of seven fifth-grade teachers in the district, she was the only one who had purchased those materials. She was committed to having the children participate in science activity and use the materials, as well as others she created herself. She used a variety of small group activities and large group demonstrations, which she and the children prepared, and alternated these with a minimum reliance on whole-class textbook lessons. In all of the science activities observed prior to the experimental sessions, the enthusiastic participation of the all the children was noteworthy.

From observations of science learning in the classroom and interviews with the teacher we learned that the children had received explicit instruction in scientific classification. In particular, instruction focused on the distinctions between plant and animal, between vertebrate and invertebrate, and on their hierarchical relationships. Within the set of vertebrates, the children had studied the categories *mammal, reptile, amphibian, bird,* and *fish,* and they had learned that insects are invertebrates. The game Animal-Vegetable-Mineral had figured prominently in the instructional unit and had remained a recurrent activity in the subsequent months. In all of their classroom science activity, the teacher tried to stress hands-on activity and process- rather than product-oriented tasks. She used the Animal-Vegetable-Mineral game to involve the children in scientific classification in a way that they viewed as fun. She noted that the students often had difficulty with these classifications, and she found this somewhat puzzling since a posttest after the classification unit showed that most of the students had "learned" the categories.

Although the game Animal-Vegetable-Mineral does not use actual scientific taxonomy, it relies on the same underlying structure. In order to succeed at the game, one must be able to use a hierarchic structure with nonoverlapping categories and to manipulate the structure in a logical and progressive or sequential way. During observations of the class playing the game, some of the children asked questions that contradicted the underlying structure, and other children commented on those questions in ways that showed they noted the contradiction, saying things like, "But he [the student 'leading' the game] already said it didn't have wings, so how could it be a bird?" Thus children commented in ways that could have helped others to understand the game better. In addition, after a solution was reached, the teacher often followed up by commenting on various strategies that had been used or others that could have been used so that children could improve their skill. Messages about the logic of classification, then, were communicated both explicitly and implicitly, and the children were given frequent opportunities to put this information into practice.

The design of the study was minilongitudinal in the sense that the students were asked to perform the classification tasks on two occasions at roughly a 1-month interval. As Adams (1987) has argued, "Vygotsky's work revolves around the concepts of internalization and transition, which are processes which unfold over time. . . . Cross-sectional data can play an important role in a Neo-Vygotskian design, but it is by itself insensitive to developmental processes." We were interested in the issue of internalization. The teacher had found the children capable of accurate recall at the end of the classification unit, but as Vygotsky theorizes, learning precedes development. We wanted to try to differentiate between the actual internalization of scientific concepts and the intermediate stage of "pseudoconcepts." In Vygotsky's view, pseudoconcepts look like true concepts but their structure is actually different, and they are not assembled on the basis of an abstract logical system.

As should be clear from our discussion and approach, this was an exploratory study, so the experimental activities were designed as our observations progressed. In addition, we wanted the activities to be "non-testlike" and to "fit in" with the classroom climate.

Tasks and procedure

Our intent was to monitor the way that children were learning with tasks that they considered to be appropriate in school but that were not testlike. In attempting to make the activities as natural and nonthreatening as possible, we took an approach similar to Vygotsky and Luria's in their field study in Central Asia (Luria, 1976). Rather than designing our tasks for a single, correct solution, we made them "open to several solutions, each of which indicated some aspect of cognitive activity. . . . they could be solved either in a functional-graphic way, based, for example, on how things look or work, or in an abstract categorical way" (Luria, 1979, p. 64). The activities seemed to generate a playful climate in the classroom, and children several times asked if there were extra sets of experimental materials that they might take home.

Two experimental activities in this work are of most importance to this discussion: a set of concept-sorting tasks and a film-retelling task.

The concept-sorting tasks were based on materials prepared for this study, but which at the same time related to content the students had been working with all year in their science curriculum. The children were asked to do three classification tasks, two in an initial session and one several weeks later. At the first session, the children were given a set of 20 pictures, 6 of plants and 14 of animals. This set of pictures came with supplementary materials which accompanied the class text but which had not been purchased by the school district; thus the choice of items was

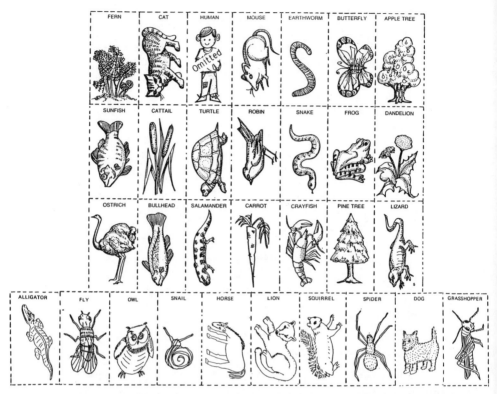

Figure 10.1. Pictures for sorting task. The top three rows are reprinted by permission from V. N. Rockcastle, B. J. McKnight, F. R. Salomon, and V. E. Schmidt, *Science,* Teacher's Edition, Addison-Wesley Science, Grade 5 (Reading, MA: Addison-Wesley, © 1980), p. 5. The pictures in the bottom row were prepared for this project by Janet Stein Romero.

perfectly matched to classification instruction that the children had earlier received. First, we asked the children to sort the pictures into two piles, to put each pile into an envelope, and to write on the envelope something that explained why those items "belonged together." Next, the children were given a second set of identical materials but with seven empty envelopes; they sorted the pictures into as many groups as they wanted (additional envelopes were readily available) but no fewer than three. Several weeks later, the children were asked to sort 23 animal pictures into at least three groups. The 23 animals included 13 of the original group (with the fish changed to the local "perch" and "trout") plus 10 new ones; one of the original 14 was deleted because none of the children had correctly classified it; the 10 added animals were chosen because they had been exemplars in subsequent instruction. The plants and animals are shown in Figure 10.1, with the 10 added animals presented in the bottom row.

The second activity to be discussed was a film-retelling task in which we adapted a narrative retelling technique to the recall of a film (Osterreich & John-Steiner,

1979). This task was useful in acquiring data that converged with the data collected through the more structured sorting task and because it helped to reveal the imme- diate effects of prior knowledge on new input. In addition, the use of an instruc- tional film (on videotape) offered the opportunity to monitor the processing of both verbally and visually encoded material, presented in the high-interest medium of television, without the confounding effect of differential reading abilities.

The entire class viewed a short (15-minute) science film and participated in a follow-up discussion. During viewing, the children's attentiveness to the film was monitored by a videocamera, which the children did not know was recording. The resulting tape was used to measure attentiveness to successive segments of the film. After viewing the film, the children participated in a discussion which gave nondi- rective closure to the film viewing, with children sharing "favorite parts" from the film. Following the discussion, one-third of the students participated in the experi- mental retelling task. This subsample of nine students was chosen based on the results of the earlier sorting tasks. The objective was to identify an equal number of students who in the sorting tasks had produced a predominance of taxonomic re- sponses, a predominance of script responses, and a balanced mixture of the two kinds of response. Each child from the subsample retold the film to a child from a lower grade who had not seen it. The retellers had no foreknowledge of this activity. During the retellings, the experimenter interjected script and taxonomic questions to probe the reteller's memory and maintain the activity.

Results and discussion

The sorting task

In the first sort, 82% of the children separated the pictures taxonomically into dis- crete plant and animal categories and labeled the envelopes accordingly. In the second classification, only 19% used an exclusively taxonomic approach. In the third sort 3 weeks later, 25% of the students used an exclusively taxonomic ap- proach.

Children's responses were categorized on the basis of the type of groupings a child used, that is, all taxonomic, a combination of script and taxonomic, or all script-based groupings. The frequency of response categories differed significantly across the three tasks ($X^2 = 29.016$, df $= 4$, P $< .001$). These results are presented in Table 10.1.

Our primary interest is in the approach taken by children who did not use a taxonomic system. As indicated above, many of the children used a combination of taxonomic and script categories for the second or third task or for both. For ex- ample, Student 1 used a combination of categories; in the second sort he relied on ecological categories familiar in his region. However, in the third sort, in the later session, he abandoned his knowledge of taxonomic categories and constructed cat- egories on the basis of information he had assimilated from the science film that

Table 10.1. *Distribution of responses by category*

	Script	Script/ taxonomic	Taxonomic	Total
Sort 1	1	4	22	27
Sort 2	9	13	5	27
Sort 3	11	7	6	24

was presented to the class by the experimenters. His sorting of *sunfish* into the plant group was probably unintentional, since the picture of a fish was unambiguous and he did have an appropriate category. (Children's wording and spelling is reproduced exactly as it was written.)

Student 1
Sort 2

All plants	Fern, apple tree, cattail, dandelion, carrot, pine tree, sunfish
All kinds of crabs	Crayfish
Animals that live in water	Turtle, frog, bullhead (fish), salamander
All birds	Robin, ostrich
All insects	Earthworm, butterfly
Mostly live on land	Cat, mouse, lizard, snake

Sort 3

It has a cuver to protect its eye	Alligator
They all have eyes just like humans	Lion, owl, cat, dog
Its has eyes on its entenas	Snail
They all have a lot of lenes	Spider, grasshopper, fly
They all have eyes at the side	Mouse, snake, salamander, squirrel, earthworm, turtle, frog, ostrich, horse, lizard, butterfly, perch, robin, trout

Some students relied on categories that evidently derived from another aspect of their experience: hunting. In this instance, Student 2 used a combination of taxonomic and ecological categories in the second sort but changed some of his ecological categories when sorting the larger collection in the third sort.

Student 2
Sort 3

Birds	Ostrich, robin
Water animals	Alligator, salamander, turtle, frog, perch, trout
Insects	Earthworm, grasshopper, snail, butterfly
Animals that hunt	Lion, snake, owl, cat, dog
Animals that are hunted	Mouse, squirrel, horse, lizard

Some children's categories showed an increase in the ability to use taxonomic categories from the second to the third sort, yet their mixing of logical levels shows that their understanding is what Vygotsky would identify as pseudoconcepts, as exemplified by Student 3. This student's third sort has the added interest of no misclassifications, despite the conflicting levels of abstraction.

Student 3	
Sort 2	
All birds	Butterfly, robin, ostrich
All plants	Ferns, apple tree, cattail, dandelion, carrot, pine tree
Live in water	Crayfish, earthworm, sunfish, snake, frog, bullhead, salamander
All have backbones	Cat, mouse, turtle, lizard
Sort 3	
All birds	Owl, ostrich, robin
All animals with backbones	Mouse, lion, squirrel, cat, horse, dog
All fish	Perch, trout
Animals without backbones	Earthworm, snail
All insects	Spider, grasshopper, butterfly, fly
All reptiles	Alligator, snake, turtle, lizard
Both amphibians	Salamander, frog

Often, when children used taxonomic labels they were not applied appropriately, as when *frog* or *earthworm* was categorized as a reptile on the basis of perceptual similarities with other members of that class, such as "They're all slimy." As often noted in the literature on concept development, perceptual features are significant to young children (Nelson, 1974). More common than static features in these data, however, were habitats and movements, such as "Things that go underground/live in water" and "Things that crawl/swim/fly."

In terms of logical structures, there were several interesting findings. A number of children adopted the category structure strategy of positive and negative exemplars, perhaps from the vertebrate/invertebrate distinction. This strategy generated categories such as "They all do/don't have legs." Sometimes a child included a negative category without its positive counterpart. In addition, children were willing to use overlapping or combined categories, as in "Plants and animals that hang around plants," or "Fish or animals that live in the sea." Such examples show that children are not using classification in the way that educated adults understand and are often not using concepts in their abstract sense. As mentioned earlier, the child's approach to the task often fluctuates: Only one-fifth of the children who used a taxonomic approach in the easier first task continued to do so in the subsequent sortings. Most of those who shifted strategy combined taxonomic and script categories, though a few shifted to an exclusive script approach. In contrast, several who had used a combined approach on the second task were able to employ all taxonomic categories, though with a few misclassifications, on the more difficult third task. Whether this more academically advanced strategy represented a stable development is not certain.

Thus, as the task increased in difficulty by requiring more groupings, by supplying more items for groupings, and by including more items that were less representative or prototypic (Mervis & Rosch, 1981), fewer children were able to use systematic strategies, as predicted. Environmental and cultural factors seem to play a part here. For example, the high desert environment in which these children live does not afford familiarity with some of the animals (such as the snail) presented in the stimulus material. Similarly, some animals (especially the snake and salamander) were less familiar to girls than to boys, reflecting cultural patterns in play.

The ability of the children to operate with conceptual labels was not firmly developed, although, as discussed earlier, they had been explicitly instructed in this area. At the beginning of the school year the children spent 6 weeks of instruction exploring the notion of scientific classification, including the distinctions *plant/animal, vertebrate/invertebrate, animal/vegetable/mineral,* and *mammal/reptile/amphibian/bird/fish/insect.* In addition, the teacher had continued the classificatory theme by frequently playing the game of Animal-Vegetable-Mineral.

Many of the responses in the sorting tasks demonstrate that the children were attempting to use newly learned concepts, or struggling to produce coherent groupings. One child's set of six categories for Sort 3 particularly illustrates the attempt to utilize scientific concepts from instruction (italicized) before internalizing the system in which such knowledge fits:

They have backbones	Lion, horse
They don't have backbones	Spider, grasshopper, fly, butterfly
They swim	Turtle, frog
They all fly	Owl, ostrich, robin
They all go without legs	Snake, earthworm, snail, perch, trout
They make up a food chain	Dog, cat, mouse

At the same time, the inappropriateness of such solutions illustrated the transformations in understanding that result during the transition from reliance on spontaneous concepts to an elaborated scientific system.

The combination of script and taxonomic categories represents an intermediate phase in the child's transition from using concepts that are highly experientially embedded to those that are systematically organized and transmitted concepts. Children appear to have different ways of mixing concepts, but all of these have a kind of explanatory power for the child. Such mixtures are not just stopping points on the way to acquiring the adult and mature form. Rather, they reflect an active and frequently creative exploration by the child looking to the way things are connected. Their categories reflect connections in terms of setting, in terms of function, in terms of appearance – linkages between diverse objects which require an active process of analysis. Frequently, the amount of intellectual work children are engaged in is underestimated because observers ignore children's own constructions of these connections and groupings, focusing instead on the direct impact of adult instruction. Consequently, the way children group and link things is not very well understood.

The film task

Results from monitoring the children while they viewed the film suggest that it held their interest most of the time. Samples taken at 15-second intervals indicated that 80% to 90% of the students were looking at the film at all times. One part of the film was particularly interesting to the students: In seven consecutive samples 100% of the children were looking at the film. In addition, the students' participation in the follow-up discussion was quite lively: They raised their hands eagerly to participate and expressed disappointment when it was time to end.

The information in the film was analyzed in terms of the script/taxonomic distinction. The film consisted of information about kinds of eyes and their general structural and functional differences, which was classified as taxonomic, and information about particular animals exemplifying the taxonomic content, which was classified as script information. Each of the retellings was studied in order to tabulate the units of script and taxonomic information recalled. Chi-square analysis revealed a statistically significant difference between the retellings and the film (X^2 = 13.29, df = 1, P < .001). That is, amounts of information recalled differed significantly from the proportions of script and taxonomic information presented in the film.

Inspection of the individual retellings suggests a correlation between recall and concept organization. Children who had utilized taxonomic sorting strategies produced the most extensive recalls. Not only did these children recall more information units from the film, they also recalled a greater proportion of the taxonomic units. In addition, the data suggest a relationship between concept organization and the development of discourse production strategies. Children who used taxonomic grouping exceeded the others in the quantity of discourse produced; both their unaided utterances and their responses to probe questions were lengthier. Overall, for both amount of recall and length of utterances, children who used taxonomic grouping exceeded those who used script/taxonomic grouping, who in turn recalled and uttered more than those who used script categories. These data are summarized in Figure 10.2.

Overall, the children's retellings showed wide variation in level of functioning. Two of the children operated independently, in the sense of producing lengthy, continuous discourses (between 150 and 300 words) in response to the most open-ended and nonspecific of questions. Other children required many more probes and produced much shorter responses; their level of functioning was much more dependent on adult assistance, and their style of discourse indicated far less assimilation of strategies for cohesion and logical connection. The utterances of the taxonomic group differed in quality as well as quantity from the others. These speakers used strategies more characteristic of written language (Chafe, 1982; Ochs, 1983; Tannen, 1982). In their recalls they used a number of devices that enable one to create greater coherence and to pack more information into fewer words: explicit topical-

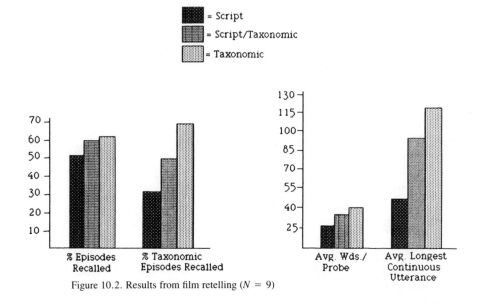

Figure 10.2. Results from film retelling ($N = 9$)

Table 10.2. *Examples of film retelling by a child who uses script categories and a child who uses taxonomic categories*

Script:	"We watched the film about eyes. That grasshopper has a lot of eyes, that they could look in any direction. Flies, they have eyes that could look around themselves." [Silence] [Probe] "The snail. He's so small he can only look close. The alligator." [Silence] [Probe] "When you turn off the light his, this thing opens. When you open the light, it closes."
Taxonomic:	"It was about how animals see. Like the first kind was the snail. You know those things sticking up from their heads, I forget the name. It has a lens on it. Further down it has these kinds of cells which were sensitive to light. Then they went to the alligator. It has like an extra eyelid. They had these tests where if you turn the light on it goes real small. Then they turned the light off, so you couldn't tell if his eyes were all big. Then when they turned the light on again after it was dark, its eyes closed."

ization (such as "the first kind of eye . . ."); elaboration (relative clauses and attributive adjectives such as "cells which were sensitive to light"); transitions and connectives (such as "then" and "so," which are used to help the hearer understand), which were used much less frequently or not at all by the other participants. The use of such strategies in spontaneous speech implies that a speaker is able to plan both the form and the content of his or her speech. Prior knowledge may facilitate production of content, thus freeing capacity for formal and audience considerations. Table 10.2 presents excerpts from two of the retellings, one by a child who had used script grouping and one who had used a taxonomic approach.

Because of the small sample size, such data can only be suggestive. Nevertheless, too little is known about the kinds of relationships between speaking and thinking that we have touched on. In most research, matters of recall, concept organization, and speech production are dealt with separately, without exploring their relationships. Analyses of these domains have become more sophisticated since Vygotsky's time, but the focus on the interrelationships between language and thought is still missing in much contemporary work. The emphasis within Vygotsky's writings can alert researchers to looking at these processes within contextualized settings of everyday cognitive activity, and the use of a variety of methods of investigation may contribute to our understanding of these complex interrelationships.

Conclusion

This study of the acquisition of scientific concepts in elementary school-age children highlights the importance of the organization of knowledge according to consistent and powerful categories. The children who are more advanced in this regard have a twofold advantage: They use their taxonomic knowledge in responding to specific school-related questions, and they appear to rely upon such knowledge in efficiently processing new information, a task that is crucial in school. When children do not know this structural system, they probably cannot process new information as efficiently. Yet the transformation from the organization of information in scriptlike frames to more powerful taxonomic structures is slow, laborious, and usually hidden. In consequence, focused assistance is rarely given to children who are not proceeding to acquire new structures effectively.

This study reveals that children are actively engaging in grouping and sorting but that their particular categorizations are frequently unavailable to teachers and parents. Even in this classroom, where the teacher was well informed about the teaching of science, the outcomes of instruction were mixed. The process of weaving together scientific and everyday concepts is lengthy and demanding and may require longer immersion than can be provided in classroom settings.

Yet there are several important instructional factors which may be more productive than the best conventional approaches. Instruction in taxonomic categories should involve active problem solving, should rely substantially on peer interaction, and should be connected with varied media and experiences (such as films and field trips). When children are involved in active field explorations, as shown in the work of Heath (1983) and Aidarova (1982), we see significant movement toward the systematization of knowledge, but according to the parameters of children's own conceptions. Although a game such as Animal-Vegetable-Mineral provides practice at a kind of problem solving, the inappropriate guesses of some children after many sessions show that additional kinds of activities and activities in peer interaction were needed. One alternative is to make classification systems an object of study. Questions for investigation might include the organization of objects in space – such as how items are arranged in kitchens or workshops – and comparative analyses of differing findings by peers investigating similar domains. Such investigations should lead to the development of active strategies for sorting or categorizing, which can be effectively applied as a system of discourse rather than in a rote fashion.

Just as students should explore thinking in the world, teachers should explore thinking in students. If educators are to assist the development of conceptual thinking, that assistance will be most valuable if children's own groupings and sortings are understood. In that way, teaching can be focused on the active mental work that a child is already doing. As Vygotsky wrote, for teaching to be effective "child thought must be known, [but not] as any enemy must be known in order to be fought successfully" (1962, p. 85); rather, child thought must be known and understood so that teachers can work effectively within the child's zone of proximal development to maximize the effectiveness of instruction.

Note

1 We believe Vygotsky's view requires some modification for those learners whose acquisition of scientific concepts or a second language occurs in everyday life settings, rather than in formal schooling. Examples are children growing up in a multilingual environment or in homes where school-like scientific explanations are routinely produced, so that the development of this knowledge in everyday contexts is less reliant on "previous" concepts.

References

Adams, A. (1987). *Vygotskian approaches to semantic development: Implications for design and analysis*. Paper presented at the Fourth International Congress for the Study of Child Language, Lund, Sweden.

Aidarova, L. (1982). *Child development and education*. Moscow: Progress.

Chafe, W. (1982). Integration and involvement in speaking, writing, and oral literature. In D. Tannen (Ed.), *Spoken and written language*. Norwood, NJ: Ablex.

Frauenglass, M. H., & Diaz, R. M. (1985). Self-regulatory functions of children's private speech: A critical analysis to recent challenges to Vygotsky's theory. *Developmental Psychology, 21,* 357–364.

Gruber, H. E., & Vonèche, J. J. (1977). *The essential Piaget*. New York: Basic.

Heath, S. B. (1983). *Ways with words*. Cambridge: Cambridge University Press.

Luria, A. R. (1976). *Cognitive development: Its cultural and social foundations*. Cambridge, MA: Harvard University Press.

Luria, A. R. (1979). *The making of mind*. Cambridge, MA: Harvard University Press.

Mervis, C. B., & Rosch, E. (1981). Categorization of natural objects. *Annual Review of Psychology, 32,* 89–115.

Nelson, K. (1974). Concept, word, and sentence: Interrelations in acquisition and development. *Psychological Review, 81,* 267–285.

Nelson, K. (1983). The derivation of concepts and categories from event representations. In E. K. Scholnick (Ed.), *New trends in conceptual representation: Challenges to Piaget's theory*. Hillsdale, NJ: Erlbaum.

Ochs, E. (1983). Planned and unplanned discourse. In E. Ochs & B. Scheiffelin (Eds.), *Acquiring conversational competence*. London: Routledge & Kegan Paul.

Osterreich, H., & John-Steiner, V. (1979). A study of story retelling among young bilingual Indian children. In O. Garnica & M. King (Eds.), *Language, children, and society*. Oxford: Pergamon.

Scribner, S., & Cole, M. (1981). *The psychology of literacy*. Cambridge, MA: Harvard University Press.

Tannen, D. (1982). Oral and literate strategies in spoken and written narratives. *Language, 58*(1), 1–21.

Vygotsky, L. S. (1962). *Thought and language*. Cambridge, MA: MIT Press.

Vygotsky, L. S. (1987). *The collected works of L. S. Vygotsky* (Vol. 1). New York: Plenum.

Wertsch, J. (1985). *Vygotsky and the social formation of mind*. Cambridge, MA: Harvard University Press.

Part III

Instructional applications

11 Changes in a teacher's views of interactive comprehension instruction

Kathryn H. Au

Although most research on teaching has centered on teachers' observable behaviors and their effects upon students, there has been an increasing emphasis on the study of teachers' thinking. In a major review of research on teachers' thought processes, Clark and Peterson (1986) outline a model of teacher thought and action. This model shows how different parts of the research on teachers' thinking relate to one another as well as to the much larger body of research on teachers' behaviors and effects on students. Clark and Peterson note that there is a reciprocal relationship between the domain of thought and the domain of action and argue that a full understanding of the process of teaching will come about only when the two domains are studied in relation to one another.

This general line of reasoning is supported by Vygotsky's work. One of Vygotsky's major contributions to psychological theory is the proposal that mind and behavior be reconceptualized so they can be studied in an integrated way (Minick, 1986). In the terms used by Clark and Peterson (1986), this proposal implies that the actual object of study should be the reciprocal relationship between teachers' thoughts and behavior, rather than either the domain of thought or the domain of action. From a Vygotskian perspective, it is argued that teaching behavior cannot be understood apart from the thought processes of the teacher.

The present study demonstrates but one of the many possible applications of Vygotsky's work to research on teaching (for other examples related to the same model of teaching, see Au & Kawakami, 1984, 1986; Gallimore, Dalton, & Tharp, 1986). This study falls into the category of research on teachers' implicit theories of teaching and learning. According to Clark and Peterson (1986), researchers who conduct studies in this category take the view that a teacher's actions are guided by a personally held system of beliefs and principles. The researcher's task is to arrive at an explicit description of this implicitly held belief system, one that is faithful to the teacher's own feeling for the system.

Studies of teachers' implicit theories, in common with other approaches to the study of teaching, have tended to focus on experienced teachers rather than novices. The present study departs from this tendency in focusing on the development of expertise in teaching, viewed as the evolution of a novice teacher's concepts about instruction.

271

Vygotsky's formulations in three areas have direct relevance to this study. The first area is that of theory development. Di Bello and Orlich (1987) examine the implications of Vygotsky's ideas for theory development by taking as their starting point the distinction between *spontaneous* or everyday concepts and *scientific* concepts (see Panofsky, John-Steiner, & Blackwell, this volume). Spontaneous concepts are ontological categories forming the basis for an individual's own intuitive theories of the world. They develop informally as products of the individual's life experiences, apart from formal schooling in systematic bodies of knowledge.

Scientific concepts, on the other hand, are systems of relations between objects, as defined in formal theories. Scientific concepts are formulated by the culture rather than the individual. Individuals acquire scientific concepts through instruction in a process of cultural transmission.

In the course of development, there is a dynamic relationship between spontaneous and scientific concepts. Scientific concepts do not emerge smoothly and directly from spontaneous concepts. Rather, the two types of concepts follow different courses and play different roles in theory development.

> [Spontaneous concepts] create a series of structures necessary for the evolution of a concept's more primitive, elementary aspects, which give it body and vitality. Scientific concepts, in turn, supply structures for the upward development of the child's spontaneous concepts toward consciousness and deliberate use. Scientific concepts grow down through spontaneous concepts and spontaneous concepts grow up through scientific concepts. (Vygotsky, 1962, p. 116)

There is a dialectic interaction between spontaneous and scientific concepts. As a result of this interaction, "true concepts" emerge. What Vygotsky refers to as true concepts, or deeper understandings, may be viewed as the basis for expertise in a particular domain.

In the case of teaching, a teacher demonstrates expertise by acting upon true concepts, not just by holding them. In other words, the teacher needs to integrate spontaneous and scientific concepts to form what Elbaz (1981) calls *practical knowledge*. Elbaz sees the teacher as confronting a wide variety of tasks and problems. To deal with these problems, the teacher draws upon practical knowledge. Practical knowledge is seen as knowledge *of* practice, as well as knowledge mediated *by* practice. Elbaz conducted a case study examining the practical knowledge of an experienced high school teacher. In Elbaz's study the central questions were: How is practical knowledge held? How is it being used? In the present study the central question is: How does practical knowledge grow and change over time?

If changes in thought are to be studied, a second area of Vygotsky's thinking becomes important. This area has to do with the role of speech in development. For both children and adults, Vygotsky (1978) suggested that development in a particular domain begins by being externally and socially regulated (see Díaz, Neal, & Amaya-Williams, this volume). Speech serves to make a person's thoughts accessible to the processes of social influence.

Di Bello and Orlich (1987) suggest that the very act of speaking about one's current understanding makes one's understanding explicit. Often, an individual may have a sketchy or partial understanding of aspects of a formal theory but be unaware of exactly what is understood or not understood. In the course of a discussion or conversation, the individual has the chance to verbalize understandings as well as misunderstandings. The process of putting thoughts into words allows the individual to become aware of his or her own understandings and misunderstandings. When these understandings and misunderstandings have been verbalized, they can also become known to an instructor who may be participating in the discussion. The instructor then has the opportunity to explain and clarify concepts that have remained unclear to the individual. As the process of discussion continues, it has the potential for promoting the individual's acquisition of scientific concepts. Thus, once a person's concepts have become explicit, they are open to discourse processes which can promote reorganization and refinement.

In examining the reorganization of a novice teacher's practical knowledge, it is necessary to have a framework for looking at the structure of thought. Here again, Elbaz's work proves helpful. Elbaz (1981) recognized the importance of studying the organization or structure of the teacher's practical knowledge as well as its content. Elbaz used the terms *rule of practice, practical principle,* and *image* to describe three degrees of generality in the teacher's knowledge. Rules of practice are clear statements of what to do in specific, commonly occurring situations. In Elbaz's study, an example is seen in the teacher's saying, ''I certainly try very hard to listen very actively to the kids, to paraphrase, to encourage them to paraphrase, and at most times to allow them to express their concerns without judging them.'' Practical principles are broader than rules and emerge at the end of a process of thinking through a problem. An example of a principle, consistent with the rule stated above, is ''that students should be provided with a class atmosphere in which they are able to take risks and thereby come to communicate more openly.'' Images, the most inclusive level, incorporate the teacher's beliefs in brief, metaphoric statements. The teacher used the image of ''having a window onto the kids and what they're thinking'' and spoke of wanting her own window to be more open.

Elbaz characterized rules as guiding action in a methodical way, principles as guiding action in a reflective way, and images as guiding action in an intuitive way. Of the three, Elbaz found images to be the most powerful in organizing the teacher's knowledge and in applying it to practice. For the teacher in Elbaz's study, images served as the means for summarizing areas of practical knowledge.

By extending Elbaz's approach, it should be possible to detect changes in the structure of a novice teacher's practical knowledge. These should appear as changes in levels of generality. For example, early on practical knowledge may largely be organized as rules and principles, whereas later it may largely be organized as principles and images.

In the present study, the novice teacher participated in conversations about her own teaching with the researcher. In these conversations, the novice teacher's thinking became explicit, and the researcher had the opportunity to influence her thinking.

An analysis of statements made by the novice at different times should reveal changes in the structure of her practical knowledge and the emergence of scientific concepts about instruction.

Finally, a third area of Vygotsky's work provides a perspective for understanding the significance of changes in the structure of thought to the individual's development. Of relevance here is the whole idea of consciousness, or awareness. Roter (1987) points out that Vygotsky viewed consciousness as the major issue in psychological theory. From a Vygotskian perspective, consciousness is seen as a highly complex system based on the interrelationships among all mental functions. These functions include both lower-level functions, such as memory, and higher-level functions, such as reasoning. They also include motivation and affect. Consciousness was central in Vygotsky's view because it offered a way of treating mind as a whole. In fact, he believed the study of consciousness to be the central problem for psychology and the basis for psychological research on all topics. In keeping with Vygotsky's efforts to promote the study of mind in nonatomistic, holistic ways, Roter argues for the integration of research on areas of consciousness normally studied separately, including awareness, automaticity, volition, and verbalizability.

As Roter indicates, consciousness represents the highest of the three levels of mental functioning. The second or intermediate level of mental functioning, just below consciousness, includes two types of cognitive components, one having an explicit function and the other a tacit function. The remaining or lowest level of mental functioning incorporates basic cognitive processes such as memory, attention, and perception.

The intermediate level of mental functioning is the primary focus in the present study, because this is the level at which changes in practical knowledge can be witnessed. As implied earlier, explicit functions are those with the potential to enter into conscious awareness. They can be verbalized and so are subject to change through discourse processes. In contrast, tacit functions cannot enter into conscious awareness. Initially, for any particular domain, tacit functions dominate. When the individual achieves a certain level of knowledge, however, explicit functions dominate.

Vygotsky's perspective on consciousness serves to frame this study of changes in a novice's practical knowledge of teaching. Through a novice's statements, aspects of knowledge should be seen to move from a tacit to an explicit status. Furthermore, as knowledge deepens, some aspects of knowledge should be combined into larger, more inclusive components. Specifically, in the case of a novice teacher's practical knowledge of teaching, the emergence of images, in the place of rules and principles, would signal the forming of more inclusive components. The appearance of these components can be said to mark the beginning of expertise. Central to the development of expertise is the movement of some aspects of practical knowledge into consciousness, the highest level of mental functioning.

Scientific concepts of instruction

In the present study, the scientific (as opposed to spontaneous) concepts were those of an interactive model of instruction, designed to improve young children's reading comprehension. The model of instruction includes four principles: (1) an emphasis on higher-level thinking, (2) active, systematic instruction, (3) responsiveness, and (4) theme development (for a full description of the model, refer to Au, 1985). Lessons incorporating these dimensions are at the heart of the effective reading program developed for Polynesian-Hawaiian children at the Kamehameha Elementary Education Program in Honolulu, Hawaii (for evidence of the program's effectiveness, see Tharp, 1982). The model of instruction is complex, and teachers typically require 2 years to master it.

To conduct interactive comprehension lessons successfully, teachers need to know how to plan lessons, how to structure them, and how to shape student thinking through responsive questioning. In planning lessons teachers must identify a central theme or main idea to be used for focusing the discussion and making the story meaningful to students. They must identify concepts likely to be unfamiliar to the students and also divide the story into chunks for guided reading and discussion. In structuring lessons, teachers follow the experience–text-relationship approach (Au, 1979), moving discussion through three phases: an experience phase, for accessing relevant prior knowledge and for concept development; a text phase, for clarifying and interpreting text information; and a relationship phase, for drawing relationships between text ideas and the students' prior knowledge. In interacting with students during the lessons, teachers formulate questions on the basis of students' responses (Gallimore et al., 1986). Teachers attempt to shift the cognitive work load over to students by eliciting information, rather than telling them the answers (Au & Kawakami, 1984).

Methods

The teacher, who taught home economics at the high school level, volunteered to participate in the study because of her interest in professional development and in becoming knowledgeable about the instruction of younger students. The teacher was not a novice to teaching as a whole, but she was a novice with respect to the model of teaching described above. She taught one small-group, 20-minute lesson almost every week from October through March, for a total of 24 lessons. The six children in the reading group were third-graders reading at grade level. Most of the students were of Polynesian ancestry and from low-income families.

All of the lessons were videotaped. The series of lessons ended when the teacher and researcher decided that the teacher had learned how to teach in ways consistent with the model of instruction. Analyses of the videotapes verified that the teacher eventually mastered most of the instructional behaviors associated with the model (Au, Oshiro, & Blake, 1986).

Following most of the lessons, the teacher and researcher held a meeting, often about 45 minutes long. In the course of the study, 23 meetings occurred. At the very beginning of each meeting, the researcher asked the teacher about her general impressions of the lesson just taught. The teacher was then encouraged to initiate discussion and ask questions on issues of immediate concern. The researcher responded and also provided advice and information on related issues. The researcher's original intention was to offer advice only in response to needs expressed by the teacher, but because the teacher experienced considerable difficulty in the early lessons, advice was freely given. Both management and instructional issues were discussed at length. In later meetings the teacher tended to use much of the meeting time to plan future lessons with the assistance of the researcher.

Although most data on the teacher's thinking were collected by the method of thinking aloud, stimulated recall was used on several occasions when the teacher and researcher viewed videotapes of the lessons. The teacher also watched several lessons taught by a master teacher and commented on these observations during the meetings. The meetings were audiotaped and transcripts shared with the teacher.

Teacher and researcher statements in the transcripts were classified in three domains: instruction, management, and attitudes and beliefs. Some statements were placed in two domains, a few in all three. The term *statement* is used here to connote portions of a turn of speaking judged to reflect practical knowledge on a certain issue or topic. Thus a turn of speaking could incorporate several different statements. Not counted as statements were brief comments serving primarily to encourage the other speaker to continue.

Statements showing practical knowledge of the model of instruction were categorized according to the specific issue or topic addressed. Statements bearing on more than one issue were included under the two issues that seemed dominant. Statements were further categorized as rules of practice, practical principles, and images, following operational definitions based on Elbaz's work (1981) but modified for the purposes of this study. For example, the level of principles included cause–effect analyses and contrasts between present and former views.

Results

The term *issue* will be used to describe the cluster of statements on the same topic, because discussion was almost always initiated and further stimulated by particular instructional problems the teacher encountered. A total of 24 different issues were discussed by the teacher and researcher. To be reported here are the results for the five issues most often discussed by the teacher:

> Pacing
> Planning
> Controlling the topic of discussion
> Drawing out relevant prior knowledge
> Teacher responsibility

For each issue, representative statements are included to illustrate changes over time in the teacher's practical knowledge. The content and structure of her practical knowledge of each issue are then discussed.

Pacing

The teacher often spoke of the importance of "keeping the lesson going" or "keeping it moving." She used these phrases to refer to the idea of moving the discussion forward in a brisk manner.

During Meeting 7, which occurred following a lesson the teacher viewed as a disaster, she agreed for the first time to watch the videotape of her lesson. The teacher realized that she needed to move the lesson forward more quickly. She observed that

> it seemed like a lot of time there too. Maybe I should have started in with the questions right away. Because I made them wait so long and think, then they got bored already.

She concluded that "Things have got to be going faster" and that one of her goals would be to "keep it going."

At Meeting 8, after having observed a master teacher, the teacher commented that it

> just seems like she had questions, questions, questions, you know. And she'd take little things to bring out. What about this, or what about this, or what about this? And [she] keeps it going.

At Meeting 10 the teacher referred to having "frozen" and completely stopped the story discussion during a previous lesson, displaying the very opposite of the behavior she wanted to achieve. At Meeting 16 the teacher saw being in tune with the children as an aspect of this goal.

> It's just [that] I've got to be able to read them a little bit more, and keep it going, and pull from them, and keep going.

She also introduced the idea of smoothness in keeping lessons going. Contrasting herself to the master teacher, the teacher said:

> It just seems so smooth when she does it. And I'm just looking at my questions and thinking, "Wait just a minute, now let's see."

During Meeting 22 the teacher described having felt "breaks" in the lesson, which had not gone as well as she had wanted. At Meeting 21 she contrasted the view she now held with her previous view:

> My hardest time is the start, because I'm so glad to see them and I just feel so good and relaxed, but you just can't be that way. You just can't relax. And you have got to right away get them going. You know, I just dream that I can just sit down and everything will go, and "okay, open your books, now do this," but you can't. You've got to just come in and be ready to go, ready go, ready go, ready go, right on them all the time.

Content and structure. The teacher appeared to have a general goal in mind from early in the study. By Meeting 7 this goal had crystallized in the phrase "Keep it going." The concept of what it meant to keep the lesson going was gradually elaborated, until by Meeting 16 it included being able to "read" the students (know what they were thinking and understanding about the text) and to "pull from them" (elicit answers). This level of knowledge seemed to be that of practical principles.

Emerging simultaneously were other aspects of knowledge about keeping lessons going which resembled Elbaz's rules of practice. For the most part these were specific procedures, such as starting to ask questions right away.

At the level of images, a continuity or smoothness metaphor seemed to emerge. The teacher conceptualized "freezing" and "letting it die" as the opposite of keeping it going, admired the master teacher's "smooth" questioning, and expressed concern about feeling "breaks" in her own lesson. For the issue of pacing, then, the teacher's knowledge appeared to be organized at all three levels of generality, being structured simultaneously as rules, principles, and images.

Planning

The teacher's initial ideas about planning centered on use of the teacher's guide. In Meeting 2 she stated that she had "just read that guide" and used its suggestions for discussion. In Meeting 5 the teacher stated that she had changed the way she planned the lessons. Now she was deciding to teach some stories and not others and identifying a theme to develop in discussions.

> The first two times I used the first story in this book and the first story in the other book, just because it was there. And now I know that it's easier to teach too, if – this is what you taught me last time – you have a purpose. Like I wrote down *responsibility* – well, I wrote down three things but, you know, you said I should have one in mind.

In Meeting 9 she spoke of reading the story over about five times. She repeated the idea that it was important to set a goal for oneself. In Meeting 10 the teacher said she could only be successful if she was well prepared with questions. In Meeting 13 she continued to associate planning with knowing which questions to ask and indicated that she was continuing to use the teacher's guide as a source of questions.

But during Meeting 14 the teacher commented that, by knowing the stories well, she could teach without relying on a set list of questions or on suggestions in the teacher's guide. In Meeting 17 she stated that her own ideas should take priority. Then she could use the guide as a supplement.

> Usually, when I pick a story I read all those suggestions, you know, the little teacher's guide. . . . But I should pick my story first, see what my own ideas are, and then go compare and see if I can get more ideas from them. Just go from what I think, from knowing the kids and things too.

Finally, in Meeting 23, the teacher concluded that good planning was a necessary but not sufficient condition for successful lessons. The teacher also had to be able to think on her feet.

> You know, you can plan so much, but I think a lot of this teaching, too, has to be off the top of your head. I mean, you know, you have to be so you can just think of things.

Content and structure. The teacher's knowledge of planning seemed to be largely at one level of generality, that of rules of practice. At first these rules related to use of the teacher's guide. Gradually, the teacher moved toward rules about picking and choosing the selections she would teach, instead of following the order of selections in the basal readers. She also stated rules about setting her own purposes for the lessons, choosing themes she wanted to explore with the students. The teacher felt it was important to read the selections over several times so she would know them well. However, the teacher continued to maintain that she needed to prepare a list of specific questions to ask.

It was not until the last meeting that the teacher spoke of limitations in conceptualizing planning as the mapping out of a lesson in advance, question by question. At this point she recognized the importance of being able to teach in a responsive way, that is, by formulating questions on the basis of students' answers. The practical principle or goal was that of being thoroughly familiar with the story, arming oneself with a theme to be developed in discussion, while at the same time being able to come up with questions or shift to another theme, depending on the students' own ideas.

Controlling the topic of discussion

The teacher introduced the issue of controlling the topic or "getting the students to stay on the subject" in Meeting 3. She was concerned that the children "rambled on and on." In Meeting 5 she realized that she might need to stop students from continuing on at length. She observed that a student who held the floor would start moving off the topic. She also wondered if she should begin ignoring extraneous questions from the students. She said:

> I waste an awful lot of time, I can tell now, with the back-and-forth stuff. You know, talking to Barbara and then Melinda, you know, about stuff that I should just say, "I don't want that," and then continue.

In Meeting 10 the teacher began to see the problem of keeping the children on the subject in a slightly different way. She worried about the children's acting silly during the discussion, although they seemed to be giving answers to her questions. In Meeting 13 the teacher described the issue in these terms:

> And that's a hard point for me too, Kathy, because . . . sometimes they're kind of on the subject even though they're a little bit off, but they're still thinking.

In Meeting 17 the teacher seemed to be aware that she could keep the students on the subject by asking them well-focused questions. In thinking of how to tap into the children's prior knowledge for reading a selection on the Loch Ness monster, the teacher said:

> I don't want to get too much into *monster* monsters, because that would really go way out. Because I was going to say, "Tell me about some monsters that you know about." But then they could get into anything; that might be too vague.

During Meeting 18, on a day when several new students had joined the group, the teacher spoke of the importance of keeping a tight rein on conversation during the reading lessons.

> The mistake I made at the first is, I thought, "Oh, they just want to talk and get to know each other and get to know me and I know them," because that's how we do with the high school kids. . . . But these kids, you can't let it go very long. You talk just a little bit, and then you've got to move right on to business or they take advantage.

Content and structure. From early in the study, the teacher had the goal of keeping the students on the subject. Over time the teacher's knowledge of how to accomplish this goal seemed to evolve along two lines. First, she became more knowledgeable of the tactics the students used to sidetrack the discussion. Second, she understood that she would need to respond differently, and this led directly to the formulation of some rules of practice. For example, she noticed that she needed to cut children off immediately after they had given a good answer. If she did not, some children would take the opportunity to elaborate upon their answers and eventually move the discussion off the subject. Because the children did this playfully, the teacher referred to the phenomenon as their "acting silly." The teacher also recognized that some children tried to distract her by asking her questions, and she knew that she would have to ignore their queries. Later, the teacher seemed to be moving toward an understanding of how to choose topics for discussion that would not lead the children away from text-relevant issues. For example, for a selection about the Loch Ness monster, she realized that asking the children to talk about monsters in general might lead them to "get into anything." The teacher also began to see a relationship between controlling the topic of discussion and keeping the lesson going. Thus she spoke of how a teacher could talk (i.e., socialize) only "just a little bit" before moving "right on to business" (i.e., discussion of the text).

Drawing out relevant prior knowledge

During Meetings 3 and 4, the teacher alluded to the children having missed the main points she had wanted to establish during the discussion. She realized that the story and discussion had to "mean something" to the students. The teacher's early thoughts in this area centered on selecting a story the children might be able to relate to.

By Meeting 6, however, she became aware that she needed to do more than simply select a good story:

> That's why I really worked on picking a good [story]. I just thought this story would really go, you know, this would really relate to them, and then it seemed like it bombed out right at the first. But then they just weren't getting into it today.

She attributed some of her difficulties in this lesson to the fact that most of the students had never faced the same problem as the story's main character.

In Meeting 8 the teacher again spoke of the idea of introducing the new story by "relating it to something they've done." The issue did not surface again until Meeting 15, but at this point the teacher showed that she had specific ideas about how to achieve this goal. In Meeting 16 the teacher described the point that she had been trying to get across in discussion of a story entitled "William's Wish":

> just mostly that we just wish for fun, but that if you really want something then maybe you should let someone know and then your wish might come true. Like, if William would have told his parents, they would have had hot dogs and watermelon for him.

She went on to speak of how several of the students had been able to relate to the story:

> And then Gregory [said], "Well, wishing's junk." And I said, "Well, it's fun." And he said, "Fun for nothing." Because he's the one that said he wished for an electronic game and he didn't get it. But then Josephine said . . . she wished for something and she told somebody and so she got it.

In Meeting 17 the teacher described the general idea in the following words:

> Everything try to relate to them and to their own experience, and then it means something to them, rather than just a bunch of concepts and, what?

Content and structure. With the issue of drawing out relevant prior knowledge, the teacher again began by recognizing an instructional problem, that the students weren't "catching on" to the main points she was trying to teach. Early on she understood that the lessons needed to be related to the students' own interests and experiences. One of her practical principles, then, was to make the lessons meaningful to the students by relating the stories to them. However, it took the teacher quite some time to grasp how this could actually be accomplished. Gradually, she concluded that it was primarily a matter of thinking of a central theme, or slant on the story, that would link the text to something the students already knew. The teacher and researcher spent considerable time brainstorming about how to set up the discussions so the students would be lured into making these personal connections to the stories. Most of the teacher's later statements on this issue had to do with charting the general course of discussion in a future lesson or with how her approach had worked in a lesson just taught. She did not come up with any rules of practice, perhaps because application of the principle necessarily varied with the content of each story.

Teacher responsibility

While watching the videotape of the lesson she felt to be her worst, the teacher commented:

> But I think they still don't think of this as a lesson. But that's what I've got to communicate, if this is important, that we do have a purpose here and something to do. It's all me – like they're there and I've got to do something with it.

In Meeting 19 the researcher joked that the teacher was making it sound as if her lesson had been terrible. The teacher answered:

> No, no, but I mean, like you said, it wasn't a bad lesson, it was a good lesson, but why not make it good every time? That's what we work for.

At this point, then, the teacher wanted to achieve a high degree of consistency in her teaching.

The idea of being responsible for the success or failure of a lesson was associated in the teacher's mind with the need for intense concentration while teaching. The teacher first mentioned this idea during Meeting 15, saying that the problem was

> just mostly me. . . . I think I just feel like I need to think more, I've got to think, think, think to stay ahead of them.

In Meeting 21 she commented:

> I felt worn out after it too. I think if you teach a good lesson you're worn out because you have to keep going; you know you have to really go, and I felt like I was getting louder and they were getting louder.

Here the idea of responsibility was associated with keeping the lesson going. The teacher added:

> Probably, if you feel too relaxed after a lesson, that means you didn't put your whole self into it. You missed something somewhere. But I felt real good about it even though I felt it was real hectic.

Teaching a good lesson meant not having "your mind on anything else."

Finally, during Meeting 23, the teacher stated:

> One thing I think I've found, too, is the story doesn't matter really that much if you get them interested in it. . . . If it's a great story and you're not having any control, then they're going to miss it.

Content and structure. The teacher's knowledge of the issue of responsibility seemed to follow yet another course of evolution. On several occasions, the teacher attributed problems in the lessons to her own behavior. Reflecting upon these errors led her to the practical principle that the success or failure of a lesson rested largely on the teacher's shoulders. For example, she eventually concluded that students could miss the point even in lessons based on a great story, if the teacher didn't have any control (good management). She elaborated upon the principle when she spoke of what she needed to accomplish to fulfill her responsibility to the students. The teacher felt the lessons should always be good ones, that the discussions should be lively and interesting to the students. She also spoke of the need to concentrate ("think, think, think") and to make a commitment to doing a good job ("put your whole self into it"). She did not state any specific rules of practice. However, she saw an association between taking responsibility and keeping the lesson going. She had the sense that a good lesson would feel hectic and that teaching with a high degree of commitment would leave a teacher feeling worn out. She appeared to be moving toward images capturing the "feel" of an interactive comprehension lesson, as it would be experienced by a teacher who had assumed personal responsibility for its success.

Discussion

The teacher's recognition of instructional issues or problems served as the starting point for the development of practical knowledge about conducting interactive comprehension lessons. In some cases the teacher had an implicit goal from the start (e.g., to have students stay on the subject). In other cases, she set a goal for herself (e.g., to keep the lesson going) after recognizing the problem. In formulating goals, the teacher showed that she was gaining a sense of what she wanted and needed to do. She had to have practical knowledge of certain issues to solve instructional problems and achieve her goals.

The content of the teacher's statements on all five issues changed over time. Changes in the teacher's understanding of an issue could be seen both in her more detailed analysis of a problem and in her formulation of more precise and elaborate goals. For example, the teacher gained an awareness of the various tactics students used to move the discussion off the subject. At the same time, she developed a goal of having them keep strictly to the topic, rather than starting on the topic and then veering off. Changes in the teacher's understanding were also revealed when she made connections among issues. For example, she began to associate keeping the students on the subject with keeping the lesson going.

As time went on, the teacher's statements reflected greater knowledge of the model of instruction. In Vygotskian terms, scientific concepts interacted with spontaneous ones to result in some true concepts or deeper understandings. Also, more of the teacher's understandings moved from being tacit to being explicit.

The structure of the teacher's practical knowledge (i.e., its being held as rules, principles, and images) seemed to differ from issue to issue and to follow different courses of development. However, knowledge of all five issues began in the same way, in the teacher's recognition of an instructional problem. The starting point for development of practical knowledge of all issues, then, was at the level of practical principles.

Rules of practice or specific procedures seemed to evolve as solutions to problems. For example, the teacher developed rules for keeping the lesson going. This issue lent itself to the formulation of specific goals and actions. However, practical knowledge at the level of rules of practice did not develop for all issues, just for the

	Initial levels		*Later levels*
Issue	*of generality*		*of generality*
1. Pacing			
	principles ——————————————————————————————→		
	rules ———————————————————————————————————→		
	images ——————————————————————————————————→		
2. Planning			
	rules ———————————————————————————————————→		
3. Control of topic			
	principles ——————————————————————————————→		
	rules ———————————————————————————————————→		
4. Drawing out prior knowledge			
	principles ——————————————————————————→ applications		
5. Responsibility			
	principles ——————————————————————————————→ images		

Figure 11.1. Development of knowledge of different issues

more concrete ones. The teacher did not arrive at rules for relating the story to the students or for assuming responsibility, both more abstract issues.

Images seemed to develop for two issues: keeping the lesson going and teacher responsibility. As seen in the teacher's statements, images emerged gradually and became clearer and stronger over time. Images served to summarize the teacher's practical knowledge of the two issues. Furthermore, the images for each issue appeared general enough to encompass knowledge of other issues as well.

One possibility is that images may function, first, to summarize knowledge about a particular issue and, later, to merge a teacher's knowledge about a number of different issues. For example, the continuity or smoothness metaphor, developed in the context of keeping the lesson going, probably was broad enough to encompass the issue of controlling the topic of discussion. Although the merger of these two issues did not take place during the period of time covered by the study, the teacher had begun to see a relationship between the two.

Practical knowledge of the five issues seemed to follow at least three courses of development, as shown in Figure 11.1. For the issue of *pacing,* practical knowledge involved the elaboration of principles, proceeding more or less simultaneously with the emergence of rules and images. Knowledge of *planning* developed in the form of a series of rules. The rules seemed in some cases to reflect practical principles, but these were unstated except at the very end of the study. No images seemed to be present. With knowledge of *controlling the topic,* principles and rules developed side by side without the appearance of images. Knowledge of *drawing out relevant prior knowledge* did not seem to be structured either as images or as rules. It began largely at the level of principles and then moved into the level of applications. Applications were even less general than rules and were determined by the content of particular texts and the teacher's sense of how these could be made personally meaningful to the students. Finally, knowledge of *teacher responsibility* seemed at first to be structured at the level of principles, moving eventually toward the level of images.

In short, the novice teacher's practical knowledge of interactive comprehension instruction seemed eventually to be organized at four rather than three levels: images, practical principles, rules of practice, and applications. Knowledge at the level of principles seemed always to be present. The structuring of knowledge at other levels of generality seemed to be related to the nature of the issue itself.

When the nature of an issue precludes the formation of rules, as in the case of planning or teacher responsibility, the teacher's behavior cannot be routinized. With complex models of instruction, then, even expert teachers cannot proceed automatically but must continue to engage in thoughtful analysis and reflection. Unlike novices, experts will have rules for the routine handling of certain instructional issues. More importantly, though, experts will also possess sophisticated principles and images. These well-elaborated structures allow experts to analyze problems in depth and to develop better applications or solutions.

The findings of this study point to the importance of viewing consciousness from a Vygotskian perspective, as Roter (1987) suggests, recognizing its complex and dynamic qualities. The teacher's thinking was complex in both content and organization. Practical knowledge was structured simultaneously at different levels of generality. Apparently, some aspects of a teacher's expertise may rest in images, which guide action in an intuitive way. Other aspects may rest in principles or rules, which guide action reflectively or methodically. Still other aspects of expertise may rest in applications, which provide guidance by serving as examples.

The organization of the teacher's thinking was not static but in a constant state of change. In fact, the teacher came to be aware of the evolution in her own understanding and made statements contrasting her present views with those she had held before. As seen in this case study, the development of practical knowledge appears to proceed in a complex yet understandable manner, in which reasons, whys and wherefores, are as important as how-tos. The results of this study suggest that the development of practical knowledge of teaching is an intellectually demanding process. Vygotsky's work provides a theoretical framework that allows researchers to acknowledge and deal with these complexities while still seeking general principles of development.

A practical implication of this study is that it calls into question the wisdom of leaving novice teachers to learn about teaching on their own, as they do in many school settings. For the teacher in this study, becoming expert seemed to be largely a matter of knowing how to deal with a wide variety of instructional problems. The opportunity to discuss these problems seemed to be highly valued by the teacher, and meetings may have hastened the teacher's discovery of solutions. This idea is consistent with Vygotsky's recognition of the role of speech in development, although more research is needed to gain an understanding of the discourse processes that support the development of a teacher's practical knowledge. In the experience of the teacher in this study, the importance of these discourse processes generally goes unrecognized, even by other teachers. The teacher explained why, in many school settings, a novice may be reluctant to seek another teacher's advice:

> I don't know if some [other teachers] would admit that maybe things didn't go too well. You're real prideful of your teaching and what you do. And the only thing you hear from other teachers [is] "oh, I did this and it was great." You know, all you hear are the good things. . . . But you don't want to go and say, "you know, I really bombed," . . . because then you think they're going to think, "well she's not a good teacher," when it's really just, you know, teaching's a hard thing.

References

Au, K. H. (1979). Using the experience–text–relationship method with minority children. *Reading Teacher, 32*(6), 677–679.

Au, K. H. (1985, April). *Instruction: The implications of research on the Kamehameha approach to developing reading comprehension ability.* Paper presented at the annual meeting of the American Educational Research Association, Chicago.

Au, K. H., & Kawakami, A. J. (1984). Vygotskian perspectives on discussion processes in small group reading lessons. In P. L. Peterson, L. C. Wilkinson, & M. Hallinan (Eds.), *The social context of instruction: Group organization and group processes* (pp. 209–225). New York: Academic Press.

Au, K. H., & Kawakami, A. J. (1986). Influence of the social organization of instruction on children's text comprehension ability: A Vygotskian perspective. In T. E. Raphael (Ed.), *Contexts of school-based literacy* (pp. 63–77). New York: Random House.

Au, K. H., Oshiro, M., & Blake, K. M. (1986, April). *The development of expertise in the teaching of reading; A case study.* Paper presented at the annual meeting of the American Educational Research Association, San Francisco.

Clark, C. M., & Peterson, P. L. (1986). Teachers' thought processes. In M. C. Wittrock (Ed.), *Handbook of research on teaching* (3rd ed.) (pp. 255–296). New York: Macmillan.

Di Bello, L., & Orlich, F. (1987). How Vygotsky's notion of "Scientific concept" may inform contemporary studies of theory development. *Quarterly Newsletter of the Laboratory of Comparative Human Cognition, 9*(3), 96–99.

Elbaz, F. (1981). The teacher's "practical knowledge": Report of a case study. *Curriculum Inquiry, 11*, 43–71.

Gallimore, R., Dalton, S., & Tharp, R. G. (1986). Self-regulation and interactive teaching: The effects of teaching conditions on teachers' cognitive activity. *Elementary School Journal, 86*(5), 613–631.

Minick, N. (1986). The early history of the Vygotskian school: The relationship between mind and activity. *Quarterly Newsletter of the Laboratory of Comparative Human Cognition, 8*(4), 119–125.

Roter, A. (1987). The concept of consciousness: Vygotsky's contribution. *Quarterly Newsletter of the Laboratory of Comparative Human Cognition, 9*(3), 105–110.

Tharp, R. G. (1982). The effective instruction of comprehension: Results and description of the Kamehameha Early Education Program. *Reading Research Quarterly, 17*(4), 501–527.

Vygotsky, L. S. (1962). *Thought and language.* Cambridge, MA: MIT Press.

Vygotsky, L. S. (1978). *Mind in society.* Cambridge, MA: Harvard University Press.

12 Learning to read and write in an inner-city setting: A longitudinal study of community change

Gillian Dowley McNamee

This is a story about a group of people who want to provide their children with better educational opportunities. The people are black and live in an inner-city neighborhood of Chicago. Many of the children attend the local public school and join the ranks of peers who statistically do not do well in school and who fall below the national reading scores by the time they are in eighth grade. Many of the parents try to enroll their children in other public schools that tend to graduate children with better grades and higher reading scores, but community residents are still bothered by the fact that their local public school cannot seem to offer neighborhood families more promise for their children's education. Six years ago, leaders from the neighborhood community center sought help in finding out what they could do to improve education, particularly in the area of literacy development, both while their children attend Head Start and day-care programs at the community center and when they go to public school.

This research tells several stories. It is the story of the unique partnership between community people and myself, a university professor, established to facilitate change. It is the story of how storytelling and dramatics as conceived by teacher and author Vivian Paley have become the core of a literacy program for the Head Start and day-care programs. It is the story of how this community is developing a "voice" in written language – that is, how these people are developing the confidence and skill to read and write, with each other and with members of society at large. It is also a story about building zones of proximal development (ZPDs) and how this concept guides my intervention and understanding of the changes that we are working on.

Vygotsky: ZPDs and literacy development

L. S. Vygotsky's concept of the zone of proximal development examines human development in relation to individuals' interactions with others around them over time. For Vygotsky (1981), "development does not proceed toward socialization

The research reported here has been funded by Chicago Tribune Charities, the Field Corporation Fund, the Field Foundation of Illinois, Northern Trust Company, the Spencer Foundation, and Woods Charitable Fund, Inc. The community and this author are grateful for their generous support.

287

but toward the conversion of social relations into mental functions'' (p. 165). Mental functions ''are first formed in the collective as relations among children, and then become mental functions for the individual. . . . Relations among higher mental functions were at some earlier point actual relations among people'' (p. 165, 158). The ZPD is a concept that explains how thinking that is initially carried out among people in groups becomes reorganized, with individuals gradually taking over more control and direction of their own thinking and relationships in a world with which they always remain interdependent. Vygotsky's theory of development leads researchers to examine systems change: changes in thinking among people as a function of shared group life, not just dyadic interactions that might facilitate change in an individual's thinking.

For literacy development, this means that written language is a social-cultural construct whose development is highly related to people, their patterns of communication, and their use of written language to mediate activities in day-to-day life. Language, both spoken and written, embodies the ties that people have with one another, their culture, and their own thinking. I will briefly describe the building of ZPDs in relation to literacy and schooling with the people who invited me to work with them. We shall see how ZPDs can be built among people, how data can be collected on systems change in ZPDs, and how the concept of zones of proximal development can guide the interpretation of data.

Two important conditions are necessary for change in a ZPD. The first is the capacity for play, the capacity for imagination. Vygotsky says that play creates a ZPD; he meant that in order to grow and develop people need to be able to think of themselves in a way that is different from the way they are now. ''A child's greatest achievements are possible in play, achievements that tomorrow will become her basic level of real action and morality. . . . It is the essence of play that a new relation is created between the field of meaning and the visual field – that is, between situations in thought and real situations'' (1978, pp. 100, 104). The quality of playfulness has been strong in the thinking and relationships of adults and children in the community since I met them, and it has become one of the foundations on which our work is built.

The second condition for change in a ZPD is the capacity to make use of the help of others (Bruner, 1962), the capacity to benefit from give-and-take in experiences and conversations with others. This community has an unusual capacity to ask questions, to seek help, and to make use of it. This was evident from the beginning, as it was the community center staff who requested help in addressing the question, ''What are we doing now in our programs that helps prepare our children for school, and what might we do differently?'' As I tried to help them think about their questions and how to answer them, a long-term partnership in education and research developed, in which they and I have grown and changed enormously.

The partnership has stipulations from both sides. The community leaders said from the very first meeting – and they have reiterated this request yearly – that any help, ideas, or program changes that might come from me and the research had to come with documentation and training that would make changes "stick," whether I was present or not. The staff did not want to depend on my being able to achieve something for and with parents, children, or teachers, only to leave them unable to carry on. Their stipulation seemed a beautiful articulation of what Vygotsky had in mind for change in a ZPD. They wanted help, but they wanted it in order to become more independent in leading and controlling their interactions with the larger world.

My stipulation concerned the content of our work. In line with a Vygotskian perspective of literacy as a social-cultural activity, I was not going to advocate or recommend a more academic approach to teaching children to read or teaching them basic skills per se. Rather, I would explore with the community an approach that would study literacy development as a process of "acquisition" as opposed to a process of "learning" (Gee, 1987). Gee defines acquisition as

> a process of acquiring something subconsciously by exposure to models and a process of trial and error, without a process of formal teaching. It happens in natural settings which are meaningful and functional. . . . This is how most people acquire their first language. (p. 4)

My work with the adults in the community would look for the roots of literacy in conversations with children, fantasy play, and activities involving books, paper, and writing tools that were or could become an integral part of daily classroom and home life.

Robert Gundlach (1983) has described the resources that children need in order to develop into readers and writers. He cites one of the most important ingredients to this learning process as belonging to a "community of writers":

> If a person participates in a community of active readers and writers, if he reads and writes regularly, and if his reading and writing put him in touch with other people, he stands a reasonably good chance of forming notions of genre and style, of developing a general sense of the literary enterprise, and of becoming increasingly sophisticated about the act of writing itself. . . . We ought to ask first how teachers can assemble true communities of active readers and writers, and how teachers can give even the most reluctant students a clear shot at participating in such communities. (185–186)

This chapter provides an anatomy of building a community of writers by analyzing some of the stories and dialogues that have been taking place among program staff, parents, and children for evidence of the changes the community members are going through. What we are finding is that literacy and its development in this community depend on arrangements of relationships among people around stories – those of fantasy play and those of books.

The agreement made between community center staff and me, as a representative of a university, was to begin by establishing program practices that would nurture and support children's interests in books, paper, and pencils while in community center Head Start and day-care programs. We would then begin to track children's progress in learning to read and write both at the community center and when they entered their local public school. The second phase of our work would involve efforts to bring the local public school into the process of working with community residents to improve educational opportunities for neighborhood children.

Problems: What needed changing

The Head Start teachers have a daunting list of requirements to stay in compliance with program guidelines. There are two meals served in the 3-hour half-day program, and three meals and naptime are required for the full-day 6–8-hour program. There are requirements for language arts, science and math, physical exercise, music, and art. There is a strong emphasis throughout the program on nutrition and health care. Teachers are pressured by parents and by public school teachers to be sure that children know their numbers, alphabet, colors, days of the week, months of the year, their parents' names, their address, and they must also be able to print their own names, be able to use a scissors, and be able to color relatively neatly. The teachers are hard-pressed to know how to organize the short school day to achieve these goals as well as helping the children leave home and adjust to group life in a place called school. Observations during the first few weeks of our work together demonstrated how teachers struggled with the pressures.

Yolanda Stevens has taught Head Start at the community center for 16 years. In my initial meeting with the staff, her questions were: "What are the limits of what a child can learn? How do I know when I've done all I can to teach them?" I was excited by the questions. They represented the kind of problem I sensed Vygotsky worried about – not what the child has already learned but how a teacher knows if she is providing optimal learning opportunities for children to benefit from in the near and longer-term future.

Yet, 5 years ago, when children entered Ms. Stevens's classroom for the start of their 3-hour session, they sat on a rug as a group to begin their school day with several large-group activities. The first was taking attendance. Ms. Stevens decided to get two tasks done at the same time: teaching the children to respond when she called their names, and having them learn the days of the week. She instructed the children to listen for their names and then to say, "Today is Thursday" (or whatever day it was). The routine proved unsuccessful because the children either did not respond at all or responded by saying, "Yes?" or "Here." Ms. Stevens asked me to help her figure out how to get the children to respond by naming the correct day of the week. When we spoke of the problem, I noted that the children's responses made sense and questioned whether there was a way to make naming the days of the week a sense-making activity also. She responded that there was too little time in these few short hours to fit everything in.

As we began our work, the administrators, teachers, and I agreed that the teachers would forgo any activity such as this attendance naming-the-day-of-the-week routine, which was frustrating and counterproductive, until we could build a basis for deciding how to organize the classrooms and the schedules to meet the children's needs and the program requirements. I then began to focus our work on establishing classroom environments that emphasized making sense and making connections in activities and teacher–child interactions. "Basic activities" as defined by Cole and Griffin (1983) became the criteria for evaluating classroom practices.

Basic literacy activities are a concrete representation of ZPDs: They have a purpose and a goal that children can comprehend, and they allow children at various levels of skill and understanding to participate with more competent peers and adults in the processes of writing and reading. Basic literacy activities also allow children to take over more responsibility and control for the carrying out of the task as they are ready to do so. Basic activities utilize basic skills, and thus children are exposed to the use of skills for a variety of purposes and in a variety of contexts that make sense to them. Fantasy play and activities such as reading to the children at least once a day, taking time to write down stories the children tell, acting out storybooks, nursery rhymes, and the children's own stories represent basic activities and have become the basis of community life in the classrooms and the basis for promoting literacy development (McLane & McNamee, 1990).

When our work first began, the basic ingredients of book-oriented literacy were missing from the classrooms. There were few children's books, and those that were available were usually informational, for example, describing a visit to the dentist or to a hospital. There were few storybooks or fairy tale or nursery rhyme collections. In addition, no paper or writing tools were available for children to use on a daily basis for their own purposes. Classrooms had crayons, pencils, and paper in storage cabinets which were used for designated art projects.

In staff meetings I led discussions with the teachers on stories that the teachers had heard as children – some were from books; others were not. I took the teachers to the local library and to children's bookstores to build a collection of storybooks in the community center that they would like to read to the children and that the children would enjoy hearing and seeing. The program directors ordered bookshelves along with rugs and pillows to create a library/book area in each classroom. We simultaneously purchased abundant supplies for a drawing/writing table, which would be in a central place in each classroom, equipped with paper of different colors, sizes, shapes, textures, as well as scissors, glue, tape, crayons, markers, pencils – different tools that would invite children to experiment and to explore different ways to represent their ideas on paper.

Classroom schedules were designed to allow a rhythm between free-choice activity periods and teacher-directed group times. Children found books and writing materials around them in their play areas, and they saw them woven into group times. Every day, teachers read at least one storybook to the class, and these books along with nursery rhymes and poems were acted out in impromptu dramatizations at group time.

When these basic activities were in place, I took them one step farther; I introduced the idea of having the children dictate a story that they made up to a teacher, who wrote it down, read it to the class at group time, and helped the author act it out with friends. At the time when I first met the staff of this community center, I had just completed a study of this arrangement of activities (first described by Vivian Paley, 1981) and the unique contribution it can make to building a foundation for children's literacy development (Gundlach, McLane, Stott, & McNamee, 1985; McNamee, 1987; McNamee, McLane, Cooper, & Kerwin, 1985).

I wanted to know how story dictation and dramatization activities carried out in a literacy-rich preschool classroom environment that emphasized play as the main context and approach to learning might help children considered at risk for school failure and illiteracy. It was this package of ideas that the community center staff eagerly endorsed when we began our work 5 years ago.

Creating and building ZPDs

ZPDs with Head Start and day-care teachers needed to include a common set of experiences where the teachers and I could engage in joint efforts working with children, where we could teach children from the "interpsychological plane of development"; and we needed opportunities to observe each other working more independently with children from our own "intrapsychological plane" (Vygotsky, 1981). In addition, we needed to be able to discuss and analyze the help we would give each other in the classroom and how best to give it in order to achieve our goals. These ZPDs were built in three ways: (1) by a partnership teaching arrangement in the classrooms; (2) by talking over all aspects of our work together; and (3) by documenting all aspects of our work in writing. During the year, I spent a half-day per week in each of the five classrooms working as the teacher's assistant. I helped with whatever was scheduled for the day but particularly with implementing activities related to literacy.

When new activities such as story dictation and dramatization were being introduced, I would take the lead in carrying out the activities with the teacher as my assistant so that the teacher could watch and learn from my efforts and facilitate the success of the activity. In time we switched roles, and the teachers took the lead in these activities while I served as assistant. In this way, activities were introduced and carried out; initially, I provided an image of the possibilities we were working toward, implemented them with their help, and then gradually shifted control of the activities to the teachers.

At the end of every morning or afternoon of work together, the teachers and I discussed what had happened. Every 3 to 4 weeks there was a staff meeting devoted solely to issues, problems, and progress with children and literacy activities in the classrooms. Every 2 to 3 months, the monthly parent night would be devoted to exploring topics in literacy development with the parents. Written notes formed the basis of discussion for these different meetings. I wrote continuously while I was in the classrooms, and I wrote my observations in the form of a letter to the teachers with carbon paper so that we each had a copy to keep. In this way, the teachers knew what I was noticing, what I was worried about, and what I wanted to bring up for discussion. The teachers quickly grew to love their weekly letters and missed them when occasionally I did not get one written.

In the third year of our work together, they too began to write as part of our work. They wrote up observations and children's comments from class discussions, and they brought copies of stories that children had dictated for discussion in staff meetings. Thus most of our interactions have been supplemented and supported by written communications. Relationships in our ZPD had been built around speaking and listening in oral and written language.

These relationships have taken a great deal of time to develop. When we first began our work, the teachers were quite reticent and not forthcoming in conversations. I was a white doctor from an institution they had heard about frequently, and I came from a very different home and cultural life. The challenge for establishing a ZPD with them was to create a sense of "our" work in order to create a joint venture. Working alongside them in their classrooms, the weekly letters, and our discussions in different kinds of meetings contributed to the building of a close working relationship where we could observe, question, and discuss our separate and common ways of working with children. We began to help each other achieve things with children that neither party could do alone. I did not know the children, their families, and the more subtle cultural practices in this community regarding ways of interacting, speaking, writing, and reading. They were unsure about what they were doing or not doing that might make a difference to the long-term literacy development of their children. ZPDs took shape between us as we acted together, spoke together, and wrote with and for each other.

Data: How do we know that change is occurring?

Over the past few years I have been collecting systematic data related to literacy development on the children, on the classroom environments, and on the teachers' activities with the children and their parents. I have extensive field notes, mostly in the form of teachers' letters, which help in interpreting the data. For this discussion, stories are presented from several levels of community life focused around one classroom, Ms. Stevens's, in order to illustrate the kind of changes that are taking place in this community's ZPDs. First, stories that Head Start children dictated to their teacher, and that were shared with the class in a group time, are introduced, and their significance in terms of literacy development is discussed. Following this are some "stories" that Ms. Stevens and the children's parents exchanged about the children in a teacher–parent written dialogue journal. Finally, Ms. Stevens tells her own story about change in her classroom.

Children's stories

One morning in May of the school year, several 4-year-old children dictated the following stories to Ms. Stevens's assistant teacher during free play time. The stories were later dramatized at a teacher-directed group time.[1]

Three Little Bears

Ariana

Mama Bear went to the store. Daddy Bear went to the store. And Baby Bear stayed home. Baby Bear went to the store on his own and he saw Mommy and Daddy Bear. So they both got into the car together. And the little girl went in the house. Baby Bear left the door open. She thoughted and thoughted. She wasn't hungry. She sat on Daddy's hard chair and she sat in Mama's hard chair and she sat on Baby's soft chair and she broke it. And the little girl was really upset. She slept in Daddy's bed and Mama's bed. They all came upstairs and they all saw the little girl in Baby Bear's bed and they saw the chair was broke and she ran home.   The End.

Evan's Story

Once upon a time I saw a bird. He was running up in the air, and the bird came down. When he came down he was dead. He was dead because he had fell, he had fell on the concrete. Then the bear came and he ate the bird up too.   The End.

Shanica's Story

The Papa Bear and the Uncle sat down and looked at wrestling. And the baby bear have to go to school. The baby bear made him some friends. And the teacher whopped the baby bear cause he was actin bad and his mother came up to the school. And he had come over to the auntie's house and stay all day. And he was getting tired from coming home. The mother was asking the uncle to come to her house tomorrow.   The End.

Loretta's Story

The sun came out and it talked to the boy. It says, "Hi, little boy." The sun said, "I'll come out every day." The sun said, "The grass come out with the flowers. All different flowers."

And then the father came and said to the boy, "Could you go to the store with me?" And the man said, "You might as well cook food cause here comes the wolf."   The End

Joseph's Story

Mickey Mouse go with his girlfriend. Goofy came. He walkin' with Donald Duck. Then Mickey Mouse, his birthday was today. Then Donald Duck had an Easter egg. Then Goofy drivin his car. A bird came. The bird made a house. And then he fly away. Mickey Mouse, he go for a walk. Donald Duck, he go with Big Bird. Then a red heart came. That's the end.

These stories are a celebration of many achievements for the children. The logic of their thinking, the clarity of their expression, and their understanding of narrative structure are readily evident in their stories. They understand and can make connections to stories that are read to them, the stories in their private fantasies, and the stories they play out each day together in the classroom. Each child has a clear sense of how to formulate an idea into a story that has a clear beginning, middle, and end. The children present their ideas phrase by phrase to the teacher, who transforms their message into written text. The months of experience with story dictation over the school year have familiarized them with the rhythms of translating spoken words into written sentences. They watch with rapt attention as the teacher prints their words one after another, checking phrasings and clarifying meanings as she goes.

This particular class of children loved the story *The Three Bears*. The teacher read the book often, the children acted it out, and the children incorporated its themes and characters into many of their stories. In the first story, Ariana savors memories of the original story by reconstructing the main ideas in her own words, but in her own homespun version of the fairy tale. Evan and Shanica have bear characters in their stories, but these two authors bring to life unique and powerful ideas of their own. Evan's story is an effort to explain the death of a bird, perhaps one that he saw or one that he is just thinking about. Shanica's story suggests the kinds of comings and goings of family members around her – watching television, going to school, relatives coming by to visit. Loretta's story is an outpouring of joyous feeling, a day when everything seems to be going well, but it also signals the coming of danger, difficulty, or trouble lurking around the corner (the wolf coming).

Joseph's story has another host of characters that the children love and find comfort in thinking about. Walt Disney friends are reliable; they come and go, have nice adventures, but usually stay clear of serious worries. The red heart that comes at the end, after nice events such as a birthday and Easter, is Joseph's symbol for the comfort and good feeling these story friends embody. He gives the role of the red heart to his best friend while he plays the role of Goofy when the story is acted out.

Ms. Stevens notices all these details of significance in the children's stories and talks about them as she narrates and helps bring their stories to life through dramatization at group time. The children in Ms. Stevens's classroom are active members of a community of writers and readers, long before they know how to write and read conventionally. The children listen to each other and their teacher, to stories that she reads and stories that their peers tell in and out of school, and then each contributes to the community his or her own unique point of view, variations on ideas and responses to ideas that have been portrayed and discussed. Every child has a story to dictate, and as Mrs. Paley discovered, every child wants to tell a story if it will be acted out in order to share it with others.

When Ms. Stevens's class moved up to the kindergarten room the following September, a new girl, Sharice, joined the class. She was a quiet, soft-spoken child who was well liked by the children but very shy of talking to the teachers or talking in group times. She stayed on the fringe of community life for many months. Finally, at the end of January, she told her first story:

> The lady was coming home. She had went out. The kids came home from school. And then Daddy came home from work. Then the kids had went outside. They looked in the sky and saw some hearts. They were happy. The End.

There were several other stories about hearts dictated that day, and Valentine's Day was not far away. Sharice's story fit right in with the rhythm of other children's stories, but her teacher said that there was a special message represented in it: Sharice was saying that she goes home from school happy and that she is part of a close family community at home. Her story marked her more active participation in the community life at school – a community where stories bind people together in friendship, embody their many diverse relationships, and hold literacy in a way that makes it accessible to members of the classroom community.

Parents' stories

Helping parents to understand how the Head Start program was introducing their children to a love for reading, writing, and stories was the topic of many parent meeting discussions but was also conveyed in an unusual teacher–parent dialogue that took place in writing. The teachers were given a small notebook for each child. Every week, the teacher wrote one or two sentences in the notebook about the child and sent it home with the child for the parents to read. Parents were requested to do the same and send the notebook back to school. All comments had to be positive; problems or difficulties were handled in person or over the phone.

The notebook dialogue proved very successful for parents, teachers, and children. The teachers and parents utilized the opportunity to mention and highlight small, yet pleasurable moments in the child's week. The children knew that their teacher and parents were writing about them in the notebook, and they loved hearing the entries read, sometimes over and over again. Below are excerpts from notebooks on three children in Ms. Stevens's classroom. The entries are presented exactly as written. Much work went into helping staff and parents overcome self-conscious feelings about their own literacy skills and reminding them of the purpose of the dialogue. The long-term goal was to build a partnership between home and school that would support the child's development. The goal was not to make school more like home or home more like school but rather to build a shared understanding of who the children were and what helped them grow and learn. The more each knew what the child was like at home and school, the more connections and bridges could be made for the children in moving between the two settings.

The teachers were motivated to write in order gradually to reinforce and emphasize the educational goals of their programs and to reassure parents that their children were learning in developmentally appropriate activities. The parents readily responded to the good feelings embodied in the dialogue, as can be seen in the following journal entries.

> Dear Parent
> Today Natalie was the leader during our large motor activity, with her the children had a lovely time.
> > Ms. Stevens

> Natalie made a car out of a box for me two days it was very pretty with her real car in it
> > sign Carla

> Dear Parents
> Natalie played a game showing her favorite letter from a chart, and saying the letter.
> > Ms. Stevens

Natalie went and played in the snow with her girl friend after school and make little snow man.

Dear Parents
Natalie played a new game with her friends.
Thank you
Ms. Stevens

Natalie played with her girl friend and help make cake with me and Joyce little girl

Dear Parents:
Natalie was very helpful today. She straighten the puzzle's in the puzzle rack.
Thank you
Ms. Stevens

Natalie went outside and played with friend and played game

Dear Parent:
Natalie drew a beautiful picture of a tree with blueberries on it at the easel.
Ms. Stevens

Natalie played with her friend out door all day with her doll

Dear Parents:
Natalie sung a beautiful
song to her teacher
that she made up
I love you
Ms. Stevens

Natalie went to the store with me and had lots of fun playing on the bus and singing

This parent–teacher dialogue reflects several important messages being conveyed and shared understandings being built. First, both teacher and parent comments are full of affection for the child; Natalie's achievements are cherished by caretakers at home and at school. Helping others, taking good care of belongings, and contributing to the group – be it family or classmates – are important values in both settings. The appreciation of what Natalie is learning in the context of play is strong and not an issue for this child's parent.

With the next parent Ms. Stevens emphasizes play a bit more as the parent conveys a stronger "academic" concern for her daughter: the desire to see her daughter master identifiable school-related knowledge. Ms. James is Shanica's mother, the child who told a story about bears, which included a baby bear who goes to school, makes friends, and gets into a bit of trouble.

Dear Parent
Today Shanica had a very happy day, and worked well with her peers.
Ms. Stevens

Dear teachers
I can see that you are doing a great job with Shanica. Everyday I ask her what

she's learned, and she tells me her colors, ABC's and counts too. Keep up the good work!

Ms. James

Dear Parents
Shanica played well in the sandbox with her friends

Ms. Stevens

Dear teachers,
Shanica was very helpful, she put away all of her toys and cleaned our bedroom. She was very happy when I gave her a surprise for doing it.

Ms. James

Dear Parents
Shanica did a great job cleaning up the dramatic play area.

Ms. Stevens

Dear Teacher,
Shanica says enjoys helping me wash the dishes after dinner.

Ms. James

Dear Parent:
Shanica dramatized a beautiful story about the three bears with her friends

Ms. Stevens

Dear teachers:
Shanica told me all about the story she dramatized with her friends also!

Ms. James

Dear Parents:
Shanica share with the class that she wants to help save money to help her mother buy a car.

Ms. Stevens

Dear teachers,
I'm so proud that shanica wants to help me. I love her she's so sweet. She always tell me she's going to do special things for me.

By their fourth exchange of comments, the teacher and parent are focusing on the same event, Shanica's bear story, and appreciating its contribution to the group life at school and at home. The joy in acknowledging the child's daily successes and accomplishments is contagious, and the child heard all of this!

Mrs. Stevens's dialogue with a third parent illustrates again how successful she was in convincing parents of the staying power of children's learning in play. Ms. Stevens's gift for sharing her joy and love of children with parents comes through in all three sets of these journal entries. She communicates and elicits from parents good feeling, confidence, and respect for their child, which then become a strong part of the context of learning for the child at home and school.

Dear Parents
Arthur share with the classroom what he had for Christmas Arthur was very happy today.

Ms. Stevens

Dear teachers.
Arthur was Very Good this Week at Home. Arthur Helped Make his Bed and take out the Trash.
Ms. Abott

Dear Parents
At the animal show Arthur felt the skin of a real snake.
Ms. Stevens

Dear Teachers,
Arthur has been very good. He made angels in the snow. He also is trying to make a square, circle, triangle and a cross.
Ms. Abott

Dear Parents:
Arthur was very helpful today he ask if he could help tidy the classroom up. Thank you.
Ms. Stevens

Arthur is doing very good this week. He knows how to make the letters B, D, G. He is also trying to write his name.
Ms. Abott

Dear Parent:
Arthur enjoy talking with his friends and teachers. He was very happy today.
Ms. Stevens

Dear Teachers:
Arthur enjoyed going to the museum. Very much and all the animal
Ms. Abott

Dear Parents:
Arthur shared with the class that he went to the candy lady and that he still had candy at home.
Ms. Stevens

Dear Ms. Stevens Arthur did go to the candy lady. And yes he still have some candy
Ms. Abott

It was surprising how simple and yet how powerful, satisfying, and interesting this written conversation could be for all involved. For the adults in the community to feel that they could begin to write and read in this more public sort of way, even though their skills might need improving, was an important step in their ongoing literacy development as well as their children's. Head Start children watched the important adults in their lives talk about their growing up in positive and playful ways, and a good deal of it was done through writing and reading.

A teacher's story

One day, after 18 months of work together, we were having a staff meeting, and as it was coming to a close Ms. Stevens said that she had an experience she wanted to

share with the group. She said that she was not sure if it had anything to do with
our work on literacy and storytelling but said she could not stop thinking about it.
It involved a set of events that she had not discussed with me or the others all year.
Her story was as follows.

> I had a number of four-year-old girls this year who were very picky about who
> they would play with and who they would be partners with. Several mothers con-
> tributed to the problem by only inviting this select group to their daughters' birth-
> day parties. They would pass out invitations in the classroom to some children,
> and would talk about the parties in front of everyone. I made it very clear to them
> that no arrangements for birthday parties could be made in the classroom because
> it was upsetting to the children who were not invited.
>
> There was one girl in particular who I worried about. She had a hard time making
> friends, and usually was left out of this "in-group." I talked to the class repeatedly
> about being good friends to one another. I would speak sharply to children when I
> saw them being unkind or excluding each other from games. But my talking did
> not seem to do any good. The problems were there day after day, week after week.
>
> But one day in early May I did something without thinking about it ahead of
> time. The children were out on the playground, and as I called them to line up to
> go inside, I noticed that the one girl I often worried about did not have a partner. I
> asked someone to be her partner, and the child said, "I don't want to." I was so
> angry and upset. I took the girl's hand myself and told the class to go inside and
> sit on the rug.
>
> When they were seated, I said, "I have a story to tell you. It's about me when I
> was a little girl growing up in the South. I grew up in a small town and I always
> loved to be with other children. I wanted them to be my friends. We would play
> games and go for walks together in the farm fields. I hated to see another child sad,
> and when the other children did not want to share with me or play with me, it
> would make me feel so bad. I always took care of other children and made sure
> that they were good friends to each other because I knew how bad it made me feel
> when others would not play with me."
>
> I then said to my class, "You know, boys and girls, I love each one of you. You
> know that I hug you every day when you come to school, and I let you sit on my
> lap if you need to. You know that I will always be your partner. I never push
> anyone away from me, and I never ignore you because I care about each one of
> you. I always hope that you will be a friend to each other the way that I am a friend
> to you."

Ms. Stevens said,

> The children sat very quietly as I talked. They listened without moving a muscle,
> and some even looked a little sad. I did not refer to what had just happened on the
> playground or to any of the past incidents where the children had been unkind to
> this child. When I finished, a number of the children said that they would be friends
> with each other. I let them go back to their play activities, and it seems like the
> most remarkable thing happened from that day on. The children who had been such
> a tight clique seemed to loosen up and play with other children, and I never saw
> this one little girl left out of activities again. It was one of the most amazing things
> I have ever seen happen with one of my classes. The year ended with such good
> feeling for all of us.

Ms. Stevens's story was very moving; it had a great deal to do with our work
together on literacy development, and we spoke of it that afternoon. Literacy, like
speaking and listening, is a process of using words to communicate meanings and

intentions and to explore new ideas. The contrast between this story and the attendance-taking response, "Today is Thursday," that she was working on 18 months earlier was dramatic and glaring. Ms. Stevens had been listening to her children's stories, had been reading books to them, and was beginning to listen to her own stories that needed to be told – stories that could be woven into the school day. Words and their meanings were making a difference to this teacher, and her story for the children and the group in staff meeting reflected a belief in the power of words to communicate and eventually change the way people think and behave toward one another. She had discovered for herself a unique way with words in her teaching: storytelling.

When Ms. Stevens told the children her story of growing up in the South, she spoke in the language of play, the language of ZPDs, the language of possible worlds. When she reprimanded the children and told them what they should or should not do, the children maintained a defensive stance and remained closed to learning. When she said, in effect, "Let's pretend we are in a world where I grew up, and let's look at the way things used to be and the way things can be between us now," the children became open and receptive to new ways of seeing themselves and others.

This same discovery was made by teacher Vivian Paley, just a few short years before this. In her book *Boys and Girls: Superheroes in the Doll Corner* (1984), she described a boy in her kindergarten class, Franklin, who had a great deal of difficulty participating in group fantasy play with other children. He had a strong sense of artistic integrity and perfection, which made it impossible for him to tolerate other children's ideas when, for example, a group was building in the block area. Mrs. Paley worked hard to reason with him about his tendency to want to have things his own way. He denied any such difficulty and was frustrated that she and the others could not appreciate what he was trying to do when building something. She too one day intuitively decided to tell the class a story (which the group acted out) about a boy named Franklin who knows how to share. The story made Franklin, the other children, and his teacher very happy.

> Suddenly I recognize the difference between telling a child he must share and instead saying, "Pretend you are a boy who knows how to share." The first method announces that a child has done something wrong. "Pretend" disarms and enchants; it suggests heroic possibilities for making changes, just as in the fairy tales. (1984, p. 87)

Like Mrs. Paley, Ms. Stevens had discovered a way of speaking that helped her and the children establish a footing from which to change and grow in their classroom ZPD.

Ms. Stevens's story provides an indication that her teaching was undergoing change, and she provided evidence that her children as a group underwent a change. Relationships in our various ZPDs were slowly changing the climate and the quality of group life together in classrooms and staff meetings and changing the individuals who were a part of the community of teachers and children.

Problems in our ZPDs

There are serious problems in this work. I have not fully kept my part of the bargain with the community; they are still dependent on my presence in various ways to keep some of the classroom literacy activities going. There are several reasons why.

The first has to do with stress in the community; it is pervasive, destructive, and frequently related to meager financial resources. Head Start and Title XX day-care programs are funded at bare minimum levels; the teachers are underpaid, over-worked, and given little time to reflect on problems or on the significance of their work. The teachers, like the families they serve, live in the community and fight for adequate housing, struggle to make ends meet financially, and put up with poor health-care facilities and high crime rates. The community center classrooms are frequently closed down because of freezing pipes, loss of heat, or vandalism, which forces classes of children and teachers to double up and work in overcrowded con-ditions. When there is too much stress, old habits take over and progress seems to backslide.

The second major factor has to do with literacy itself. Most community members are literate; they read and write frequently in the course of their daily lives. Their work with government-funded programs requires a large amount of paper work: writing reports, lesson plans, and budgets. However, a number of the staff and parents are not used to or comfortable with the kind of writing and reading they long for: literacy that will sustain community members through a college education, which will then put them in a position to operate more independently with busi-nesses and professionals in the larger urban community of which they are a part. For the time being, teachers, parents, and children need to continue participating in writing and reading with people like me while they acquire the skills and confidence to carry on in the future the work we have been engaged in.

The third major area of difficulty concerns the question: Do the literacy-rich preschool experiences make any difference in children's experiences in learning to read and write in public school? Going to school for all children requires an adjust-ment process as they make the transition from home-based care to a new cultural institution whose instructional practices and roles for adults and children bear little resemblance to those they have experienced in their first 5 years of life (Alexander & Entwisle, 1988). The research of Alexander and Entwisle demonstrates that this transition is particularly difficult for black children. Black children are at risk due to the many layers of cultural discontinuity between their home environment and that of many schools as they now exist. It is not clear yet whether the early literacy experiences of this new generation of children will have any identifiable influence on their public school experiences in learning to read and write. This is the focus of our current work.

My understanding of this work with the community has changed substantially over the years. I realize now that this community may need me or similar educa-tional support for many years to come, along with other forces for community economic and social change. Outside support is needed to remind the community members of how far they have come, to support and suggest possibilities for future changes, to help remind them of their goals, and to reinforce their faith that they can get there. This community is unusual because it has a vision. But reaching its goals will take longer than any of us had realized. The ebb and flow of giving and receiving help continue; we are still exploring how to give every child in this community a shot at becoming a participating member of the larger world of writers and readers in American society. The ZPD at work in this community is just now beginning to include the local public school, and we continue to work at understanding what kind of long-term arrangement of resources can help a group of people bring about the educational as well as economic and cultural change that they want for themselves. In the meantime, we continue to play and work together, to talk about these efforts, and to write about them.

Note

1 Stories are presented here exactly as the text appeared on paper. Teachers were encouraged to write down the children's words as accurately as they could in order to capture the child's voice and train of thought. Through questions of clarification during dictation, and in the dramatization of stories where the meanings of words were brought to life, the form and structure of children's language moved toward that of standard written exposition.

References

Alexander, K., & Entwisle, D. (1988). Achievement in the first 2 years of school: Patterns and processes. *Monographs of the Society for Research in Child Development, 53*(2, Serial No. 218).
Bruner, J. (1962). Introduction. In L. Vygotsky, *Thought and language.* Cambridge, MA: MIT Press.
Cole, M., & Griffin, P. (1983). A socio-historical approach to re-mediation. *Quarterly Newsletter of the Laboratory of Comparative Human Cognition, 5*(4).
Gee, J. P. (1987). *What is literacy?* Preprint, Mailman Foundation Conference on Families and Literacy, Harvard Graduate School of Education, Cambridge, MA.
Gundlach, R. (1983). The place of computers in the teaching of writing. In A. M. Lesgold & F. Reif (Eds.), *Computers in education: Realizing the potential.* Washington, DC: U.S. Department of Education.
Gundlach, R., McLane, J. B., Stott, F., & McNamee, G. D. (1985). The social foundations of children's early writing development. In M. Farr (Ed.), *Advances in writing research: Vol. 1. Studies in children's writing development* (pp. 1–58). Norwood, NJ: Ablex.
McLane, J. B., & McNamee, G. D. (1990). *Early literacy.* Cambridge, MA: Harvard University Press.
McNamee, G. D. (1987). The social origins of narrative skills. In M. Hickmann (Ed.), *Social and functional approaches to language and thought* (pp. 287–304). Orlando, FL: Academic Press.
McNamee, G. D., McLane, J. B., Cooper, P. M., & Kerwin, S. M. (1985). Cognition and affect in early literacy development. *Early Childhood Development and Care, 20,* 229–244.
Paley, V. (1981). *Wally's stories.* Cambridge, MA.: Harvard University Press.
Parley, V. (1984). *Boys and girls: Superheroes in the doll corner.* Chicago: University of Chicago Press.
Vygotsky, L. (1978). *Mind in society.* Cambridge, MA: Harvard University Press.
Vygotsky, L. (1981). The genesis of higher mental functions. In J. V. Wertsch (Ed.), *The concept of activity in Soviet psychology.* Armonk, NY: Sharpe.

13   Writing as a social process

Joan B. McLane

Several months after the establishment of a writing program in an after-school day-care program in Chicago, an 8-year-old girl wrote the following story:

> *Three Little Scarycats*
> Once upon a time there were
> 3 little scarycats, there name's
> were Manuel, Kevin and Simon. They were
> scared of the dark, a cat, a dog, a little
> bird, and a little baby. They slept with
> their parents because they are to
> scard of the dark. They always screamed
> when they saw a cat, a dog or a baby
> bird. They always started to cry
> when they saw a little baby
> smile.

This story represents a considerable achievement for both its young author and the adults in charge of the writing program. It illustrates one child's discovery that she can use writing for playful and social purposes of her own devising, and it had an impact on the small community of 16 children and two group workers in the after-school room when it was read aloud and then dramatized (McLane & Graziano, 1987).

In the course of this informal after-school writing program, children discovered that they could use writing to enhance and extend activities that were already interesting and important to them, such as playing, drawing, and speaking. They could use writing in their play, and they could play with their writing; they could incorporate writing in their drawing, and they could use writing to elaborate on their drawing; they could use writing in their social relationships, to express themselves and to communicate with people who mattered to them. They discovered that writing could be used to amplify and elaborate on many of the communicative functions

This research was carried out in part with grants from the General Service Foundation, the Spencer Foundation, and the Field Foundation of Illinois. The author wishes to thank Deirdre Graziano for her part in implementing and analyzing the after-school writing program, and Robert A. Gundlach for his help in thinking through many of the ideas in this chapter.

Portions of this material appear in J. B. McLane and G. D. McNamee, *Early literacy*, Cambridge, MA: Harvard University Press, 1990.

304

already served by speech and that it could be used as an effective and powerful means of expressing and asserting themselves, of pleasing, amusing, teasing, joking, showing off, displaying competence, provoking, offending, and apologizing. Thus writing offered them a new and challenging means of interacting with the people around them and made some interactions more interesting than they otherwise would be.

In ''The Prehistory of Written Language'' (1978), Vygotsky argued that ''teaching [writing] should be organized in such a way that reading and writing are necessary for something. . . . Reading and writing must be something the child needs.'' Vygotsky went on to lament ''the contradiction that appears in the teaching of writing . . . namely that writing is taught as a motor skill and not as a complex cultural activity. . . . the issue of teaching writing . . . necessarily entails a second requirement: writing must be 'relevant to life' '' (pp. 117–118). Vygotsky's criticisms of writing instruction are still applicable in many schools today where writing continues to be taught as a set of mechanical and technical skills – with the result that children's writing experience in the primary grades is often limited to worksheet exercises in handwriting and spelling. This emphasis on basic skills may mean that many children acquire a narrow and restricted view of writing as a set of academic techniques that are unconnected to their needs and interests.

With Robert Gundlach, Gillian D. McNamee, and Frances Stott, I have been engaged in exploring resources and supports for children's writing outside of formal school settings – in private homes and in urban institutional settings such as a children's program in a museum, a child-life program in a children's hospital, and an after-school day-care program (McLane, McNamee, Stott, Graziano, Lipshultz & Geocaras, 1986). We assumed that it would be worth while to pay close attention to writing in nonschool settings, where writing is supported but not directed by adults, and that it would be worthwhile to ask children in these settings to write in order to see what kind of writing they would produce and how they would use it – and to see how writing could fit the purposes of the particular setting. We were interested in Vygotsky's idea that ''make-believe play, drawing and writing can be viewed as different moments in an essentially unified process of development of written language'' (1978, p. 116) and in Gundlach's suggestion that ''children first use writing to serve and perhaps to extend functions already served for them by certain kinds of speech, by drawing, by various forms of play'' (1982, p. 134).

When we began our observations (in September 1985), we found very little writing being done by children in any of these settings, and little interest among the adults in charge in finding a place for it. However, as we worked with the adults in each setting, we were able to identify potential occasions and opportunities for children's writing that meshed with the goals and purposes of the particular program and then gradually to introduce a range of writing activities adapted to the needs of each setting.

In this chapter I will consider some of the issues related to young children's writing that emerged in the course of finding and securing a place for writing in an after-school day-care program. This is the setting in which I was most involved, and it is also the only one in which the researchers had a long-term relationship with a stable, consistent group of children and their adult caretakers. I will explore some of the implications of Vygotsky's ideas about writing as an extension of children's play and drawing, and about writing as a "complex cultural activity," in conjunction with his ideas about the importance of social mediation in negotiating and constructing zones of proximal development in which learning and development can take place (Vygotsky, 1978).

Children's writing in an after-school program

The after-school program is located in a community social service agency in a poor inner-city neighborhood of Chicago whose residents include blacks and recent Hispanic and Asian immigrants. At the time of this study, the after-school program served 16 children, most of them between the ages of 6 and 8 (one girl was 9, and one was 11). All of these children came from low-income families who were qualified for Title XX (a state-funded entitlement program). All but two children were Hispanic; one was Ethiopian, and one was an American black. Most of the children attended the local public school (the two older girls attended a parochial school). The after-school program was administered by two female "group workers," one black and one Hispanic. One group worker had finished high school and 1 year at a community college, and the other had completed high school. The basic purpose of the program was to provide the children with after-school care, recreation, and activities that would foster their school success. The schedule of daily activities included teacher-directed activities such as art projects (making paper pumpkins for Halloween, red hearts for Valentine's Day, free drawing), group games as well as free choice of board games and puzzles, and the "Strong Club." The Strong Club had been devised by the group workers to improve the children's performance in math, reading, and writing and consisted of school-like lessons in reading, spelling, and arithmetic and activities such as fill-in-the-blank work-sheet exercises in these subjects.

Starting in October 1985, Deirdre Graziano (graduate student and research assistant) and I began observing in the after-school room several afternoons a week in order to see how writing was used and how we might introduce new writing activities into the program. When we began, we found that the children were doing very little writing other than the occasional school-like exercises of the Strong Club. We also discovered that they did very little writing at home and little writing in school other than work sheets and spelling lists.

In November, we gradually introduced a range of writing activities. Our method was to initiate activities with the children ourselves and then meet at a later time with the group workers to evaluate the activities and to encourage them to try implementing some of these themselves. When they tried out new activities, we were available to provide assistance and feedback. Our purpose was to see if we could establish writing activities that would engage the children's interest by helping them find ways to use writing that would serve their needs, interests, purposes – so that, from their perspective, writing would be ''necessary for something'' (other than meeting a school requirement). We were hoping to exploit the essentially social nature of the writing process and to capitalize on potential links among writing, play, and drawing. In doing this, we hoped to establish zones of proximal development with the children in relation to writing, and with the group workers in relation in supporting and facilitating the children's writing.

Our approach to facilitating children's writing was based in part on the story dictation and dramatization activities described by Paley (1981) and McNamee (Gundlach, McLane, Stott, & McNamee, 1985; McNamee, 1987) and on the methods for teaching writing in elementary school developed by Graves (1983) and Calkins (1986). Paley and McNamee found that story dictation and dramatization are effective ways for adults to involve young children in the writing process and to demonstrate that children can use written language to express themselves and communicate with each other. With adult support, children learn to use stories ''to inform one another of social preferences and private fantasies. . . . the stories, when shared, form part of the fabric of their relationship with one another'' (Gundlach et al., 1985, pp. 37–38; and see McNamee, this volume).

Graves and his colleagues have developed a collaborative approach to teaching writing that has been adopted by a number of elementary schools in recent years (Calkins, 1986; Graves, 1983). Teachers implementing Graves's approach emphasize writing as a complex process as well as a final product. This represents a departure from more traditional writing instruction, which is usually a one-shot affair in which the child is told to write something (typically, a list of words or sentences), which is then corrected for handwriting, spelling, and grammar, graded – and forgotten. Teachers using a traditional, product-oriented approach often focus on the technical aspects of writing and pay little attention to the writer's communicative purposes, with the result that, for many children, writing becomes an exercise in formal mechanics divorced from personal content and intentions.

Teachers using Graves's ideas encourage children to write frequently, on the grounds that the only way to learn to write is to write. Graves has noted that most elementary classrooms do not allow nearly enough time for writing. (This also appears to be true in most secondary school classrooms, where Applebee found only about 3% of students' time was spent on ''writing of at least paragraph length'' [1981, p. 30].) Following this approach, children are urged and encouraged to write and are allowed to choose their topic and mode of writing. Teachers try to respond to children's writing as interested readers first, paying attention to the writer's meanings and intentions and, second, as critics and collaborative editors. This means that teachers accept what children write – their choice of content and style, as well as their often rough approximations of spelling and conventional grammar – as serious communications. The teacher's role is that of a friendly editor who teaches children how to revise their writing in the context of trying to communicate more effectively.

Graves urges teachers to "publish" what children write in order to make it available to classmates, so that children can write with the expectation that they will be read by their peers. Children like to read each other's writing, and they are likely to write with more purpose, and to try to write more effectively, if they know their writing will be shared (Gundlach, 1983). Children, like most writers, need some kind of interested audience to read and respond to what they write; they need – as Gundlach (1983) has put it – to be part of a "community of readers and writers."

Although the Graves and Calkins approach to teaching writing is not explicitly Vygotskian, it appears to mesh with some of Vygotsky's ideas about writing, particularly in its emphasis on the importance of contextual supports for motivating and sustaining writing and in stressing the collaborative nature of the writing process itself. Adults in nonschool settings can use an interactive, process-oriented approach such as this one to emphasize the social, communicative aspects of writing and to create a supportive social context in which children can obtain the kinds of assistance they need to learn to communicate with writing.

In the after-school program, we began by trying to get the children interested in writing. We did this by taking down their dictated stories and then helping them to dramatize them; we asked children about their drawings and asked if they would like us to write labels or stories to go with them; we set up a "mailbox" and wrote notes to the children and encouraged them to write back, and for a while there was a flurry of note writing. At the beginning of March 1986, we gave the children large spiral notebooks and asked them to write in them at least twice a week, with the promise that we (Deirdre Graziano and I) would respond in writing. The children were told that they could write about anything they wanted to but that we wanted them to write something.

Perhaps because of their school experience with writing, several children appeared hesitant and uncertain about what to write about and about their own writing competence. Some children were very concerned about making mistakes – such as poorly formed letters or misspelled words – and they needed a lot of adult reassurance that their writing was okay. For example, 7-year-old Manuel was reluctant to write more than brief labels for his intricate drawings. These labels were often evaluative; for example, a page of carefully drawn boats was labeled "dum boats" and "smart boats." In response to a note from me urging him to write more, he commented, "I write ugly." Eventually, after much encouragement from the researchers, he wrote his first story, entitled "The Six Dummies." Although this story is about some of the other children in the group, it may have reflected his continuing concern about his writing competence:

> *the six dummies*
> Once upun a time there
> lived 6 dummies there [their] names
> where Rosa Nina
> Maria Diana Stephany Luz
> One day their mother told
> them to look for

> something they look
> all around they said
> we are such dummies
> even in school we are
> more dumb then
> animals and cats.
>   the End

By January, we found that the children were increasingly willing – and sometimes eager – to write under certain conditions: *if* they were allowed to control their
own writing, and *if* an adult was available for encouragement and support while
they wrote. Allowing children to control their writing meant allowing them to choose
their own subject matter and write about it as they wished and as they were able to.
For the adults sponsoring the writing, this meant accepting the children's choice of
topic, however bizarre it might seem, and accepting messy handwriting and unconventional spellings and punctuation. It also meant establishing expectations that the
children would write, providing assistance when requested, and serving as interested readers of what the children wrote. When these conditions prevailed, the
children used writing in a variety of playful and social ways not generally encountered or encouraged in school writing programs: They use writing to elaborate on
their drawings; to extend the functions of sociodramatic play; to experiment and
play with the forms and conventions of written language; and to conduct and comment on their social relationships with each other and with the group workers and
the researchers.

Playful uses of writing

Many of the children filled the first pages of their notebooks with drawings, punc-
tuated with occasional words as labels for their drawings. For example, the first
entry in 8-year-old Kevin's notebook was a drawing of a figure in a black costume
holding a sword, surrounded by an assortment of vividly colored swords; on the top
of the page, Kevin had written ''Ninja stuff.'' The prevalence of drawing over
writing may have reflected, in part, some of the children's uncertainty about their
writing competence and in part their greater comfort and familiarity with drawing
as a graphic means of expression. As Howard Gardner (1980) commented, ''Until
the task of writing has been mastered, the system of drawing is the only [graphic
means] sufficiently elaborated to permit the expression of inner life'' (p. 155).

For many young children, drawing and writing are closely linked, serving as
equivalent and complementary means of self-expression (Dyson, 1982; Gundlach,
1982). Young children combine drawing and writing in many different ways, sometimes using them interchangeably, creating their own ''mixed medium'' to convey
meaning (Gundlach, 1982). Often, children who are beginning to use conventional
writing (conventional letter formation, invented and/or conventional spelling) will
use writing to label, identify, and explain their drawings and use drawing to explain
or elaborate on their writing. Some children's earliest written stories are mostly

drawing, probably because for most children drawing is more familiar and easier to control.

Gradually, the children in the after-school program expanded their use of writing to communicate their ideas, sometimes creating products in which drawing and writing are fairly evenly distributed and equally important in conveying meaning. For example, when 6-year-old Jose used his notebook to compose his first (unfinished) story, it consisted of brightly colored drawings of four figures, each with a comic-strip-style caption over its head bearing a name: Ana, Deborah, Joan, and Deirdre (the names of the group workers and the researchers); underneath the drawings, Jose had written: "They were walking down the road."

Jose's story also shows the connections between pretend play and writing that the children discovered as they began to use writing to pursue their own interests and purposes. Some of the children began to use their pretend play experience as a resource for writing, writing to create imaginary situations and to imagine someone else's experience in another time and place. Sometimes they used writing as a form of role play, casting themselves, their friends, the group workers, and the researchers in a variety of roles as they experimented with taking different voices and points of view. In her first story, 6-year-old Karla made Deborah (the lead group worker) the central character:

> *The Little Deborah*
> Onec upon a time there lived a Gril named
> Deborah. She was in a Plane hihn in sky.
> She a very good Gril. She was very
> nice to her parents and she liked to
> Play Barbies with
> her friends.
>   The End.

Here, Karla was engaging in role play with Deborah, making the group worker – a large and powerful figure in her world – into a little girl who likes to do the same kinds of things that she, Karla, does. Thus Karla did with writing what children so often do in pretend play when they reverse everyday role and power relationships and subject important adult figures to their imaginative control.

These children also used writing to explore, experiment, and play with some of the literary forms and conventions they encountered in their reading (including being read to). When Karla wrote "The Little Deborah," she used her knowledge of literary structure, language, and conventions: She gave her story an appropriate title and opened with a typical storybook beginning, "Onec apon a time [Once upon a time]"; she continued with language clearly acquired from book experience – "there lived a Gril [girl] named Deborah" – and closed with a conventional ending, "The End." We found many children writing stories that began with "once upon a time" and ended with "they lived happily ever after"; and we found some children playing with being different speakers and using different voices, writing sentences such as "oh no she cryd ['oh no,' she cried]" and "then she said 'oh, my donkey is missing.' "

Some children experimented with the visual and graphic features, formats, and conventions of written language – playfully exploring the way language looks on the page, using different colors, different kinds of handwriting, and different spatial arrangements for letters and words. Karla wrote her own variation on an old favorite of elementary school children, using different (and appropriate) colored markers for each line:

> Roses are red
> Violets are blue
> Flowers are purple
> Pumpkins are orange
> The sky are blue
> grass is green
> shoes are black.

Here, Karla was using one of the literary forms available to her as an object for playful exploration and experimentation: a rhyme she has heard her school friends recite which begins ''Roses are red, violets are blue.'' This playful, exploratory use of a literary form is one way children can learn about different literary forms as they discover what they can do with them. Children also experimented with titles, with stylistic conventions such as beginnings and endings, and comic-book-style captions; we observed one 6-year-old girl writing a page of titles, then a page of story beginnings, then a page of story endings. In addition, some children played with the mechanics of writing, writing with their eyes closed or with their left hand.

Such playful uses of writing are worth paying attention to for several reasons. The fact that children play at and with writing indicates they consider writing important, interesting, and worth investigating. Playful writing activities can also serve as ways for children to practice, refine, extend, elaborate, or assimilate their knowledge about written language. Jerome Bruner has noted that to play with something is ''to open it up for consideration'' (personal communication; and see Bruner, 1976), because play allows the freedom to use materials and ideas in a nonliteral, hypothetical, creative, ''as-if'' manner. The player does not have to worry about the risk of failure because in play the focus is on exploring and manipulating means rather than accomplishing predetermined goals; in play there are no pressures or constraints to produce correct answers or final products. Play thus confers a sense of freedom and control, encouraging the player to try out materials, activities, roles, and ideas in new and inventive ways. Playing at and with writing – playing with forms and conventions, using writing as an extension of dramatic play – may serve to open up the activity of writing for consideration and exploration.

In discussing children's oral language acquisition, Bruner (1984) argued that ''children's language use . . is most daring and most advanced when it is used in a playful setting'' (p. 196). This may well be true of children's written language acquisition as well. The playful uses of written language described above are similar to children's play with spoken language. When children play with oral language, words, sounds, and meanings are treated as objects to be explored and manipulated. Courtney Cazden (1976) has argued that play with language helps children develop "metalinguistic awareness" – the awareness and understanding that language is a system that can be manipulated and exploited in a variety of different ways. It seems likely that play with written language can help children develop greater awareness and understanding of how it can be manipulated – of what can be done with it and of what they can do with it.

Finally, play encourages the player to act as if he or she were already competent in the activity under consideration, to act, in Vygotsky's words, "as though he were a head taller than himself" (1978, p. 102). Playing with the processes and forms of writing seems likely to give children a sense of "ownership" of – or "entitlement" to – this complex cultural activity. Through playful uses and approaches to writing, children may come to feel that they are writers long before they have the necessary skills and knowledge to produce mature, fully conventional writing. Such positive and proprietary feelings are likely to nourish assumptions and expectations about learning to write, as well as the motivation to work at developing increasing competence in writing.

Writing and social relationships

The children in the after-school program also discovered that they could use writing as a means of exploring, testing, conducting, and commenting on their social relationships. Once the children realized that they were expected to write – and that they were free to write about whatever they wanted to in whatever manner they chose – they began experimenting with writing as a means of offering friendship, cementing alliances, and declaring hostility. They wrote to and about each other, to the researchers, and to the group workers; they wrote notes of friendship; they wrote "lists of friends"; they wrote stories, poems, and essays, some of which were about their peers and the group workers (as did Stephany and Jose in their stories).

As the children grew more comfortable with using writing for these purposes, they began using it in increasingly provocative ways, writing playful tests and challenges to the adults and jokes and insults to and about each other. For example, 7-year-old Maria wrote a "test" for one of the researchers:

> Deirdare is not goig to gess it ———
> [Deirdre is not going to guess it ———; the test was to guess a particular number.]

Maria (who speaks Spanish at home) challenged the other researcher as follows:

> I Love all the
> Techers epset Joan Ha
> Ha Ha for you I am
> Jest kidteing Joan
> So you Better Not
> feal good if you
> Do you are going
> to get it OK"
> HA" HA" HA"
> lets see if you know

> Thes numbers uno dos
> trees cuatro if you do
> NOT know it you ar Not
> The Techer.

Maria appeared to take great pleasure in playfully reversing roles with the adults in the program (all of whom were categorized by the children as "teachers") – much as Stephany did in "The Little Deborah."

Eight-year-old Rosa initiated an interchange of written insults between the girls and the boys when she wrote the "Three Little Scarycats" (quoted at the beginning of this chapter). The protagonists in this story were three boys in the group, Manuel, Kevin, and Simon, whom Rosa described as "little scarycats" who were "scared of the dark, a cat, a dog, a little bird," and even of a little baby's "smile." When Rosa's story was read to the group and then dramatized, the three boys were outraged. Kevin retaliated by putting Rosa and two other girls into a story in which they became "The livig [living] dead":

> *The livig dead*
> The livig dead eat
> peploe [people]. They are sick.
> They are dead pepole.
> They ate Rosa, Nina and
> Mara [Maria]. Rosa is the living dead
> now.

A few days later, Kevin wrote about Rosa and two other girls in the program:

> *The Pigs That Liked Mud*
> Once upon a time There live three
> Pigs. Their names were, Karla, Luz and
> Rosa. They liked mud. They ate
> mud. One day they were killed.

The children found these stories either hilarious or infuriating, depending on their relationship to the writer and the characters in the story – and they always found them exciting and provocative. Notebook writing had been a noisy activity from the beginning, and composing and delivering insults and challenges made it more so. Gradually, the children's insults grew more direct; for example, when Maria was annoyed at Karla she wrote:

> Karla is dum . . . She dos not know her taim taibles.
> [Karla is dumb. She does not know her time (multiplication) tables.]

Some children found that they could use more forceful language when they wrote than they could in face-to-face verbal encounters; utterances that would be considered rude if spoken were sometimes acceptable in print. They also discovered that writing could allow them a certain distance and safety to express ideas and feelings that might be embarrassing or risky to say. This point was illustrated most vividly when one child flung an insult she had written at the feet of the intended recipient and hastily retreated to another part of the room.

On occasion, the insults went too far for some of the adults, and the children learned that putting ideas into writing may entail some risks and sanctions. This happened when Oscar, a 6-year-old boy with poor writing skills but with great interest in writing, wrote a note to Ana, the group worker he was most attached to. He asked a researcher how to spell *nosey* and then wrote "NOSEY ANA" on a scrap of paper and handed it to Ana. (When asked why Ana was "nosey," he said "because she looks too much.") Ana was offended by the note and told Oscar to write her an apology. Oscar then wrote a note saying "SORRY ANA." He gave it to Ana, who said, "Thank you, Oscar." In this case, the group worker was also using writing to manage – and control – social relationships in the group. Eventually, the group workers put a stop to the writing of insults, which they considered unacceptable social behavior.

Thus, within the small community of an after-school program, children discovered playful and communicative uses for writing, which they found interesting and personally meaningful. They found that writing could serve their own interests and purposes; they could do things with writing that they could not do – or could not do as effectively or that would not be as interesting – without it. In this sense, they were discovering that writing is a "complex cultural activity."

This may by particularly important for children who have few opportunities either at home or at school to discover their own uses and purposes for writing. When children's experience with writing is limited to classroom exercises in handwriting and spelling, it is much harder for them to understand the potential power of writing in their own lives and much harder for them to develop a sense of potential control and authorship. This is worth emphasizing because it is not immediately obvious why young children might want to write. Writing is not easy and, particularly for young children, it presents numerous mechanical and technical difficulties, such as letter formation, spelling, and punctuation. Because school writing instruction often emphasizes these aspects of writing, it is difficult for many children to discover that writing can be a means of self-expression and communication with other people. This may be especially difficult for those children who find little support for writing outside of school and who have not yet discovered reasons and purposes for writing – other than meeting the demands of their classroom teacher. If children can be helped to find their own uses for writing, it may help them to construct zones of proximal development which can enable them to find entry points to this complex cultural activity.

Writing as a social process

Not only did the children in the after-school program use writing for social purposes, but the process of writing itself was an intensely social one. During scheduled writing times, children talked to themselves, to each other, and to the group workers and researchers about what they were writing; they requested help with spelling from the adults and from each other, offered each other help with spelling and editing, and asked for responses to what they had written. Sometimes more competent writers acted as scribes for less competent ones. Children plagiarized each other's ideas freely, so that similar themes and characters would appear in several notebooks simultaneously. They reacted to each other's writing with interest, enthusiasm, amusement, and sometimes with outrage.

We soon discovered that this social process needed a particular kind of social support: Writing flourished in the after-school room on the days when we, the researchers, were present; however, even during the months when the children seemed most interested in writing, there was very little writing on the days when we were not present. Indeed, it seemed that the children's writing was closely tied to their relationships with the researchers and to the kinds of support we provided; even the children with the most interest and confidence in their writing appeared to need a specific kind of "supportive adult presence" in order to write. This suggests an interesting paradox: Even to write to pursue their own interests and purposes, children need adult support, from adults with particular conceptions about writing.

The kind of support that we provided, and which the children seemed to need in order to write, consisted of the following: First, at the most basic level, we provided the children with a time and place for writing, as well as the necessary tools and materials (paper, pens, markers, crayons). Second, we communicated our expectations that the children would write – which meant encouraging, urging, cajoling, and sometimes insisting that they write something, however minimal. Third, we tried to respond as interested readers to whatever the children wrote. This meant demonstrating our interest in what they had written by reading it, talking about it, and writing something in response. Fourth, we accepted the children's choice of topic and style and generally ignored mistakes in letter formation, spelling, and punctuation, except when the children wanted and could use help with such matters; we tried to provide technical assistance as a means to help the children accomplish their specific communicative purposes more effectively. In addition, we sometimes made metacognitive comments on the children's writing ("That's a good beginning"), offered definitions ("That looks like a poem"), and made editorial suggestions ("You could explain how that happened"). When the children were writing, all of the adults (researchers and group workers) were constantly engaged with one or more children in one of these capacities. As this suggests, the role of adults in establishing and sustaining children's writing can be complex and demanding.

It is important to recognize that our approach to facilitating writing (as well as the approach to teaching writing developed by Graves and Calkins, on which it was based) is *not* easy for most adults to implement. To work well, this approach requires adults who are both comfortable with writing and knowledgeable about the writing process, and who are willing to allow children to take a considerable degree of control. To do this, some adults may have to redefine their ideas about writing and how children develop as writers in order to make it work. Adults will find, for example, that they must become sensitive readers of writing that is not always easy to interpret or understand, and at times they may find it quite difficult to discern a beginning writer's communicative intentions (Florio-Ruane, in press).

What seems to be most difficult about implementing the approach to writing described here, however, is that it means allowing children a substantial amount of control in the writing process – which, in turn, means that adults have to relinquish some control. Many adults are not comfortable with allowing children to choose their own topics and to develop their own ideas, which they may find bizarre or disconcerting (for example, children may choose to write about monsters and superheroes engaged in fighting and killing) and which perhaps seem inappropriate to the classroom or child-care setting. Adults may have difficulty responding with enthusiasm to writing that contains as many pictures as it does words and/or tolerating writing that is full of formal imperfections such as unconventional spellings and punctuation. This does not mean, of course, that adults abdicate all control; rather, their energy is focused on keeping the writing process going in the ways described above, providing expectations that children will write, and responding to children's writing with interest, enthusiasm, and encouragement. This redistribution of control, then, involves a delicate balancing act for the adults sponsoring children's writing. (See Florio-Ruane, in press, for a discussion of some of these difficulties in relation to implementing writing conferences in school settings.)

The group workers had expressed a strong interest in having the children write and generally appreciated the writing that the children did when we were present, working with us to facilitate their writing. However, on the days when we were not present, writing languished. For several reasons, our approach to writing may have seemed particularly alien and difficult for the group workers. Like many adults, the group workers were not themselves comfortable with the activity of writing, and they tended to avoid it. They were uncertain about spelling, punctuation, and grammar, as well as the structure of literary forms such as poems, stories, and essays. For them, writing – and responding to children's writing – threatened to reveal what they didn't know or couldn't do well.

We tried to share the ideas about the value of playful and social uses of writing described earlier in order to help the group workers develop new perspectives on the nature, uses, and possibilities of children's writing, as well as new approaches to facilitating children's writing. We were only partially successful in these efforts. The kinds of writing being done by the children, as well as the ways in which my research assistant and I supported it, appeared to violate the group workers' beliefs about what writing is and what writing should be used for, as well as their notions of how to help children learn to write. Like play, our approach may have seemed too casual, too frivolous, not serious enough for what is perceived as a difficult, even unpleasant task. For adults with little confidence in their writing skills, and for those whose previous experiences with writing have been painful and unrewarding, our approach to children's writing may have seemed both alien and possibly suspect, as well as complex and difficult.

Through sporadic contact with the after-school program since the spring of 1986, we have found that the group workers will support and facilitate some playful and social writing by the children in their care as long as someone is available to provide *them* with support in doing this. It appears that they need a supportive relationship in order to implement activities that are as unfamiliar and remote from their own experience as the children's writing activities described here, and which require such multifaceted support.

Conclusion: Educational implications

The writing activities in the after-school program illustrate several of Vygotsky's ideas about early writing. They indicate that children will, with adult involvement and support, use writing as a resource for extending their interests in drawing, in pretend and exploratory play, and as a means of exploring and conducting social relationships. This suggests that adults in nonschool settings can support children's writing by helping them discover connections between more familiar symbol-using activities such as drawing, play, and talking, and the less familiar one of writing.

In order for this to happen, children are likely to need considerable support from adults, especially in the early stages, even in writing as unschool-like as the writing in the after-school program. Children need adult mediation in order to understand the uses and purposes of written language, as well as to master its mechanics and techniques (Gundlach et al., 1985). It seems probable that most beginning writers will continue to need such support for some time. How much support they will need, and how long they will need it, probably will depend on individual children's experience with writing, on their writing competence, on their confidence in their writing, and on whether or not there are peers who can take on some of these adult functions for them.

From the perspective of program administrators who want to implement similar writing programs for children, this means finding ways to support the adults who work with the children to help them to develop new perspectives on the nature, use, and purposes of writing, and new perspectives on their relationship to the writing process. In other words, this means considering how to negotiate zones of proximal development with the children *and* with the adults who work with them.

Finally, it is not clear precisely what connections there may be between such uses of writing and the kinds of writing children are generally expected to do in school. The fact that many children found these writing activities interesting and engaging suggests that teachers might consider allowing and encouraging more playful kinds of "unofficial writings" (Dyson, 1985). Also, it seems likely that, at least for some children, using writing in the ways described here will help them in traditional school writing tasks. In part, this seems likely because children should benefit from the additional experience with the activity of writing. When they do write, most children want to do it well; they want to use what they recognize as an important cultural tool competently and effectively, so that there is a push toward mastery. In addition, by writing in a responsive and supportive environment, children can develop more confidence in their ability to write and to use writing to communicate their ideas and feelings.

Whether there is a connection with school writing or not, it seems worthwhile to sponsor children's writing outside of formal school settings because it provides opportunities for children to learn what they can do with writing, which is likely to motivate them to want to learn more about writing and to want to develop their competence as writers. It seems likely that children's realization that written language offers them an interesting, useful, and powerful means of expression and communication – and one that is potentially accessible and available to them – will fuel their interest in writing and their motivation to want to learn to write or to learn to write more effectively.

References

Applebee, A. N. (1981). *Writing in the secondary school: English and the content areas* (NCTE Research Report No. 21). Urbana, IL: National Council of Teachers of English.

Bruner, J. S. (1976). The nature and uses of immaturity. In J. S. Bruner, A. Jolly, & K. Sylva (Eds.), *Play: Its role in development and evolution* (pp. 28–64). Harmondsworth: Penguin.

Bruner, J. S. (1984). Language, mind, and reading. In H. Goelman, A. Oberg, & F. Smith (Eds.), *Awakening to literacy* (pp. 193–200). Portsmouth, NH: Heinemann.

Calkins, L. (1986). *The art of teaching writing.* Portsmouth, NH: Heinemann.

Cazden, C. B. (1976). Play with language and metalinguistic awareness. In J. S. Bruner, A. Jolly, & K. Sylva (Eds.), *Play: Its role in development and evolution* (pp. 603–608). Harmondsworth: Penguin.

Dyson, A. H. (1982, autumn). The emergence of visible language: Interrelationships between drawing and early writing. *Visible Language, 16*(4), 360–381.

Dyson, A. H. (1985, October). Research currents: Writing and the social lives of children. *Language Arts, 62*(6), 632–639.

Florio-Ruane, S. (in press). Instructional conversations in learning to write and learning to teach. In B. Jones (Ed.), *Dimensions of thinking: A framework for curriculum and instruction: Vol 2. Cognitive instruction.* Hillsdale, NJ: Erlbaum.

Gardner, H. (1980). *Artful scribbles: The significance of children's drawings.* New York: Basic.

Graves, D. H. (1983). *Writing: Teacher and children at work.* Portsmouth, NH: Heinemann.

Gundlach, R. A. (1982). Children as writers: The beginning of learning to write. In M. Nysrand (Ed.), *What writers know: The language, process, and structure of written discourse* (pp. 129–147). New York: Academic Press.

Gundlach, R. A. (1983). The place of computers in the teaching of writing. In A. M. Lesgold & F. Reif (Eds.), *Computers in education: Realizing the potential* (pp. 173–188). Washington, DC: U.S. Department of Education.

Gundlach, R. A., McLane, J. B., Stott, F. M., & McNamee, G. M. (1985). The social foundations of children's early writing development. In M. Farr (Ed.), *Advances in writing research* (Vol. 1, pp. 1–58). Norwood, NJ: Ablex.

McLane, J. B., & Graziano, D. (1987). *Writing in an after school program.* Unpublished report, Erikson Institute, Chicago, IL.

McLane, J. B., McNamee, G. D., Stott, F. M., Graziano, D., Lipshultz, D., & Geocaras, H. (1986). *Writing in nonschool settings: Final report.* Unpublished report, Erikson Institute, Chicago, IL.

McNamee, G. D. (1987). The social origin of narrative skills. In M. Hickmann (Ed.), *Social and functional approaches to language and thought* (pp. 287–304). Orlando, FL: Academic Press.

Paley, V. (1981). *Wally's stories.* Cambridge, MA: Harvard University Press.

Vygotsky, L. S. (1978). *Mind in society.* Cambridge, MA: Harvard University Press.

14   Creating zones of possibilities: Combining social contexts for instruction

Luis C. Moll and James B. Greenberg

> Of great value, in both scientific and practical respects, would be the pedagogical-psychological investigation of the reciprocal relation between learning activity and the productive labor that pupils undertake together with adults. This problem has received precious little attention by developmental and pedagogical psychology in the Soviet Union, although the development of learning activity is closely tied precisely to productive activity.
>
>   V. V. Davydov (1988, p. 34)

One of the most interesting and important contributions of Vygotskian psychology is the proposal that human thinking must be understood in its concrete social and historical circumstances. As Luria (1982) explained it, to understand thinking one must go beyond the human organism. One must search for the origins of "conscious activity," not in the "recesses of the human brain or in the depths of the spirit, but in the external conditions of life." "Above all," Luria continued, "this means that one must seek these origins in the external processes of social life, in the social and historical forms of human existence" (p. 25). He later reiterated as follows:

> The basic difference between our approach and that of traditional psychology will be that we are not seeking the origins of human consciousness in the depths of the "soul" or in the independently acting mechanisms of the brain. . . . Rather, we are operating in an entirely different sphere – in humans' actual relationship with reality, in their social history, which is closely tied to labor and language. (1982, p. 27)

In what follows we describe a research project that studies households' social histories, especially their labor and language, and attempts to derive instructional innovations from such an analysis. In line with the quotation from Davydov (1988), a leading Soviet psychologist, our focus is on the labor-related activities that occur within and among households and on the participation of students in these activities. Additionally, we experiment with how to create the reciprocal relations that Davydov mentions between such activities and instruction in schools. As in the Soviet Union, this connection between productive (labor-related) and learning (school-related) activities has received little attention in this country (but see, e.g., Heath, 1983; Laboratory of Comparative Human Cognition, 1986; Trueba & Delgado-Gaitán, 1988; Weisner & Gallimore, 1985).

319

Our research project, still in progress, consists of three main, interrelated activities conducted simultaneously as part of a research/teaching system: (1) an ethnographic analysis of the transmission of knowledge and skills among households in a Hispanic community of Tucson; (2) creation of an after-school laboratory where researchers and teachers use community information to experiment with literacy instruction; and (3) classroom observations in which we examine existing methods of instruction and explore how to change instruction by applying what is learned at the after-school site (see Moll, Vélez-Ibáñez, & Greenberg, 1988). We build on the idea that every household is, in a very real sense, an educational setting in which the major function is to transmit knowledge that enhances the survival of its dependents. The content and manner of this transmission, the households' zones of proximal development, if you will, are the central feature of the ethnographic study. In order to examine the instructional potential of these household activities, we have created an after-school "lab" within which researchers, teachers, and students meet to experiment with the teaching of literacy. We think of this lab setting, following Vygotsky, as a "mediating" structure that facilitates strategic connections, multiple paths, between classrooms and households. The goal of the lab is to support new teaching practices that make ample use of both the school's and the community's resources.

We start by presenting key elements of our household analysis. In particular, we highlight the social sharing of knowledge as part of the households' functioning, what we have labeled the exchange of "funds of knowledge" (Greenberg, 1989; Vélez-Ibáñez, 1988a). We then contrast these household events with the usual social organization of instruction in classrooms and follow with two case studies that attempt to combine strategically household and classroom contexts to develop innovations in literacy instruction. Throughout, we indicate how we are using Vygotskian concepts in our investigation. We are influenced by his emphasis on the interdependence of children's learning with the socially provided resources to support that learning. We have found his ideas on mediation particularly fruitful in helping to create more advanced social circumstances for teaching and learning (Vygotsky, 1978, 1987).

Zones of knowledge

Our household study[1] examines what Milardo (1988) has called the complex "interconnections bonding families to their social environments of kin, friends, neighbors, co-workers and acquaintances" (p. 9). More specifically, we are studying families within a Hispanic, predominantly Mexican,[2] working-class community in Tucson, Arizona. Economically and socially, Tucson can be described as a highly stratified city with a dual class structure. For example, 75% of the Mexican population may be found in the lower-paid craft, assembly, service, and laborer occupations. Mexican wages are 80% that of Anglos, and Mexicans are twice as likely as Anglos to be below the poverty line. The working-class segment of the Mexican population is three times larger than both the middle and upper economic class segments, whereas the opposite relationship is true of the Anglos' class distribution. Further, 75% of Mexicans have incomes (average annual income of $14,500) that are within the lowest 25% of the Anglo incomes. In fact, Mexicans earn less even when the effects of education are controlled statistically. This dual economy in great part determines where people live and contributes to the geographic separation and ethnic concentration of the populations. Residentially, about 75% of the Mexican population is concentrated in "barrios" located in the city's south side. This social and economic stratification is also reflected educationally. For example, only 27% of Mexicans have a median education level above 13.3 years, in contrast to 73% for the Anglo population (see Vélez-Ibáñez, Greenberg, & Johnstone, 1984).

Our analysis concentrates on a pervasive and significant sociocultural practice or activity that we have called *confianza* (mutual trust) (see Greenberg, 1984, 1989; Vélez-Ibáñez, 1983a, 1983b, 1986, 1988a, 1988b; also see, e.g., Aguilar, 1984; Lomnitz, 1977; Stack, 1974; Wellman, 1985). This term refers to reciprocal exchange relations that form social networks among households. These networks, often developed in response to difficult economic conditions, facilitate at least three important socioeconomic functions. First, they serve as a buffer against uncertain and changing economic circumstances. In particular, the networks facilitate different forms of economic assistance and labor cooperation that help families avoid the expenses involved in using secondary institutions, such as plumbing companies or automobile repair shops. Second, although not well understood, these networks function to "penetrate" labor markets. That is, these relations often serve as a pipeline to jobs in both the formal and the informal economy and as a way to bring labor markets "into" the networks. For example, several of the men and women in our sample obtained their jobs through family and non-kin contacts that form part of their networks. Finally, these networks serve important emotional and service functions, providing assistance of different types, most prominently with child care and rearing. In brief, these networks form *social contexts* for the transmission of knowledge, skills, and information, as well as cultural values and norms (Vélez-Ibáñez, 1986, 1988a).

Our work highlights the multiple, "thick" social relationships that constitute household life within this Mexican working-class community. Consider the following example taken from case study analyses we are currently developing of the Aguilar and the Morales (pseudonyms) families.

In the dense social networks in which the Aguilar and Morales households are embedded as central nodes, exchange of mutual help not only occurs constantly but is a defining feature of social relations and even shapes household composition. The Aguilar household, for example, is an extended household which, in addition to Mr. Aguilar's immediate family, includes his brother, his brother's wife, and his nephew, who works in construction but is temporarily out of work. Aguilar's brother came to live with them when he fell ill and could no longer work. The Aguilars also have four married children who have their own households. Their eldest son,

Carlos, lives nearby and works in construction, even though he has a degree in bookkeeping from Mexico. Susana, their eldest daughter, works in a factory that produces telephones and is a divorced mother with two daughters. Another of Mrs. Aguilar's daughters, Ana, is a bookkeeper. Still another, Maria, lives in Coolidge, Arizona, and works as a secretary for the Department of Transportation. Mrs. Aguilar's daughters come to visit or for babysitting almost daily. Susana's household, in particular, is a satellite to that of her parents. Her mother babysits for her while she is at work, and they spend hours together almost daily. Not only are Mrs. Aguilar's children regular visitors, but Mr. Morales, his wife, and their children come over frequently. The Aguilars' neighbors also visit them almost daily. As well, the Aguilars receive visitors regularly from Sonora (Mexico), and not just relatives but often friends of relatives. Mrs. Aguilar is central to the maintenance of these relationships. She serves as a channel for communicating messages, babysits her grandchildren, takes care of her sick brother-in-law, and gives advice. As Mrs. Aguilar expressed it, ''I was molded the old way in a united family. We used to live close to one another and get together often; now we live in different towns, so we stay close by helping each other in times of need.''

Obviously, not all household relations are as complex, multistranded, or reciprocal; many, if not most, family relations are based on simple acquaintance. We have focused on the more intimate and complex relationships because of their importance in obtaining and providing a variety of resources to families (see Vélez-Ibáñez, 1988a). As Wellman (1985) has suggested, densely knit networks may be structurally better suited for conserving and controlling existing resources. Each household in our sample consists of approximately six members and has about six related (kin) households in the general community (some as many as 16). Approximately 90% of our sample reports assisting others with tasks or chores, including household repairs and child care, which suggests an ongoing exchange. These exchange relations, we should note, are not limited to kin or to any particular ethnic group; they also incorporate nonrelatives and different age groups. These families' multiple relationships contrast with the singular, narrow teacher–child relationship common in classrooms (see, e.g., Goodlad, 1984). In contrast to household networks, classrooms are relatively isolated entities, something quite uncommon outside the classroom.

The most important function of these clustered households, and the reason why they are the object of our analysis, is that they share or exchange what we have termed *funds of knowledge*. Greenberg (1989) has suggested that one way to understand this concept is in relation to other household funds. For example, Wolf (1966), in his discussion of household economy, identified several funds that households must manipulate for subsistence and development. The most basic are caloric funds, needed to furnish minimum caloric intake to sustain life. He also mentioned other funds such as funds of rent, a charge on the households' production resulting from a superior claim on the land or housing. This charge, depending on the situation, may be paid in money, labor, or produce. There are also replacement funds, which represent the amount needed to replace or maintain minimum equipment for production and consumption, and ceremonial funds, used to sustain symbolic aspects of social relationships, such as marriage ceremonies and other rituals found in the social order. Each of these funds, and others we have not mentioned, entails a broader set of activities which require specific knowledge of strategic importance to households. These bodies of knowledge are what we call funds of knowledge. Greenberg (1989) has referred to funds of knowledge as an "operations manual of essential information and strategies households need to maintain their well being" (p. 2).

As part of our analysis we are tracing the social history of specific funds of knowledge. Within our study sample much of the knowledge is related to the households' rural origins. Many of the families have members who were farmers and ranchers, relatives involved in these activities, or are themselves engaged in these activities around Tucson. The knowledge and skills in these households are extensive. For example, we have visited families that know about different soils, the cultivation of plants, and water management. Other families know about animal husbandry, veterinary medicine, ranch economy, and mechanics, as well as carpentry, masonry, electrical wiring, and fencing. We also find families that employ folk remedies and herbal cures or other first-aid procedures, or that practice midwifery. Obviously, not every household in our sample possesses knowledge about all of these matters. But that is precisely the point. It is unnecessary and unfeasible for individual persons or households to possess all this knowledge; when needed, such knowledge is available and accessible through social networks.

This social distribution of knowledge is especially important in urban settings within a wage economy, as the funds of knowledge required of workers may become much more narrow and specialized than, for example, in a rural, farm environment. Households in our sample share not only knowledge regarding repair of homes and automobiles, home remedies, planting and gardening, as mentioned, but funds of knowledge specific to urban living, such as access to institutional assistance, school programs, transportation, occupational opportunities, and other services. In short, *households' funds of knowledge are wide-ranging and abundant.* They are central to home life and to the relationship of the families to others in their community. As Vélez-Ibáñez (1988b) has observed, funds of knowledge are the "nuts and bolts for survival."

Besides depicting their origins and content, we are also analyzing how specific household activities make use of these funds of knowledge, that is, the domains within which they may be learned, organized, and transmitted. We have found there are identifiable household pedagogies, identifiable social organizations to learning (cf. Greenfield & Lave, 1982). These strategies for teaching and learning must be understood in context, that is, in relation to the social history of the families, the content of the funds of knowledge, and the goals of teaching. Consider the following example from our case studies.

Many of Mr. Zavala's (a pseudonym) funds of knowledge have their roots in his father's skills: mechanics, construction, washing machine and refrigerator repair. Zavala's father worked for many years in a gasoline station; later he worked in construction and also repaired washers and refrigerators. When they were growing up, Zavala and his brothers often helped their father with these tasks. Unlike the elder Zavala, who had little use for education and bragged that he had gotten ahead without it, his son has had to rely more on formal training, schooling, and self-study to acquire the skills he has needed to get ahead. Whereas his father who had little education could become a jack-of-all-trades through skills learned on the job, as urban labor markets have become increasingly segmented and highly specialized it has become harder and harder to follow the path his father followed. Unlike his father, the younger Zavala believes that education is essential. For example, to get extra training while working as an airplane mechanic, he went to welding school. Again, when he had his repair shop – though he had learned something of how to repair appliances from his father – he needed to study books and manuals on how to repair the ever more complex new washing machines and refrigerators. Like his father, Zavala has taught practical skills to Juan (his son) by including him in domestic chores and other activities. For example, when Zavala repairs the car, he asks Juan to bring him the tools he needs. Even such minimal inclusion in these tasks allows Juan to learn by observing the whole task and by asking questions about what his father is doing. In this way Juan has learned enough to do simple repairs around the house, such as fixing the toilet by himself.

Also consider an example from the Aguilar family. Mr. Aguilar's son Alfredo often helps with (household) chores, especially when they are cooperatively organized, as is common in activities involving exchange. His help in fixing cars is typical of the way in which children are taught in these contexts. In activities like fixing cars, there are many potential entry points, and Aguilar lets Alfredo contribute by doing things he likes to do; at the same time, Aguilar may exclude him from other tasks. Thus Aguilar takes his cue from the child about what he would like to do and then decides whether or not he is capable of it. If he is not, the father may suggest things that he feels are within the child's scope. Even though Alfredo's help is minimal – helping to put in screws, checking the oil – and often ends in a mess – as Mrs. Aguilar put it, *le gusta empuercarse* ("he likes to get dirty") – his efforts are not discouraged. There seems to be an implicit understanding that, even though it might be easier not to have the child's help, his participation in the whole task is an essential part of learning.

A particularly powerful strategy is the creation by a family of special circumstances within which the children or others have ample opportunities to acquire skills or values the family wants them to learn. A good example is the Morales family: The Aguilars and the Moraleses are typical cross-border families with rural roots, part of an extended family – Mrs. Aguilar is Mr. Morales's sister – which came to Tucson from the northern Sonoran (Mexico) towns of Esqueda and Fronteras. The Moraleses had a parcel of land on an *ejido*. Mr. Aguilar's father had been a cowboy and had worked on a large ranch owned by the descendants of a governor of Sonora in the 19th century. Like his father, Aguilar is a cowboy. Although he worked for a time in construction after coming to the United States, he is currently employed on a cattle ranch near Pinal, Arizona, where he spends 5 or 6 days a week, coming home only on Tuesdays. Like Mr. Aguilar, Mr. Morales initially found work in construction, but unlike his brother-in-law, he eventually formed his own company: Morales Patio Construction. This family concern also employs his son as well as his daughter-in-law as their secretary/bookkeeper. Nevertheless, the Moraleses's rural roots remain strong, even idealized. In their back yard, the Moraleses have re-created a "rancho" complete with pony and other animals. Moreover, the family owns a small ranch north of Tucson that serves as a "recreation center" and locus for learning. They take their children and grandchildren not just to help with the chores (running the tractor, feeding animals, building fences) but, more importantly, to teach them the funds of knowledge entailed in these old family traditions, which cannot be learned in an urban context.

Another compelling example comes from the Zavala family, discussed above. Notice that they don't share the social origins of the Aguilar and Morales families, so the content of their funds of knowledge and the preferred modes of transmission differ. The Zavalas are an urban working-class family, with no ties to the rural hinterland. They have seven children. Their eldest daughter, however, is no longer at home but lives with her boyfriend and son. Mr. Zavala is best characterized as an entrepreneur. He works as a builder, part-time, and owns some apartments in Tucson and properties in Nogales (a nearby border town). Mrs. Zavala was born in Albuquerque, New Mexico, in 1950 but came to Tucson as a young child; she left school in the 11th grade. Mr. Zavala was born in Nogales, Sonora, in 1947, where he lived until he finished the sixth grade. His father too was from Nogales. His father had little education and began to work at the age of 9 to help support the family. His family then moved to Nogales, Arizona, where he went to school for another 2 years. When he was 17, Zavala left home and joined the army and spent 2 years stationed on military bases in California and Texas. After his discharge, he returned to Nogales, Arizona, and worked for a year installing television cable and heating and cooling ducts. In 1967 Zavala came to Tucson, first working as a house painter for 6 months, then in an airplane repair shop where he worked for 3 years. In 1971 he opened a washing machine and refrigerator repair shop, a business he had for 3 years. Since 1974, Zavala works in construction part-time, builds and sells houses, and owns four apartments (two of which he built in the back yard of his home).

Everyone in the Zavala household, including the children, is involved in informal-sector economic activities to help the family. Juan, for example, who is in the sixth grade, has a bicycle shop in the back of the house. He buys used parts at a swap meet and assembles them to build bicycles, which he sells at the yard sales his family holds regularly. He is also building a go-cart and says he is going to charge kids 15 cents a ride. His sisters Carmen and Zoraida sell candies, which their mother buys in Nogales, to their schoolmates. The children have used the money they have earned to buy the family a video cassette recorder.

What is important about these activities is not necessarily that a youngster can fix a car or a toilet, use farm equipment, or build a bicycle, but the social matrix in which these skills are acquired. In the Zavala family, as in the Aguilar and Morales families, contexts for assisted performance are constantly generated by their productive activity and by their relations of exchange. These social relations provide a motive and a context for applying and for acquiring knowledge. The key point is that *funds of knowledge are manifested through events or activities*. That is, funds of knowledge are not possessions or traits of people in the family but characteristics of people-in-an-activity. Our household observations suggest the importance of taking into account not only visible, apparent knowledge, where contexts of application, such as cooking a meal, are ubiquitous, but more latent, hidden knowledge, displayed in helping or teaching others or as part of the families' production. Within these activities, much of the teaching and learning is initiated by the children's interests and their questions. That is, children are active in creating their own activities or are active within the structure of the tasks created by the adults. In either case, knowledge is *obtained* by the children, not imposed by the adults.

What are some implications for instruction of the sketch provided above? In our terms, there are various household zones of proximal development, manifested in different ways depending on the social history of the family and the purpose and goal of the activity. These zones are clearly content- or knowledge-based and rarely trivial. They usually matter; that is, they are authentic. It is when the content of the interactions is important or needed that people are motivated to establish the social contexts for the transfer or application of knowledge and other resources. It follows that it is by creating similar authentic activities in schools that we can access these funds of knowledge and investigate their relevance for academic instruction.

These household zones are also adaptive in that they are organized in many ways, often diffuse, and involve multiple persons. In our terms, they are multistranded. A key characteristic of the social exchanges is their *reciprocity*. In fact, reciprocity is the glue maintaining the structure of these important social relationships. As Vélez-Ibáñez (1988a) has observed, reciprocity represents an "attempt to establish a social relationship on an enduring basis. Whether symmetrical or asymmetrical, the exchange expresses and symbolizes human social interdependence" (p. 142). That is, reciprocal practices establish serious obligations that are not only based on the assumption of *confianza* (trust) but lead to the reestablishment of trust with each exchange and the development of long-term relationships. Each exchange with kinsmen, friends, and neighbors not only entails many practical activities (everything from home and automobile repair to animal husbandry and music) but constantly provides contexts in which proximal development can occur – contexts where children have ample opportunities to participate with people whom they trust. There are, as Valsiner (1988) puts it, redundant ways of constructing zones of proximal development (ZPD):

> The ZPD can be constructed not only by the purposeful efforts of the instructor of the child, but also by cultural structuring of the environment in such ways that the developing child at any time is guided by his/her environment to make use of the parts of that environment that are currently within the ZPD. . . . not only instruction but also the individual learner can define the ZPD, given the culturally structured life environment that provided the "stimulus means" for the child's own construction of the ZPD and, by that, of the child's own future development. (p. 147)

Without a focus on social relationships and persons-in-activities, it is very easy for outsiders (educators) to underestimate the wealth of funds of knowledge available in working-class households. Funds of knowledge are available in these households regardless of the families' years of formal schooling or prominence assigned to literacy. Yet this knowledge and its forms of transmission, as we discuss in the next section, rarely make their way into classrooms in any substantive way. From our perspective, then, funds of knowledge represent a major, untapped resource for academic instruction.

Zones of possibilities

In what follows we describe two case studies developed collaboratively with teachers. Both case studies, or modules, as we call them, originated through our discussions with teachers at the after-school lab. These modules are intended to facilitate a connection among the household analysis, work at the after-school lab, and classroom practices. That is, these modules are ways to conduct "formative" or "teaching" experiments in classrooms, and their development is closely monitored, especially through participant observations (see Hedegaard, this volume; Moll & R. Diaz, 1987). The modules take into account the specifics of each classroom, the teacher and the students, and instructional constraints the teachers may face and specific goals they may want to attain. Additionally, each module allows for in-depth study of a topic or theme. This theme of study must be conducive to plenty of reading and writing and to going beyond current instructional practices. Finally, it must be a theme that is relevant to the classroom curriculum.

The first case study started as a classroom demonstration intended to motivate the children to write. The children's activities, however, quickly became elaborate, extending far beyond the classroom, with important consequences for their writing. The second case study involved a teacher's attempts to organize instruction in ways that connect with households' funds of knowledge. In implementing these activities, and in developing others, we have come to realize fully the difficulty of introducing innovations into practice (see Gallimore & Tharp, this volume). Teachers face various constraints, including district goals that must be accomplished, a curriculum to follow, tests to administer, in-services to attend, and what seems an overwhelming amount of paper work to complete. In addition, current instructional practices, with the usual requirements of following a specific curricular sequence with its emphasis on the teacher as the holder and transmitter of knowledge, represent a formidable obstacle to implementing instructional innovations. We have come to appreciate better Langer and Applebee's (1986, 1987) conclusion that traditional instructional practices make introducing innovations into classrooms a very difficult task. That is, the majority of school tasks, with their rote recitation requirements, provide students "little room to claim *ownership* for what was being written or read" (Langer & Applebee, 1986, p. 196, italics added). These instructional practices also provide teachers and researchers little room to maneuver in trying out new methods of instruction.

In our classroom observations we have found many of the rote and reductionist instructional elements that characterize working-class schooling in general (see, e.g., Anyon, 1980; Oakes, 1986). Lessons rarely extend beyond the classroom or incorporate ideas, interests, or activities of the students and their families. Literacy instruction is heavily dependent on basal readers, and what is read or written is usually imposed; student interests are rarely considered. Furthermore, with important exceptions, the intellectual level of the lessons is low; we have observed infrequently activities that are clearly intellectually challenging to the students or activities requiring research or investigation on the part of the students. It is these social arrangements for learning that prompted Greenberg (1989) to call classrooms "zones of underdevelopment."

Nevertheless, classrooms are not uniform in their practices. In all of the classrooms we have observed some lessons that were advanced, interesting, or demanding of the students. We borrow from the notes of one of our classroom observers.[3]

> Instruction in this [third-grade, bilingual] classroom . . . occurs through a structure that encourages children to be responsible and independent. There was no whole group instruction or teacher directed activity. Rather, the students know what to do and proceeded with very little help from the teacher. The students were working on individual contracts for this [Ancient Egypt] theme so they each made decisions about what to do for the extended period of time, set about doing it and only conferred with the teacher about free time requests or help with materials. . . . The concept of negotiation is strong in this classroom. Present in the negotiation process is the attitude that the students are very involved in developing their own curriculum. The teacher verbalized the negotiation process with the students both in a large group and individually and checked that the students kept their end of the bargain. . . . The intellectual level is quite high and challenging in this classroom and the teacher feels it is better to have high expectations for all the students than to limit their progress. The expectation is set for the highest abilities and then the teacher and the aide help the students achieve their best given that expectation. The teacher says there are very few children who have difficulty meeting her high goals. The curriculum involved in the current Ancient Egypt theme was impressive in that the amount of content is so high. The [students'] contract represents that content in its depth and difficulty. It appears to me that the intellectual level of this third grade classroom is higher than many classrooms at the 4th, 5th and 6th grade levels.

These more advanced lessons, although unusual, are clearly not unique (see Moll, 1988). There exist in every classroom opportunities for change. That is, all lessons are not automatically rote learning, and not all teachers' questioning requests some form of factual recitation from the students; the teachers try to create variety within their classrooms. It is upon this variety that we build in creating social conditions that engage students in more advanced instructional activities.

Therefore, an important goal of the lab was to develop a collegial, working relationship between the teachers and researchers. We wanted to turn the lab into a place where we could provide the teachers with strategic assistance in developing and implementing innovations (cf. Berliner, 1985; Laboratory of Comparative Human Cognition, 1982). In our work with teachers we emphasized the need for students to assume more control over their own learning, in ways similar to the classroom described above. We introduced the idea of students deciding their own units of study, seeking answers to their own questions, and using themselves and their peers as resources for thinking. The role of the teachers, we proposed, was to facilitate or mediate the students' activities but not to control them by imposing a required sequence or task or by providing answers. From our perspective, teachers must trust (and assist) students to make appropriate decisions and grow into self-responsibility (see Goodman & Goodman, this volume; Langer, 1987; Moll, 1989).

The first case study

This first case study[4] started from two teachers' concerns about their students' lack of writing. The students in both classrooms (fourth and fifth grades) are predominantly Mexican, all of them being bilingual or monolingual Spanish speakers. There is a wide range of literacy abilities within these classrooms, including students in the beginning stages and proficient students performing above grade level. The child we feature in the case study, Elena (a pseudonym), is in the fifth grade and classified as Spanish monolingual. A quiet and soft-spoken child, Elena formed part of a small group of students who preferred to write in Spanish. We concentrate on Elena's activities and writing because the details of her work help illustrate essential elements of our study. However, Elena is not unique; in fact, she is representative of several other students in these classrooms.

The module was organized around three activities. The first was the formation of a study group between the teachers and the researchers. In these study groups the participants read research articles on literacy instruction and discussed how to apply some of these ideas in practice. These meetings, held weekly with the teachers as part of the after-school lab, also served to plan the modules and evaluate their progress. The second activity involved demonstration lessons. The teachers invited the researchers to implement lessons in their classrooms that would interest the students in writing. In particular, they were interested in eliciting topics from students and organizing lessons to help the students address those topics in writing.

After the demonstration lessons, one of the teachers identified 11 students who were interested in developing a video that would explore in more depth specific topics of interest to the students. This combination writing/video development activity became too elaborate to be confined to the classroom. The students, therefore, agreed to work with the researchers on the lessons at the after-school lab, and it became one of the regular lab activities.

We will summarize the module by describing three phases in its development: the initial writing, the extension to the household, and writing to develop the video. For each phase, we provide examples of Elena's writing. It is important to understand the changes in her writing in the context of the specific module activities. We will show how Elena drew on the available resources to develop her writing and her ideas, and how her writing was shaped by the goals and structure of the activity. Particularly important for our purposes is how Elena used writing as a tool to extend and organize her thinking and plan her activities, how Elena assumed ownership of the activity and the writing process. The key role of the adults in this process was in *mediating* the activities, especially in helping the students to be active in creating and shaping their tasks. The adults did not control the writing, as is common in classrooms; instead, they oriented the students to the use of other persons and materials in developing their writing. That is, following our household analysis, they obtained funds of knowledge by connecting the literacy activity to parents, community organizations, and libraries, among other resources.

The module also shows that by studying children in diverse circumstances we gain a more sophisticated perspective on what they are capable of doing. The students themselves initiated most of the writing and the accompanying activities. In the case of Elena, none of the writing, except the initial writing, was required by the instructor. As such, both the students' and the instructor's activities departed considerably from the usual classroom practices.

Initial writing. As part of the demonstration lessons, the children in the classroom brainstormed a list of topics for writing, discussed topics of special interest to them, and began writing on one of the topics. Some of the students, including Elena, were particularly interested in developing further their computer communications with a school in Ponce, Puerto Rico, one of the lab's ongoing activities.[5] Elena formed part of a group of students who preferred the lesson in Spanish. Although most of these children understood much of the demonstration lessons, conducted in English, they felt more confident discussing their topics and writing in Spanish. During the first lesson, Elena, like many of her classmates, appeared unsure. She did not seem confident in sharing her responses and writing and did not actively participate in the lesson; she appeared unresponsive. When it was time to write, Elena said, ''Pero Miss, no se que escribir.'' The instructor encouraged Elena to select one of her topics and write about it. After some hesitation, she began to write about her ideas of what a school in Ponce (Puerto Rico) might be like. This draft serves as Elena's first writing sample. She wrote as follows:

> Las escuelas an decer como un cuarto chico son como echas comodamente para los alumnos y los maestros tambien ande tener acientos echos de madera y pintados tambien an de estar limpias y acomodada ande ser como un techo de lamina luego como sacate encima para que de sombra tambien los usan para que es te fresca en el calor y caliente en el frio ellosan de estar my agusto en las escuelas porque a ellos les gusta el modo decer las escuelas tambien las escuelas estan echas de lodo y queda un poco asperas Las . . . (E.O., 3/20/89)

> (The schools must be like a small room they are like made comfortably for the pupils and the teachers also they must have seats made of wood and painted also they must be clean and orderly they must be like a tin roof later like grass on top to give shade also they use them so that it will stay cool be very comfortable in the schools because they like they ways the schools are also the schools are made of mud and remain a bit rough The . . .)

Note that Elena selected the topic because it was of interest to her, and she revealed some prior knowledge of the topic. For example, she discussed how a building may be adapted to changes in climate and possibly assumed that the materials used in construction may be indigenous to Puerto Rico's tropical region. Elena may also be using her own knowledge of adobe construction in Tucson and Mexico to guess about how schools are constructed in Ponce. An analysis of Elena's writing shows that her intent was to write an informational piece of writing. She begins with the statement "Las escuelas an decer . . ." (The schools must be . . . ; *Las escuelas han de ser*), indicating with this opening that the text will inform about the topic of schools. The text is also not in the form of an outline, list, or story but in a narrative paragraph similar to those found in content-area textbooks. It appears that Elena is aware of or borrowing from a textbook organizational structure. Textbooks organize content into groups of sentences that inform about a particular concept. Once that concept has been explained, a new concept is described with a new group of sentences delineated by a paragraph. Elena attempted to do the same, although she did not utilize new paragraphs to begin new concept descriptions.

Perhaps what is most noticeable in the text is Elena's spelling and lack of punctuation. Elena spelled phonetically, the way words sounded, and used no conventional punctuation. Yet, in parts of the text her ideas flowed, and she used words that indicated the connection between her thoughts. For example, she used "tambien" (*también;* also) instead of punctuation to inform the reader that one sentence had ended and another had begun. When her description changed from the interior to the exterior of the classroom, she did not use any punctuation but again used the word "tambien" to connect her sentences conceptually and provide the text with some semantic coherence. By focusing on these surface difficulties in her writing, however, difficulties that can be corrected with instruction, we may underestimate greatly what Elena is capable of doing with print.

Extending beyond the classroom. After her first writing Elena decided she wanted to develop a video about Tucson to send to the students in Puerto Rico. In developing ideas for the video, she interviewed her father about Tucson, and together

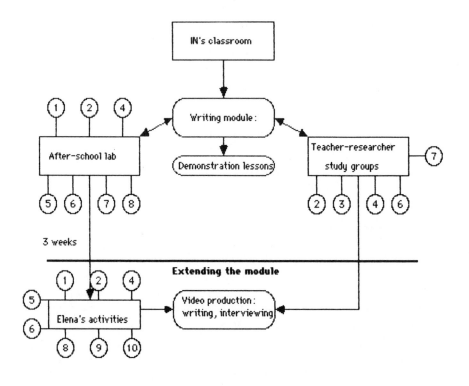

Figure 14.1. The classroom's social networks

they looked in encyclopedias for suggestions. They also contacted an aunt who had been a longtime resident of Tucson to obtain additional information about the city. This research, we should mention again, was self-initiated, not assigned by the instructor. This extension of the literacy activity beyond the classroom was also not unique to Elena; it formed part of the general structure of the module. Figure 14.1 depicts the various social networks that formed part of the study groups and the after-school lab. Also included in the figure are the specific social relations Elena used in developing her activities. These social relations represent resources, new means to accomplish the goals of her project, that are not usually found or used in classroom instruction. Here we highlight what Elena wrote at home with her father's assistance. She decided to visit a local museum and depict its content as part of a video documentary:

> ir al museo con una gia para que me enseñe esplique lo que significa cada cosa y que mediga más o menos cuando hicieron cada cosa y ir apuntando lo que me va diciendo la gia de cada cosa asi les doy enformasion a los niños de Puerto Rico para que vean como hera antes Tucson Arizona y enseñar como se vestian los indios que vivian en Tucson. Como eran las camas, y las casas donde vivian. Enseñar que hacian las casas de soquete y que aun esiste una casa hecha por los indios y de soquete eso creo que les va a interesar a los niños de Puerto Rico como de mi hedad porque ami me interesa mucho saber del tiempo pasado como vivian y lo que usaban para vivir que comian y como hacian las casas de soquete para que no se cayera enseñar la cosas que hay en la cosina como las piedras donde molian la comida y la estufa de dos placas. Y el baño la vañera era una bandejas y habia la ropa como votas y camisas pantalones de cuero que se ponian los indios nativos y sus maletas. La sala era como tenia unos muebles de madera y unos libreros y en medio abia una alfombra muy antigua tejida (E.O., 5/4/89)

> (go to the museum with a guide so that he can show explain to me what each thing signifies and tell me more or less when each thing was made and write down each thing the guide tells me that way I can give information to the children from Puerto Rico so that they can see how Tucson Arizona used to be and show how the Indians that lived in Tucson used to dress. How the beds were, and the houses where they lived. Show that they made their houses from mud and that even now there exists a house made by the Indians and from mud that I think will interest the children from Puerto Rico about my age because I am very interested in knowing about times past how did they live and what they used to live what did they eat and how did they make the mud houses so that they wouldn't fall show the things that there are in the kitchen like the stoves where they ground food and the two burner stove. And the bathroom the bathtub was some pans and there was the clothes like boots and shirts suede pants which the native Indians wore and their suitcases. The living room had some wooden furniture and some bookshelves and in the middle there was a very old knitted rug)

The text seems to take the form of a list of ideas that Elena's father may have shared with her. Elena recognizes that there is no need to write a complete narrative because the purpose of the text is to provide suggestions to herself and a plan of action during her upcoming video sessions. What is most interesting is that Elena used the text to communicate with herself, *to regulate her own behavior,* to plan her activities. For example, she starts the list by directing herself, as the reader, through each step of the tour, beginning with a general statement about the museum, then progressing through each room. She's also very conscious of her audience, specifying what type of information she thinks the children in Puerto Rico, her eventual audience, will find interesting and why. Along with the detailed description, Elena prepared a storyboard for the videotaping. The storyboard consists of step-by-step video instructions and corresponding audio segments accompanying the video. Elena even drew sketches of what the camera should be focusing on and underneath each sketch wrote a brief description of what she would say.

It is also evident that Elena's spelling improved, which may be because of her father's help. In contrast to her previous writing, she also begins to use some punctuation, for example, periods at the end of some sentences and capital letters at the beginning of sentences. The text, for its purposes, has unity and hangs together coherently; it is grammatical despite the lack of conventional punctuation. This is not to say she does not need assistance with the conventions for writing, such as punctuation, which would enhance the communicative power of her writing. But this assistance can be provided by the instructor or a more capable peer in the context of using writing for communication.

Video preparation. Preparation of the video was a major undertaking. Elena had carefully planned the visit and written questions to ask the tour guide, the expert on the site. Elena chose the Fremont House as her site, one of the first and few remaining homes still standing in one of Tucson's original barrios. The house is now a museum that contains many artifacts of its time. She chose the date to go to the museum and film her video and asked others to do the videotaping while she interviewed the guide and toured the historical site. Elena produced this final writing sample as an outline to guide the sequences of her video:

> Boy a presentar al gia para ve si me ayuda
> Boy a decir de que vamos hablar durante la pelicula
> Despues boy a entrar ala casa y empesar a esplicar cada cosa
> Enseñar las recamaras con todo adentro
> Enseñar las armas que usaban para matar animales
> Enseñar la cosina con la mesa, las sillas y las estufas
> (E.O., 5/10/89)

> (I will introduce the guide to see if he will help me
> I will say what we going to talk about during the film
> Afterward I will enter the house and begin explaining each thing
> Show the bedrooms with everything inside
> Show the arms which they used to kill the animals
> Show the kitchen with the table, the chairs and the stoves)

Armed with her plans and outlines, Elena was very confident throughout the videotaping and interview. Her questions were well thought out and clear. For example, she asked the guide what was done to protect the structure from erosion. Although Elena encountered some obstacles in her interview – for example, the guide was not completely fluent in Spanish – she was undaunted by the experience and completed, through her own volition, the task she set for herself at the beginning of the module.

Despite the brief writing sample, we can detect improvements in spelling and vocabulary. For example, Elena is using the aspirated *h* (as in *hablar,* speak) and does not overgeneralize by using it with words such as *empezar* (to begin) and *enseñar* (to teach) as she did in her previous writing. For an outline, her sentences are well designed and grammatically acceptable, and her description of events is coherent and clear. But what is impressive is Elena's use of writing over the course of the module to help her think, plan, conduct, and successfully complete her activity. She went from a tentative, reluctant writer to a student who used writing to accomplish her intellectual goals.

It seems obvious that Elena has already internalized the actions and knowledge to participate fruitfully in a creative activity and to use literacy not only to communicate with others but to communicate with herself – to mediate and regulate her own actions. We are not claiming she developed these abilities working in our module; she probably already had this literate capacity. However, we created the supportive circumstances and facilitated the resources and tools, the new means, that allowed her to display her competence. We created a zone of proximal development that led to the student's utilization of social resources to accomplish her goals. Elena's displaying what she knew provided us, and the teacher, with a good indication of what Vygotsky called the child's potential for instruction; in this instance, the child's potential to benefit from instruction that is more complex and challenging than what she is currently offered. These opportunities to observe students "showing off" what they can do with print are rare in classrooms as presently organized, especially if the students are working-class and Spanish-speaking (but see Moll, 1988). These students, and their teachers, are provided with little room to maneuver or to deviate from the standard curriculum. How can we organize lessons to facilitate for these children continuous or multiple displays of competence? How can teachers and students take maximum advantage of existing social resources to reorganize instruction? The second case study addresses these issues.

The second case study

One of the initial activities in the lab centered around construction and building, a theme of interest to the students. Construction, it also turns out, is one of the most prominent funds of knowledge found in the homes. We, therefore, viewed this "construction module" as an important opportunity to extend our ideas about integrating home and school knowledge. We started the work by showing the students slides of a group of men constructing a home in rural Mexico, as a way of eliciting their comments on the building process. We also asked the children to develop models of buildings or houses and provided them with wood, paper, and other materials with which to construct.

One of the teachers who attended the lab, Ina A. (a pseudonym), decided she wanted to develop a similar construction module in her classroom.[6] Ina teaches sixth grade in a bilingual program; she has approximately 30 students in her class, and they are predominantly Spanish-dominant, Mexican children. Along with another teacher, she is responsible for Spanish reading for the intermediate students in her school. This is Ina's fourth year of teaching. She is a native of Mexico and has been living in the Tucson area for approximately 5 years.

Although Ina followed the assigned curriculum, she deviated often to implement supplementary activities. For example, she used the assigned basal reader but supplemented it with novels, newspaper and magazine stories, and poems. She also

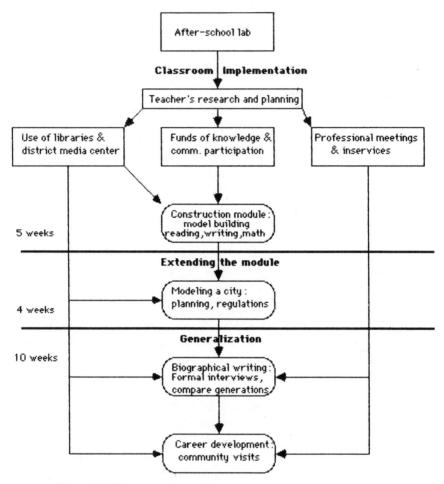

Figure 14.2. The construction module

had the class write often, including poems, short stories, narratives, and descriptions, but reported that the children were reluctant writers, not an unusual situation. The teacher started her module sharing our belief that the use of outside, community resources could give more meaning to the learning experiences of the students. She mentioned that the "parents and children will see the role of the community [in education] as something that is worthwhile." She was concerned with how parents perceived the school and believed that parents felt that they didn't belong. However, she also believed that parents were interested and willing to help. The module and its extensions are depicted graphically in Figure 14.2. We will discuss its development, highlighting the use of social resources for teaching and learning.

Beginning. The teacher introduced the idea of the construction module to the class and discussed with the students possibilities for research on this topic. The students accepted the idea of the new research. The teacher believed, however, that the work required to conduct the module would be more in-depth and extensive than anything they had done before. For the teacher, the module clearly represented a new challenge for her and for the students.

After introducing and clarifying the idea of the module, the teacher asked the students to visit the library and start locating information on building or construction. In particular, the students obtained materials on the history of dwellings and on different ways of constructing structures. Through her own research in a community library and in the school district's media center (see Figure 14.2), the teacher identified a series of books on construction and on different professions, including volumes on architects and carpenters, and decided to use them as part of the module. The initial module was successful. The students followed their library research by building a model house or other structure as homework and wrote brief essays describing their research and explaining their construction. The students wrote in different ways. Some described in detail how they built the model; two students collaborated on a story based on the details of their model, inventing a character named Maria, whose father constructs houses:

> La casa de María está en un pueblo lejano y está hecha por su padre. La casa de María tiene dos cuartos un cuarto para su mamá y papá. El otro de azul es de ella. Su cuarto no tiene nada ni de sus padres. La sala tiene dos sillones y una mesita en el medio. El baño es chico y es ancho no es lujoso lo unico lujoso es un espejo chico. La cocina tiene una estufa poco lujosa y tiene una mesa. La casa fue hecha de troncos de árboles muy buenos y bonitos. María y su familia estan contentos en su casa tienen dos cuartos, un baño, la sala y la cocina. También tienen electricidad gas y agua. Por fuera de la casa esta lujoso y bonito. Tiene un río tres árboles con piedritas alrededor. Ellos tienen poco dinero pero su papá trabaja haciendo casas. Asi que viven bien. A nosotros nos gusto la cocina, la sala, las camitas, los árbolitos y nos gusto como la hicimo estuvimos una hora haciendo la casita. Nos gusto y aprobechamos el tiempo que estuvimos haciendola. Nosotros creemos que ustedes también aprobecharon su tiempo en la de ustedes.   Fin.

> (Maria's house is in a far away town and was made by her father. Maria's house has two rooms a room for her mom and dad. The other blue one is hers. Her room has nothing nor her parents'. The living room has two couches and a small table in the middle. The bathroom is small and is wide it is not luxurious the only luxurious thing is a small mirror. The kitchen has a stove lacking in luxury and has a table. The house was made from very good and pretty tree trunks. Maria and her family are happy in their house they have two rooms, a bathroom, the living room and the kitchen. They also have electricity gas and water. On the outside the house is luxurious and pretty. It has a river three trees with little rocks around them. They have little money but her dad works making houses. So they live well. We liked the kitchen, the living room, the little beds, the little trees and we liked how we made it we spent an hour making the little house. We like it and we made good use of the time that we spent building it. We believe that you all also made good use of your time in making yours.   End.)

Another student compared his model to the human body; note the use of metaphors and precise construction terms, such as *hormigón armado* (reinforced concrete).

> Sin barillas, no podrias mantener en pie una casa. Caerías al suelo como una mareoneta sin hilos que la sostenga. Una casa sin esqueleto se caería del mismo

modo. Sin embargo, el esqueleto de una casa no esta constituido por huesos como los nuestros, Sino por hormigón armado. Para Construir una casa necesitas, antes que nada, hacer los cimientos, es decir, una sólida base de hormigón. Sobre ésta se levanta el esqueleto de la casa y lla está construida. Nosotros utilisamos carton goma y picadientes para hacer una casita primero estabamos pegando los puros picadientes y se caian entonces decidimos ponerle carton y luego le pegamos los picadientes y no se cayo.

(Without steel rods, you couldn't maintain a house upright. It would fall to the ground like a puppet without strings to sustain it. A house without a frame would fall the same way. Nevertheless, the frame [*esqueleto,* skeleton] of a house is not constituted by bones like ours, but by reinforced steel. To construct a house one needs, first of all, to make the foundations, that is to say, a solid base of reinforced steel. On top of this the frame is built and now it is constructed. We utilized cardboard glue and toothpicks to make the little house we were first glueing only the toothpicks and they would fall then we decided to add carton and then we glued the toothpicks and it did not fall.)

In short, the teacher was able to get the students to write about their experiences and in the process improved the activities she learned at the lab.

Mobilizing funds of knowledge. The teacher, however, did not stop there; she extended the module beyond what we had accomplished in the lab. The teacher proposed to the class inviting parents as experts to provide information on specific aspects of construction and mentioned that she had already invited one father, a mason, to describe his work. She was particularly interested in having the father describe his use of construction instruments and tools and tell how he estimated or measured the area or perimeter of the location in which he works. The teacher reported that the children were surprised by the thought of inviting their parents as experts, especially given some of the parents' lack of formal schooling, and were intrigued by the idea.

The visit by the first parent was a key to the module. Neither the teacher nor the students were sure what to expect. The teacher described it as follows:

> The first experience was a total success. . . . We received two parents. The first one, Mr. S., father of one of my students, works at [the school district] building portable classrooms. He built his own house, and he helped my student do his project. He explained to the students the basic details of construction. For example, he explained about the foundation of a house, the way they need to measure the columns, how to find the perimeter or area. . . . After his visit, the children wrote what they learned about this topic. It was interesting to see how each one of them learned something different: e.g., the vocabulary of construction, names of tools, economic concerns, and the importance of knowing mathematics in construction.

Building on her initial success, the teacher invited other parents or relatives to make their expertise available to the class. We quote again from the teacher's notes:

> The next parent was Mr. T. He was not related to any of the students. He is part of the community and a construction worker. His visit was also very interesting. He was nervous and a little embarrassed, but after a while he seemed more relaxed. The children asked him a great number of questions. They wanted to know how to make the mix to put together bricks. . . . He explained the process and the children

were able to see the need for understanding fractions in mathematics because he gave the quantities in fractions. They also wanted to know how to build arches. He explained the process of building arches through a diagram on the board, and told the students that this was the work of engineers.

The teacher also invited people she knew to contribute to the class. What is important is that the teacher invited parents and others in the community to contribute *substantively* to the development of lessons, to access their funds of knowledge for academic purposes. Theirs was an *intellectual* contribution to the content and process of classroom learning. The parents came to share their knowledge, expertise, or experiences with the students. This knowledge, in turn, became part of the students' work or a focus of analysis, as illustrated eloquently in the following English writing sample from one of the girls in the class:

> Mr. S. came today and in a way he taught us how to build a house. He taught us how to measure for the materials and which materials we needed and how to get the best only. He also taught us that if you buy an expensive house from a company it may be made from real cheap stuff and just maybe it might fall apart. And that if you build a house without a ridge or varillas it may tip over and just fall apart. When you are putting the ridge you must put an joist hanger or the ridge will fall. Also you must put cement first then you put in the varillas. For the wall the plywood fir is better than the waffle board. But the waffle board is cheaper than plywood fir. And that for the door and the window you put a metal board for it could hold the material or blocks. He also said that if you paid another worker that isn't from the company he might cheat you, like tell you to pay by the hour. And then they'll take a long time. So then you have to pay them more because they worked more hours. If you do it yourself you might save, I said you might because if you don't know you will be wasting a lot of money because will not be knowing what you are doing . . . and if you are paying the worker how much both of you decided they might do it real fast. He also said that you'll need to put at least 3 or 4 feet of cement above the ground so that termites do not go in. And that the bottom of the plywood or what ever you are using people put some termite poison. But well it is better to have a brick house and to build it yourself because you might save a lot of money.
>
> If you do not know how to make your own home or just a storage room like Mr. S. you might want a friend to help. You should also know the size or amount of the wood, bricks, nails, or any other supply that you might need so that you don't spend a fortune or a lot of money on some dum storage room that you didn't even do right and that in a week it'll fall down.
>
> So if you are wanting a house or just a room make sure you know what you're doing. Take my advise I listened to someone who does know. Don't try to do it yourself because you'll probably end up with nothing because it'll probably fall. He also showed the size of some nails and other supplies.

Another girl wrote, although in less detail, about the same visit, and the visitor happened to be her uncle.

> My tio Mr. S. came to our class to talk about the facts of house making. My tio is a carpenter. He told us about how some people are Honest and some people are not Honest. Most honest people are like your family and friends. After you put some bricks you put some fiber glass and then put tirmite liquet and then some serock. My tio said its better to build a house out of brick instead of wood. There are some word he told us I only remember is Ridge, Fiber glass, Stager, Bolts, Joist Hanger,

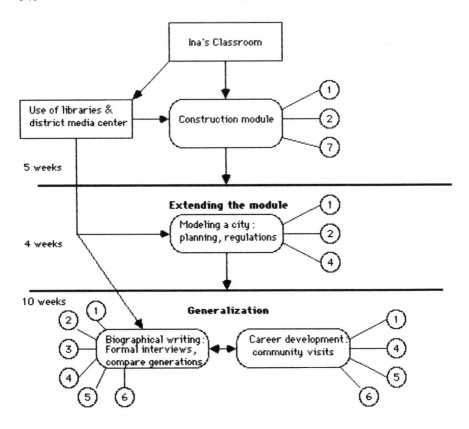

Code:
1-Students' own knowledge
2-Students' parents & relatives
3-Other students' parents or relatives
4-Teacher's own network

5-School & district staff
6-Community members
7-University faculty & students

Figure 14.3. Social networks for teaching

Serock, plywood, waffle board, and panel. The elictricion and pluming gos threw the bottom of the ground. these days houses are made easy and cheap. I think it is better to make a house out of brick.

Obviously, these visits were not trivial; they mattered for the development of the lessons. As such, these invitations and classroom visits helped create a new instructional routine in this classroom, which helped the teacher and students exceed the curriculum, stretch the limits of their writing, and expand the knowledge that formed lessons. Figure 14.3 illustrates this mobilization of funds of knowledge through the creation of social networks for teaching. In total, about 20 people visited the classroom during the module implementation. The teacher utilized at least seven different sources of funds of knowledge, listed below.

1. The students' own knowledge: The first step in the module activities was for the students to discuss and present what they knew about the topic and to visit the library to search for written sources that would help them elaborate their knowledge.
2. The students' parents and relatives: The first visitor to the classroom was one of the students' parents, and in subsequent activities the parents became a regular source of information and assistance with the academic tasks.
3. Other students' parents or relatives: The teacher also invited parents of students not in her class, thus extending beyond her classroom the immediate network of knowledge available to her and to the students.
4. The teacher's own network: In extending the module the teacher used her own social network as a resource of knowledge, inviting relatives and friends to participate in the lessons.
5. School staff and teachers: The teacher also used the expertise of others in the school, including teachers and other staff.
6. Community members without school-age children: The teacher also invited other members of the surrounding community who were not necessarily part of the children's or her immediate social network.
7. University faculty and students: This group includes the lab staff and other university personnel.

As we will show next, these social networks became a regular feature of classroom instruction.

Extending the module. Establishing social networks to access funds of knowledge for academic learning generated important secondary activities in this classroom that went far beyond the initial module. For example, the class invited the brother of one of the students, who was studying to be a draftsman, to present construction plans to the class and explain how he developed them. Stimulated by the presentation, the students decided to extend the module by going beyond the building of individual structures and combining them to form a community. But developing a community with its streets, services, parks, and private and public buildings required considerable research. The students and the teacher followed two strategies: They returned to the library to do research, acquiring additional information on what a town or city requires for its development, for example, obtaining water and providing electricity. To supplement the library research, the students conducted observations in their own communities to determine what other aspects of urban life they might need to incorporate into their model. The teacher provided the class with a large poster of a town, which she found during her own research, and the students placed it on the side wall of the classroom, near their models. As was now a routine, part of the classroom task, the students presented their research in writing and shared it orally with the class or with others in the school. Consider the following example:

> There are many people that work in construction. First there is a designer. She designs the way the inside of the building will look like. She finds the best quality furniture to match the color of the room, she also gets the rugs, curtains etc. to match the color. The architecture designs the building. He must figure out the length, width and how many rooms there will be.
>
> The estimators figures out how much everything will cost. he tries to find the

best, least expensive tools for the job. he also has to extimate how long will it take to finish, because every day they must pay money.

The carpenter does all the wood work. He designs all the wood work. He designs the frame to start the building. He also does sticks so when they pour the concret it is straight. The electrician puts the wires inside the walls for electricity. he also does the outlets for connecting things, to have lights and other needs.

The plumber is someone who does drains. He does bathroom wires and he puts a hose like, so that water can come out of a fountain.

An important consequence of the module was the way it shaped the students' and the teacher's perception of the parents and the community in general. In a sense, the teacher convinced herself that valuable knowledge exists beyond the classroom and that it could be mobilized for academic learning. She also understood that teaching through the community, as represented by the people in the various social networks and their collective funds of knowledge, could become part of the classroom routine, that is, part of the "core" curriculum. We describe next this generalization of the activities into the curriculum.

Generalization. The two activities we describe below were developed by the teacher and students, independent of our assistance. As such, they represent a generalization of the construction module activities into the curriculum. This is a key point. The module started as a temporary and supplementary activity, but as the teacher extended the module, it became more central to the classroom's activities, a vehicle to accomplish the teacher's curricular goals. The teacher generalized the module by incorporating the core curriculum within the module's activities. This generalization illustrates the extent to which the teacher and her class had taken over, appropriated, in the Vygotskian sense, the initial module's activities and created something new to address the needs of this specific classroom. An example will illustrate this process of appropriation.

The teacher had attended an in-service on writing and was provided with a package of materials on possible writing activities. She noticed that one of the activities concerned writing biographies and deliberately chose this topic as a theme to reinforce the instructional process involving funds of knowledge which the class had started with the construction module. The logic of developing this new module is what is of interest here. It depicts how the teacher re-created her own version of the module and suggests the way she was acquiring ownership of the procedures and goals of the activity. What follows is the sequence of the module's activities:

1. The goal of the activity was for the students to write a biography. The procedures included the students' writing about the lives of people from different generations. The study materials included questions about people's activities as children, a topic that particularly interested the students. The teacher used the available language-arts materials to train the children in how to interview others. The students also started to identify whom they wanted to invite to the classroom for the class to interview and persons they could interview outside the classroom.

2. As an extension of the materials, the students developed questions in Spanish and English that they could ask the interview subjects, among them questions about

different jobs that people had done. This topic had become quite salient in the previous module, when the students analyzed the division of labor that goes into constructing a building. The topic is also related to the identification of people's or households' funds of knowledge.

3. The teacher and the students invited people from three different generations, representing the decades of the 1940s, 1960s, and 1970s. The teacher discussed with those invited the types of questions they could expect the students to ask.

4. During a 4-week period, a total of 12 people visited the class. These people were identified and contacted through the social networks previously discussed (see Figure 14.3). In this instance, the class drew people from all of the sources available to them. The children interviewed the people in both Spanish and English.

5. The students wrote summaries of the interviews, highlighting specific questions or areas of interest to them.

6. The students were then asked to interview two other people in the community who represented two different generations and to write a comparison based on their interviews.

7. Finally, the students brought pictures from their families depicting different generations. These pictures were discussed in class and posted on the front board as a symbol of the students' research and the theme of study.

This process represents how the teacher reapplied in her instructional practice the principles that guide the activities of the lab, and she was able to do so independently, without our assistance. She picked a theme that was significant to the children and helpful to her in achieving the curricular goals. She also adjusted the packaged curriculum to include funds of knowledge not available within the classroom. This incorporation of funds of knowledge was accomplished by bringing into the classroom community people who could be reached through the available social networks, but the teacher also used homework assignments to tap the funds of knowledge of the students' homes and other locations.

All of the activities, from the planning and interviewing to the preparation of a final product, involved considerable reading and writing in both languages on the part of the students. As the students' writing samples suggest, literacy in English and Spanish occurred as a means of analysis and expression, not as isolated reading and writing exercises. To support the development of writing, and to enable individual assessments, the teacher organized peer-editing groups that focused on how to improve the writing to facilitate the clear expression of ideas, whether in English or Spanish. The teacher evaluated the students' progress by their ability to deal with new and more complex activities, and by their ability to read and produce more sophisticated writing to accomplish those activities. As Langer (1987) has suggested, it is necessary

> to look for successful literacy learning not in isolated bits of knowledge, but in students' growing ability to use language and literacy in more and broader activities. It will also be necessary to judge progress in learning by students' ability to successfully complete those activities. When we do this, the nature of instructional activities will change dramatically – from pretend to real tasks, from parts to wholes, from practice to doing, and from recitation to thinking. (p. 17)

Following this module, the teacher organized yet another module, this time – coinciding with the end of the school year – on career development. The topic evolved from the children's questions and work during the previous modules, as they came into contact with diverse jobs and family labor histories. Their guiding question was: What do you see in your future? Next to the board displaying the family pictures, the students and teachers developed posters depicting various jobs and professions. Through the social networks, they invited high school and university teachers and students to discuss various careers and how to enter them. They also visited local schools and interacted with professors and students. As with other modules, the children used their reading and writing to mediate and analyze their interactions with the "living knowledge" brought into the classroom by their social networks or encountered in the community during their visits.

Discussion

"For Vygotsky," Bakhurst (1986) has suggested, "the identity of psychology as a science depended on the degree to which it could contribute to the transformation of the object it investigates. Its task was not simply to mirror but to *harness* reality" (pp. 122–123, italics in original). It is this "harnessing" of social resources for the transformation of teaching and learning that is the essence of our project. Our analysis shows that families control their resources through social relations that connect households to each other and facilitate, among other functions, the transmission of knowledge among participants. We have termed these diverse, socially mediated transactions *the exchange of funds of knowledge*. It is how these social systems of knowledge operate – these extended zones of proximal development – that has attracted our attention. These social relations of exchange are multistranded and flexible in that they involve many people and can be arranged or rearranged depending on the specific needs of the participants. These exchanges are also reciprocal. It is this reciprocity that establishes and maintains the necessary trust among participants to keep the system active and useful.

We have come to think of both the content and process of exchange of funds of knowledge as enormously useful in *mediating* instruction. Our claim is that by developing social networks that connect classrooms to outside resources, by mobilizing funds of knowledge, we can transform classrooms into more advanced contexts for teaching and learning. The first case study showed that by developing units of study that connect literacy to the social world teachers can provide students with practice in a wide range of oral and written language uses. The study featured the work of a girl who was very reluctant to participate in class. Through the activities that formed part of the module, activities she initiated, she actively created her own learning situations by involving her father in the research, visiting a local historical site, producing a videotape, and interviewing a tour guide. These activities, in turn, created many opportunities to write and to use writing to guide her thinking. Regardless of the limitations in the writing of any specific student, teachers can develop many circumstances within which to assess students' strengths and weaknesses and within which to provide instruction to develop their writing.

The second case study shifted the analysis from an individual lesson and showed how a teacher changed her classroom from a relatively self-contained entity, as is the case with most classrooms, with little or no interaction with the outside world into a classroom whose learning activities were enhanced by the participation of community members. Through the development of social networks for teaching, the teacher facilitated the intellectual contribution of parents and other adults to academic lessons. This parental participation, in turn, provided the teacher and students not only with an appreciation of the knowledge of the parents but with an additional context for learning. As with the households, the key to these networks was their reciprocity. Parents and other persons readily agreed to contribute to lessons because of the implicit assumption that the students would benefit academically. These networks could not be sustained if the parents, teachers, or students believed them to be educationally insignificant. For most classrooms, this infusion of funds of knowledge would mean reorganizing the context of literacy instruction from a passive recitation model to an interactive, more holistic approach that would make full use of student and parental experiences. To be successful, the introduction of funds of knowledge into the classroom must facilitate the development of new, more advanced literacy activities for the students.

In both case studies, we refrained from imposing a curriculum on teachers; that is a recipe for failure. Instead, we worked collaboratively with teachers and built on their needs or interests. In our first case study, the teachers were motivated by their concerns about the students' writing. We found they needed considerable support before they began experimenting with instruction. The formation of study groups as part of the after-school lab greatly facilitated these teachers' participation in the project by creating a setting where they could think, question their own teaching, plan activities, and address practical concerns. The teacher in the second case study was motivated to develop new activities in her classroom and willing to re-create and extend in her class the module she observed in the lab. That she was already testing the limits of her curriculum by including in her classroom supplementary activities facilitated implementing the innovation. Her efforts show that teachers can develop literacy activities that exceed in sophistication, intellectual level, and scope what is currently being taught in schools.

Vygotsky (1987) wrote that in "receiving instruction in a system of knowledge, the child learns of things that are not before his eyes, things that far exceed the limits of his actual and even potential immediate experience" (p. 180). We hardly believe that rote instruction of low-level skills is the system of knowledge that Vygotsky had in mind. We perceive the students' community, and its funds of knowledge, as the most important resource for reorganizing instruction in ways that "far exceed" the limits of current schooling. An indispensable element of our approach is the creation of meaningful connections between academic and social life through the concrete learning activities of the students. We are convinced that teachers can establish, in systemic ways, the necessary social relations outside classrooms that will change and improve what occurs within the classroom walls. These social connections help teachers and students to develop their awareness of how they can use the everyday to understand classroom content and use classroom activities to understand social reality.

Notes

1 A total of 35 families are participating in the household study. All are families of fourth-graders (bilingual classrooms) participating in the implementing and comparison schools of our project, except for 6 families of fifth- and sixth-grade children participating in the after-school lab. Our goal was to sample families as follows: 10 students from the "treatment" classroom who also participate in the lab; 10 students from the "treatment" classroom who do not participate in the lab; 10 students from the comparison classroom. Attrition has forced us to modify our sample to include fifth- and sixth-graders. However, the distribution of students representing the treatment and comparison classrooms remains faithful to the original design. We are currently recruiting additional families into the study. Our thanks to our colleagues, Carlos Vélez, Gerardo Bernache, Javier Tapia, and Claudina Cabrera, all of the Bureau of Applied Research in Anthropology, University of Arizona, who have conducted most of the participant observations in the households and helped to elaborate the analysis presented herein. The project is funded by a contract from the Office of Bilingual Education and Minority Language Affairs, Department of Education, Washington, DC, as part of the Innovative Approaches Research Project, directed by Charlene Rivera, Development Associates, Inc.

2 Following Vélez-Ibáñez (1988), we are using the term *Mexican* to designate native-born of Mexico as well as those of Mexican parentage born in the United States. This designation is also consistent with the self-descriptions of the persons, regardless of generation, in our study sample. The present study builds directly on our previous work addressing social and educational issues of Latino families and students (see, e.g., Moll, 1988; Moll & S. Díaz, 1987; Vélez-Ibáñez, 1983a, 1988a).

3 Kathy Whitmore conducted these observations.

4 Rosi Andrade and Elizabeth Saavedra, in collaboration with the teachers, developed this case study and were the instructors in the examples described here. They also helped develop the analysis presented in this chapter.

5 As part of the lab's activities, we communicated by computer with students in Ponce, Puerto Rico, San Diego, California, and New York City. These written communications were conducted in both English and Spanish. Our thanks to Dennis Sayers and Project Orillas for facilitating the link-up with Puerto Rico and New York.

6 Arminda Fuentevilla and Hilda Angiulo helped develop the analysis presented herein.

References

Aguilar, J. (1984). Trust and exchange: Expressive and instrumental dimensions of reciprocity in a peasant community. *Ethos, 12*(1), 3–29.

Anyon, J. (1980). Social class and the hidden curriculum of work. *Journal of Education, 162*(1), 67–92.

Bakhurst, D. J. (1986). Thought, speech, and the genesis of meaning: On the 50th anniversary of Vygotsky's *Myslenie i Rec'* [Speech and thinking]. *Studies in Soviet thought, 31,* 102–129.

Berliner, D. C. (1985). Laboratory settings and the study of teacher education. *Journal of Teacher Education, 36*(6), 2–8.

Davydov, V. V. (1988). Learning activity: The main problems needing further research. *Multidisciplinary Newsletter for Activity Theory, 1*(1–2), 29–36.

Goodlad, J. (1984). *A place called school.* New York: McGraw-Hill.

Greenberg, J. B. (1984). *Household economy and economic sector participation in Douglas, Arizona, and Agua Prieta, Sonora.* Unpublished manuscript.

Greenberg, J. B. (1989, April). *Funds of knowledge: Historical constitution, social distribution, and transmission.* Paper presented at the annual meetings of the Society for Applied Anthropology, Santa Fe, NM.

Greenfield, P., & Lave, J. (1982). Cognitive aspects of informal education. In D. Wagner & H. Stevenson (Eds.), *Cultural perspectives on child development* (pp. 181–207). San Francisco: Freeman.

Heath, S. B. (1983). *Ways with words: Language, life, and work in communities and classrooms.* Cambridge: Cambridge University Press.

Laboratory of Comparative Human Cognition. (1982). A model system for the study of learning difficulties. *Quarterly Newsletter of the Laboratory of Comparative Human Cognition, 4*(3), 39–66.

Laboratory of Comparative Human Cognition. (1986). The contributions of cross-cultural research to educational practice. *American Psychologist, 41*(10), 1049–1058.

Langer, J. (1987). A sociocognitive perspective on literacy. In J. Langer (Ed.), *Language, literacy, and culture: Issues in society and schooling* (pp. 1–20). Norwood, NJ: Ablex.

Langer, J., & Applebee, A. (1986). Reading and writing instruction: Toward a theory of teaching and learning. In E. Z. Rothkopf (Ed.), *Review of research in education* (pp. 171–194). Washington, DC: American Educational Research Association.

Langer, J., & Applebee, A. (1987). *How writing shapes thinking: A study of teaching and learning* (NCTE Research Report No. 22). Urbana, IL: National Council of Teachers of English.

Lomnitz, L. (1977). *Networks and marginality: Life in a Mexican shantytown.* New York: Academic Press.

Luria, A. R. (1982). *Language and cognition.* New York: Wiley.

Milardo, R. (Ed.) (1988). *Families and social networks.* Beverly Hills, CA: Sage.

Moll, L. C. (1988). Key issues in teaching Latino students. *Language Arts, 65*(5), 465–472.

Moll, L. C. (1989). Teaching second-language students: A Vygotskian perspective. In D. Johnson & D. Roen (Eds.), *Richness in writing: Empowering ESL students* (pp. 55–69). New York: Longman.

Moll, L. C., & Díaz, R. (1987). Teaching writing as communication: The use of ethnographic findings in classroom practice (pp. 195–221). In D. Bloome (Ed.), *Literacy and schooling* (pp. 55–65). Norwood, NJ: Ablex.

Moll, L. C., & Díaz, S. (1987). Change as the goal of educational research. *Anthropology and Education Quarterly, 18*(4), 300–311.

Moll, L.C., Vélez-Ibáñez, C., & Greenberg, J. (1988). *Project implementation plan. Community knowledge and classroom practice: Combining resources for literacy instruction* (Technical Report, Development Associates Subcontract No. L-10). Tucson: University of Arizona, College of Education and Bureau of Applied Research in Anthropology.

Oakes, J. (1986). Tracking, inequality, and the rhetoric of school reform: Why schools don't change. *Journal of Education, 168*, 61–80.

Stack, C. (1974). *All our kin: Strategies for survival in a black community.* New York: Harper Colophon.

Trueba, H.T., & Delgado-Gaitán, C. (Eds.) (1988). *School & society: Learning content through culture.* New York: Praeger.

Valsiner, J. (1988). *Developmental psychology in the Soviet Union.* Sussex: Harvester.

Vélez-Ibáñez, C. G. (1983a). *Bonds of mutual trust.* New Brunswick, NJ: Rutgers University Press.

Vélez-Ibáñez, C. G. (1983b). *Rituals of marginality.* Berkeley: University of California Press.

Vélez-Ibáñez, C. G. (1986). *Incorporating mechanisms of exchange among Mexicanos in the U.S. borderlands.* Paper presented at the Fourth Symposium of Mexican and United States Universities, "One border: Two nations," Sante Fe, NM.

Vélez-Ibáñez, C. G. (1988a). Networks of exchange among Mexicans in the U.S. and Mexico: Local level mediating responses to national and international transformations. *Urban Anthropology, 17*(1), 27–51.

Vélez-Ibáñez, C. G. (1988b, November). *Forms and functions of funds of knowledge among Mexicans in the southwest.* Paper presented at the annual meeting of the American Anthropological Association, Phoenix, AZ.

Vélez-Ibáñez, C., Greenberg, J., & Johnstone, B. (1984). The ethnic, economic, and educational structure of Tucson, Arizona: The limits of possibility for the Mexican Americans in 1982. *Proceedings of the Meetings of the Rocky Mountain Council on Latin American Studies, 1*, 154–164.

Vygotsky, L. S. (1978). *Mind in society.* Cambridge, MA: Harvard University Press.

Vygotsky, L. S. (1987). Speech and thinking. In L. S. Vygotsky, *Collected Works* (Vol. 1, pp. 39–285) (R. Rieber & A. Carton, Eds.; N. Minick, Trans.). New York: Plenum.

Weisner, T., & Gallimore, R. (1985, December). *The convergence of ecocultural and activity theory.* Paper presented at the annual meetings of the American Psychological Association, Washington, DC.

Wellman, B. (1985). Domestic work, paid work, and net work. In S. Duck & D. Pearman (Eds.), *Understanding personal relationships: An interdisciplinary approach* (pp. 159–185). Beverly Hills, CA: Sage.

Wolf, E. (1966). *Peasants.* Englewood Cliffs, NJ: Prentice-Hall.

15   The zone of proximal development as basis for instruction

Mariane Hedegaard

This chapter describes a teaching experiment combining psychological theory development with school teaching. The project took place in a Danish elementary school and followed the same class from third to fifth grade. Here I will report only on the activities of the first year of our experiment, which was carried out in cooperation between researcher and teacher in a social science subject (biology, history, and geography).

The aim of the project is to formulate a theory of children's personality development that considers development from a comprehensive point of view in a cultural and societal context and to formulate a related theory of instruction. We base our work on the methodology of the cultural-historical school, as formulated for Vygotsky (1985–1987) and developed by Leontiev (1978, 1981), Elkonin (1971, 1980), Davydov (1977, 1982), and Lompscher (1980, 1982, 1984, 1985).

In this chapter, I will focus on those aspects of the project that illustrate the importance of Vygotsky's concept of the zone of proximal development. I will show that, as an analytic tool for evaluation of school children's development in connection with schooling, this concept is of great value.

The theoretical basis

Vygotsky's zone of proximal development connects a general psychological perspective on child development with a pedagogical perspective on instruction. The underlying assumption behind the concept is that psychological development and instruction are socially embedded; to understand them one must analyze the surrounding society and its social relations. Vygotsky explained the zone of proximal development as follows:

> The child is able to copy a series of actions which surpass his or her own capacities, but only within limits. By means of copying, the child is able to perform much better when together with and guided by adults than when left alone, and can do so with understanding and independently. The difference between the level of solved tasks that can be performed with adult guidance and help and the level of independently solved tasks is the zone of proximal development. (1982, p. 117)

Vygotsky wrote that we have to define both levels in the child's development if we wish to know the relation between the child's process of development and the

349

possibilities of instruction. He pointed out that the main characteristic of instruction is that it creates the zone of proximal development, stimulating a series of inner developmental processes. Thus the zone of proximal development is an analytic tool necessary to plan instruction and to explain its results.

> From this point of view, instruction cannot be identified as development, but properly organized instruction will result in the child's intellectual development, will bring into being an entire series of such developmental processes, which were not at all possible without instruction. Thus instruction is a necessary and general factor in the child's process of development – not of the natural but of the historical traits of man. (1982, p. 121)

The zone of proximal development includes the normative aspects of development. The direction of development is guided by instruction in scientific concepts considered important by curriculum planners and the teacher. Through instruction, the scientific concepts relate to and become the child's everyday concepts. Leontiev describes the relation between scientific and everyday concepts as follows:

> The degree to which the child masters everyday concepts shows his actual level of development, and the degree to which he has acquired scientific concepts shows the zone of proximal development. (1985, pp. 47–48)

At the same time, this relation describes the connection between learning and development; the everyday concepts are spontaneously developed in a dialectical relation to the scientific concepts, which are mediated through the instruction. However, if the scientific concepts are not included, the child's entire development will be affected. Leontiev quotes Vygotsky to point out this relation:

> But when scientific concepts result in development of a developmental stage through which the child has not yet passed . . . we will understand that the mediation of scientific concepts may play an important role in the child's psychic development. The only good instruction received in childhood is the one that precedes and guides development. (1985, p. 48)

Vygotsky's methodological basis

Vygotsky's theory integrates several approaches to form a comprehensive agenda for research of the genesis, development, function, and structure of the human psyche. These approaches include (1) an activity approach, (2) a historical societal approach, (3) a mediating instrumental approach, and (4) an interhuman genetic approach.

1. Vygotsky's successors have posited practical activity as a unit of analysis that allows for a comprehensive approach to the description of the development of the human psyche. This unit comprises all aspects of the genesis of the human psyche: social, cognitive, motivational, and emotional (Davydov & Radzikhovskii, 1985; Leontiev, 1985).

2. Vygotsky's methodology is based on the application of the Marxist historical societal approach. In psychology this approach emphasizes the concept of work

activity: the relation between human beings and the world as mediated through tools (Leontiev, 1985, p. 33).

3. According to Vygotsky, the development of psychic tools determines humans' relations with their environment and with themselves. Psychic tools are analogous to industrial tools and are also characterized by being produced through social activity, rather than arising organically (Vygotsky, 1985–1987, p. 309). Psychic tools may be very complex systems; as examples, Vygotsky mentioned spoken language, systems of notation, works of art, written language, schemata, diagrams, maps, and drawings.

4. The interprocessual aspect of the human psyche first appeared as practical activity between human beings. Shared and collective tool use is part of this inter-human practical activity. The interpersonal procedures for tool use gradually became acquired intrapsychic procedures. Through the procedures for tool use, humans are bearers of societal historical traditions; consequently, the interhuman activity, as it forms the child's inner activity, is always societal, historical, and cultural. Therefore, in order to understand the human psyche it is necessary to analyze it genetically as a societal and historical phenomenon (Hedegaard, 1987; Markova, 1982; Wertch, 1985).

Development, teaching

According to Vygotsky, human development is characterized by the ability to acquire psychic tools. Vygotsky does not deny biological development (cf. Scribner, 1985); however, human biological development is shaped and concretized through societal and historical development. In a specific culture, it may be historically characterized as the development of traditions through human activity. The development of traditions has its parallel in ontogenetic development (cf. Elkonin, 1971), although the ontogenetic development is never identical with the development of traditions in a culture. Ontogenetic development can be characterized by stages of activity determined by the child's biological capacity as well as by the historical traditions in which the culture involves the child.

According to Elkonin, the child's development is characterized by three periods, each including a motivational and a cognitive stage of development. The first period, the infant and early play period, includes the development of motives for emotional contact, methods for socializing, and situational mastery. The second period includes the age of role play and early school age. This period is dominated by the development of motives for mastery of the adult world and acquisition of analytic methods and related goals and means. The late school and youth period is characterized by the development of motives for social and societal involvement and methods for mastery of personal relations as well as work and societal requirements (see Figure 15.1).

At every stage, the child's development is related to one of the societally determined activities and traditions. During the first stage, the tradition for child care,

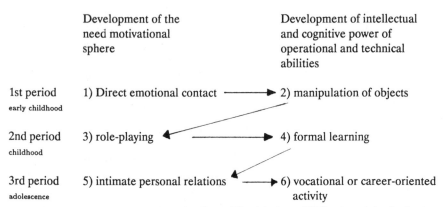

Figure 15.1. The stages that, according to Elkonin's theory (1971), characterize the dominant forms of child development in Western society

the building of emotional bonds, especially with the mother, is the determining activity for development. The next stage is characterized by traditions for creating supportive surroundings for the child's explorative and imaginary play activity. Kindergarten and school are the institutionalized traditions for determining the dominant activities for the following two stages: development of motives and development of skill and knowledge for relating theoretically and reflectively to the world. The fifth stage is characterized by traditions for peer activities institutionalized in different forms of after-school activities. Work activity is the determining activity for the last stage described by Elkonin. By analyzing the tradition we can critically evaluate whether the stages are relevant descriptions of child development today in Western society. For instance, one could argue that the period between late school age and work in today's society has become institutionalized as education for work. This evaluation of the stages underlines Leontiev's description of stages in child development as societally and historically determined.

The zone of proximal development can be related to Elkonin's developmental stages (Griffin & Cole, 1984). As stated, the qualitatively new structures that arise in the course of a child's development are related to the changing demands made on children by social institutions.

When children enter school, the teacher confronts them with the zone of proximal development through the tasks of school activity, in order to guide their progress toward the stage of formal learning. These tasks help children acquire motives and methods for mastery of the adult world, as mediated by the teacher.

The zone of proximal development can also be viewed from the aspect of action within a certain activity. To the school child, action is related to the learning/teaching activity (cf. Engestrom, 1986; Rogoff & Wertsch, 1984; Schneider, Hyland, & Gallimore, 1985; Wertsch, 1985). The teacher's role is to direct action within school activity in a manner appropriate to the child's present level of development, the cultural and social context, and the teacher's theories of what central subject matter is. For instance, the teacher's theory of what language and reading are – and what characterizes the logic of language and reading – will influence the teaching and learning actions of mother-tongue instruction.

Empirical knowledge, theoretical knowledge

The child is born into a society in which knowledge is available as the standard procedure for dealing with persons and things. It is important to distinguish between knowledge that exists independently of the child and the child's acquisition and development of this knowledge.

In a specific society, the standard procedures for solving societal problems can be seen as the culturally developed skills acquired and developed by each generation. Knowledge is accessible through different media, for example, language and pictures, and is the result of culturally and societally developed procedures for solving societal problems. The development of medicine is a typical example. According to Juul Jensen (1986), societal practices exist prior to societal knowledge, leading to a rejection of the assumption that knowledge is the essence of environmental phenomena and things existing independently of human societal practice. Societally developed skills are thus the basis for societally developed knowledge. Davydov has separated this societal knowledge into two forms of knowledge – empirical knowledge and theoretical knowledge – each with its associated epistemological procedures.

Empirical knowledge deals with differences and similarities among phenomena; has arisen via observation and comparison of phenomena; can be ordered hierarchically on the basis of formal characteristics; and the word or a limited term is the medium whereby it is communicated. Through empirical epistemological procedure, the individual object is grasped by isolating it from its spatial and chronological connections so that it can be observed, compared, categorized, and remembered. Imagery and language are the media used to this end. In the empirical exposure the individual object functions as an independent reality.

In contrast, theoretical knowledge deals with a connected system of phenomena and not the separate, individual phenomenon; arises through the development of methods for the solution of the contradictions in a societally central problem area; develops understandings of the origins, relations, and dynamics of phenomena; and models are the medium whereby this knowledge is communicated. Through the theoretical epistemological procedure, the object is observed as it transforms. By re-creating the object in its relation to other objects, these relations are revealed. This reproduction has the character of experimental exploration of relations and changes, through both concretely changing the world and mentally imagining changes. Theoretical knowledge cannot be acquired via its verbal or literary form alone, even though it does appear primarily in verbal and literary forms at the scientific level.

Societal knowledge and skills are inseparably bound together. In the same way, the child's concept acquisition is tied to the acquisition of cognitive procedures. In teaching, if one wants children to acquire theoretical knowledge in the form of the fundamental relations in a subject or a problem area, then the cognitive method in instruction must also characterize theoretical knowledge. If, on the other hand, one applies the epistemological method that characterizes empirical knowledge – that is, observation, comparison, categorization, and memory – together with a subject area's fundamental concepts, then knowledge acquisition will remain on the empirical level. School children have already learned the empirical epistemological procedure in their practical everyday activities; they have yet to acquire the theoretical epistemological procedure.

Theoretical knowledge must be acquired through exploratory activity. In school, this activity is controlled activity, consisting of the exploration of problems that contain the fundamental conflicts of the phenomenon. A prerequisite for theoretical knowledge acquisition is teaching activity built on tasks that illuminate the contrasts found in a phenomenon's fundamental relations. Through this exploration it becomes possible to gain insight into the development of the phenomenon.

As an example, I will discuss the problem area on which our teaching experiment is based: "the evolution of species." Darwin's theory of species and its elaboration in the more modern synthetic theory of evolution (Gould, 1977; Mayr, 1976, 1980; Simpson, 1962) demonstrate how knowledge has developed through problems that, for science, have been urgent.

The phenomenon of the evolution of species contains a fundamental conflict which has stimulated scientific development: How can an animal population adapt to changes in its habitat while many individual animals cannot manage this adaptation and die? This conflict has been of central importance to a theory of the evolution of animal species and is therefore useful as the basis for instruction in the evolution of species. However, such a conflict cannot be presented abstractly to pupils; rather, it must be presented via analyses of concrete animal species. For example, pupils can analyze how the polar bear adapts to its arctic surroundings to survive as an individual, how it breeds and ensures the survival of its young. Students can analyze limits to this adaptation as well. The teacher must set tasks for pupils so that they become aware of the adaptations of the polar bear as well as the different ways in which other animals in the Arctic survive, breed, or die. Through the resulting insights children can arrive at the formulation of general laws about the survival and change of an animal species.

Theoretical knowledge as psychic tool

The tool character of theoretical knowledge becomes especially evident when formulated in a model. The model may become the tool that guides the teacher's instruction activity. This type of model is characterized as a germ-cell model (Davydov, 1982; Engestrom & Hedegaard, 1986), which implies a model that grows in complexity from a set of basic central relations. It also implies that every time the model becomes complicated by new relations it not only adds to the concepts already modeled but influences and changes their meaning, because the concepts are defined through their relations. The basic concepts in a germ-cell model are complementary in their explanatory value for the problem area being modeled. This means that the relation between the basic concepts in a germ-cell model is contradictory, and through explicating this contradiction related concepts are developed. This can be illustrated by the growth of the germ-cell model in the teaching experiment. The problem area to be modeled and explained was the evolution of animals. The basic concept relation in the modeling of this problem area was the relation animal–nature (see Figure 15.2).

The pupils may first acquire an external, auxiliary model that gives a general impression of the area taught. The auxiliary model then functions as a basis of information for the pupils' further work with the subject and for the development of their own models of understanding, which in turn will become psychic tools for the pupils. Through experiencing the contradiction of their modeling of the problem area in their concrete problem solving, the pupils' concepts of their models become richer and new conceptual relations are included.

The school's task is generally considered to be the passing on of knowledge and skills, but the children do not necessarily develop a theoretical orientation toward reality. Their orientation may remain on an empirical level. The difference between theoretical and empirical orientation is connected with Vygotsky's differentiation between everyday concepts and scientific concepts (see Figure 15.3). These pairs of concepts are not identical because scientific concepts can also be empirical; for example, the periodic system in chemistry can be empirically presented.

Theoretical knowledge that has become everyday knowledge can be found, for example, among young people who have both the electronic skill and the knowledge to build their own music equipment, or the mechanical skills and knowledge needed to repair their motorcycles, or the knowledge of both the composition and the history of their preferred type of music. Unfortunately, it is very difficult to find school knowledge that has become everyday theoretical knowledge and can be used as a tool for reflection and skilled activities. Most school knowledge is empirical knowledge, which means knowledge in the form of facts or text knowledge, and as such it never becomes very useful in the pupils' everyday life, either during their school years or later.

The school's task should be to teach children scientific concepts in a theoretical way by applying a theoretical epistemological procedure. Children's everyday concepts are thereby extended to include scientific theoretical concepts. If scientific concepts are learned as empirical concepts, children will have difficulty in relating what they learn at school to the surrounding environment. Only by learning concepts theoretically can this development take place. As mentioned earlier, teaching should create zones of proximal development through involving children in new kinds of activity. By relating scientific concepts to everyday concepts, teaching provides children with new skills and possibilities for action.

The concept of the zone of proximal development can be used to guide children

from the learned and understood scientific concepts to the spontaneously applied
everyday concepts through a method of teaching I have called a *double move*.

The double move in teaching

Development of a theoretical basis requires that teachers, when planning instruction, have a profound knowledge of the concepts and general laws of the subject.
This knowledge guides planning of the different steps of instruction. The teacher's
planning must advance from the general laws to the surrounding reality in all its
complexity. In order to explain these laws the teacher must choose concrete examples that demonstrate the general concepts and laws in the most transparent form.

Stage I: The relation between nature and animal life, and animals' adaptation
                    to a given/specific/particular nature

Stage II: The adaptation of different animal species to the specific nature which
                    is characteristic of a particular biotope (the relation between genetic
                    and functional inheritance)

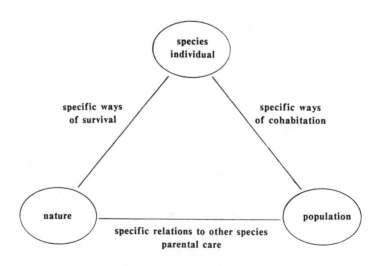

Stage III: The development of a species is determined by changes in the nature and by changes in the estate of the offspring

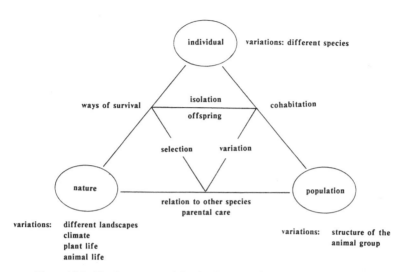

Figure 15.2. The three stages of the development of the germ-cell model (these stages are also present in the teaching process)

Whereas the teacher's planning must advance from the general to the concrete, the children's learning must develop from preconceived actions to symbolization of the knowledge they obtain through their research, finally resulting in a linguistic formulation of relations. Initial activities must be oriented toward concrete exploration. In our teaching experiment such activities include exploratory analysis of objects, museum visits, and films. In the next step, the children must be able to symbolize the relations they perceive through their research activity. In our experiment, drawings and modeling of the initial findings were used to this end. Finally, the children must be able to formulate the relations they have perceived.

Thus there is a double move in instruction: The teacher must guide instruction on the basis of general laws, whereas the children must occupy themselves with these general laws in the clearest possible form through the investigation of their manifestations. This is why practical research activities with objects, films, and museum visits are such an important part of instruction, especially during the early periods.

The basis for instruction is the division of the learning activity into three different types of actions: (1) delineation of the problem; (2) problem solution and problem construction, which implies acquisition of capacities; and (3) evaluation and control. Davydov (1982) has described six steps in the learning activity, which can be seen as differentiating the phases in learning activity based on the use of models as learning tools. These steps are produced through the different structures of the in-

Vygotsky's theory of knowledge: Davydov's theory of knowledge:

The conceptual world of the child   The conceptual world of society

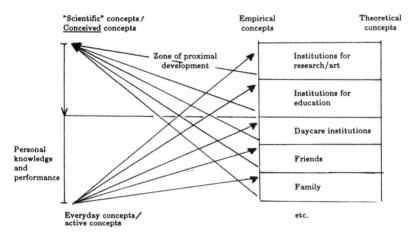

Figure 15.3. The zone of proximal development, illustrated as the relation between empirical and theoretical knowledge, according to Davydov's and Vygotsky's theories of everyday and scientific concepts

structional tasks. The steps are: (1) change or production of a problem so that the general relations are clearly seen, (2) modeling of these relations, (3) transformation of the model relations so that the connection is clear, (4) creation of new problems and tasks from the model, (5) control of one's own learning actions, and (6) evaluation of the model's sphere of application. As will be shown, these steps have influenced the planning of instruction in our experiment.

Children's learning activities may be characterized as guided investigations. Through working with the central conceptual relations and procedures that characterize a subject area, the children acquire the scientific concepts of the subject. The children acquire the concepts as active concepts when they have completed all six instructional steps, that is, when they are able to relate themselves to their own learning activity as well as to the sphere of application of the concepts they have worked with. The scientific concepts will have become everyday concepts, allowing the children to orient themselves theoretically to the surrounding world.

The teaching experiment

The following teaching experiment is based on the idea of using germ-cell models as tools in instruction and the idea of the double move in instruction, which implies that the instruction goes from specific concrete examples and the children's daily-life conceptions to general conceptualizing and modeling of the phenomena studied.

The model should then become a research tool for the children, which can be used for analyzing and explaining the concrete world's phenomena in all their variation and complexity; in other words, the modeled concept relation should be a tool for the child in his or her daily life and thereby become usable and changeable as daily-life concepts.

As the content of teaching we chose social science subjects taught from third to fifth grade in the Danish elementary schools. The subjects include biology, history, and geography. As problem areas we chose "the evolution of species," "the origin of man," and "the historical change of societies" to integrate and relate the three subjects and emphasize their developmental aspect and the relations between the development of nature and society. The results of the teaching experiment presented here deal only with the first year of teaching the evolution of species. The next phase of the teaching experiment is still in progress.

The concepts forming the basis for instruction are demonstrated in the germ-cell model shown in Figure 15.2. The content of instruction included the following subthemes:

Accounts of creation
Prehistoric nature, animal life
Research method: the use of fossils and analogies
Visit to the Department of Denmark's Prehistory at the Natural History Museum
Evolution of species
Arctic nature, animal life
Desert nature, animal life
Desert hare, polar hare
Moving the polar hare to the Faroe Islands
Moving chimpanzees to Estonia
Arctic nature, animal life
Project work: Africa's animals
Wolves: summer and winter living conditions
Evolution from wolf to dog
Evolution of the horse
The catastrophe: the extinction of the saurians

The procedure for attaining theoretical concepts

One approach was based on the "scientific work" procedure described by Aidarova (1982) and also found in Kurt Lewin's work (1946) (see Figure 15.4).

The children were told to work exploratively like scientists. A goal-result board was used to record the steps attained in this exploration. Each teaching period started with a summary of the exploration related to the general problem area of research: the evolution of animals and the origin of humans. Furthermore, the teaching was built around the children's analysis of the concrete themes according to the questions in the scientific work procedure. For instance, in exploring the life of the polar bear, we wanted to address the following issues: What do we know and what do we not know about the polar bear's survival in Greenland? How can we model what we know, and how are we going to explore what we do not know? We developed

Scientific Work

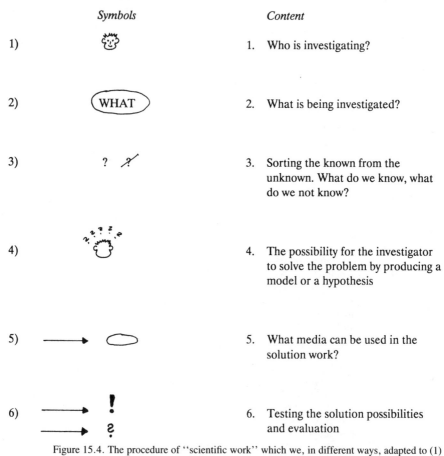

	Symbols		Content
1)		1.	Who is investigating?
2)	WHAT	2.	What is being investigated?
3)	?	3.	Sorting the known from the unknown. What do we know, what do we not know?
4)		4.	The possibility for the investigator to solve the problem by producing a model or a hypothesis
5)		5.	What media can be used in the solution work?
6)		6.	Testing the solution possibilities and evaluation

Figure 15.4. The procedure of "scientific work" which we, in different ways, adapted to (1) keep track on the goal-result board of the steps in exploring the main problem "evolution of animals," and (2) analyze subproblems, which were steps in exploring the main problem

specific questions based on the relations depicted in the germ-cell model at the start of this theme and by studying books and films about polar bear life. Through class discussions, we evaluated the germ-cell model and considered how it fit with our knowledge; we also analyzed what our knowledge so far about the polar bear could tell us about why some animals survive, why some animals die, and why some change into new species.

Research method

The teaching experiment is a concretization of Vygotsky's statement that the formative genetic method is a necessary research method for investigating the formulation and development of the conscious aspects of humans' relation to the world. The experiment included the total planning of instruction in the social science subjects during a 3-year period.

The teaching experiment was characterized by the following procedures:

1. Developing a general plan for the entire school year
2. Continuous and detailed planning of each lesson (3 hours), based upon the observation protocol from the previous lesson. This planning was formulated as a written sequence worked out in cooperation between the teacher and the researcher. It contained:
   a. the goal of instruction
   b. the concept in the instruction
   c. teaching materials used
   d. plans for teacher activities
   e. plans for pupil activities

The teaching of the theme "the evolution of species" required 32 periods of planned instruction over a 9-month period. The teaching process was documented through participant observations (cf. Hedegaard, 1987) and through the collection of pupils' written tasks.

The planning of instruction was based on the following six primary principles:

First, each child must be taken into consideration when planning for the class as a collective. On the face of it, it appears contradictory to ensure the development of the individual pupil as well as to work with the class as a whole. However, it is my impression that no contradiction exists; children's development takes place through their relation to the class and to the groups in the class. Thus we used group solving processes to develop the children's intellectual processes, instead of isolating each child to work on tasks in a trial-and-error fashion. We attempted several times to produce a division of work in which the children would work on a number of different tasks in a group with a shared motive for the entire activity. This activity, in principle, is intended to develop a zone of proximal development for the class as a whole, where each child acquires personal knowledge through the activities shared between the teacher and the children and among the children themselves.

Second, the general content of the teaching must be related to the children's experiences. Class dialogue and children's drawings were the media through which children's experiences with the different subthemes were expressed in the class situation. Also, through the activity associated with these media their experiences were extended. The teaching was planned so that the children were active in investigating the themes of instruction. It was not intended, however, that the children's investigations would result in blind trial and error or in an activity they had already mastered. We must emphasize that the teacher planned and gave direction to the activities to a certain extent but did not determine the concrete form of the activity or the results.

Third, the content of instruction must be clearly related as a whole to the general themes "the evolution of species" and the "origin of humans." The integration of the subjects into a whole was achieved through consistent emphasis on the themes that guided the teaching through the 3-year period. Each teaching period began with a class dialogue focused on the goal-result board. This goal-result board provided a permanent instrument for helping the children to record their progress in researching the evolution of species and the origin of man. The board was revised and expanded by the teacher when necessary through class dialogue and the use of the model.

Fourth, motivation and interest in the content of teaching must be developed in the children. In order to motivate their interest in the subjects, we utilized three main techniques. We took advantage of their interest in the big questions of life. Where do we come from? Where does the universe stop? Have the animals always looked like they do today? Have there always been human beings? How were humans created? We tried to maintain their interest through activities involving them in the procedure or researching the problems. Finally, in order to develop the children's motivation, we explored the following contrasts, problems, and conflicts:

1. The conflicting explanations for and descriptions of the origin and development of animals and humans
2. The contrast between the animals in the Kalahari Desert (Africa) and the animals in Greenland, and the problems that would arise if the animals' habitats were exchanged
3. The contrast between animal life in Denmark and animal life in Greenland and the Kalahari Desert
4. The problem of survival that arose when the polar hare was moved to the Faroe Islands
5. The problems that would occur if reptiles were moved from the desert to Greenland
6. The problems that occurred when a group of chimpanzees were moved to an island in Estonia
7. The contrast in the wolf's living conditions between winter and summer and the problems that would occur if either season disappeared.

Fifth, the children's capacities for modeling knowledge must be developed so that the models can become tools for analyzing the diversity of problems encountered in the world they live in. The tasks given to the children were intended to guide them through the central concepts of the subjects. These concepts were integrated in a germ-cell model, which was to function, first, as an external tool for the children's analyses of the relations between animal and nature and, second, as a psychic tool for the children's understanding of these relations in all their complexity. The model becomes a psychic tool when a child can use it for analyzing, solving and creating new problems (when Steps 3 and 4 in the structure of learning activity are acquired).

Sixth, knowledge must be integrated with performance in the children's acquisition of the subjects biology, history, and geography. The integration of knowledge and performance was made possible through the children's modeling of their knowledge and, later, their use of this model for analyzing and producing questions. This integration was based on the six steps in learning activity described earlier. These steps move from actions connected to the general aspects of reality to actions connected to the concrete complexity of reality. At the same time, an opposite movement occurs in the children's learning, from exploration based on action activities to symbolizing and, finally, describing the concept relation explored (see Figure 15.5).

Analysis and results

Our qualitative analysis is based on the observation protocols and on the children's task solutions throughout the year. The focus of the analysis of the teaching activity will be the problems encountered in the teaching process. In the learning activity, the focus will be on the concept learning of the children and the solution of motivational problems.

Problems in the teaching activity

Two different types of problems were identified in our analysis. The first is connected to the content of the teaching and concerns the children's problems with understanding the concepts introduced in the teaching process. These problems emerged as important because they lead to insights into the nature of obstacles encountered by children in the learning activity and the strategies utilized for overcoming them. The teacher who seeks to deal with this type of problem develops teaching which, in our opinion, reaches into the zone of proximal development.

An example is the problem some children had in understanding the time dimension and in separating animals' adaptation from animals' development. There were also problems with categories in the model connected to the introduction and proper placement of new dimensions; for instance, when the categories *food seeking, parental care, cohabitation* were introduced the children did not quite know how to use them, and when the concept of desert was introduced they did not know what desert conditions were. The children had no problems, however, in accepting modeling or in modeling their knowledge. The problems concerning time and evolution are, then, the central problems related to the children's acquisition of content. Very few of the problems were related to using the model.

The second type of problem is connected with the planning and realization of the teaching and concerns the problems that arise when instruction is not at an appropriate level. Some examples are the problems we had in achieving a balance between providing an overview of the general problem during each period and becoming too repetitive. In addition, we had to choose between sticking to the goals of the class and following up on the children's comments. Most importantly, we found that it was extremely difficult to capitalize on the children's knowledge of heredity. They were not able to relate what they know about heredity in their family relations with their investigation of heredity of animals.

The problems have shown us that we must reject the common assumption that concretization will facilitate children's understanding of problems. On the contrary, the result is often confusion for the children. Features such as self-centeredness and concretization are commonly used to explain children's performance because it is

CONTENT	LEARNING ACTIVITIES
Animals' historic development (the origin of man)	Formulation of the aim via conflict
Parallelization to the researcher's work. Exploration as a method.	Method formulation
Development – historical time The time concept The nature concept	Analyses of texts, pictures, films, museum visits

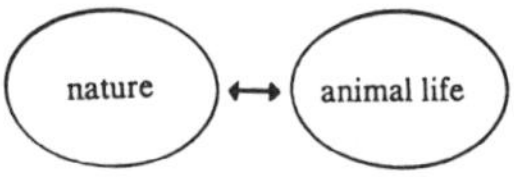

nature ←→ animal life   **Formulation of what we know**

Why some animal species died out	Formulation of what we don't know

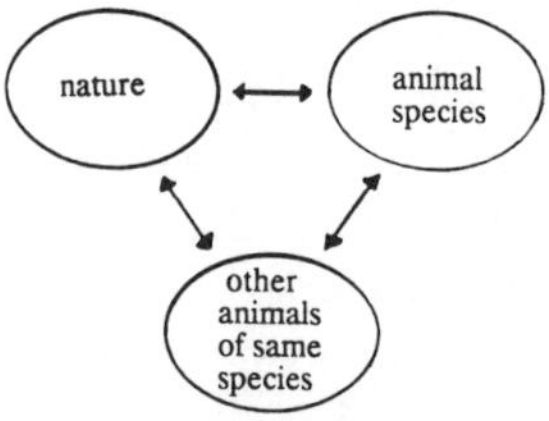

nature ←→ animal species → other animals of same species

Different forms of adaptation: survival via food seeking, animal relations, parental care, defence against enemies.

Model formulation and application of the model

The mutual relations among food seeking, cohabitation, parental care, defence against enemies.

Hypothesis-formulation

Transformation of the model

Limits of functional adaptation

Variation among members of a species
Selection

Question formulation via application of the model

The evolution of new species

Control of explanation in relation to the initial problem

Figure 15.5. Plan for integrating the two aspects of knowledge and performance in the whole-teaching experiment

generally assumed that children's thoughts are concrete and self-centered. Our results indicate that the children's dialogues and use of models and task solutions contradict this widely held assumption. Moreover, children did have problems understanding when they were allowed to be self-centered and were asked to use themselves and their families as examples in the lessons on heredity.

Analysis of children's learning

We can obtain knowledge about the children's concept learning through analyses of the observation protocols. Furthermore, the children's learning can be checked by analyzing their written task solutions.

One type of analysis focused on the children's learning actions as they acquired the conceptual relations of the germ-cell model. For example, we identified 12 types of learning actions during students' work with the evolution-of-animals theme. These actions are grouped under three headings: delineation of the problem, acquisition of capacities, and evaluation. They occurred in the following order:

Delineation of the problem
1. The children's comments are relevant to the themes of teaching.
2. The children precede the process of teaching in their comments.
3. The children keep each other and the teacher to the topic.
4. The children pose questions regarding the *why* of a phenomenon.

Acquisition of capacities in model use
5. The children look for relations instead of categorial solutions.
6. The children work with modeling of their knowledge.
7. The children want reasons for the relations in the model.
8. The children accept that the model changes and that they contribute to the changes.
9. The children's imagination and fantasy production increase.
10. The children produce tasks themselves.

Evaluation
11. The children become critical and evaluative of their own performances and capacities.
12. The children become critical and evaluate the content of teaching.

When the children's task solutions are analyzed and evaluated, it is important to remember that these tasks have been assigned not as part of the research procedure or as tests but as educational devices in the teaching process. The two most informative series of tasks were given in the middle of the teaching period just before and immediately after Christmas (December 12 and January 9). The tasks in these two series included the following:

First series
What do we know about the evolution of animals?
What do we not know?
What is important for the survival of a species?
What do we mean when we speak of nature?
What do we know about the origin of man?
Draw a model for the polar hare.
Draw a model for the desert hare.

Second series
Draw a model for the polar bear.
Draw a model that is valid for all animals.
Draw a model for the sperm whale.
When we write nature in the model, what does that mean?
What does the model show as important for the survival of species?
Why can't a single member of a species survive without other members of the same
      species?

A conclusion from our observations is that the children did not solve the tasks connected to the procedure (the questions about what they know and do not know) as well as the tasks connected to the model. All the children could draw the models for the animals, and they could also draw the general model. Of 16 children, 10 could draw a model of the sperm whale, which had not been addressed in the teaching. From the tasks given immediately prior to completion of the theme, it was quite clear that the children understood that changes in nature mean change for the reproduction and survival of a species and that changes in species are always reflected in their offspring (see Figure 15.6).

Development of motivation

The results from the first year of the teaching experiment demonstrate a development in the ways in which the children related to the theme and subthemes in the evolution of species. A qualitative change occurred in their interest in the content of the teaching. These changes in interest can be characterized sequentially as follows:

1. Interest in the problem formulation and the research method
2. Interest in the relationship between nature and animals in relation to the specific living conditions of the animals introduced in the teaching
3. Loss of interest in specific animals when they became too familiar
4. Interest in formulating general models for the adaptation of animals to their living conditions
5. Interest in sticking to the general problem formulation in their research
6. Interest in influencing the process and content of instruction as related to problem formulation
7. Critical evaluation of the content of teaching
8. Desire to finish the evolution-of-animals theme and to start something new

These changes in interest can be seen as a developmental shift in the children's motivation, moving from interest in concrete material to interest in developing principles that can be applied to new concrete material. The development of motivation has its parallel in the development of concepts, delineation of the problem, model formulation/model use, and evaluation. And both the structure in concept development and development of motivation can be seen as derived from the steps of instruction (cf. Figure 15.5).

This result supports the conceptions in activity theory (Hedegaard, 1989; Leontiev, 1978) that motives and concepts are dialectically related. The concepts are the content and specify the object of the motives at the same time that the motives create the images and the objectives of concept learning.

Conclusion

The double move in teaching

Teaching that promotes children's theoretical concept learning must occur on a basis of profound teacher knowledge of the central concepts of the subject area. Knowledge of the general laws can guide the planning of the steps through which instruction must proceed. The teacher must guide the learning from student involvement with general laws in the clearest possible form. Clearly, practical activities are an important part of teaching; however, these activities must, as mentioned, contain the general laws in their most transparent form. The conclusion from the teaching experiment based on this principle of the double move in teaching can be summarized as follows:

1. Teaching can be based on the central concepts of evolution whereby it integrates the different subthemes into an exploration of the general problem *the evolution of animals*.
2. Furthermore, the children learn to integrate their knowledge into a general model, a germ-cell model, and to use this model on new and unknown animals. We found that the children had very few problems in modeling their knowledge; it was much more troublesome for the teacher and the researcher to do this.
3. The teaching resulted in qualitative changes in the children's capacities and interest in solving problems connected to the theme of the evolution of animals.

The zone of proximal development

To work with the zone of proximal development in classroom teaching implies that the teacher is aware of the developmental stages of the children and is able to plan for qualitative changes in the teaching toward a certain goal. Although each child is unique, children obviously share common traits with other children. Being of the same tradition, children in the same class have a lot of knowledge and skills in common. Instruction can build upon these common features if it takes into account that the children vary in their speed and form of learning. In this way, we have worked with the zone of proximal development as a relation between the planned instructional steps and the steps of the children's learning/acquisition process.

Elkonin (1971) pointed out that the stages in children's development are determined by the societal historical development. The conception of childhood as differentiated into separate life periods and as a quite large part of human life is only a couple of hundred years old. Before that, children were taught to behave like adults; Ariès (1982) describes how, in the 18th century, children behaved like adults at the age of 4.

The fact that children have common traditions, prior to school and at school, in

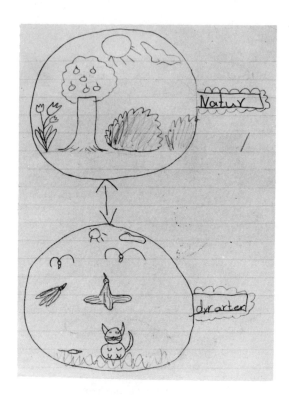

A

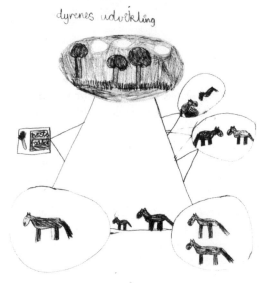

B

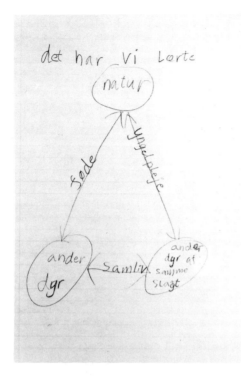

C

Figure 15.6. Examples of the children's models: *A* is a pupil's generalization in symbol form of the relation between nature and animal species. In *B,* the generalization is differentiated and the relation of an animal to other animals of the same species is represented; the model symbolizes the relations for the horse. *C* is a pupil's representation of the relations in general form for animal species.

the form of shared knowledge and procedures for activities enables them to communicate and interact in shared concrete activities. The content and form of this interaction and communication should then be developed further in school.

A child is unique and individual, but children's individualities have common features. If these features are not developed, we tend to regard the child as deviant and offer special instruction. It should not be the function of school pedagogy to offer special instruction to each child in a class. Instead, instruction must be based on development of common knowledge and skills.

Consequently, the zone of proximal development must be used as a tool for class instruction. In our teaching experiment, we saw that it is actually possible to make a class function actively as a whole through class dialogue, group work, and task solutions. The teaching experiment differed from traditional instruction in that the children were constantly and deliberately forced to act. The children's research activity was central in these guided actions, which gradually led the children to critical evaluations of the concepts. We can conclude, therefore, that we have succeeded in building a common basis for the children in the class from which future teaching can be developed.

We are quite certain that the teaching has built a common foundation in the children; however, we also recognize that some children achieved a more differentiated content in their concepts than other children. For the fast learners, our teaching experiment neither destroyed their interest nor inhibited their development of motivation. For the slow learners, our instruction has encouraged insight into and capacities for understanding the theme related to the evolution of animals.

References

Aidarova, L. (1982). *Child development and education*. Moscow: Progress.
Ariès, P. (1982). *Barndommens historie* [The history of childhood]. Copenhagen: Nyt Nordisk Forlag.
Davydov, V. V. (1977). *Arten der Verallgemeinerung im Unterricht* [The art of generalizing instruction]. Berlin: Volk & Wissen.
Davydov, V. V. (1982). Ausbildung der Lerntätigkeit [Development of learning activity]. In V. V. Davydov, J. Lompscher, & A. K. Markova (Eds.), *Ausbildung der Lerntätigkeit bei Schülern* (pp. 14–27). Berlin: Volk & Wissen.
Davydov, V. V., & Radzikhovskii, L. A. (1985). Intellectual origins of Vygotsky's semiotic analysis. In J. W. Wertsch (Ed.), *Culture, communication, and cognition* (pp. 35–65). Cambridge: Cambridge University Press.
Elkonin, D. B. (1971). Toward the problem of stages in the mental development of the child. *Soviet Psychology, 10,* 538–653.
Elkonin, D. B. (1980). *Psychologie des Spiels* [The psychology of play]. Berlin: Volk & Wissen.
Engeström, Y. (1986). The zone of proximal development as the basic category of educational psychology. *Quarterly Newsletter of the Laboratory of Comparative Human Cognition, 8,* 23–42.
Engeström, Y., & Hedegaard, M. (1986). Teaching theoretical thinking in elementary School. In E. Bol, J. P. P. Haenen, & M. A. Wolters (Eds.), *Education for cognitive development* (pp. 170–193). Proceedings of the Third International Symposium on Activity Theory. Den Haag: SVO/SOO.
Gould, S. (1977). *Ever since Darwin*. London: Penguin.
Griffin, P., & Cole, M. (1984). Current activity for the future: The Zo-ped. In B. Rogoff & J. V. Wertsch (Eds.), *Children's learning in the "zone of proximal development"* (pp. 45–63). New Directions for Child Development, No. 23. San Francisco: Jossey-Bass.
Hedegaard, M. (1987). Methodology in evaluative research on teaching and learning. In F. J. Zuuren, F. J. Wertz, & B. Mook (Eds.), *Advances in qualitative psychology* (pp. 53–78). Sweetz North America INC/Berwyn.
Hedegaard, M. (1989). Motivational development in schoolchildren. *Multidisciplinary Newsletter for Activity Theory, 1,* 30–38.
Juul Jensen, U. (1986). *Practice and progress: A theory for the modern healthcare systems*. Oxford: Blackwell Scientific Publications.
Leontiev, A. N. (1978). *Activity, consciousness, and personality*. Englewood Cliffs, NJ: Prentice-Hall.
Leontiev, A. N. (1981). *Problems in development of mind*. Moscow: Progress.
Leontiev, A. N. (1985). Einleitung: Der Schaffensweg Wygotskis [Introduction: Vygotsky's Works]. In L. S. Wygotsky, *Ausgewählte Schriften I* [Selected writings, Vol. 1]. Cologne: Pahl-Rugenstein.
Lewin, K. (1946). Behavior and development as a function of the total situation. In L. Carmichael (Ed.), *Manual of child psychology* (pp. 918–983). New York: Wiley.
Lompscher, J. (1980). Ausbildung der Lerntätigkeit durch Aufsteigen vom Abstrakten zum Konkreten [Development of learning activity through advancing from the abstract to the concrete]. In A. Kossakowski (Ed.), *Psychologie im Sozialismus* [Psychology in socialism]. Berlin: VEB Deutscher Verlag der Wissenschaften.

Lompscher, J. (1982). Analyse und Gestaltung von Lernanforderungen [Analysis and form of learning requirements]. In V. V. Davydov, J. Lompscher, & A. Markova (Eds.), *Ausbildung der Lerntätigkeit bei Schülern* [Development of learning activity in school children] (pp. 36–50). Berlin: Volk & Wissen.

Lompscher, J. (1984). Problems and results of experimental research on the formation of theoretical thinking through instruction. In M. Hedegaard, P. Hakkarainen, & Y. Engeström (Eds.), *Learning and teaching on a scientific basis* (pp. 293–357). Aarhus: Aarhus University.

Lompscher, J. (Ed.) (1985). *Persönlichkeitsentwicklung in der Lerntätigkeit* [Personality development through learning activity]. Berlin: Volk & Wissen.

Markova, A. K. (1982). Der ausbildende Experiment in der psychologischen Erforschung der Lerntätigkeit [The developmental experiment in psychological research of learning activity]. In V. V. Davydov, J. Lompscher, & A. Markova (Eds.), *Ausbildung der Lerntätigkeit bei Schülern* [Development of learning activity in school children] (pp. 28–35). Berlin: Volk & Wissen.

Mayr, E. (1976). *Evolution and the diversity of life*. Cambridge, MA: Harvard University Press.

Mayr, E. (1980). Some thoughts on the history of the evolutionary synthesis. In E. Mayr & W. B. Provine, *The evolutionary synthesis* (pp. 1–48). Cambridge, MA: Harvard University Press.

Rogoff, B., & Wertsch, J. V. (Eds.) (1984). *Children's learning in the "zone of proximal development."* New Directions for Child Development, No. 23. San Francisco: Jossey-Bass.

Schneider, P., Hyland, J., & Gallimore, R. (1985). The zone of proximal development in eighth grade social studies. *Quarterly Newsletter of the Laboratory of Comparative Human Cognition, 7,* 113–119.

Scribner, S. (1985). Vygotsky's uses of history. In J. V. Wertsch (Ed.), *Culture, communication, and cognition* (pp. 119–145). Cambridge: Cambridge University Press.

Simpson, G. G. (1962). *The major features of evolution*. New York: Columbia University Press.

Vygotsky, L. S. (1978). *Mind in society*. Cambridge, MA: Harvard University Press.

Vygotsky, L. S. (1982). *Om barnets psykiske udvikling* [On the child's psychic development]. Copenhagen: Nyt Nordisk.

Vygotsky, L. S. (1985–1987). *Ausgewählte Schriften, I & II* [Selected writings, Vols. 1 & 2]. Cologne: Pahl-Rugenstein.

Wertsch, J. W. (1984). The zone of proximal development. In B. Rogoff & J. V. Wertsch (Eds.), *Children's learning in the "zone of proximal development."* New Directions for Child Development, No. 23. San Francisco: Jossey-Bass.

Wertsch, J. W. (1985). *The social formation of mind: A Vygotskian approach* (pp. 7–18). Cambridge, MA: Harvard University Press.

16 Detecting and defining science problems: A study of video-mediated lessons

Laura M. W. Martin

At five years old, mortals are not prepared to be citizens of the world, to be stimulated by abstract nouns, to soar above preference into impartiality; and that prejudice in favour of milk with which we blindly begin, is a type of the way body and soul must get nourished at least for a time. The best introduction to astronomy is to think of the nightly heavens as a little lot of stars belonging to one's own homestead.

> George Eliot, *Daniel Deronda*

According to many educators, the core concern of teaching elementary science is maintaining children's interest in how the world works (Hawkins, 1983; National Science Teachers Association, 1982; Rowe, 1978). When they are curious, children are willing to go below the surface appearance of events and learn about the less self-evident properties of matter. It is hoped that, as they explore deeper explanations and relationships, children learn analytic and critical skills to apply creatively to novel events they encounter later, in school and out.

Encouraging such creative thinking among students is another goal of science educators. Related to this concern is the problem of motivating learning or discovery of scientific concepts when the school environment functionally does not demand a higher level of analysis and prediction (Horton, 1967), except for the purpose of getting a passing grade. Teachers have attempted to satisfy these demands of science teaching, for example, by defining science problems or tasks that are related to children's experiences in interesting ways, yet require higher levels of understanding and analysis for completion.

In the study reported here, classroom discussions about identifying and defining science problems that centered around a videotape stimulus were examined to get a sense of the ways in which elementary teachers might organize the conjunction of children's untutored experiences with more restricted or definable problem domains. We also wanted to know how that conjunction may have served to define what a problem is and what a solution is at a new level from the students' points of

This work was conducted as part of the Bank Street College Mathematics, Science, and Technology Teacher Education Project (NSF No. TE18319705). Roseanne Flores, Mary McGinnis, and Maxine Shirley helped collect and code the data. Thanks go to the teachers and students who allowed us into their classrooms and to Seth Chaiklin, Jan Hawkins, and Sol Magzamen for their comments on the manuscript.

view (see Engeström, 1987). The results illustrate a set of possibilities for pairing what Vygotsky (1987) regarded as systematic thinking with the "everyday."

In particular, we examine what happens to children's questions and observations about the world around them, within the structured setting of a science lesson. The lessons are unique in that they center on a dramatic video science story, but they are not unusual in that the elements of intuition (the familiar or everyday) and consciously organized systematicity are present, as they often are in science classes. As we shall see, the teacher's role in discussion is the critical link between the information presented and the children's responses to it. From our observations, we can imagine what happens to children's motivation to tackle the world with mental tools.

Children's everyday questions

Children, of course, ask dozens of questions about their world. They are constantly conjecturing and formulating hypotheses. Parents who were interviewed reported that a wide variety of private experimenting routinely goes on in kitchens, bathrooms, and back yards, where their children mix and build, probe and sample, in an effort to understand the world around them. "How do animals live in the park?" "Why when you hold your finger does it turn red?" "Where does glass come from?" These are a few of the questions some 8-year-olds we know generated recently on a questionnaire.

Children, who are good inductive thinkers (Carey, 1985), acquire or infer information by asking adults, by consulting various reference materials, and by developing theories together. Somewhere along the way, however, children tend to stop asking "how come" questions in class. Simultaneously, children's interest in school science begins to decline sometime around sixth grade and escalates downward thereafter (National Science Foundation, 1987).

If given the opportunity, children show that they still ask themselves questions even if they don't do so during school. When we asked sixth-graders to keep records of what they wondered about (Martin, Chang, & Flores, 1988), a myriad of questions emerged touching on a wide range of topics, disciplines, and concerns: "I wonder how clouds form shapes." "I wonder if animals know anything about humans." "Why do people kill themselves?" "Why can't scientists find a cure for AIDS?" "Why was writing invented?"

The everyday and the scientific

Educators have recommended several ways to stimulate or maintain students' questioning in classrooms. One is for the teacher to produce or point out discrepant events by confronting children's expectations of phenomena directly. Another is to emphasize more generally children's experiences as the basis for the science inquiry. These approaches may place special burdens on teachers, who may have to monitor children's particular understandings while they attempt to present science subject matter meaningfully and effect conceptual change (Neale, Smith, & Wier, 1987).

A related trend in instruction is to present science (and mathematics) principles embedded in problems, to be discovered, construed, or solved. This approach provides children with linguistic and visual cues that are likely to enrich the problem-solving process. For example, in the present study the videotaped science drama used was explicitly designed to capture children's interest; to show the working context of a science investigation; and to present opportunities for the teachers to build hands-on activities, by raising questions in the children's minds (Martin, Hawkins, Gibbon, & McCarthy, 1988). Problem solving under such instructional conditions may be practiced with respect to elements more characteristic of non-school, or everyday, environments, for example, with functional outcomes for the solutions devised. If the problem setting is designed well, these activities can be highly stimulating, and the application of formal knowledge is likely to be encouraged and, it is hoped, transferred to new situations.

The motivational issue in science problem solving is having school children want to elaborate upon their solutions when they are dealing with both new and familiar events; that is, to think systematically about particular situations for which there was previously an unreflective (although pressing) set of responses. An experience must be planned by the teacher that gives rise to a question, one posed by the children and leading to a new level of conceptualization – let us hope, a reflective one. Vygotsky (1987) distinguishes between everyday and scientific concepts.[1] For him, scientific thinking involved the conscious manipulation of relations among objects. For the researcher in schools, this entails thinking about what becomes defined as a problem realm for students as they interact with authoritative sources (Goodnow, 1987).

To elaborate further on this issue: apprehending the everyday as opposed to the scientific, though equally motivated by a desire to make the world predictable (Horton, 1967), may involve different thinking strategies. The difference between the two is not merely quantitative, such as a change in the number and depth of questions one can ask in two domains, but involves a qualitatively different kind of question. In his studies of development, Vygotsky (1987) observed that understandings based on empirical comparisons were, for children, less general than understandings based on abstract notions about two sets of objects.

In schools, systematicity of thinking rests on an explicitly verbal though abstract relational structure. Reflectivity, on the other hand, which is both a characteristic and a precursor of "scientific" thought, must be built upon concrete experience as well as on abstract notions originating in the scientific community. But instruction in this kind of thought within the present school system has been problematic. Further, the process of learning systematicity and learning what is to be considered "systematic" according to the culture involves socialization of a particular kind (Goodnow, 1987). Like all development of "higher psychological functions" (Vygotsky, 1978), it involves a selection process in which the social transactions between individuals, in this case teacher and students, will be transformed into inner thought processes by each. But, in addition, it involves the particular lesson of approaching the everyday world as a kind of problem text. This approach is value-laden in that only certain practices or problem realms are defined as legitimate (Goodnow, 1987). For instance, in the lessons described herein, the affective side of science problems was not marked as a valid topic for discussion.

Following Vygotsky's (1987) observation that scientific concepts grow down to the concrete and spontaneous concepts grow up to the abstract, several educational questions arise concerning what happens to the everyday content of children's experience in school. Does it comprise latent systematicity that can be labeled, or does its systematicity merely result in "pseudoconcepts"? Does scientific thought transform the everyday? If "curiosity" arises first in conjunction with everyday phenomena, how can children's impelling questions about objects in the world be transferred and applied to an abstract body of knowledge? Finally, from a given shared or collective school activity, can children develop what Engeström (1987) calls "explosive knowledge," or individual creative thinking, within a domain? We wonder, too, about the role of teachers' own everyday thinking in the science lessons.

Video technology as a mediator of the everyday and scientific

In an effort to examine this socialization process which results in scientific thinking, we begin with a theory about the materials that may mediate between the cultural body of knowledge (interpreted through the teachers' framework) and the everyday experience of the children. In particular, we posit that children's growing sophistication about life can be linked to more formal knowledge systems through the use of audiovisual technology.

"Good technology," argues Christiansen (1987), "leaves room for interpretation." A technological tool can help generate creative mental activity because it can instantiate formally construed relationships that can then be acted upon by children in unique ways as they encounter it. Instances of this can be found in certain computer microworld environments, where children can manipulate elements of formal rule systems to discover their relationships and properties (Levin & Waugh, 1988).

For older children, who can more readily construct generalities and abstractions than younger primary school children, bridging the familiar and the unexpected may be powerfully accomplished through the use of audiovisual media (Gibbon, 1987). Links from the classroom to the great outdoors, exotic climes, and various remarkable people and phenomena can be introduced through film and video because older children are familiar with the formats of these media (Greenfield, 1984). In fact, in many ways, organizing lessons around the wider world of their experience seems to be more motivating to upper elementary students than dwelling exclusively on the more contained world of the here and now (Mitchell, 1963).

Video, as we have seen in work around the country (Martin, 1987), can be used as the basis for organizing science activities. Here, we were interested in how teachers incorporated material covered in the videotape into class discussions. We were curious to see how teachers chose to define "problems" involving science as an object of study: Did they tend to construct definitions from everyday or prepackaged instances?

Using visually informative examples as mediators for classroom activity is helpful for several reasons. One is the inherent power of images to communicate information. A graphic depiction of an event can set a context for questioning or experimentation in a compelling and age-appropriate way. Around the fourth grade, children become quite adultlike about the way they categorize the world (Carey, 1985) and about the questions they have. They can make reference to information extracted from complex visual images (Brown, 1986). Role models, too, can be presented more explicitly on film than in print. Characters, for instance, can be portrayed tackling problems and searching for solutions vividly yet in a focused way. Links can be made from this somewhat idealized version of the world to what children know from their own experience.

Developers of educational television assume that didactic content can be pleasantly and memorably conveyed when it is embedded in a gripping story. These assumptions have been supported by research on the structure of narrative. A well-formed story can assist in recall and comprehension of content (Mandler & Johnson, 1977; Salomon & Cohen, 1977); images are more helpful in comprehension of material than verbal or textual presentation of the same content (Levin & Lesgold, 1978); and, in conjunction with discussion (Greenfield, 1984), the processing of video narrative can lead children to greater comprehension than using print.

Children's sophistication with audiovisual media, particularly television, means that the information source can more readily become an object of analysis itself (see Díaz, 1984). We observed that video-viewing sessions in schools can lead to rather marked shifts in ordinary discourse patterns in the classes: Children show authority and critically discuss video content (Martin, 1987). This is important in the case of science literacy, where we would like to encourage children to question sources, analyze techniques of presenting information, and discuss the constraints of format on communicating information. Watching video is a basis for mental activity, because students already have considerable practice with it in nonschool settings.

Finally, video can be a powerful link between the everyday and the extraordinary because it offers teachers relevant examples of issues to refer to in class. Until now, teachers have not been asked to scan the environment for problems and solutions directly related to their students' experience. Theoretical and illustrative material has been most often guided by textbook examples and curriculum topics. If teachers have difficulty creating a context for their science programs or detecting problem configurations within their immediate environment, video sequences can vividly suggest, model, and motivate them. In some cases, it can even provide factual information when the teacher is uninformed.

Examining the socialization process: The interface of the everyday and the scientific

The mediating role of materials in educational activity has consequences for the development of thinking, according to Vygotsky (1978) and others (Newman, Griffin, & Cole, 1989; Scribner & Cole, 1981). Mental tasks are carried out by the learner based on interactions with materials provided in the culture. The interactions, however, are not determined by the materials; they arise from goals that are socially constructed. It is therefore important to look at particular situations involving the use of a medium to understand how it may influence learning.

In order to study the concomitant mediated processes of socialization and scientific concept acquisition that may have been promoted by the use of video technology, we needed to focus on what was marked as important during interactions in the discussion setting and on what is then transformed by children as their own.

The study of the interface of the everyday and the scientific in schools, as mediated by an audiovisual experience, entails the examination of four interrelated components of instruction. First, attention must be paid to group processes of information exchange. Vygotsky's notion of a zone of proximal development (1978), for instance, focuses importance on what children can accomplish in conjunction with adult guidance. Student–teacher interchanges are interesting to study because they provide clues to the structure of the child's concepts and to the goal of the adult's instruction. Although there are many methods of capturing elements of interindividual behavior, science educators have identified several forms of exchange that relate to the likelihood of children acquiring science concepts. One of these forms of exchange involves the types of questions asked by a teacher and the kinds of responses made by children (Rowe, 1978). Particular types of exchanges have been associated with different qualities of question asking by children.

Second, the nature of the collective experience that forms a basis for more systematic inquiry is important. One aspect of this that was of great interest here was how teachers' use of the television narrative could serve as a device for connecting the characters' problem-solving experiences to what the children know about their own experiences. Rather than look for overlap in the content of the children's and video characters' experience, we felt it would be important to watch for the ways in which teachers juxtaposed the examples of each and for how the points of view adopted by speakers changed, as indicators of the relative meshing of the teachers' and children's conceptual systems. Changes in viewpoint may also be indications that examples are being generalized or that principles are being tied to examples (Davydov, 1988).

Third, in addition to local-level analysis of dialogic exchange, the structure of an entire lesson's discussion is also critical to describe. The full sequence not only conveys the meaning of discourse in science class but permits us to see possible changes in meaning among the interlocutors. For instance, we need to look at what teachers, who are charged with the academic socialization of their students, admit as acceptable contributions to a discussion at different times, thereby selecting and shaping the children's patterns of communication and establishing the parameters of what constitutes systematic thought (Goodnow, 1987).

Fourth, the role of written symbols in the classroom interchange is important. As Vygotsky remarked, the verbal community provides common cultural mediators of individuals' perceptual experience in the written symbol. With its introduction, the means for reflection and application of systematicity is provided. Such schematic representations can indicate something of the nature of the scientific system being applied and of the meaning being derived.

Looking at these four elements can help us assess the ultimate interface of the everyday and scientific systems and perhaps allow us to infer the extent of internalization of the scientific.

The study

Background

Three teachers and their students in three elementary schools in the New York metropolitan area participated in the study. Each school served an ethnically mixed and predominantly working-class population. Carol, who had been a teacher for 6 years, taught fifth grade in Brooklyn; Scott, a 15-year veteran, taught fourth grade in a suburban Long Island school; and Charlie, in his fourth year of teaching, worked with a fifth grade in Manhattan.

Each teacher had participated in a staff development program in mathematics, science, and technology carried out by Bank Street College and supported by the National Science Foundation. A multimedia science and mathematics package, *The Voyage of the Mimi*,[2] served as a vehicle for conveying the training ideas and methods. The package includes a 13-episode video drama concerning scientists studying whales. The *Mimi* is their boat. The training consisted of one week of intensive workshops, demonstrations, and discussions at Bank Street in February 1985. Follow-up meetings and classroom visits during the rest of the year were conducted by project personnel and by district staff, who had also been trained.

During the year following their training, teachers continued to receive assistance if they needed it from their local staff developers and, to a lesser extent, from the project staff. The focus of this staff development project was on assisting teachers to organize science inquiry lessons with their classes, to integrate mathematics into the science curriculum, and to make use of both new and old technologies in conducting lessons. Carol and Scott had each taken a science methods course and at least one college-level science course. Charlie had taken neither.

Materials

The materials used in this study consisted of Episode 3 of *The Voyage of the Mimi* video drama, a 15-minute segment.

Episode 3 begins with the captain of the *Mimi* wondering if the knotmeter might be malfunctioning, as he believes that the boat is traveling at a rate faster than the speed indicated. One of the student crew members, Arthur, is feeling seasick. Ann, the oceanographer, exclaims below deck that her computer keeps crashing. Another student crew member, Rachel, who has had a lot of experience on boats, provokes the seasick teenager to vomit by offering him a peanut butter/banana/raisin/chocolate sauce sandwich. The captain, meanwhile, sets out to verify the speed of the boat. With the help of Rachel, he times how long the boat takes to travel past a piece of bread he has thrown into the water. Knowing the length of the boat from the bow to a dowel affixed to the railing and measuring the time with a stopwatch allows him to calculate the speed per second and then the knots. His calculations tell him they have been traveling at a faster rate than the knotmeter indicated. He then asks Ann for a check of the ocean depth, only to discover that the echo sounder, which measures signal return rates from the ocean floor, also seems to be misreading. Suspecting that something is wrong with the boat's electrical system, the captain must quickly check the water depth because of the danger of sailing onto shoals. He and Rachel use a lead line to find that they are indeed in shallow waters. The captain knows they have to change course. He orders the rest of the crew to lower the sails and organizes a check of the boat's location with Arthur, who is feeling better now. To do this, they use a radio direction finder that works on batteries, a compass, a map, a compass rose, and a parallel ruler. After they get their bearings, the captain orders the anchor dropped. He says that they must return to port the next day to fix the electrical problems and that the scientific expedition will have to be scrapped.

While the *Mimi* crew members are adjusting to their disappointment, Arthur decides to locate the electrical problem himself. He begins by checking the wiring and ends up at the fuse box, which is sending off sparks. He throws a switch to disconnect it and pinpoints the fault: A piece of copper tubing had been used to replace a fuse, and this, he surmises, has caused a short circuit somewhere. Using a voltmeter, Arthur locates the short in the electric winch. He and the captain disconnect the winch and replace the fuse, and the scientists are back in business.

Figure 16.1 diagrams the science-related events that occur during Episode 3 and indicates their chronological sequence. The lightbulb indicates the moment when the captain realizes that the instruments have been misreading and that there is an electrical problem. Three modes of utilizing evidence, formulating hypotheses, and resolving problems are exemplified in the video drama: inductive, causal, and deductive reasoning. Interpersonal problems also arise between characters and are resolved during the episode, but those are not discussed in the present chapter.

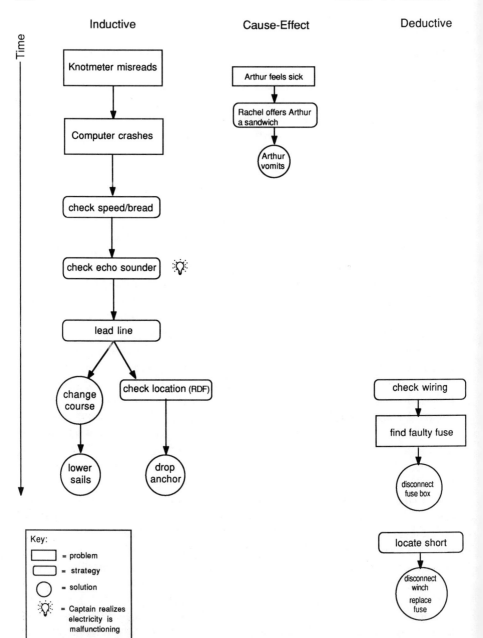

Figure 16.1. The structure of the Episode 3 narrative

Procedure

This study was conducted during the second semester that the teachers used the materials. The teachers had agreed to work the lesson we suggested into their regular classroom use of the *Mimi* materials. They each planned the experimental lesson alone, within the constraints provided by the researchers.

Teachers were asked to show Episode 3 of the *Mimi* drama and to conduct a discussion with their class afterward. We asked that class discussions be organized around the following questions:

1. What problems did the *Mimi* crew have to solve?
2. What did the crew have to know in order to solve their problems?
3. What problems have you encountered in your experience that may be like the ones you saw in the show?
4. What possible problems might be anticipated for the crew in the future?

Teachers discussed the purpose of the lesson with the researchers and were given written copies of the questions in advance of the day of the lesson. However, teachers were given little guidance in the actual orchestration of the lesson. They were asked to structure the lesson any way they wanted because our interest was in studying the possible configurations of use teachers might develop using video as a basis for a lesson about problem detection and problem solving.

A class discussion prior to presentation of the *Mimi* video episode and the postviewing discussion segment of the lessons lasted between 11 and 16 minutes. Lessons were videotaped by a researcher familiar to the teacher and the children but who did not otherwise participate in the lesson. Several weeks after they had conducted the ''experimental'' lessons, each teacher was invited to review his or her lesson tape with the researcher so that more could be learned about the teachers' decision making during the lesson. Two of the teachers were able to attend the sessions; the third canceled appointments a few times so we decided not to press the issue. These sessions were audiotaped.

The videotapes were transcribed and coded according to a scheme derived from Rowe (1978). Questions and statements were distinguished first as either inferential, descriptive, informative, expansive, identifying, or applicational. Inductive and deductive frames of talk were identified, as was the character of utterances, such as soliciting, probing, leading, reacting, or structuring (see Appendix). Changes in types of questions were noted since varying question types has been shown to be effective for children's learning in science discussions (Holdzkom & Lutz, 1984). The numbers of questions teachers asked requiring comprehension, application of knowledge, and analytic skills were also counted, as were the kinds of focusing devices teachers used to organize the discussion, because both of these are indicators of effective instructional practices (Holdzkom & Lutz, 1984).

Findings

The analysis of the lessons shows that local features of information exchange, that is, those relating to the scientific nature of remarks (inferential, descriptive, and so forth), were not immediately useful in capturing the differences between the lessons. Rather, we found that descriptions of the structure of the discussions proved more powerful for capturing distinctions between the lessons. When the properties of the video material were matched with the structures of the lessons and with the teachers' strategies for introducing information to the children, some inferences could be made about what the children were learning. Use of written symbols in class also reflected differences in the approaches of the teachers.

In order to examine the convergence of the everyday and scientific, we mapped the sequence of discussion topics concerning the video program and related the topics to other events in the teacher/student dialogue. In addition, we coded the problem solving depicted in the video drama, children's own personal problem solving, hypothetical problems and solutions as they arose in class discussion, and the sequence of teacher- and student-initiated topics.

Carol's lessons: In which the use of narrative causes a separation of the personal and the scientific. Carol's class met in the library – a classroom with bookshelves along the walls – to watch the videotape and have their discussion. The class began with Carol giving a brief introductory lesson in which she prompted the children to recall the characters in the story and the purpose of the scientific expedition. After the children viewed the episode, Carol began the discussion by asking the children to identify problems encountered by the *Mimi* crew. Figure 16.2 shows the sequence in which the problems were mentioned superimposed on the narrative structure of the videotape. The numbers represent the order in which the crew's dilemmas were discussed, so that the first problem mentioned was the knotmeter misreading; the second, the malfunctioning computer; and so forth. Broken lines indicate that a cluster of incidents, in this case the whole sequence of checking and rechecking the ship's instrumentation to determine its speed, was offered as a topic. Circled numbers were teacher-initiated topics; squares were child-initiated. Numbers with slashes indicate that Carol refused the bid for that topic of conversation. She did this by such statements as, "Not yet. You're ahead." In all, during the discussion of the crew's problems, Carol initiated the topic under discussion eight times and the children four.

Instead of remembering incidents chronologically, children instead seemed to remember salient visual events such as sparks coming out of the fuse box or the lights in the cabin going out when the circuits are broken. With two exceptions (the computer crashing and checking the speed of the boat with the bread), Carol directed the flow of discussion topics to match the narrative sequence.

Seasickness was not mentioned, nor were the solution steps taken by the crew. Instead, Carol separated the four original questions (see section on Procedure) into

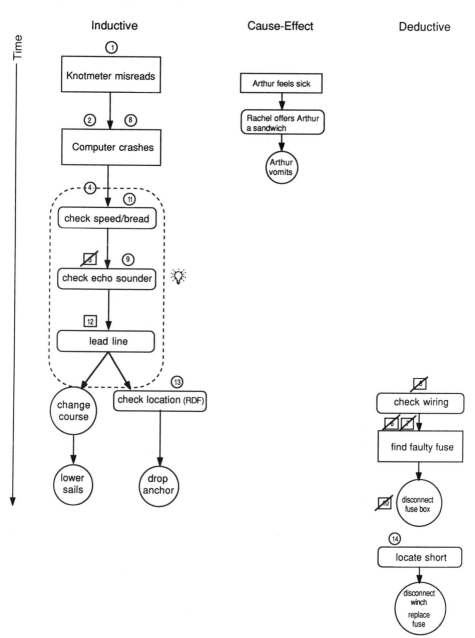

Figure 16.2. The sequence of discussion of Episode 3 in Carol's class

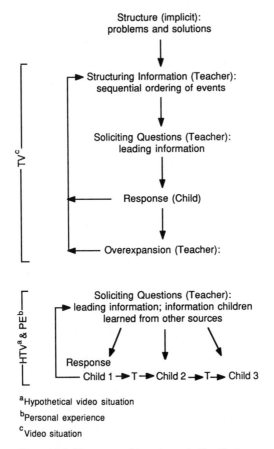

Figure 16.3. The pattern of interchange in Carol's class

four sections of discussion so that what the crew encountered and had to know, students' personal anecdotes, and hypothetical problems aboard the *Mimi* were dealt with in distinct segments. Toward the end of the lesson, however, Carol asked the children to imagine some possible problems the *Mimi* crew could encounter. At that point, Carol initiated only three topics compared to the children's 20. This sequence ended with children being asked to imagine themselves on board. Then, children generated some solutions to the hypothetical dilemmas.

If we map out the nature of the instructional events during Carol's lesson (see Figure 16.3), we can see that the pattern for discussing the crew's experience (TV) is different than that for discussing personal (PE) and hypothetical (HTV) problems.

Carol structured the discussion without explicitly telling the children what the structure would be. Before the viewing, however, she told the children that she wanted them to think about the science and math problems that they would be seeing. She used these terms to direct their thinking during the discussion too. This is important to note because it is known that explicit set induction can facilitate students' understanding of the point of a lesson (Holdzkom & Lutz, 1984). In Carol's class, the purpose of the viewing and of the dilemma was stated. During the first segment of the post-viewing discussion Carol began writing a problem list on the board; however, she stopped writing after notating one problem.

Carol proceeded by offering an open invitation for children to volunteer their observations. This technique mostly failed, so she solicited ideas by leading with references to the narrative content:

a29. Carol: Next problem. (*Pause*) A biggie. (*Pause*) I'll give you a clue. It has to do with Ann. Ann is working . . .
a30. Child: The computer has a failure.
a31. C: And what happens to the computer?
a32. Child: They see it's flat [referring to the image on the echo sounder that isn't registering].
a33. Carol: No, that's different. We'll get to that.

If the child responded by naming a problem, some additional information was elicited and the problem-detection cycle began again. Most often, the child's response provided an occasion for Carol to elaborate the child's comment with additional information. These types of utterances were longer than the initial soliciting comments and contained a lot of factual information. She also drew on the connection to the narrative flow in order to begin the next questioning sequence. In contrast, children's statements in this portion of the lesson, measured by mean length of utterance (MLU), were succinct, averaging 4.2 words per turn.

After the discussion reached the end of the video narrative, Carol asked for ideas about "what they can do to take care of these problems," which was immediately recast as: "Let's do one problem at a time. How did the crew solve the problem of how fast the boat was going?" Carol maintained the viewpoint of the television viewer. The students responded as Carol named the problems in turn. In this segment, she elicited from the children the names of the different instruments used and different measurements mentioned in the episode but did not discuss particular calculations involved in navigating and estimating speed. The structure and nature of the questioning sequence in the second segment were the same as in the problem-detection segment.

As Carol's lesson moved to a discussion of the children's personal experiences (PE) and of hypothetical problems (HTV), the dialogic structure shifted (see Figure 16.3). Although she continued to solicit the students' comments with the leading information from the drama, Carol also mentioned sources of information in the children's experience; for example, "How many of you have ever been driving with your parents and you got lost?" In this part of the lesson, a child's response could be followed by another child's, sometimes after minor redirection by Carol. At a couple of points, there was evidence of one child having been reminded of something by another. Children reported their own experiences of problem resolution.

In recounting the stories of their own past – being lost, blowing fuses, a motor

dying – children's expressions expanded to 31.3 words on the average. Their stories
were well formed, detailed, humorous, and dramatic. For example:

> a99. Child: Once I was going down the basement to get something and I opened the
> lights and I saw water all over the floor. And then I called my father and he came
> down and was trying to look where the water was coming from but it wasn't com-
> ing from those tubes. And then my baby brother, we found out that my baby
> brother had opened the pump from outside and the window is right next to that and
> the window was open and all the water came in.

In all, five children volunteered such personal accounts. Carol offered absolutely
no elaborations of the content of the children's experiences.

When no more personal stories were forthcoming, Carol asked the children to
think of problems the *Mimi*'s crew might have in the future (Segment 4). In short
statements, they generated a list of mishaps and disasters (without solutions): for
example, "A mouse might eat the wires"; "a hurricane blowing in the other direction"; "a blizzard coming"; "tidal waves"; "They might hit land"; "Maybe they'd
run out of food"; "How about if they run out of water?"; "a tornado"; "What if
lightning comes and catches?"; "The rudder might come off"; and "falling over-
board," "the ship being split by a whale," "fire," "something falling into the fan
of the motor," and "leaks." The ideas are imaginative and pertinent, although the
observer had the sense that, because no solutions to these dilemmas were offered or
requested, the class had become focused on disasters. At one point, however, Carol
asked one child what she would have done if she had been on the *Mimi* and there
was an electrical problem. A brief discussion then evolved among Carol and several
children (with Carol directing but the children responding to each other as well)
about other solutions they would have tried if they had been on the boat. Solutions
were usually generated by the same child who posed the problem. The lesson concluded with the bell.

Carol's decision to address, point by point, the questions of the experimenter,
led to a segmented discussion and, perhaps, reinforced the distinction of two domains of thinking, the everyday and the scientific, or schooled. On viewing the tape
of her lesson, Carol felt the class had been acting up because they weren't in their
home room, and for that reason she had to do a lot of directing. She also remarked
that she needed to assist them because they "have no skills in problem-solving
techniques," including word problems. She said if she did it again, she would give
the children work sheets with headings: a chart to fill out (similar to what we shall
see Scott constructed), possibly including their own experiences. She much preferred the later segments of the lesson, wondering if the children didn't have much
to say earlier because she was "looking for answers."

Scott's lesson: Wherein points of view mingle and concepts are revealed. Scott's
lesson is characterized by a directed mixing of points of view among the children,
himself, the television characters, reality, and possibility. Before showing Episode
3, Scott reviewed the previous *Mimi* episode with the children, eliciting comments

about the purpose of the scientists' voyage. He asked the class if there had been any problems for the scientists in accomplishing their tasks. The sequence of questions and answers placed the children in the scientists' perspective:

b35.1. Scott: Did they have any trouble with the boat while they were going out? Did they have any problem with the boat? Nicole?
b36.1. Child: Yes.
b37.1. Scott: They did! What?
b38.1. Child: They had trouble putting up the sails.
b39.1. Scott: They were having trouble putting up the sails. What happened? Tell me about it.
b40.1. Child: . . . when he tied the rope . . . then it came apart. . . .
b41.1. Scott: Okay, very good. He had a problem with tying the rope correctly. If you were out on a boat, Derek, would you know how to tie the rope correctly?
b42.1. Child: No.
b43.1. Scott: No, I wouldn't either. So when he was told to tie the rope what should he have said?
b44.1. Child: That I don't know how.
b45.1. Scott: Sure! I don't know how. Why do you think he didn't say anything?
b46.1. Child: Because he didn't want them to think that he didn't know about it. . . .
b47.1. Scott: That's a very good answer. Why else might he not have said anything?
b48.1. Child: Because he might think that people like might get mad at him. . . .
b51.1. Scott: So we see the captain does not seem like the world's easiest person to get to know. Okay. So we see already they had a bit of a problem. Now what other problems do you think people could have on a boat? Let's put that word up here [chalkboard]: *problems.*

Scott then wrote these problems mentioned by students on the board and told them this was to "get our mind on the whole idea of a problem." He told them what they should look for in the episode, what he wanted them to think about: the problems and what one has to know to solve them.

Immediately after the viewing, Scott took up the discussion. But he said:

b1.2. Before we add any new problems to the list – because we have too many problems, and Jennifer's going to get depressed and we don't want that. We don't want to get depressed, do we, Jen? What would you have to know to solve this problem?

As a child generated an answer, Scott created a table on the board, saying:

b8.2. Look at this. Problems. Solutions. We want solutions to our problems. We don't want to be all with a list of problems nobody can solve.

And he wrote down the solutions that correspond to the problems based on the children's responses, creating a table on the blackboard (see Figure 16.4).

If we map out the sequence of topics discussed in Scott's class (see Figure 16.5) with respect to the drama narrative we can see several striking differences from Carol's map. First, problems were discussed in the order in which they are generated, not in chronological order of the story. Boxed numbers on the extreme right indicate topics arising from personal experiences.

The children generated five of the eight problem topics. Rather than conveying that the lesson is about recall, this structure legitimates what the children find salient. Children's statement length during the sequence, which constituted the entire

PROBLEM	SOLUTION
Knowing where to go	Map reading, compass reading: navigation
Storm	Emergency procedures
Getting back	Navigation
Seasickness	Medical equipment, walking around, going on deck, to vomit
Electrical	Knowing about electricity, tools, wires, and fuses
Boat sinking	Lifeboats
Instruments don't work	Fix power supply, use other equipment that works without electricity

Figure 16.4. Scott's problem/solution chart

lesson, showed less variance according to topic than in Carol's class. The children's utterances, however, were comparable in length to the nonpersonal statements made in the class (MLU = 4.3), perhaps because they are all made in a teacher-centered school-discussion format.

Although children's utterances were short, the problem/solution-detection framework Scott set up is based not on the "given" of the video but on the fact that a type of experience was shared between the children and the characters. This conceptual level represents the commonality among the personal, video, and hypothetical instances.

Second, because the problems are introduced always in conjunction with their possible solutions, the problems become something to be solved, rather than dilemmas per se. The problems, in other words, were presented and treated as conceptual action-based wholes. Even solutions to particular problems were cast and discussed as general principles, for example, "emergency procedures."

Third, the personal human element – seasickness – is included as a legitimate

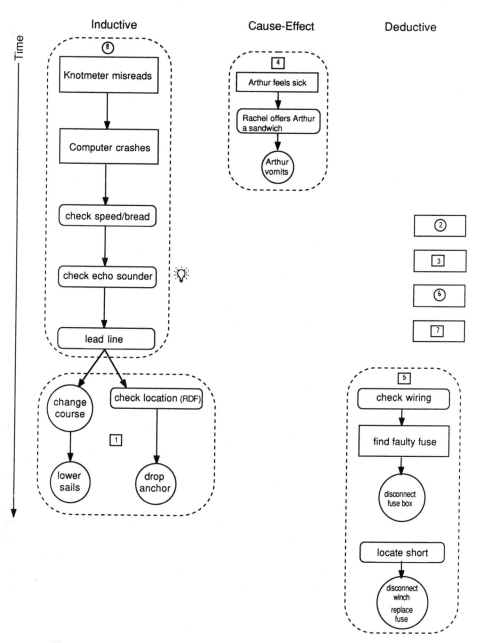

Figure 16.5. The sequence of discussion topics in Scott's class

albeit somewhat humorous problem for which emergency actions may be necessary. This, too, expands the problem/solution construct beyond technological problems alone. It thus crosses an important conceptual boundary, to which, one could argue, the children are very likely to relate easily: getting sick versus needing to fix a computer.

If we look, then, at the sequence of instructional dialogue during the lesson, a recursive pattern emerges wherein children's responses are consistently related back to the overarching and abstract framework of the problem/solution chart (see Figure 16.6).

Scott's class, though highly teacher-directed, sets its agenda early and carries it out. In a later interview, Scott explained that he prepared the structure beforehand and that he intended to have the children come away from the lesson knowing that "you have to have relevant knowledge to solve a problem." He also "planted things" to get "specific-level" problems, not simply electrical problems, for example, but general classes of problems – ones that call for skills, ones that call for emergency procedures, and ones that call for logic in order to be solved. He "planted" not the problems themselves but, rather, elements of framing solutions.

Charlie's lesson: In which the scientific dominates and children's logic is unraveled. Charlie planned his lesson on Episode 3 in yet a different way than Carol and Scott. He informed us that he would use the lesson to get his students to attack the problem of calculating rate of travel from distance and time. We can characterize his intent as one of organizing an activity to introduce children to working within a scientific system. The problems they were to detect and think about solving related to a particular and formal class of problems.

In his pre-viewing session, Charlie prepared the children specifically for the problem he wanted them to attend to in the video. He first went over some nautical terms with his class. He demonstrated the definition of *shoals* by drawing a diagram on the board and of *channel* by pointing to the rows between the desks. He had children define *navigation, heading, chart,* and *knot,* which a child defined as "a nautical mile." With this definition – which is incorrect because a knot represents nautical miles per hour, a rate measure – Charlie concurs: "It's a nautical mile. It's a measure of distance." He then asked the children if they thought it was important to know how fast the boat is going and why, and what is controlled by the boat's electrical system. After eliciting a few examples and more definitions, Charlie told the children:

c95.1.   We're going to be presented with some kinds of problems here. They are going to present you with some kinds of mathematical problems. One is called a speed, distance, time problem. That I want you to be aware of when it comes up.

This certainly could be called inducing the set. However, after the viewing, Charlie began the lesson by trying to get the students to reconstruct the *context* of the rate problem, asking them, "What's the first thing you know that went wrong? That

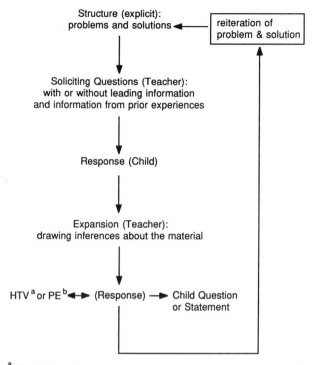

Structure (explicit):
problems and solutions ◄——— reiteration of
problem & solution

Soliciting Questions (Teacher):
with or without leading information
and information from prior experiences

Response (Child)

Expansion (Teacher):
drawing inferences about the material

HTV[a] or PE[b] ◄—► (Response) —► Child Question
or Statement

[a] Hypothetical video situation
[b] Personal experience

Figure 16.6. The pattern of interchange in Scott's class

caused everything else?'' This is a very ambiguous question because, as the mapping of the episode problems shows, many of the causal elements of the problems
become known by the characters through induction, and so initial cause is not the
first thing that is seen to precipitate the problems. When a student responded to this
question by saying, ''They were lost,'' Charlie sought to recover his intent by
asking:

   c5.2.   Why did they get lost? Why didn't they know where they were going? What hap-
          pened? It doesn't work chronologically in the story, but what happened that caused
          the other problems? The first thing that really went wrong was what?

Because the children didn't answer, Charlie made the questions simpler. Carefully verifying selected responses of the children's, he gradually constructed a set
of problem elements so that the class arrived at the fact that the knotmeter was
malfunctioning. Here, he remarked that, ''on a boat where you measure speed in
knots, it [the instrument that tells how fast you're going] is called a knotmeter.''
The lesson was a fishing expedition for the students, who were not thinking
chronologically about the underlying problem components but were asked to take

part in constructing causal reasoning. They, instead, tended to remember images (e.g., the stopwatch, the lead line, the radio direction finder), which in many cases did in fact answer the teacher's question but were not acceptable to the teacher. (Charlie: "What tools was he using [to keep from going aground]?" Child: "The lead line." Charlie: "Well, before that.")

When Charlie asked the class what the captain replaces the knotmeter with, one child answered, "a piece of bread." Charlie then said, "This is where I want to stop and spend a little time." "What else did the captain use?" he asked. "Stopwatch" was the answer. But there was one more thing Charlie wanted them to say, one more "thing" the captain used. The responses of the class began by being reasonable. The first response was a "a pin," which is what the captain calls the dowel on the rail that he uses to mark the length of the boat. This response, however, was not accepted. Charlie hinted, "Remember . . . there's speed, there's time, and there's . . ." As Charlie continued to elicit guesses, the children volunteered "that pole," "steering wheel," "multiplication," "shortwave radio," "the boat," "speed," with the answers becoming less reasonable, less associated figuratively with the video event, and more random, although still related to the nature of the event (e.g., "a protractor," which is a kind of measurement tool). The answer turned out to be "the length of the boat," which no one guessed, although one suspects "the pin," "the pole," "halfway," and "the width" were guesses proffered that were all fairly close in meaning.

In the second segment of the lesson, Charlie went over the formula for rate problems, writing them on the board, and had the children do some sample calculations. Once again, however, he confused the meaning of *knot*. He said, "A knot is 6,211 feet. . . . If your speed is 6 knots and you're traveling for 3 hours, how far have you gone?" He then defined knots as a distance unit and knots per hour as the speed unit until one point when he said, "A knot is essentially a mile per hour, a nautical mile per hour." Later, he switched back to using the distance definition. From this confusion, we suspect that this technical term is essentially unimportant to Charlie and the children because they are dealing with a rote formula, not trying to understand the meaning of rate. Interestingly, Charlie has experience sailing. This suggests that for him, too, the school definition of the term is not practically relevant.

The children seemed to have been already introduced to the $S \times T = D$ formula because they can fill in Charlie's lead-in, "feet times time equals . . ." After giving them three hypothetical problems using easy numbers to calculate distance, he then attempted to have them calculate the formulas for speed and time. "If speed times time equals distance, what in relationship to what gives us speed?" The children seemed to know mechanical ways to interpret and balance equations, because one child answered "*D* divided by *S*" to Charlie's question about time, and because they generally failed to use unit names when reporting their calculations. Charlie wrote the formulas and numbers on the board. At the very end of the lesson, he had the children write the formulas down in their "math section."

It is not possible to map out the sequence of the topics covered in this discussion vis-à-vis the video narrative because Charlie organized the discussion abstractly. That is, he began by eliciting what the captain's worries were, what the tools were the captain usually used and what he had to replace them with, and finally, how he measured the rate of the boat. Charlie selected the topics to be developed in discussion by negating the various contributions of the students (as in ''No, what else?''). He did this on the basis of a kind of general logical sequence just outlined, designed to focus on the calculation of rate.

Charlie's pattern of eliciting responses from the class changed character during the lesson (see Figure 16.7). In the first part, he was attempting to define the legitimate problem under discussion so that later the children could apply this concept to mathematical calculations. It should be noted that no personal information about the children's experiences emerged during the lesson. The children's utterances averaged 2.2 words overall.

That the children's lesson participation consisted of guessing and rote manipulation of the rate formula is ironic, because this lesson was supposed to encourage systematicity in their thinking. There was systematicity of a sort, but its nature is predictable from Davydov's (1975) and Gal'perin's (1969) observations that introducing terminology without an experiential base will result in its rigid conceptual application. The net effect of guessing what the acceptable answer is teaches a lesson that ''problems'' are defined outside the student's perceptions and responses to the world. The children's systematicity lies in their supplying the right type of answer to this teacher rather than in applying a content-based conceptual scheme to the problem domain. Thus we have an example of ''scientific'' thinking being introduced in a way that is not generalizable to the concrete (Davydov & Markova, 1983) for children.

The lessons described illustrate that there is a systematicity to children's ''spontaneous'' knowledge and that it can be brought into congruity with a more formal pattern. In Charlie's class, we see how, without the stuff of the everyday, the scientific stays arbitrary in content and can promote detached responding. The children learn to respond to the question form, not the conceptual material.

Discussion

The study conducted investigated how a single, potentially rich mediating device – the video drama – might be used to define a connection between clear examples of science problem solving and more intuitive knowledge that is based on personal and haphazard experience.

We asked about the ways the regularities of the everyday and the scientific can be interleaved so that the otherness of an abstract conceptual system is internalized as part of the child's thinking and questioning. The present data do not yield a definitive answer, but they suggest that the use of commonplace experience as well as the formal content of the commonplace information can actually facilitate learning the scientific. At the same time, whereas the empirical content of experience

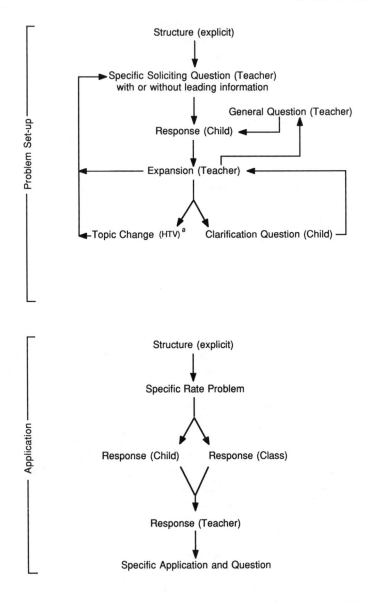

[a] Hypothetical video situation

Figure 16.7. The pattern of interchange in Charlie's class

provides an image that can be assigned a term, the conditions of the linking process form a relational structure. Eventually, these relations can be internalized (Davydov, 1988).

We saw that, however fixed the mediating material is, its content is still open to a wide range of interpretations. If we had filmed more teachers doing the same lesson, we undoubtedly would have witnessed even more uses of the video and the researcher's questions. The variations we did see, though, exemplified three positions: elaborating the everyday; merging the everyday and the scientific; and emphasizing the scientific. The variations emphasize the critical nature of the teacher's conceptualization of the everyday as well as of the scientific for the development of scientific meaning among children. This is because such a development process is essentially one of socialization, not merely learning. As Vygotsky stresses (1987), the origins of conceptual thinking are interpersonal; thus the matter is best accounted for as a shaping process rather than as individual construction.

Earlier research associated with the teacher-training project showed us that variation among teachers in use of materials was the rule with video, computers, and, to a less extreme degree, print (Martin, 1987). The particular set of science and math materials used, however, sought to accommodate that kind of variation and to build good science into their use in general ways. The fact that the package included several media added strongly to the adaptability of the *Mimi* materials into so many settings.

This interpretability is argued to be an important feature of the technology. Its value lies in its ability to be comprehensible to the teacher, to interest and motivate the students, and at the same time to foster interactions in which conceptual bridges among experiences can be constructed and original connections created. This is not, as we have seen, inevitable, even with the best of materials. In some cases, the interactions that arose reproduced distinctions between what is experienced everyday and what is scientific, in Vygotsky's sense.

There are many routes to detecting problems in the everyday world or in a video presentation of it. Some routes, such as the abstract, the purely empirical, or the repositioned empirical, appear to lead one more easily toward conceptual systematicity whereas others present obstacles. Some may result in the reinforcement of "pseudoconcepts" (Vygotsky, 1987). For example, in the many instances where we observed children watching this episode and discussed it with them, they identified strongly with the tension, the efforts to help, and the excitement (and amused disgust, in the case of seasickness) of finding solutions. Children's recall of the video material, however, was most often of visually salient events. They had difficulty organizing their recall along logical lines of causation or inference. In the sample of teachers studied here, we witnessed a set of instructional variants in which the adults defined acceptable instances of problems and, over the course of a lesson, brought children's responses into conformity with their own vision. Because the teacher's understandings did not necessarily include connections between the spontaneous thinking of the children and the formality of the material, the spontaneous often remained unchanged.

Interfacing techniques

Each of the lessons we observed was traditionally teacher-centered. Remarks most often flowed so that each child's comment was followed by the teacher's. Alternative lesson structures that nonetheless do not dilute the leading role of the teacher have been suggested elsewhere (Lampert, 1985; Rowe, 1978). One is found in the Investigative Colloquium Model (Lansdown, Blackwood, & Brandwein, 1971), in which the teacher carefully chooses materials that facilitate observations of specific scientific principles and organizes discussion around the children's observations. Another model asks teachers to assist in structuring communication between children in such a way that an experience-based conceptual schema is revealed (Rubtsov, 1981). Scott's lesson resembled this last model as he focused on the diagram while prompting the children's observations.

Each teacher was able to use the video to construct a problem-detection theme for the lesson. Encouraging the children to discuss phenomena below the surface of events rested upon the teacher's ability to connect them to the everyday. The explicitness of the connection between realms of everyday and scientific experience related to the teachers' own sense of connectedness of the two. The explicitness was operationalized in a variety of ways.

1. Differences in lesson structures are characterized by *the ways in which the personal and "other" are made to overlap*. We saw that unguided expression of the everyday is richer in form and content than expressiveness concerning formally structured concepts for children in this age range. In two classes (Carol's and Charlie's), as children answered questions about material with which they had no direct experience, their responses were collapsed in form and connectivity. In the case where the teacher facilitated expressiveness irrespective of the topic source (Scott's class), the utterances also tended to be underdeveloped.

Though the teachers were controlling the interactions closely, the balance within the working arena of discussion could be tipped in several ways. Carol and Scott, for instance, managed to integrate the children's own recollections into the lesson discussion, albeit to differing degrees, whereas Charlie kept the focus on story recall. Scott brought his own as well as the children's experiences into the discussion.

2. *Juxtaposing everyday experience with the video examples,* as Scott did, allowed him logically to bring metainformation to the foreground of the discussion. Because of his somewhat controlling style, however, there was a trade-off in the richness of the individual contributions within the class discussion: The children spoke about their own knowledge in the same brief terms as they did about the video examples. At the same time, the technique of equating enacted and observed experiences created a collective base for analyzing both. That is, in repositioning children's everyday experiences and responses he formed a superordinate category level: problems and solution, an explicitly verbal, abstract identity (Vygotsky, 1987). Scott, who had taken a workshop in inferential questioning, thought he had talked too much during his lesson. When he saw his classroom tape, he was surprised at the brevity of the children's answers. He nonetheless felt his role as teacher requires efficiency in telling the children what is expected and in not letting discussion become tangential. He believes in preparing lessons with "specifics," that is, with clear concepts to convey.

The emphasis for discussion in Charlie's class was on the abstract problem that the teacher had in mind. There, the scientific, such as it was, predominated. Furthermore, despite Charlie's having some of the scientific information wrong and glossing over some inaccuracy, we conclude it was the unrelatedness of the information to students' experience that contributed to the deterioration in the students' guessing. Charlie failed to accept the children's bids to respond and to work with them. Instead, he waited for the one answer that only he, it turned out, knew and, later, for the mechanical answers that no one quite grasped.

3. Asking children to identify with characters and situations seems to be a strategy that can promote conceptual connections. *Mix of pronominal point of view* in the lessons was another particularly interesting technique for linking reference frames. Scott intermingled *they, you,* and *we* within discussion about the same event, saying, for example, "What would you have to know?" when asking about the video characters, whereas Carol used separate types of pronouns in each lesson segment ("What did they have to know?"). Charlie never asked the children to put themselves in the shoes of the characters or even to relate events from their own perspective.

4. Each teacher, at least once, used *notation* to enhance the points of the lesson. Such notations can be tools for juxtaposing problem elements that don't literally co-occur in the world and for introducing a universal language to describe them. The teachers used them as graphs, demonstrations, and examples.

Carol, who intended to write a list of problems on the board, did not continue writing after the first item. We might say that writing the list was only taking up time and not serving to clarify any abstract relationships among the examples elicited in the class. Although a list distills and equates information, in this case it was merely redundant with the discussion, which itself was recapping the videotaped information.

Scott appeared to represent the data of discussion in a way that highlighted superordinate organization of information. His use of a chart seemed to come closest to creating a framework of systematicity from which one can generalize to new problem sets and to new instances. Though it too was partly redundant with the discussion, it illustrated the reorganization of the video, personal, and hypothetical information.

Charlie's use of notation was dual: He drew schematic representations of shoals and channels, which might have helped the students to visualize the navigation problem, and he wrote permutations of the rate formula on the board. The latter seemed to underscore that invoking the fact of the rate formula was the object of the lesson, rather than having the students achieve understanding of the formula.

5. Differences in the use of graphic or external representations were paralleled by *differences in the evocation of internal imagery* of everyday knowledge during the lessons. Here again, Scott frequently evoked recall of experiences all the children have had (e.g., the school custodian fixing something; how to get to McDonald's if you don't know the way; what would happen if you were on a rocking

boat). On two occasions Carol asked the children in her class to reflect on particular experiences ("Has anyone had an electrical problem?" "Has anyone gotten lost when driving with your parents?"). Charlie invoked no recall of personal or everyday knowledge and only asked the children to remember what the characters did in the video story.

6. Knowing the stance adopted by teachers vis-à-vis the group and the lesson goal seemed to be more useful for describing the lessons than knowing any particular question or response category frequency differences here. So, although small differences can be found among the teachers in information-based measures such as question-type distribution, it is not clear that these are causal rather than symptomatic of the different ways discourse developed in the classes. For instance, Carol asked a total of eight questions requiring comprehension, application, or analysis skills, according to Rowe's criteria, and Scott nine (e.g., "What might the salt do if we drank it?" "Why did they get lost?" "Why do you think he didn't say anything?"), whereas Charlie asked two such questions during his lesson. Despite differences, these did not amount to a very large proportion of the total questions asked.

Neither did teachers differ strongly in the relative frequency of their comments about the thinking process itself, a reflection, perhaps, of their feelings about the learning task. Teachers' remarks about the children as thinkers (e.g., "That's something nobody thought of") were used fairly liberally by all teachers, although Charlie described his own processes more often than the other teachers did (e.g., "I'm not making myself clear"; "Let me ask it this way"). However, Scott's comments, often interspersed with humor, were inflected in a pointed way to emphasize the children's participation in the thinking process ("You know, I don't think anybody before we saw this episode thought much about electricity being on the boat"). In the case of the other two teachers, one senses in such comments a more automatic response (e.g., "Think about it"; "What's a word you've learned . . ."). Scott, furthermore, used praise to clarify aspects of the thinking process (e.g., "I like that Michelle used that word *saloon,* because we learned the different parts of the *Mimi* and she knew they were sitting in a saloon"; "And I'm glad you knew that he was seasick. He wasn't sick from bad food or from germs").

What may have been learned

The focal questions of the lesson, as proposed by the researcher, were chosen to illuminate ways in which teachers could use a common experience (the video and video viewing) to form conceptual connections between everyday experience and knowledge of a system of experience for students.

The children in each class learned, at least for the day, what it means to identify a problem and to solve it. Carol might be said to have encouraged interaction that "taught" that problems exist in particular contexts, that they may or may not have solutions that can be figured out, and that the everyday and the more formally systematic coexist. Scott selected a different version of "problem" from among his students' responses. His choices in developing their examples of problems served to integrate the familiar and the novel. Although his students' expressiveness was restricted with regard to the elaboration of their answers, they did control the topic choices within the frame established by the teacher. His organization did not teach the logic of inductive or deductive inference. Instead, getting students to think about what the crew did, using what the students themselves knew, may have resulted in a critical prior awareness: that problems have structure in the first place. Finally, Charlie developed the steps in his lesson based on answers from the children that corresponded to what he and a mathematical community defined as problem elements. The students' approximations of answers were not acknowledged. Their contributions became more restricted and lost coherence. Those students probably learned that one is told how the world works.

All the children worked to construct logical connections between the teacher's questions and their answers. Their interindividual responsiveness is what ultimately allows them to internalize the particular model of problem detection they encountered in class, because the children engage with the teacher, who organizes the use of examples, instances, and generalities (Martin, 1983).

Systematicity of the examples, however, is not simply what is at issue. Each teacher worked systematically in his or her own way, either by following the narrative chronology and experimenter's directions, by creating a problem/solution chart, or by presenting variations on rate problems. The teachers, working with the same instructions and the same materials, created different instructional goals and different conceptual frameworks for their lessons. Their own experiences determined their definition of the "problem." In fact, this work shows that different versions of systematic thought were presented, illustrating what Vygotsky implies: that canonical systematicity is culturally determined; it is not just "how adults think."

Though everyday knowledge, defined by familiar problems and solutions, seemed to allow access to the scientific, the teacher's working assumptions were the central mediating principle determining the affordance. Total separation of the content of everyday problems and video-based examples, as Carol achieved, resulted in the students describing their home knowledge quite nicely, but there were no moves to use this in the service of enriching the discussion of the more generic examples of problems. Children can generate endless examples without arriving at resolution or an overarching scheme, as we also saw in Carol's lesson, where children produced an imaginative list of hypothetical disasters. The disasters generated by Carol's students remained exactly that, a list of images, until almost the very end when the teacher helped the children imagine their own solutions to two of the dilemmas they posed for the *Mimi* characters. Carol noted later, of one of her students who suggested the crew could call for help, that "usually his thinking is black and white. Concrete." She couldn't believe he'd "think that abstractly." Being asked to imagine problem solutions, though briefly, seemed to result in some new thinking on the part of at least one student.

That the children truly assimilated the object lesson of the day is not likely. According to Soviet and Piagetian theory, assimilation is not immediate. It is an act upon an image that is based on the empirical (Davydov, 1988). We would argue that in class the lesson of the day is probably repeated sufficiently often to give the children a good idea of what "science" and "problems" are according to the operative norm.

Conclusion

The content of the video drama provided a fertile field for detecting and defining problems and solution patterns. Two teachers interpreted the problem solving to be about practical matters, that is, literally handling dilemmas. One of these teachers, Scott, gave us a good clue as to how television as a communal but prepackaged experience can help our own experiences become general cases, as the commonality between others' and our own becomes explicit. For the third teacher, Charlie, the video provided a problem prototype whose underlying mathematical representation became the focus of the lesson. In the way he used the video, though, this event became something to be explicated because the teacher said so.

The fate of the children's "curiosity" is not known, but their interest and creative thinking are suggested to be alive and well by Carol's disaster discussion segment. Only at the end of her lesson do the enthusiasm and the idea of problem attack come together when she "puts" the children on the boat. In Scott's class, curiosity could be said to have been harnessed to the explorations of solutions. In Charlie's class, unfortunately, probing the fathoms of the teacher's mind became the object of curiosity.

What has been presented is an illustration of a dialectic described by other educators (e.g., Davydov, 1975): Principles of systematicity detectable in the lesson material – in this case the chronological narrative – must, like our own life encounters, be divorced from one sort of everyday logic and dubbed into a formal, culturally derived framework that lies in some sense apart from natural experiential unfolding. On the other hand, symbolic notation (such as $S \times T = D$) and the structure of such frameworks, unmanifest in narrative and in our everyday doings, need to be tied to an unfolding personal experience (see Lampert, 1985) to be discovered and acted upon and thereby acquire an identity in the problem/solution-detection process.

Appendix: coding scheme

    I.   Topic

        TV: pertaining to the videotaped episode
        PE: pertaining to personal experiences
        HTV: pertaining to hypothetical events that could arise for the video characters

    II.   Conversational moves (based on Rowe, 1978)

        Structuring information: a question or statement in which the teacher or student gives directions, states procedures, and suggests changes

A procedural statement

Open-ended soliciting (probing): a question or statement that prompts for additional data or relationships, or that encourages explanation

Leading information: questions or statements that clue students either to answers or to processes that could be used to find answers, apply inference

Fact information: a question or statement in which teachers or students communicate or look to elicit factual information

Reacting: student or teacher evaluation of statements made by others

III. Utterance content

Expansion: prompting the joining of at least two ideas to explain how a system works or to compare to systems

Identification: identifying a problem

Information: giving information previously learned, stating observations

Inference: prompting the use of conjecture for stating relationships between pieces of evidence

Application: encouraging interpretation of new material, using concepts already identified

Notes

1 Vygotsky viewed the scientific as synonymous with school-like thinking. According to this model, verbal terms are given to label conceptual structures and regularities. These labels make possible verbal, or true conceptual, thinking. Everyday concepts may reflect systematicity in perceptions or actions, but such regularities are undefined verbally and hence are not truly conceptual or generalizable.

2 *The Voyage of the Mimi* was funded by the U.S. Department of Education, with additional funding by CBS, Inc., Samuel Y. Gibbon, Jr., Executive Producer. Copyright, Bank Street College of Education.

References

Brown, L. K. (1986). *Taking advantage of media: A manual for parents and teachers*. Boston: Routledge & Kegan Paul.

Carey, S. (1985). *Conceptual change in childhood*. Cambridge, MA: MIT Press.

Christiansen, M. (1987). *The impact of IS design on knowledge in work*. Unpublished manuscript. Department of Humanistic Computer Science, University of Aalborg, Aalborg, Denmark.

Davydov, V. V. (1975). Logical and psychological problems of elementary mathematics as an academic subject. In E. G. Begle, J. Kilpatrick, J. W. Wilson, & I. Wirszup (Eds.), *Soviet studies in the psychology of learning and teaching mathematics* (Vol. 7). Chicago: University of Chicago Press.

Davydov, V. V. (1988). Problems of developmental teaching: The experience of theoretical and experimental psychological research. *Soviet Education, 30*.

Davydov, V. V., & Markova, A. K. (1983). A concept of educational activity for schoolchildren. *Soviet Psychology, 21*, 50–76.

Díaz, E. (1984, November). *Bilingual, bicultural computer experts*. Paper presented at the meeting of the American Anthropological Association, Denver.

Engelström, Y. (1987). *Learning by expanding: An activity-theoretical approach to developmental research*. Helsinki: Orienta-Konsultit Oy.

Gal'perin, P. Y. (1969). Stages in the development of mental acts. In M. Cole & I. Maltzman (Eds.), *A handbook of contemporary Soviet psychology*. New York: Basic.

Gibbon, S. Y. (1987). Learning and instruction in the information age. In M. A. White (Ed.), *What curriculum for the information age?* Hillsdale, NJ: Erlbaum.

Goodnow, J. J. (1987, November). *The socialization of cognition: What's involved?* Paper presented at the conference on Culture and Human Development, Chicago.

Greenfield, P. M. (1984). *Mind and media: The effects of television, video games, and computers.* Cambridge, MA: Harvard University Press.

Hawkins, D. (1983). Science closely observed. *Daedalus, 112*, 65–89.

Holdzkom, D., & Lutz, P. B. (1984). *Research within reach: A research-guided response to the concerns of educators.* Charleston, WV: Research and Development Interpretation Service, Appalachian Education Laboratory.

Horton, R. (1967). African traditional thought and Western science. *Africa, 37*, 50–71.

Lampert, M. (1985). Mathematics learning in context: *The Voyage of the Mimi. Journal of Mathematical Behavior, 4*(2), 157–168.

Lansdown, B., Blackwood, P. E., & Brandwein, P. F. (1971). *Teaching elementary science through investigation and colloquium.* New York: Harcourt Brace Jovanovich.

Levin, J. R., & Lesgold, A. M. (1978). On pictures in prose. *Educational Communication and Technology Journal 26*, 233–243.

Levin, J. A., & Waugh, M. (1988). Instructional simulations, tools, games, and microworlds: Computer-based environments for learning. *International Journal of Educational Research, 12*(1), 71–79.

Mandler, J., & Johnson, N. (1977). Remembrance of things parsed: Story structure and recall. *Cognitive Psychology, 9*, 111–151.

Martin, L. W. M. (1983). *Children's problem solving as inter-individual outcome.* Unpublished doctoral dissertation, University of California, San Diego.

Martin, L. M. W. (1987). Teachers' adoption of multimedia technologies for science and mathematics instruction. In R. D. Pea & K. Sheingold (Eds.), *Mirrors of minds: Patterns of experience in educating computing.* Norwood, NJ: Ablex.

Martin, L. M. W., Chang, H.-h., & Flores, R. (1988). *Linking science and literacy.* Final Report to the Department of Education. New York: Bank Street College of Education.

Martin, L. M. W., Hawkins, J., Gibbon, S., & McCarthy, R. (1988). Integrating information technologies into instruction: *The Voyage of the Mimi.* In J. Ellis (Ed.), *1988 Yearbook.* Colorado Springs: Association for the Education of Teachers in Science.

Mitchell, L. S. (1963). *Young geographers: How they explore the world and how they map the world.* New York: Basic. (Original work published 1934)

National Science Foundation (1987, June). *Opportunities for strategic investment in K–12 science education* (Vol. 1). Washington, DC: National Science Foundation.

National Science Teachers Association (1982). *Science–technology–society: Science education for the 1980s.* Washington, DC: National Science Teachers Association.

Neale, D. C., Smith, D. C., & Wier, E. A. (1987, April). *Teacher thinking in elementary science instruction.* Paper presented at the annual meeting of the American Educational Research Association, Washington, DC.

Newman, D., Griffin, P., & Cole, M. (1989). *The construction zone: Working for cognitive change in school.* Cambridge: Cambridge University Press.

Rowe, M. B. (1978). *Teaching science as continuous inquiry: A basic.* New York: McGraw-Hill.

Rubtsov, V. V. (1981). The role of cooperation in the development of intelligence. *Soviet Psychology, 19*, 41–62.

Salomon, G., & Cohen, A. A. (1977). Television formats, mastery of mental skills, and the acquisition of knowledge. *Journal of Educational Psychology, 69*, 612–619.

Scribner, S., & Cole, M. (1981). *The psychology of literacy.* Cambridge, MA: Harvard University Press.

Vygotsky, L. S. (1978). *Mind in society.* Cambridge, MA: Harvard University Press.

Vygotsky, L. S. (1987). *Collected works* (Vol. 1). New York: Plenum.

17   Assisted performance in writing instruction with learning-disabled students

Robert Rueda

In recent years, there have been many theoretical advances in the conceptualization of the processes involved in childrens' development and learning. This includes, for example, much greater emphasis on the social and interactive nature of these processes, as emphasized in the work of the sociohistorical tradition (Vygotsky, 1978). These developments have begun to influence, in a profound way, the conceptualization and teaching of literacy, one of the major objectives of formal education. For a variety of historical and other reasons, these developments have only very recently begun to infiltrate the instruction of mildly handicapped students.[1] However, these theoretical notions have the potential to reshape radically the nature of literacy instruction for students whose academic achievement is sufficiently low that they come into contact with the special education system.

In this chapter, the Vygotskian approach to one aspect of literacy, namely written language, will be explored with special attention to mildly handicapped and learning-disabled students and compared with other prominent theoretical approaches. Following this, the chapter will briefly review the literature on mildly handicapped students and writing, including the use of microcomputers, with a critical analysis of traditional instructional practices. In addition, the implications of a Vygotskian approach for mildly handicapped students will be discussed. Finally, examples will be provided of the application of the Vygotskian approach to writing, including an interactive writing experience with learning-disabled students.

A sociohistorical perspective on writing

Although social and cognitive processes are often conceptualized as separate areas of investigation, there is increasing evidence that they are intimately related (Laboratory of Comparative Human Cognition, 1983). One theoretical framework that

Special thanks are extended to Interlearn, Inc., in particular Bud Mehan and Margaret Riel, for use of the programs and for technical assistance in various aspects of the author's study. In addition, the assistance of various members of the Laboratory of Comparative Human Cognition in the early stages of conceptualization of the study is appreciated, especially Jim Levin and Mike Cole. Other valuable ideas were contributed by Dennis Sayers, Joy Peyton, and Mitzi Cholowenski, and especially the members of the TEECH Microcomputer Research Team at the University of California at Santa Barbara. Thanks is extended to Diane Alvarado for assistance in data collection.

403

explicitly acknowledges this interdependence is found in work developed by the Soviet investigators of the sociohistorical school (e.g., Vygotsky, 1978), adapted and expanded upon here in the United States, especially regarding the relationship between culturally organized experiences and learning (LCHC Newsletter, 1982; Rogoff & Wertsch, 1984; Tharp & Gallimore, 1988; Wertsch, 1979; Wertsch, 1985a, 1985b). These ideas are particularly useful because they emphasize how interactions between people become the principal mechanism by which learning and development occur.

A key assumption of the sociohistorical approach is that the intellectual skills that children acquire are considered to be directly related to how they interact with adults and peers in specific problem-solving environments. That is, children internalize the kind of assistance they receive from more capable others and eventually come to use the means of guidance initially provided by another to direct their own subsequent problem-solving behaviors. In this framework, an explicit and direct connection is posited between interactions among people and individual psychological processes. Given this orientation, the role of the teacher, peers, and others in the learning process is extremely important, that is, as agents capable of driving development and learning by means of providing assisted performance (Tharp & Gallimore, 1988).

The specific path by which activities are moved from the level of social experience to that of individual experience consists of a series of transformations (Vygotsky, 1978), the result of a number of developmental events. These events occur in learning situations, which Vygotsky called the "zone of proximal development."

In general, the student's entering level of development is perceived as a major determinant of the zone. The activity organized by the teacher provides the necessary practice to move the child from the initial, assisted level to the final, independent level. Note that in contrast to instruction that breaks learning into small, discrete steps this approach suggests that the activity (learning task) remain whole throughout the instructional process until independent functioning is finally attained. It is only the level of the child's participation (not the task) that changes over time.

Zebroski (1981) has summarized major aspects of the sociohistorical school with special relevance to writing. First, children are viewed as active participants in their world and their learning. Second, language and culture are viewed relationally. That is, language processes should be studied in terms of their use, history, and connections to other parts of social life. These theorists suggest that, just as oral language is learned with another person in a functional context, so too must writing be acquired in a context in which it has a meaningful function (Vygotsky, 1983). Third, language and cognitive processes are viewed dynamically, that is, as always in change. A major focus of study, therefore, is what changes and how it changes rather than "what is." Implicit in this view is that effective instruction organized by the teacher should be goal-directed, meaningful, and in advance of current levels of development.

Although the sociohistorical approach is best known for the emphasis on socio-cultural and interactional factors as the forces driving development, one important principle with respect to children's acquisition of literacy is the notion that writing begins much prior, developmentally speaking, to the production of recognizable print. This developmentally based approach has been suggested in the work of Luria (1983) and Vygotsky (1978, 1983). As one example, Vygotsky (1934/1962) suggests that early writing cannot simply be said to serve no function, as is commonly assumed in early writing instructions. Rather, it is functionally associated at first with other symbolic activities. In addition, Luria (1983) has reported on the development of children's early markings as mediators in the recall of events and objects. In general, the assertion is that there is some regularity and logic in children's conceptualization of the meaning and functions of print, which largely reflects current cognitive developmental levels.

Consistent with this framework, various investigators in the area of writing have argued that its development is best viewed as an interaction between cognitive processes and educational and cultural contexts that influence these processes (Collins, 1981, 1984; Elsasser & John-Steiner, 1977; Erickson, 1984; John-Steiner & Tatter, 1983; Kroll, 1980). This influence, furthermore, is accomplished through the functions of writing in particular contexts, which can vary. As an example, Heath (1983), Scollon and Scollon (1981), and Trueba, Moll, and Díaz (1982) have identified different orientations to literacy as well as patterns of literacy used as a result of various cultural orientations and understandings. Rueda (1988) has termed theoretical approaches, including the Vygotskian perspective, that are consistent with these developmental principles *functional/interactive approaches.*

What are the instructional implications of such an approach to writing? A functional/interactive approach to writing suggests that at the initial stages writing should be structured to be interactive, building upon the oral language proficiency and other knowledge bases that students already have. Further, beginning writing should be functional (for a purpose other than teacher evaluation or "correct" form) and meaningful to the student, should provide for self-selection of topics by the student, and should include dynamic support, which is adjusted according to the individual and changing developmental levels of the student.

It is only recently that the sociohistorical approach has been widely disseminated in the United States and has begun to influence scholars and practitioners. How does it relate to other major frameworks that have been used as a basis for the instruction of written language? These questions will be explored in the following paragraphs.

Cognitive/developmental approaches to writing

A significant amount of current research in writing focuses on the development of writing in very young children, tracing the roots of later writing behavior (Collins, 1984; Grinnell & Burris, 1983). Some of this work has consisted of carefully documented, extended case studies of young children learning to write (Baghban, 1984; Bissex, 1980). Other researchers have focused on the functions of writing at the early stage and its relationship to other areas of development. For example, King and Rentel (1979) suggest that writing shows a sequential development, and Gundlach (1981) suggests that early writing shows a functional association with other activities, such as symbolic play (Pellegrini, 1980). The association between writing and drawing is particularly strong. Several researchers have pointed out that children begin to distinguish between drawing and writing at very young ages and that they view their marks as communication (Baghban, 1981; Graves, 1975; Grinnell & Burris, 1983; Harste, Burke, & Woodward, 1981).

An important influence in this work has been Piagetian developmental theory. As an example, work on invented spelling (children's inventions of systematic but unconventional ways of spelling words before receiving formal instruction) has been used to argue that children actively construct hypotheses about written language consistent with understanding of writing at different developmental stages (Clay, 1983). Clay (1975) and Read (1975) have shown that children know a lot about literacy before they can write and read in an "adult" conventional sense. That is, they are active developers of principles, which they use for writing before they have learned the conventional system of their language (Bissex, 1980; Ferreiro & Teberosky, 1982). This work is based upon the Piagetian notions of children as active constructors of such principles as a result of interactions with the world and their qualitatively different understandings of literacy as a function of developmental level.

In addition to the preceding developmentally based approaches, some researchers have adopted cognitive approaches related more closely to information-processing models (Lachman, Lachman, & Butterfield, 1979; Schank & Ableson, 1977). An important part of this work is a model of the writing process as a cognitive activity best explained with concepts such as planning, decision making, and problem solving (Gerber, 1984; Hall, 1980). For example, Hayes and Flower (1980a, 1980b) have used the analysis of verbal protocols, and Matuhashi (1981) has used videotape records of pause times of writers at work. This work suggests that the cognitive processes involved in writing appear to occur simultaneously and interactively rather than in discrete and neatly defined stages. The writer appears to operate like a busy switchboard operator trying to juggle a number of demands on his or her attention and constraints on what he or she can do. This "switchboard" model emphasizes the active role of the writer in attempting to juggle the demands of writing in the face of a finite amount of cognitive resources. Performance, then, can be seen as a result of the interaction of individual cognitive processes with the task itself. It is easy to see the importance of "executive" or monitoring processes, which are needed in order to regulate and coordinate the task demands with available (and finite) cognitive resources.

Scardamalia and Bereiter (1986), in a recent review, consider the hypothesis that immature writers are handicapped by having to focus attention on writing mechanics and other low-level production problems. In the face of limited cognitive processing capacity, some researchers have attempted to ease the "cognitive burden" as a means of facilitating writing. One series of studies (Scardamalia, Bereiter, & Goelman, 1982) used dictation to discover whether composing would be facilitated when low-level production problems were eased. These studies showed a positive effect on length but not necessarily quality of text generated. In addition, Bereiter and Scardamalia (1982) reported on several experiments on the effects of procedural facilitations, that is, teaching strategies designed to ease the cognitive demands of writing. Generally, they found that these types of approaches eased the cognitive burdens of writing and facilitated the oral-to-written transition for fourth- and sixth-grade writers. Finally, as further support for this hypothesis, Graves (1975) has reported that self-selection of topics of interest significantly increases the amount written by primary-grade students. Scardamalia and Bereiter (1986) suggest that this can be viewed as compensating for students' lack of metamemorial and heuristic search abilities.

Scardamalia and Bereiter (1986) have pointed out some characteristics of expressive writing that meet some of the aforementioned conditions:

> From a processing standpoint, expressive writing would seem to have the following characteristics: (a) readily available content, so that heuristic search of memory is not required, (b) little need for intentional framing of the discourse, since content may be adequately presented in the form given to it in memory, and (c) little need for goal-related planning, since the goal of the activity is to a large extent realized through the very act of expression. All of this serves to explain why expressive writing should be easier for novices than other kinds of writing. . . . Thus there is reason, from an instructional viewpoint, to regard expressive writing as a preliminary or bridge to other kinds of writing. (p. 793)

Summary of theoretical perspectives

What are the instructional implications of the preceding theoretical frameworks? Does a Vygotskian approach to written language suggest instructional practices that deviate from the other approaches just discussed? Interestingly, although these frameworks embrace different assumptions and premises, and are often considered as very distinct, there is a surprising yet significant convergence with respect to instructional principles. At the most basic level, for example, early writing instruction should take into account the early developmental and social roots of language as a tool, as well as existing connections to a larger complex of previous developmental achievements such as oral language.

Although each of the perspectives reviewed emphasizes different aspects of the teaching/learning process, in each case a major component is the key role of the social agent (especially the teacher) in advancing development. The classroom teacher can be hypothesized to play a critical role in assisting students to internalize the concept of written language as a medium for expressive and communicative purposes. Teachers should provide authentic contexts for written expression, focus on writing as meaningful communication, provide guided assistance by structuring input just above students' present developmental levels, and attempt to bridge present levels of proficiency (such as in oral language) to future levels of written proficiency.

Having reviewed Vygotskian principles regarding the instruction of writing and compared them to other major approaches, we will now consider the literature on mildly handicapped students and written language, including traditional instructional approaches.

Mildly handicapped students and written language

An extensive body of research suggests that mildly handicapped students have significant problems in the acquisition and use of written expression. For example, Deno, Marston, and Mirkin (1982) found that samples of third- to sixth-grade learning-disabled students were performing approximately 3 years behind nonhandicapped comparison groups in the development of writing skills. Similarly, Myklebust (1965, 1972) reported that learning-disabled (LD) children performed more poorly on syntax, ideation, total number of words, and words per sentence than did non-LD children. In addition, Hermeck (1979) found learning-disabled students wrote an average of 42% fewer words per composition than nonlabeled peers, and Poteet (1979) found learning-disabled students wrote significantly fewer words and sentences and made more punctuation errors and word omissions than their nonhandicapped peers. Finally, Poplin, Gray, Larsen, Banikowski, and Mehring (1980) and Weiner (1980) have found the performance of mildly handicapped children to be significantly poorer than that of nondisabled children on a variety of indicators.

Although not exhaustive, these and other studies (Cartwright, 1968; Gerber & Hall, 1984; Moran, 1981; Morris & Crump, 1982; Sedlak & Cartwright, 1972) suggest that mildly handicapped students encounter a number of difficulties in the use of written language skills. Traditionally, it has been assumed that these difficulties were entirely attributable to within-child defects (see, e.g., Coles, 1987, for a discussion of this issue with respect to learning-disabled students). In fact, mildly handicapped students have been described as exhibiting certain cognitive characteristics that may interfere with the development of written language proficiency, and these will be described in the following paragraphs. Nevertheless, as will be argued, a more likely hypothesis is that a more significant part of these students' difficulty may be traced to problematic approaches to writing instruction (Graham, 1982), which may interact with cognitive factors or which may independently affect the development of writing ability. These cognitive and instructional factors will be discussed briefly in the following paragraphs.

Cognitive factors

Since writing is clearly a developmental process, it is logical to assume that the quality of written communication will be hampered by developmental delays (Litowitz, 1981) such as those which the psychological and educational literature has described as characteristic of mildly handicapped students. Although generalized, nonspecific developmental delays might affect the acquisition of written language proficiency, more specific characteristics of mildly handicapped students are reported in the literature that might influence writing competence as well. These include, for example, difficulties in strategic and self-regulatory behaviors, difficulties in taking into account a listener's perspective, and difficulties in sustained attention and motivation.[2]

Current conceptualizations of problem solving in a wide variety of tasks suggest the importance of various self-regulatory mechanisms for successful performance, for example, checking, planning, monitoring, testing, revising, and evaluating strategies (Brown, Bransford, Ferrara, & Campione, 1982). Yet it is precisely in these areas where mildly handicapped students appear to have particular difficulty. Torgeson (1977), Hall (1980), Brooks, Sperber, and McCauley (1984), and others, for example, have written about the difficulties of mildly handicapped students in these areas during problem-solving situations. It is evident that there are several stages in the writing process where these behaviors are essential and that problems in these areas will be reflected in written expression (Martlew, 1983). As Martlew indicates, "Writing is a more deliberate and conscious act than speech, and requires the ability to reflect upon language. . . . In writing, an awareness of the reader, in relation to style and content, has to be sustained solely by internal prompts throughout the entire exercise" (pp. 306–307). Consistent with this hypothesis, Deshler (1978) found that disabled learners detected only one-third of the errors made in a writing task.

In addition to metacognitive skills, an essential part of successful writing is the ability to take into account one's audience. In Piagetian terms, this is referred to as decentration, or the ability to view situations or events from the perspective of another. There is some evidence that mildly handicapped students find this type of task especially problematic as well. For example, Greenspan (1979) and Simeonsson (1978) have described the relatively poor performance of mildly handicapped students on social problem-solving situations that entail having to anticipate the views or perspective of others. It is not difficult to hypothesize how limitations in perspective-taking ability might interfere with the development of written communication proficiency.

A third area in which it has been suggested that mildly handicapped students tend to perform poorly is based on research on attention and its relation to task performance (see, e.g., Carr, 1984, for a review). When the sustained effort required by the editing and revising process is considered, problems can be anticipated, especially where attentional and motivational deficits are present (Polloway, Patton, & Cohen, 1981). This is especially true where composing, editing, and revising take place through the medium of paper and pencil, which are relatively unforgiving of errors and corrections. This problem might be further exacerbated in a context where the teacher emphasizes error-free or "correct" writing.

Upon close examination of commonly reported learner-related characteristics of mildly handicapped students, it is clear how difficulties in acquiring written proficiency are often attributed to within-child defects. Nevertheless, consideration of commonly used instructional practices, briefly outlined in the following paragraphs, suggests that other factors may be important as well.

Instructional factors

One of the factors mitigating against the development of writing in mildly handicapped students is the fact that often only minimal instructional time is provided. One reason for this is based on early but now outdated conceptualizations of the development of writing. For example, there has been some controversy regarding the nature of the relationship among oral language, reading, and writing, which has been under investigation for some time. One of the first researchers to examine this issue with special education students was Myklebust (1965, 1972), who hypothesized a hierarchy of language abilities. This hierarchy started with Oral Receptive ability (listening) and proceeded to Oral Expressive ability (speaking), then to Written Receptive ability (reading), and finally to Written Expression (writing). Instruction based on this presumed developmental hierarchy concentrated on these areas, following this order. Although this assumed progression of language abilities has been challenged by a number of investigators (Bissex, 1980; De Ford, 1980; King & Rentel, 1979; Read, 1980), both Barenbaum (1983) and Poplin (1983) point out that instruction resulting from this framework has tended to dominate special education classrooms. For example, since mildly handicapped students frequently exhibit delays in acquiring listening, speaking, and reading abilities, "higher-order" activities involving writing are rarely taught in special education classrooms.

In addition to the fact that little instructional time is devoted to writing, questions have been raised regarding the theoretical assumptions of prevailing educational practices (Laine & Schultz, 1985). Much of this criticism is directed at the decontextualized, "discrete step" style that characterizes most instruction (Edelsky, Draper, & Smith, 1983; Erickson, 1984; Ferreiro & Teberosky, 1982; Graves, 1983; Laine & Schultz, 1985; LCHC Newsletter, 1982; Riel, 1985), and which is often even more pronounced in special education settings as part of a remedial approach. As Vygotsky has pointed out, psychology (which education and special education in particular have drawn on as a parent discipline) has tended to conceive of writing as a complicated motor skill, and this has been translated into many writing programs. Laine and Schultz (1985) have described the role of the teacher in this widely used type of mechanics-oriented writing curricula and instructional materials:

> Rather than encouraging clear, vivid, and honest language, teachers emphasize mistake-free writing, workbook exercises, drills on usage, and analyzing existing prose. Negative correction and prescription replace positive instruction. Students may master grammar and correct usage, but may also adopt a sterile objectivity and disinterest. (p. 14)

In contrast to instructional approaches that are reductionist in nature, advocates of holistic approaches argue that meaningful, authentic communication should be the central focus of both reading and writing (De Ford, 1981; De Ford & Harste, 1982; Goodman & Goodman, 1981; Harste & Burke, 1977). From this perspective, decontextualized, discrete-skill, hierarchical approaches to reading and writing reflect fundamentally incorrect conceptualizations of literacy as a process. More recently, Poplin (1988) has outlined the rudiments of a holistic approach to learning with respect to teaching and learning for learning-disabled students.

Given an instructional orientation that decontextualizes and breaks apart the components of writing such that they are detached from meaningful and functional activities, it is understandable that mastery of written language as a functional communicative tool would be problematic for many students. For instance, one important hypothesis is that some students have problems in reading and writing at least in part because their conceptualization of reading and writing is basically incorrect (Edelsky et al., 1983; LCHC Newsletter, 1982). It appears that, rather than defining reading and writing as integrated, functional activities that allow one either to gain useful information about the world or to communicate with others, many poor writers view these activities as discrete, isolated skills to be performed for teacher approval.

Mildly handicapped students, microcomputers, and writing

In light of the problems of mildly handicapped students with written language, the rapid growth of microcomputer use for writing has sparked a great deal of interest in possible applications with learning-disabled students. Given the problems that LD students have with written language, it is reasonable to hypothesize that microcomputers might be an important tool in increasing the quality and amount of writing. For example, Graves (1984) has discussed the negative consequences of revising when using paper and pencil (e.g., erasures, cross-outs, recopying, etc.), which tends to discourage playing and experimenting with writing. Such consequences might be overcome with a word processor. Nevertheless, the initial results of studies of microcomputer-based writing with learning-disabled students have been less than enthusiastic.

As an example, Kerchner and Kistinger (1984) found facilitating effects on the standardized writing test scores of learning-disabled students, in comparison to two control groups, when word-processing experience was combined with an interactive and motivating approach to writing. However, the pattern of results suggested that it was not computer use per se but rather the combination of computer use and the interactive approach to writing that produced the gains in test scores.

There are at least two possible explanations for these initial findings. First, there is evidence that some groups, such as females, minority students, and special education students, simply have less access to computers and therefore less time to develop proficiency. Various investigations have pointed out how access to computers is differentially distributed such that, for members of these groups, the actual amount of time spent using the computer is less (Boruta et al., 1983; Christensen & Cosden, 1984; Cosden, Gerber, Goldman, Semmel, & Semmel, 1984).

A second and more important explanation, however, can be found in the ways that these students interact with computers. These studies show, for example, that the kind of experiences provided are "low-order" computer literacy skills (keyboard entry, disk placement, etc.) or repetitive drill and practice activities. In contrast, students not in these groups tend to spend more time with the computer and tend to be exposed more to "higher-order" activities, such as programming and problem solving.

Unfortunately, when the instructional uses of computers are analyzed carefully, it is apparent that the ways in which they are utilized are characteristic of more general and problematic instructional patterns (Cosden, Gerber, Semmel, Goldman, & Semmel, 1985). As discussed earlier, commonly used approaches to writing instruction characteristically conceptualize writing as multileveled skills and abilities which can be separated for instructional purposes and taught sequentially and hierarchically, and it appears that this tends to transfer to educational uses of microcomputers as well. Students with learning problems are provided extensive instruction in the basic, low-order steps assumed to lead to higher-order proficiency in literacy. Continued failure in reading and writing leads to more intensive drill and practice in the elemental steps thought necessary for continued development.

Application of the theory: Assisting written performance

The earlier discussion of theoretical approaches to writing suggests that beginning writing and/or writing activities for learning-handicapped students should be structured to minimize the cognitive demands in the face of their limited cognitive-processing capacity. For example, the teacher should attempt to minimize, where possible, the low-level production problems in complex writing tasks so that resources can be directed toward meaningful communication. Yet this emphasis needs to be tempered by the Vygotskian principle of providing input and guidance just above the current developmental level. That is, the role of the teacher is best conceptualized as facilitating writing as a developmental process. Since writing begins very early in development, an optimal approach should provide a bridge from already existing to current levels of development.

One major implication of the Vygotskian approach for learning-disabled students is that mild learning or developmental delays should not preclude the introduction of and stress on writing at an early point in the curriculum. Further, the preceding suggests that errors are not simply mistakes and should not be taken as evidence of lack of readiness to begin receiving instructions. Rather, they represent a given developmental level of understanding of print, which is part of normal development. More importantly, however, within the framework children are seen as active constructors, rather than passive learners, in their attempts to make sense of the nature and uses of print. One of the primary motivating forces driving an ever more complex organization of writing as a tool for the child is interaction with the environment and others in it. Especially in the early stages of the acquisition of writing, the teacher is a key part of the process, who must actively engage the child and provide feedback in activities involving print.

Interactive writing approaches

Recently, various investigators have begun to incorporate the above principles in an attempt to develop children's written communication. For example, one line of research has attempted to examine the role of the teacher in creating functional writing environments for students of English as a second language (ESL) and for hearing-impaired and mentally retarded students (Farley, 1984; Kreeft, Shuy, Staton, Reed, & Morroy, 1984; Staton, 1981a, 198b, 1985; Staton, Shuy, Kreeft, & Reed, in press) through the use of classroom-based dialogue journals.

Staton (1981a, 1981b, 1985) has described dialogue journals as interactive, written conversations carried on by student and teacher frequently and continuously over an extended period of time. In essence, the journal provides a means for maintaining private written conversations with the teacher on a regular basis. Distinguishing characteristics of journals include the freedom of the writer to select topics and to communicate real and meaningful concerns and issues, a focus on meaning and mutual understanding rather than correct form, and communication that is private and not subject to public inspection without the writer's consent.

In addition to drawing on the sociohistorical and ''whole-language'' approaches to instruction, these investigators have been influenced by research on the natural acquisition of oral language. An important aspect of this work has been the attempt to provide an authentic and meaningful context for writing, as well as to create a bridge between competence in oral language and developing proficiency in written expression (Peyton, in press; Shuy, in press; Staton, 1984). One assumption in this research is that learning to read and write can and should emulate the natural, functional, interactive process of oral language acquisition as it occurs between parent and child in nonschool settings without the benefit of formal training. This learning is accomplished primarily through meaningful interaction with adults and peers, with a great deal of nonevaluative assisted performance. These investigators have attempted to use journal writings as a bridge to incorporate and expand what young children can already accomplish with oral language. As Shuy (in press) points out, most types of school-based written language assignments strictly limit the range of acceptable language functions, often emphasizing the reporting of facts. For example, narrative writing encourages sequencing of ideas, descriptive writing encourages description, and essays encourage introductions, explanations, and conclusions. However, young children are apparently capable of much more extensive variety, at least in oral language contexts. The more formal types of writing are not necessarily bad, but they do not appear to assimilate already existing competence in oral language during the *initial* stages of development. In this work, then, optimal teacher input should include interactional features comparable to those encountered by young children learning oral language in natural contexts, including the maintenance of topics of mutual interest and knowledge over time.

In one analysis, Staton (1984) demonstrated that teacher input in a dialogue journal situation varied markedly across a number of linguistic and interactional features. In addition, Kreeft (1984) found that, with the same teacher, the patterns of question asking resembled face-to-face conversation rather than typical classroom interaction patterns, and that questions were adjusted to the language level of individual students and changed as students became more fluent. Kreeft (1984) also traced the development of a single student, a native English speaker, in the areas of topic focus and elaboration, creation of context, and interaction with audience through daily written interaction with a teacher over 10 months' time.

Farley (1984) examined the written communication between himself (the teacher) and six educable mentally retarded teenagers over a 40-day period. Although there was considerable variability in the students' performance in the production of correct linguistic structures, all students demonstrated the acquisition of mature topic maintenance which was chronological-age (not mental-age) appropriate. Further, all participants were able to produce functionally relevant, interactive written communication.

In an important extension of this type of work, Morroy (1984) argued that the written products of dyadic journals must be considered on a level larger than either the individual student or the teacher. That is, the *dyad* and not the individual student or teacher should be the unit of analysis. He suggested one useful method, the analysis of extended topic chains, as a means of quantifying the effectiveness of teacher input in initiating and/or sustaining written interaction around topical areas. The idea underlying the topic chain is that the teacher actively assists the student in the dialogue journal interaction to link together topically related ''moves'' within student entries. A *move* consists of one or more topically related acts. For example, the following is an example of a move made up of three acts:

1. I went to school today.
2. It was fun.
3. I saw my friends there.

Moves can be either initiating or responding, depending upon whether the move introduces a new topic or is a response to a topic raised previously by the journal partner. Finally, an *extended topic chain* is a series of topically related moves. More specifically, these chains consist of at least two moves by the initiator of the topic, for example, student–teacher–student, or teacher–student–teacher. Given the goal of emulating everyday conversational ability, these chains provide a way of examining the partners' ability or willingness to maintain topics on an extended basis. It should be noted that, since journal interactions take place in nonreal time, participants typically produce more than one move at a sitting, and therefore multiple topics can be introduced or responded to simultaneously.

Using this analytical scheme with the written journals of six sixth-grade students, Morroy (1984) found that most extended topic chains were student-initiated. On the average, 9.3% of all student topic initiations developed into extended topic chains as opposed to 2.7% of teacher topic initiations.

Computer-based functional learning environments

Although little of the work reviewed has focused on the use of microcomputers for writing, there is no reason to hypothesize that the addition of the computer substantially changes any of the principles involved. For example, attempts have been made to develop software that allows the amount of assistance provided by the computer to be decreased systematically by the novice user as expertise is gained. This "dynamic support" is based directly on the interactional notions of learning presented earlier (Mehan, Moll, Riel, et al., 1985; Riel, Levin, & Miller-Souviney, 1984).

Another approach has concentrated on attempting to organize microcomputer-based *functional learning environments*. These environments are described as those in which writing (and reading) activities are organized for communicative purposes, rather than just as an exercise for teacher evaluation (cf. Edelsky et al., 1983; LCHC Newsletter, 1982). As one example, Levin, Riel, Boruta, and Rowe (1984) created a "Computer Chronicles Newswire," which connected students in geographically distant areas, enabling communication by computer. Students in each classroom in the network (Alaska, Hawaii, and California) wrote and edited stories about local events, which were then sent on disk to all participating sites. This collection of stories was then edited, and each site published local versions of a computer-based newspaper. The intent was to create meaningful, functional, and authentic contexts for the development of writing; that is, the teaching of writing was embedded in a context where writing was used to accomplish goals important to the students.

Naiman (1988) has reported the use of microcomputers to facilitate an interactive approach to literacy in a 3-year study of 91 special education students between the ages of 12 and 18, in 10 schools. The various disability groups represented included deaf, learning-disabled, emotionally disturbed, and mentally retarded students as well as students with cerebral palsy. Microcomputer-based activities included electronic mailbox correspondence; an electronic school bulletin board for posting stories, news, and so on; and a dialogue journal writing conference in which teachers and students communicated on an individual basis. Overall, students were able to demonstrate progress in their ability to communicate, and in addition there were positive changes over time with respect to both the structural aspects of the students' writing and their attitudes toward writing. Most importantly, these findings were most characteristic of students who were high-frequency users, and especially when students were engaged in ongoing correspondence with a mature writer.

It should be recalled that in Vygotsky's work the role of the "more competent other" is central in providing "assisted performance" (Tharp & Gallimore, 1988). From this perspective, the teacher's role is best conceived as organizing the learning context to create a scaffold and draw upon existing levels of development while providing input and feedback within the upper ranges of the zone of proximal development. How do teachers of learning-disabled students attempt to engage them and "draw out" what they can do with written language? In those instances when this happens, are some interactional strategies more successful than others?

Preliminary answers to these questions are provided in some of my work (Rueda, 1986, 1988), which has attempted to utilize a Vygotskian approach to interactive writing in microcomputer environments with learning-disabled students. In this work, a major goal has been to investigate microcomputer-based, interactive written communication (dialogue journals) between special education teachers and learning-disabled students in everyday classroom settings.

Each of seven special education teachers selected three to four learning-disabled students for participation in the study for a total of 27 students. The mean chronological age was 10.8 (sd = .85) and mean IQ was 97 (sd = 5.09). Although all of the students were judged by their teachers to be proficient English speakers at the time of the study, 11 (41%) of the resource room students were from non-English-language backgrounds (Spanish, in all cases).

As part of the study, teachers were provided with specially created software designed to facilitate interactive dialogue journal writing with students. As with paper-and-pencil dialogue journals, the *Dialog Maker* (1985) attempts to foster the major interactional characteristics of face-to-face conversation in a written interaction that takes place over an extended period of time. For example, the *Dialog Maker* allows the teacher to write his or her part of the conversation to a student sequentially, characteristically carrying on multiple threads of conversation at the same time, leaving "pauses" for the student to write back. This part of the dialogue is then saved in a file, which the student can access at any time. When the student signs on, each part of the teacher "message" is presented to the student in the order in which it was written, and the student can then respond. Although there are some similarities between these written dialogues and face-to-face conversation, the pauses between the different multiple threads of the written interaction, which allow the student time to think and respond to the message, represent a basic difference between this form of discourse and oral conversation. When a student has responded to one part of the message, or if the student chooses not to respond to a particular point, the program automatically presents the next part of the message written earlier by the teacher (if any). The completed dialogue can then be printed out, including both teacher and student entries, so that a completed journal entry is available for review. This permits the student to reflect, at a later time, on the *whole* body of the written discourse for one or more sessions.

The following example, taken from one of the early journals, when the "ground rules" were being negotiated and established, characterizes some of the unique features of this type of interaction. The excerpt, reproduced exactly as written, illustrates several features, such as multiple threads of discourse carried on at the same time, the use of invented spellings and other "mistakes" by the student, the teacher's use of modeling of "correct" form while focusing on the message and not the errors. (It should be kept in mind that the teacher's entries were completed all in one sitting at the computer, and the student then responded, at a later time, to these entries, which were presented sequentially by the program):

> Ms. P: Jose, I didn't know you were so interested in football. Are you in a league? Do you play on a team? I'm wondering if you will have a hundred girlfriends because you'll be a handsome football player.
>
> Jose: Yes Ms P I do have a girlfriend called Virginia but please dont tell nobody. And I wish to play for the Raiders.
>
> Ms. P: Jose, I just want you to know that nobody reads these dialogs except you, me and Dr. Rueda. We keep this information very private because we want to be able to write about ourselves too! So the info about your girlfriend, Virginia, is totally secret and protected. You know I think that Main Street should have an ongoing football team. I wish you weren't in the sixth grade and we could start one next year. What do you think about this whole idea?
>
> Jose: I think thats a great idea Ms P Today I'm going to play football with my consoler so someday I will be in a real football team. Ms P by for now Ms P.

Since the role of the "more capable other" is so important in the Vygotskian framework, the input of the teacher was seen as especially important. Over the approximately 3-month period that the program was used, a completed journal interaction was produced, on the average, every third day. Although teachers tended to write more than students (the mean ratio of student-to-teacher words was .73, sd = .45), much of this appeared to be due to students' lack of previous experience with computers and keyboarding skills as well as classroom disruptions, which occur frequently for special education students.

One especially interesting aspect of teacher input is the use of questioning, one of the main vehicles used by teachers for assessing student understanding, promoting or sustaining discussion, and so on. Although teachers tended to dominate the amount of discourse in the journals, the use of low-level questions was relatively infrequent. From a Vygotskian standpoint, a preponderance of low-level yes/no-type questions would indicate that teachers were probably inappropriately simplifying input to the students' lower end of the zone of proximal development. However, only 4% of the 581 teacher questions analyzed were low-level "tag" questions (a statement with a question contained in the final clause and requiring only a yes/no answer) or "choice" questions (providing two or more possible responses from which to choose). In contrast, 61% of the teacher questions were "statement" questions (having the form of a declarative but eliciting an opinion) or questions eliciting information regarding who, when, where, what, why, or how, indicating that these teachers did not appear to simplify input indiscriminately. Although the teachers in this particular study preferred to use high-level questions in these interactions, apparently this practice is not universal. For example, Kreeft (1984) reported that teachers in her study with ESL sixth-grade students rarely used "higher-order'' questions but frequently used low-order yes/no questions. The following example shows the excessive use of low-level questions by one teacher and the resulting low-level responses of the student:

> Mrs. C: Good morning, Adalbert. How are you today? What did you do last night? I played racketball. Have you ever played? It is fun! Have you ever played smashball? I played at some friends house for the first time on Sunday. It is fun and easy. What is your favorite game? Are you getting your homework done? I hope so. How is everything else? Is there anything you want to talk to me about? Please try to write more than you have been.
> Adalbert: No. Yes. Softball. No. And yes. Fine. No. No. Thanks.

It is evident that this student is attempting to respond in machine-gun fashion to a barrage of questions which stimulate little more than the yes/no-type answers he has provided. In the example given earlier, however, the teacher uses yes/no questions but then integrates a statement question that elicits the student's opinion and prompts him to disclose a secret bit of information which he chooses to share with the teacher:

> Ms. P: Jose, I didn't know you were so interested in football. Are you in a league? Do you play on a team? I'm wondering if you will have a hundred girlfriends because you'll be a handsome football player.
> Jose: Yes Ms P I have a girlfriend called Virginia but please dont tell nobody. And I wish to play for the Raiders.

In addition to teachers' use of questions, other interactional aspects of the journals were examined as well, using Morroy's (1984) analytical scheme, which was described earlier. It will be recalled that this scheme provides a system for coding initiating and responding moves as well as extended topic chains. In general, there were more initiating moves by teachers than students (teachers produced 538 initiating moves, whereas students produced only 127). Again, this does not appear to be a universal feature of this type of interaction. Data presented by Morroy (1984) for sixth-grade ESL students, for example, showed that the majority of initiating moves were student-generated. However, the teachers of these learning-disabled students were not engaging in discourse that went unheeded. Interestingly, students responded to 97% of teachers' initiating moves. Moreover, in 9 of 27 cases resource room students had a higher percentage of initiating moves that led to extended chains than did their teachers. This is an encouraging finding, as it suggests that, even though students tended to produce substantially fewer initiating moves than teachers, in several cases students were successful not only in participating in but in actually initiating interaction. This attests to the role of creating a context and structuring learning to take existing abilities into account.

Of particular interest for the present discussion were the extended topic chains found in the dialogue journals. Although these are joint productions by teachers and students, examination of the teacher input provides some insight into the ways in which teachers attempted either to initiate or to sustain written conversation with these students. Overall, 39 of these chains were initiated by teachers (initiating chains), and 48 were initiated by students and responded to by teachers (responding chains).

In order to examine more closely the strategies that teachers incorporated in promoting extended topic chains, the language functions associated with the teachers' initiating and responding moves within extended topic chains were coded. Morroy (1984) has termed these *local strategies,* and the various categories represent the functional uses of language that teachers employed while attempting to engage their students in written interaction. One assumption in this analysis is that journals build upon what students already know, in this case proficiency in oral language and everyday conversational ability. One indicator of "success" in this type of everyday conversation is the ability to sustain an interaction over a period of time or series of interactions. Therefore, since the journals attempted to emulate this activity, it was assumed that an important indicator of successful journal interaction was the production of extended topic chains. In this regard, these extended chains provide a unique opportunity to examine the local strategies that either initiate or sustain this interaction and therefore represent key elements of "successful" teacher input. The 19 categories used to classify these were adopted from examination of the written journals, as well as from Morroy (1984) and Shuy (1984). They included a variety of pragmatic functions from school-like forms, such as evaluating, giving directives, and requesting academic information, to more conversational functions, such as reporting personal facts and requesting personal information. (Although there are two teacher moves in such a chain, only sentences within the first teacher move were coded, under the assumption that the first move was the stimulus for the resulting student response.)

Analysis of the extended topic chains produced by the teachers and students showed that the most common local strategies associated with those topic chains initiated by the teachers were reporting opinion or expressing feeling and requesting personal information.

In addition to the local strategies associated with topic chains initiated by teachers, the local strategies associated with sustaining topic chains, where teachers responded to student initiations, were also analyzed. These are especially important from a Vygotskian perspective, as they demonstrate a sensitivity to student input and can be conceptualized as the teacher's informal theory of how to engage the student in further interaction. The most frequently used local strategies in these data were reporting opinion/expressing feeling and requesting personal information. In general, these results were not markedly different from those that emerged from the initiating topic chains.

In the following example, from Rueda (1988), the teacher engages a student during a discussion of the army by disclosing very personal information and then asking an open-ended question:

> Ms. P: Jose, I never met a boy who was so excited about going to the army. When I lived in Israel, I was there during a war in 1973. My boyfriend was hurt, and it wasn't fun. What do you think about that?

> Jose: Yes I think youre right Was is not a game Was is when people looses familys
> and when peoples suffers because people dont like their familys Ms. P wore
> you their when was was in Israel How does it feel Ms. P And wore you hurt . . .

In spite of the fact that the student's response is replete with invented spellings, lack of punctuation, and other grammatical problems, it is evident that the student is engaged and has begun to grasp the notion of written language as a communicative tool.

What do these findings mean with respect to the questions posed earlier regarding teachers' strategies? It should be recalled that there are many routinized interactional features of typical classrooms which are not commonly found in other settings, such as initiation–reply–evaluation sequences (Mehan, 1979). In contrast, the extended topic chains examined were best described as initiation–reply–reply sequences. It is not often that language functions such as reporting personal opinion, expressing personal feelings, and requesting personal information from students form a significant part of ordinary classroom discourse, whereas evaluation of student performance through questioning does. At the points in time when the teachers used the non-teacherlike patterns, they appear to have implicitly adopted a pattern of interaction that led to "personalization" of the input. For example, reporting opinion or expressive feeling requires personal self-disclosure and openness on the part of the teacher. Although teachers used a range of strategies in interacting with their students, it is clear that they tended to avoid strategies that are most often associated with classroom teacher talk, that is, requesting academic information, giving directives, and, most importantly, evaluating. Providing a nonevaluative, non-school-like context, then, seemed to be an effective way of assisting performance in this writing activity.

It must be recalled that, although the use of these language functions or local strategies were associated with student responses more often than the others, and in this sense can be considered as more "successful," it cannot be concluded that they "caused" students to respond. Moreover, the extended topic chains formed only a part of the dialogue journals. That is, there were many instances where initiating moves by the teachers did not result in responses by students. There were also many instances where teachers' replies to student initiations did not result in continuation of the topic by the students. However, the fact that there were relatively few of these chains makes careful analysis of those instances where these interactional sequences did occur all the more important, since they provide preliminary clues to teachers about directions to explore in assisting the beginning writing performance of students with writing difficulties.

Summary and conclusion

One important aspect of Vygotsky's approach to learning and development is the notion of primary defect and secondary defect (Gindis, 1988). The former refers to organic impairment due to both hereditary factors and biological factors acquired after birth. The latter, on the other hand, refers to a disruption of the development of higher psychological functions due to social factors. That is, social activity and social relationships, which form the basis for learning and development, can be distorted due to social reactions to real (or, more importantly, perceived) handicaps, with a resulting decay in developmental progress. As Gindis (1988) notes,

> Social deprivation, as a result of society's response to a child's organic impairment, adversely affects the whole developmental process. Crucial in a chain of social exclusions are adequate communications with adults, distorted relationships with peers, and failure in acquisition of "role games." From this point of view, many symptoms of mental retardation . . . may be considered as typical secondary defects acquired . . . in the process of social interaction. (pp. 381–382)

It is well documented that learning-disabled students experience problems in acquiring written language proficiency. Often, these difficulties are conceived as mainly due to within-child deficiencies. However, whatever the state of a child's biological or neurological makeup,[3] the Vygotskian framework emphasizes that learning handicaps can be exacerbated or minimized by subsequent social interaction, specifically those in school-based contexts. In the case of learning-disabled and other mildly handicapped students, who make up over 90% of the special education population (Forness & Kavale, in press), the nature of these interactions can be especially critical. From an educational perspective, aiming learning activities at a level too low within the zone of proximal development, or underestimating learning potential due to inappropriately or poorly organized instructional activity, is certain to result in further difficulties. As the earlier review suggests, it is very possible that many instructional approaches used with special education students for teaching writing may be doing just that.

The interactional characteristics of the journals just described, as well as the other work examined, provide a unique look at written interaction, which has yet to be explored as an important part of the classroom context, especially in special education settings. This is probably due to the fact that written interaction occurs relatively infrequently; in addition, writing is usually conceptualized and taught as an individual academic event and not as a social and communicative tool. Most often, once the basic mechanics have been mastered, this communicative aspect of writing is left for students to arrive at independently. Nevertheless, the theory and research reviewed here suggest that there are interesting possibilities for development when this notion is reversed, that is, when the social and communicative aspects of written language are given primary emphasis before mastery of basic skills. The work just described suggests that learning-disabled students are able to engage appropriately in written interaction with their teachers, given the appropriately organized context. As the Vygotskian framework suggests, the role of the teacher can be one of the more important factors in stimulating the development of beginning writing ability. Moreover, as a theoretical framework, Vygotskian theory offers significant potential for major changes in how literacy is taught to handicapped students.

Notes

1 The terms *mildly handicapped* and *learning handicapped* are generic terms most often used to characterize students traditionally labeled learning-disabled, mildly mentally retarded, or behavior-disordered. The use of the term *mildly handicapped* reflects increasing recognition that the common characteristic of these students is academic underachievement and that the separation of these students into distinct categories may not be educationally relevant. See MacMillan, Keogh, and Jones (1986) for further discussion of this issue.

2 Although various characteristics, cognitive or otherwise, are attributed to mildly handicapped students, there is increasing evidence that cognitive abilities are much more contextually specific than commonly assumed, and caution must be exercised in generalizing inappropriately. See, for example, Donaldson (1978) and Laboratory of Comparative Human Cognition (1983) for more comprehensive treatment of this issue.

3 There is a great deal of controversy regarding the role of biological and neurological factors in learning disabilities. Some argue that learning disabilities are the direct result of neurological impairments, whereas others assert that they are merely a special case of undifferentiated low achievement. See Coles (1987) for a review of this issue.

References

Baghban, M. (1981). *Language development and early encounters with written language.* Paper presented at the annual meeting of the National Council of Teachers of English, Boston. (ERIC Document Reproduction Service No. ED 211 975)

Baghban, M. (1984). *Our daughter learns to read and write: A case study from birth to three.* Newark, DE: International Reading Association.

Barenbaum, E. (1983). Writing in the special class. *Topics in Learning and Learning Disabilities, 3*(3), 12–20.

Bereiter, C., & Scardamalia, M. (1982). From conversation to composition: The role of instruction in a developmental process. In R. Glaser (Ed.), *Advances in instructional psychology* (Vol. 2). Hillsdale, NJ: Erlbaum.

Bissex, G. L. (1980). *GNYS at work: A child learns to write and read.* Cambridge, MA: Harvard University Press.

Boruta, M., et al. (1983). Computers in schools: Stratifier or equalizer? *Quarterly Newsletter of the Laboratory of Comparative Human Cognition, 5*(3), 51–55.

Brooks, P. H., Sperber, R., & McCauley, C. (Eds.) (1984). *Learning and cognition in the mentally retarded.* Hillsdale, NJ: Erlbaum.

Brown, A. L., Bransford, J. D., Ferrara, R. A., & Campione, J. C. (1982). *Learning, remembering, and understanding* (Tech. Rep. No. 244). Urbana: University of Illinois.

Carr, T. H. (1984). Attention, skill, and intelligence: Some speculations on extreme individual differences in human performance. In P. H. Brooks, R. Sperber, & C. McCauley (Eds.), *Learning and cognition in the mentally retarded.* Hillsdale, NJ: Erlbaum.

Cartwright, G. (1968). Written language abilities of educable mentally retarded and normal children. *American Journal of Mental Deficiency, 72,* 499–505.

Christensen, C. A., & Cosden, M. A. (1984). *Instructional software for microcomputers: Differences in use across regular and special education environments* (Project TEECH Tech. Rep. No. 12.0). Santa Barbara: University of California.

Clay, M. M. (1975). *What did I write?* London: Heinemann.

Clay, M. M. (1983). Getting a theory of writing. In B. M. Kroll & G. Wells (Eds.), *Explorations in the development of writing: Theory, research, and practice.* New York: Wiley.

Cohen, M. (1984). Exemplary computer use in education. *Sigcue Bulletin: Computer Uses in Education, 18*(1), 16–19.

Coles, G. (1987). *The learning mystique: A critical look at learning disabilities.* New York: Pantheon.

Collins, J. L. (1981). *Spoken language and the development of writing abilities.* Paper presented at the Conference on College Composition and Communication, Dallas. (ERIC Document Reproduction Service No. ED 199 729)

Collins, J. L. (1984). The development of writing abilities during the school years. In A. D. Pellegrini & T. D. Yawkey (Eds.), *The development of oral and written language in social contexts*. Norwood, NJ: Ablex.

Cosden, M. A., Gerber, M. M., Goldman, S. R., Semmel, D. S., & Semmel, M. I. (1984). *Survey of microcomputer access and use by mildly handicapped students in Southern California* (Project TEECH Tech. Rep. No. 4.0). Santa Barbara: University of California.

Cosden, M. A., Gerber, M. M., Semmel, D. S., Goldman, S. R., & Semmel, M. I. (1985). *Observational study of microcomputer use by special day class, resource room, and mainstream handicapped and nonhandicapped students* (Project TEECH Tech. Rep. No. 8.0). Santa Barbara: University of California.

De Ford, D. (1980). Young children and their writing. *Theory into Practice, 19*, 157–162.

De Ford, D. (1981). Literacy: Reading, writing, and other essentials. *Language Arts, 58*(6), 652–658.

De Ford, D., & Harste, J. (1982). Child language research and curriculum. *Language Arts, 59*, 590–600.

Deno, S., Marston, D., & Mirkin, P. (1982). Valid measurement procedures for continuous evaluation of written expression. *Exceptional Children, 48*, 368–370.

Deshler, D. O. (1978). Psychoeducational aspects of learning-disabled adolescents. In L. Mann, L. Goodman, & J. L. Wiederholt (Eds.), *Teaching the learning disabled adolescent*. Boston: Houghton Mifflin.

Dialog Maker (1985). Interlearn, Inc., Cardiff by The Sea, CA.

Donaldson, M. (1978). *Childrens' minds*. New York: Norton.

Edelsky, C., Draper, K., & Smith, K. (1983). Hookin' 'em in at the start of school in a "whole language" classroom. *Anthropology and Education Quarterly, 14*(4), 257–281.

Elsasser, N., & John-Steiner, V. P. (1977). An interactionist approach to advancing literacy. *Harvard Educational Review, 47*, 355–369.

Erickson, F. (1984). School literacy, reasoning, and civility: An anthropologist's perspective. *Review of Educational Research, 54*(4), 525–546.

Farley, J. (1984). An analysis of written dialogue journals of educable mentally retarded writers. *Education and Training of the Mentally Retarded, 21*(3), 181–191.

Ferreiro, E., & Teberosky, A. (1979). *Los sistemas de escritura en el desarrollo del nino*. Mexico, D.F.: Siglo XXI. (English, 1982)

Ferreiro, E., & Teberosky, A. (1982). *Literacy before schooling*. Exeter, NH: Heinemann.

Forness, S. R., & Kavale, K. A. (in press). Identification and diagnostic issues in special education: A status report for child psychiatrists. *Journal of the American Academy of Child and Adolescent Psychiatry*.

Gerber, M. M. (1984). Orthographic problem-solving ability of learning disabled and normally achieving students. *Learning Disability Quarterly, 17*, 157–164.

Gerber, M., & Hall, R. (1984). *The development of spelling in learning disabled and normal students* (Monograph No. 1). Austin, TX: Society for Learning Disabilities and Remedial Education.

Gindis, B. (1988). Children with mental retardation in the Soviet Union, *Mental Retardation, 26*(6), 381–384.

Goodman, K., & Goodman, Y. (1981). *A whole-language comprehension-centered view of reading development* (Occasional Paper No. 1). Tucson: University of Arizona, Program in Language and Literacy.

Graham, S. (1982). Composition research and practice: A unified approach. *Focus on Exceptional Children, 14*(8), 1–16.

Graves, D. (1975). An examination of the writing processes of seven year old children. *Research in the Teaching of English, 9*, 227–241.

Graves, D. (1983). *Writing: Teachers and children at work*. Exeter, NH: Heinemann.

Graves, D. (1984). Microcomputers and writing. *Classroom Computer Learning, 4*(8), 20–24.

Greenspan, S. (1979). Social intelligence in the retarded. In N. R. Ellis (Ed.), *Handbook of mental deficiency: Psychological theory and research* (2nd ed.). Hillsdale, NJ: Erlbaum.

Grinnell, P. C., & Burris, N. A. (1983). Drawing and writing: The emerging graphic communication process. *Topics in Learning and Learning Disabilities, 3*(3), 21–32.

Gundlach, R. A. (1981). On the nature and development of children's writing. In C. H. Frederiksen and

J. F. Dominic (Eds.), *Writing: The nature, development, and teaching of written communication* (Vol. 2). Hillsdale, NJ: Erlbaum.

Hall, R. J. (1980). An information processing approach to the study of learning disabled and mildly retarded children. In B. Keogh (Ed.), *Advances in special education* (Vol. 2, pp. 79–110). Greenwich, CT: JAI Press.

Harste, J., & Burke, C. (1977). A new hypothesis for reading teacher research: Both teaching and learning of reading are theoretically based. *Claremont Reading Conference Yearbook*. Claremont, CA.

Harste, J. C., Burke, C. L., & Woodward, V. A. (1981). *Children, their language and world: Initial encounters with print* (NIE-G-79-0132). Bloomington: Indiana University.

Hayes, J. R., & Flower, L. S. (1980a). Identifying the organization of writing processes. In L. W. Gregg & E. R. Steinberg (Eds.), *Cognitive processes in writing*. Hillsdale, NJ: Erlbaum.

Hayes, J. R., & Flower, L. S. (1980b). The dynamics of composing: Making plans and juggling constraints. In L. W. Gregg & E. R. Steinberg (Eds.), *Cognitive processes in writing*. Hillsdale, NJ: Erlbaum.

Heath, S. B. (1983). *Ways with words: Language, life, and work in communities and classrooms*. Cambridge: Cambridge University Press.

Hermreck, L. A. (1979). *A comparison of the written language of LD and non-LD elementary children using the inventory of written expression and spelling*. Unpublished master's thesis, University of Kansas, Lawrence.

John-Steiner, V. P., & Tatter, P. (1983). An interactionist model of language development. In B. Bain (Ed.), *The sociogenesis of language and human development*. New York: Plenum.

Kerchner, L. B., & Kistinger, B. J. (1984). Language processing/word processing: Written expression, computers, and learning disabled students. *Learning Disabilities Quarterly, 7*, 329–335.

King, M. L., & Rentel, V. (1979). Toward a theory of early writing development. *Research in the Teaching of English, 13*, 243–253.

Kreeft, J. (1984). Dialogue writing: Bridge from talk to essay writing. *Language Arts, 61*(2).

Kreeft, J., Shuy, R. W., Staton, J., Reed, L., & Morroy, R. (1984). *Dialogue writing: Analysis of student–teacher interactive writing in the learning of English as a second language* (NIE Final Report). Washington, DC: Center for Applied Linguistics. (NIE G-83-0030)

Kroll, B. M. (1980). Developmental perspectives and the teaching of composition. *College English, 41*, 741–742.

Laboratory of Comparative Human Cognition (1983). Culture and cognitive development. In W. Kessen (Ed.), *Mussen's handbook of child psychology: Vol. I. History, theory, and method* (4th ed.). New York: Wiley.

Lachman, R., Lachman, J. L., & Butterfield, E. (1979). *Cognitive psychology and information processing*. Hillsdale, NJ: Erlbaum.

Laine, C., & Schultz, L. (1985). Composition theory and practice: The paradigm shift. *Volta Review, 87*(5), 9–20.

LCHC Newsletter (1982). Model systems for the study of learning disabilities. *Quarterly Newsletter of the Laboratory of Comparative Human Cognition*, pp. 42–65.

Levin, J. A., Riel, M., Boruta, M., & Rowe, R. (1984). Muktuk meets jacuzzi: Computer networks and elementary schools. In S. Freedman (Ed.), *The acquisition of written language* (pp. 160–171). Norwood, NJ: Ablex.

Litowitz, B. E. (1981). Developmental issues in written language. *Topics in Language Disorders, 1*(2), 73–99.

Lunsford, A. (1979). Cognitive development and the basic writer. *College English, 41*, 39–46.

Luria, A. R. (1983). The development of writing in the child. In M. Martlew (Ed.), *The psychology of written language: Developmental and educational perspectives*. New York: Wiley.

MacMillan, D. L., Keogh, B. K., & Jones, R. L. (1986). Special educational research on mildly handicapped students. In M. W. Wittrock (Ed.), *Handbook of research on teaching*. New York: Macmillan.

Martlew, M. (1983). Problems and difficulties: Cognitive and communicative aspects of writing. In M. Martlew (Ed.), *The psychology of written language: Developmental and educational perspectives*. New York: Wiley.

Matsuhashi, A. (1981). Pausing and planning: The tempo of written discourse production. *Research in the Teaching of English, 15*(2), 113–134.

Mehan, H. (1979). *Learning lessons.* Cambridge, MA: Harvard University Press.

Mehan, H., Moll, L., Riel, M., et al. (1985). *Computers in classrooms: A quasi-experiment in guided change* (NIE Final Report). San Diego: University of California. (NIE 6-83-0027)

Moran, M. (1986). *A comparison of formal features of written language of learning disabled, low-achieving, and achieving secondary students* (Research Report No. 34). Lawrence: Kansas Institute for Research in Learning Disabilities.

Morris, N., & Crump, W. D. (1982). Syntactic and vocabulary development in the written language of learning disabled and non-learning disabled students at four age levels. *Learning Disability Quarterly, 5*(2), 163–172.

Morroy, R. (1984). Teacher strategies: Their effect on student writing. In J. Kreeft, R. W. Shuy, J. Staton, L. Reed, & R. Morroy, *Dialogue writing: Analysis of student–teacher interactive writing in the learning of English as as second language* (NIE Final Report). Washington, DC: Center for Applied Linguistics. (NIE-G-83-0030)

Myklebust, H. (1965). *Development and disorders of written language: Vol. 1. Picture Story Language Test.* New York: Grune & Stratton.

Myklebust, H. (1972). *Development and disorders of written language: Vol. 2. Studies of normal and exceptional children.* New York: Grune & Stratton.

Naiman, D. W. (1988). *Telecommunications and an interactive approach to literacy in disabled students* (Project Report). New York: New York University.

Pellegrini, A. (1980). The relationship between kindergartners' play and achievement in prereading, language, and writing. *Psychology in the Schools, 17,* 530–535.

Peyton, J. (in press). Dialogue writing: Bridge from talk to essay writing. In J. Staton, R. Shuy, J. Kreeft, & L. Reed (Eds.), *Dialogue journal communication: Classroom, linguistic, social, and cognitive views.* Norwood, NJ: Ablex.

Polloway, E. A., Patton, J. R., & Cohen, S. B. (1981). Written language for mildly handicapped students. *Focus on Exceptional Children, 14*(3), 1–15.

Poplin, M. (1983). Assessing developmental writing abilities. *Topics in Learning and Learning Disabilities, 3*(3), 63–75.

Poplin, M. (1988). Holistic/constructivist principles of the teaching/learning process: Implications for the field of learning disabilities. *Journal of Learning Disabilities, 21*(7), 401–416.

Poplin, M., Gray, R., Larsen, S., Banikowski, A., & Mehring, T. (1980). A comparison of components of written expression abilities in learning disabled and non-learning disabled children at three grade levels. *Learning Disability Quarterly, 3,* 46–53.

Poteet, J. (1979). Characteristics of written expression of learning disabled and non-learning disabled elementary-school students. *Diagnostique, 4,* 60–74.

Read, C. (1975). *Children's categorization of speech sounds in English.* Urbana, IL: National Council of Teachers of English.

Read, C. (1980). What children already know about language: Three examples. *Language Arts, 57,* 144–148.

Riel, M. (1985). Functional learning environment for writing. In H. Mehan et al. (Eds.), *Computers in classrooms: A quasi-experiment in guided change* (NTE Final Report). San Diego: University of California. (NIE 6-83-0027)

Riel, M. M., Levin, J. A., & Miller-Souviney, B. (1984). *Dynamic support and educational software development.* Paper presented at the annual meeting of the American Educational Research Association, New Orleans.

Rogoff, B., & Wertsch, J. V. (Eds.) (1984). *Children's learning in the "zone of proximal development."* San Francisco: Jossey-Bass.

Rueda, R. (1986). *A descriptive analysis of teacher input strategies in microcomputer-based, interactive writing with mildly handicapped students* (Project TEECH Tech. Rep. No. 46.0). Santa Barbara: University of California, Special Education Program, Graduate School of Education.

Rueda, R. (1988). *The role of the teacher in computer-based interactive journal writing with learning disabled students: A descriptive study.* Manuscript submitted for publication.

Rueda, R., & Goldman, S. (1988). Developing writing skills in bilingual exceptional children. *Exceptional Children, 54*(6), 543–551.

Scardamalia, M., & Bereiter, C. (1986). Research on written composition. In M. Wittrock (Ed.), *Handbook of research on teaching.* New York: Macmillan.

Scardamalia, M., Bereiter, C., & Goelman, H. (1982). The role of production factors in writing ability. In M. Nystrand (Ed.), *What writers know: The language, process, and structure of written discourse* (pp. 183–210). New York: Academic Press.

Schank, R., & Abelson, R. (1977). *Scripts, plans, goals, and understanding.* Hillsdale, NJ: Erlbaum.

Scollon, R., & Scollon, S. (1981). *Narrative, literacy, and face in interethnic communication.* Norwood, NJ: Ablex.

Sedlak, R., & Cartwright, G. (1972). Written language abilities of EMR and nonretarded children with the same mental age. *American Journal of Mental Deficiency, 77,* 95–99.

Shuy, R. (1984). The function of language functions in the dialog journal interactions of nonnative English speakers and their teacher. In J. Kreeft, R. W. Shuy, J. Staton, L. Reed, & R. Morroy, *Dialogue writing: Analysis of student–teacher interactive writing in the learning of English as a second language* (NIE Final Report). Washington, DC: Center for Applied Linguistics. (NIE-G-83-0030)

Shuy, R. (in press). The oral language basis for dialogue journals. In J. Staton, R. Shuy, J. Kreeft, & L. Reed (Eds.), *Dialogue journal communication: Classroom, linguistic, social, and cognitive views.* Norwood, NJ: Ablex.

Simeonsson, R. J. (1978). Social competence: Dimensions and directions. In J. R. Wortis (Ed.), *Annual review of mental retardation and developmental disabilities* (Vol. 10). New York: Brunner/Mazel.

Staton, J. (1981a). Analysis of writing in dialogue journals as a communicative event. In A. Humes, B. Cronnell, J. Lawlor, & L. Gentry (Eds.), *Moving between practice and research in writing.* Los Alamitos, CA: SWRL Educational Research and Development.

Staton, J. (1981b). Literacy as an interactive process. *Linguistic Reporter, 24*(2), 1–5.

Staton, J. (1984). Dialogue journals as a means of enabling written language acquisition. In J. Kreeft, R. W. Shuy, J. Staton, L. Reed, and R. Morrow, *Dialogue writing: Analysis of student–teacher interactive writing in the learning of English as a second language* (NIE Final Report). Washington, DC: Center for Applied Linguistics. (NIE-G-83-0030)

Staton, J. (1985). Using dialogue journals for developing thinking, reading, and writing with hearing-impaired students. *Volta Review, 87*(5), 127–152.

Staton, J., Shuy, R., Kreeft, J., & Reed, L. (Eds.) (in press). *Dialogue journal communication: Classroom, linguistic, social, and cognitive views.* Norwood, NJ: Ablex.

Tharp, R., & Gallimore, R. (1988). *Rousing minds to life: Teaching, learning, and schooling in a social context.* Cambridge: Cambridge University Press.

Torgesen, J. K. (1977). The role of nonspecific factors in the task performance of learning disabled children: A theoretical assessment. *Journal of Learning Disabilities, 10,* 27–34.

Trueba, H., Moll, L. C., & Díaz, S. (1982). *Improving the functional writing of bilingual secondary school students* (Context No. 400-81-0023). Washington, DC: National Institute of Education.

Vygotsky, L. S. (1978). *Mind in society: The development of higher psychological processes* (M. Cole, V. John-Steiner, S. Scribner, & E. Souberman, Eds.). Cambridge, MA: Harvard University Press.

Vygotsky, L. S. (1983). The prehistory of written language. In M. Martlew (Ed.), *The psychology of written language: Developmental and educational perspectives.* New York: Wiley.

Vygotsky, L. S. (1962). *Thought and language* (E. Hanfmann & G. Vakar, Eds. & Trans.). Cambridge, MA: MIT Press. (Original work published 1934)

Weiner, E. (1980). Diagnostic evaluation of writing skills. *Journal of Learning Disabilities, 13,* 43–48.

Wertsch, J. V. (Ed.). (1985a). *Culture, communication, and cognition: Vygotskian perspectives.* Cambridge: Cambridge University Press.

Wertsch, J. V. (1985b). *Vygotsky and the social formation of mind.* Cambridge, MA: Harvard University Press.

Wertsch, J. (1979). From social interaction to higher psychological processes: A clarification and application of Vygotsky's theory. *Human Development, 22,* 1–22.

Zebroski, J. T. (1981). Soviet psycholinguistics: Implications for teaching of writing. In W. Frawley (Ed.), *Linguistics and literacy.* New York: Plenum.

Name index

Ableson, R., 406
Adams, A., 257
Aguilar, J., 321
Ahlbrand, W., 182, 188, 196, 201
Aidarova, L., 265, 359
Alexander, K., 302
Alonson, J., 81
Althusser, L., 61
Altwerger, B., 243
Alvarez, A., 5
Amaya-Williams, M., 11, 272
Ambrogio, I., 49
Ames, G., 159
Anderson, R., 196
Anyon, J., 8, 11, 328
Appel, G., 2
Applebee, A., 201, 328
Archambault, R., 238, 239
Ardila, R., 39, 50
Argan, G., 36
Ariès, P., 367
Arns, F., 155, 190
Au, K., 9, 13, 190, 191, 271, 275
Ausubel, D., 80
Azcoaga, J., 39, 49, 50, 53
Azmitia, M., 168

Baghban, M., 406
Bain, B., 44
Bakhtin, M., 45, 112, 117, 118, 119, 120
Bakhurst, D., 4, 5, 6, 16, 24, 344
Balibar, E., 61
Bandura, A., 179
Banikowski, A., 408
Barenbaum, E., 410
Bauer, A., 68, 69, 70, 71
Baumrind, D., 138
Bearison, D., 159
Benjamin, W., 39
Benson, D., 128
Bereiter, C., 406, 407
Berk, L., 24, 136, 186
Berliner, D., 198, 329
Bernal, J., 40

Berry, J., 101
Bissex, G., 406, 410
Blackwell, P., 9, 272
Blackwood, P., 396
Blake, K., 275
Blanck, G., 2, 3, 4, 5, 24, 31, 40, 44, 45, 47, 49, 51
Blom, G., 143, 144
Bloom, B., 208
Bloome, D., 229, 245
Boruta, M., 412, 415
Brandwein, P., 396
Bransford, J., 183, 409
Braswell, L., 141, 142
Brooks, P., 409
Brown, A., 24, 80, 81, 123, 183, 220, 221, 409
Brown, J., 8, 9
Brown, L., 376
Brownell, C., 160
Bruner, J., 1, 3, 14, 15, 31, 39, 43, 49, 80, 98, 102, 114, 139, 210, 221, 288, 311
Budwig, N., 114, 140
Buhler, K., 51
Bullock, D., 200
Burke, C., 240, 406, 411
Burris, N., 405, 406
Butterfield, E., 406

Calkins, L., 180, 307, 315
Camp, B., 141, 142, 144
Campione, J., 80, 81, 183, 409
Carey, S., 373, 376
Carr, E., 35, 66
Carr, T., 409
Cartwright, G., 408
Caruso, D., 167
Carver, C., 180
Cazden, C., 3, 11, 13, 14, 24, 80, 168, 169, 195, 206, 211, 221, 224, 311
Chafe, W., 263
Chalmers, A., 60, 63
Chang, H., 373
Childs, C., 102
Childs, J., 223

427

Christiansen, M., 375, 412
Ciborowski, T., 102
Cicourel, A., 122
Clark, C., 271
Clark, K., 112, 116
Clay, M., 13, 14, 24, 206, 208, 217, 218, 219,
       221, 224, 406
Clift, R., 201
Cohen, A., 376
Cohen, G., 34, 145
Cohen, S., 409
Cole, M., 1, 2, 3, 5, 7, 8, 11, 12, 23, 24, 40,
       42, 49, 52, 54, 78, 90, 97, 100, 101, 102,
       103, 104, 112, 119, 121, 122, 141, 156,
       178, 179, 189, 255, 291, 352, 377
Coles, G., 408
Collins, A., 8
Collins, J., 405
Comenius, J., 224
Cook, T., 112
Cooper, P., 292
Cosden, M., 411
Counts, G., 223
Cranstoun, Y., 197
Crowell, C., 191
Crump, W., 408

Dalton, S., 24, 186, 271, 275
Damon, W., 168
D'Andrade, R., 100, 105
Dasen, P., 98
Davydov, V., 11, 52, 319, 349, 350, 354, 357,
       377, 393, 394, 400
Dawson, J., 101
De Ford, D., 410, 411
De Forest, M., 101
Delgado-Gaitán, C., 319
del Río, P., 5
Deno, S., 408
Descartes, R., 37
Deshler, D., 409
De Vries, R., 167
Dewey, J., 223, 226, 248
Díaz, E., 376, 405
Díaz, R., 327
Díaz, R. M., 11, 136, 137, 145, 272
Di Bello, L., 272
Dillon, R., 80
Dobkin, S., 32, 33, 34, 36, 37, 42
Doise, W., 159, 160
Donaldson, M., 96
Downing, J., 65
Drabman, R., 144
Draper, K., 410, 411, 415
Duckworth, E., 243
Duffy, G., 24, 182, 183, 201
Dugid, P., 8
Durkin, D., 175, 182, 196, 201
Dyson, A., 309, 317

Easley, J., 99
Eastman, B., 145
Eccles, J., 49
Echeíta, G., 80
Edelsky, C., 8, 224, 225, 410, 411, 415
Ehrenburg, I., 36
Elbaz, F., 272, 273, 276
Elkonin, D., 49, 196, 217, 349, 351, 366
Ellis, S., 156
Elsasser, N., 405
Engestrom, Y., 2, 8, 352, 354, 373, 375
Entwisle, D., 302
Erickson, F., 405, 410
Ervin-Tripp, S., 181

Farley, J., 413, 414
Farr, M., 24
Fernandez, R., 81
Ferrara, R., 24, 80, 81, 183, 220, 221, 409
Ferreiro, E., 243, 406, 410
Feuerstein, R., 81
Filardo, E., 159
Fischer, K., 200
Fitzpatrick, S., 36
Flores, R., 373
Florio-Ruane, S., 316
Flower, L., 406
Fodor, J., 84
Forman, E., 24, 80, 168, 169
Forness, S., 421
Fortes, M., 178
Frauenglass, M., 137
Freire, P., 238
Freud, S., 47
Fromm, E., 53

Gallimore, R., 2, 5, 6, 7, 9, 10, 11, 24, 50, 175,
       177, 178, 180, 181, 182, 183,184, 186,
       188, 189, 190, 191, 192, 194, 196, 198,
       199, 200, 201, 271, 275, 319, 327, 352,
       404, 416
Gal'perin, P., 186, 393
Gardner, H., 84, 111, 140, 309
Gardner, W., 156
Garvin, R., 163, 186
Gaskill, M., 145
Gay, J., 78, 100, 122
Gearhart, M., 155
Gee, J., 289
Geocaras, H., 305
Gerber, M., 406, 408, 412
Gergen, K., 82
Germond, J., 156
Gibbon, S., 374, 375
Gilbride, K., 156
Gilligan, C., 120, 122
Gilman, R., 169
Gindis, B., 420, 421

Glick, J., 78, 100, 122
Godwin, D., 80
Goelman, H., 243, 407
Goldman, S., 412
Gollasch, F., 239, 240
Goldstein, A., 201
Goldstein, K., 49
Good, T., 199
Goodlad, J., 6, 8, 175, 188, 196, 197, 201, 322
Goodman, K., 8, 9, 13, 14, 24, 230, 239, 240, 241, 329, 411
Goodman, S., 141, 142, 143, 144
Goodman, Y., 8, 9, 13, 14, 24, 224, 230, 239, 240, 241, 243, 329, 411
Goodnow, J., 374, 375, 378
Goody, J., 49, 93, 95
Gorbachev, M., 43
Gordon, D., 139
Goudena, P., 136
Gould, S., 354
Graham, L. 66, 72
Graham, S., 408
Graves, D., 307, 309, 406, 407, 410, 411
Gray, R., 408
Graziano, D., 304, 305, 306
Greenberg, J., 7, 8, 13, 320, 321, 322, 323, 328
Greenfield, P., 97, 102, 323, 375, 376
Greenspan, S., 409
Griffin, P., 2, 5, 7, 8, 24, 103, 156, 201, 291, 352, 377
Grinnell, P., 405, 406
Gruber, H., 253
Guberman, S., 155
Guguernidze, G., 78, 85
Gundlach, R., 289, 292, 305, 307, 308, 309, 317, 406
Guzmán, R., 169

Habermas, J., 121
Hakkarainen, P., 2, 8
Hall, R., 406, 408, 409
Halliday, M., 225, 231, 239
Hallpike, C., 98
Hanesian, H., 80
Harris, R., 95
Harste, J., 406, 411
Hasan, R., 225, 239
Hawkins, D., 372, 374
Hayes, J., 406
Heath, S., 122, 197, 265, 319, 405
Hedegaard, M., 2, 5, 7, 8, 9, 13, 50, 327, 351, 354, 361, 366
Helwig, C., 145
Henderson, R., 8, 24
Henriques, J., 83
Herbert, F., 143, 144
Hermeck, L., 408
Hiebert, E., 196

Hoetker, J., 182, 188, 196, 201
Hoffman, M., 139
Holdzkom, D., 381, 385
Hollway, W., 83
Holquist, M., 112, 116, 117
Homme, L., 179
Horton, R., 372, 374
Hubner, K., 61, 62, 86
Hughes, L., 237
Hyland, J., 352
Hynd, G., 128

Iaroshevsky, L., 78
Inhelder, B., 98
Inkeles, A., 102
Isaac, W., 128
Israel, A., 144
Ivanov, V., 49, 123

Jackson, P., 201
Jahoda, G., 98, 99, 100, 103
Jakobson, P., 37
Janet, P., 114
Johnson, D., 168
Johnson, K., 139
Johnson, N., 376
Johnson, R., 168
John-Steiner, V., 9, 79, 178, 258, 272, 405
Johnstone, B., 321
Jordan, C., 178
Joyce, B., 201
Juul Jensen, U., 353

Kahneman, D., 122
Kamara, A., 99
Kamii, C., 167
Kaur, B., 169
Kavale, K., 421
Kawai, A., 92
Kawakami, A., 271, 275
Kazdin, A., 141
Keller, J., 80
Kendall, P., 141, 142
Kerchner, L., 411
Kerwin, S., 292
Kilpatrick, W., 223
King, M., 406, 410
Kistinger, B., 411
Knoblock, P., 201
Koch, S., 51
Kol'tsova, V., 168, 169
Kopp, C., 128, 129, 130, 131
Kozulin, A., 24, 34, 44, 75, 85
Kraker, M., 169
Kreeft, J., 413, 414, 416
Kroll, B., 405
Kuhn, T., 84
Kuhnian, A., 50

Lachman, J., 406
Lachman, R., 406
Laine, C., 410
Lakatos, I., 60
Lambert, W., 90
Lampert, M., 396
Langer, J., 24, 201, 328, 329, 434
Lansdown, B., 396
Larsen, M., 95
Larsen, S., 408
Latour, B., 99
Lave, J., 97, 101, 111, 112, 323
Leahey, T., 85
Lemke, J., 195
Leont'ev, A., 111, 189, 193
Leontiev, A., 2, 11, 24, 44, 46, 47, 48, 50, 62,
    63, 78, 80, 90, 91, 92, 349, 350, 351, 366
Lerner, D., 102
Lesgold, A., 376
Levin, J. A., 375, 415
Levin, J. R., 376
Levitin, K., 2, 33, 41
Lewin, K., 359
Light, P., 168
Linell, P., 120
Lipshultz, D., 305
Litowitz, B., 409
Lomnitz, L., 321
Lomov, B., 168
Lompscher, J., 349
Lubovsky, V., 221
Lukacs, G., 51, 121
Luria, A., 2, 11, 24, 33, 37, 38, 39, 40, 42, 45,
    46, 47, 48, 49, 52, 53, 89, 90, 99, 102,
    113, 121, 122, 128, 136, 137, 257, 319,
    405
Lutz, P., 381, 385
Lyons, C., 206

McCarthy, R., 374
McCauley, C., 409
McGurk, H., 100
McLane, J., 8, 13, 14, 114, 140, 291, 292, 304,
    305, 307, 317
McMahon, L., 197
McNamee, G., 8, 13, 14, 114, 140, 291, 292,
    305, 307, 317
McPhail, J., 169
Magzamen, S., 159
Makarenko, A., 36
Malkin, C., 156
Maltzman, I., 78
Mandler, J., 101, 376
Marchesi, A., 81
Markova, A., 2, 351, 393
Marshak, A., 93
Marston, D., 408
Martin, L., 9, 13, 168, 169, 373, 374, 376, 395,
    399

Martlew, M., 409
Maruyama, G., 168
Marx, K., 45, 62
Matuhashi, A., 406
Mayr, E., 354
Mead, G., 47, 114
Meador, A., 141
Mecacci, L., 38
Mehan, H., 105, 122, 123, 415, 420
Mehring, T., 408
Meichenbaum, D., 141, 142, 143, 144, 186
Meloth, M., 183
Meredith, R., 8, 230
Mervis, C., 262
Meshchernyakov, A., 49
Middleton, D., 139
Milardo, R., 320
Miller, G., 39, 85, 160
Miller-Souviney, B., 415
Minde, K., 145
Minick, N., 3, 4, 5, 10, 11, 12, 13, 15, 78, 121,
    155, 190, 194, 195, 196, 271
Mirkin, P., 408
Mischel, W., 129, 141
Mistry, J., 156
Mitchell, L., 376
Moll, L., 4, 5, 7, 8, 9, 11, 13, 14, 38, 320, 327,
    329, 335, 405, 415
Montero, I., 2, 3, 4, 5, 24, 79, 81
Moran, M., 408
Morawski, S., 49
Morris, N., 408
Morroy, R., 414, 415, 416, 419
Mosier, C., 156
Mugny, G., 159, 160
Murray, F., 159
Myklebust, H., 408, 410

Naiman, D., 415
Nazarova, L., 65, 66
Neal, C., 11, 272
Neale, D., 374
Neimark, E., 99
Nelians, T., 144
Nelson, D., 168
Nelson, K., 253, 261
Nerlove, S., 178
Newman, D., 2, 377
Ngini, L., 98
Novak, J., 80, 145
Nowicki, S., 139
Nunn, G., 2
Nyiti, R., 99

Oakes, J., 6, 11, 328
Ochaita, E., 81
Ochs, E., 197, 263
Oesterreich, H., 178, 258
Olberg, A., 243

O'Leary, K., 144
Ollendick, T., 141
Olson, D., 12, 120
Olver, R., 102
Ong, W., 193
Orlich, F., 272
Oshiro, M., 275

Padilla, K. 145
Palacios, J., 5
Paley, V., 301, 307
Palincsar, A., 24, 123
Panofsky, C., 9, 272
Pardo, A., 80
Paris, C., 62
Passler, M., 128
Patterson, C., 129, 141
Patton, J., 409
Pellegrini, A., 406
Penton, J., 223
Perlmutter, M., 168
Perret-Clermont, A.-N., 159, 168
Peterson, P., 271
Pettit, G, 178
Peyton, J., 413
Pfeiffer, J., 94
Phelps, E., 168
Piaget, P., 98, 99, 114, 131, 160, 229
Pinkus, T., 51
Pinnell, G. 206
Plejanov, G., 64
Polloway, E., 409
Pontecorvo, C., 228
Poplin, M., 408, 410, 411
Popper, K., 49
Potenbnya, A., 37
Poteet, J., 408
Pozo, J., 80
Premack, D., 1, 92
Price-Williams, D., 199
Prigogine, I., 83
Puzirie, A., 34, 49

Radzikhovskii, L., 350
Radziszewska, B., 155
Raleigh, M., 246
Rasbury, W., 145
Read, C., 406, 410
Reed, J., 36
Reed, L., 413
Reeve, R., 140
Reigeluth, C., 80
Rentel, V., 406, 410
Reschitzki, L., 98
Riel, M., 410, 415
Rivière, A., 1, 2, 39, 49, 81, 84
Roehler, L., 24, 182, 183, 201
Rogoff, B., 5, 50, 78, 97, 105, 111, 140,
    155,156, 169, 178, 179, 352, 404

Rommetveit, R., 120, 220
Rosa, A., 2, 3, 4, 5, 24, 81
Rosch, E., 262
Ross, S., 139, 210, 221
Roter, A., 274, 285
Rowe, M., 372, 377, 378, 396, 400, 416
Rozanova, T., 221
Rubtsov, V., 168, 169, 396
Rueda, R., 8, 13, 14, 405, 416, 419

Salomon, G., 376
Sánchez-Vásquez, A., 36
Sarason, S., 196, 200, 201
Saxe, G., 155
Scardamalia, M., 406, 407
Schank, R., 406
Schedrovitsky, G., 38, 39, 45
Scheier, M., 180
Schmandt, D., 94
Schneider, P., 352
Schultz, L., 410
Scollon, R., 405
Scollon, S., 405
Scribner, S., 1, 12, 40, 46, 49, 52, 54, 59, 78,
    97, 100, 101, 104, 105, 112, 113, 120, 121,
    178, 179, 255, 351, 377
Searle, J., 105
Sedlak, R., 408
Semmel, D., 412
Semmel, M., 412
Serpell, R., 101, 102
Sève, L., 40, 50
Shakhlevich, L., 38
Sharp, D., 78, 100, 101, 102, 122
Shklovsky, V., 36
Shuy, R., 413, 419
Siegler, R., 160
Siguán, M., 84
Silvestri, A., 45
Simeonsson, R., 409
Simpson, G., 354
Skon, L., 168
Slavin, R., 168
Smirnov, A., 113
Smith, D., 102, 374
Smith, E., 8, 230
Smith, F., 231, 243, 245
Smith, K., 410, 411, 415
Snipper, A., 178
Souberman, E., 79
Sperber, R., 409
Spindler, G., 104
Spinoza, B. de, 37
Spitalnik, R., 144
Staats, A., 50, 179
Stack, C., 321
Stagner, R., 85
Stanovich, K., 206
Stanton, J., 413, 414

Sternberg, R., 80, 128
Stevenson, H., 101
Stone, C., 146, 177
Stone, I., 237
Stott, F., 292, 305, 307, 317
Street, B., 93
Stuss, D., 128
Suchodolsky, B., 39
Sullivan, J., 145
Sulzby, E., 243

Tafoya, M., 178
Tannen, D., 263
Tater, P., 405
Teale, W., 197, 243
Teberosky, A., 228, 243, 406, 410
Tharp, R., 2, 5, 6, 7, 9, 10, 11, 24, 50, 175,
    177, 178, 179, 180, 181, 182, 183, 184,
    186, 188, 189, 190, 191, 192, 194, 196,
    198, 199, 200, 201, 271, 275, 327, 404,
    416
Tomasello, M., 92
Torgeson, J., 409
Tough, J., 197
Toulmin, S., 39, 40
Triandis, H., 90
Trimbur, J., 24
Trueba, H., 319, 405
Tudge, J., 5, 7, 11, 50, 160, 163, 167, 169, 228
Tulviste, P., 100, 121

Urwin, C., 83
Uspensky, V., 119

Valsiner, J., 2, 4, 5, 24, 155
Van Der Veer, R., 24, 37, 44, 47, 80
Van Doornick, W., 143, 144
Vavrus, L., 183
Vélez-Ibáñez, C., 320, 321, 322, 323, 326
Venn, C., 83
Vogt, L., 178
Voloshinov, V., 45, 118

Voneche, J., 253
Vucinich, A., 67, 68, 71
Vygodskaya, G., 32, 33, 35, 36, 41, 42, 43

Wagner, D., 101
Waitz, T., 92
Walberg, H, 199
Walkerdine, V., 83
Wason, P., 100
Watson, D., 180, 186, 206, 218, 240
Watson, R., 61
Waugh, M., 375
Weiner, E., 408
Weinstein, R., 199
Weisner, T., 190, 319
Wellman, B., 321, 322
Wells, G., 197
Wertsch, J., 2, 5, 6, 7, 9, 11, 12, 24, 33, 35, 39,
    40, 42, 45, 46, 50, 52, 78, 80, 113, 114,
    115, 119, 120, 121, 122, 128, 135, 140,
    146, 155, 156, 177, 185, 193, 219, 234,
    235, 254, 351, 352, 404
Wetzel, R., 179
White, S., 178, 191
Whiting, B., 190
Whiting, J., 190
Wichern, F., 139
Wier, E., 374
Wilde, S., 239
Wittrock, M., 195, 198
Wolf, E., 322
Wood, D., 139, 194, 197, 200, 210, 221
Woodward, V., 406

Yashima, T., 225

Zebroski, J., 2, 404
Zeigarmik, B., 39, 43, 53
Zinchenko, V., 52, 113
Zivin, G., 136
Zucchermaglio, C., 228
Zukier, H., 60

Subject index

ability grouping, 6
accent, in speech, 117
acoustic factors, speech, 137
activity settings
    design of, 189–90
    KEEP program, 190–192
    in reading comprehension, 195–196
activity theory
    and concept development, 366–367
    and motivation, 80–81, 366–367
    role of culture, 91–92
    in teaching experiment, 358–370
"adult–child problem-solving systems," 114,
    140
affect, 37
African children, 99
agricultural societies, 102–103
arousal, 131
artifacts, 92
assessment, process models, 81
assessment question, 182
assistance question, 182
assisted performance
    and activity settings, 189–192
    learning disabled, 412–420
    vs. recitation script, 188, 197
    and teaching, 176–183, 199–201, 412–420
    theory of schooling, 187–192, 196–199
    zone of proximal development, 184–187
atomistic theory, 48
attentional processes
    in writing, 409–410
    zone of proximal development, 184
audiovisual technology, 372–401
auditory deficiency, 81
"authentic" events
    in households, 326
    in text comprehension, 239–242
    whole-language approach, 9
authoritarian parents, 138–139
authoritative parents, 139
autism, 81
automatized performance, 186
auxiliary signs, 133

Bakhtin, M., 45, 116–120
banking pedagogy, 238–239
"basic activities," 291
basic skills approach, 6–9
behavioral curricula, 224, 246
blindness, 81
Bullock committee, 223

calendar systems, 93–94
Cartesian dualism, 37, 49, 79
cerebral cortex, 47–49
cerebral palsy, 81
change, 12–15
    metaphysics, 82–83
    models of, 102–105
Chomskian theory, 52–53
classification ability, 101–102
cognitive conflict, 159–165, 168–169
cognitive development
    context effects, 103–107
    cross-cultural research, 89–107
    formal schooling effects, 97–107
    and writing, 406–410
cognitive science, 84
cognitive strategies, 104, 106
cognitive structuring
    and assisted performance, 182–183
    vs. instruction, 183
collaborative performance, 12–13
communication
    Bakhtin's theory, 116–120
    in learning process, 80
"community of writers," 289
comprehension instruction, 191
computers, 411–412, 415–420
concept development (*see also* everyday con-
    cepts; scientific concepts)
    and motivation, 366–367
    Vygotsky vs. Piaget, 252–253
concept formation, 101–102
concrete operations
    cultural variation, 98–99
    schooling effect, 98
concretization, 363–365

433

confianza, 321, 326
confidence, and peer collaboration, 160–165
"conjunctural urgency," 62
conscious realization, 219–220
consciousness, 274–286
conservation tasks
    cultural variation, 98–99
    peer collaboration, 159
    schooling effects, 98
conservation training, 98
"construction module," 335–336
context-specific theory
    cognitive development, 103–107
    and rationality, 120–122
contingency management, 179–180
"copycat" method, 143
creativity, 49
critical assimilation, 52
Critical Theory of Frankfurt, 40
culture, 89–107 (*see also* sociohistorical perspective)
    and cognitive development, 89–107
    general vs. specific effects, 102–107
    influence on development, 46–47
    language as tool of, 45–46
    Piagetian tasks, 98–100
    sociohistorical perspective, 89–107
    Vygotsky's theory, 43–49
    Wundt's theory, 89–90
cuneiform writing, 95
curriculum, 243–245

deafness, 158
deautomatization of performance, 186–187
decentration, 409
decontextualized rationality
    reification of, 121–122
    voice of, 120–122
defectology, 40–41, 49
delay of gratification, 139
dense practice, 99
depth perception, 100–101
developmental processes, 46–47
Dewey, John, 226–227, 248
dialectical materialism, 67, 72, 74
"dialecticians," 68
Dialog Maker, 416
dialogue, Bakhtin's theory, 116–118
dialogue journals, 413–414, 416
dictation, 407
discourse
    in schooling, 193–196, 199–201
    social interaction importance, 195–196
    Vygotsky's approach, 115
    and word meaning, 192–193
"discrete step" model, 410–411
Dostoevsky's "polyphonic" novel, 118
double move method, 356–358, 367
dramatization activities, 292–303, 307–318

drawing, and writing, 406
dualism, 37, 44, 49, 79, 83
dyadic journals, 413–414, 416

eclecticism, 52
education psychology, 78–82
elaboration concept, 50
Elkonin's developmental stages, 351–352
embedded-figures test, 101
emotion, 79–80
empirical knowledge
    Davydov's model, 353–358
    and everyday concepts, 355–358
    model of, 81
"empirical" thinking, 100
entropy, 83
error, 239, 242–243
"E-T-R sequences," 190–191
everyday concepts
    Davydov's theory, 358
    and empirical concepts, 355–358
    mediative function, 9–10
    in science teaching, 373–375
    and scientific concepts, 9–10, 251–252, 272, 350, 358
    video technology mediation, 375–377, 393–400
    Vygotsky's theory, 252–253, 272
    zone of proximal development, 350
experimental psychology, 89–90
"expert pedagogy," 198
"explication," 86*n*
explicit mental functions, 274–286
expressive writing, 407
extended topic chain, 414, 418–420

feedback
    and assisted performance, 180
    in peer collaboration, 165–167
    in teacher training, 191
field explorations, 265
folk concepts, 230
"folk psychololgy," 90
foreign language learning, 230–231
formal operations
    cultural variation, 99–100
    schooling effect, 99–100
formal schooling, *see* schooling
fossilized performance, 186
functional/interactive approach, 405–422
"functional method of double stimulation," 4–5
functional systems, brain, 48–49
Functions of Language in the Classroom (Cazden, John, & Hymes), 122
"funds of knowledge," 320–346

generalization of effects, 141–147
generalization principle, 77
"The Genesis of Higher Mental Functions" (Vygotsky), 132–133

genetic psychology
    social influences, 113–116
    Vygotsky's terminology, 46–47, 113–116
germ-cell model, 354–358, 367
group discourse, 196
group learning, peers, 169

handicapped, 403–422
    mainstreaming, 157–158
    Vygotskian educational theory, 81–82, 157–158
Head Start, 287–303
hearing deficiencies, 81
"hidden processes," 5
hierarchical language model, 410–411
Hispanics, 319–346
Historical Meaning of the Crisis in Psychology
    (Vygotsky), 41, 51, 75, 77
history of science, 60–65
holistic approach (*see also* whole language approach)
    cerebral cortex function, 47–48
    vs. reductionism, 5–9
households
    funds of knowledge, 320–346
    zones of proximal development, 326–327
hyperactivity, 141–147

identity formation, 99
illusions, 101
illustration-explanation method, 11
imagination, 288
impulsive behavior, 141–147
independent performance, 12–13
independent problem solving, 139–140
individual differences, 137–138
induction, 139
industrial societies, 103
information-processing psychology, 84
initiation-reply-evaluation sequence, 105
innate ability approach, 5–6
instruction, *see* teaching
instructional conversation
    vs. recitation script, 197
    as task of teaching, 196–199
instructional discourse, 105
instrumental competence, 139
"instruments," 45
integrated day, 223
intelligence, assessment models, 81
intention, and speech, 117
interactive training, 142–143
internal locus of control, 139–140
internalization
    longitudinal data, 257
    and private speech training, 146–147
    self-regulatory function, 133–135
    Vygotsky's theory, 47, 133–135
interpsychological functioning, 114

"intersubjectivity," 140
invented spelling, 406
Investigative Colloquium Model, 396
IQ measures, 3, 81

Janet, Pierre, 114
joint learning conditions
    inner-city study, 293
    peers, 169, 189
    teacher training, 191–192
jointness, 192

"kairological principle," 62, 73
Kamehameha Early Education Project, 18–19
    activity settings, 190–192
    teacher thought processes, 275–286
Kazaki people, 103
known-answer questions, 105

language (*see also* whole-language approach)
    Bakhtin's theory, 116–120
    development of, 229–235
    hierarchical instructional model, 410–411
    self-regulatory function, 135–136
    social theory, 231
Latinos, 319–346
learning by discovery, 80
learning by doing, 227
learning disabilities, 403–422
    computer-based instruction, 411–412, 415–420
    social interaction importance, 421
    writing instruction, 403–422
Leontiev, A. N., 80–81, 350
letter–sound relationships, 218
Lewin, Kurt, 43, 359
liberating pedagogy, 238–239
literacy (*see also* writing)
    cultural mediation, 93
    development of, 405
    inner-city studies, 287–318
    social–cultural basis, 289, 304–318
    theory of, 192–199, 405
    whole-language approach, 225
"the literacy club," 226, 245
localization of function, 47–49
logical syllogisms
    cultural effects, 98–100
    schooling effect, 100, 105
Luria, A. R.
    attack on, 71
    literacy development theory, 405
    schooling effects theory, 102–107
    self-regulation theory, 136–138
Lysenkoism, 72

"manifest program," 78
Marxism
    influence on Vygotsky, 40, 74, 114

Marxism (*cont.*)
   and practical psychology, 82
   and psychology, 74
materialistic psychology, 74
maternal style
   and child's self-regulation, 139–140, 148–152
   private speech effect, 148–152
mathematical balance beam, 160–165
Mead, G. H., 47, 114
meaning
   importance in learning, 7–9, 13–15
   and motivation, 80–81
"mechanicists," 68
mechanistic materialism, 68–69, 79
mediation, 9–12
   function of text, 240–241
   role of adults, 330
   role of culture, 91, 114
   social network role, 321–346
   Vygotsky's approach, 9–12, 114–115
memory, 101
mentally retarded (*see also* learning disabilities)
   mainstreaming, 157–158
metaphysics of change, 82–83
metaphysics of permanence, 82–83
methodology
   and philosophy, 85
   Vygotsky's program, 76–78
Mexican students, 319–346
microcomputers, 411–412, 415–420
microgenetic development, 103–107
"microteaching," 199
Mills, Wright, 47
miscue analysis, 240–242
modeling technique
   and assisted performance, 178–179
   private speech training, 141–147
mothers, *see* maternal style
motivation
   development of, 366–367
   educational importance, 80–81
   relation to concepts, 366–367
   role in peer collaboration, 168
   techniques for, 362
   Vygotsky's model, 79–80
   in writing, 409–410
Mozart and Salieri (Pushkin), 33
"mutation," 86*n*
mutual trust, 321

Navajo teacher, 176–177
Nelson, Katherine, 253–254
neurolinguistics, 49
neuronal constellations, 48
neuropsychology, 47–49
notation, 397
novelistic discourse, 118
numeracy, 93

observation-and-inference activity, 191–192
obuchenie, 24*n*
ontogenetic development, 47, 97–107

pacing issues, teaching, 277–278
paired-associate learning, 101
parenting styles, 138–140
Pavlov, I. P.,67
peer collaboration
   and feedback, 165–167
   joint activity setting, 189
   motivational factors, 168
   vs. peer tutoring, 168
   in play, 228
   regression in, 162–167
   role of confidence, 160–165
   in taxonomic learning, 265–266
   and zone of proximal development, 155–170
perceptual tasks, 101
permissive parents, 138–139
personal concepts, 229–230
phonics program, 217–218
phylogeny, 92–93
Piagetian tasks
   cultural variation, 98–100
   effect of schooling, 98–99
   peer collaboration, 159
   and writing, 406
Piaget's concept theory, 252–253
planning issues, teaching, 278–279
play
   and change, 288
   Vygotsky's influence, 49–50, 227–228
   and writing, 309–312, 406
"polyphonic" novel, 118
Ponzo illusion, 101
practical knowledge, 272–286
practical psychology, 82, 85
pragmatics, 115
preschool children, private speech, 145–146
Prigogine, Ilya, 83–84
primary defect, 420–421
private speech
   individual differences, 137–138
   internalization, 146–147
   Luria's theory, 137
   self-regulatory function, 135–137
   social dialogue effects, 147–152
   training of, studies, 141–152
privileging, 122
problem solving
   adult–child systems, 140
   transfer effects, schooling, 106
"procedural display," 229
pronominal point of view, 397
"pseudoconcepts," 257, 375, 395
psychic tools, *see* tools
psychoanalytic method, 118
psycholinguistics, 49

psychological processes, 4–5
psychology
    cultural historical school, 349
    sociocultural approach, 112, 116–123
    theoretical crisis of, 50–53
    Vygotsky's theory, 43–49, 74–78
The Psychology of Art (Vygotsky), 37, 41, 75
public concepts, 230

qualitative assessment, 81
questioning, 181–182

rationality
    reification of, 121–122
    voice of, 120–122
reading
    hierarchical model, 410
    social interaction role, 195–196
    theory of, 206–207
    whole-language approach, 8–9
Reading Recovery, 19, 206–221
receptive-reproductive method, 11
"reciprocal teaching," 123
reciprocity, 326
"recitation" approach
    vs. assisted performance, 188
    vs. instructional conversation, 197
    Vygotsky's critique, 6, 11
recursion of performance, 186–187
reductionism, 5–9
"referentially semantic content," 118–119
reflective thinking, 238, 374
regression, 158, 162–167
reinforcement, 180
risk taking, 239
rote learning, 11
rules of practice, 273–286

"scaffolding"
    in Reading Recovery program, 212, 219
    teacher's role, 139–140
schemas
    learning of, 229
    social norm internalization, 62
scholarly concepts, 193
schooled concepts, 193
schooling
    assisted performance theory, 187–192, 199–201
    context-specific effects, 103–107
    decontextualized rationality, 121–122
    discourse in, 193–194
    effect on cognitive development, 97–107
    origins of, 94–97
    social interaction importance, 195–196
    social speech internalization, 121–123
    transfer effects, 106
    word meaning function, 193–194

science
    history of, 60
    methodology, 85–86
    theory of, 60–65
    video-mediated teaching, 372–401
scientific concepts, 251–266
    Davydov's theory, 358
    development of, 251–252
    ethnographic study of, 255–266
    and everyday concepts, 9–10, 251–252, 272, 350, 358
    folk concept contrast, 230
    meaning of term, 193
    mediative function, 9–10
    and personal concepts, 229–230
    and schooled concepts, 193
    in science teaching, 373–375
    video technology mediation, 375–377, 393–400
    Vygotsky's theory, 252–253, 272, 350
    zone of proximal development, 350
"scientific work" procedure, 359
"scribes," 95–96
scripts
    acquisition of, 253–254
    social norm internalization, 62
second-language learning, 230, 413
secondary defect, 420–421
self-control
    development of, 131–132
    self-regulation contrast, 129–132
self-directed speech, 186
self-guidance, 186
self-regulation, 127–152
    and child-rearing styles, 138–140
    development of, 131–138
    function of signs, 133–135
    individual differences, 137–138
    Luria's theory, 136–138
    private speech function, 135–137, 141–147
    self-control contrast, 129–130
    social origins, 127–152
    teaching for, 138–147
    training of, 141–152
    Vygotsky's contribution, 132–136
    and writing, 409–410
    zone of proximal development, 185–186
semantics, 137
semiotic mediation, *see* sign mediated activity
short-term memory, 101
sign-mediated activity
    and Bakhtin's theory, 119
    and decontextualized rationality, 120
    development of, 133–134
    mediation function, 115–116
    self-regulatory function, 133–135
    vs. tools, 134–135
    Vygotskian ideas, 3–5, 45–46, 114–116, 133–134

skills-based approaches, 6–9
social interaction
    importance in comprehension, 195–196
    and language learning, 228–231
    in schooling, 244–245
    and writing, 312–318
social networks
    in classroom, 332
    functions, 321
    funds of knowledge access, 341
    Hispanic households, 321–346
social processes
    video technology application, 377–378, 395
    and writing, 304–318
social speech type
    Bakhtin's theory, 116–120
    internalization of, 122–123
social support, 315–317
social systems
    and concept formation, 253
    importance in learning, 12–15
    influence on development, 46–47, 113–116
    and instruction, Latinos, 319–346
    in schooling, 244–245
    Vygotsky's theory, 43–49
    and zone of proximal development, 3–15
Socialist Academy, 66
socialization, 83
Society of Militant Materialist Dialecticians, 67
sociocultural approach, 111–123
sociohistorical perspective, 59–86
    basic postulates, 90
    child development role, 367
    contributions to educational psychology, 78–82
    and cross-cultural research, 89–107
    holistic aspects, 8
    mental functioning, 111–123
    and psychic development, 350–351, 367–368
    Vygotsky's theory, 40, 52, 113–116, 350–351
    and writing, 403–422
special education
    computer-based instruciton, 415–421
    instructional models, 410–411
speech
    Bakhtin's theory, 116–120
    and concept development, 272–273
    dialogicality, 118
    hierarchical model, 410
    Luria's theory, 137
    mediation function, 115
    self-regulatory function, 135–137
"speech genre," 117
spontaneous concepts, *see* everyday concepts
Stalinism's effect, 70–72
static measures, 3
stimulus-response model, 5, 45
story dictation activities, 292–303, 307–318

"Strong Club," 306
Studies in the History of Behavior (Vygotsky), 42
syllogisms, *see* logical syllogisms
symbolic play, 406

tacit mental functions, 274–286
teacher training
    activity settings, 191–192
    assisted performance goal, 199
    and self-directed speech, 186
teaching, 271–286
    assisted performance theory, 176–183, 196–199
    development of expertise in, 271–286
    double move method, 356–358, 367
    instructional conversation task, 196–199
    interactive approach, 271–286
    and mediation, 236–238
    and social networks, 340–341
    thought processes, change, 271–286
    whole-language approach, 235–239, 242–243
    zone of proximal development basis, 349–370
testing, 81
text
    authenticity importance, 239–242
    mediator function, 240–241
    in whole-language approach, 225
    zone of proximal development, 239–242
theoretical knowledge
    Davydov's model, 353–358
    as psychic tool, 354–356
    and scientific concepts, 355–358
    teaching experiment, 359–370
"theoretical thinking," 100, 102
Think Aloud program, 143–144
Thinking and Speech (Vygotsky), 42, 115
Tohono O'odham Indians, 239
token-based systems, 94–95
tools
    and psychic development, 351
    role of culture, 91
    vs. signs, 134
    theoretical knowledge as, 354–356
    Vygotsky's theory, 45, 114, 351
transfer effects, 106
trust, 321, 326
two-dimensional pattern perception, 100–101

unit of study, 6–9, 16, 92–93, 97–98, 360–363
utterance, 116–120
Uzbekistan investigation, 46, 71, 103

Vai people, 104
"ventriloquation," 117–118
video-mediated lessons, 372–401
voice
    Bakhtin's theory, 116–120

decontextualized rationality, 120–122
formal schooling, 121–122
Volkerpsychologie, 89–90
voluntary acts, 136
vowels, 218
The Voyage of the Mimi, 378
Vygotsky, L. S., 31–58
    biographical information, 31–42
    educational theory, 49–50
    interest in pedagogy, 38
    vs. Piaget, concept formation, 252–253
    play theory, 227–228
    and self-regulation, 132–136
    sociohistorical theory, 40, 52, 113–116
    theory of knowledge, 358
    theory of psychology, 43–49, 74–78
Vygotsky–Luria–Leontiev troika, 39, 67

weekly conference, 191
whole activities, 6
whole-language approach, 19–20, 223–248
    authenticity, 9, 239–242, 247–248
    collaborative aspects, 235–243
    curriculum, 243–245
    definition, 223–225, 229
    vs. hierarchical approach, 410–411
    importance of meaning, 8–9
    personal invention in, 231–235
    Reading Recovery program difference, 217–218
    role of teacher, 235–239, 245–248
    social context, 229–235, 244–245
word meaning
    and discourse, 192–193
    and holistic approach, 7–9
    literacy basis, 192–199
    schooling function, 193–194
working brain, 49
working-class classrooms, 11
writing
    cognitive theory, 406–410

computer-based instruction, 411–412, 415–420
development of, 405–422
and dramatization, 292–303, 307–318
functional/interactive approach, 405–422
hierarchical vs. holistic model, 410–411
inner-city programs, 287–318
learning disabled students, 403–422
in Reading Recovery program, 216–217
social network use, 329–346
social process, 304–318
sociohistorical perspective, 403–422
story dictation role, 292–303, 307–318
whole-language approach, 8–9
written discourse, 194
written notation systems, 93
    in formal schooling, 104
    history, 93–97
    regulatory function, 93–94
Wundt, Wilhelm, 89–90

Zone of proximal development
    adult–child intersubjectivity, 140
    and assisted performance, stages, 184–187, 200
    as basis for instruction, 349–370
    conditions for change, 288–289
    as "connecting" concept, 3
    and holistic approach, 5–9
    in households, Latinos, 326–327, 335
    inconsistencies in concept of, 227
    inner-city study, 287–303
    literacy development, 287–303
    peer collaboration, 155–170
    progression through stages, 184–187
    relevance to education, 50, 81–82
    and social systems, 3–15
    in text comprehension, 239–242
    theoretical basis, 349–358
    Vygotsky's definition, 50, 156–158, 349–353